D1227102

The urban challenge in Africa

Note to the reader from the UNU

The objective of the United Nations University Programme on Mega-cities and Urban Development, initiated in 1990, is to examine the social, economic, and environmental consequences of the development of large metropolitan agglomerations, particularly in developing countries.

Following the release of *Mega-city Growth and the Future* (Tokyo: UNU Press, 1994), *Emerging World Cities in Pacific Asia* (Tokyo: UNU Press, 1996), and *The Mega-city in Latin America* (Tokyo: UNU Press, 1996), this book provides new insights into emerging mega-cities and urban development trends in Africa.

The urban challenge in Africa: Growth and management of its large cities

Edited by Carole Rakodi

WARNER MEMORIAL LIBRARY
EASTERN UNIVERSITY
ST. DAVIDS, PA 19087-3696

**United Nations
University Press**

TOKYO · NEW YORK · PARIS

2-10-05

HT 384 .A35 U728 1997

The urban challenge in
Africa

© The United Nations University, 1997

The views expressed in this publication are those of the authors
and do not necessarily reflect the views of the United Nations
University.

United Nations University Press
The United Nations University, 53-70, Jingumae 5-chome,
Shibuya-ku, Tokyo 150, Japan
Tel: (03) 3499-2811   Fax: (03) 3406-7345
Telex: J25442   Cable: UNATUNIV TOKYO

UNU Office in North America
2 United Nations Plaza, Room DC2-1462-70, New York, NY 10017
Tel: (212) 963-6387   Fax: (212) 371-9454   Telex: 422311 UN UI

United Nations University Press is the publishing division of the
United Nations University.

Cover design by Andrew Corbett

UNUP-952
ISBN 92-808-0952-0

Library of Congress Cataloging-in-Publication Data

The urban challenge in Africa : growth and management of its
   large cities / edited by Carole Rakodi.
        p.   cm.
   Includes bibliographical references and index.
   ISBN 9280809520 (pbk.)
      1. Cities and towns—Africa—Growth.   2. Urbanization—
   Africa.   3. Urban policy—Africa.   I. Rakodi, Carole.
   HT384.A35U728   1997
   307.76′4′096—dc21
                                                97-4603
                                                CIP

Contents

Tables and figures

Tables

Figures

Acknowledgements

The preparation of this volume has been a collective effort. In addition to the cooperation received from the contributors themselves in my repeated requests for more information or clarification, the assistance of a number of others is acknowledged. The United Nations University funding made the whole endeavour possible, but thanks are due in particular to Fu-chen Lo and Jacob Park. Assistance with the organization of the planning meeting was given by Professor Mahmoud Yousry and with the mid-project meeting by Professor Alan Gilbert and Keith Rudkin of the Department of Geography, University College London. I am indebted to the referees, Professor Akin Mabogunje and Dr. Tony O'Connor, whose comments were invaluable, but who cannot be held responsible for the final product. Technical assistance with the production of maps and diagrams and other support were provided by the technical and administrative staff of the Department of City and Regional Planning, University of Wales, Cardiff, and Catherine Jele competently and quickly translated between French and English where necessary.

Foreword

With contributions from prominent urban planning scholars and experts in Africa, *The Urban Challenge in Africa: Growth and Management of Its Large Cities*, edited by Professor Carole Rakodi of the University of Wales, Cardiff, represents the latest in a series of books from the United Nations University Programme on Mega-cities and Urban Development.

Africa, long thought of as one of the least urbanized continents, will likely have over one half of its population in urban areas by 2020. *The Urban Challenge in Africa* introduces and highlights many important development issues in Africa. In addition to chapters on individual cities including Cairo, Johannesburg, Kinshasa, and Lagos, the book also explores important sectoral issues such as property markets, urban governance, and urban–rural linkages.

With the goal of examining the social, economic, and environmental aspects of large metropolitan centres, the UNU launched its research programme by organizing an international conference on Mega-city Growth and the Future in cooperation with the United Nations Population Division and the Tokyo Metropolitan Government in 1990. The UNU later initiated an ambitious study of evolving urban systems at the regional level addressed to Pacific Asia, Latin America, and, of course, Africa. *Mega-city Growth and the Future* (the first volume in the series), *Emerging World Cities in Pacific Asia*, and *The Mega-city in Latin America* have already been released.

Foreword

As the Rector of the United Nations University, I am proud that the UNU has been involved in research and dissemination on the issues of mega-cities and urban development since the early 1990s. I believe we have made a valuable contribution to related academic fields and the preparatory work for the United Nations Habitat II Conference held in Istanbul, Turkey. It is my hope that this work will continue well into the next century through the UNU/Institute of Advanced Studies (UNU/IAS), the new research and training centre that started its activities in 1995 and is located next to the University headquarters in Tokyo, Japan.

Heitor Gurgulino de Souza
United Nations Under-Secretary-General and Rector
United Nations University

1

Introduction

Carole Rakodi

By now it is almost a truism that the planet's future is an urban one and that the largest and fastest-growing cities are primarily in developing countries. Even in Africa, long thought of as one of the least urbanized continents, it is expected that over half the population will be urban by 2020 (UN, 1993). The largest cities "serve simultaneously as national and regional engines of economic growth, centres of technological and cultural creativity, homes of the poor and deprived, and the sites and sources of environmental pollution" (Fuchs, 1994, p. 2). As yet, our understanding of the dynamics of these cities and the urban systems of which they form part, and our capacity to manage them effectively, are limited. To help redress the deficiencies in our systematic knowledge and experience, the United Nations University is carrying out a research project on Mega-cities and Urban Development. The objective of the project is to examine the growth of large metropolitan agglomerations, especially in the developing world, with regard to the patterns and projections of their growth, the demographic and economic causes, and the social, economic, and environmental consequences. It was launched in 1990 with a conference at which a range of issues related to the global mega-city phenomenon were explored: the demographic and economic causes of mega-city growth, the economic and social consequences of this growth, and alternative management issues and approaches (Fuchs et al., 1994).

1

Subsequently, projects to examine large city growth in Asia and Latin America have been undertaken (Lo and Yeung, 1996; Gilbert, 1996). It was early recognized that the initial concern with mega-cities according to one UN definition (a population of 8 million or more) was neither conceptually adequate nor likely to result in an improved understanding of relationships between the largest cities and economic systems, or between these cities and international and national urban systems. In 1990 it was agreed that it was necessary to conceptualize and define the mega-city along a greater range of dimensions than size alone (Fuchs, 1994). The Asian project focused on the changing functional relationships between the largest cities and the economy, both national and international, in particular the emergence of interlinked systems of cities within and across urban boundaries.

Aims of the research project

In Africa, it was clear that to adopt a definition of mega-cities based on size alone would be inappropriate, as at the time of writing only two African cities (Greater Cairo and the Pretoria–Witwatersrand–Vereeniging region centred on Johannesburg) had populations of over 8 million (fig. 1.1). A more nuanced approach to the selection of cities and design of a project that would address priority issues in the African context led to the adoption of a set of research objectives specifically designed for the purpose.

The aims of the project are:
  (i) to analyse the dynamics of urbanization in Africa, with special emphasis on the largest cities;
  (ii) to assess the performance of urban management systems in coping with rapid urban growth in a deteriorating situation;
  (iii) to explore the implications of the trends observed for the future.

The first of these aims is addressed by considering, firstly, the influence on cities of changing patterns of integration into the global economy; secondly, how cities function, in economic, political, and administrative terms; and, thirdly, how people function in cities, in terms of obtaining access to economic, political, and social resources and providing each other with mutual support. In order to achieve these aims, a balance between case-studies of particular urban settlements and thematic analyses was considered desirable, especially in view of the availability of a recent volume that analyses urbanization in Africa in terms of historical periods and country studies (Tarver,

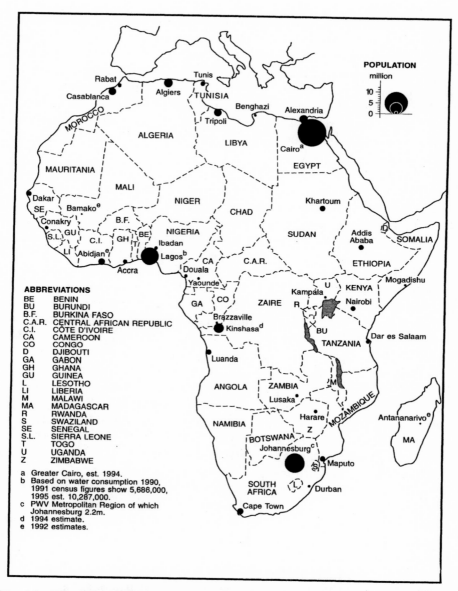

Fig. 1.1 **The cities of Africa (Source: 1995 estimates – UN, *World Urbanization Prospects, 1994*, United Nations Department for Economic and Social Information and Policy Analysis, New York, 1995; exceptions based on relevant chapters from UNCHS, *Global Report on Human Settlements*, draft, UNCHS, Nairobi, table 4)**

3

1994). Urbanization, of course, includes all settlements classified as "urban." Here the focus is on significant and representative cities and metropolitan areas, and the role of secondary cities and small urban centres has not been considered (but see Hardoy and Satterthwaite, 1986; Baker, 1990; Pedersen, 1991). The aims of the research will be further elaborated below, and the structure of the remainder of the book related to these aims. In the final part of this introduction, some of the particular difficulties faced by researchers working in Africa will be described.

Cities are essentially locations for economic activity. They are, therefore, inextricably linked both to the economies of their hinterland regions (especially national economies) and to the wider global economy, via trade and investment. Changing forms of organization of production and consumption have significant spatial effects, particularly on urban settlement systems. As capital is reconstituted in response to falling profit margins and other crises, the composition of economic activity, the technology used, the organization of production processes, and patterns of labour use also change. The new phase of globalization is generally held to have begun in the decades after World War II and to be characterized by progressive but uneven integration of different parts of the world into a global economic and financial system distinguished by increasingly transnational organization of production, greater openness of national economies, changes in production systems impelled by technological innovation, and greater integration of financial markets. Changing transport and telecommunications technologies have facilitated greater mobility of capital, goods, and people (Dicken, 1992). The global economy is more integrated than ever before and the volume of trade larger. However, the extent and pattern of integration, and the results for countries, regions, cities, and their inhabitants, are highly uneven over time and space. Increased mobility of capital and production has been one of the main driving forces behind the evolution of many national economies, especially those in the North and some of the more buoyant Asian and Latin American countries. For these countries, globalization is generally regarded as a positive stimulus to economic growth, although this does not mean that the results for all regions and social groups or for the environment are positive. Just as the phenomenon of "world cities" is a product of this new phase of globalization at the global level (Sassen, 1994), so evolving regional systems of cities in Asia are a product of flows of investment largely emanating from Japan (Lo and Yeung, 1996). One of the results of the increasing transnationalization of production is the globalization of patterns of consumption, supposedly leading to greater homogeneity of patterns of work, living, taste, and culture. However, global forces interact with local circumstances to produce unique socio-economic, political, and spatial results at national, regional, and city levels. This interaction takes a variety of forms, including resistance and adaptation as well as accommodation. In addition, countries and localities have differential abilities to compete with each other for mobile investment, resulting in heterogeneity rather than homogeneity.

Integration into the world economy is, of course, nothing new for Africa. However, the characteristics of global changes in production and consumption in the past 25 years are considered to differ from those of earlier rounds of globalization, and their effects to be different. We will argue that the manifestation and impact of global forces in Africa are more contradictory than in many other parts of the world and are often negative. The aims of chapters 2 and 3 are to assess the ways in which globalization has impacted upon the development of Africa and upon the process of rapid urbanization that is occurring in that continent. To distinguish the current forms of globalization from earlier phases, these phases will be outlined and the urbanization processes associated with them described in chapter 2. More attention is then given to global forces in the past two decades: deteriorating terms of trade, indebtedness, exclusion from emerging profitable forms of production, and dependence on international assistance. Although unimportant to the global economy as a whole, these relationships with the global economy are significant and often damaging to African countries. The final section of the chapter examines what, in the context of the continent's external dependence and vulnerability, marginalization, and aid dependence, has happened to cities. Have "world cities" emerged in Africa? In the context of economic deterioriation, has urbanization continued? What form has it taken? What have the implications of aid dependence been for approaches to urban management?

The theme of Africa's exclusion from those forms and sectors of production that are most profitable at present and are likely to be so in future is taken up again by Rogerson in chapter 10, where its implications for the vitality of urban economies are further explored. In chapter 3, David Simon elaborates on the extent and nature of globalization, the relationship of this to economic development trends, and the relationship of the latter to trends in urbanization.

He examines the connections between African cities and the global economy, in terms of multinational investment, trade, debt, and international organizations, concluding that, although these connections are limited and tenuous, they often have important implications for the cities concerned. The marginality of African cities to international systems of manufacturing production, finance, and politics is contrasted with the spread of global patterns of consumption. Although these have made an impact throughout Africa, Simon stresses the limits of this impact, firstly because of the strength and diversity of local cultures and, secondly, owing to the impoverishment both of the continent as a whole and of those excluded from the benefits of such economic growth as has occurred.

In part II of the book, a number of case-studies of some of the largest and most significant cities in the continent are presented, in order of population size (fig. 1.2). The largest cities (Cairo, Lagos, and Johannesburg) are included. What has led to their growth, what is continuing to drive their expansion today, and what are the prospects for the future? Cities that at present or potentially have more than a national or regional role are included: Nairobi, Johannesburg, and Cairo. Are any of these, or could they potentially be, "world cities"? Cities from the main cultural regions are represented: Cairo from Arabic, Muslim north Africa; Lagos and Nairobi from anglophone west and east Africa; Johannesburg from anglophone settler southern Africa; Abidjan and Kinshasa from francophone Africa. What differences have these varied colonial and cultural heritages made to patterns of urban development, modes of urban governance, and the lives of urban people, and can processes of divergence or convergence be detected today? Finally, cities with different experiences of urban management are included, along a continuum from Johannesburg, with its significant financial and human management resources, at one end, to Kinshasa, where recognizable public sector management has completely broken down, at the other. What accounts for the relative success of some cities and the failure of others to generate the resources needed to manage and service their growth? How can a city the size of Kinshasa sustain itself and its residents without any formal administration?

In each of the case-studies, written in 1994, authors review recent and likely future trends in the growth of the city, with particular reference to its global links and the emergence of a city region; analyse urban characteristics; and assess the extent to which its development is being adequately managed. They consider economic and demographic trends, the structure of the urban economy, sources of capital and labour, the components of population growth, and the extent and nature of urban poverty. They examine the forms that political and social organization has taken in recent years and the implications of these for residents and urban administration. They describe processes of land development, the production of the built environment, and the changing spatial structure of the city and its region that results. Arrangements for planning and management are reviewed, urban policies and their outcomes examined, and finally issues and promising approaches for the future identified. The chapters do not cover all the above areas in equal detail or in the same order: contributors have concentrated on the features of a particular city that are most crucial to understanding it, and have presented material in an order appropriate for the case in hand. Together, however, they offer a rich source of insights and a fertile basis for comparison.

In the third part of the book, a series of themes are explored in chapters that draw on the case-studies and on a much broader range of examples. The themes have been selected to provide between them the basis for a fuller understanding of both the dynamics of city growth and functioning and the experience of urban planning and management. They are concerned with how cities function and how people function in cities – the first three chapters emphasize the former and the fourth the latter, but these two aspects of urban life are, of course, interrelated. In chapter 10, Christian Rogerson examines how cities function in economic terms: he analyses the changing structure of urban economies, the different scales and sources of investment, and the resulting economic opportunities for residents. The aim of chapter 11 is to review what is known about the process of urban development, with particular reference firstly to transactions in land and residential/commercial property, and secondly to the outcomes of attempts to intervene in this process through the instruments of land policy. Tade Aina, in chapter 12, explores the interrelated areas of political and social organization and analyses their implications for urban management. Changes in governance, administration, social organizations, and informal networks are analysed, and their influence on the political economy of the city and on the lives of its citizens described. Themes from each of these chapters are picked up by Deborah Potts in chapter 13, which focuses on the nature of people's lives, as they live in cities, move between cities and rural areas, and deal with the shocks resulting from policy changes associated with structural adjustment. Potts considers whether "urban"

7

The PWV Metropolitan Area,
South Africa

0   10   20

N

Built-up Areas

Fig. 1.2 **The case-study cities compared**

is an artificial construct in the context of the movement patterns of
many urban residents, and examines the ways in which people are trying to cope with increased economic hardship.

Inevitably, the selection of themes results in the neglect of some
areas – there are no chapters on housing, infrastructure, transport,
or the environment, although related issues have been picked up in

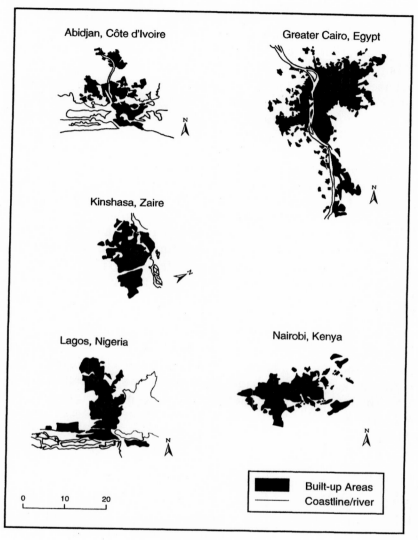

Fig. 1.2 **(cont.)**

some of the thematic chapters and in many of the city case-studies. Some of these areas have been more adequately dealt with elsewhere than others. Compared with other aspects of urban life, work on housing is well developed (see, for example, Amis and Lloyd, 1990). An important comparative research project at the end of the 1980s examined infrastructure and services, including transport, in a number of African cities (Stren and White, 1989). Cities make continuing demands on natural resources for inputs of energy, water, food, building materials, etc., and disposal of waste. Natural resource availability may influence both the rate and direction of growth, and cities have impacts on areas far outside their boundaries, while the urban environment influences the quality of life for all residents. Some of these issues are raised in the city case-studies. However, the dearth of published work militated against the production of a significant thematic chapter as part of a study based on the compilation of existing knowledge rather than new empirical research.

In the final part of the book, issues and approaches for the future are identified. In chapter 14, Salah El-Shakhs draws on evidence presented in parts I–III about the current problems faced by large cities and the effectiveness of recent policies and administrative arrangements in order to suggest ways forward. He examines likely future trends, identifies promising innovations, and suggests desirable approaches. His emphasis is on planning, administration, spatial patterns, and physical improvements. In chapter 15, Kadmiel Wekwete reviews recent experience with managing urban growth, in order to reveal how and why approaches have changed in recent years and to assess their effectiveness. The themes of the book are drawn together in the concluding chapter, which briefly considers the future of Africa in general terms and then in terms specifically of urbanization. Finally, some of the themes of the recent debates over how to manage Africa's cities are reviewed and future research priorities identified.

Constraints

One of the most significant problems in addressing urbanization issues and in assessing the performance of urban management systems in Africa is the dearth of information. The reasons for this lack of data and the unreliability of information that does exist are well known: economic deterioration has reduced the resources for research and data collection (Stren, 1994); economic difficulties combined with political turmoil have reduced the capacity of governments to lead development and ensure that administrative procedures are adhered to; war and civil unrest have prevented or invalidated data collection; and a combination of overcentralization and an emphasis on rural development has led to a weakening of city-based administration.

In effect, in Africa, we have to study urbanization in the absence of reliable and up-to-date demographic information and in the face of enormous gaps in the research that has been carried out. How, it might be asked, is it possible to understand the dynamics of urbanization when it is not known what proportion of the population is living in urban areas, what the population of many cities is, and what has happened to rates of natural increase and patterns of migration during the 1980s and early 1990s? Although there was a round of censuses in many countries around 1990, few have managed to process and make available the results in a suitably disaggregated fashion. To fill the gap, the United Nations Centre for Human Settlements is attempting to collect city-level information. However, this information was not available in time for use by the researchers reporting here. Nevertheless, the urgent need to improve our understanding of the dynamics of urbanization and of the outcomes of attempts to manage urban growth means that we must proceed, by assembling what data are available, drawing on personal experience, and reaching conclusions with care.

An additional hindrance to the ability of authors in this volume to reach definitive conclusions and to generalize with confidence is the heterogeneity in the geographical area covered. The desire of the United Nations University to define Africa in continental terms has had the effect of increasing a level of heterogeneity that is already hard to deal with across north Africa or within sub-Saharan Africa. Reflecting and encompassing both diverse and common characteristics have posed real problems for the contributors of thematic chapters. One way of dealing with a vast continent is to identify the characteristics of regions, defined in terms of geographical contiguity. However, in Africa this gives rise to anomalies where the colonial history of adjacent countries was different. Mozambique has more in common with Angola than with its neighbours, South Africa, Zimbabwe, and Tanzania. Francophone central African countries have characteristics in common with anglophone central African countries, as well as with francophone west African countries. The Muslim countries of north Africa have more in common with the Middle East than with most sub-Saharan African countries, a problem illustrated by the internal tensions of countries such as the Sudan and Nigeria.

Most scholars working in Africa confine their area of expertise to a particular part of the continent, partly because of its size, and partly for language reasons. Exchange of material between scholars working in French, English, Portuguese, and indigenous languages, including Arabic, is difficult and limited. In addition, statistics are often produced for sub-Saharan Africa whereas North Africa is included in the Middle East. Inevitably, the authors of the thematic chapters in this volume draw primarily on their own knowledge and the work of other researchers in the parts of the continent with which they are familiar. Despite their best efforts to review material in other languages and ensure coverage of all parts of the continent, the obvious difficulties caused by linguistic and cultural differences, as well as limitations on space, have inhibited this. This book is being published in English, a language that is foreign to many Africans interested in urban issues. In a wholly inadequate attempt to make the material more accessible, French abstracts have been included for each of the chapters.

Despite the difficulties, it is hoped that the assembly of knowledge and expertise facilitated by the United Nations University and represented in this volume will increase understanding of urbanization in general, and large city growth in particular, in the continent of Africa. Given the patchy nature of the data and recent research, an exercise such as this has inevitably thrown up as many questions as it has answered. It is to be hoped that the agenda for research outlined in the final chapter of this volume (alongside that identified in Stren, 1994) will provoke researchers and funders to undertake the substantive studies of urban processes and evaluations of past policies necessary to underpin future attempts to meet the challenge of urban growth in Africa more effectively.

References

Amis, P. and P. Lloyd, eds. 1990. *Housing Africa's Urban Poor*. Manchester University Press, Manchester.

Baker, J., ed. 1990. *Small Town Africa: Studies in Rural–Urban Interaction*. Scandinavian Institute of African Studies, Uppsala.

Dicken, P. 1992. *The Internationalization of Economic Activity*. Paul Chapman, London.

Fuchs, R. J. 1994. Introduction. In: R. J. Fuchs, E. Brennan, J. Chamie, F.-C. Lo, and J. I. Uitto, eds., *Mega-city Growth and the Future*. United Nations University Press, Tokyo, pp. 1–13.

Fuchs, R. J., E. Brennan, J. Chamie, F.-C. Lo, and J. I. Uitto, eds. 1994. *Mega-city Growth and the Future*. United Nations University Press, Tokyo.

Gilbert, A., ed. 1996. *The Mega-city in Latin America*. United Nations University Press, Tokyo.

Hardoy, J. and D. Satterthwaite, eds. 1986. *Small and Intermediate Urban Centres:*

Their Role in National and Regional Development in the Third World. Hodder & Stoughton, London.

Lo, F.-C. and Y.-M. Yeung, eds. 1996. *Emerging World Cities in Pacific Asia.* United Nations University Press, Tokyo.

Pedersen, P. O., ed. 1991. The role of small and intermediate urban centres in planning in Africa. *African Urban Quarterly* 6(3/4): 171–303.

Sassen, S. 1994. *Cities in a World Economy.* Pine Forge Press, Thousand Oaks, Calif.

Stren, R. F. and R. R. White, eds. 1989. *African Cities in Crisis: Managing Rapid Urban Growth.* Westview, Boulder, Colo.

Stren, R., ed. 1994. *Urban Research in the Developing World, Vol. 2 Africa.* University of Toronto Press, Toronto.

Tarver, J. D., ed. 1994. *Urbanization in Africa: A Handbook.* Greenwood Press, Westport, Conn.

UN. 1993. *World Urbanization Prospects: The 1992 Revision.* United Nations Department of Economic and Social Information and Policy Analysis, New York.

Part I
Globalization and Africa:
The challenge of urban growth

2

Global forces, urban change, and urban management in Africa

Carole Rakodi

Abstract

Il est possible de distinguer en Afrique diverses phases d'urbanisation partiellement liées à l'évolution des conditions suivant lesquelles
le continent s'est intégré dans l'économie mondiale. S'il existe de
grandes disparités en termes de ressources naturelles et de passé his-
torique, il est néanmoins possible d'établir une distinction d'ensemble
entre les périodes pré-coloniale, coloniale et celle suivant immédi-
atement l'indépendance et les vingt dernières années. Pour chacune
de ces phases, les tendances et modèles d'urbanisation peuvent être
mis en relation avec la nature des relations politiques extérieures
en même temps que la situation physique, sociale, politique, économique et culturelle intérieure. Ce sont aussi bien des forces extérieures que la situation interne qui ont influencé les choix de méthodes
de gestion et d'aménagement urbain. Après avoir brièvement passé
en revue les périodes pré-coloniale et coloniale, l'on étudie de façon
plus approfondie la période allant des années 50 au milieu des années
70, puis les 20 années suivantes. L'examen porte d'abord sur l'impact
des influences politiques et économiques extérieures sur les pays
d'Afrique, puis sur les tendances de l'urbanisation et enfin sur les
politiques et gestions urbaines. Malgré l'ouverture économique de
l'Afrique, le continent ne présente qu'une importance marginale
pour l'économie mondiale; tout en étant vulnérable à des forces

économiques extérieures, il est exclu des récentes tendances à la mondialisation qui ont enrichi un nouveau groupe de pays aux revenus jusqu'alors inférieurs. C'est ce qui le fait dépendre de l'aide extérieure et lui impose d'accepter des conditions en matière de politique économique et aussi de politique urbaine. L'on démontre ici à quel point les résultats des réformes de politique économique et d'urbanisation préconisées par les donneurs d'aide, en particulier les institutions multilatérales, sont loin des objectifs visés par les donateurs comme par les bénéficiaires. Il ressort notamment de cet examen qu'une mauvaise compréhension des problèmes suscités par les réformes et l'incapacité de les surmonter que ce soit aux niveaux international, national ou local, l'insuffisance des données de référence, la faiblesse des remèdes aux erreurs politiques et les contradictions entre les ensembles de politiques recommandées par les institutions de financement risquent de se combiner pour continuer de freiner une croissance économique plus équitable, la stabilité socio-politique et une meilleure gestion des villes.

Introduction

The aim of this chapter is to assess the ways in which global forces have impacted upon the development of Africa and upon the process of rapid urbanization that is occurring in that continent. Africa has been integrated into the world trade system on unfavourable terms and has become dependent on international assistance. Phases of urbanization can be distinguished which are related in part to the shifting terms on which Africa has been integrated into the world economy. The pre-colonial phase will be dealt with briefly, before examining the colonial phase, the results of which, in terms of economic development, settlement patterns, and urban form, are relatively well known. Ending in most countries in sub-Saharan Africa in the 1960s, a transitional period ensued in which the achievement of autonomous economic and political status was attempted by means of state-centred, interventionist strategies paralleled by a regulatory approach to urban development. By the 1970s it became clear that the endeavours of the central and local state were far from achieving economic or urban development goals. The debate over the relative roles of the terms of Africa's integration into the world economy, state weakness, and domestic policy mistakes in explaining Africa's continued underdevelopment is ongoing. What is clear is that the continent's economic difficulties have made it reliant on and thus vulnerable to the policy dictates of the international agencies, especially the International Monetary Fund (IMF) and the World Bank. Rapid urbanization in a situation of continued poverty has outpaced the financial and administrative capacity of governments to ensure that cities provide efficient locations for economic activity and satisfy the basic needs of all their citizens. Much of the chapter will be devoted to an examination of trends in the past 20 years. The role of global forces in Africa's development, including trade, foreign investment, flows of international finance capital, and flows of Official Development Assistance (ODA), will be explored. The latter have been accompanied by policy conditionalities that have affected economic development paths, urban development processes, and urban management strategies. The appropriateness of current national and international urban policies and management approaches will be assessed.

As has been noted in chapter 1, Africa is a continent of enormous contrasts. North Africa, with its political, economic, and cultural ties to Europe and the Middle East, is frequently dealt with separately from sub-Saharan Africa (SSA). Distinctions can be drawn between countries based on their colonial histories (colonial power, system of rule, date and means of achieving independence), their natural resource base, their geographical location (especially coastal/landlocked), their cultural composition (ethnicity, religion), and their political history (form of the state, significance in global politics, nature of the political system). These have affected the way in which countries have been integrated into the world economy; the domestic policies they have adopted; the interests represented in the state, and the ability of these interests to advance their own causes and of the state to pursue policy goals consistently; and the urbanization process. Generalizations are, therefore, dangerous, but common trends, problems, and pressures can be identified. These will be emphasized in this chapter, although, to avoid overgeneralization, and within the usual constraints on space, attention will be drawn to contrasting features as well.

Pre-colonial Africa

Urban settlements have been widespread in Africa for centuries. In North Africa, Greek colonialism dating from the fourth century BC interacted with local kingdoms: cross-Mediterranean trade encouraged the emergence of flourishing ports, such as Carthage and Alexandria (Bonine, 1983). Many of these remain significant settlements today. In most of SSA, towns were the seats of kings, political rulers with religious overtones. They accommodated courts and gave rise to the production of arts and crafts, but remained small because of their dependence on locally produced food. Royal power involved some control over exchange, although trade also seems to have occurred independently of urban settlements. The prevalence in many areas of shifting agriculture and the close association of urban settlements with kingship meant that the sites of many towns shifted. Some cities and kingdoms were ephemeral, linked to the reign of a particular ruler; others, such as the Yoruba towns of south-west Nigeria, prospered through many regimes and continue to be important today (Mabogunje, 1968). Some kingdoms, especially in West Africa, expanded into empires, in which cities emerged as seats of government and trading centres – for example, Mali between the twelfth and fourteenth centuries, Songhay in the Sudan in the fifteenth and sixteenth centuries, and Benin between the twelfth and eighteenth centuries (Gugler and Flanagan, 1978; Mehretu, 1983; Winters, 1983; Coquery-Vidrovitch, 1991; Chandler, 1994).

Islam was spread across North Africa in the seventh century and Arab neighbourhoods were generally established outside existing ancient cities (Bonine, 1983). Tunis, for example, was founded 15 km from the site of the ancient city of Carthage (Findlay and Paddison, 1986). By the Middle Ages, Cairo was the capital of an alien dynasty, the Mamelukes, who were interested only in collecting taxes (see also Chandler, 1994). It was only by the eleventh or twelfth centuries that most of the inhabitants of North African cities had converted to Islam. Integration of relatively self-contained kingdoms elsewhere in Africa into wider economic systems seems to date from the extension of medieval Muslim trade into the Sudan, southwards along the Nile Valley and Africa's eastern coast, and across the Sahara. Trans-Saharan trade initially focused on gold and salt (Amin, 1972). The empire of Ghana, whose power peaked in the ninth century, was based on control of the gold trade (Gugler and Flanagan, 1978). Trade was followed by religion. At break-of-bulk points, on the northern and southern fringes of the Sahara, where savannah met forest (for example, Timbuktu), where water and land routes crossed (in the Niger and Nile valleys), or at ports, trade stimulated urban growth. The Hausa towns of northern Nigeria, such as Kano, Katsina, and Maiduguri, were state capitals and trading centres. These settlements focused on the mosque and the market and were controlled by a merchant élite. The East African coastal settlements, such as Zanzibar, Lamu, and Mombasa, were closest in character to the Muslim cities of the Middle East, while in the Sudan and the Sahel Muslim influences on earlier African settlements were partial and varied (Winters, 1983). The fall of the Songhay empire to Morocco at the end of the sixteenth century marked the close of an era, although trans-Saharan trade continued and Arab mercantilism (and trade in slaves) continued in East Africa until the second half of the nineteenth century (Amin, 1972; see also Chandler, 1994). The pre-colonial cities of North Africa sometimes reached considerable sizes: Cairo is estimated to have had a population of 300,000 in the eleventh century and 500,000 at the beginning of the fourteenth century, although, as Yousry and Aboul Atta show in chapter 4, it subsequently declined; Marrakesh and Fès probably each had 100,000 inhabitants in the eleventh century and grew to 150,000 and over 200,000, respectively, in the thirteenth and fourteenth centuries (Chandler, 1994). Urban settlements in SSA, although significant in administrative and trade terms, were generally small, few exceeding 100,000.

Portuguese mercantilism expanded into Africa from the mid-fifteenth century; it was followed by British and French traders in the next century. The West African coastal trade was initially in gold and was carried on by leave of local rulers, although the Europeans played one kingdom off against another to prevent the emergence of powerful states (Gugler and Flanagan, 1978). Benin, for example, had been engaged in regional trade until the late fifteenth century, when trade with the Portuguese in slaves, pepper, etc. developed. Although control over trade was a royal monopoly on both sides, it was carried on by merchants, those from Benin acting as intermediaries between the Europeans and hinterland cities (Onokerhoraye, 1975). The slave trade became increasingly important from the sixteenth century, drawing more and more African leaders into it and having a devastating effect on the economies and political structures of the coastal and forest kingdoms (Amin, 1972; Gugler and Flanagan, 1978). An estimated 12 million slaves were taken from Africa in Christian- and 7 million in Muslim-owned ships (Chandler, 1994). Evidence on the impact of the slave trade on urbanization patterns is scarce and contradictory. Algiers was, according to Chandler and Tarver (1993), the largest slave port, following the appointment of a Turkish governor in 1520.

Inland, earlier patterns of urban development evolved slowly (Chandler, 1994). In the interior of Ghana, small city-states developed that were later absorbed by the Ashanti empire, centred on Kumasi. The power of this empire lasted until 1873–74, when it was finally defeated in a clash with the British over its attempts to assert control over smaller coastal states (Gugler and Flanagan, 1978). Although urbanization continued in Ghana in the seventeenth century, the earlier urban culture was weakened as the slave trade peaked in the eighteenth and nineteenth centuries. Yoruba urbanization also continued, in response to the insecurity caused by internal conflicts over control of channels for slave trading (Coquery-Vidrovitch, 1991).

Successive waves of European traders gradually shifted the focus of economic activities from the northern savannah areas of West Africa towards the forest belt and the coast, leading to stagnation for earlier trading centres (Salau, 1990). From the first Portuguese contact at the mouth of the Senegal River in 1445, they extended trading networks down the west coast and eventually round to East Africa. During the sixteenth century they founded Bissau in Guinea; Luanda, Benguela, and São Salvador in Angola; and Lourenço Marques, Sena, and Mozambique in Mozambique; as well as temporarily wresting control of Zanzibar and Mombasa from Arab traders. The Dutch founded Cape Town in 1652 and the French and British a number of West African ports, including Conakry, Accra, Sekondi, Cape Coast, and Calabar (Mehretu, 1983). Napoleon invaded Egypt, the brief French occupation (1798–1802) being a precursor of greater European influence (Bonine, 1983). In 1830 the French invaded Algeria, and then Tunis and Morocco. However, the European presence was generally confined to defence and trade in coastal settlements and there was little penetration inland. Meanwhile, Egyptian incursions into Sudanese sultanates aimed at extracting slaves and other wealth and establishing political control (Amin, 1972).

Colonial Africa

The economic role of colonialism

The mercantilist period evolved into colonialism proper in the second half of the nineteenth century. The development of capitalism in Europe gave rise to a search for cheap raw materials and agricultural produce and for markets for manufactured exports. In West Africa, the destructive effects of the slave trade on pre-existing social formations made it possible to shape a system of large-scale production of goods such as cocoa, palm oil, timber, and rubber by organizing a trade monopoly, taxing peasants, providing support to local rulers, and forced labour. In southern and parts of central and eastern Africa, colonial capital wished to exploit minerals and engage in agriculture. To obtain a cheap labour force, for mining, settler agriculture, and later manufacturing, land was expropriated, taxes imposed, and African agriculture discriminated against. In contrast with Africa of the colonial-trade economy and Africa of the labour reserves, large parts of central Africa were opened up to plunder by concessionary companies. The colonial system thus organized African societies so that they produced exports that provided only minimal returns to local labour (Amin, 1972). It restructured peasant agriculture, introduced new administrative systems, and changed the pattern of urbanization.

While economic competition was responsible for the penetration of African economies, it was paralleled by political competition. Belgian and German annexation of territory upset the balance of power, and the scramble for partition and political control that followed coincided with and was related to economic and social transformation. Colonial rule was established by a combination of persuasion and coercion, often arbitrary boundaries were drawn, and interaction between the colonial administration and indigenous rulers had an important influence on the type of administrative system established. Generally, British paternalist philosophy found expression in decentralized administrative practice, which was adapted to existing local institutional and political structures, while the doctrine of assimilation underlay direct centralized control in French, Portuguese, and Belgian territories. In practice, the distinction was less clear cut than this and perhaps greater contrasts can be seen between the colonial and settler societies. Settlers demanded not only opportunities for colonial accumulation, but also political and other rights, giving rise to more extensive influence and tighter control over indigenous economies, cultures, and socio-political systems, seen above all in South Africa, Southern Rhodesia, and Algeria, and to a lesser extent in the Portuguese colonies and Kenya (Bell, 1986).

Colonial urbanization

Colonial cities developed not as industrial centres, but to facilitate the extraction of commodities and the politico-administrative system on which this depended. Many coastal settlements that were already engaged in international trade expanded. Lagos is an important example in west Africa and Tunis in north Africa (see chap. 6; Findlay and Paddison, 1986). In order to fulfil their functions as administrative and commercial centres, transport infrastructure, especially railways, was developed to connect the ports to their hinterlands (Gugler and Flanagan, 1978; Mehretu, 1983; Coquery-Vidrovitch, 1991). In some parts of Africa, earlier urban systems had decayed and "new" colonial settlements were established, sometimes from scratch and sometimes on the sites of earlier settlements (O'Connor, 1983). Elsewhere, colonial settlements were superimposed on and attached to existing towns and cities, while the choice of transport routes gave a boost to or bypassed existing settlements. Port cities thrived at the expense of inland settlements (Bonine, 1983; Findlay, 1994).

Although traditional manufacturing survived in some parts of the continent, especially in the north, rarely was industrialized manufacturing introduced, except in the settler societies, where import-substituting industry designed to meet the needs of the substantial European populations was developed with government help, and reinforced the new pattern of urban settlements that had been established. Even in the parts of Africa that were never directly colonized, links between their economies and the outside world grew and European influences on urban form can be detected, for example in Addis Ababa in Ethiopia (O'Connor, 1983). Within an increasingly global economy, King (1990) suggests, a capitalist–industrialist urban culture grew, overlaying or replacing the more culture-specific pre-industrial and pre-capitalist urban forms of the mercantile era. Metropolitan cities were increasingly linked to colonial cities through their relative roles in the international division of labour.

In the early period, the trading fort model was the best tool for coercion, surveillance, and exploitation, but colonial officials' conceptions of "civilisation and power clashed with the sordid realities they created" (Coquery-Vidrovitch, 1991). Health concerns and the need to provide colonial administrators and early settlers with an acceptable living environment gave rise to environmental sanitation measures and the establishment of rudimentary local government (King, 1990). Until the 1930s, rural–urban migration was typically temporary and seasonal. This suited both employers, enabling them to pay wages insufficient to meet the full costs of reproducing the labour force (Gregory and Piché, 1982), and peasant farmers, whose needs for cash were still limited. However, especially in the labour reserve economies, shortages of labour led to the strengthening of mechanisms designed to ensure an adequate labour supply. The collapse in commodity prices in the 1930s' depression had knock-on effects in the African colonies. Urban property markets slumped, unemployment rose, and African residents returned to their villages (Skinner, 1986). From the 1920s on in the Belgian Congo and the 1940s onwards in South Africa and Southern and Northern Rhodesia, the desire of mining and manufacturing capital for a more stable labour force led to changes in government policies (Coquery-Vidrovitch, 1991; Rakodi, 1986a, 1995a). Although older patterns of migration persisted, it became acceptable for a man and his family to live in urban areas for the duration of his working life. Acceptance of a more stable labour force and growing urban population had a variety of impacts on urban policy and management, in particular:

(a) A desire to ensure land for urban development and the provision of services, especially to the European population, led to the strengthening of local government, under the control of appointed administrator-mayors in the French colonies (Skinner, 1986) and the European population in the British colonies, with sufficient revenue-raising capacity not to be a drain on central or metropolitan government funds and based on an imported legislative framework.

(b) The need to stimulate provision for and maintain control over the labour force led to public sector provision of rental housing, often subsidized. Such housing was often physically separate from areas of indigenous urban development, where the newly enacted legislation did not apply and forms of government and/or access to land and housing were based on existing local structures and mechanisms (Chandler and Tarver, 1993). Elsewhere, existing tenure systems were swept away or the colonial state became the main landowner (King, 1990).

(c) A desire to restrict the urban African population to that necessary to provide a labour force for colonial enterprises led in some of the colonies to (mostly unsuccessful) attempts to control and eradicate other types of economic enterprise (the informal sector) and housing development (squatter areas or other unauthorized settlement).

(d) For political, social, and cultural reasons, the residential areas and social lives of urban residents (Europeans, Syrian-Lebanese traders, an imported Asian commercial class in eastern and southern Africa, mixed race people, and Africans) were segregated, despite the essential but differently valued contribution of each to the urban economy (Simon, 1992; see also Christopher and Tarver, 1994).

By 1950, at the beginning of the main decolonization period, Cairo (population 2.41 million) and Johannesburg (915,000) were the largest cities, followed by Casablanca, Cape Town, Durban, the East Rand, Tunis, Algiers, and Ibadan, each with over 400,000. Overall, only 15 per cent of the continent's population lived in urban areas and in most countries the urban population was heavily concentrated in one or two cities, normally including the colonial capital.

The independence decade

In a sense, it is misleading to speak of the independence decade as the 1960s and early 1970s. Liberia's independence was recognized in 1847, South Africa became independent but minority ruled in 1910, Egypt has been independent since 1922, Libya gained its independence in 1951, followed by Morocco, Tunisia, and the Sudan in 1956, Ghana in 1957, and Guinea in 1958. The Portuguese colonies, Namibia, and Eritrea have gained their independence, and Zimbabwe and South Africa majority rule, since the mid-1970s. Nevertheless, of over 50 African countries, the great majority gained their independence in the 1960s. For this reason, and because this was a decade of relative economic prosperity before major changes occurred in the world economy in the mid-1970s, as a transitional period it is significant for both national political economies and the process of urbanization. Although for Egypt, because of its longstanding self-rule, this period is not of such dramatic importance, the economic pressures were similar. The settler societies of Zimbabwe and South Africa commenced the period with more developed commercial agricultural and industrial sectors than other African countries did, but faced increasing internal resistance and external ostracism.

Political independence: Reality or myth?

Independence implies autonomy to make political decisions and the capacity to carry them out. By the 1950s, it was in the interests of both France, following the Algerian war, and Britain to hand over political rule. In juridical terms the new states were strong, but politically and socially they were weak:

in the great majority of states there was no shared culture ... and the typical state was characterised by ethnic pluralism, linguistic diversity, the strength of communal ties and loyalties, and an educational system which hitherto had benefited only a minority of the population. (Tordoff, 1984, p. 77)

Nationalist movements had incorporated divergent interests, and the initial problem for the inexperienced politicians who took power, on the basis of political systems modelled on those of the metropolitan powers, was to establish their legitimacy and balance conflicting ethnic and economic interests. The inherited bureaucracies were generally fairly well developed (except in the ex-Portuguese and ex-Belgian colonies), but they were costly to run and hard to manage without expatriate expertise. However, heavy demands were placed on the political and bureaucratic structures, while the uncertain relationship between them gave rise to misunderstanding and conflict (Tordoff, 1984; Chazan et al., 1988). The apparent need for state economic development planning and, in the absence of foreign control of major economic sectors, for it to take on productive roles led to the establishment of planning machinery and large parastatals, which further strained the capacity of the state to manage its affairs (Tordoff, 1984). An additional problem has been the role of the military – only 18 countries had escaped successful military coups by the end of the 1980s. Once constitutional rules have been discarded, the conditions in which factionalism, mutual distrust, fear, and counter-coup flourish are reinforced (Wunsch and Olowu, 1990). Many countries have been subject to military repression, civil war, and ethnic pogroms.

For a variety of reasons, including economic management and resource allocation to fulfil developmental goals, the need to foster a sense of national unity, fear of strong or opposition-controlled local government, and scarcity of skilled and experienced public servants, strong government has been equated with centralization. However, this has facilitated the abuse of power, increased the propensity to error, slowed down and bureaucratized responses to changing circumstances, and made access to the central state the prime source of opportunities for personal accumulation. Except in "strong man" governments, there have been attempts at decentralization, but these have typically been flawed and unsuccessful (Wunsch and Olowu, 1990). The relative weakness of state structures in the first decades of independence is thus attributed by Chazan et al. (1988, p. 62) to "scarcity of resources, politicized patterns of social differentiation, overexpanded state structures, insufficient state legitimacy, inadequate state power and the lack of adaptation of alien institutions to local conditions." Politics has been characterized by personal rule and political domination and political life has pivoted around individual leaders, while domination by particular social groups has been resisted. In some countries, a degree of continuity, stability, and accountability has been achieved, but more commonly political processes have been marked by repression, instability, inequality, dishonesty, ineffectiveness, and disorder (Chazan et al., 1988).

In addition to state weakness, political autonomy has been eroded by superpower interest, continued identification with the ex-colonial powers, and the relationship between political and economic dependence. The United States and the USSR sought to channel post-colonial change in their own interests, the former to contain Soviet influence and the latter to establish a presence in the continent. The USSR tried to extend its influence by supporting regimes that asked for assistance, not all of them sporting socialist ideologies, and a reliance on arms supply as the main lever, especially in its areas of strategic interest in the Horn and North Africa. US policy has been anti-communist, leading to support of reactionary and repressive governments, especially in Zaire and the Horn, and assistance to friendly capitalist regimes, especially Egypt, Morocco, and South Africa (Chazan et al., 1988). Other external interference with national sovereignty has originated within the continent itself, most notably the destabilizing activities of South Africa in the front-line states, but also the activities of Algeria in supporting anti-colonial activity and of Libya in the trans-Saharan region. Ties to ex-colonial powers, for example by membership of the Commonwealth, have remained strong. France in particular has deliberately maintained its influence in its ex-colonies by political, technical, and military support, especially for conservative and moderate regimes (Chazan et al., 1988). It has been able to do so because of the economic dependency of most of the states, their small size and political fragility, and the longstanding policy of cultural assimilation. In return, "most of the Francophone states show solidarity with France in voting at the UN General Assembly" (Tordoff, 1984, p. 275). Tordoff argues that, despite these dependencies, African regimes have exercised political autonomy and that their ruling classes cannot be portrayed merely as puppets on strings pulled by external forces. However, a distinction can be drawn between political influence based on continuing economic dependency and political interference during crises, during which African élites have been ready and willing to exploit superpower rivalry in their own interests (Chazan et al., 1988).

Economic autonomy and progress: A mirage?

The economies inherited by African countries at independence imposed considerable constraints on policy choices. Exports were overwhelmingly of raw materials and agricultural products (93 per cent from SSA in 1965 – World Bank, 1992, p. 249), most economies depended on fewer than three products for over three-quarters of their export earnings, rendering economies very vulnerable to fluctuations in world commodity prices, and trade was often monopolized by large European companies. In SSA, industry accounted for only 9 per cent of GDP in 1965 and manufactured exports were unimportant. Trade was largely with the colonial powers, an industrial base was almost non-existent except in some of the settler economies, and education and training had been exceptionally poor.

The favoured development strategy during the independence decade was based on modernization, industrialization, economic diversification, and indigenization of the economy. Given the heavy reliance on imported manufactures – both consumer goods and capital equipment (76 per cent of SSA imports in 1965; World Bank, 1992, p. 247) – the logical place to start was with import substitution. Given the obstacles (inadequate infrastructure oriented mostly towards colonial trade, absence of an industrial workforce, small domestic markets, dearth of indigenous capital), high levels of protection, a substantial role for the state, and a search for external assistance were inevitable.

External assistance was obtained mostly from transnational corporations (TNCs). The colonial trading and mining companies were international firms. However, the search within capitalism for increased rates of profit results in tendencies for monopoly, vertical integration, expansion, and concentration. These forces, and the role of developments in telecommunications and transport technology in facilitating central control and coordination of worldwide operations, have led to growth in the scale, reach, and significance in the world economy of TNCs (Jenkins, 1987). Said to offer scarce capital, technology and know-how, employment creation, tax revenue, and access to export markets, their share of mining and manufacturing investment and world trade was increasing. Although foreign direct investment (FDI) underestimates the role of TNCs, much of whose investment is financed from local profits and borrowing, published data refer to it.

FDI in Africa grew in the 1960s, and by the mid-1970s was concentrated in Nigeria, Liberia, Zaire, Gabon, Kenya, and the Côte d'Ivoire. Although starting from a small base, investment in countries such as Botswana, the Gambia, Niger, Tanzania, and Malawi grew rapidly in the decade. In 1972, 20.7 per cent of all FDI was in Africa (excluding South Africa, for which information was not available), but by 1975 still over half (52.2 per cent) of all the FDI stock in Africa (excluding South Africa) was invested in the primary sector compared with 26.5 per cent of FDI in all developing areas, and only a third (32.3 per cent) in the secondary sector compared with 53.2 per cent overall (Cantwell, 1991, p. 188). In practice, TNC investment in manufacturing had a number of disadvantages: restrictive practices often prohibited local subsidiaries from production for export, to prevent them from competing with other subsidiaries of the same TNC; the use of capital-intensive techniques generated relatively few jobs; and the goods produced were often considered to be inappropriate for local markets, using advertising to promote luxury items and imported brand names over local products. Despite increasing insistence on local public or private sector participation, import substitution industrialization did not live up to its promise. It proved to be import intensive, because capital equipment, components, and spare parts had to be imported; quasi-monopolistic behind protective walls and thus inefficient, resistant to reducing protection, and unable to compete in export markets; high cost and thus discriminatory against other economic sectors dependent on it for inputs and a drain on what local capital was available for investment. Policies associated with import substitution industrialization included an overvalued exchange rate, inefficient public ownership, and inappropriate choice of industries and technologies (Chazan et al., 1988). Although increases in manufacturing output and urban employment were recorded for the continent as a whole, economic diversification based on industrialization proved elusive, especially in SSA.

The capital requirements of mineral extraction were clearly beyond indigenous entrepreneurs or most of the smaller African governments and so mining was dominated by TNCs. From its traditional base in South Africa, multinational investment in mining rapidly grew after independence. US-based TNCs, for example, invested in copper in Zaire, bauxite in Guinea and Ghana, iron in Gabon, and copper-nickel in Botswana, increasing the American share in total FDI and challenging the older colonial-based interests, such as copper in Zaire and Zambia (ROAPE, 1975). Soon the disadvantages of TNC operations – repatriation of profits and reluctance to develop in-country processing – were seen to outweigh the supply of capital, technology, and export outlets. The only alternative open to governments appeared to be nationalization, either by expropriation or by acquisition of majority shareholdings. By no means discomfited by such moves, TNCs have maintained a high degree of control by licensing agreements, management contracts, provision of refining and manufacturing facilities, and overseas marketing.

Chazan et al. (1988) argue that SSA's agriculture at independence was relatively healthy. Cash crop production was widespread, in most places it had not been established at the expense of food crops, and there was scope for increased production of both. However, the slow rise in agricultural production combined with rapid population growth turned a food surplus into a deficit by the mid-1970s. Explanations for the poor performance of the agricultural sector were complex: they included environmental constraints, as well as anti-agriculture government policies aimed at extracting surplus as taxes and subsidizing urban food. Exacerbating these were lack of recognition of the strengths of peasant agriculture, leading to disastrous and wasteful experiments with large-scale mechanized state farms, bias in favour of plantation agriculture in research and development, allocation of inputs, and extension, and failure to develop adequate infrastructure (Chazan et al., 1988). Declining per capita food production led to increased dependence on food imports and, even more damagingly, food aid.

Overall, the real value of many significant exports, such as cotton, iron, and cocoa, did not rise as rapidly as that of imported manufactured goods. In addition, reliance on one or two exports rendered countries particularly vulnerable to price fluctuations, for commodities such as copper, and Northern protectionism, for crops such as sugar. The pattern of development in most newly independent countries was regarded as "neo-colonialism," signifying the impossibility of formulating and implementing development policy based on local resources when economic growth depended so heavily on external conditions of demand and foreign capital (Amin, 1971; Williams, 1981; Jamal and Weeks, 1993). Within this overall perspective, however, views differ on both the scope for indigenous industrial development and the extent to which incipient national bourgeosies played and continue to play a comprador role with respect to foreign capitalist interests (Bell, 1986).

Rapid urbanization

At the beginning of the 1960s less than a fifth of Africa's population lived in urban areas (table 2.1). Although the proportion of southern Africa's population that was urban was twice this (42 per cent) and levels of urbanization were also relatively high in North Africa (30 per cent), the remainder of African countries, with few exceptions, had very low levels of urbanization. In East Africa, Somalia and Zambia were relatively highly urbanized, with 17 per cent of their populations in urban areas, while Zimbabwe had 12 per cent, compared with the regional average of 7 per cent and the predominantly rural nature of the two countries with the largest populations in the region, Ethiopia (6 per cent) and Tanzania (5 per cent). In Middle Africa, 31 per cent of Congo's population was urban, nearly double the regional average. In North Africa, levels of urbanization varied from 10 per cent in the Sudan to 38 per cent in Egypt; while, in West Africa, Ghana (with 23 per cent) and Senegal (with 32 per cent) far exceeded the regional average, the latter heavily influenced by the most populous country, Nigeria (14 per cent). Despite the extractive nature of colonial economies, the limited development of manufacturing, and attempts at influx control, however, urban areas had been growing at between 4 per cent and 6 per cent per annum in the 1950s, except in southern Africa.

The rate of urban growth, which had been accelerating prior to the main wave of countries attaining independence, continued to do so. Although rates of natural increase also steadily increased, reaching 2.5 per cent per annum for Africa as a whole in the early 1960s, 2.6 per cent per annum later in the decade, and 2.7 per cent per annum in the early 1970s, the urban growth rate was nearly double this (UN, 1993). The most marked increases in urban growth rates occurred, on the whole, in the least urbanized countries, including those that attained independence without significant urban centres, such as Mauritania (which was previously governed from Senegal) and Rwanda (previously administered from Burundi). In contrast, slower rates of urban growth were experienced in some countries that inherited oversized capitals, for example Congo and Senegal, where Brazzaville and Dakar had been the administrative centres for the whole of French Equatorial and West Africa, respectively

Table 2.1 **Urbanization in Africa**

	1950–55	1955–60	1960–65	1965–70	1970–75	1975–80	1980–85	1985–90	1990–95
% urban at the beginning of period									
Africa	14.5	16.3	18.3	20.6	22.9	25.0	27.3	29.6	32.0
East	5.3	6.3	7.4	8.8	10.3	12.3	14.6	16.9	19.1
Middle	14.2	15.9	17.9	21.1	24.8	26.6	28.2	29.8	31.9
North	24.5	27.1	30.0	33.6	36.2	38.4	40.2	42.1	43.8
South	38.2	40.0	41.9	42.8	43.6	44.1	44.5	45.0	46.2
West	10.2	12.2	14.5	16.9	19.7	22.7	26.0	29.5	33.2
Average annual rate of growth									
Africa	4.55	4.69	4.92	4.75	4.46	4.59	4.54	4.51	4.53
East	5.63	5.79	6.07	6.04	6.05	6.50	5.71	5.55	5.62
Middle	4.11	4.29	5.51	5.68	3.86	3.98	4.07	4.39	4.64
North	4.28	4.35	4.64	4.04	3.58	3.61	3.70	3.42	3.41
South	3.21	3.32	3.00	2.86	3.02	2.89	2.84	3.01	3.22
West	5.85	5.93	5.73	5.77	5.78	5.73	5.64	5.52	5.27

Source: UN (1993), p. 74.

(O'Connor, 1983). In the later 1960s urban growth rates reached 8 per cent per annum or more in Uganda, Tanzania, Zambia, Libya, Botswana, Lesotho, Swaziland, Benin, and Mauritania. By the early 1970s these had been joined by, for example, Kenya, Mozambique, Cameroon, and Gabon. In the eight, mostly francophone, countries of West Africa examined by Zachariah and Condé (1981), almost half the urban growth between the mid-1960s and the mid-1970s came from migration, mostly from the rural areas, but some from smaller urban centres and some international. The anticipated inhibiting effect of urban residence on fertility was outweighed by the relatively young age profile of migrants, the lower mortality rates in urban areas, and the increase in family migration (Standing, 1984; Salau, 1990).

In 1950, there were only two cities in Africa with more than 1 million inhabitants (Cairo and Alexandria). By 1960, Casablanca and Johannesburg had also reached 1 million, while by 1970 there were eight cities of this size – four in north Africa, two in South Africa, and only two elsewhere in the continent: Lagos and Kinshasa, which had grown, insofar as it was possible to tell in the absence of reliable census results, at about 10 per cent per annum consistently throughout the 1950s and 1960s. Other large cities with particularly rapid rates of growth (10+ per cent per annum) in the 1960s and early 1970s included Abidjan, Conakry, and Tripoli, and Dar es Salaam after 1965, along with many of the smaller capital cities. A pattern of increased concentration of rural–urban migration in the largest city within a country was widely evident (Zachariah and Condé, 1981).

Early migration theories suggested that the volume of migration was related to urban–rural income differentials. Faced with continued rapid migration in the face of increasing unemployment and the inability of formal sector job creation to keep up with growth of the urban labour force, the model was modified to consider not only urban wages but also the probability of obtaining a formal sector job. This theory underlay the belief that urban bias in investment and policy, backed by a politically powerful élite and wage labour force paid above market wages, discriminated against agriculture and rural areas, thus encouraging out-migration (Lipton, 1977). The assumptions underlying these theories have been subjected to serious criticism by Jamal and Weeks (1993), amongst others.

Migration is an extremely complex process, comprising a variety of different patterns of migration movement (see chap. 13) and influenced by underlying structural causes, immediate explanations for household and individual behaviour, and the presence of facilitating conditions. Any explanation of the rapid rates of urbanization and urban growth observed in African countries must take into account a wide range of structural factors. Incorporation of the African peasantry into the national and international economy started in the mercantilist era, was consolidated in the colonial era, and was desired both by governments reliant on extracting foreign exchange and revenue from cash crop exports and food for their urban populations from food crop surpluses and by farmers, who had become used to and dependent on cash purchases. The role of subsistence agriculture in meeting part of the costs of reproduction, as a way of maintaining low wages for colonial enterprises, has already been mentioned. As long as migrants retain rural ties, they can remain permanently in the urban areas, but the effect, it is suggested, is to withdraw surplus from the rural economy to maintain the urban labour force. Eventually the effect is to reduce rural incomes to the point that out-migration occurs despite a lack of urban opportunities (Standing, 1984). In some areas, population growth and environmental deterioration placed pressure on land and other means of production, while increasing life expectancy and larger families reduced the prospects of access to land. Although migration was not the only response, it was a common one (Gugler and Flanagan, 1978; Standing, 1984). While there are examples of unemployment rates being decreased by out-migration, it may also have an impact on the productivity of the household unit, forcing other members to enter the wage labour market and even creating a labour shortage (Standing, 1985). An example of the latter is amongst the Mossi in Burkina Faso, where out-migration to the Côte d'Ivoire and Ghana forced all adults to work in collective fields, with the result that individual fields, weaving cloth, and capital formation such as the digging of wells were neglected (Gregory and Piché, 1982). In some areas, commercialization of agriculture and changes to tenure led to increased differentiation and landlessness, although this was not widespread in the years under discussion (Oberai and Bilsborrow, 1984). Elsewhere the rural economy broke down because of civil strife, for example in Zaire, where the urban population rose from 1.2 million in 1955 to nearly 6 million in 1975, while numbers in Kinshasa rose by 350,000 to 1.7 million (O'Connor, 1983; see chap. 7). Finally, it was suggested that government policies reduced producer prices in the interests of exports and cheap urban food, reducing the returns to agriculture.

All cities yield economies of agglomeration for secondary and tertiary economic activities, producing growth and increased concentration in the largest cities, as illustrated in the continued growth of already well-established cities in the continent. In African countries, a number of changes associated with independence in the 1950s and 1960s increased the attraction of cities. The growth of civil services, attempts to industrialize, and the abandonment of remaining relics of influx control gave a boost to rural–urban migration. The centralization of politics and bureacracy formed a further attraction to investors who needed access to the state machinery. The process of decolonization resulted in the emergence of many new states, each generating a new or enlarged national bureaucracy. Thus the former colony of French West Africa, for example, was dissolved into eight new states (Standing, 1984). What urban centres there were became the locus of power and investment and new states invested heavily in infrastructure and amenities in their capitals because of their international and national visibility (Gugler and Flanagan, 1978; Mehretu, 1983; Skinner, 1986). The creation of additional subnational units (states) in Nigeria gave rise to a further impetus to develop state capitals, while construction of the first of the new capitals was started in this period. Nigerian National Development Plans in the 1970s, for example, devoted over 80 per cent of non-agricultural public capital investment to urban areas (Salau, 1990, p. 163). The exploitation of new resources led to new growth in cities such as Port Harcourt, centre of Nigeria's oil industry, while other mining centres declined in relative terms, for example in Zaire and Zambia (Rakodi, 1992a).

Both Todaro's migration model (1994, p. 268) and the belief that urban bias accounts for the perpetuation of poverty rest on the concept of a labour aristocracy, paid above-market wages in a substantial formal sector. In some countries, for example Kenya, Zimbabwe, Zambia, Morocco, and Tunisia, the large-scale sector dominated urban employment and the availability of wage jobs attracted migrants. In others, however, small and intermediate enterprise accounted for a large proportion of urban employment even at independence, for example Kumasi with 60 per cent and Accra with 45 per cent in 1960, Kaduna with 44 per cent in 1967, Abidjan with 44 per cent and Brazzaville with 37 per cent in 1974 (O'Connor, 1983, p. 143). In addition, despite the concentration of a large proportion of all manufacturing in countries' capital cities (one-third in Accra and Lagos, half in Conakry, two-thirds in Abidjan, three-quarters in Freetown, 87 per cent in Dakar, and 100 per cent in Banjul and

Monrovia – O'Connor, 1983), the empirical evidence that wages were higher and employment more secure than in the informal sector was said to be scarce (O'Connor, 1991; Jamal and Weeks, 1993). Where colonial labour policies had resulted in an urban age–sex structure dominated by men of working age, the trend toward convergence with national age–sex structures that had begun with labour stabilization policies 20 or more years before intensified, as increasing numbers of women either joined their husbands in the cities or migrated in their own right. In South Africa, however, apartheid policies and the use of migrant labour from surrounding countries maintained a relatively slow rate of urban growth and a gender imbalance. A secondary attraction in some places was the better access to social and educational facilities available in town, while transport improvements and greater awareness of opportunities because of better access to education and the media facilitated the process. Remittances by urban migrants to rural areas were significant and complicated the relatively simple picture portrayed by Todaro (1994, p. 268) and Lipton (1977).

The inherited philosophy, legal and financial basis, and institutional system for planning and managing urban development changed only incrementally in most countries in the early years after independence. The balance between continuity and change, Simon (1992) suggests, was influenced by the nature of the anti-colonial struggle; the fate of the ex-colonial élite; the policies pursued by the new élite with respect to national integration and relations with the world economy; national modes of production and means of social reproduction; and the extent to which urban legislative change was instituted. Governments were preoccupied with national political and economic issues and generally paid relatively little attention to urban administration. Where centralized structures existed, these persisted, especially in francophone Africa (Stren, 1989a). Where urban local government on the British model had been established, apart from a rapidly enlarged franchise at independence, it was retained more or less intact. However, the scope of urban local government functions was reduced before independence in some cases by the establishment of separate statutory bodies. In other cases, previously local functions were taken on by central government after independence for ideological and practical reasons, particularly education and the police (Rakodi, 1986a). The potential contradiction inherent in central–local government relations led to the erosion of local government autonomy in most post-colonial societies (although the extent to which this occurred and the form it took varied between and even within countries). This erosion was exacerbated by the lack of administrative capacity at the local level. The inherited British ideology of impartial officials guided by notions of technical rationality, advising elected councillors who viewed the exercise of power as a moral non-political activity – a poor description of the authoritarian and self-interested reality even in colonial times – was particularly inappropriate in a post-independence situation in which political office was used to fulfil traditional social obligations, further personal interests, and increase popular support and power bases (Rakodi, 1986b).

Local institutional systems were designed to facilitate accumulation by capital, much of which was in foreign hands, by ensuring an environment conducive to business and the maintenance of lifestyles for European residents. This was achieved by infrastructure provision; by land-use planning in the parts of the settlement used for trade, administration, and European residence (and sometimes manufacturing); and also, in many settlements, by the public sector provision of housing for African residents. The urban spatial structure and built environment that resulted reflected the underlying ideology of separate development, based on racially segregated residential areas and radically different standards of service provision and construction. The imported land administration system survived independence, but the speed of urban growth far outpaced its capacity to cope, and the years after independence were marked by a proliferation of unauthorized residential development. The problems arising from the superimposition of an imported system on indigenous tenure systems, its role in producing the segregated colonial built environment, its considerable administrative and skill requirements, and its function as one of the main bases for local revenue generation, were not resolved. The system of private individualized land tenure, with the opportunities it presented for accumulation, was extended on independence to many more indigenous urban residents, entrenching their interest in maintaining and extending private property ownership. These issues are taken up and analysed in more detail in chapter 11.

The extension of unauthorized development, central government expenditure constraints, and the lack of a buoyant local revenue base together resulted in infrastructure provision and maintenance falling further and further behind demand. Even where inherited administrative structures were changed after independence, as, for example, in the nationalization of the British private monopoly company that ran the public transport system in Dar es Salaam, the change more often led to a deterioration than to an improvement in services. The philosophy underlying colonial housing policy in some countries, that of providing housing for temporary urban residents (Africans and, in many countries, Europeans too), which had led to a system of contractor-built tied subsidized rental housing, was apparently not reconsidered. Most post-independence housing policies were based on similar assumptions; they proved to a greater or lesser extent unable to keep pace with the housing needs of the growing urban population and rapidly gave rise to vested interests in their continuation (Rakodi, 1986a; Stren, 1989b). In the countries where pre-colonial settlements existed, and elsewhere, the public sector had much less of a role, and private sector construction was relied upon to a greater extent to provide houses for low-income residents, for example in Zaire, Uganda, the Sudan, and Nigeria until the mid-1970s (Stren, 1989b). In these, as in the former cases, the continuation of spatial planning as a technical/regulatory activity undertaken by a section of the bureaucratic élite and/or foreign consultants and the failure to reconsider land administration meant that a large proportion of urban development occurred without reference to any guiding framework. Resources that were available for investment in infrastructure, service provision, and regulatory activities, to produce basic environmental standards for all urban residents rather than high standards for a few, were not used to best effect.

Global forces in the past two decades of African development

It has been important to sketch the history of African globalization because the impress of mercantilist trade and above all of colonial control left an enduring political, economic, and spatial legacy which not only determined countries' room to manoeuvre on their attainment of independence but also, as seen in the recent history of the continent, is far from spent. The global forces that impact upon African countries and cities today have their origins in the historical relationship between the continent and the world economic system. However, the character of globalization has continued to evolve and its differential effects have become more marked. In this section we will explore how Africa is situated with respect to these global economic forces, before concluding the chapter with a more detailed examination of their implications for urban development and urban management.

Trade

The nature of Africa's continued integration into the world trading system was revealed by a number of incidents and trends in the 1970s, above all the deteriorating terms of trade for primary commodities and the oil price increases of 1973/74 and 1979. In 1965, 93 per cent of SSA's merchandise exports were primary commodities. By 1990, this was unchanged, although the range of primary products from which export earnings were derived had changed (see also Adedeji, 1993; Husain, 1993): 91 per cent of export earnings were still from primary products, although fuels, metals, and minerals accounted for two-thirds of this compared with a quarter in 1965. Unlike low- and middle-income countries elsewhere in the world, therefore, which had increased the share of manufacturing in their export earnings from 26 per cent to 50 per cent, and had increased their share of world trade, Africa remained marginal to the world trade system. Africa's marginal position was not, as often implied by the IMF, for want of effort – export volumes from SSA grew at 6.1 per cent per annum between 1965 and 1980 and 0.2 per cent per annum in the 1980s (World Bank, 1992) and from Africa as a whole by 1.9 per cent per annum between 1971 and 1993 (IMF, 1993, p. 70) – but because demand for primary commodities has weakened in developed countries. Because of deteriorating terms of trade, the volume of imports that can be purchased with the earnings has decreased. Even the IMF admits that the terms of trade for African countries as a whole deteriorated in six out of the eight years between 1984 and 1992 (IMF, 1993).

Imports to SSA countries were, inevitably, dominated by manufactured goods in 1965 (76 per cent), much as imports of low- and middle-income countries as a whole were (66 per cent) and this continued to be the case in 1990. However, despite Africa's position as an exporter of agricultural products, food continues to constitute 16 per cent of imports (World Bank, 1992). Exports grew at a faster rate (6.1 per cent per annum) than imports (5.6 per cent per annum) between 1965 and 1980, but during the 1980s, while exports continued to grow slowly, imports fell by −4.3 per cent per annum (World Bank, 1992). The slow growth of export earnings resulted in reduced capacity to import and this in turn resulted in under-utilization of manufacturing capacity and constraints on economic growth and economic diversification throughout the later 1970s and 1980s, with adverse effects on urban employment opportunities (IMF, 1993).

Perhaps the most crucial incidents affecting Africa's trading position have been associated with oil prices. The fourfold increase in oil prices in 1973/74 and further increases in the later 1970s, which resulted in an overall real price increase of over threefold between 1973 and 1980, had differential effects: the terms of trade of the only high-income oil-exporting country, Libya, improved by 241 per cent in the seven years after 1973 and those of the other oil exporters (including Algeria, Egypt, Nigeria, and Cameroon) by 195 per cent, whereas those of the great majority of countries, which were oil importers, declined to 85 per cent of 1973 levels (Nafziger, 1990, p. 52). The immediate impact on transport, energy, and agriculture forced countries to borrow to foot the increase in import bills. At the time, the massive influx of petrodollars into the world financial system was resulting in negative real interest rates and the strategy seemed both necessary and rational.

The OPEC countries used about three-quarters of the oil revenue for imports, but were also determined to use the wealth to finance their own industrialization, again with differential results. Libya increased its manufacturing production from 3 per cent of GDP in 1965 by 13.7 per cent per annum in the following 15 years (World Bank, 1992). The Middle Eastern countries had insufficient indigenous labour for industry and construction and so imported between 40 and 85 per cent of their labour forces, mostly from the Indian subcontinent, parts of East Asia, and North Africa. Remittances constituted a major flow of capital, much of which was invested in urban property. In 1986, for example, workers' remittances were equivalent to over half the earnings from merchandise exports in Morocco and Egpyt (Nafziger, 1990, p. 360), or 6.0 per cent and 13.1 per cent of GNP in 1989, respectively, as well as 3.7 per cent of GNP in the Sudan and 4.8 per cent in Tunisia (UNDP, 1992). Significant impacts on urban property markets followed (see also chaps. 4 and 11). However, these flows proved vulnerable when later oil price falls and world recession led to labour shedding.

Nigeria benefited from increased oil prices and its economy grew by 7.0 per cent per annum between 1965 and 1975. The boom, however, stimulated extravagant investment and the use of the state machinery by the élite, civil servants, and intermediaries for foreign capital to further their own interests. The naira was allowed to appreciate, leading to a decline in the volume and relative significance of agricultural exports, so that, when the oil-based boom came to an end at the end of the 1970s, not only did Nigeria have little other than increased inequalities, increased concentration of activity in the south of the country including Lagos (see chap. 6), and wasteful prestige projects to show for it, but also alternative sources of export earnings had not been developed. As a result, Nigeria rapidly entered the slow-growth group of economies and its GDP actually fell by 2.5 per cent per annum between 1975 and 1986. Cameroon, although a smaller producer, was equally dependent on oil exports. Better-managed economic policies, however, enabled it to avoid the worst effects of the oil price falls (Nafziger, 1990).

Debt

For the majority of African countries, their additional borrowing in 1973/74 was to have adverse effects in the longer term, because real interest rate increases coincided with yet higher oil prices at the end of the decade, producing the debt crisis of the early 1980s. By world standards, Africa is not a major borrower. By 1986, Egypt was the seventh-largest debtor country, Nigeria the fourteenth, and Algeria the eighteenth amongst less-developed countries (LDCs), with the Côte d'Ivoire not far behind (Nafziger, 1990). A few countries, including Nigeria, Gabon, and the Congo, have been the main commercial borrowers, mainly for oil exploitation. Another reason for borrowing has been to cover current account deficits (which for Africa as a whole averaged between 4.5 and 5.4 per cent of GDP between 1985 and 1988, although they have, under IMF and World Bank pressure, been steadily reduced since then, to 3.5 per cent of GDP in 1992 – IMF, 1993, p. 154).

By 1992, Africa's debt : GDP ratio was over 70 per cent and its debt : export ratio over 400 per cent. Its debt service ratio had, as a result, doubled as a proportion of GDP from 2 per cent in 1980/81 to 4.5 per cent in 1990/91, and repayments consistently absorbed 25 per cent of export earnings between 1985 and 1992, even though 67 per cent of the debt in 1992 (excluding IMF loans) was owed to official, mostly bilateral, concessional creditors and only 33 per cent to commercial lenders. In SSA, official debt formed an even larger proportion of the debt overhang (78 per cent) and commercial bank debt (13 per cent) was even less significant (IMF, 1993, p. 187; see also Husain, 1993). The burdensome nature of this debt to the countries concerned is illustrated by comparing SSA, which had outstanding debt equal to 324 per cent of exports of goods and services and 109 per cent of GNP in 1990, with East Asia and the Pacific (91 per cent and 27 per cent, respectively) or Latin America and the Caribbean (257 per cent and 42 per cent) (World Bank, 1992).

Africa's indebtedness is variously a result of necessity, extravagance, and the opportunities offered, as noted above, by its strategic importance. In the poorest countries, heavy reliance on aid has been unavoidable. However, much of the money has been squandered, especially in countries such as Zaire, Ghana, and Nigeria (Nafziger, 1990). Growing aid dependence and its implications will be discussed below. Most African countries have not been able to borrow at all extensively from commercial banks since the early 1980s, because they have been unable to repay debts incurred earlier. The extent to which the continent's earlier share of FDI has been maintained since the mid-1980s will be examined in the next section.

Foreign direct investment

On average over 95 per cent of investment in any developing country is financed from domestic savings (IMF, 1993). As discussed above, however, FDI is sought for its anticipated advantages in giving access to technology and export markets (Jenkins, 1987). Much has been concentrated in a small number of countries with large domestic markets, rich natural resources, or advantages as a base for export-oriented production. In 1975, 19 per cent of the world's stock of FDI was in LDCs. By 1982, the proportion of global FDI that was in LDCs had increased to 24 per cent but Africa's share of it had decreased from 21 per cent to 11 per cent (Cantwell, 1991, pp. 187–189). Its share of new FDI was even less (Cantwell, 1991). The IMF acknowledged that, even when the smaller, resource-poor African countries offered substantial incentives and imposed few restrictions, they were unsuccessful in attracting investment (IMF, 1985, p. 4). Thus between 1976 and 1986 significant net inflows occurred to only half a dozen countries. Most countries experienced net disinvestment, not least because of the effects of structural adjustment (see below; Cockcroft, 1992, p. 337).

The sectoral composition of worldwide FDI changed over the period, initially away from oil, mining, and agriculture to manufacturing. Nationalizations and the effect of policies to restrict entry of new foreign capital lessened TNC interest even in oil and mining in Africa (IMF, 1985; UNCTC, 1991). Nevertheless by the early 1980s half the total stock of FDI was still in the extractive sectors, compared with about 20 per cent in non-African LDCs, and almost 40 per cent of foreign-owned primary commodity enterprises, concentrated in oil extraction and the mining of copper, iron, bauxite, and uranium, were in Africa. To the extent that FDI occurred in manufacturing (about a quarter of the stock in Africa by the beginning of the 1980s compared with half in Asia and over half in Latin America), it has been in import substitution and resource-processing industries in the larger, more developed economies and so has been of only limited importance to urban economies (Cantwell, 1991).

Between 1983 and 1989, FDI outflows worldwide increased 29 per cent per annum, as the global economy recovered from the early 1980s' recession, although the share of LDCs in this investment fell to about a fifth (UNCTC, 1991). The destination for over three-quarters of these flows continued to be 10 countries, of which only Egypt was in Africa. Although Africa's share of worldwide FDI remained stable, at just over 2 per cent throughout the 1980s, and its share of FDI in LDCs increased slightly in the second half of the decade, the volume of investment was minute by world standards and concentrated on oil-related investment in Egypt and Nigeria (UNCTC, 1991). Low-technology, low-value-added import substitution (IS) industries continued to dominate most countries' industrial structure, yielding lower rates of return to foreign investors than manufacturing elsewhere in the world (Bennell, 1990). Only a tiny share of investment originating in Japan and the United States goes to Africa. Most FDI in the continent originates in the former colonial powers (UNCTC, 1985), although Bennell concludes that, for British industrial capital as a whole, Africa is now of only marginal and decreasing interest (Bennell, 1990).

FDI in manufacturing worldwide has continued to grow over the past 10 years. However, a further sectoral shift, which had started in the 1970s, gathered pace in the 1980s. Services FDI, including business and financial services, trade, tourism, and construction, grew to comprise over half of all annual flows of FDI and 40 per cent of FDI stock worldwide. Intermediate services, such as financial, business, and professional services, and those competing for the discretionary income of consumers, are concentrated in developed countries, whereas FDI in services in LDCs traditionally concentrated in trade and construction, and has more recently diversified into tourism and banking, especially in those countries offering "tax haven" facilities (UNCTC, 1989). Recent growth in FDI in services in Africa has been concentrated once again in a few countries (Egypt, Morocco, Nigeria) and in the traditional areas of trade and construction, rather than the financial services sector, which has been so important globally. However, a very high proportion of the tiny but growing Japanese investment is in trade and financial services (UNCTC, 1989). Although Africa has shared in the increased global flows of investment in services, as with manufacturing its position is marginal.

Development in Africa has been held back not only by limited flows of FDI but also by low levels of domestic savings and investment, which fell from 27 per cent of GDP between 1971 and 1975 and 30 per cent between 1975 and 1981 to 21–22 per cent in the 1980s and early 1990s (IMF, 1993; see also Husain, 1993). Reinforcing the shortage of capital for investment, FDI has had a negative effect on the balance of payments: outflows of dividends, royalties, management fees, etc. exceed inflows of new investment and are financed from commodity exports, while the investment in manufacturing is generally for the domestic market and absorbs rather than earns foreign exchange (Cockcroft, 1992). The limited volume of FDI in manufacturing has exacerbated the difficulties experienced by African countries in generating sufficient wage jobs for growing urban labour forces.

Aid dependence

External and internal shocks, a general deterioration in the terms of trade for many of Africa's most important products, and economic mismanagement have, as we have seen, led to a continued need for foreign exchange, which is not satisfied by earnings from exports, commercial bank borrowing, or FDI. As a result, Africa became the largest recipient region of Official Development Assistance (ODA) by the 1980s, accounting for 43 per cent of all bilateral and multilateral development assistance by 1990 (12 per cent to north Africa and 30 per cent to SSA) (Simon, 1995). Aid receipts as a percentage of GNP were 9.6 per cent for SSA as a whole in 1990 or US$34 per capita. The poorest and most aid-dependent countries were Mozambique, its economy wrecked by civil war, in which 66 per cent of GNP in 1990 came from aid (US$60/head), Tanzania (48 per cent of GNP, US$47/head), and Somalia (46 per cent of GNP, US$55/head). Although other countries were less aid dependent, in several between a fifth and a third of GNP came from aid. The recipients of the largest volume of aid per capita, however, were not the poorest countries: the level in Mozambique was exceeded by four other countries, none among the poorest (Egypt US$108/head, Mauritania US$107/head,

Senegal US$100/head, and the Congo US$92/head) and that in Tanzania by a further four, with relatively rich countries such as Morocco and Tunisia not far behind (US$39/head) (World Bank, 1992). Aid receipts, clearly, are related to factors other than need. It should also be noted that, whereas net credits from the IMF were positive in the early 1980s, they were negative later in the decade (Bird, 1993; ODI, 1993).

The reliance of African countries on aid has rendered them vulnerable to policy conditionality, both by the multilateral agencies, which supplied just under one-third of ODA to SSA during the 1980s (although a much smaller proportion to north African countries), and, in their wake, by the bilateral donors, especially the United States. Policy conditions have affected both general economic management and approaches to urban development. The latter will be considered in the next section.

The difficulties caused for African countries by the external shocks of the 1970s and early 1980s (oil price increases, world recession, and increased interest rates) were initially seen as temporary trade crises and tackled by IMF stabilization packages. However, endogenous shocks (drought, civil strife) and economic mismanagement combined with external vulnerability showed that the economic crisis had deeper roots, resulting in the addition of structural and sectoral adjustment programmes to the stabilization programmes. By the end of the 1980s, 30 African countries had adopted structural adjustment policies, many implementing a succession of programmes. Only a few small countries had no IMF/World Bank programmes and several had introduced some kind of "home grown" programme (Jesperson, 1992). As a result, 29 per cent of IMF commitments by value were to SSA countries in April 1989 (ODI, 1993, p. 2).

The Structural Adjustment Programmes (SAPs) adopted by most countries comprised three basic components:
(1) "[A] reform of the system of economic incentives with the objective of changing the structure of incentives in favor of tradeables versus nontradeables, accompanied by measures to liberalize economies so that factors of production can seek their highest returns" (Seralgeldin, 1989, p. 5). Thus the strategies advocated are typically export led, aiming above all to increase export earnings in order to foster economic growth and enable the repayment of outstanding debt. The main macroeconomic policies urged on countries are:

- devaluation, to encourage exports and discourage imports;
- trade liberalization, by removing controls on imports, foreign exchange, and foreign investment;
- price decontrol, to remove distortions that discriminate against export sectors and agriculture and protect inefficient industry. This includes decontrol of the price of labour. The intention is to increase the efficiency of industry by ensuring appropriate prices for the factors of production and by shedding labour where overmanning has occurred, thus enhancing domestic and export competitiveness. In addition, price subsidies are to be removed, *inter alia* to remove the bias in favour of urban consumers;
- strict control of money supply and credit expansion, by increasing real interest rates. The latter is also intended to fight inflation, promote saving, and allocate investment capital to the highest bidders;
- tax reform to replace taxes on production with taxes on consumption and value added.

(2) "[S]treamlining the public sector ... while directing scarce public financial resources toward the provision of basic infrastructure; supporting vital economic services; and developing human resources ... and freeing of domestic resources for private sector investment and production" (Seralgeldin, 1989, p. 5). This is to be achieved by:

- reduction of public expenditure. Although the World Bank holds that this can be achieved by improving revenue generation, in practice streamlining of the civil service is required, based on reducing the number of civil servants employed and freezing wages;
- privatization of government enterprises and parastatals, to reduce the size of the public sector and increase efficiency;
- reorientation of public sector investment towards fostering productive sectors, especially agriculture, and providing basic services in education and health. In a climate of general expenditure cutbacks, the provision of basic services is to be accompanied by the introduction or raising of user charges and the removal of subsidies.

(3) "[A] comprehensive restructuring of external debt with the objective of relieving the resource constraint" (Seralgeldin, 1989, p. 5); restructuring debt (rather than writing it off, although

some write-offs may be negotiated) and improving repayment are intended to encourage new flows of aid and commercial investment.

To achieve these aims, macroeconomic policies aimed at removing distortions in markets are needed, in particular to favour trade, as well as sectoral policies to encourage the development of productive sectors and resources, and policies to improve resource mobilization, both private investment (domestic and foreign) and public resources, by a balance between improved revenue generation and public expenditure cut-backs. By the end of the 1980s, the Bank's emphasis had shifted from stabilization and growth to place rather more emphasis on equity, stressing the need for programmes to foster the participation of the poor in the process of economic growth, by improving their access to jobs, income-generating assets, and basic services, and to "provide for action programs to avoid social distress in the short term" (Seralgeldin, 1989, p. 7). The latter, generally termed the "social aspects of adjustment," are compensatory transitional provisions to protect vulnerable groups' access to services and to compensate redundant workers and enable them to make a new start (Ribe et al., 1990). SAPs have continued to evolve in response to both donor and country experience and the negotiations between them as programmes are extended (Green and Faber, 1994).

Despite the difficult circumstances in which, it is acknowledged, most countries have adopted and pursued SAPs (fluctuating and/or declining terms of trade, high real interest rates exacerbating the debt burden, and droughts), Seralgeldin detected a number of positive experiences in the first two-thirds of the 1980s. Between 1980 and 1985, in 20 countries relatively little affected by unusual weather or external shocks, World Bank figures suggested that real GDP growth rates (allowing for inflation and population growth) of 1.5 per cent per annum on average were experienced. However, in 1986/87, GDP growth more than doubled to about 4 per cent per annum in countries that were considered to have had sustained adjustment programmes, whereas it fell by half in non-adjusting countries. In addition, in adjusting countries inflation and the fiscal deficit are said to have been reduced, and real interest rates to have become positive (Seralgeldin, 1989, pp. 3–4).

Not all assessments are so positive, and some reach contrary conclusions. Mosley and Weeks (1993) concluded that, contrary to World Bank assertions, Africa as a whole did not recover after 1985, although there was some improvement for some countries; countries with Bank-supported structural adjustment did no better than those without; and "there may have been no significant difference between the economic performances of 'strong' and 'weak' adjusters that can be attributed to structural adjustment packages" (p. 1588). Difficulties in assessing the outcomes arise from methodological problems, differences in definitions, and disagreement over the relative roles of domestic policy reform and exogenous shocks or the effects of war and civil disorder (Green, 1993). As a result, adjustment measures have not been disaggregated and assessed in a way that is useful to improving policy. In partial recognition of these and other criticisms, the World Bank's most recent assessment (World Bank, 1994) is more measured in its conclusions.[1] It notes that there has been more progress with liberalizing trade than with reforms in the agricultural, financial, and public sectors, and, although it acknowledges external constraints on achieving economic growth, it attributes growth in per capita GDP, exports, and industrial and agricultural production in those countries that have achieved these primarily to far-reaching and consistent domestic policy reforms (see also O'Brien, 1994).

Killick, however, in an assessment of the outcome of IMF programmes, concludes that the effects of Fund programmes and their ability to influence macroeconomic policy (with the exception of exchange rates) are overrated. High programme failure rates and lack of clear evidence that objectives are being achieved throw doubt on the Fund's ability to operate in low-income countries. Although the programmes have, he acknowledges, raised awareness amongst some governments of the importance of financial discipline, the increased inflow of private capital expected to result has not, as noted above, materialized (Killick with Malik, 1992; ODI, 1993). Riddell (1992), Stewart et al. (1992), and Jesperson (1992) are even more critical:

Broadly speaking, stabilisation achieved positive but modest results in Sub-Saharan Africa in the 1980s ... [but] [w]ith few exceptions, stabilisation was accompanied by sharp losses in GDP growth, investment and human capital development ... The belt-tightening undertaken by most African countries would perhaps have been acceptable if adjustment had triggered the desired changes in economic structures and eventually led to expansion in food production, manufacturing activities and non-traditional exports. However, from this perspective also, the improvements realised in the 1980s were not satisfactory, despite profound reforms in privatisation, the liberalisation of prices and foreign trade and the mobilisation of external resources. (Jesperson, 1992, p. 14).

An analysis of 24 countries that initiated adjustment programmes in the 1980s showed that:

   (i) capital accumulation slowed in 20 of the countries, owing to low rates of public and private (domestic and foreign) investment;

 (ii) the share of manufacturing in GDP increased in only 6 of the countries (in 10, industrial output declined and in a further 9 it stagnated or grew very slowly; Stewart et al., 1992);

(iii) export volumes increased in only 11 countries, although even in these countries "the impact on the balance of payments was almost always negligible because of the fall in the export prices of primary commodities" (Jesperson, 1992, p. 14). In the other 13 countries, export volumes stagnated or diminished.

Overall, in SSA in the 1980s, only 12 countries (representing less than a fifth of the region's population) recorded positive rates of growth of per capita GDP. Per capita GDP fell in the remaining 21 countries, including many that had achieved growth in the previous 15 years (see also Stewart, 1991; Helleiner, 1992; Stoneman, 1993). Even including the more buoyant economies of north Africa, IMF figures show that, whereas real GDP growth was positive between 1973 and 1992 (increasing at about 3 per cent per annum in the 1970s and 2 per cent per annum in the 1980s), *per capita* real GDP was stagnant or negative in seven out of the eight years between 1983 and 1990 (Bird, 1993). There was little change in the overall picture in the first half of the 1990s. These conclusions conceal marked variations in implementation and outcomes, which themselves need careful explanations related to political and institutional as well as economic factors (Harvey, 1993).

SAPs have also had uneven impacts on economic groups within countries. It was hoped, for example, that increased producer prices and reduced food and services subsidies would benefit rural populations, especially small farmers, redressing the perceived anti-agriculture and anti-rural bias in government policy. In practice, these impacts have been more complex than anticipated by the multilateral agencies and in many cases strongly negative, despite half-hearted compensatory programmes and lip-service paid to integrating anti-poverty measures into SAPs (Gibbon, 1992). Many of the impacts have affected urban populations in particular and will be analysed in more detail below. An even more recent aspect of policy conditionality has been the association of political liberalization with economic reform. However, as has been shown in ODI (1994) and Simon (1995), the relationship between type of political system and economic policy is complex and the nature and significance of democratization imperfectly understood in either theoretical or practical terms.

Although policy reform was needed in African countries, their increased dependence on external assistance in the 1980s made them susceptible to uniform policy prescriptions, determined, despite apparent opportunities for negotiation, largely by outside agencies. Although the donors claim that there is now evidence of improved macroeconomic performance as a result, few others are convinced. Instead, the policy formulation hegemony of the colonial powers to which Africa was subjected in the first half of the twentieth century seems to have been substituted by a new hegemony which no less clearly has the interests of transnational capital and northern countries at heart (Biel, 1994). Such a hegemony, it is argued, is illustrated by the lack of influence of alternative agendas for reform, such as that of the UN Economic Commission for Africa (UNECA, 1989; Stewart et al., 1992; Parfitt, 1993; Simon, 1995).

Urban change and urban management

What, in the context of Africa's external dependence and vulnerability, marginalization and aid dependence, has happened to cities? What effects has the economic deterioration precipitated by the first oil price increases and reinforced by subsequent exogenous and endogenous forces had on the rate of urbanization, on the economic structure of cities, and on urban management? In the first part of this section, urban trends will be related to the internationalization of capital and their manifestation in Africa will be explored. Aid dependence, and especially the implementation of SAPs, have had particular implications for urban populations, in terms of both incomes and access to jobs and services. Finally, the donors, especially the UN, the World Bank, and the United States Agency for International Development (USAID), have adopted a series of policies related to lending for urban development which reveal congruences and contradictions with their wider policy stances.

Global cities and urbanization in Africa

One of the manifestations of the internationalization of capital has been the emergence of a hierarchy of cities with particular roles in the capitalist economic system. At the apex of the system are the so-called "world cities," sites for the control and management of TNC operations, specialized business services to back these up, and nodes in the world banking and commercial system (Friedmann and Wolff, 1982; Sassen-Koob, 1985; Thrift, 1987; Sassen, 1994). Second to these global cities are regional or continental cities, which perform similar functions within the world capitalist system to global cities, but within a more restricted geographical region (Sit, 1993). LDC cities of most obvious regional significance are those in the newly industrialized countries (NICs), which are increasingly integrated into functional networks of economic linkages with global or core cities, especially in Asia, where TNC headquarters and R&D functions remain in Tokyo but investment occurs in a regional network of cities in East and South-East Asia. Within these regional networks, "growth triangles" have been identified based on complementarities across national boundaries and urban corridors based on mega-cities (Yeung and Lo, 1996). At the third level in the hierarchy are national cities, which are foci for national accumulation but also provide a location for transnational offices and operations, banks, and corporate services, and are thus linked into the world economic system (Sit, 1993; Simon, 1992, 1993).

Not unexpectedly, as Simon shows in earlier work (1992, 1993) and in chapter 3, given Africa's marginality to the world economic system, none of the world cities is located in the continent, although Cairo, Nairobi, and increasingly Johannesburg have regional roles. Africa is not even part of the semi-periphery, and the functional city systems linked across national borders that have begun to emerge in Asia are not evident in Africa except insofar as cities in the interior must use ports in other countries for trade. Most large African cities are centres of national economies, although they are connected to the world economy through the unequal trade, investment, and aid relationships analysed above.

Despite its marginal position in the world economy and the economic difficulties experienced more or less consistently since the mid-1970s, urbanization has continued (table 2.1). By 1990 it was estimated that a third of Africa's population was urban compared with a quarter in 1975. The rate of urban growth was about the same in the 1980s, it was suggested, as in the post-independence decade, running at just under 5 per cent per annum. As in the earlier period, rates of growth in the least urbanized regions (east and west Africa) were above the average for the continent as a whole, while those in the most urbanized regions (south and north Africa) were below (UN,

1993). However, there are major difficulties with these figures: of the 53 countries included, only two-thirds had had a census since 1980 (14 in the early 1980s and 17 since 1985); figures for 19 were based on censuses carried out in the 1970s and 3 in the 1960s. Not only the recency but also the reliability of the figures varies widely: of the five largest countries (20 million+ in 1980), only three have had reasonably recent semi-reliable censuses (Ethiopia, South Africa, and Egypt[2]), while Zaire appears to have had only one (1984) and Nigeria's last reliable one was in 1963, because there are some doubts even about the most recent (1991) census: these latter two countries account, on 1980 estimates, for 22 per cent of the continent's total population and 23 per cent of its urban population.

The inability of so many African countries to carry out regular and reliable censuses is a symptom of their poverty and under-development, as well as of civil war and political instability. Much of the data on recent urbanization trends is, therefore, unreliable and many of the apparently precise figures are mere estimates, based on extrapolations of earlier trends. This is a theme that is developed in more detail by Simon and taken up again in later chapters, especially chapter 13. In addition, given the series of exogenous and endoge-nous shocks that have affected the development of most African countries, it is risky to make assumptions based on previous patterns.

By 1970 there were eight cities of 1 million+ in Africa, and by 1990 there were estimated to be 24, in 18 countries (UN, 1993). So far, the number of very large cities is limited. The emergence of Cairo in Egypt, as elaborated upon by Yousry and Aboul Atta in chapter 5, owes much to the country's geography (the limited stock of fertile, watered agricultural land, the significance of the Nile as a source of water and transport route), as well as to its long urban history and the economies of agglomeration which operate in any major city (Ron-dinelli, 1988). However, efforts to encourage urban and industrial growth elsewhere, especially in Alexandria and also to some extent in the new towns, have borne some fruit and the proportion of Egypt's urban population that lives in Cairo is expected to decline from a peak of 39 per cent in 1980 to 34 per cent by 2000. Lagos has never been as dominant in Nigeria as Cairo has in Egypt. It accounted for only 8.5 per cent of Nigeria's urban population in 1950, but has increased its dominance in succeeding decades and now is estimated to accommodate a fifth of the country's urban population (UN, 1993). From its colonial origins as a port and administrative centre, a history of concentrated public and private sector investment underlain by poor communications with the rest of the country, political and administrative dominance combined with a politics of patronage, and dependence on imported inputs for industry and construction has, as Abiodun shows in chapter 6, reinforced its early dominance. Beavon (chap. 5) describes the early mining and later manufacturing economic base of Johannesburg which, together with its services functions, accounts for its growth and agglomeration into the Pretoria–Witwatersrand–Vereeniging conurbation. Even in countries that do not have very large cities, the proportion of the urban population that lives in the largest city is high and increasing, while secondary cities and small urban centres continue to be underdeveloped (Rondinelli, 1988).

The relationship between economic and urban growth, as Simon shows in chapter 3, is complex and far from direct. Despite Africa's economic difficulties, many large cities have continued to grow – they are communications and transport hubs, and often the seats of government, and rates of natural increase are high despite the spread of AIDS. Their location as the place of residence for politicians, senior civil servants, and diplomats has helped to bias public expenditure on specialist health and other services and infrastructure towards them; this and the need for access to government offices has in turn made them the most likely locational choice for both transnational and domestic investment in manufacturing and for the offices of TNCs with mining or agricultural enterprises elsewhere in the country. Even though transnational investment in services in African countries is limited, what there is occurs in the largest cities, the fulcrums of flows of international capital, travel, and communications (Thrift, 1987). FDI is even more concentrated than domestic investment in the largest cities, because of executives' greater knowledge of the city economic environment and the presence of commercial facilities to intermediate between extraction/production and the international market where necessary (Sit, 1993). In 1988 over half of all urban wage employment in Kenya was in Nairobi (Simon, 1992, pp. 94–97; see chap. 9).

The locational attractions of the city are often magnified by policy with respect, for example, to transport tariffs, energy and service prices, and incentives for industrial development. Official policies to encourage decentralization are often counteracted by the spatial effects of non-spatial policies: Oberai (1993) quotes the example of Nigeria, where over 90 per cent of total net subsidies granted to industries benefited those located in Lagos.

The leading economic functions in the international and national economy have a multiplier effect, generating both formal and informal sector employment in wage and consumer goods and services industries. Despite the decreasing ability of the formal sector to absorb increased numbers in the labour force, as described by Rogerson in chapter 10, the cities continue to exert an attraction for migration. Many rural areas provide few economic opportunities for their growing populations, despite the pro-agriculture policy changes which have formed part of SAPs. Although the deterioration in infrastructure and services that has resulted from public expenditure cut-backs has been countrywide, rural areas started in a disadvantaged position. The chance of a better life in the cities, however much of a gamble, continues to attract migrants (Dogan and Kasarda, 1988). The evolving economic, social, political, and physical characteristics of these cities, marked as they are by so-called "informalization," are the subject of both the city case-studies and the thematic chapters in parts II and III of this volume.

Aid dependence and urban management

Rapidly growing urban populations place increasing demands on land, housing, services, and infrastructure, but weak revenue bases, lack of technological and administrative capacity amongst the agencies responsible for urban development, and vulnerability to evasion or exploitation by those with political and economic power prevent provision keeping pace with need. The result is environmental damage, deteriorating living conditions, especially for the urban poor, and lack of the political legitimacy needed to improve revenue collection and regulatory processes. Recognition of urban bias in spatial investment and non-spatial policies by the 1970s led to an over-reaction. Aid flows switched almost entirely to rural development, with the partial exception of those from the World Bank and USAID. Governments, despite the political power of urban populations, had declining volumes of resources and often misdirected them into ineffective or prestige investment. The result was that local administration and services deteriorated. In this chapter, the particular role of external agencies is the focus of attention and, as a result, the analysis applies predominantly to the most aid-dependent countries. Urban management more broadly will be considered both in the course of the city case-studies and also in part III.

Africa's aid dependency has brought with it policy conditionality not merely for economic policies but also for spatial investment. The World Bank's first attempt to tackle urban problems started in the early 1970s (World Bank, 1972). Although it had previously funded some macro-infrastructure projects, its new interest in urban problems coincided with its president's attempts to reorient its lending towards poverty-focused priorities, in particular the needs of the bottom 40 per cent of the income distribution. Its search for appropriate locations for pilot projects based on the principles of affordability, cost recovery, and replicability coincided with the dawning realization in low-income countries that traditional methods of catering for newly formed urban households by the construction of complete conventional housing units for rent or sale were unrealistic in situations of rapid population growth and strained resources. In Senegal and Zambia, the World Bank identified promising locations for its first two projects, both based on sites and services, with the latter also incorporating upgrading of unauthorized areas. Although the Bank envisaged the first projects as both pilot and demonstration projects, and located them in the capital cities of the respective countries in the hope that they would later be replicated throughout the urban system, their large scale, the conditions of World Bank lending, and other problems slowed their implementation and prevented modifications being made as design problems emerged. For various reasons, neither project was replicated, although some of the lessons were fed into later projects of the same type in other African countries. Other early projects were located in Botswana and Tanzania, and between 1972 and 1978 there were 12 altogether in SSA (Okpala, 1990) and by 1984 a further 13 (World Bank, 1986). Few, however, were 100 per cent successful with respect to the principles on which they were based: most sites and services projects were not affordable by the poorest, hidden subsidies were common, cost recovery problems were widespread, and replication rare. Other funders, especially USAID, which was funding 14 projects in 1984, adopted similar approaches (World Bank, 1986). Thus in 1985, out of the 72 projects identified for the International Year of Shelter for the Homeless in 28 African countries, 60 per cent were externally funded (Okpala, 1990).

By the later 1970s it was clear to many observers that there were problems associated with project-based lending, some of which resulted from the external funding and some from the process of project planning and implementation. The requirement for most of the significant decisions with respect to project design, implementation, and cost recovery to be agreed at the appraisal stage, prior to loan approval, and for agreed schedules of implementation to be adhered to, firstly deterred participation in project planning even in unauthorized areas and where local political and official forces were sympathetic and, secondly, made it difficult to modify project components that proved inappropriate or unworkable in practice. The establishment of separate project units to implement externally funded projects was a mixed blessing: they permitted external agencies to keep track of funds and insist on their correct use, and local implementors were able to avoid red tape and recruit appropriate staff, but they also led to problems of integrating newly serviced areas into ongoing systems of administration and service operation and maintenance. In addition, few of the projects resulted in an improved capacity with respect to land delivery, infrastructure provision, operation and maintenance, building materials production and supply, or housing finance (Rakodi, 1991; see also Rakodi, 1992b).

By 1983 the World Bank had also begun to recognize some of these problems (World Bank, 1983; Cohen, 1983, 1990) and the emphasis of its lending programmes and those of USAID shifted. Inadequate local revenue generation and the limited volume of mortgage funding that the public sector was able to make available were perceived to be major constraints on the larger-scale provision of serviced plots. Attention was paid to local revenue generation from the mid-1980s, when, for example, a USAID study in Burkina Faso was carried out (Mabogunje, 1990). A desire to tap into private sector funds for low-income housing, an ideological belief that private sector institutions would be more efficient in disbursing and recovering loans than public sector institutions, and an underlying desire to extend the reach of international and domestic large-scale capital led to a major focus on housing finance. USAID had established a Housing Guarantee programme in the early 1970s, which mobilizes private bank funding in the United States through a Congressionally sanctioned government loan guarantee. Attempts were made to create self-supporting financial intermediaries capable of making loans to low- and moderate-income households and to reduce and restructure housing subsidies (especially to eliminate subsidized interest rates) (World Bank, 1993). This was much easier in Asia and Latin America, with their more developed financial sectors, than in Africa and, although the worldwide volume of Bank shelter-related lending increased, it also shifted towards higher-income countries (World Bank, 1993, p. 57). The limitations of the approach and its vulnerability to economic downturn are revealed by the Zimbabwe experience (Rakodi, 1995b; see also Pugh, 1994). Following an overall review of experience (UNCHS, 1987), the new emphasis was nevertheless endorsed by the UN (UNCHS, 1990) and the World Bank (1993) as a strategy for housing based on enabling and facilitating the private sector to address the housing needs of all income groups including the poor.

Parallel with this attention to the housing sector was a recognition that most cities were so poorly serviced that they could not maintain their roles in national economies as the centres of administration and suppliers of rural inputs, let alone satisfy the basic needs of their inhabitants. By the mid-1980s, in the face of "worldwide economic stagnation, the economic benefits of urbanization were revisited" (Stren, 1993, p. 127) and the inhibiting effects on private sector investment of infrastructure neglect recognized (Peterson et al., 1991; Lee, 1993; Becker et al., 1994). In Tanzania, for example, while the economy stagnated, the per capita decline in expenditure on infrastructure and services was −11 per cent per annum between 1978/79 and 1986/87. As a result, large firms had to lay off workers sporadically in response to irregular water and electricity supplies; this in turn resulted in lower production, lower profits, and lower yields from taxation (Stren, 1993, p. 128). Simon examines urban basic needs satisfaction in chapter 3, using the example of Maputo in Mozambique.

In 1991 a World Bank policy document set out a new agenda designed:

(i) to improve urban productivity by remedying infrastructure deficiencies, rationalizing regulatory frameworks, strengthening local government, and improving the financing of urban development;

(ii) to alleviate urban poverty by increasing demand for the labour of the poor, investing in health and education, and supporting safety nets and compensatory measures to deal with transitional problems caused by SAPs; and

(iii) to protect the urban environment by raising awareness, improving the information base, and developing city-wide environmental strategies and programmes of action (World Bank, 1991a; Cohen, 1992; Cohen and Leitmann, 1994).

To implement this agenda, an increase in World Bank lending was anticipated, and a shift in emphasis from neighbourhood investments in shelter and infrastructure to city-level policy reform, institutional development, and city-wide investment in infrastructure. The Urban Development Cooperation Strategy of the UN Development Programme (UNDP), "Cities, People and Poverty," shares the goals of making cities economically viable and productive, as well as environmentally sustainable, and strengthening the capacity of local government. It apparently places much more emphasis than the World Bank on the need for social justice and participation, by means of poverty alleviation measures, including assistance to small-scale enterprises; enabling and participative strategies for the provision of infrastructure and services; and support for initiatives by non-governmental organizations to improve the environment (Cheema, 1992).

Together with the UN Centre for Human Settlements (UNCHS) and UNDP (and later some bilateral donors too), an urban management programme (1986–1999) was agreed that aims to work with developing countries to strengthen the contribution that cities and towns make toward economic growth, environmental quality, and the reduction of poverty. The programme now works in five areas: land management, infrastructure management, municipal finance and administration, environmental management, and poverty alleviation (World Bank, 1991b). It operates in Africa through a regional office, initially in Accra and now in Abidjan, using city and country consultations as a basis for policy formulation and regional networks of expertise to provide technical advice on the implementation of action plans. The programme is underpinned by earlier World Bank research (for example, Bahl and Linn, 1992, on urban finance) and an ongoing research programme as part of which a series of research and advisory publications are being produced. By the late 1980s, lending to strengthen municipal finance, infrastructure investment and management, and land management had increased (Wegelin, 1994).

As yet, there have been neither published in-house evaluations nor independent external evaluations of the World Bank's new urban agenda and the urban management programme (UMP). However, concerns have been expressed about the assumptions upon which it is based, the gap between policy and implementation, and its relationship to the wider economic policies advocated by the same institutions (Jones and Ward, 1994). Harris (1992), for example, considers that the measures intended to increase urban productivity are not based on an adequate understanding of the structure, competitive advantages, and disadvantages of city economies. Stren (1993) criticizes the agencies' failure to define what is meant by urban management, although he recognizes that this is in part to retain organizational flexibility. The term has become popular, Stren suggests, because of its ideological appeal, given its association with business management, and the desire of the funding agencies to harness private sector resources. Nevertheless, it can be used to encapsulate conceptual and practical advances in approaches to planning for urban growth (Devas and Rakodi, 1993). There is, in addition, a certain political naivety in the published documents (Jones and Ward, 1994). For example, the mentions of participatory approaches seem to be made with little understanding, as exemplified by the suggestion by UNDP's programme manager that "we [*sic*] must organize the urban poor at the community level to increase their capacity to make demands on the urban system" (Cheema, 1992, p. 27). It is unclear if he is implying that the international donor agencies intend to adopt a more proactive role in local political systems, from which they have typically distanced themselves. Harris (1992) also points out that many World Bank and UMP projects are still concerned with traditional land management, household services provision, and housing rather than city-wide institutional strengthening.

Structural adjustment lending, with its economic and political conditionalities, forms the context within which the new emphases in urban lending will be implemented. Although the municipal development funds being established in a number of countries as part of World Bank-funded projects promise a more regular supply of capital funds, they do not of themselves solve all the difficulties in the political relationships between the central ministry responsible and local councils. The ability of local authorities and other agencies to achieve good yields from a variety of revenue sources is threatened by the pressure on them to lay off staff and the likelihood that, in a situation of declining real wages, staff are likely to have to continue and diversify the survival strategies they have already developed. Without adequate administrative capacity, service delivery is often not good enough to persuade users to pay their charges or taxes; poor service delivery in turn diminishes the political legitimacy of local authorities and makes it more difficult to enforce regulatory instruments and tax collection.

By the end of the 1980s, the World Bank (1991a) was more explicit about the expected impacts of adjustment on urban populations. Firstly, urban labour markets were expected to contract and unemployment to increase as a result of civil service cut-backs and labour shedding by industries adversely affected by import liberalization. Secondly, there would be what was hoped to be only a short-term decline in real incomes, as wages stagnated and prices of imports and subsidized goods and services rose. Thirdly, cuts in expenditure on and increased charges for education and health services might reduce access to them by the urban poor, unless compensatory mechanisms were introduced. It was also thought likely that the slow-down in formal sector employment and wages was likely to hurt the informal sector, although it was considered that this might be partly compensated for by increased demand for informal sector products and services both when these substitute for imports and where rising rural incomes lead to increased demand. It was considered possible that rates of rural–urban migration would decline as employment opportunities shrank in urban areas, and that the transition would be eased by reliance on extended family networks. The realities of economic and social trends are analysed by Rogerson in chapter 10 and Potts in chapter 13 respectively.

Adjustment programmes in African countries have typically been associated with very slow growth or a decline in formal sector employment; reductions in public sector employment, even if less extensive than planned (World Bank, 1994), have not been compensated for by increases in private employment, because rapid trade liberalization has undermined local industries given too little time to adjust to changed local circumstances. Real (non-agricultural) average and minimum wages fell 25 per cent between 1980 and 1985 in two-thirds of the countries for which data are available (ILO-JASPA, 1989, quoted in Jesperson, 1992), and country studies show a continuation of this trend in the later 1980s. Although deliberate policies aimed at reducing labour costs were intended to increase competitiveness, lower real wages have a dampening effect on consumer demand and thus on domestic markets for formal and informal sector products. They also have adverse effects on efficiency in both the public and private sectors when they fall below the amount necessary to support a household. What evidence there is shows that urban populations in most cases have responded by devoting increased time to a diversified set of informal economic activities, rather than by return migration to the rural areas (O'Connor, 1991; see chap. 13). The informal sector has expanded to absorb increasing numbers of people, but many of the economic opportunities yield limited returns, especially those available to people without access to capital (Jesperson, 1992; see also Stewart, 1991, and chap. 10). The unstructured markets favoured for capital, it has been pointed out, do not level the playing field between large and small enterprises; they discriminate against the latter (Stewart et al., 1992). The optimism with which the agencies expect the informal sector to absorb additional labour is threatened by shrinking demand as the formal wage bill shrinks, while former civil servants and formal sector employees do not necessarily have the skills and qualifications necessary to be successful in self-employment. The shrinkage of the formal sector may also decrease tax revenue, since any form of tax is harder to collect in informal systems of marketing, employment, or housing development. However, municipalities need a sound financial base, well-trained staff, and political legitimacy in order to improve their administrative procedures and service delivery.

Real government expenditure per capita stagnated or fell in most countries in the region, as required by SAPs, and the pattern of expenditure also changed. Despite World Bank encouragement for appropriate micro-credit schemes, expenditure on public works for upgrading and maintenance of urban infrastructure, and "shielding public expenditure on key health, education, nutrition and other basic welfare services" (Seralgeldin, 1989, p. 50) in order to protect those most vulnerable to cuts, spending on health care, education, economic services, and infrastructure was disproportionately cut (Stewart, 1991; Logan and Mengisteab, 1993). Such cuts reflected not government policy changes but the resources available once increased debt repayments had been allowed for (Jesperson, 1992). Some governments made efforts to redirect expenditure towards primary education and basic health care, but these efforts were threatened or negated by reduced resources and the introduction of user charges. In theory, prices for water, energy, health, education, etc. can be structured progressively. In practice, the balance of interests in most countries has militated against political commitment to progressive price structures (Jones and Ward, 1994), while measures to protect the poor from price increases have often been badly designed and under-resourced (Rakodi, 1995c). As a result, and exacerbated by falling real wages and increased unemployment, defaults have increased, so that the flow of revenue is insufficient to build up local capacity to provide the quality of service people will be willing to pay for. Although evidence is patchy, and sometimes contradictory and inconclusive, there is some indication of worsening nutritional and health status among vulnerable groups, declining school enrolment, and deteriorating basic educational achievements. The pressures have had a particularly adverse impact on women (Stewart, 1991). Reduced expenditure on education and training adversely affects the quality of the available workforce, as does the poor health associated with deteriorating infrastructure, inhibiting the mobilization of private sector investment in manufacturing, while poor health reduces the ability of children to absorb education (Harris, 1992; Stewart et al., 1992).

Programmes introduced to compensate the newly unemployed (severance payments, retraining, credit, etc.) have generally absorbed most of the available funds without reaching the poor, while programmes to assist the chronically poor (public works schemes, nutrition support, and targeting of subsidized education, health care, and food) may mitigate some of the immediate adverse effects of impoverishment but do not address its structural causes. Meanwhile, basic SAP policy packages have not been redesigned either to eliminate these adverse effects or to reduce poverty (Stewart, 1991). Whether lessons from better-designed programmes, such as the GAPVU programme in Mozambique (Schubert, 1995), or recent work at the Bank (Moser et al., 1993) will succeed in improving these programmes remains to be seen.

The blanket faith in the private sector on which SAPs have been based has also been subject to criticism. We have noted above that FDI is unlikely to show any marked increase in volume. It cannot be relied on for the development of manufacturing and is even less likely to be interested in investment in infrastructure and housing. Development will, therefore, depend on the level of domestic savings and investment, which, it is hoped, will increase with interest rate reforms. Some doubt, however, has been thrown on the expectation that higher interest rates will generate increased investment (Helleiner, 1992). It is by no means certain that the funds will be there for local authorities to borrow from the private sector or that the housing finance system will be able to rely on private sector savings. Investment is a function of household income and, as long as incomes are depressed, it is unrealistic to expect savings – for investment in formal sector financial institutions, owner-occupied housing, or small enterprises – to increase at the cost of consumption (Jamal and Weeks, 1993).

The new approaches to housing and urban development are, in many respects, to be welcomed. This brief and incomplete assessment has shown that many of the assumptions on which they are based fit logically with the premises of SAPs. However, not only can many of these assumptions be challenged (Jones and Ward, 1994), but there are notable inconsistencies between the effects of SAPs and the aims of the new urban agenda, as recognized even by some World Bank staff (Cohen, 1990).

Conclusion

The main foundations for Africa's incorporation into the world economic and political system were established during the colonial period, which left a political, economic, and urban legacy that survived the 1960s, despite the attempts of African countries to secure both political independence and economic autonomy. Political independence did bring a degree of autonomy, but this was eroded by superpower interest and continued economic dependence. In addition, with respect to domestic politics, states were beset by a wide range of difficulties, resulting in political instability and administrative weakness. Both took a variety of forms and in many cases influenced patterns of urbanization and adversely affected the capacity of the public sector, especially local government, to manage urban development. The colonial period was marked by a reorientation of urban patterns to serve the needs of trade and administration. Some existing settlements prospered, while others stagnated or decayed, and a series of new centres was established. There has been relatively little change to this pattern since independence, and what change has occurred has been associated with administrative rather than economic change. The rate of urban growth increased, owing, *inter alia*, to expansion of public sector employment, attempts to industrialize, an increased rate of natural increase, and relative neglect of rural areas. Per capita economic growth was fairly widespread in the 1960s and some progress was made in some countries towards economic diversification and indigenization.

However, the 1970s and 1980s were marked by a series of setbacks, many, but not all, of which were outside the control of African governments. Some, for example oil price increases and deteriorating terms of trade for primary commodities, were exogenous and some, such as drought, endogenous. They are a crucial element in the explanation of Africa's continued underdevelopment and its inability to break free of the vicious circle into which it is locked. The structure of production in north Africa has become more industrialized, with a reduction in the role of agriculture from about a quarter to less than 20 per cent of GDP in most countries, while manufacturing is now just under a fifth and services a half. However, in SSA, despite a relative decline in the importance of agriculture (from 40 per cent of GDP in 1965 to 32 per cent in 1990) and minerals, services and especially manufacturing are still relatively unimportant. This failure to industrialize can partly be explained by external factors, but a variety of domestic factors must also be taken into account, including economic policies, the effects of personal rule, historical and social structure, the role of the state, and low levels of literacy and skills (Killick with Malik, 1992).

The globalization of manufacturing has been reflected in the emergence of a new international division of labour, which has provided a basis for industrialization in the early and more recent NICs. African countries sought FDI in order to develop their manufacturing sectors, and in a number of countries considerable progress with import substitution industrialization was made. However, the desired progression from import substituting to export industry has been elusive. Although some aspects of the reforms advocated by the IMF and World Bank are desirable to counteract previous biases against export industry, these will not necessarily enable countries to gain access to markets, while import substitution industry has been adversely affected, at least in the short–medium term, by rapid trade liberalization. The main thrust of SAPs has, however, been to encourage increased primary commodity exports to earn foreign exchange and repay debt. This has, firstly, by flooding world markets with increased volumes of certain commodities, exacerbated the problem of declining terms of trade and, secondly, re-emphasized colonial trade patterns (static rather than dynamic comparative advantage) (Jamal and Weeks, 1993). Meanwhile, the increased flow of FDI in manufacturing anticipated following liberalization has not materialized and even the international agencies now recognize its volume is unlikely to grow in most countries (Husain, 1993).

In part because of the financial demands of internationalized manufacturing capital, the globalization of services has also occurred and has contributed to the emergence of "world cities," pre-eminent in financial and business services. The congruence of a global services sector and dynamic export-oriented manufacturing in the West Pacific Rim countries has given rise to rapid development of systems of cities with Tokyo at the apex (Yeung and Lo, 1996). Although there has been some increase in services FDI in Africa, it is mostly in the trade and construction sectors, and the FDI stock as a whole remains concentrated in the primary sector and in relatively few countries. Most of the continent remains marginal to the interests of global capital, the economic underdevelopment and political instability of African countries interacting to perpetuate their marginalization. FDI has an influence on patterns of urban economic activity and development and is crucial to many African economies, because of its interlinkages with trade, technology, and financial flows, despite its low volume in world terms (UNCTC, 1991; Helleiner, 1992). However, it cannot be relied upon to provide the necessary impetus to enable Africa to break out of the vicious circle of under-development, and dependence on aid is likely to continue.

This chapter has reviewed how such dependence renders countries vulnerable to the imposition of doctrinaire economic policies, which have tried to achieve rapid adjustment at the cost of longer-term development goals (Stewart et al., 1992). The agencies promoting such policies have also failed to recognize that economics can never be divorced from politics, social processes, and culture, and that individual countries cannot be treated as if they are independent of their neighbours and of the global political economy (Logan and Mengisteab, 1993). Further, the policies have had adverse impacts on the well-being of a variety of social groups, notably the urban poor (Stren, 1992). In the absence of recent census results, the impact of Africa's economic difficulties on urban growth is uncertain, a point that Simon also emphasizes. Despite policy reforms intended to redress a perceived anti-agricultural, anti-rural policy bias, and some efforts to encourage investment in secondary cities and small urban centres, further concentration in the largest cities has probably occurred, because they continue to provide the most profitable locations for investment and the best prospects for migrants, despite the decline in formal sector employment resulting from recession and SAP implementation. Increased unemployment is seen by the funding agencies as a temporary problem, its effects cushioned by the anticipated expansion of informal sector activity and reliance on extended family networks. However, not only is future growth in formal sector employment at best unpredictable and at worst unlikely, but reductions in the number of employees and declining real wages have a knock-on effect on the ability both of those in informal sector occupations to earn reasonable incomes and of local authorities to collect adequate revenue.

Recognition of the adverse impacts of SAPs on welfare and productivity, together with a realization that cities without adequate infrastructure and services do not provide an efficient location for economic activity, has given rise to a new aid agenda which aims to strengthen the capacity of public and private sector institutions to manage urban growth. Aid for urban development in the past has been influential on policy despite its small volume because much of it has taken the form of technical assistance, although reliance on consultants has given rise to a variety of problems (Meikle, 1988; Okpala, 1990). Aid has also been biased towards the larger cities (Blitzer et al., 1983), perhaps reinforcing their dominant position. Some aspects of the new policy approaches are desirable, but experience with earlier lending gives rise to some doubt about whether the policy packages offered are either appropriate or feasible in the African context, especially given the contradictions between the urban policies being promoted and the design and outcome of SAPs. Further, in the absence of debt write-off, neither the economic nor the urban problems of African countries are going to be solved by increases in lending, which have consistently been less than promised.

Notes

1. Although the classifications and methodology adopted are not consistent with its earlier analyses.
2. Ethiopia 1967, 1984, and 1989; South Africa 1951, 1960, 1970, and 1985; Egypt 1947, 1960, 1966, 1976, and 1986.

References

Adedeji, A. 1993. The case for remaking Africa. In: *Action in Africa: The Experience of People Involved in Government, Business and Aid.* James Currey, London, pp. 43–57.

Amin, S. 1971. *Neo-colonialism in West Africa.* Penguin, Harmondsworth (transl. 1973).

——— 1972. Underdevelopment and dependence in black Africa – origins and contemporary forms. *Journal of Modern African Studies* 10(4): 503–524. Reprinted in D. L. Cohen and J. Daniel, eds., *Political Economy of Africa.* Longman, London, 1981, pp. 28–44.

Bahl, R. W. and J. F. Linn, 1992. *Urban Public Finance in Developing Countries.* Oxford University Press for the World Bank, Oxford.

Becker, C. M., A. M. Hamer, and A. R. Morrison. 1994. *Beyond Urban Bias in Africa: Urbanization in an Era of Structural Adjustment.* Heinemann, Portsmouth, NH.

Bell, M. 1986. *Contemporary Africa.* Longman, London.

Bennell, P. 1990. British industrial investment in Sub-Saharan Africa: Corporate responses to economic crisis in the 1980s. *Development Policy Review* 8(2): 155–177.

Biel, R. 1994. *Role of the IMF and the World Bank in Developing Countries.* Quaker Peace and Service, London.

Bird, G. 1993. Sisters in economic development: The Bretton Woods institutions and developing countries. *Journal of International Development* 5(1): 1–25.

Blitzer, S., J. E. Hardoy, and D. Satterthwaite. 1983. The sectoral and spatial distribution of multilateral aid for human settlements. *Habitat International* 7(1/2): 103–127.

67

Bonine, M. E. 1983. Cities of the Middle East and North Africa. In: S. D. Brunn and J. F. Williams, eds., *Cities of the World*. Harper & Row, New York, pp. 280–322.

Cantwell, J. 1991. Foreign multinationals and industrial development in Africa. In: P. J. Buckley and J. Clegg, eds., *Multinational Enterprises in Less Developed Countries*. Macmillan, London, pp. 183–224.

Chandler, T. 1994. Urbanization in medieval and early modern Africa. In: J. D. Tarver, ed., *Urbanization in Africa: A Handbook*. Greenwood, Westport, Conn., pp. 15–32.

Chandler, T. and J. D. Tarver. 1993. Urbanization in colonial Africa. *Africa Insight* 23(4): 250–254.

Chazan, N., R. Mortimer, J. Ravenhill, and D. Rothchild. 1988. *Politics and Society in Contemporary Africa*. Macmillan, London.

Cheema, G. S. 1992. The challenge of urbanisation. In: N. Harris, ed., *Cities in the 1990s: The Challenge for Developing Countries*. UCL Press, London, pp. 24–33.

Christopher, A. J. and J. D. Tarver. 1994. Urbanization during colonial days in Sub-Saharan Africa. In: J. D. Tarver, ed., *Urbanization in Africa: A Handbook*. Greenwood, Westport, Conn., pp. 33–48.

Cockcroft, L. 1992. The past record and future potential of foreign investment. In: F. Stewart, S. Lall, and S. Wangwe, eds., *Alternative Development Strategies in SubSaharan Africa*. Macmillan, London, pp. 336–367.

Cohen, M. A. 1983. The challenge of replicability. *Regional Development Dialogue* 4(1): 90–99.

—— 1990. Macroeconomic adjustment and the city. *Cities* 7(1): 49–59.

—— 1992. Urban policy and economic development – the agenda. In: N. Harris, ed., *Cities in the 1990s: The Challenge for Developing Countries*. UCL Press, London, pp. 9–24.

Cohen, M. A. and J. Leitmann. 1994. Will the World Bank's real "new urban policy" please stand up? *Habitat International* 18(4): 117–126.

Coquery-Vidrovitch, C. 1991. The process of urbanization in Africa (From the origins to the beginning of independence). *African Studies Review* 34(1): 1–98.

Devas, N. and C. Rakodi, eds. 1993. *Managing Fast Growing Cities: New Approaches to Urban Planning and Management in the Developing World*. Longman, Harlow.

Dogan, M. and J. D. Kasarda. 1988. Introduction: How giant cities will multiply and grow. In: M. Dogan and J. D. Kasarda, eds., *The Metropolitan Era. Vol. 1, A World of Giant Cities*. Sage, Newbury Park, Calif., pp. 12–29.

Findlay, A. M. 1994. *The Arab World*. Routledge, London.

Findlay, A. M. and R. Paddison. 1986. Planning the Arab city: The cases of Tunis and Rabat. *Progress in Planning* 26(1): 1–82.

Friedmann, J. and G. Wolff. 1982. World city formation: An agenda for research and action. *International Journal of Urban and Regional Research* 6(3): 309–343.

Gibbon, P. 1992. The World Bank and African poverty, 1973–91. *Journal of Modern African Studies* 30(2): 193–220.

Green, R. H. 1993. Neo-liberalism and the political economy of war: Sub-Saharan Africa as a case-study of a vacuum. In: C. Colclough and J. Manor, eds., *States or Markets? Neo-liberalism and the Development Policy Debate*. Clarendon, Oxford, pp. 238–259.

Green, R. H. and M. Faber. 1994. The structural adjustment of Structural Adjustment: Sub-Saharan Africa 1980–1993. *IDS Bulletin* 25(3): 1–8.

Gregory, J. W. and V. Piché. 1982. African population: Reproduction for whom? *Daedalus*, Spring: 179–209.

Gugler, J. and W. G. Flanagan. 1978. *Urbanization and Social Change in West Africa*. Cambridge University Press, Cambridge.

Harris, N. 1992. Productivity and poverty in the cities of the developing countries. In: N. Harris, ed., *Cities in the 1990s: The Challenge for Developing Countries*. UCL Press, London, pp. 173–195.

Harvey, C. 1993. Recovery from macro-economic disaster in Sub-Saharan Africa. In: C. Colclough and J. Manor, eds., *States or Markets? Neo-liberalism and the Development Policy Debate*. Clarendon, Oxford, pp. 121–147.

Helleiner, G. K. 1992. Structural adjustment and long-term development in Sub-Saharan Africa. In: F. Stewart, S. Lall, and S. Wangwe, eds., *Alternative Development Strategies in SubSaharan Africa*. Macmillan, London, pp. 48–77.

Husain, I. 1993. Trade, aid and investment in Sub-Saharan Africa. In: *Action in Africa: The Experience of People Involved in Government, Business and Aid*. James Currey, London, pp. 75–106.

IMF (International Monetary Fund). 1985. *Foreign Private Investment in Developing Countries*. IMF Occasional Paper 33, Washington D.C.

——— 1993. *World Economic Outlook*. IMF, Washington D.C.

Jamal, V. and J. Weeks. 1993. *Africa Misunderstood: Or Whatever Happened to the Rural–Urban Gap?* Macmillan for the ILO, London.

Jenkins, R. 1987. *Transnational Corporations and Uneven Development*. Methuen, London.

Jesperson, E. 1992. External shocks, adjustment policies and economic and social performance. In: G. A. Cornia, R. Van der Hoeven, and T. Mkandawire, eds., *Africa's Recovery in the 1990s: From Stagnation and Adjustment to Human Development*. St Martin's Press, New York, pp. 9–90.

Jones, G. A. and P. M. Ward. 1994. The World Bank's "new" urban management programme: Paradigm shift or policy continuity? *Habitat International* 18(3): 33–51.

Killick, T. with M. Malik. 1992. Country experiences with IMF programmes in the 1980s. *The World Economy* 15(5): 599–632.

King, A. D. 1990. *Urbanism, Colonialism, and the World-Economy: Cultural and Spatial Foundations of the World Urban System*. Routledge, London.

Lee, K. S. 1993. How Nigerian manufacturers cope with infrastructural deficiencies: Private alternatives to public provision. In: G. S. Cheema, ed., *Urban Management: Policies and Innovations in Developing Countries*. Praeger, Westport, Conn., pp. 253–260.

Lipton, M. 1977. *Why Poor People Stay Poor: Urban Bias in World Development*. Temple Smith, London.

Logan, I. B. and K. Mengisteab. 1993. IMF-World Bank adjustment and structural transformation in Sub-Saharan Africa. *Economic Geography* 69(1): 1–24.

Mabogunje, A. L. 1968. *Urbanisation in Nigeria*. University of London Press, London.

——— 1990. Urban planning and the post-colonial state in Africa: A research overview. *African Studies Review* 33: 121–203.

Mehretu, A. 1983. Cities of SubSaharan Africa. In: S. D. Brunn and J. F. Williams, eds., *Cities of the World*. Harper & Row, New York, pp. 243–279.

69

Meikle, S. 1988. The performance of aid-funded human settlement projects. *Habitat International* 12(4): 125–133.

Moser, C. O. N., A. J. Herbert, and R. E. Makonnen. 1993. *Urban Poverty in the Context of Structural Adjustment: Recent Evidence and Policy Responses.* World Bank, Transportation, Water and Urban Development Department DP 4, Washington D.C.

Mosley, P. and J. Weeks. 1993. Has recovery begun? "Africa's adjustment in the 1980s" revisited. *World Development* 21(10): 1583–1606.

Nafziger, E. W. 1990. *The Economics of Developing Countries.* Prentice-Hall, Englewood Cliffs, N.J.

Oberai, A. S. 1993. Urbanization, development and economic efficiency. In: J. D. Kasarda and A. M. Parnell, eds., *Third World Cities: Problems, Policies and Prospects.* Sage, Newbury Park, Calif., pp. 58–73.

Oberai, A. S. and R. E. Bilsborrow. 1984. Theoretical perspectives on migration. In: R. E. Bilsborrow, A. S. Oberai, and G. Standing, eds., *Migration Surveys in Low Income Countries.* Croom Helm, London, pp. 14–59.

O'Brien, S. 1994. Some reflections on country experiences with Structural Adjustment. *IDS Bulletin* 25(3): 51–54.

O'Connor, A. 1983. *The African City.* Hutchinson, London.

———— 1991. *Poverty in Africa: A Geographical Approach.* Belhaven, London.

ODI (Overseas Development Institute). 1993. *Does the IMF Really Help Developing Countries?* ODI Briefing Paper, London.

———— 1994. *Political Liberalisation and Economic Reform in Developing Countries.* ODI Briefing Paper, London.

Okpala, D. C. I. 1990. The roles and influences of external assistance in the planning, development and management of African human settlements systems. *Third World Planning Review* 12(3): 205–229.

Onokerhoraye, A. G. 1975. Urbanism as an organ of traditional African civilization: The example of Benin, Nigeria. *Civilisations* 25: 294–305.

Parfitt, T. W. 1993. Which African agenda for the 'nineties? The ECA/World Bank alternatives. *Journal of International Development* 5(1): 93–106.

Peterson, G. E., G. T. Kingsley, and J. P. Telgarsky. 1991. *Urban Economies and National Development.* USAID, Office of Housing and Urban Programs, Washington D.C.

Pugh, C. 1994. Development of housing finance and the global strategy for shelter. *Cities* 11(6): 384–392.

Rakodi, C. 1986a. Colonial urban policy and planning in Northern Rhodesia and its legacy. *Third World Planning Review* 8(3): 193–217.

———— 1986b. State and class in Africa: A case for extending analyses of the form and functions of the national state to the urban local state. *Society and Space* 4: 419–446.

———— 1991. Developing institutional capacity to meet the housing needs of the urban poor: Experience in Kenya, Tanzania and Zambia. *Cities* 8(3): 228–243.

———— 1992a. *Urbanization in Zambia.* Papers in Planning Research, Department of City and Regional Planning, University of Wales, Cardiff.

———— 1992b. Housing markets in third world cities: Research and policy into the 1990s. *World Development* 20(1): 39–55.

―――― 1995a. *Harare. Inheriting a Settler-Colonial City: Change or Continuity?* Wiley, London.

―――― 1995b. Housing finance for lower income urban households in Zimbabwe. *Housing Studies* 10(2): 199–227.

―――― 1995c. The household strategies of the urban poor: Coping with poverty and recession in Gweru, Zimbabwe. *Habitat International* 19(4): 447–472.

Ribe, H., S. Carvalho, R. Liebenthal, P. Nichalos, and E. Zuckerman. 1990. *How Adjustment Programmes Can Help the Poor: The World Bank's Experience.* World Bank DP 71, Washington D.C.

Riddell, J. B. 1992. Things fall apart again: Structural Adjustment Programmes in Sub-Saharan Africa. *Journal of Modern African Studies* 30(1): 53–68.

ROAPE (editors of the Review of African Political Economy). 1975. The multinationals in Africa. Reprinted in D. L. Cohen and J. Daniel, eds., *Political Economy of Africa.* Longman, London, 1981, pp. 67–74.

Rondinelli, D. A. 1988. Giant and secondary city growth in Africa. In: M. Dogan and J. D. Kasarda, eds., *The Metropolis Era. Vol. 1, A World of Giant Cities.* Sage, Newbury Park, Calif., pp. 291–321.

Salau, A. T. 1990. Urbanization and spatial strategies in West Africa. In: R. B. Potter and A. T. Salau, eds., *Cities and Development in the Third World.* Mansell, London, pp. 157–171.

Sassen, S. 1994. *Cities in a World Economy.* Pine Forge Press, Thousand Oaks, Calif.

Sassen-Koob, S. 1985. Capital mobility and labour migration: Their expression in core cities. In: M. Timberlake, ed., *Urbanization in the World Economy.* Academic Press, Orlando, Fla., pp. 231–265.

Schubert, B. 1995. Poverty and poverty alleviation programmes in the urban areas of Mozambique. *Habitat International* 19(4): 499–514.

Seralgeldin, I. 1989. *Poverty, Adjustment and Growth in Africa.* World Bank, Washington D.C.

Simon, D. 1992. *Cities, Capital and Development: African Cities in the World Economy.* Belhaven, London.

―――― 1993. *The World City Hypothesis: Reflections from the Periphery.* Research Paper 7, Centre for Developing Areas Research, Department of Geography, Royal Holloway, University of London, Egham, Surrey.

―――― 1995. Debt, democracy and development: Sub-Saharan Africa in the 1990s. In: D. Simon, W. van Spengen, C. Dixon, and A. Närman, eds., *Structurally Adjusted Africa: Poverty, Debt and Basic Needs.* Pluto, London.

Sit, F.-S. 1993. Transnational capital flows, foreign investments, and urban growth in developing countries. In: J. D. Kasarda and A. M. Parnell, eds., *Third World Cities: Problems, Policies and Prospects.* Sage, Newbury Park, Calif., pp. 180–198.

Skinner, E. P. 1986. Urbanization in Francophone Africa. *African Urban Quarterly* 1(3–4): 191–195.

Standing, G. 1984. *Population Mobility and Productive Relations: Demographic Links and Policy Evolution.* World Bank Staff Working Paper 695, Washington D.C.

―――― 1985. Circulation and the labour process. In: G. Standing, ed., *Labour Circulation and the Labour Process.* Croom Helm for the ILO, London, pp. 1–45.

Stewart, F. 1991. The many faces of adjustment. *World Development* 19(12): 1847–1864.

Stewart, F., S. Lall, and S. Wangwe. 1992. Alternative development strategies: An overview. In: F. Stewart, S. Lall, and S. Wangwe, eds., *Alternative Development Strategies in SubSaharan Africa*. Macmillan, London, pp. 3–46.

Stoneman, C. 1993. The World Bank: Some lessons for South Africa. *Review of African Political Economy* 58: 87–98.

Stren, R. E. 1989a. Urban local government in Africa. In: R. E. Stren and R. R. White, eds., *African Cities in Crisis: Managing Rapid Urban Growth*. Westview, Boulder, Colo., pp. 20–36.

———— 1989b. The administration of urban services. In: R. E. Stren and R. R. White, eds., *African Cities in Crisis: Managing Rapid Urban Growth*. Westview, Boulder, Colo., pp. 37–68.

———— 1992. African urban research since the late 1980s: Responses to poverty and urban growth. *Urban Studies* 29(3/4): 533–556.

———— 1993. "Urban management" in development assistance: An elusive concept. *Cities* 10(2): 125–139.

Thrift, N. 1987. The fixers: The urban geography of international commercial capital. In: J. Henderson and M. Castells, eds., *Global Restructuring and Territorial Development*. Sage, London, pp. 203–233.

Todaro, M. P. 1994. *Economic Development*, 5th edn. Longman, New York and London.

Tordoff, W. 1984. *Government and Politics in Africa*. Macmillan, London.

UN. 1993. *World Urbanization Prospects: The 1992 Revision*. United Nations Department of Economic and Social Information and Policy Analysis, New York.

UNCHS (United Nations Centre for Human Settlement – Habitat). 1987. *Global Report on Human Settlements, 1986*. Oxford University Press for UNCHS, Oxford.

———— 1990. *The Global Strategy for Shelter to the Year 2000*. UNCHS, Nairobi.

UNCTC (United Nations Centre on Transnational Corporations). 1985. *Transnational Corporations in World Development: Third Survey*. Graham & Trotman for UNCTC, London.

———— 1989. *Foreign Direct Investment and Transnational Corporations in Services*. UNCTC, New York.

———— 1991. *World Investment Report 1991: The Triad in Foreign Direct Investment*. UNCTC, New York.

UNDP. 1992. *Human Development Report 1992*. United Nations Development Programme, New York.

UNECA (United Nations Economic Commission for Africa). 1989. *African Alternatives to Structural Adjustment Programmes: A Framework for Transformation and Recovery*. UNECA, Addis Ababa.

Wegelin, E. 1994. Everything you always wanted to know about the urban management programme (but were afraid to ask). *Habitat International* 18(4): 127–137.

Williams, G. 1981. Nigeria: The neo-colonial political economy. In: D. L. Cohen and J. Daniel, eds., *Political Economy of Africa*. Longman, London, pp. 45–66.

Winters, C. 1983. The classification of traditional African cities. *Journal of Urban History* 10(1): 3–31.

World Bank. 1972. *Urbanization Sector Working Paper*. World Bank, Washington D.C.

———— 1983. *Learning by Doing: World Bank Lending for Urban Development 1972–82*. World Bank, Washington D.C.

———— 1986. Aid flows for urban projects remain relatively low. *Urban Edge* 10(2): 4–5.

———— 1991a. *Urban Policy and Economic Development: An Agenda for the 1990s.* World Bank Policy Paper, Washington D.C.

———— 1991b. *Urban Management Program: Revised Prospectus. Capacity Building for Urban Management in the 1990s.* World Bank, Washington D.C.

———— 1992. *World Development Report.* World Bank, Washington D.C.

———— 1993. *Housing: Enabling Markets to Work.* World Bank, Washington D.C.

———— 1994. *Adjustment in Africa: Reforms, Results and the Road Ahead.* Oxford University Press, Oxford.

Wunsch, J. S. and D. Olowu. 1990. *The Failure of the Centralized State: Institutions and Self-Governance in Africa.* Westview, Boulder, Colo.

Yeung, Y.-M. and F.-C. Lo. 1996. Global restructuring and emerging urban corridors in Pacific Asia. In: F.-C. Lo and Y.-M. Yeung, eds., *Emerging World Cities in Pacific Asia.* United Nations University Press, Tokyo, pp. 2–47.

Zachariah, K. C. and J. Condé. 1981. *Migration in West Africa: Demographic Aspects.* Oxford University Press, Oxford.

3

Urbanization, globalization, and economic crisis in Africa

David Simon

Abstract

Ce chapitre examine, dans le contexte d'une mondialisation accélérée, les différentes facettes des relations entre urbanisation et situation économique. Il faut absolument démonter les notions simplistes concernant la mondialisation, surtout parce que d'apparentes similitudes de formes ne se traduisent pas forcément par des similitudes de même ordre dans les formes et processus sous-jacents. C'est pourquoi la situation et le rôle des villes africaines dans le contexte de l'économie mondiale sont mis en rapport avec la situation contemporaine dans les autres régions du monde. Les liens le plus souvent ténus de ces villes avec le reste du monde et le rôle périphérique qu'elles y jouent sont en relation directe avec la marginalisation croissante de l'Afrique. Les implications de ce constat sont ensuite examinées en termes de relations entre les tendances de l'urbanisation et la situation socio-économique prévalante. Malgré l'insuffisance des données et les dangers de généralisation, il semblerait bien que le rythme de l'urbanisation se soit quelque peu ralenti depuis la fin des années 80 et le début des années 90 du fait de l'aggravation de la crise économique, de l'augmentation des coûts et de la difficulté de la vie dans les grandes villes d'Afrique. Mais ces relations sont complexes et ne sont pas toujours absolument cohérentes ni prévisibles. Examinant la qualité de la vie urbaine, la dernière partie du chapitre illustre les différentiations socio-économiques et l'ampleur de la pauvreté et de l'insuffisance des infrastructures dans de nombreuses villes. Quoiqu'en termes absolus il y ait peu de véritables mégapoles en Afrique, les problèmes des grandes zones urbaines du continent sont, d'un point de vue relatif, aussi graves qu'ailleurs.

Introduction: Globalization, identity, and difference

Over the past millenium, Africa's peoples and cultures have been subject to dramatic external interventions and influences enmeshing them firmly within the emerging world system. The successive conquests, colonizations, and associated cultural imperialisms of Arab and European, Islam and Christianity, the haemorrhaging of literally millions of Africans constituted by the slave trade, and more recently the rapid modernization and spread of capitalist consumerism have all transformed and internationalized cultures, conceptualizations, and commodities. This increasingly powerful process of convergence has captured the popular imagination to the extent that "globalization" is as much a subject of media interest as of academic enquiry.

Yet convergence and globalization are not all-embracing, unidirectional, and homogenizing processes, as Robertson (1991, 1992) has claimed. Rather, their impact varies greatly in extent and intensity over time, across space, and within and between cultures and social classes. Moreover, counter-movements, both conscious and unpremeditated, are occurring simultaneously. Divergence, economic and social counter-penetration, the emergence of new syncretic forms of social and material culture, including deviance (that ultimate social construct for non-conformity), are constantly emerging. Furthermore, as discussed in greater detail below, globalized consumerism and industrial production for global markets often occur to very different extents in particular regions. Africa is a classic case in point: its increasing marginalization within the world economy reflects, as pointed out in chapter 2, the paucity of inward foreign direct investment and exports of secondary or tertiary output. The continent's exports remain overwhelmingly primary commodities, while a high proportion of manufactured goods are still imported or produced purely for the local market.

"Globalization," except in a superficial, journalistic sense, therefore has little meaning and analytical utility in general terms. It is precisely the kind of totalizing or universalizing construct being called into question by postmodern modes of social enquiry. As the contributions in King (1991) reveal clearly, globalization even has very different meanings in the cultural arena for various academic disciplines.

More specifically, too, we need to highlight the difference between form and content or substance. The term "Coca Cola culture" illustrates this extremely well. Facilitated by increasing transnationalization and global organization of production in an array of manufacturing industries and categories of services such as finance and telecommunications, together with high-profile advertising, it has acquired widespread international currency as a symbol of a supposedly healthy, carefree, recreationally oriented, middle-class and consumerist lifestyle. Until comparatively recently, the use of European models and actors in worldwide advertising promoted images and constructions of Western material sophistication and the desirability of such lifestyles. However, in poorer regions, not least Africa, the demonstration effect was constrained by the unattainability of any aspirations that might have been stimulated in the majority of the population. Increasingly also, nationalist sentiment, resentment at the perpetuation of images of (implied) European superiority, and the reassertion of indigenous values and roles – albeit in an overtly modernizing context – led to increasing use of indigenous models and actors. This change – crafty, subtle, or driven by necessity according to one's perspective – served the dual purpose of assuaging such hostile ("unhelpful") sentiments and simultaneously conveying new images of local acceptability, desirability, and wider attainability. The demonstration effect of élite Westernized lifestyles and consumerism was thus enhanced for the growing middle classes and also the poor, especially in urban areas. Coca Cola and similar brand names are no longer the sole preserve of urban affluence but are readily obtainable and widely consumed even in remote villages across rural Africa. They are disproportionately expensive in relation to average money incomes, and are nutritionally of little value. Particularly for the poor, the high opportunity cost and potential dietary and health consequences count for little in relation to the real or imagined prestige acquired.

What has this apparent evidence *for* globalized consumption patterns got to do with form versus content or substance? Simply this. Although Coke, McDonald's, and even Toyotas in varying states of decrepitude are now common commodities from Greenland to Mount Kilimanjaro, and are having an impact on lifestyles, we cannot assume that this is necessarily evidence of social and cultural convergence in a unidirectional, linear sense with a predetermined or universally predictable outcome. Adoption may lead to adaptation and innovation, to different forms of diversity rather than to global homogenization. This process can also be contradictory with respect to different commodities, cultural forms, and identities. This should hardly be surprising, given that such ambiguities and contrasts are commonly evident in the character of individual people, despite the misplaced assumptions of (economic) rationality and consistency of behaviour in still-influential paradigms ranging from modernization to Marxism. Much recent anthropological and social psychological research into identity, difference, and senses of self has highlighted people's multiple – and often contradictory – identities arising from domestic and non-domestic roles, as well as differential identification with a number of relevant socially or territorially defined groups and contexts. As I have argued previously,

Moreover, changes and the identities which emerge are inherently likely to overlap and perhaps even conflict. People can and do operate simultaneously in very different social, cultural and material environments, often also at different geographical scales. The most obvious examples are the national elites and bourgeoisies, which operate nationally and internationally in professional terms or for leisure purposes by means of the jumbo jet, (mobile) telephone, fax, laptop computer with modem, satellite dish, electronic bank transfer, credit card and a lingua franca like English or French, while often still retaining an active role in indigenous traditions and activities. They often own or even work part-time on rural plots or *shambas*, which may be home to parents and other members of the extended family, quite possibly living and working in largely "traditional" ways and speaking only the local vernacular. (Simon, 1992, p. 102)

In the context of the theme of this chapter, the implications of the foregoing are important. We cannot assume that Africa, and in particular its large cities, are increasingly similar to other continental regions of the third world, simply because of evidence of global material culture and the physical appearance of central business districts or because, increasingly, the city centre pavements have become as much the preserve of the beggar as of the suited businessperson and civil servant. Our concern must be with underlying process rather than purely with external appearances. Processes of urban convergence and divergence have been documented in Africa (O'Connor, 1983; Simon, 1992), Latin America and Asia (Armstrong and McGee, 1985), and the Caribbean (Potter, 1993), but, although they have many comparable aspects, there are also significant regional and local differences. These reflect the intensity of integration into, and role(s) within, the changing international divisions of labour of any particular country or region. The European colonial impact was clearly of fundamental importance in this process and, especially in now peripheral regions where decolonization occurred only recently, as in most of Africa, the aftermath of this experience and the persistence of neo-colonial relations are still keenly felt (see chap. 2). Nevertheless, it would be unhelpful and deterministic merely to attribute the situation to external forces in a manner reminiscent of the *dependistas*. What we can assert, however, is that the nature of urbanization (strongly influenced by colonial policies as it was), and the relative extent and dimensions of wealth and poverty, indebtedness or prosperity are inextricably linked, and the rest of this chapter explores these interrelationships.

The positions and role of African cities in the world economy

It is now well established that Africa, and especially sub-Saharan Africa (SSA), has become the world's poorest continent, with per capita income levels in many countries now back roughly to what they were during the early 1960s. Food production increases have not kept pace with the average population growth of 3 per cent per annum, with the result that food imports have been rising by 10 per cent per annum since the 1980s. This situation cannot be more than partially attributed to the succession of droughts and famines experienced in the Sahel, Horn of Africa, and central–southern Africa. Because of their reliance on primary exports, as noted by Rakodi, African countries have suffered a longstanding deterioration in their terms of trade. For these as well as internal reasons, the debt crisis has increased, Structural Adjustment Programmes have had a profound effect, and absolute poverty has afflicted progressively more people in urban as well as rural areas. As discussed in greater detail in the next section of this chapter, the 1980s proved so disastrous in development terms that they have been dubbed "the Lost Decade." Most people elsewhere now associate the continent with images of starvation, war, refugees, and general human misery even more than with the traditional exotic "otherness" of graceful tribespeople and stunning environments, scenery, or wildlife. There have, however, been a few bright spots, perhaps most notably Botswana's buoyant mineral-led economic growth and social development, the end of apartheid rule in South Africa, and moves towards apparent democratization in countries across the continent.

Nevertheless, Africa has acquired the unwanted status of being the outer periphery of the world economy. Although there are certainly some attractive investment opportunities, particularly in the minerals sector and other forms of primary production, as discussed in chapter 2, there was sustained disinvestment from the continent during the 1980s. Africa now accounts for no more than 4–6 per cent of net global foreign direct investment (FDI) by most major Western transnational corporations (Bennell, 1990; Simon, 1992). As Bennell's work clearly shows,

The importance of Africa as a location of British overseas investment in global terms declined considerably since the mid-1970s. In fact, net industrial investment in Africa by UK companies has become relatively inconsequential, amounting to less than 0.5% of total industrial FDI in 1986 compared with around 4% in the mid 1970s ... The percentage of total net earnings derived from African industrial investments has declined somewhat less – from 4.7% in 1978 to 3.4% in 1986 – but it will undoubtedly continue to fall in the future, given the already dramatic fall in the relative size of British net investments in Africa. For British industrial capital as a whole, therefore, Africa is now of minor interest. (Bennell, 1990, p. 159)

Moreover, the most recent data available show that Africa's share of total new global FDI averaged 13 per cent for 1981–1985 but fell to 11 per cent for 1986–1990, despite the implementation of structural adjustment and economic recovery programmes (UNCTAD, 1994). In 1991, investment inflows totalled US$2.5bn, a 21 per cent increase over 1990 but still below the 1985–1990 average of $2.7bn. The bulk of this FDI went to oil-exporting countries, although a marked increase to Morocco helped raise the proportion attracted by non-oil exporters to 28 per cent for the 1989–1991 period, compared with only 20 per cent for 1986–1988. With the exception of South Africa, investment outflows from Africa were negligible during 1991 (UNCTAD, 1993).

Unfortunately, the one recent attempt (of which I am aware) to address the relationship between FDI and urbanization in developing countries is unhelpful, relying on very dated literature and data, failing to mention Africa at all, and throwing little new light on the relationships (Sit, 1993). In the past few years, some signs of industrial and especially manufacturing recovery in Africa have emerged (table 3.1). The picture remains mixed, however, with countries

Table 3.1   **Growth of manufacturing value added at constant 1980 prices, 1975–1985 and 1985–1990 (selected countries)**

Country or area[a]	Total MVA					
	Growth rate (%)		Index (1980 = 100)			
	1975–1985	1985–1990	1987	1988	1989	1990
Algeria	9.0	2.1	166	174	170	170
Angola	1.5	3.2	106	110	122	123
Benin	3.3	−4.6	110	116	110	115
Botswana	4.1	9.7	174	183	194	203
Cameroon	15.2	−2.7	286	246	231	238
Chad	−7.0	4.5	80	87	93	91
Congo	9.6	2.1	188	201	209	212
Côte d'Ivoire	3.7	−1.6	116	116	109	103
Egypt	7.1	3.6	154	161	159	166
Gabon	2.5	−9.0	68	62	62	64
Ghana	−7.7	6.1	98	103	104	109
Kenya	6.9	5.8	135	143	151	159
Lesotho	13.2	13.6	241	288	328	315
Libyan Arab Jamahiriya	14.0	4.6	226	231	240	249
Mauritania	8.0	6.2	175	188	194	208
Mauritius	5.4	10.4	206	222	233	251
Nigeria	5.0	5.2	94	106	108	116
São Tomé and Príncipe	−2.1	2.8	86	88	89	92
Senegal	1.3	6.7	147	162	166	174
Seychelles	7.9	8.4	125	138	142	157
Somalia	2.0	6.1	96	106	111	111
Swaziland	5.4	7.0	139	163	155	167
Tanzania, U. Rep. of	−2.6	5.1	78	83	89	96
Tunisia	9.2	6.3	153	163	173	192
Uganda	−6.5	13.7	111	136	161	173
Zambia	0.9	7.6	121	143	142	153
Zimbabwe	3.2	4.1	118	124	132	137

Source: UNIDO (1993), table 3.3.

a. The countries listed have been selected to highlight the range of performances as well as of changes in growth rates of MVA between the two periods. Data on South Africa are not given in the original source.

such as Benin, Côte d'Ivoire, Cameroon, Libya, and Mali showing a continued deterioration. Given the continuing political uncertainty and instability in many countries, coupled with the overall economic climate, especially in relation to the far higher rates of return in Pacific Asia, parts of Latin America, and central Europe, there can be little realistic prospect of a substantial increase in FDI in the foreseeable future. In any case, only a comparatively small percentage of this would be attracted to the major cities for key infrastructural and prestige developments and the opening of offices by foreign investors, given the predominance of resource-based production across the continent and the concentration of FDI in agriculture, mineral exploitation, and infrastructure (Simon 1992, p. 49). This spread is, in turn, hardly surprising in view of Bennell's (1990, p. 167) data, which show that rates of return on non-industrial FDI by British firms in anglophone Africa (outside South Africa and Namibia) were nearly double those on industrial investment between 1978 and 1984.

Despite the central importance of agriculture and mineral exploitation (especially to exports), South Africa has important urban industrial complexes, making it the principal exception to Africa's heavy primary sector dominance. Yet, even here, full data on FDI are not published – probably because of its political sensitivity until early 1994. From the evidence that a recent study managed to assemble for the period from the final quarter of 1989 to the second quarter of 1993 (Garner, 1993), it is not possible to say with any degree of accuracy what proportion would have accrued directly to the principal urban areas. However, the sectoral breakdown suggests that it was actually very high, since 21 per cent of inward investments were in the motor industry, 21 per cent in electronics, 11 per cent in chemicals, 9 per cent in building, over 5 per cent in pharmaceuticals, and 4 per cent in engineering, all of which have high urban concentrations. How representative these data are of total FDI in South Africa, or of other time-periods, is not clear.

One characteristically urban-based form of economic activity is the business and personal service sector, and it has been the most rapidly growing element of African economies of late. However, although several countries, including Kenya, Zimbabwe, Botswana, and Namibia, have recently established stock exchanges, most of the continent's 14 active stock markets still trade almost exclusively in local stock. More generally, capital markets also remain very limited. South Africa is the principal exception, because the long-established Johannesburg Stock Exchange is well established in the top international league. This is evident in the difference between its market capitalization and that of Cairo, its nearest rival (table 3.2).

Other dimensions of Africa's peripherality are illustrated by the level of foreign diplomatic representation, and the location of headquarters and secretariats of international organizations. These are

Table 3.2 **Africa's active stock markets, March 1994**

Country	No. of companies listed	Market capitalization (US$ m.)	Average P/E[a]
Botswana	10	280	7.5
Côte d'Ivoire[b]	30	423.3	N/A
Egypt	674	1,487	5.1
Ghana	15	191	7.5
Kenya	56	1,800	10.0
Mauritius	30	960.5	N/A
Morocco	60	3,500	14.0
Namibia	5	75	9.8
Nigeria[b]	174	1,029.2	6.3
South Africa	703	216,650	18.2
Swaziland	4	290.86	N/A
Tunisia	20	1,291	15.8
Zambia	New	New	New
Zimbabwe	62	1,810	12.6

Source: *Kencom Digest* 12(3), July 1994, Kenya Commercial Bank, Nairobi.
a. P/E = price to earnings ratio.
b. Data for December 1993.

closely related, since foreign missions located in the strategic cities commonly have accreditation in several adjacent countries of lesser importance. Overall, the number of embassies, high commissions, and consulates in African capitals is smaller than in politically and economically powerful regions. Nevertheless, the relative numbers within Africa provide a good indication of external perceptions of the importance of individual cities and countries. Small, peripheral states such as Lesotho (9), Guinea-Bissau (17), and Malawi (19) have tiny diplomatic communities. Most African states have between 30 and 45 foreign legations. Atop the list are Ethiopia (70), Kenya (72), Nigeria (82), and Egypt (109) (Europa, 1992). Although South Africa had only 44 in 1992, these had the largest staff complements in Africa of many Western countries on account of the large white population of European origin and the strength of economic ties. Moreover, the number of embassies has risen dramatically since then, with the end of apartheid and South Africa's full re-admission to the international community.

Addis Ababa owes its standing primarily to the location there of the Organization of African Unity, the UN Economic Commission for Africa, and several associated organizations. Nairobi benefits from hosting the UN Environment Programme (UNEP), the UN Centre for Human Settlements (UNCHS), and numerous satellite intergovernmental and non-governmental organizations, as well as being the economic hub of East Africa. Lagos is the ex-capital of Africa's most populous country, which has considerable oil resources and experienced dramatic economic growth during the 1970s (see chap. 6). Cairo, an ancient city, remains in effect the headquarters of the Arab world, as the seat of the Arab League and related bodies, and also serves as a gateway between Africa, the Middle East, and Europe (see chap. 4).

Table 3.3 shows the extent to which major African cities host the headquarters of international organizations of various types. This provides another good indication of the strength of insertion into global networks of contacts, communications, and leverage. Although the principal cities come out well in aggregate terms relative to the hubs of other world regions of the South, when principal secretariats of *global* membership organizations are considered separately (Category A), African cities are very poorly represented. In the main, therefore, they host regional or continental secretariats of global bodies, and the headquarters of African organizations. This again reflects peripherality. It is interesting but unsurprising that there was little change in the position of African cities relative to other regions from 1990 to 1993, although all the African cities increased their total number of secretariats (cf. Simon, 1992, 1993). Such increases were not recorded in any other region. It is also noteworthy that Cairo and Nairobi, now hosting the largest numbers of secretariats in Africa, registered the most significant increases. Moreover, the Nairobi data omit the headquarters of the UNEP and UNCHS, both global membership organizations, an important anomaly probably explicable in terms of note (b) to table 3.3. The table also shows the extent to which Europe and North America remain the primary fulcrums of decision-making power in these terms.

Although, to the best of my knowledge, such an investigation has not been done, I believe that research into the extent of core metropolitan dominance over African cities in terms of international bank corporate structures and representation would reveal findings very similar to those of Meyer (1986) in respect of Latin America. If anything, the dominance–dependence links would be clearer and more concentrated, given the relative lack of economic dynamism on the continent and the strong recent colonial roles of Britain, France, and (to a lesser extent in continental terms) Portugal. Examining patterns

Table 3.3 **African cities with the greatest number of secretariats of international organizations,[a] 1993**

City[b]	Principal secretariats[c]				Secondary secretariats[c]				Grand total
	A	B	C	Total	A	B	C	Total	
Nairobi	0	30	83	113	1	2	11	14	127
Dakar	0	21	43	64	0	3	4	7	71
Addis Ababa	0	8	38	46	0	1	7	8	54
Tunis	0	13	11	24	1	0	1	2	26
Abidjan	0	16	20	36	1	1	1	3	39
Cairo	5	29	34	68	1	2	4	7	75
Lagos	2	16	16	34	1	2	3	6	40
Accra	0	14	14	28	0	1	2	3	31
Ouagadougou	0	8	12	20	0	0	4	4	24
Harare	0	11	13	24	4	0	7	11	35
Yaoundé	0	13	9	22	0	1	0	1	23
Some comparisons:									
Asia									
Bangkok	3	11	73	87	1	0	8	9	96
Manila	2	26	44	72	3	3	8	14	86
Kuala Lumpur	3	14	28	45	1	3	2	6	51
New Delhi	4	13	24	41	1	1	1	3	44
Jakarta	2	6	25	33	1	1	2	4	37
Seoul	1	13	10	24	3	3	2	8	32

of control within the world system of cities, Meyer found – unsurprisingly – that a clear hierarchy emerged, with core metropolises dominating Latin American cities. Moreover, the dominance by the leading core metropolises was more intense than that by second-level metropolises in the core. In 1980/81, 53 and 25 per cent of the international banks with offices in Latin America had their headquarters in European and North American metropolises, respectively. Given the centrality of international financial institutions, both corporate and intergovernmental, to global circuits of capital in these days of flexible accumulation and instantaneous international electronic transactions, such findings are very important. Moreover, unlike other activities of transnational corporations in Africa, such banking functions are specifically urban in location.

Many other variables can provide pertinent insights, as revealed in a far more extensive study (Simon, 1992). Although these often reveal a high level of congruence, because dominance–dependence

Table 3.3 **(cont.)**

City[b]	Principal secretariats[c]				Secondary secretariats[c]				Grand total
	A	B	C	Total	A	B	C	Total	
Latin America and Caribbean									
Buenos Aires	3	47	29	79	2	7	2	11	90
Mexico City	1	28	23	52	1	1	8	10	62
Santiago	0	16	58	74	2	2	5	9	83
Caracas	0	25	41	66	2	5	5	12	78
Bogatà	2	16	10	28	0	3	3	6	34
São Paulo	1	15	7	23	1	3	2	6	29
Europe									
Brussels	83	351	657	1,091	10	71	98	179	1,270
Paris	135	215	348	698	68	45	54	167	865
London	118	140	257	515	14	13	32	59	574
Rome	20	23	430	473	4	4	12	20	493
Geneva	68	36	243	347	19	9	28	56	403
North America									
New York	18	22	188	228	11	4	33	48	276
Washington, D.C.	14	15	131	160	6	3	19	28	188
Montreal	12	10	24	46	2	1	8	11	57
Ottawa	5	5	12	22	3	2	4	9	31

Source: Union of International Associations (1993: table 10).

a. International organizations include all non-profit bodies, whether governmental or non-governmental.

b. Secretariats located in differently named suburbs/districts are not always included.

c. A: International organizations with global or intercontinental membership (i.e. *Yearbook* categories A–C).

B: Regionally defined membership organizations, representing at least three countries in a particular continent or subcontinent region (i.e. *Yearbook* category D).

C: Other (including funds, foundations, religious orders, etc. (i.e. *Yearbook* categories E, F, R).

and core–periphery relationships are mutually reinforcing, there is no necessary direct correlation. For example, although Cairo followed by Johannesburg are Africa's busiest airports in terms of aggregate passenger flows, the balance between international and domestic passengers is more revealing in terms of connectivity with the world economy. Cairo's passengers are overwhelmingly international, and scheduled flights serve a far wider range of destinations around the world than is the case with any other African airport. Although Johannesburg has high domestic flows, international traffic has always been considerable and it has risen markedly since the late 1980s as the demise of apartheid approached. By contrast, Lagos has surprisingly low international passenger throughputs, deriving the bulk of its flows from domestic traffic. Nairobi's high international passenger flows have suffered over the past few years as a result of political unrest deterring some foreign tourists, coupled with the far smaller number of flights between Europe and South Africa stopping to refuel since the introduction of the Boeing 747-400 at the beginning of the 1990s. This example serves as a reminder that the relative positions of individual cities (especially within a single world region) in the world system, on one or more specific variables, can change rapidly in response to political, economic, and/or technological developments (Simon, 1992). It is important not to regard relative positions, as shown by indicators such as those used here, as immutable, and thus to assume too deterministic a perspective.

Overall, though, Africa has been becoming more, rather than less, peripheral in global politico-economic terms over the past two decades or so. This is symbolized by the fact that there is no true world city, however defined, on the continent, and no immediate prospect of there being one in the foreseeable future (Simon, 1992, 1993; see also chap. 2). However, the actual picture is more complex. The process of globalization has been operating extremely unequally, having its principal impact in capital and other major African cities. In key respects, therefore, these pivots between domestic and international relations, these basing points for international transactions, are as well integrated into the continental and even global system of cities as into their domestic space economies. But intra-urban inequalities are probably even sharper than the urban–rural disparities discussed in detail in the following section. The accumulation of capital and the sophistication and often ostentatious Western lifestyles of the national élites and bourgeoisies are built on exploitation. The majority of residents in Cairo, Johannesburg, Lagos, Nairobi, Addis Ababa, Abidjan, or Dar es Salaam have little stake in this globalizing, materialistic culture. As Friedmann and Wolff (1982, p. 322) put it, "The juxtaposition [of extreme wealth and poverty] is not merely spatial; it is a functional relation: rich and poor define each other." This applies as much to Africa's mega-cities and others with important supranational roles as to world cities *per se*. In the next section, I move on to explore the relationships between economic performance and urbanization, with respect particularly to rural–urban disparities and prevailing politico-economic conditions.

Urbanization trends and their relationship to economic and social conditions

Urbanization levels and rates since 1960

With an aggregate urbanization level of only 31 per cent in 1991, sub-Saharan Africa (SSA) is the least urbanized continental region in the world, although there is considerable diversity between its constituent countries. At 54 per cent, the average figure for the Maghreb was rather higher than for SSA (table 3.4). These UN Development Programme (UNDP) data[1] show that altogether only five African states had over half their populations recorded or estimated as "urban" in 1991: Djibouti (81 per cent), Libya (70 per cent), South Africa (58 per cent), Tunisia (54 per cent), and Algeria (52 per cent), while the Zambian figure was exactly 50 per cent. The first two are both exceptional – Djibouti as a micro-state and Libya as a vast tract of desert with its population concentrated in Tripoli and Benghazi. Potts (1994, p. 6, and chap. 13) argues that the Zambian data are spurious, since the 1990 census showed an urbanization level of only 42 per cent, a mere 2 per cent higher than in 1980.

According to UNDP (1993), another 11 countries fell in the 40–49 per cent range, namely Egypt, the Congo, Gabon, Cameroon, the Central African Republic, Côte d'Ivoire, Liberia, Mauritania, Mauritius, Morocco, and Zaire. The majority of countries had levels of between 20 and 39 per cent, while the least urbanized were Malawi (12 per cent), Burkina Faso (9 per cent), Rwanda (8 per cent), and Burundi (6 per cent) (table 3.4). As noted in chapter 2, given the significant differences between countries in terms of the definition of an urban area, not to mention the recency, coverage, and accuracy of the most recent census, these figures should be treated with caution, i.e. as ballpark estimates rather than as totally reliable.

Given the low *levels* of urbanization, it is hardly surprising that urban growth *rates* have been consistently among the highest in the world over the past 30-odd years, approximately the period since most African countries were decolonized and colonial restrictions on rural–urban mobility and migration rescinded. The annual average for SSA has been 5–6 per cent, compared with 3–4 per cent per annum for total national population growth. At the upper extreme, many of the principal (usually primate) cities have grown by 9–11 per cent per annum. According to table 3.4, Botswana (13.5 per cent), Swaziland (10.5 per cent), and Tanzania (10.3 per cent) experienced

Table 3.4   **African urbanization trends, 1960–2000**

Human Development Index rank	Country	Urban population (as % of total)			Urban population annual growth rate (%)	
		1960	1991	2000^a	1960–1991	1991–2000^a
Medium human development		25	42	54	4.0	4.0
56	Mauritius	33	41	42	2.3	1.3
85	South Africa	47	58	66	3.2	3.2
87	Libyan Arab Jamahiriya	23	70	76	8.1	4.5
93	Tunisia	36	54	59	3.6	2.7
104	Botswana	2	28	42	13.5	7.9
107	Algeria	30	52	60	4.7	4.3
109	Gabon	17	46	54	6.3	4.9
Low human development		16	28	34	4.2	4.5
Excluding India		15	29	36	4.7	4.9
114	Cape Verde	16	29	36	4.1	5.6
117	Swaziland	4	33	45	10.5	6.7
119	Morocco	29	48	55	4.3	3.8
120	Lesotho	3	20	28	8.6	6.3
121	Zimbabwe	13	28	35	5.9	5.4
124	Egypt	38	47	54	3.1	3.6
125	São Tomé and Príncipe	–	33	–	–	–
126	Congo	32	41	47	3.6	4.9
127	Kenya	7	24	32	7.7	7.0
128	Madagascar	11	24	31	5.6	6.0
130	Zambia	17	50	59	7.1	5.5
131	Ghana	23	33	38	3.9	4.6
133	Cameroon	14	41	51	6.5	5.7
135	Namibia	15	28	34	4.8	5.4
136	Côte d'Ivoire	19	40	47	6.5	5.5
138	Tanzania, U. Rep of	5	33	47	10.3	7.5
140	Zaire	22	40	46	4.8	5.0
142	Nigeria	14	35	43	6.3	5.4
144	Liberia	19	46	57	6.2	5.5
145	Togo	10	26	33	6.2	6.0
146	Uganda	5	10	14	6.1	6.6
149	Rwanda	2	8	11	7.4	7.6
150	Senegal	32	38	45	3.5	4.4
151	Ethiopia	6	13	17	4.8	5.8
153	Malawi	4	12	16	6.5	6.5
154	Burundi	2	6	7	5.5	6.1
155	Equatorial Guinea	25	29	33	1.5	4.0
156	Central African Rep.	23	47	55	4.8	4.6
157	Mozambique	4	27	41	9.5	7.2
158	Sudan	10	22	27	5.4	4.8

Table 3.4 **(cont.)**

Human Development Index rank	Country	Urban population (as % of total)			Urban population annual growth rate (%)	
		1960	1991	2000[a]	1960–1991	1991–2000[a]
160	Angola	10	28	36	5.9	5.4
161	Mauritania	6	47	59	9.8	5.3
162	Benin	9	38	45	7.4	5.0
163	Djibouti	50	81	84	7.3	3.5
164	Guinea-Bissau	14	20	25	3.2	4.7
165	Chad	7	30	39	7.1	5.4
166	Somalia	17	36	44	5.8	4.7
167	Gambia	13	23	30	5.2	5.3
168	Mali	11	19	23	4.4	5.2
169	Niger	6	20	27	7.4	6.7
170	Burkina Faso	5	9	12	4.6	6.3
172	Sierra Leone	13	32	40	5.2	5.1
173	Guinea	10	26	33	5.3	5.8
	All developing countries	22	37	45	4.0	4.0
	Least developed countries	8	20	26	5.3	5.8
	Sub-Saharan Africa	15	31	38	5.2	5.3

Source: UNDP (1993).
a. Projected.

the most rapid rates of urban growth, which explains their average current urbanization levels in relation to the negligible figures recorded in 1960. Only four other countries – Lesotho, Libya, Mauritania, and Mozambique – experienced urban growth of 8–10 per cent per annum. These seven countries were among the poorest in Africa in 1960. Four of them still are, but Swaziland has experienced a marked improvement in economic and social conditions (attested to by its Human Development Index rank of 117) and Libya and Botswana have benefited from dynamic economic growth precipitated by oil and diamond exploitation, respectively, which in turn has been utilized to increase overall social well-being commendably.

At the other end of the spectrum, countries with relatively high urbanization levels in 1960, including Egypt, Tunisia, South Africa, the Congo, and Equatorial Guinea, experienced modest urban growth rates of 3–4 per cent annually, apart from a mere 1.5 per cent in the last-mentioned. Even here, though, caution is needed, as South Africa's urban growth rate was systematically depressed by the notorious excesses of "influx control" and the pass laws, which persisted until 1986 under apartheid rule (see chap. 5). Since then, the rate of rural–urban migration has accelerated dramatically – although no accurate figures are available. Despite apartheid, however, it is no coincidence that South Africa has the highest urbanization level in SSA, because it is the continent's most industrialized and economically sophisticated country.

Is there a link between economic and urban growth?

Unfortunately the average urbanization rates over a 31-year period provided by UNDP (1993), as reflected in table 3.4, conceal significantly different trends over shorter sub-periods for many countries, even assuming a reasonable degree of accuracy in the data, something that is frequently not the case. Generally, as shown in the previous chapter, the rates were highest during the immediate post-colonial period, coinciding with the economic boom years of the 1960s and early 1970s. Thereafter, the process slowed down somewhat in many countries, before accelerating again. Economic crisis, growing indebtedness, and the impact of structural adjustment during the 1980s and early 1990s have created a more complex and diverse picture. Some support for this contention is derived from the urbanization rates presented in World Bank (1992), which do distinguish the 1965–1980 period from 1980–1990. For 19 of the 43 African countries included, urban growth was faster during the 1980s than during the preceding period, whereas for 21 it was slower. For the remaining 3, it remained virtually constant. The lowest growth rates in Africa cited for the 1980s were 0.4 per cent in Mauritius (down from 2.4 per cent), 2.9 per cent in Tunisia (down from 4.0 per cent), and 3.1 per cent in Egypt (up from 2.7 per cent). In all the other countries, the figures imply that urban growth remained faster than the total population growth rates, which were overwhelmingly between 3 and 3.5 per cent annually. This implication is open to question, as will become clear below.

However, as also stressed by Rakodi and other contributors in this volume, the lack of detailed and reliable data makes it difficult to write with confidence. Many UN and World Bank figures are estimates, modified data, or projections made on various assumptions. One reason for this is the inadequacy of data produced by national statistical offices. This problem is arguably most acute in Nigeria, where all censuses since 1963 have been officially repudiated as untenable (Simon, 1992, p. 171). The most recent, in November 1991, was carefully designed and executed with the aid of a dusk-to-dawn curfew in an effort to be above reproach. However, the total population figure of approximately 88.5 million, being some 20–30 million lower than previous estimates and extrapolations (*The Independent*, 20 March 1992), has again proved very controversial and contested. It is also widely felt to be inaccurate and the census may yet be cancelled after all (*Nigerian Tribune*, 23 November 1994).

It appears that some but by no means all of the primate cities have continued to grow very rapidly, especially in poor countries. This is probably on account of a relative lack of attractive alternative destinations for migrants and the prospects of access to facilities and income-earning opportunities, even during recession and structural adjustment, which have reduced traditional rural–urban income disparities (Jamal and Weeks, 1988, 1993). The Tanzanian case illustrates these issues well. Suggestions that the growth of Dar es Salaam declined during the 1978–1988 intercensal period (Barke and Sowden, 1992), have been sharply criticized by Briggs (1993) on the grounds of deficient and incomplete data and misinterpretation of the available data. Whereas both these papers rely on preliminary census data, Potts (1994, pp. 6–7; see also chap. 13) uses the rather different final census figures in arguing that Dar grew by 4.8 per cent per annum from 1978 to 1988, a significant reduction from the 9.7 per cent rate recorded during the previous intercensal period. Nevertheless, even the slower rate is well above the total population growth rate, implying that net in-migration to Dar remained significant. Barke and Sowden (1992) assert that secondary cities continued to grow very rapidly, but Potts cites the final census report, showing that only four grew faster than Dar es Salaam while seven grew more slowly. Evidence from the census and primary fieldwork by Holm (1995) suggest that Tanzania's intermediate towns grew faster than either large cities or small urban centres during the 1980s, although these rates seem to have slowed since the late 1980s as infrastructure and general living conditions there deteriorated steadily. Even here, the balance between the cost of living and income-earning opportunities was unfavourable. The continued urban residence of migrants is therefore explicable in terms of economic diversification and risk-minimizing strategies by "multi-active" households and extended families divided between town and the rural *shamba*. Access to services unavailable in rural areas remains a vital part of their equation.

Accra, the Ghanaian capital, was reputed to be experiencing significant net out-migration during the worst period of economic hardship in the early to mid-1980s, as people returned to their traditional stool or family lands. Informed Ghanaian sources suggest (pers. comm.) that this trend reversed again once conditions improved under the second Structural Adjustment Programme and PAMSCAD (the much-criticized Programme of Actions to Mitigate the Social Costs of Adjustment). Clear documentary evidence either way is still hard to come by, but Jeffries (1992, pp. 210–213) highlights how dramatically purchasing power and the real value of the legal minimum wage fell between 1974 and 1984 and from 1988 to 1990, with only a very modest recovery over the intervening years. Only a small proportion of the 46,000 civil servants retrenched between 1987 and 1990 took PAMSCAD loans, but of these, Jeffries suggests, a large proportion used them to facilitate a return to farming. Potts (1994, p. 10) reports census data as suggesting that some urban centres have been experiencing net out-migration to rural areas over a considerable period. The 1984 census data reveal a 3.2 per cent annual national urban growth rate for 1970–1984, a marked decline from the 1960–1970 rate of 4.8 per cent and seemingly consistent with deteriorating urban conditions. Curiously, the World Bank (1992) estimates the 1980–1990 urban growth rate at 4.2 per cent annually, a marked *increase* over its 3.2 per cent figure for 1965–1980. This does not seem likely.

Returning to the Zambian case, Potts (1994, and chap. 13) reports a steady decline in the overall urban growth rate over the three decades, from 8.9 per cent (1963–1969) to 5.8 per cent (1969–1980) to no more than 3.7 per cent (1980–1990) according to the respective censuses. This she attributes, plausibly enough, to the country's economic decline in the wake of the collapse of the world market price of copper, from which Zambia derives over 90 per cent of its export revenues. The Copperbelt towns have experienced the most dramatic decline in their growth rates and experienced net out-migration, in some cases already since the late 1970s. By contrast, World Bank urban growth estimates for Zambia were 7.2 per cent per annum for 1965–1980 and 6.7 per cent annually for 1980–1988, apparently ignoring the evidence.

Although the economic situation in Zimbabwe is arguably less severe than in the countries cited above, the World Bank (1992) estimates overall urban growth in Zimbabwe for 1980–1990 to have been 5.9 per cent per annum, virtually unchanged from the 6.0 per cent rate for 1965–1980. The latter is close to the census-based growth rate of 5.8 per cent per annum for 1969–1980. Harare's annual growth rate during the 1980s was recorded as 6.1 per cent in the 1992 census, although this was somewhat lower than expected in view of restrictions on rural–urban migration and the under-enumeration of urban Africans in censuses taken before independence in 1980. It may not, however, last into the 1990s, as several studies, for example Tevera (1995), indicate clearly how serious the impact of public expenditure cut-backs and other measures adopted under Zimbabwe's intensified Structural Adjustment Programme since 1991 has been upon the ability of Harare's urban poor to meet their basic needs.

The foregoing discussion shows clearly how difficult it is to be precise about any demographic and urban trends in Africa. The same is often true with economic data. Seeking clear relationships is therefore no easy task. Everything is contingent. Much depends on the particular data source, the statistical base used, the accuracy and coverage of surveys and censuses, and the method of inter- or extrapolation used for projections. African censuses have – justifiably in the main – acquired a reputation for being notoriously inaccurate on several of these counts (see chap. 2 and above). Whereas populations and growth rates were commonly underenumerated or under-estimated during the 1970s, it is plausible that the reverse was the case during the 1980s and in the 1990/91 census round. The World Bank is known to adjust national census data in line with other evidence and possibly its own preconceptions. Conversely, and without wishing to question her contentions, it seems that Potts, in her 1994 paper, placed great reliance on national census figures, just as she pointed to the uncritical use of 1990 World Bank data by Jamal and Weeks (1993).

The wide disparities between different sources are extraordinary. Part of the problem seems to be that data from different years and for somewhat different periods are being juxtaposed. The importance of comparing like with like is underlined by the rapidity with which the World Bank updates some of its data and estimates. For example, Potts's criticisms are based on Bank estimates for 1980–1988 used by Jamal and Weeks (1993) – presumably taken from the 1990 *World Development Report*, although Potts does not cite the original source. However, as indicated above with respect to Zimbabwe, for example, the Bank's estimates in its 1992 *World Development Report* cover the whole decade 1980–1990, are substantially lower than its earlier figures, and are close to the 1992 census data. On the other hand, as suggested earlier, the Bank's 1992 figures for Ghana are less plausible.

The 1980s were a period of unprecedented economic hardship for Africa. The combination of sustained depression in world market prices for the continent's principal primary export commodities, deteriorating terms of trade (especially for non-oil producers), and the long-term effects of inappropriate economic policies and expenditures and corruption proved unsustainable. As has been noted in chapter 2, more countries in Africa than anywhere else had adopted IMF/World Bank structural adjustment and economic recovery programmes (with differing degrees of voluntarism and coercion). Government expenditures were slashed, with the result that many social programmes and sectors suffered declining provision. The impact of these cuts was particularly serious for the most vulnerable groups but also for the middle classes, many of whom lost their jobs. At the same time, sub-Saharan Africa's level of indebtedness increased roughly threefold over the decade, making it the world's most indebted region relative to economic size and structure. In 1990, total debt stood at roughly the value of three years' exports of goods and services. By contrast, the position of the key Latin American debtor countries, such as Mexico and Brazil, which precipitated the "debt crisis," improved markedly (Simon, 1995). The majority of African countries suffered a decline in per capita GNP of up to 2 per cent per annum over the decade, but the most serious fall (−4.6 per cent annually) was recorded in Côte d'Ivoire, the World Bank's erstwhile model of market-oriented economic growth in West Africa (table 3.5). Very few countries recorded positive economic growth over the decade. Mauritius and Botswana head the list at 6.1 and 5.6 per cent per annum, respectively, but it is noteworthy that some of the poorest countries, e.g. Burundi (1.3 per cent), Chad (3.8 per cent), and Burkina Faso (1.2 per cent), also appear on it. Egypt recorded an annual rate of 1.9 per cent.

War, political turmoil, and periodic famine in rural areas have constituted another important source of urban growth in several African countries since the late 1970s, despite economic crisis and hardship. The floods of displaced people into Maputo, Luanda, Addis Ababa, and Monrovia exacerbated already difficult urban conditions in some of the continent's poorest states. Conversely, urban-based insurrections, as in Mogadishu and most recently in Kigali, precipitated large-scale exoduses of urban residents. How temporary or otherwise these flows prove varies in accordance with local conditions and the duration of fighting. In a similar context, the growing toll of the HIV/AIDS pandemic, being concentrated disproportionately among the younger, most economically active – and often best-educated – age cohorts, will have a marked impact upon economic performance and perhaps even on urbanization rates, while the social and health costs and burdens of care will mount rapidly.

One other (admittedly very crude) way to explore the relationship between urbanization rates and economic conditions is to compare the World Bank's (1992) estimates of urbanization rates for 1980–1990 and the average annual growth rates of GNP in 1980–1991 contained in World Bank (1993) (table 3.5). Not only are the data subject to inaccuracies and anomalies as already discussed, but many GNP figures omit the important "informal" sector and often also peasant production for domestic consumption. These sectors provide employment and forms of income for a high proportion of Africa's population at the best of times; during economic hardship, though, reliance on them increases still further as people engage in risk-spreading and survival strategies (see also chaps. 10 and 13). In recent years it has become more common to include GNP *estimates* for the subsistence sector, but these figures are often crude and tend to underestimate the actual position (Simon, 1992). The world's three lowest-income countries in terms of GNP per capita (Mozambique, Tanzania, and Ethiopia) all recorded negative economic growth of between −0.8 per cent and −1.6 per cent per annum during the 1980s, yet their urban growth rates remained extremely high (but see the discussion above regarding data on Tanzania). That of Ethiopia actually increased to 5.3 per cent per annum from 4.9 per cent between 1965 and 1980. Chad (3.8 per cent) and Burundi (1.3 per cent) both experienced positive economic growth rates, but these were still several per cent below their rates of urban growth, which nevertheless had declined modestly since the 1965–1980 period. There is thus considerable diversity, but nowhere did the rate of economic growth outstrip that of urban centres. The most extreme indicators of possible crisis are Niger, Rwanda, Côte d'Ivoire, and Gabon, which experienced economic growth rates of −4.1, −2.4, −4.6, and −4.2 per cent per annum simultaneously with urban growth rates of 7.6, 8.0, 4.5, and 6.2 per cent per annum respectively. These four countries span the World Bank's low-income, lower-middle-income, and upper-middle-income categories. Egypt and Tunisia represent the least unfavourable balances, with economic growth and urbanization rates of 1.9 and 1.1 per cent versus 3.1 and 2.9 per cent,

Table 3.5 **Urbanization and GNP growth rates, 1980–1990/91**

		Average annual growth rate (%)		
		Urban population		GNP per capita
		1965–1980	1980–1990	1980–1991
Low-income economies		3.5[a]	–	3.9[a]
	China and India	2.9[a]	–	5.6[a]
	Other low-income economies	4.7[a]	5.0[a]	1.0[a]
1	Mozambique	10.2	10.4	−1.1
2	Tanzania	11.3	10.5	−0.8
3	Ethiopia	4.9	5.3	−1.6
4	Somalia	5.4	5.6	–
6	Chad	8.0	6.5	3.8
9	Malawi	7.4	6.2	0.1
11	Burundi	6.9	5.5	1.3
12	Zaire	4.9	4.8	–
13	Uganda	4.8	4.4	–
14	Madagascar	5.2	6.4	−2.5
15	Sierra Leone	5.2	5.3	−1.6
16	Mali	4.4	3.7	−0.1
17	Nigeria	5.7	6.0	−2.3
18	Niger	7.2	7.6	−4.1
19	Rwanda	7.5	8.0	−2.4
20	Burkina Faso	4.1	5.3	1.2
22	Benin	8.9	5.1	−0.9
25	Kenya	8.1	7.9	0.3
27	Ghana	3.2	4.2	−0.3
28	Central African Republic	4.3	4.8	−1.4
29	Togo	6.6	6.9	−1.3
30	Zambia	6.6	6.2	–
31	Guinea	4.9	5.7	–
33	Mauritania	10.6	7.5	–
34	Lesotho	7.5	7.0	−0.5
37	Egypt	2.7	3.1	1.9
40	*Liberia*[b]	6.2	6.1	–
42	*Sudan*[b]	5.9	3.9	–

respectively (table 3.5). Again, Egypt is classified as a low-income and Tunisia as a lower-middle-income country. It therefore seems apparent that no *particular* relationship exists between a country's level of GNP per capita (a proxy for formal economic development) and the rate of either recorded economic growth or urban growth rates.

Table 3.4 also contains UNDP projections of urban growth rates during the final decade of the twentieth century. In the majority of cases, these are lower than for the 1960–1991 period; in only 18 is the

Table 3.5 **(cont.)**

		Average annual growth rate (%)		
		Urban population		GNP per capita
		1965–1980	1980–1990	1980–1991
Middle-income economies		3.9[a]	3.4[a]	0.3[a]
	Lower-middle-income economies	3.7[a]	3.6[a]	−0.1[a]
45	Zimbabwe[c]	6.0	5.9	−0.2
46	Senegal	3.3	4.0	0.1
48	Côte d'Ivoire	7.6	4.5	−4.6
52	Morocco	4.3	4.3	*1.6[b]*
53	Cameroon	7.6	5.9	−1.0
56	Congo	3.5	4.7	−0.2
63	Tunisia	4.0	2.9	1.1
71	Botswana[c]	12.6	9.9	5.6
72	Algeria	3.9	4.8	−0.7
74	Mauritius	2.5	0.4	6.1
79	*Angola[b]*	6.4	5.8	–
82	*Namibia[b]*	4.6	5.3	−1.2
Upper-middle-income economies		4.2[a]	3.2[a]	0.6[a]
86	South Africa	3.2	3.7	0.7
93	Gabon	7.3	6.2	−4.2
100	Libya	9.8	6.3	–
Low- and middle-income economies		3.7[a]	6.6[a]	1.0[a]
Sub-Saharan Africa		5.8[a]	5.9[a]	−1.2[a]
Middle East & North Africa		4.6[a]	4.4[a]	−2.4[a]

Sources: World Bank (1992, 1993).
a. Weighted average.
b. Data for years other than those specified.
c. In 1993, Zimbabwe was classified as a low-income country and Botswana as an upper-middle-income country.

rate expected to rise. The underlying assumptions and basis for projection are unclear, but are likely to be a combination of improved economic growth prospects and increasing rural poverty. The limitations of using past trends as the basis for making projections are now more widely appreciated (Hardoy and Satterthwaite, 1989).

The foregoing discussion indicates that, although there are clearly relationships between urbanization rates and prevailing economic and social conditions, they are complex and neither entirely consistent nor always predictable. Trying to "read off" current or future urbanization trends from economic data is a risky undertaking. For example, the evidence presented in the discussion above on individual countries and cities broadly supports Jamal and Weeks' (1988, 1993) thesis on the "vanishing rural–urban gap" in Africa in certain periods and in certain localities. But the Zambian and Tanzanian data also show that the fortunes of individual urban centres within a single country can vary considerably over the same period. In other words, one cannot automatically assume that falling in-migration and rising out-migration will occur simultaneously or in similar proportions. Holm's (1995) findings in two Tanzanian intermediate towns are significant in this context. Furthermore, economic and political crises need not necessarily reduce the rate of urbanization; there are several examples of the opposite being true, particularly if the immediate problems are concentrated in rural areas. In extreme conditions, such as those afflicting Mozambique during the 1980s, war and economic collapse combined to increase the rate of urban growth considerably.

Meeting urban basic needs

It is extremely difficult to obtain reliable and up-to-date estimates of the extent of basic needs fulfilment in many third world countries. The data on rural–urban disparities in access to basic health facilities, potable water, and adequate sanitation facilities included in the Human Development Report (UNDP, 1993) are thus useful as broad indicators (table 3.6), despite the many gaps and possible questions of accuracy. Access to safe water and sanitation is defined as "reasonable," i.e. within or in close proximity to the dwelling. Access to health services means within one hour's travel on foot or by other means. Unfortunately, there is no time series available to enable direct correlation with economic trends and urban growth rates as discussed in the previous subsection. However, the disparities in the late 1980s (the data are for some time in the 1987–1990 period in each case) are quite marked across Africa, with only a few exceptions. The figures for rural areas are on a par with the poorest countries and/or those with low levels of human development as measured by the Human Development Index.

For the countries with medium human development levels, the urban figures for all three variables are generally over 90 per cent; in rural areas accessibility may be as low as one-third to one-quarter of the urban figure, especially in respect of potable water, for which urban provision is particularly good. In the low human development category, the picture is more patchy and varied. Several countries, surprisingly including very poor ones such as Mali, Niger, and Burundi, apparently manage 100 per cent accessibility to urban water supplies. Notwithstanding the many gaps, especially in respect of health services, the lowest accessibility is commonly for rural sanitation facilities. Rural–urban disparities on this variable may be as high as 1 : 13 (Niger) but as low as 1 : 1.25 (Angola). Given the war devastation in Angola, however, the figure can be little more than notional, probably based on the pre-war situation. Egypt is one country in this category with extremely good provision in both urban and rural areas (apart from rural sanitation). These figures are borne out by recently published results of a 1992 national demographic and health survey. Unsurprisingly, provision in the four urban governorates of Cairo, Alexandria, Suez, and Port Said was marginally higher than for all urban areas (National Population Council et al., 1993, pp. 21–23). Overall, the data in table 3.6 provide some concrete evidence for the superior access to social services and basic needs in urban areas, undoubtedly one of the contributory causes of sustained rural–urban migration, as discussed above. We cannot, however, adduce anything direct about how such aggregate statistics relate to the preferences and priorities of individual citizens, or about relative provision in different categories of cities and towns. It is the largest centres on which the next section focuses.

Urbanization and the quality of life in large cities

Disproportionate attention – both academic and in terms of policy and resources – is still conventionally lavished on the primate and other largest cities in national settlement systems. This reflects the concentration of political and economic power there, their generally far more complex economic and physical structures, and the sheer scale of urban growth and its attendant resource requirements. There is almost universally a severe inadequacy of public resources relative to need, while in Africa the rate of growth in formal economic employment opportunities has never kept pace with population increase. For reasons of scale, intensity, and visibility, phenomena such as urban unemployment, shelter deficiency, increasing pollution, and inadequate infrastructure, social facilities, and management capacity in large cities still tend to displace concern with smaller urban centres to a significant extent (e.g. Stren and White, 1989; Gilbert and Gugler, 1992; Harris, 1992; Simon, 1992; Devas and Rakodi, 1993; Drakakis-Smith, 1993; Kasarda and Parnell, 1993).

Table 3.6 **Rural–urban disparities in access to basic services**

		Population with access to services (%)				
	Health		Water		Sanitation	
	Urban	Rural	Urban	Rural	Urban	Rural
HDI rank	1987–90	1987–90	1988–90	1988–90	1988–90	1988–90
Medium human development	–	81	90	59	90	72
56 Mauritius	100	100	100	100	100	96
85 South Africa	–	–	–	–	–	–
87 Libyan Arab Jamahiriya	100	100	100	80	100	85
93 Tunisia	100	80	95	31	72	15
104 Botswana	–	–	98	46	98	20
107 Algeria	100	80	85	55	80	40
109 Gabon	–	–	90	50	–	–
Low human development	98	–	78	56	47	11
Excluding India	94	59	77	40	54	18
114 Cape Verde	–	–	87	65	35	9
117 Swaziland	–	–	100	7	100	10
119 Morocco	100	30	100	50	100	19
120 Lesotho	–	–	59	45	–	–
121 Zimbabwe	–	–	–	14	100	22
124 Egypt	100	99	96	82	100	34
125 São Tomé and Príncipe	–	–	–	–	–	–
126 Congo	–	–	42	7	–	–
127 Kenya	–	–	61	21	75	39
128 Madagascar	–	–	81	10	12	–
130 Zambia	100	50	76	43	77	34
131 Ghana	–	–	93	39	63	15
133 Cameroon	–	–	47	27	35	16
135 Namibia	–	–	–	–	–	–
136 Côte d'Ivoire	–	–	100	75	69	20
138 Tanzania, U. Rep of	94	73	75	46	76	77
140 Zaire	–	–	59	17	14	14
143 Nigeria	87	62	100	20	30	5
144 Liberia	–	–	93	22	24	8
145 Togo	60	60	100	61	42	16
146 Uganda	–	–	45	12	40	10
149 Rwanda	–	–	66	64	–	–
150 Senegal	–	–	79	38	–	–
151 Ethiopia	–	–	70	11	97	7
153 Malawi	–	–	82	50	–	–

Table 3.6 **(cont.)**

| | Population with access to services (%) | | | | | |
| | Health | | Water | | Sanitation | |
HDI rank	Urban 1987–90	Rural 1987–90	Urban 1988–90	Rural 1988–90	Urban 1988–90	Rural 1988–90
154 Burundi	–	–	100	34	80	–
155 Equatorial Guinea	–	–	–	–	–	–
156 Central African Rep.	–	–	14	11	36	9
157 Mozambique	–	–	44	17	61	11
158 Sudan	–	–	–	–	40	5
160 Angola	–	–	75	19	25	20
161 Mauritania	–	–	67	65	34	–
162 Benin	–	–	79	35	60	31
163 Djibouti	–	–	50	21	94	20
164 Guinea-Bissau	–	–	–	–	30	18
165 Chad	–	–	–	–	–	–
166 Somalia	50	15	58	55	41	5
167 Gambia	–	–	92	73	–	–
168 Mali	–	–	100	36	94	5
169 Niger	–	17	100	52	39	3
170 Burkina Faso	–	–	–	–	35	6
172 Sierra Leone	88	–	83	22	59	35
173 Guinea			56	25	–	–
All developing countries	90	–	85	60	76	40
Least developed countries	85	–	61	45	45	15
Sub-Saharan Africa	87	–	79	28	47	18

Source: UNDP (1993).

Although these phenomena are conventionally constructed as "problems" by national élites and professionals, it is far from clear that all urban residents, especially some of the urban poor, would share such sentiments. After all, if migrants found conditions significantly worse than in their (rural or other urban) areas of origin, many would return there. This is not to say that people are necessarily happy with their lot, or that they do not suffer hardship and very real threats to their health and well-being, or to argue for official inaction instead of seeking to improve conditions. Rather, I am merely reminding us that people in different positions and from different backgrounds may have very different world-views, sets of ambitions and options, and scales of measuring good versus bad, acceptable versus unacceptable. "Substandard" dwellings, labelled a "slum" by officials and planners intent on demolition and rebuilding in the image of imported and often inappropriate urban layouts and building standards, may nevertheless represent a significant improvement over what the inhabitants lived in previously, not least in terms of their access to certain urban facilities. On the other hand, the rational choice thesis so dear to the neo-liberal orthodoxy that directs structural adjustment and economic recovery programmes will be a totally alien concept to most urban dwellers in Africa and elsewhere. Politico-economic forces often act to preclude or constrain individual choice and even world-views. For example, urban unemployment and poverty have risen markedly as a result of recession and the implementation of structural adjustment and economic recovery programmes since the early 1980s. This has had a substantial impact on the quality of life of many urban residents.

It has become commonplace to label all large cities "mega-cities." This is a very imprecise term, used with different meanings. Literally it refers to great size: the UN adopts a definition of a population of 8 million or more in some cases, but the recent UNEP/WHO (1992) study of urban pollution in mega-cities adopted a minimum population threshold of 10 million. Clearly, however, pure size does not serve as an adequate proxy for economic sophistication, urban well-being, or even a supranational role as in a continental or world city. Not all mega-cities are such key global control points and, conversely, some genuine world cities have far smaller populations. I shall return to this point below. If we adopt the 10 million population threshold, Africa has no more than two mega-cities: Greater Cairo (see chap. 4) and the Pretoria–Witwatersrand–Vereeniging (PWV) metropolitan region centred on Johannesburg (chap. 5). Thereafter the largest cities include Lagos, Kinshasa, Algiers, Greater Durban, Alexandria, Tripoli, Tunis, Casablanca, Greater Cape Town, Kano, Khartoum, Abidjan, and Ibadan, with estimated 1995 populations of between 2 and 8 million each.[2] Most African capital cities are under 2 million in size, although several, including Addis Ababa and Khartoum, are fast approaching that threshold. Conversely, the smallest cities (e.g. Mbabane, Maseru, Lilongwe, Gaborone, Windhoek) still have under 200,000 inhabitants.

In absolute terms, therefore, the sheer scale of so-called "mega-city problems" is not as severe as in Latin America and parts of Asia. In relative terms, however, given the state of most African economies, the problems may be extreme. The UNEP/WHO (1992) study of air pollution in mega-cities with populations of over 10 million did not include any African cities, but this does not give cause for complacency. Already the most industrial cities and those with high numbers of motor vehicles – the two principal sources of such pollutants – such as Lagos, the PWV, Durban, and Cape Town, suffer significant problems. Cairo and the PWV, whose pollution problems are referred to by Yousry and Aboul Atta (chap. 4) and Beavon (chap. 5), would now qualify for inclusion in any updated study. The 1992 report found that, in broad terms, the mega-cities of the South now suffer from poorer air quality and the associated problems than those of the increasingly post-industrial North. Rapid urban growth in the South is certain to widen this gap unless and until serious pollution abatement measures are enforced (see also Hardoy et al., 1992; World Bank, 1992). We should also not overlook the substantial contribution of wood and charcoal burning by the urban poor, both to overall air pollution levels in winter and to these people's health problems.

As a measure of basic needs fulfilment in the primate city of one of the poorest countries, recent survey data from Maputo, Mozambique, make useful reading. In late 1991, fully 82 per cent of families considered themselves to be poor, and 61 per cent were living in absolute poverty (*estado de indigência*), i.e. their per capita incomes did not cover their minimum nutritional requirements. A mere 18 per cent of families did not consider themselves to be poor. Just over 53 per cent of the city's total population were of economically active age (15 and over), but only 58 per cent of these were economically active (60 per cent of whom were men and only 40 per cent women). The overall labour force participation rate was 32 per cent of the total population. Among the absolute poor the rate was 29 per cent, among the relative poor 35 per cent, and among those not in poverty 37 per cent – a surprisingly modest difference (Commissão Nacional de Plano et al., 1993, pp. 6, 18). This depressing situation reflects the state of economic collapse in Mozambique as a result of the extremely destructive civil war, which has also brought large numbers of displaced people (*deslocados*) into Maputo and other cities. Today, as has been noted in chapter 2, Mozambique is the world's most aid-dependent country, deriving two-thirds of its GNP from aid (Simon, 1995).

In terms of physical living conditions, 67 per cent of residents have their own homes, principally dwellings built of reed (*caniço*) or other relatively temporary materials in the poor areas. Rental (including lodging and similar arrangements) accounts for only 33 per cent of residents, the most important landlord being the state housing agency, APIE, which assumed responsibility for second homes and other residential properties nationalized after the Portuguese flight at independence. Only 39 per cent of homes in Maputo have electricity, 33 per cent have piped water, and 21 per cent an internal toilet. Given these figures and those on poverty levels cited earlier, it is hardly surprising that per capita availability of domestic electrical appliances is extremely low or that firewood and charcoal constitute the most widely used domestic fuel. Over 71 per cent of households rely on these for cooking, compared with only 17 per cent using electricity and 8 per cent gas (Mozambique Information Agency, 1993). Globally, an estimated 170 million urban residents did not have potable water in or near their homes in 1990, while 400 million lacked adequate sanitation – an increase of almost 100 million since 1980 (World Bank, 1992).

The figures for Maputo are undoubtedly more extreme than would have been the case just before independence, for example, because the condition of much of the colonial cement city (*cidade cimento*) has now deteriorated through lack of maintenance and overcrowding, economic conditions are dire, and output capacity utilization remains low. At the same time, the urban population has been swollen by large numbers of *deslocados* who would arguably not have migrated in the absence of war. The city literally doubled its population in the eight years after independence in 1975 (Simon, 1992). Its population today must be approaching 2 million. Although Maputo, and other large African cities such as Luanda, Mogadishu, Monrovia, and now also Kigali, which have been dramatically affected by war, are extreme cases, they do serve to illustrate well just how marginally they, and the national economies that they control, articulate with the world economy, except as the conduits for channelling official and NGO aid. This vulnerability and the economic liberalizations implemented under structural adjustment have also, in the case of Maputo, led to foreign purchase of the most viable investment opportunities (especially in tourist facilities) in a manner that will probably enhance the country's long-run external dependence. The most visible form of globalization here is the consequent resurrection of foreign tourism (principally from South Africa) amid the sea of poverty. However, even at the height of the war, it was possible to buy Coca Cola and beer – freighted in from South Africa – for hard currency. The future challenges of urbanization in Africa are as profound in these cities as in the metropolises of Cairo, the PWV, Lagos, or Kinshasa. It is doubtful whether many or even most *deslocados* will return to their home areas, while the prospects for reconstruction and more equitable development will depend greatly on the outcome of political negotiations and subsequent elections, the attractiveness of investment opportunities for foreigners and expatriates, and the ability to overcome the loss of a high proportion of skilled nationals through war or emigration. In Mozambique, at least, the situation appeared to be improving by late 1995.

Conclusions

This chapter has sought to explore some basic but vitally important issues with respect to urbanization in Africa and its relationships both with other components of the world system and with economic performance. We need to remind ourselves, however, that there are no universally agreed definitions, concepts, and agendas. The views from the respective ends of the kaleidoscope are very different. Globalization is often taken rather simplistically to mean convergence – usually along Western norms and on the basis of Western values. However much there may be evidence of such convergence, processes of divergence and hybridization are also occurring. In Africa, the outer periphery of the world system, the extent and rate of convergence have thus far arguably been markedly less than on many other continents. That said, there are often great differences in conditions, dominant processes, and influence over outcomes within individual cities and countries. Peripheralization, which has been clearly demonstrated, also does not mean unidirectional dependence. Interaction, albeit often unequal, is a bidirectional process. Nevertheless, the fact that London and Paris are two of the (if not *the*) most vibrant centres of African music, art, literature, and even politics is sad testimony not only to the state of the continent but also to the continued intensity and relevance of (neo-)colonial ties.

The large number of countries, with very different characteristics and experiences, makes generalization about urbanization processes and their relationships to economic conditions difficult. The problem is exacerbated by data deficiencies and inconsistencies, coupled with the fact that so much economic activity in Africa remains unrecorded. Overall, there is now a growing body of evidence that, in a significant number of countries, rates of urban growth slowed – in at least some large centres – during the 1980s in comparison with earlier periods.

This does also appear to be due, in significant measure, to the economic crisis, which dramatically altered the balance between urban and rural living standards and survival opportunities in the worst-hit countries and cities. On the other hand, a number of countries apparently showed an increase, despite economic conditions. This is certainly the case in South Africa, where apartheid previously reduced rural–urban migration through statutory fiat. It should also be stressed that by no means everyone is worse off as a result of structural adjustment and economic recovery programmes. Certain groups of agricultural producers, merchants, big businesspeople, and service providers have gained significantly.

Overall, however, the data remain far too sketchy and incomplete to offer any firm conclusions on the precise nature of the relationships between urban and economic growth, which are undoubtedly complex. Importantly, similar conditions may give rise to different responses in countries where other politico-economic situations prevail. In most cases for which some information is available, economic crisis and rising relative urban living costs seem to have resulted in reduced in-migration and even net out-migration. However, the opposite can also occur. The extent to which armed conflicts are perceived to threaten particular cities or rural areas is also important, as the very different recent experiences of Maputo and Mogadishu illustrate.

Although Africa does not possess a true world city, there are at least two mega-cities and several others with over 2 million inhabitants. Global peripherality varies in extent and nature. Urbanization is certainly continuing, albeit sometimes more slowly at present, and, given the resource constraints, it will pose no less a challenge than in other regions of the world.

Notes

1. These data drawn from the UNDP *Human Development Report* are presented here, in addition to the data given in chapter 2, to illustrate both the difficulties in arriving at agreed figures for the urban population in Africa and the discrepancies that occur between different sources.
2. The lack of reliable figures and the discrepancies between sources for data on urban growth rates also extend to population figures for individual cities, complicated by the failure of boundary revisions in some cases to keep pace with the growth of the built-up area and/or the functional integration of a city with its surrounding settlements. While the population of cities such as Durban, Kano, and Ibadan is thought by some to be less than 2 million, alternative estimates for Addis Ababa and Khartoum consider that their populations have already exceeded 2 million.

References

Armstrong, W. and T. G. McGee. 1985. *Theatres of Accumulation: Studies in Latin American and Asian Urbanisation.* Methuen, London.

Barke, M. and C. Sowden. 1992. Population change in Tanzania, 1978–88: A preliminary analysis. *Scottish Geographical Magazine* 108(1): 9–16.

Bennell, P. 1990. British industrial investment in sub-Saharan Africa: Corporate responses to economic crisis in the 1980s. *Development Policy Review* 8(2): 155–177.

Briggs, J. 1993. Population change in Tanzania: A cautionary note for the city of Dar es Salaam. *Scottish Geographical Magazine* 109(2): 117–118.

Commissão Nacional do Plano, Direccão Nacional de Estatistica, and Unidade de Populacão e Planificação. 1993. *Pobreza, Emprego e a Questão Demográfica na Cidade de Maputo.* CNP, DNE & UPP, Maputo.

Devas, N. and C. Rakodi, eds. 1993. *Managing Fast Growing Cities: New Approaches to Urban Planning and Management in the Developing World.* Longman, Harlow.

Dixon, C., D. Simon, and A. Närman. 1995. Introduction: The nature of Structural Adjustment. In: D. Simon, W. van Spengen, C. Dixon, and A. Närman, eds., *Structurally Adjusted Africa: Poverty, Debt and Basic Needs.* Pluto, London.

Drakakis-Smith, D. 1993. *The Nature of Third World Cities.* Working Paper 93.10, Centre for Development Research, Copenhagen.

Europa. 1992. *The World Directory of Diplomatic Representation.* Europa, London.

Friedmann, J. and G. Wolff. 1982. World city formation: An agenda for research and action. *International Journal of Urban and Regional Research* 6(3): 309–343.

Garner, J. 1993. *Determinants of Recent Direct Investment Flows to South Africa.* Research Paper 8, Centre for the Study of the South African Economy and International Finance, London School of Economics, University of London, London.

Gilbert, A. and J. Gugler. 1992. *Cities, Poverty and Development*, 2nd edn. Oxford University Press, Oxford.

Hardoy, J. E. and D. Satterthwaite. 1989. Urban change in the Third World: Are recent trends a useful pointer to the urban future? In: G. K. Payne and D. Cadman, eds., *Future Cities.* Methuen, London.

Hardoy, J. E., D. Mitlin, and D. Satterthwaite. 1992. *Environmental Problems in Third World Cities.* Earthscan, London.

Harris, N., ed. 1992. *Cities in the 1990s: The Challenge for Developing Countries.* UCL Press, London.

Holm, M. 1995. Rural–urban migration and urban living conditions: The experiences in a case study of Tanzanian intermediate towns. Unpublished PhD thesis, University of London.

Jamal, V. and J. Weeks. 1988. The vanishing rural–urban gap in sub-Saharan Africa. *International Labour Review* 127(3): 271–292.

———— 1993. *Africa Misunderstood: Or Whatever Happened to the Rural–Urban Gap?* Macmillan, London.

Jeffries, 1992. Urban popular attitudes towards the economic recovery programme and the PNDC government in Ghana. *African Affairs* 91(363): 207–226.

Kasarda, J. D. and A. M. Parnell, eds. 1993. *Third World Cities: Problems, Policies and Prospects.* Sage, London and Newbury Park, Calif.

King, A. D., ed. 1991. *Culture, Globalization and the World-System.* Macmillan, London, and SUNY Department of Art and Art History, Binghamton.

Meyer, D. R. 1986. The world system of cities: Relations between international financial metropolises and South American cities. *Social Forces* 64: 553–581.

Mozambique Information Agency. 1993. *Mozambiquefile*, no. 207 (October).

National Population Council and Macro International Inc. 1993. *Egypt: Demographic and Health Survey 1992*. Macro International Inc., Calverton, Md.

O'Connor, A. 1983. *The African City*. Hutchinson, London.

Potter, R. B. 1993. Urbanization in the Caribbean and trends of global convergence–divergence. *Geographical Journal* 159: 1–21.

Potts, D. 1994. Shall we go home? Increasing urban poverty in African cities and migration processes. Paper presented to the Annual Conference of the Institute of British Geographers, University of Nottingham, 5 January.

Robertson, R. 1991. Social theory, cultural relativity and the problem of globality. In: A. D. King, ed., *Culture, Globalization and the World-System*. Macmillan, London, and SUNY Department of Art and Art History, Binghampton.

——— 1992. *Globalization: Social Theory and Global Change*. Sage, London and Newbury Park, Calif.

Simon, D. 1992. *Cities, Capital and Development: African Cities in the World Economy*. Belhaven, London.

——— 1993. *The World City Hypothesis: Reflections from the Periphery*. Research Paper 7, Centre for Developing Areas Research, Department of Geography, Royal Holloway, University of London, Egham, Surrey.

——— 1995. Debt, democracy and development: Sub-Saharan Africa in the 1990s. In D. Simon, W. van Spengen, C. Dixon, and A. Närman, eds., *Structurally Adjusted Africa: Poverty, Debt and Basic Needs*. Pluto, London.

Sit, V. F.-S. 1993. Transnational capital flows, foreign investments, and urban growth in developing countries. In: J. D. Kasarda and A. M. Parnell, eds., *Third World Cities: Problems, Policies and Prospects*. Sage, Newbury Park, Calif., and London.

Stren, R. E. and R. R. White, eds. 1989. *African Cities in Crisis: Managing Rapid Urban Growth*. Westview, Boulder, Colo.

Tevera, D. 1995. The medicine that might kill the patient: Structural Adjustment and urban poverty in Harare. In: D. Simon, W. van Spengen, C. Dixon, and A. Närman, eds., *Structurally Adjusted Africa: Poverty, Debt and Basic Needs*. Pluto, London.

UNCTAD (United Nations Conference on Trade and Development). 1993. *1993 World Investment Report*. UNCTAD, New York.

——— 1994. *1994 World Investment Report*. UNCTAD, New York (cited in *The Namibian*, 2 September 1994).

UNDP (United Nations Development Programme). 1993. *Human Development Report 1993*. Oxford University Press, New York.

UNEP/WHO (United Nations Environment Programme and World Health Organization). 1992. *Urban Air Pollution in Megacities of the World*. Blackwell, Oxford.

UNIDO (United Nations Industrial Development Organization). 1993. *African Industry in Figures 1993*. UNIDO, Vienna.

Union of International Associations. 1993. *Yearbook of International Organizations 1993/94. Vol. 2*. Saur, for UIA, Munich.

World Bank. 1992. *World Development Report 1992*. Oxford University Press, New York.

——— 1993. *World Development Report 1993*. Oxford University Press, New York.

Part II
The "mega-cities" of Africa

4

The challenge of urban growth in Cairo

Mahmoud Yousry and Tarek A. Aboul Atta

Abstract

L'antique cité du Caire est devenue aujourd'hui, avec ses quelques 12 millions d'habitants, la plus grande ville d'Afrique et du Moyen-Orient, un centre administratif, culturel et économique au niveau régional comme à celui du pays. Après 70 ans d'occupation, la révolution menée par Nasser en 1952 chasse l'administration coloniale de la ville et la haute bourgeoisie égyptienne du pouvoir et inaugure une période de planification centralisée, de contrôle des loyers et de vastes projets de logements sociaux, bénéficiant avant tout aux travailleurs et aux couches pauvres des classes moyennes. Le Caire passe de 1 million d'habitants dans les années 20 à 5 millions en 1970. Quoiqu'une croissance rapide naturelle y compte pour beaucoup, l'exode rural est aussi significatif, stimulé par divers facteurs de répulsion dont notamment la difficulté croissante d'accès à des terres arables de dimensions suffisantes, et par des facteurs d'attraction des villes, en particulier le programme d'industrialisation mené par les pouvoirs publics dans les années 50 et 60. Mais la guerre de 1967 avec Israël dévore les ressources des programmes publics égyptiens, la croissance urbaine se ralentit et l'infrastructure se détériore. Lorsque le gouvernement de Sadat prend le pouvoir en 1970, sa politique de "porte ouverte" attire les investissements étrangers, donne un nouvel élan à la croissance économique et ravive l'intérêt qu'offre le Caire.

D'immenses investissements publics consacrés aux infrastructures ne réussissent cependant pas à satisfaire la demande et de nombreux aménagements se réalisent au mépris de toute planification, sans permis de construire. Les prix des terrains et des propriétés sont rendus exorbitants par la spéculation immobilière, accélérée par les rentrées de gains des nombreux Egyptiens partis travailler dans les pays producteurs de pétrole du Moyen-Orient. La croissance de la ville en termes de dimensions, de surface et de richesse s'accompagne néanmoins de disparités croissantes entre les biens, les offres de services, la qualité des logements et les normes concernant l'environnement. Les principaux problèmes d'urbanisme proviennent des très fortes densités au cœur de la vieille ville du Caire, des vastes quartiers de logements de mauvaise qualité construits récemment, de l'occupation illégale des toits et de la Cité des morts, de l'insuffisance des infrastructures et des services, des problèmes de transport persistants et de l'aggravation constante de la pollution. Ces vingt dernières années, la planification a visé à pallier ces problèmes tout en détournant les nouveaux aménagements des fertiles terres arables aux alentours de la ville vers de nouvelles villes et de nouveaux établissements de la région. De nombreuses nouvelles industries se sont installées dans ces villes nouvelles et des investissements massifs y ont été consacrés, mais en 1994, moins de 0.5 million de personnes y résidaient, soit 8 pour cent de l'objectif visé, et de nombreux logements restaient inoccupés en raison du retard dans l'apport des services. Depuis 1980, les importants investissements consacrés aux infrastructures dans la partie la plus importante de la ville ont quelque peu amélioré la situation. Mais la dispersion des responsabilités de gestion urbaine et l'insuffisance de la coordination entre les autorités régionales et les trois gouverneurs qui se partagent l'administration de la ville ont handicapé la réalisation des principaux objectifs. Au cœur de la métropole qui se constitue le long de l'axe Alexandrie–Le Caire, la domination de cette dernière sur la vie économique, politique et urbaine de l'Egypte ne risque guère de diminuer.

Introduction

Egypt, with its strategic location in the centre of the old world, has become the second most populous country in Africa after Nigeria. Owing to its specific geographic conditions, most urban development in Egypt has taken place in the Nile Valley and Delta, which represent only 4 per cent of its total area. Throughout its long history, urbanization has occurred, and great cities and kingdoms have grown up along the banks of the Nile River. Thus, population and economic activities concentrated in this narrow and limited area, and polarization became the pattern of Egyptian life.

Egypt has a long history of growth and decline over almost 1,400 years. Cairo, its capital, has grown rapidly to reach more than 12 million inhabitants in 1994. It has become the largest urban centre not only in Africa, but also in the Middle East. The city's history has been closely related to that of Egypt, which has been subject to a succession of foreign rulers in the past 2,000 years. A study of the development of Cairo cannot ignore the prevailing political, economic, and social conditions in Egypt, which have affected its growth and shaped all related development policies. Such policies, in recent decades, have led to a massive process of concentration, with the result that Cairo today is not only the capital of Egypt but also its economic, social, service, and administrative centre. The city's size and rapid growth have resulted in serious problems in most aspects of the life of its population. The government has attempted both to decentralize population and activities from Cairo and to reorganize and manage its growth at the national, regional, and local levels.

In the first part of this chapter, the historical development of Cairo will be outlined. The growth of the city in the twentieth century will then be analysed in more detail, including its population, the factors that have influenced its growth, its physical development, and the problems that have resulted. In the final part of the chapter, attempts to plan the city and their outcomes will be analysed.

Historical background

Since the dawn of civilization, the capital of Egypt has been located in the Cairo metropolitan region for long periods, in areas such as Manf, Lecht, Ono, and Babylon (see fig. 4.1). Few traces of these cities remain today. It was not until the year A.D. 641 that the existing city of Cairo was founded by Amr Ibn-Elass in El Fostat, east of the Nile River. Its location represented the centre of gravity of the whole country in terms of cultivated area, population, wealth, and power. The proximity of the fortress of Babylon (formerly the headquarters of the Roman and Greek armies in Egypt) influenced the choice of this particular site (Moselhi, 1988).[1]

Historically, Old Cairo expanded north-east of El Fostat, when the Abbacies built El Askar in A.D. 751 (fig. 4.2). Then Ibn Tolon added a

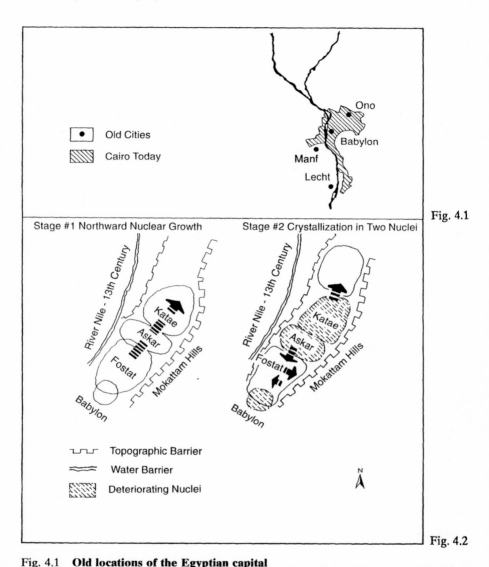

Fig. 4.1

Fig. 4.2

Fig. 4.1　**Old locations of the Egyptian capital**

Fig. 4.2　**The development of Cairo in the Islamic period (Source: based on Moselhi, 1988)**

third settlement – El Katae. After A.D. 870 Cairo El Moez (Fatimid Cairo) was built by Gawhar El Sikili along the Nile borders north-east of the previous settlements (fig. 4.2) (Selem, 1983). These four towns primarily performed the role of military settlements. A major mosque and sometimes palace were located in the centre of each settlement.

In the twelfth century these settlements were united in one agglomeration, when Salah El Din El Ayouby surrounded them with walls and built his fortress (El Qalaa). Only then did Cairo begin to perform its role as a unified city where most of the political, cultural, social, and urban developments took place in the following three centuries and its area reached more than 5 km^2 (fig. 4.3). The city expanded rapidly in the western, northern, and southern directions in the Mamlouk period (A.D. 1200–1500), reaching an area of 43,868 feddans (184 km^2). The Mokattam hills form a natural barrier blocking any eastern expansion. Most studies estimated the population of Cairo by that time at almost 1 million inhabitants (Hamdan, 1982).[2]

In the following Ottoman period (1500–1800) the city deteriorated for various economic, political, and military reasons. Economically, the transfer of eastern trade from Egyptian territories to detour around Africa deprived the country of tremendous tax resources. This period was also characterized by political instability and conflict among the remaining Mamlouks, as well as among Ottoman army sections. National revolution against the Turkish rulers and the Mamlouks ensued and many districts in Cairo were badly damaged. After having been an established capital, Cairo became only an administrative base for foreign rulers interested in exploring the country's resources. The city witnessed notable out-migration to other parts of the country, with the result that by A.D. 1800 Cairo's population had decreased to about 260,000 (Moselhi, 1988).

However, with Mohammed Ali's rule (1805–1849), Cairo began its modernization, an era that reached its peak between 1873 and 1879 in the western part of the city. The extravagant cost of this expansion led to many problems, beginning with high foreign debts and political unrest and ending with the British colonization of Egypt in 1882 (Eddin Ibrahim, 1987). During the colonial period Cairo grew as the ruling centre, to which thousands of foreigners and nationals migrated looking for wealth and power. New districts were built in the west (Garden City and Zamalek), in the north (Heliopolis), and in the south (Maadi) (see fig. 4.4). The old city was left undeveloped to face tremendous problems of high densities, lack of infrastructure, and deterioration in living conditions. At the beginning of the twentieth century the newly formed upper middle class launched a reform strategy in most fields, such as education, banking, industries, and recreation, and migrated to the new districts. Cairo expanded rapidly

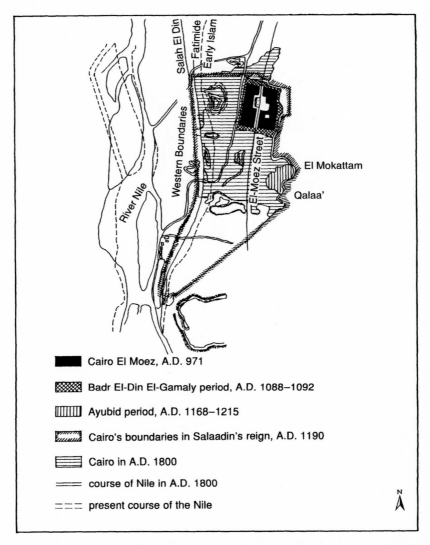

Fig. 4.3   **The growth of Cairo, A.D. 971–1800 (Source: based on Moselhi, 1988)**

and reached more than 1 million inhabitants in the late 1920s. Inter-class inequalities widened in the following decades leading to major social, economic, and political problems and laying the foundations for the 1952 revolution against British colonization and the royal regime.

Subsequently, massive industrial and housing projects were undertaken by the new government, particularly in the Cairo zone. New

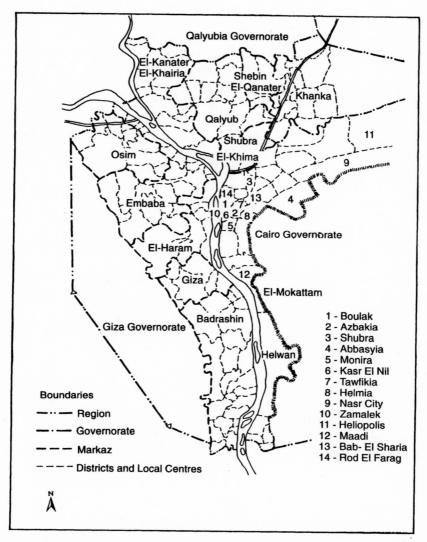

Fig. 4.4 **Districts in the Greater Cairo Region (Source: General Organization for Physical Planning)**

districts appeared in the northern, southern, and western parts of the city. The Cairo metropolitan area emerged, with a population of 5 million in 1970 (El Shakhs, 1971; Moselhi, 1988). After the 1973 war, the policy of the government moved from a socialist, centrally planned, and public-sector-dominated economy to the so-called "open-door" policy. The latter aimed at encouraging the private sector and attracting international and Arab investment. A large part of such investment was directed to Cairo and its region, fostering further rapid urban development. By 1980 the population of Greater Cairo was 8 million. Informal and illegal housing appeared in this period in many areas on the outskirts of the city and in the City of the Dead. Such trends continued in the 1980s and 1990s. It is estimated that in 1994 more than 4 million people were living in illegal settlements in the Greater Cairo Region (GCR). The efforts of the government to control the growth of the city have not been sufficient and it kept growing in most directions, particularly to the west and north, to reach an estimated population of over 12 million in 1994.

The urban growth of Cairo

Urbanization in Egypt and the development of the Greater Cairo Region

The process of urbanization itself is a result of rural–urban migration. Moreover, in Egypt, high rates of natural increase partly account for rapid urban growth rates. In 1907 the inhabitants of urban areas accounted for 19 per cent of the total Egyptian population, rising to 33 per cent in 1947, 43 per cent in 1976, and 44 per cent in 1986. UN studies suggest that the urban population in Egypt will exceed 50 per cent of the total population by the year 2010 (UN, 1993). However, such figures should be treated with care. On the one hand, the 1986 census showed that around 2.25 million Egyptians (mostly from urban areas) were at that time living outside Egypt. On the other hand, the growth rates in rural areas in the late 1980s and 1990s exceeded those of urban areas. High rates of natural increase in rural areas may be attributed to the fact that the adoption rates for birth control and family planning procedures have not been as high as in urban areas, while growth has also occurred because of the sharp increase in urban land prices, which has driven many to build on cheaper land in rural areas surrounding the cities.

Within the urban sector, large centres, particularly Cairo, have witnessed higher rates of growth than medium- and small-sized centres. Thus, whereas the population of Egypt has increased by more than 5 times in the twentieth century, Cairo's population has increased by nearly 16 times (table 4.1), with the result that its share

Table 4.1   **Population growth of Cairo and Egypt, 1800–1986**

Year	Cairo Population ('000)	Cairo % growth rate	Egypt Population ('000)	Egypt % growth rate	Cairo as % of national population
1800	200		3,000		6.7
		2.0		1.2	
1900	600		10,000		6.0
		2.3		1.3	
1920	875		13,000		6.7
		3.1		1.4	
1930	1,150		15,000		7.7
		2.2		2.3	
1940	1,525		19,000		8.0
		4.1		1.0	
1950	2,350		21,000		11.2
		4.1		2.2	
1960	4,784		26,000		18.4
		2.2		2.4	
1976	6,776		38,200		17.7
		3.5		2.8	
1986	9,514		50,500		18.8

Source: Central Agency for Population Mobilization and Statistics (CAPMAS), Population Censuses, Cairo.

of the national population increased from nearly 9 per cent in 1940 to 18 per cent or more in the 1960s and 1970s, and was estimated to be 21 per cent in 1994. It is clear that the real demographic change in Cairo's modern history began in the nineteenth century when death rates began to decline while birth rates stayed constant. The figures in table 4.1 show that the growth rate of GCR surpassed the national average except in the periods 1930–1940 (World War II) and 1960–1976 (owing to the 1967 war). Between 1976 and 1986 the open-door policy (see below) boosted economic and urban development and consequently population growth in the GCR.

A large metropolitan area was formed, encompassing the city of Cairo and its extension in Shubra El-Khima to the north and Giza city to the west of Nile. The boundaries of this conurbation were later extended to include more surrounding areas and settlements, forming the Greater Cairo Region (GCR). The population of this region was more than 9.5 million in 1986 and was estimated to be more than 12 million in 1994, in addition to about 2 million daily commuters.

This extraordinary population represents about 20 per cent of the total population of Egypt and 40 per cent of its urban population. Cairo and, to a lesser extent, Alexandria, with a population of 3.5 million, dominate the urban system and there is a wide gap between these two cities and the remaining settlements (Aboul Atta, 1985). The urban concentration index increased from 0.623 in 1965 to 0.649 in 1980 and the four-city primacy index from 2.11 in 1965 to 2.70 in 1985, indices of primacy that are among the highest in the world.

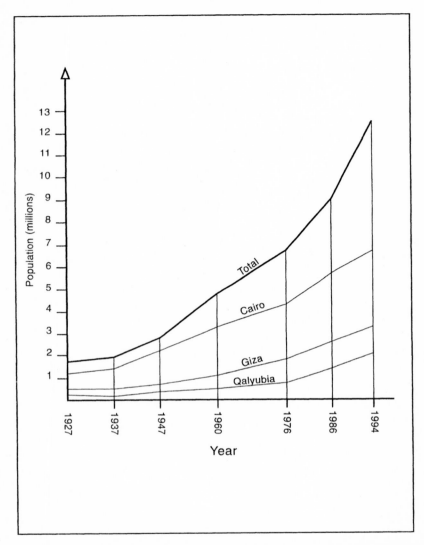

Fig. 4.5 **The population of the Greater Cairo Region, 1927–1994 (Source: Central Agency for Population Mobilization and Statistics, Censuses. Note: 1994 population estimated)**

Figure 4.5 shows the population share of the three sections of the GCR (namely Cairo, Giza, and Qalyubia) and detailed figures are given in the appendix. The population in Cairo, which includes the old city and its surrounding area, accounted for 70 per cent or more of the population of the GCR until 1960. At that time the built-up area was saturated, with very high densities. Since the 1960s growth has been directed toward the other two sections, while the proportion of the population living in the Cairo section declined steadily to reach an estimated 55 per cent in 1994. The growth rate of the population in the Cairo section declined from 5.9 per cent per annum in the 1940s to 1.9 per cent per annum in the 1970s, but subsequently increased owing to massive housing projects and expansion onto the desert land of Nasr city and Helwan (see fig. 4.4). However, its growth rate is still below those of the other two sections, which reached 5.2 per cent per annum in Giza and 7.9 per cent per annum in Qalyubia between 1986 and 1994. In the Giza section, a recent study suggests that another 2.3 million people have been added in informal areas and squatter settlements since the 1986 census (Al-Wali, 1993).

Factors of urban growth

Such rapid urban growth of the GCR has been the result of many factors, of which some are applicable to most large urban centres in Egypt and some are specific to Cairo. Some of the leading factors are demographic, economic, and political, while accessibility is also important.

Demographic factors

As already mentioned, Egypt has experienced increasingly rapid growth in the past 40 years (2.7 per cent as compared with 1.3 per cent between 1900 and 1950; see table 4.1). The birth rate during the first half of the twentieth century was among the highest in the world (45 per 1,000 inhabitants in 1952). Since 1950 it has declined, to reach 32 per 1,000 inhabitants in 1990, owing to the spread of education, rising living costs, government policies for birth control, and family planning programmes. However, these rates are still high compared with those of more developed countries. Fertility rates, which are usually higher in rural areas, were slightly higher in the late 1950s and 1960s in the major urban centres than in surrounding rural areas. In addition, death rates have decreased steadily from 20.4 per 1,000 inhabitants in 1948 to 7.5 per 1,000 inhabitants in 1990 owing to improvements in public health and a decrease in child death rates. High fertility and birth rates in urban areas have coupled with decreasing death rates to produce rapid natural population growth in urban and rural areas alike. However, the rate of natural increase seems to have reached a peak of 30.4 per 1,000 in 1985 and is now showing signs of a steady decline (24.7 per 1,000 in 1990).

Rural–urban migration has been the major driving force behind urbanization in Egypt. It has resulted from the deterioration of rural areas as well as from the concentration of economic activities (and hence employment opportunities), services, political power, and wealth in the major urban centres and mainly in Cairo. Most rural migrants have kept their traditional way of life at their urban destination, creating what has been called "ruralization of urban areas" (UN, 1961). They usually reside with or near their relatives, forming foci of interrelated families. They work mostly in the informal sector, earning low and unsteady wages. They have limited social and economic mobility. Many still keep strong contacts with their rural relatives and send them financial support.

Economic factors
Since the British colonization of Egypt in 1882, government policies have favoured urban areas and particularly large centres. In the early stage of colonialism a strongly primate settlement system was developed, primarily focusing on Cairo as the political and administrative centre. Alexandria was developed as a port to link the country with the exterior and to facilitate the export of agricultural products. After the 1952 revolution, the government directed its major resources towards these large urban centres for efficiency, political, and sometimes prestige reasons. It was argued then that it is more efficient to develop urban centres because of the availability of services, infrastructure, power, and skilled labour. Moreover, the favoured strategy, for political as well as developmental reasons, was industrialization concentrated in urban centres, especially Cairo. Rural areas did not receive much attention, with the exception of a few instances where rural development experiments have been carried out, such as in Mudiriat El Tahrir in the 1950s and Salhia in the 1970s.

There are a number of reasons for the underdevelopment of rural areas, which has been the driving force behind rural–urban migration. In addition to the lack of government investments, land issues are crucial:

• Egyptian urban development has taken place along the Nile Valley and in the Delta region, mostly on scarce agricultural land. Table 4.2 shows that the GCR alone has consumed increasing portions of the surrounding agricultural land (an average of 328 ha per annum between 1968 and 1977 and 593 ha per annum between 1977 and

Table 4.2 **Agricultural land consumed by new development in Greater Cairo, 1968–1982**

Period	Governorate	Urban		Rural		Total		Average per annum (ha)
		Hectares	%	Hectares	%	Hectares	%	
1968–1977	Cairo	850	50	–	–	850	29	
(9 years)	Giza	640	38	560	44	1,200	41	
	Qalyubia	200	12	700	56	900	30	
	Total	1,690	100	1,260	100	2,950	100	327.8
1977–1982	Cairo	500	30	–	–	500	17	
(5 years)	Giza	775	46	640	50	1,415	48	
	Qalyubia	410	24	640	50	1,050	35	
	Total	1,685	100	1,280	100	2,965	100	593.0

Source: GOPP (1983).
Note: 1 feddan = 1.06 acres or 0.38 hectares.

1982). As a result, per capita food production has declined and food has had to be imported. In 1977, food represented 23 per cent of Egyptian imports and the proportion has grown since then.

• Land reform laws were enacted in 1952 and 1961, with the aim of expanding food production, stimulating rural development, and, above all, achieving social justice. The law called for expropriation of holdings exceeding a ceiling of 100 feddans (38.2 ha) per owner. This required a transformation of traditional and deep-rooted relationships between people and the land, as well as changes to the rights and obligations of several classes, particularly landlords and tenants. Over time, it has become evident that such a transformation has not taken place and the result has been:

– absentee ownership;
– inequitable tenancy and ownership arrangements;
– an excessive fragmentation of agricultural land, by distributing expropriated land in small lots (5 feddans or less, or <1.9 ha). This has been further exaggerated owing to inheritance. The percentage of agricultural land divided into parcels of less than 5 feddans increased from 35.4 per cent in 1952 to 53.9 per cent in 1985, and parcels of more than 200 feddans decreased from 19.7 per cent in 1952 to 6.5 per cent in 1985.

The result was added inefficiency and decreased productivity in the rural areas, increasing their underdevelopment and pushing more migrants to urban centres. Invasion of agricultural land by the desert is another specific factor that threatens rural development. Although it has not been measured yet, it has had an impact on land adjacent to the western desert.

Since 1952, when Egypt began to implement its national industrial plan, the share of the industrial sector in the total economy increased from 8 per cent in 1952 to 22 per cent in 1961 and to 42 per cent in the late 1970s. Since then, it has decreased in relative terms, to 25 per cent and 28 per cent in 1980 and 1985, respectively, leaving the lead to the service sectors since 1983. Most of this industrial development was concentrated in the major urban centres and particularly in the GCR. In 1976 more than 55 per cent of Egypt's industrial establishments, 48 per cent of industrial employment, and 51 per cent of industrial output were located in the GCR. Although these percentages have fluctuated since, industries are still highly concentrated in the GCR. In the past decade major investments have been directed towards industrial development in the new cities, particularly the ones near the GCR such as 6 October and 10 Ramadan, thus decreasing the share of Egypt's industrial employment in the GCR to 35 per cent (table 4.3). However most of these investments originate in

Table 4.3 **The composition of employment in the Greater Cairo Region and Egypt, 1986**

	GCR		Egypt		GCR as % of Egypt
	No.	%	No.	%	
Agricultural	114,553	5	4,566,945	38	2.5
Industrial	826,047	35	2,346,021	19	35.2
Mining	14,696		52,769		27.8
Manufacturing	533,053		1,475,608		36.1
Construction	278,298		817,644		34.0
Commercial	474,207	20	1,492,951	12	31.8
Trade	291,322		852,124		34.2
Transport & Communications	182,885		640,827		28.5
Utilities	24,133	1	91,077	1	26.5
Services	808,663	34	2,838,538	23	28.5
Social services	701,452		2,614,477		26.8
Finance & insurance	107,211		224,061		47.8
Other	123,227	5	811,099	7	15.2
Total	2,370,830	100	12,146,631	100	19.5

Source: CAPMAS, *1986 Census of Population*, Cairo.

and profits are returned to the GCR, further pushing its economic pre-eminence. Unequal distribution of services has been an important factor in attracting migration from rural to urban areas. High levels of educational, health, cultural, entertainment, recreational, and commercial services can be found only in the GCR, as well as to some extent in Alexandria.

In Egypt, an enlarged formal sector has emerged in recent decades which has offered the prospect of material standards of living equivalent to those in the more developed countries. However, the support needed to develop this sector has created a kind of dependency on developed countries for technical and financial aid. Formal sector establishments and enterprises have concentrated in the GCR near the seat of the government and political decision makers. This locational preference has also increased the imbalance between the developed and underdeveloped regions. The formal sector is dominated by large-scale, high-technology, and capital-intensive processes imported from the more developed countries. Yet its products are characterized by limited life-spans, because they depend on the middle class for consumption of their products. Increased consumption has occurred at the expense of savings and the strategy has accentuated disparities within urban areas.

Communication and transportation networks

The transportation network in Egypt was very limited for much of its history. In the late 1970s the length of roads in the whole country amounted to 16,139 km, of which only 25 per cent were paved, with a rate of 1 km to every 8,000 inhabitants. In the late 1980s and 1990s this rate increased to 1 km per 2,000 inhabitants, which is still less than in developed countries. Other means of communication and transportation such as railways and telephones were similarly underdeveloped. Most of the transportation routes radiate from Cairo, connecting it with other major centres of the country and adding to its centrality. The lack of well-developed transportation and communication systems made it difficult to diffuse development from Cairo to other parts of the country, thus maintaining the primacy of Cairo.

Political factors

The centralization of government in Egypt is a major factor in Cairo's rapid growth. Decision makers, government ministries and institutions, central offices for all Egyptian organizations, major investors, and élite groups that possess economic and political power are con-

centrated in Cairo and particularly in its distinguished high-class districts. Many studies (for example, Todaro, 1981) have discussed the role of the élite group in the concentration process, suggesting that:
• élitism implies the concentration of power and influence over decision-making in a few hands;
• when economic planning decisions on what to produce and for whom to produce are made under élitist conditions, income generation and distribution will be biased in favour of groups influencing those decisions. Conversely, individuals and groups excluded from the decision-making process will be losers, as reflected in greater income inequality and poverty.

In Egypt before 1952, the élite consisted of those of aristocratic origin and top bureaucrats related to colonization and the ruling system. After the 1952 revolution, the élite group consisted of the top military class, which ruled the country. Over time this has been transformed into a wider élite of families and social groups with close relations with the ruling system. These relationships have facilitated political power and wealth accumulation. For these reasons, the élite has concentrated in Cairo near the ruling class.

From a prestige point of view, the government has emphasized the development of Cairo as Egypt's display window to the outside world. Extravagant services were concentrated in high-class districts and on major roads. Because public investments were concentrated in the core region (GCR) and not in peripheral regions, inequalities increased within the country.

International relationships
Recent studies suggest that a notable part of the growth of GCR is due to its international relations and its position within the world system. Egypt has been integrated into the world economy since the dawn of civilization owing to its strategic location at the centre of the old world. This integration became more evident in the nineteenth century with the opening of the Suez Canal, the expansion of the port of Alexandria, and the construction of Suez and Port Said ports. This integration was accompanied by a rapid increase in debts to foreign private banks, which ultimately led to direct intervention and occupation of the country by the British in 1882. Cairo became the administrative centre, with strong external links, especially to the colonial power.

After the 1952 revolution and independence, the government's industrial development programme was based on high-technology and capital-intensive processes imported from the USSR and Eastern countries. In the 1970s, Egypt began its "open-door" policy aiming at attracting foreign investment, particularly from the United States and Western countries, as part of the process of shifting to a mixed economy. This period was marked by high inflation rates, sharp rises in imports, significant imbalances in both the trade account and government budgets, and, above all, growing foreign debt. Within Egypt, Cairo has been the centre of financial activities, housing multinational corporations and institutions, and has, as a result, become more and more integrated into the world economy. To fulfil this role, additional high-class residential areas, infrastructure facilities, and services were developed, reinforcing Cairo's growth and primacy.

Recently, radical theorists have emphasized subsystems at the intermediate level, such as regions or a group of countries sharing similar characteristics (Wallerstein, 1974; Portes and Walton, 1981). Cairo in this respect is strongly interrelated with its surrounding regional subsystems: the Arab world, the Islamic world, and Africa. In the Arab world, Egypt is the largest country in terms of population and represents its heart. Cairo is the seat of almost half of the Arab political, economic, and cultural organizations, particularly in the Arab League, and an important banking centre. It provides military support to other Arab countries, as well as being a major source of labour (Findlay, 1994). The number of tourist nights spent in Egypt increased from under 1 million in the 1950s to an average of 18.6 million per annum in the late 1990s, and, of these, an average of 46 per cent between 1985 and 1990 were spent by Arab tourists, compared with 35 per cent in 1952 (see table 4.4). Cairo is also considered to be the cultural centre of the Arab world by most Arab states (Eddin Ibrahim, 1987). In the Islamic world, Cairo plays an extremely important role owing to the existence of Al-Azhar Mosque and

Table 4.4 **Tourist nights in Egypt by origin of tourists, 1952–1990 ('000)**

Nationality	1952	1985	1986	1987	1988	1989	1990
Arab	273	3,962	3,722	7,672	7,643	9,645	9,600
European	335	3,313	2,971	5,609	7,508	7,879	7,487
American	113	1,162	561	946	1,048	1,267	1,178
Others	69	570	592	1,635	1,665	1,793	1,677
Total	790	9,007	7,846	15,862	17,864	20,584	19,942

Source: CAPMAS, *Egypt Statistical Year Book 1991*, 1991.

University, which are the centre of Islamic knowledge. Extensive educational exchanges of students, professors, and preachers occur between Egypt and most Islamic countries. In Africa, Egypt has several times been elected as head of the Organization of African Unity, including twice in the past decade. Cairo is also the seat of many African political, economic, social, and sporting organizations. Deep-rooted economic relations tie Egypt with many African nations, particularly in the northern part of Africa. Finally, Egypt is related to many countries around the Mediterranean sea, such as Greece, France, Italy, and all the North African countries.

Physical development

The built-up area of Cairo has fluctuated throughout its history, from a low of 5 km^2 (around A.D. 1200) to an estimated 184 km^2 at the peak of the Mamlouk period (A.D. 1200–1500). The city passed through periods of recession in the following centuries, with the result that its area had declined to about 15 km^2 at the beginning of the nineteenth century and 30 km^2 50 years later. The districts adjacent to the old city, such as Boulak and El Azbakia, witnessed high rates of growth during this period and new districts appeared to the north, the north-east, and the west, such as Shubra, Abbasyia, Monira, Kasr El Nil, Tawfikia, and El Zatoon (Ibrahim, 1984; see fig. 4.4).

Bridges across the Nile River were built to link Cairo to Giza, and Zamalek and Garden City became the favourite districts for the upper classes and foreigners. The introduction of a tramway in 1896 boosted the expansion of the city. Two new districts, Heliopolis (Misr El Gedida) and Maadi, were built to the north and south of the city to absorb the overflow of high-class districts at the beginning of the twentieth century (fig. 4.4). The area of the city reached almost 100 km^2 around 1950 (fig. 4.6).

After the 1952 revolution, massive housing projects were built on the desert land east of the existing areas in Nasr city, to the south-east over the Mokattam hills, and to the south in new Maadi. The city also expanded on agricultural land to the south, linking Maadi and Helwan, and to the west of the Nile River in Giza. Helwan city was transformed from a high-class residential area to an industrial district housing most of the new heavy industries of Egypt. In Giza, new developments were planned to house middle-class professionals in single family homes, which were later torn down and transformed to high-rise buildings. To the north of the city and along major roads,

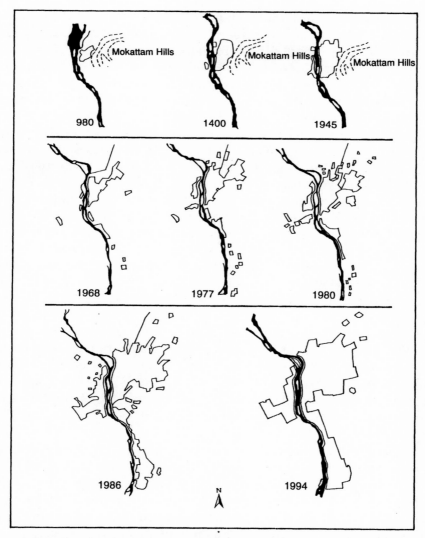

Fig. 4.6   **Urban development of Cairo and the Greater Cairo Region, 980–1994**

housing and industries grew in the adjacent Qalyubia governorate. In the late 1970s the built-up area reached 350 km² (fig. 4.6) and many villages in the surrounding area were enclosed and absorbed.

However, this physical expansion did not match the rapid population growth. Population densities rose to astounding levels. In 1966, densities in Bab-El Sharia district, situated in the oldest part of the city, reached 136,000 inhabitants per km^2; and in Rod El Farag, which was subject to heavy in-migration from the Delta, they reached 105,000/km^2. The overall density in Cairo ranged between 20,000 and 23,000 persons/km^2 between 1966 and 1970. Overall densities rose steadily in the next two decades to reach 32,000/km^2 in 1994, ranging from 109,000/km^2 in the most densely populated districts, to under 15,000/km^2 in the least (fig. 4.7). The density in the old districts has, however, not risen further during the past two decades as they have reached their ultimate capacities. There are many reasons for this astounding rise in densities. On the demand side, the majority of the population preferred to reside as near as possible to the city centre, where employment opportunities and services are available but where high housing prices led many families to share their units with others. On the supply side, the government was unable, because of financial and managerial limitations, to service sufficient urban land to keep pace with population growth. In addition, rent control laws led to slow growth of the housing stock.

Land uses

In 1982 the GCR was delineated by administrative boundaries encompassing 131,260 hectares, including the built-up area (32,609 ha), government property (11,219 ha), vacant land (839 ha), and agricultural land (86,593 ha). This area did not include the River Nile and desert land, which amounted to almost 130,000 hectares (GOPP, 1983, App. B).

Residential land use thus accounted for 67 per cent of the total built-up area in 1983. Economic activities and service facilities shared the remaining area, with 17 per cent and 16 per cent respectively (see table 4.5). A closer look at the spatial distribution of land uses shows that in 1982, when the Giza section had attracted migrants from Cairo and other parts of the country, residential land use was dominant (74 per cent). Qalyubia section was, in contrast, characterized by the number of economic activities that were located in Shubra El-Khima and Mustorod (27 per cent of the total built-up area). Most of the services needed for the GCR were located in the Cairo section, followed by Giza (where Cairo University is located). The central business district (CBD) of Cairo is located between the old city and the Nile. However, during the 1980s and 1990s, commercial, retail, and business activities expanded to the west, in Zamalek, then in Mohandissin on the other side of the river. New centres also

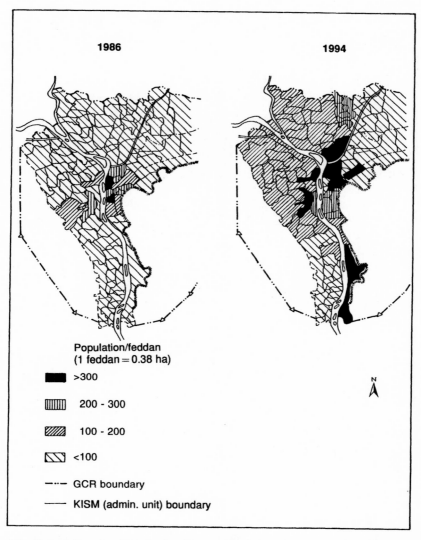

Fig. 4.7 **Population densities in the Greater Cairo Region, 1986 and 1994 (Sources: based on figures produced by CAPMAS for 1986 and Cairo governorate for 1994)**

appeared in the north (Roxy Square) and in the south (in Maadi). Industrial uses were traditionally located in the old city in Cairo near the CBD. Because of the scarcity of land in these areas, however, since the 1960s large industrial sites have been established outside the built-up area to the north (Shubra El-Khima) and south (Helwan). Most of this industrial development took place on agricultural land

131

Table 4.5 **Land use in the Greater Cairo Region, 1983 (ha)**

Governorate		Residential	Service facilities	Economic activities	Total built-up area[a]	Government property	Vacant land	Agricultural land	Total[b]
Cairo	Total of Cairo governorate	12,059	3,571	3,163	18,793	6,847	839	2,911	29,390
Giza	GC agglomeration	3,680	681	208	4,569	74	–	3,324	7,967
	Total rural[a]	2,519	369	880	3,779	4,000	–	41,177	48,956
	Total in Giza	6,199	1,050	1,088	8,348	4,074	–	44,501	56,923
Qalyubia	GC agglomeration	1,262	132	632	2,026	4	–	1,378	3,408
	Total rural[a]	2,165	431	846	3,442	294	–	37,803	41,539
	Total in Qalyubia governorate	3,427	563	1,478	5,468	298	–	39,181	44,947
Total in GCR		21,685	5,184	5,729	32,609	11,219	839	86,593	131,260
Of which:									
Greater Cairo agglomeration		17,001	4,384	4,003	25,388	6,925	839	7,613	40,765
Small towns and villages		4,684	800	1,726	7,221	4,294	–	78,980	90,495

Source: GOPP (1983).
a. Undefined buildings included in total built-up area.
b. Excluding River Nile and desert.

and along major regional roads, consuming more than 85 ha per year. Old areas became specialized in small- and medium-scale industries and crafts, while new sites housed heavy industries and large warehouses. Today, industrial investors have used up most industrial sites in the new cities built around the GCR, particularly in 6 October new city in the west and 10 Ramadan new city to the north-east.

Urban growth problems

Owing to the polarization process in Egypt, large urban centres, and particularly Cairo, have suffered from serious urban problems, both physical and social. This section highlights some of these urban problems in the GCR: housing, transportation and infrastructure, and inequality.

Housing

Housing supply was mostly by the private sector until the late 1950s, when rent control laws were applied. A sizeable proportion of developers in the housing market, as a result, shifted their investment to other fields. After that, the public sector assumed a major role in housing supply through central and local government, development agencies, and public housing companies. The semi-public agencies helped in the production of housing units through housing cooperatives, the El-Awkaf Authority, banks, insurance companies, and the construction of housing for individual workers. The private sector diminished to a few individual landlords, owner-occupiers, and small development companies. Provision of infrastructure remained the responsibility of the government (see below). The total number of housing units built per year by both public and private sectors decreased from 56,000 units in the 1950s to fewer than 30,000 in the 1960s. Low- and medium-cost housing was financed by personal and family savings, loans from the General Organization for Housing Cooperatives and the Bank of Housing, as well as low-interest loans to governorates to finance public housing.

The change in economic policy in the second half of the 1970s caused drastic changes in the housing market. The annual number of units built increased steadily to reach more than 180,000 in 1990. The role of the public sector diminished and was limited to the provision of low- and medium-cost units, mainly in the new towns and settlements around the GCR. Private investment in the housing and real estate sectors has increased continuously in the past two decades, despite the fact that these sectors are, in theory, tightly regulated and rent controlled and suffer from credit shortages. According to estimates by the Ministry of Housing and Reconstruction, private sector gross investment in housing grew from £E732 million in 1982/83 to £E2,950 million in 1991/92, representing more than 25 per cent of the total private investment in Egypt. On the other hand, public gross investment in housing fluctuated from £E67 million in 1982/83 to £E370 million in 1986/87 and back to £E91 million in 1991/92, representing less than 1 per cent of total Egyptian public investment. Similarly, gross value added in private sector housing rose from £E350 million in 1982/83 to £E2,223 million in 1991/92, whereas it increased only from £E62 million to £E127 million in public sector housing over the same period. In 1991/92, the private sector contributed 97 per cent of the total investment in housing and 95 per cent of the total value added in the housing sector.

Factors that explain the burgeoning private sector investment in housing include the high levels of demand resulting from urban population growth. In addition, private sector developers find ways around the rent control laws, such as build-to-own arrangements, and cash advances paid to developers. The illegal/informal housing that represents a large portion of the Egyptian housing market is totally financed by private investment. Given the limited choice of alternative investments in the Egyptian market (especially during periods of recession), real estate is a major outlet for domestic savings and especially for the remittances of Egyptians working in oil-exporting Arab countries (World Bank, 1994; see also chap. 11).

Informal housing, in the form of illegal subdivisions for low- and middle-income classes, is usually developed on the fringes of the built-up area. Such informal housing is built mostly on privately owned land (generally agricultural land) that is subdivided into small parcels without informing the local authorities and then sold to buyers without any legal deeds. Consequently, no building permits are issued. The magnitude of this process is far greater than the capacity of government authorities to organize or control it. The result is usually unplanned, high-density, and low-quality developments deprived of basic services and infrastructure. However, when such areas reach a population size large enough to exert political pressure, the government is forced to provide them with water, electricity, and sometimes sewerage networks.

Squatting is less common, but occurs on the fringes of the built-up area, in and around tombs in the City of the Dead, and on rooftops.

In the City of the Dead, adjacent to the Islamic core of Cairo, traditional burial places include a grave, one or two adjacent rooms, and an open yard surrounded by a fence, so that relatives of the deceased can pay extended visits. In the past four decades, the City of the Dead has been occupied by increasing numbers of permanent residents (250,000 in the mid-1980s) and the authorities have reluctantly extended services (Eddin Ibrahim, 1987). Peripheral squatter settlements, which are usually built on publicly owned or desert lands, are even worse than illegal subdivisions in terms of their lack of services and infrastructure, poor physical conditions, and high population densities.

Transportation and infrastructure
Although the road network represents nearly 25 per cent of the total GCR area, its practical capacity is inadequate owing to many problems. Lack of maintenance, poor driving habits, low vehicle occupancy, bottlenecks, and lack of parking lots and garages are among the major problems that decrease the efficiency of the network. In 1983 more than 530,000 vehicles were on the road. Owing to the sharp increase in car ownership in the GCR in the past decade, this figure has now doubled to reach more than 1 million vehicles. Amongst the most important bottlenecks are the six bridges over the Nile that link Cairo and Giza sections and are overloaded during the rush hour. Mass transportation is owned and operated by the public sector and is, by any standards, overloaded. In response to this problem, privately owned passenger vans have begun to function all over the GCR.

The General Organization for Water in the GCR provides almost 3 million m^3 of potable water per day. This amount is sufficient by international standards to supply the population. However, owing to the lack of maintenance of pipelines, equipment, and fittings, more than 25 per cent of this capacity is lost or wasted. The water network is old and pipe diameters are small, adding more problems to the distribution of water to many areas of the city. The situation with respect to the sewer network is even worse, even in districts connected to the system. Because of the sharp increase in population densities, the discharge in many districts of the GCR far exceeds the capacity of the sewerage system. This causes frequent overflows and represents a dangerous source of pollution.

In 1994, 14 per cent of the buildings in the Cairo and Giza sections were not connected to any infrastructure system. Of the remaining 86 per cent, 9 per cent are still not connected to the water system, 8 per cent have no electricity, and 38 per cent are unconnected to sewage disposal networks. Solid waste disposal is a major problem in Cairo, where more than 3,000 tons of solid waste is produced every day: 60 per cent is collected by private contractors and the remaining 40 per cent by local municipalities. Informal sector operators based in "refuse settlements" pay for the rights to collect refuse from wealthier parts of the city, using female household labour to sort it into recyclable waste for sale, organic waste for animal fodder, and unusable waste, which is burnt. An effective system, it results in very poor environmental conditions in the settlements concerned (Findlay, 1994). However, owing to the increased volume of solid waste and the geographical expansion of the city, neither private contractors nor the municipalities are able to keep up with the need.

Problems of traffic congestion and inadequate services have combined to increase environmental pollution. High levels of air pollution, due to suspended particulate matter and lead generated by traffic and industry (especially cement manufacture), are exacerbated by wind-blown dust (WHO/UNEP, 1992).

Social problems and inequality

Wage jobs in the formal sector have not kept pace with demand. As a result, the informal sector, which it was hoped would diminish over time, has shown clear signs of expansion. Levels of unemployment, real and disguised, have risen sharply, particularly during the past decade. Interclass and inter-sector disparities have widened over time to add a new dimension to the polarization process, despite protests by the urban poor and, increasingly, the lower rungs of the middle classes.

Data on income distribution in Egypt are very scarce. The only available figures are from a series of three consumer budget surveys conducted by the Central Agency for Population Mobilization and Statistics (CAPMAS) in 1958, 1964, and 1974. The 1974 surveys showed that the share of the top 20 per cent of the population was around 47 per cent of total income, while the share of the lowest 40 per cent was 17 per cent. A later study by the World Bank, in 1980, showed that the share of the top 5 per cent of the population had increased from 17 per cent of the national income in the late 1960s to 27 per cent in the late 1970s; and the share of the lowest 20 per cent had decreased from 7 per cent to 5 per cent during the same period (Abdel Khalek and Tignor, 1982). In addition, the share of wages in national income, which decreased from 50 per cent in 1967 to less than 34 per cent in 1986, indicates the shift towards an increasingly unequal distribution of wealth.

Social problems, such as lack of safety, illiteracy, and crime, have appeared in many parts of this mega-city, affecting both rich and poor areas. It has become evident, during recent decades, that government institutions are not able to cope properly with the ever-increasing rate of growth of Cairo and to manage it.

Policies, plans, and future prospects

National and Greater Cairo Region plans

Such concentrations of population, economic activities, wealth, and power have led to serious urban problems, resulting in several attempts since 1960 to manage and reorganize the growth of the GCR and to decentralize population and activities.

At the national level, the country was divided into eight homogeneous planning regions in 1975, with the aim of developing peripheral regions in order to absorb the additional expected growth of the urbanized areas. In 1982, a national urban policy study identified several goals for the future planning of the GCR (Advisory Committee for Reconstruction, 1982). First, it was suggested that Cairo's urban growth be redirected from an essentially north–south axis to an east–west orientation on vacant desert areas in proximity to the current built-up area. Secondly, it was recommended that the deconcentration of central Cairo should be pursued through the establishment of secondary and tertiary commercial, financial, industrial, and administrative centres. Thirdly, it suggested policies to promote an improvement in the general quality of life. Fourthly, it advocated the creation of appropriate instruments of governance aiming at guiding and controlling an integrated set of spatial, economic, social, and financial programmes.

At the city level, a master plan was formulated in 1970 incorporating two major concepts on which it recommended that the future management of the region be based (Ministry of Housing, 1970). First, it was suggested that a ring road surrounding the existing built-up area be constructed to control its growth and stop the invasion of agricultural areas. Secondly, it was recommended that self-sufficient new communities be established at suitable distances from the city to attract additional expected growth. Although the ideas of this plan were not fully implemented in the following years, they formed the basis for policies adopted in the 1970s and for the structural plan of 1983 (fig. 4.8), which remains the major guide for the urban development of the GCR to date.

In the 1983 plan, demographic studies produced estimates that the population of the GCR would increase from 6,700,000 in 1977 to 9,660,000 in 1982 and 16,500,000 by the year 2000 (table 4.6; GOPP, 1983), in addition to 1,400,000 people in surrounding rural areas that it expected to be included in the region by that date. This population would be absorbed both within and outside the existing built-up area. Within the existing area it was considered that population could be accommodated by incremental development, in proposed major housing projects, on vacant desert land inside the ring road to the north and east, and in pockets of agricultural land and peripheral areas to the north, east, and west (fig. 4.8). This, it was suggested, will require a restructuring of the metropolitan region using the concept of "homogeneous sectors", which will be discussed below. Table 4.6 shows the expected distribution of the population by the year 2000. It was estimated that an additional 5,055,000 could be accommodated within the built-up area and on marginal arable land. Secondly, the rest of the population will be accommodated outside the built-up area through the establishment of new satellite or independent communities on major radial axes and 10 smaller settlements adjacent to the ring road. It was estimated that 4,745,000 inhabitants would be absorbed in these communities and settlements by the year 2000.

The concept of homogeneous sectors

The concept of "homogeneous sectors" was suggested in the 1983 plan as a basis for reorganizing the existing built-up area in Cairo. It has since been developed to encompass the whole area of the GCR. It was suggested that, as Cairo is becoming too big to be managed as one unit and from a single core, it should be subdivided into smaller units within which development could be directed to ensure better living conditions, particularly in terms of the provision of job opportunities and the upgrading of existing service standards. Homogeneity in each sector was defined as meaning an equal distribution of services and access to jobs among its residents. However, it was envisaged that some sectors could specialize in particular functions, such as administration, commercial services, small-scale industries and handicrafts, or heavy industries. Such differentiation could, it was thought, strengthen the sector's identity. It was suggested that the

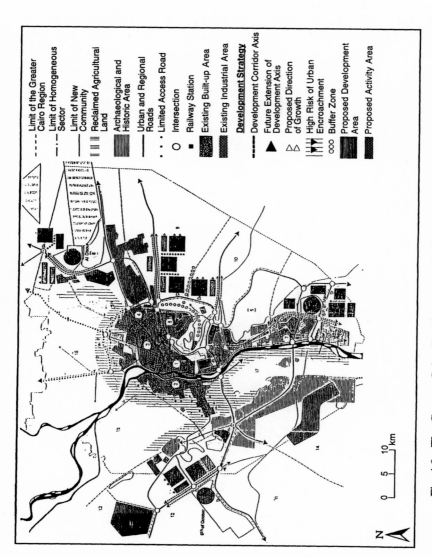

Fig. 4.8 The Greater Cairo Region Structural Plan, 1983 (Source: GOPP, 1983)

Table 4.6 Distribution of population according to homogeneous sectors and directional growth areas, 1977–2000 (population in '000)

Growth area	Sector no.	Present growth potential (1)	New projects (2)	New cities (3)	Vacant land within the ring road (4)	Marginal arable land (5)	New urban settlements (6)	Total increase 1977–2000	Total population 1977	Total population 2000
Centre	1	−140	–	–	170	–	–	30	1,700	1,730
North	3	−350	–	–	150	210	–	10	2,350	2,360
	15	–	–	–	–	–	–	–	–	–
	16	–	–	–	–	–	–	–	–	–
		−350	–	–	150	210	–	10	2,350	2,360
East	4	+300	20	–	130	90	–	540	660	1,200
	5	+230	130	–	910	–	–	1,270	80	1,350
	8	+10	410	500	–	–	375	1,295	100	1,395
	9	–	–	250	–	–	770	1,020	–	1,020
	10	–	–	250	–	–	350	600	–	600
		+540	560	1,000	1,040	90	1,495	4,725	840	5,565

South									
6	+120	160	–	750	200	–	1,230	350	1,580
7	+330	55	150	310	120	750	1,715	230	1,945
	+450	215	150	1,060	320	750	2,945	580	3,525
West									
2	+130	145	–	85	380	–	740	1,230	1,970
11	–	–	–	–	–	–	–	–	–
12	–	–	500	–	–	600	1,100	–	1,100
13	–	–	250	–	–	–	250	–	250
14	–	–	–	–	–	–	–	–	–
	+130	145	750	85	380	600	2,090	1,230	3,320
Total	+630	920	1,900	2,505	1,000	2,845	9,800	6,700	16,500

Source: GOPP (1983).

(1) = Urban area of Greater Cairo Region according to 1977 plans.
(2) = Housing projects (public and private sector) as from 1982.
(3) = Master plans by the Ministry of Reconstruction and New Communities.
(4) = Determined by Dames & Moore, 1981.
(5) = Urban growth on agricultural land.
(6) = Population excess to be settled in new settlements in the desert.

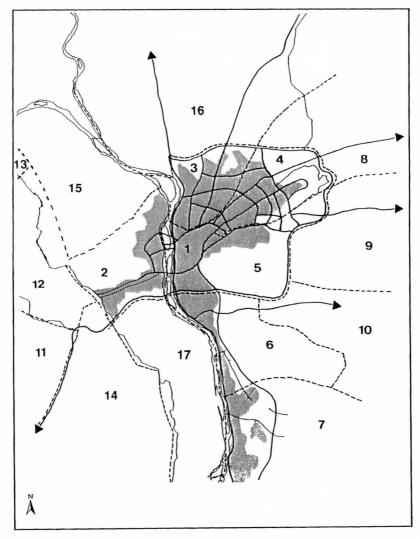

Fig. 4.9 Homogeneous sectors as defined in the 1983 Greater Cairo Region Structural Plan (Source: GOPP, 1983)

GCR could be divided into 17 homogeneous sectors, as shown in figure 4.9, according to the following criteria:
- a population range of 1–2 million inhabitants in order to provide an adequate threshold for most services;
- jobs should be available for 80 per cent of the labour force within the sector;

- at least one service centre should be provided in each sector;
- intrasectoral transportation networks should be improved to link its different parts and activities before developing intersectoral networks;
- sectors should be separated by open areas, which could also be used for public facilities on the edge of the built-up areas, such as major roads, railroads, waterways, cemeteries, and sports fields.

The new cities, satellite or independent, were intended to be developed as growth centres in order to attract economic activities and population from the core region. The cities are situated along the major regional radials to tie the GCR to other economic regions such as Suez, Ismailia, and Alexandria. Ten new settlements were suggested, primarily as an alternative to squatter and informal areas encroaching on agricultural land. These settlements were intended to be separate from the existing built-up area and to provide development affordable to the squatter population. Their size is intended to be large enough to guarantee an adequate level of self-sufficiency in terms of employment and services. It was hoped that the private sector would be the primary investor in these settlements, in order not to compete for public investment with the new towns. Finally, these settlements were to be located near existing labour pools in order to attract employment in the short and medium term. Figure 4.10 shows the proposed axes of development and the location of proposed new cities and settlements.

The present situation

The structural plan of 1983 was revised in 1991 (GOPP, 1991). New data showed a decline in the rate of growth in the city centre in favour of the middle and outer urban rings, particularly to the west. In the 1970s, most of this outer growth had taken place on agricultural land, indicating the urgency of providing desert land for urban expansion. However, the construction of new towns in the 1980s directed most of the urban growth to desert lands. The 1991 plan showed that encroachment on agricultural land decreased from 590 ha in 1980 to just under 150 ha in 1989. This was mainly due to sharp increases in land prices, declining purchasing power, and stringent legal controls.

In addition to the six new cities and satellite towns that have been established (10 Ramadan, El-Sadat, Badr, 6 October, 15 May, and El-Obour), ten new settlements along the ring road have been started

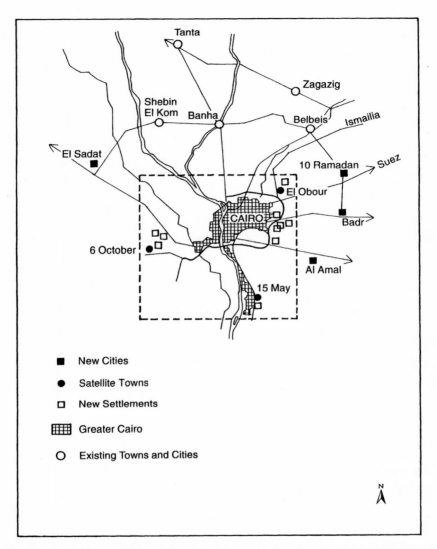

Fig. 4.10 Distribution of new cities, satellite towns, and new settlements around the Greater Cairo Region (Source: GOPP, 1983)

(table 4.7). The population capacity of the new settlements has been revised upwards to 5,382,000 from the 1983 estimate of 4,745,000. However, implementation is well short of that intended, and by 1994 only 448,850 people were living in the settlements (8.3 per cent of the planned population). Figures for the individual towns are given in

Table 4.7 **New towns occupancy in 1994 compared with year 2000 capacity**

	Year 2000 population capacity ('000)	Occupancy in 1994 ('000)	% occupancy
New cities and towns			
6 October	1,100	93	8.5
10 Ramadan	500	120	24.0
15 May	250	120	48.0
El-Obour	362	1.25	0.35
El-Sadat	500	25	5.0
Badr	280	1.5	0.5
Settlements			
El-Salhiya	60	15	25.0
New Nubaria	140	2.1	1.5
Borg El-Arab	500	10	2.0
El-Shorouk	250	–	–
New Beni-Suif	120	–	–
New Damietta	270	20	7.4
El-Shiekh Zayed	430	–	–
New Minya	120	–	–
Fifth Settlement	250	–	–
El-Kattameya	250	40	16.0

Source: Compiled from various publications of Egyptian New Towns, GOPP.

table 4.7, although the resident population figures given in this table should be treated with care because an appreciable proportion of the population have taken housing units for speculative purposes and do not live in these cities. Only 7,346 housing units have been finished in new settlements, with almost 23,000 units in the construction phase, but finished units are not yet occupied for lack of infrastructure and services.

Many infrastructure and transportation projects have been implemented in the GCR: parts of the ring road have been finished; the first line of the metro between El Marg and Helwan has been completed; two major water treatment plants with a capacity of 1 million m^3 per day have been constructed; and extensions to Cairo airport and the wholesale market in El-Obour have been completed. Other major projects are under way, such as the extension of sewage collection networks, the second line of the metro, a second wholesale market in 6 October city, and thousands of low-cost housing units in the new cities and settlements.

However, the GCR is still facing serious urban problems in terms of a lack of job opportunities; informal and illegal expansion of the built-up area; deterioration of the housing stock; and social, health, and environmental problems. It has become very evident that the major impediment to the implementation of planned projects is mismanagement and lack of sectoral and geographic integration. The GCR is still managed by three different governors (in Cairo, Qalyubia, and Giza sections), each having their own authority, local departments, and resources. At the same time, some facilities and services, such as planning, transportation, water supply, and sewage disposal, are administered by regional authorities. These local and regional institutions are not integrated and coordination of policy and implementation is poor. In addition, sectoral ministries, which are also located in Cairo, interfere in the affairs of these regional institutions. Moreover, the resources available for public investment are limited, discontinuous, and mismanaged. The result is usually the cancellation, delay, or alteration of planned urban development policies and projects. Proposals for the homogeneous sectors have also not been successfully carried out owing to management problems and lack of planning expertise at the local level. It is clear that the urban development policies for the GCR have not yet achieved their major goal of decentralizing population and economic activities. Because the government did not take appropriate measures to change the social, political, economic, and institutional structures radically, the effects of the policies are likely to be limited, or may even add to the polarization process.

Future prospects

It is expected that if the current pattern of growth continues in the future, the GCR will continue to expand rapidly along its major regional axes, particularly the Cairo–Alexandria axis. Along the road from Cairo to Alexandria, which extends for 220 km, lie five large cities, namely Banha, Tanta, Kafr El Zayat, Damanhour, and Kafr El Dawar, and a number of medium and small towns and villages (fig. 4.11). These urban centres are interrelated and affected heavily by the zone of influence of the two major poles of Cairo and Alexandria. They have experienced high rates of growth during recent decades both in population and in area. If these settlements continue to grow

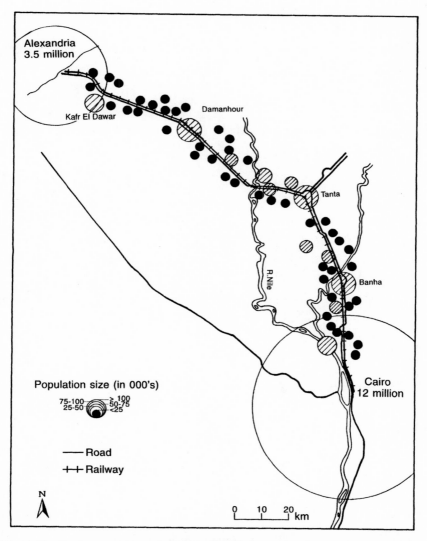

Fig. 4.11 **Settlement size and distribution on the Cairo–Alexandria road, 1994**

at the same rate, in a few years an extensive urban corridor may appear along this regional road and a new megalopolitan area may emerge either along the whole corridor between Cairo and Alexandria or, at least, between Cairo and Tanta. Such a metropolitan area would house almost half of the Egyptian population.

Notes

1. Manf, Lecht, Ono, and Babylon were in the location of the current Badrachen, south Ayat, Mataria, and Old Cairo, respectively (Moselhi, 1988).
2. Others, such as Abu-Lughod (1969) and Clerget (1934), claim that Cairo's population did not reach 1 million inhabitants at that time and estimate it at about half this size.

Appendix: Population growth in the Greater Cairo Region, 1927–1994 ('000)

Year		Cairo	Giza	Qalyubia	Region total
1927	No.	1,065	348	243	1,656
	%	64.3	21.0	14.7	100
1937	No.	1,312	409	182	1,903
	%	69.0	21.5	9.5	100
1947	No.	2,091	508	223	2,822
	%	74.0	18.0	8.0	100
1960	No.	3,349	1,035	400	4,784
	%	70.0	21.6	8.4	100
1976	No.	4,344	1,649	783	6,776
	%	64.1	24.3	11.6	100
1986	No.	5,603	2,506	1,405	9,514
	%	58.9	26.3	14.8	100
1994[a]	No.	6,849	3,467	2,133	12,449
	%	55.0	27.8	17.2	100

Source: CAPMAS, *General Census of Population and Housing*, Cairo.
a. 1994 population estimated.

References

Abdel Khalek, G. and R. Tignor, eds. 1982. *The Political Economy of Income Distribution in Egypt*. Holmes and Meier, New York.

Aboul Atta, T. 1985. Urban and economic spatial concentration in less developed countries. A reassessment of the interregional divergence–convergence hypothesis. Unpublished Ph.D. dissertation, Rutgers University, NJ.

Abu-Lughod, J. 1969. Varieties of urban experience: Contrast, coexistence and coalescence in Cairo. In: I. Lapidus, ed., *Middle Eastern Cities*. University of California Press, Berkeley, Calif.

Advisory Committee for Reconstruction. 1982. *The National Urban Policy Study*. Cairo.

Al-Wali, M. 1993. *Shacks and Squatter Settlers*. Egyptian Syndicate of Engineers, Cairo.

CAPMAS (Central Agency for Population Mobilization and Statistics). Various dates. *Egypt Statistical Year Book*. Cairo.

Clerget. 1934. *Le Caire. Géographie urbaine et d'histoire économique*. Cairo.

Eddin Ibrahim, S. 1987. A sociological profile. In: A. Y. Saqqaf, ed., *The Middle East City: Ancient Traditions Confront a Modern World*. Paragon House, New York, pp. 209–226.

El-Shakhs, S. 1971. National factors in the development of Cairo. *Town Planning Review* 42(3): 233–249.

Findlay, A. M. 1994. *The Arab World*. Routledge, London.

GOPP (General Organization for Physical Planning). 1983. *The Urban Development Plan, Year 2000: Greater Cairo Region*. Cairo (in Arabic).

――― 1991. *Evaluation of the Implementation of the Structural Plan of Greater Cairo Region*. Cairo (in Arabic).

Hamdan, G. 1982. *Egypt's Character: A Study of the Genus Loci*. Dar El Elm, Cairo (in Arabic).

Ibrahim, S. 1984. Cairo: A sociological look. In: *The Challenges of Urban Expansion: Case Study Cairo*. A Conference of the Aga-Khan Award, Cairo, 11–15 November.

Ministry of Housing. 1970. *The Preliminary Master Plan*. Cairo (in Arabic).

Moselhi, F. 1988. *The Development of the Egyptian Capital and Greater Cairo*. Dar El Madina El Mounawarah, Cairo (in Arabic).

Portes, A. and J. Walton. 1981. *Labour, Class and the International System*. Academic Press, New York.

Selem, H. 1983. Foustat City: A study in historical geography. *Arab Geography* 15: 140–145 (in Arabic).

Todaro, M. 1981. *Economic Development in the Third World*. Longman, New York.

UN. 1961. *The Myone Population Studies*. United Nations, New York (st/soa/ser a/34).

――― 1993. *World Urbanization Prospects: The 1992 Revision*. UN Department of Economic and Social Information and Policy Analysis, New York.

Wallerstein, I. 1974. *The Modern World System*. Academic Press, New York.

WHO/UNEP (World Health Organization and United Nations Environment Programme). 1992. *Urban Air Pollution in Megacities of the World*. Blackwell, Oxford.

World Bank. 1994. Private sector development in Egypt – status and challenges. Paper for the Conference on Private Sector Development in Egypt, Cairo, 9–10 October.

5

Johannesburg: A city and metropolitan area in transformation

Keith S. O. Beavon

Abstract

En 1886, la découverte de l'or déclenche la naissance de Johannesbourg et du complexe industriel environnant, la région du Witwatersrand. Dès 1895, la population de Johannesbourg dépasse celle du Cap et dans les années 20 elle devient la plus grande ville de l'Afrique subsaharienne. Aujourd'hui, Johannesbourg forme avec Prétoria au nord et le complexe industriel de Vereeniging au sud le cœur de la région du PWV. Le rôle prééminent de l'or n'a guère duré au-delà de la Deuxième Guerre mondiale, les mines s'épuisant. La guerre avait favorisé les manufactures développées au service des mines mais dès les années 90 elles perdent de l'importance tandis que le nombre d'emplois croît régulièrement dans les services. Quoique les sanctions se traduisent dans les années 80 par un début de chômage, la croissance des services financiers et d'affaires destinés au marché local se maintient. Au début, les travailleurs migrants sont logés dans l'enceinte des mines, dans les habitations pour domestiques des quartiers résidentiels et des zones isolées à l'ouest du centre ville. Au fur et à mesure que la population noire augmente, elle se regroupe dans des bidonvilles d'arrière-cour, des faubourgs à l'ouest de la ville, des banlieues établies par les pouvoirs publics au sud-ouest à proximité desquelles s'établissent, dès les années 40, des zones de squatters. Dans le même temps, le secteur privé multiplie les constructions pour loger les riches classes moyennes anglophones au nord du centre ville et un nombre grandissant de travailleurs blancs dans les autres faubourgs. Lorsque le Parti National arrive au pouvoir en 1948 avec sa politique d'apartheid un programme massif de construction au sud-ouest – Soweto – s'accompagne d'une accélération des évictions des noirs chassés des zones "blanches" de Johannesbourg et de leurs anciens quartiers. Vers le milieu des années 70, un million à un million et demi de personnes habitent les cités dortoirs du sud-ouest. La mauvaise qualité des logements, l'insuffisance des infrastructures et des services, la pénurie d'appareils sociaux et l'interdiction de toute une gamme d'activités commerciales se traduisent par un milieu appauvri et malsain. Le maintien de la discrimination réduit à néant les maigres réformes qui suivent la révolte de Soweto en 1976. Le peu de ressources dont disposent les autorités locales issues de la ségrégation leur interdit d'améliorer les services, ce qui s'ajoute aux conflits politiques pour décourager tout investissement commercial. Suite à la détérioration croissante de la situation, des mouvements associatifs locaux se mettent en place et organisent le boycott des loyers et autres paiements de service, ce qui handicape plus encore les autorités locales noires. Les cabanes de fortune et autres installations de squatters se multiplient. Ce n'est qu'en 1990, un accord étant passé avec les autorités locales provisoires annulant les arriérés de loyers, que les boycotts s'arrêtent, les tarifs des charges locales sont révisés et les réformes commencent. Les nouvelles autorités locales vont devoir se charger d'une région où l'économie est stagnante depuis une dizaine d'année et qui se caractérise par une ségrégation et des inégalités criantes entre les races en termes d'espaces et de revenus. Il va falloir restructurer le tissu urbain, la base financière et le cadre institutionnel en même temps qu'il faudra surmonter d'autres problèmes, y compris l'insuffisance de services dépassés et le terrible manque de logements.

Introduction

Given the long period during which South Africa was isolated from much of the world because of the country's apartheid policy, the city of Johannesburg was probably no more than a name to many people. Indeed it could be argued that, apart from knowing that it has an association with gold, Soweto, and periodic bouts of violence, few would recognize it if they were to see it unexpectedly! By way of illustration consider the following: suppose people from a developed country, who had never been to South Africa before, were to fly unknowingly to Johannesburg on one of the 53 international airlines that now land at its airport. Suppose that the visitors were then transported in an instant to the interior of one of the city's five-star hotels and thereafter to one of the suburban shopping malls, and asked to identify where they were. Almost certainly they would believe they were in some European, North American, or Australasian city. In effect, the concrete, chrome, and glass structures of Johannesburg, and the volume and variety of branded foods, clothes, sports goods, compact discs, as well as consumer durables in its upmarket malls are indistinguishable from those in most world cities. A carefully structured tour of the city could reinforce the perception of the visitors that they might be in any one of many large cities of the world. They could travel for hours and see no obvious signs of mining activity, they would see large, sophisticated, essentially clean-air industrial estates powered by electricity and a variety of comfortable and even luxurious housing. The skyline of the central business district (CBD) from a distance, with many tall buildings reaching up to compete with the 50-storey Carlton Centre, might well conjure up an image of Dallas. If, however, the tour inadvertently strayed to the south-western side of the agglomeration then the visitors would be immediately struck by the massive contrast between the townscape they had been observing and that of the sprawling residential townships occupied exclusively by Black people.[1] Because of the exposure on international television, the visitors should instantly recognize the "matchbox" houses as being part of Soweto and only then would they deduce that the adjacent "town" had to be Johannesburg.

The emphasis in this volume is on understanding the nature, present status, and future prospects of the largest cities of Africa. Given this objective, and the contention set out in the opening paragraph, it seems appropriate to set the scene by sketching some of the parameters that both define and characterize the modern, well-developed aspects of the city and its region. Thereafter attention will briefly shift to a consideration of other essential aspects of Johannesburg. In particular, and by way of some stark contrasts, it will be shown that the current urban crisis centres on redressing the legacy of the past whereby the indigenous population was consciously marginalized through a process of creating ghettos within the fabric of what was conceived to be a whites-only town. The chapter will conclude with a consideration of current thinking on how a new system of interim local authorities, finalized only in August 1995, might attempt to address the accumulated inequalities in the metropolis. Given restrictions of space, emphasis has been placed on circumstances and situations that embrace the Black and white populations of the Johannesburg Metropolitan Area, but similar themes have affected the Coloured and Indian populations (see, *inter alia*, Lupton, 1992, 1993a,b, on Coloured areas; and Carrim, 1990; Randall, 1973, on the Indian areas).

Setting the scene: From open veld to metropolitan giant

The real reason for Johannesburg's location and origin began 3,000 million years ago when fortuitous geological events created the Witwatersrand Basin and resulted in the world's richest deposits of gold (McCarthy, 1986). Preserved under a cap of lava and then exposed as a result of uplift and erosion (Moon and Dardis, 1988), the gold was still in place when humans with the necessary technical skills stumbled on it in the nineteenth century. Even then the mining and urbanization that followed could have been cut short, because iron sulphide in the ore body prevented separation of the gold. Only the timely discovery of a process that solved the separation problem for ore from the deeper levels where the bulk of the real wealth lay (Gray and McLachlan, 1933) ensured that Johannesburg would become a permanent feature on the highveld of the Transvaal (Richardson and Van-Helten, 1980; van Onselen, 1982a).

A little over a century ago, in early 1886, the site of Johannesburg was no more than an unwanted south-sloping remnant of ground lying between three highveld farms (Gray and Gray, 1940). There was little to commend the property for agricultural purposes, and it offered precious little prospect as a suitable place for a village, let alone a great city that would inexplicably be named Johannesburg (see, *inter alia*, Shorten, 1970, pp. 84–87; Smith, 1971, pp. 246–248; Hirschson, 1974; Appelgryn, 1984, pp. 21–30). Yet, within a mere 40 years of being founded on such an unlikely site, Johannesburg was being hailed as a "world city" (MacDonald, 1926) and was the largest and most powerful financial and commercial city in Africa south of the equator. By the time of its golden jubilee celebrations in 1936, Johannesburg had a population of 475,000 (Shorten, 1970, p. 365).

Gold not only provided the spark that ignited the development of Johannesburg, it also precipitated the growth of a string of towns along the east–west line of the gold-reef. Today they are all part of an urban industrial region known as the Witwatersrand (figs. 5.1 and

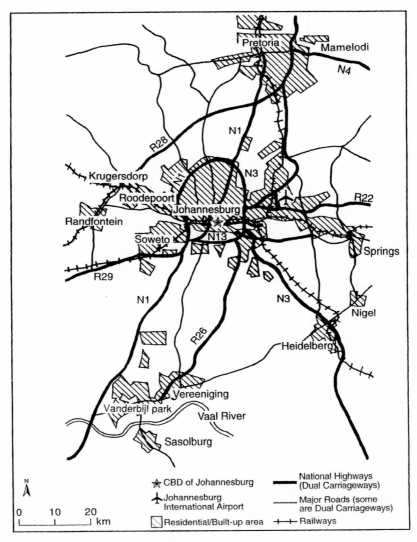

Fig. 5.1 **Johannesburg in its regional setting (Source: based on Beavon, 1992a)**

5.2). Some 60 km to the north was Pretoria, the capital of the Trans-vaal Republic, and a similar distance to the south, on the banks of the Vaal River, was the district where the settlement of Vereeniging would grow as the service centre for an industrial complex (composed of Vereeniging, Vanderbijlpark, and Sasolburg) to be known as the Vaal Triangle. As such the future Johannesburg was to find itself at

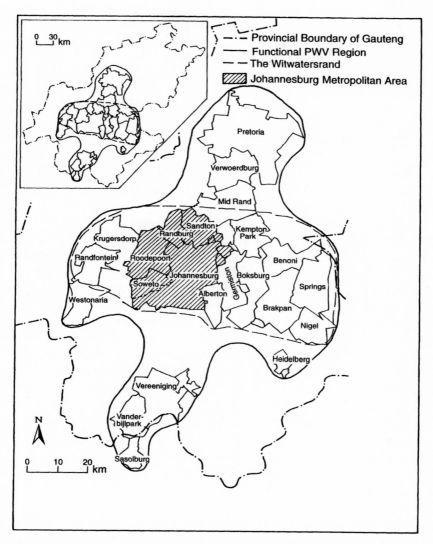

Fig. 5.2 **The functional area of the PWV and Gauteng province (Source: based on Development Bank of Southern Africa,** *South Africa's Nine Provinces: A Human Development Profile,* **DBSA, Midrand, 1994)**

the centre of a region of urban places known colloquially by the initials of its major focal points as the PWV (figs. 5.1 and 5.2). In addition, Johannesburg would be at the centre both of the Witwatersrand and of what is today the core region of the country lying in the south of the richest province of the "New" South Africa (initially, expediently, and confusingly dubbed the PWV but, since December 1994, officially named *Gauteng* – a northern Sotho colloquialism meaning "place of gold" or, in the present context, the Province of Gold).

To underscore the significance of the PWV region (in Gauteng province) it should be noted that whereas in 1990 the PWV (albeit somewhat loosely defined, see fig. 5.2) comprised only 2.5 per cent of the area of South Africa it contained between 23 and 25 per cent, or some 8.8 million, of the population. With 93 per cent of the PWV population in effect classified as urban, it is not surprising to find that the region also has approximately one-third of all the formal employment of the country. The PWV is responsible for between 43 and 40 per cent of the gross domestic product of South Africa (Urban Foundation, 1990; Department of Regional and Land Affairs, 1992; Hall et al., 1993, p. 1). It is anticipated that, by the year 2020, Johannesburg, the central but separate municipality of the metropolitan area (fig. 5.2), will be the fulcrum of a region containing an estimated 20 million people (Urban Foundation, 1990; Solomon, 1992). It is also useful to note here that initially Johannesburg, and later the Witwatersrand, have always been a focus for foreign workers, many of them actively recruited. Countries represented included China (with 63,695 mine workers between 1904 and 1907; Richardson, 1982) but the bulk of the labourers came from Malawi, Zambia, Zimbabwe, Botswana, and Lesotho (Crush et al., 1991). In 1972 foreign labour was at its highest, when it constituted three-quarters of the then 350,000 miners (although a significant proportion would have been employed in the goldfields of the Orange Free State) (Moodie, 1994). At the time of writing, claims in the local press assert that there are between 3 and 12 million foreign (and largely illegal immigrant) Black people resident in South Africa, of whom probably more than 60 per cent are resident, working, or seeking employment in the PWV. The figure now generally accepted as valid is one of 8.5 million illegal residents (CDE, 1995; van Niekerk, 1995).

In 1895, nine years after it was established, Johannesburg had a population of 80,000 and had surpassed Cape Town, which had been South Africa's primate urban place for the previous 243 years (*The Star*, 1987, pp. 7, 26). Johannesburg's position as the country's largest town, later a city, and now a commonly used tag for a metropolitan area in a metropolitan region, has never since been challenged. The definition of Johannesburg for population purposes has, however, become more all-embracing. In everyday parlance, the name Johannesburg is used of the Johannesburg Metropolitan Area, or Greater

Table 5.1 **Population of the Witwatersrand and the Johannesburg Metropolitan Area, 1970–1990**

| | Witwatersrand[a] | | | | Johannesburg Metropolitan Area[a] | | | |
| | 1970 | | 1990 | | 1970 | | 1990 | |
	No.	%	No.	%	No.	%	No.	%
Total	2,636,854	100.0	4,948,124	100.0	1,621,717	100.0	2,554,726	100.0
Black		57.7		63.0		54.5		61.1
White		36.0		30.5		37.7		30.3
Coloured		4.3		4.4		5.3		5.8
Indian		2.0		2.1		2.5		2.8

Sources: Fair and Muller (1981); DBSA (1991a).

a. Various estimates exist of the city's population. The 1991 census count given in the text (Central Statistical Services, 1992) is considered to be an underestimate, and the figures here may be more realistic.

Johannesburg roughly demarcated by the circular freeway system of the N1, N2, and N3 (fig. 5.1), whereas the City of Johannesburg refers to the old municipal area shown as Johannesburg in figure 5.2. The latter had a population in 1991 somewhat in excess of 2.2 million, whereas the core of the Witwatersrand had a total population of *at least* 4.3 million (Central Statistical Services, 1992; cf. table 5.1). Not surprisingly, because of its sizeable population, and not least because it has been the financial capital of the South African region for more than 100 years, Johannesburg has long been a general service centre not only for the Transvaal but for much of the South African and even the southern African interior.

Johannesburg's rise to regional pre-eminence began with the discovery of gold in 1886. Notwithstanding the early dominance of gold mining in the economy of Johannesburg and the central Witwatersrand, the pre-eminent role of the industry as a producer of earnings and as an employer of labour did not last much beyond World War II. In 1945 the Witwatersrand was producing 96 per cent of South Africa's gold (at a time when the country in turn was the source of about 40 per cent of the world total) and the mines of the Central Rand (lying largely in the Johannesburg metropolitan boundaries) were responsible for 34 per cent (Scott, 1951). By 1980 the contribution to national production from Johannesburg's mines had fallen dramatically to 3 per cent (Fair and Muller, 1981). As gold dropped out of the local and regional economy, owing in part to the fact that the economically viable ores had largely been worked out, and in part to the fact that new highly productive mines had opened on the Far West Rand (Randfontein and Westonaria; see fig. 5.2) and in the Orange Free State, the place of gold mining on the central Witwatersrand was taken by a variety of secondary industries. They in turn were accompanied by an expansion of tertiary services.

Both of those sectors, which had been closely associated with mining from the outset, had enjoyed a considerable boost in their fortunes during World War II when manufacturing industry in South Africa, particularly in Johannesburg, boomed, as the country manufactured *matériel* for the Allied war effort. Even so, in 1951 just over 1 in 3 members of the Witwatersrand labour force were still employed by the mining industry. That ratio had, however, dropped to 1 in 11 by 1970 and is even less at the present time. By contrast the labour force employed in secondary industry, located in what is now termed the Johannesburg Metropolitan Area, increased from 130,000 to 230,000, while employment in the services sector rose from just over 272,000 to 422,000 in the 20 years from 1951 to 1970 (table 5.2). The loss of some 200,000 mining jobs on the Witwatersrand as a whole over the same period was more than offset by an increase of 475,000 jobs in the secondary and tertiary sectors (of which 60 per cent were in the Johannesburg Metropolitan Area). Whereas the two decades from 1950 clearly marked the change from a primary industrial phase into a fully fledged secondary industrial phase, the same period was also marked by a considerable surge in services (Fair, 1977; Fair and Muller, 1981), which increasingly were located, or had office space, in the Johannesburg CBD.

By the 1990s *actual* mining activity had to all intents and purposes become insignificant in the regional economy of the Johannesburg Metropolitan Area. Manufacturing, although important in absolute terms, had dropped to a mere 18 per cent of the metropolis's gross geographic product (GGP) (Mabin and Hunter, 1993, pp. 87–88), largely as a result of centrifugal forces that pushed it over the borders of the metropolitan periphery and further afield in search of lower costs. By contrast, the trade and catering sector contributed 20 per cent of the local GGP, and the finance and business services sector made up nearly 30 per cent. Transport and communications and the general government sector each contributed 10 per cent to the GGP. Between 1980 and 1991, a period believed by some to be the one in which international sanctions against the apartheid state were biting hardest on the Witwatersrand, the Johannesburg Metropolitan Area saw a decrease in its overall formal employment of about 3.5 per cent

Table 5.2 Employment by sector in the Johannesburg Metropolitan Area and the rest of the Witwatersrand, 1951–1970

	Primary sector				Secondary sector				Tertiary sector			
	1951		1970		1951		1970		1951		1970	
	No.	%	No.	%	No.	%	No.	%	No.	%	No.	%
Johannesburg Metropolitan Area	87,408	18	35,958	5	131,131	27	230,466	34	272,368	55	422,029	61
Remainder of Witwatersrand	212,804	53	74,172	15	74,301	18	210,816	43	119,071	29	208,486	42
All Witwatersrand	300,212	33	110,130	9	205,432	23	441,282	37	391,439	44	630,515	54

Source: based on Fair and Muller (1981).

Table 5.3 **Employment by sector in the Johannesburg Metropolitan Area, 1980–1991**

Primary sector				Secondary sector				Tertiary sector			
1980		1991		1980		1991		1980		1991	
No.	%	No.	%	No.	%	No.	%	No.	%	No.	%
21,227	2.8	17,101	2.3	225,742	30	189,560	26	509,978	67	523,726	72

Source: based on Mabin and Hunter (1993), table A4.

(Mabin and Hunter, 1993, p. 71). Yet the financial and business component of the tertiary sector, although almost exclusively focused on servicing the local region and South Africa, continued to expand. There was a 30.7 per cent increase in its employment, translating into an additional 24,000 jobs (Mabin and Hunter, 1993, p. 71). The net result was that by 1991 approximately 7 out of 10 people employed in the formal sector of the Johannesburg Metropolitan Area were engaged in tertiary services (table 5.3). Notwithstanding the figures just cited, it is still extremely difficult (in 1995) to assess the true effects of the sanctions, disinvestments, and divestments that took place particularly in the 1980s. The task of detailing the effects on the country as a whole, let alone on regions within it, remains to be tackled, by searching through not only the plethora of published material (see, *inter alia*, Kalley, 1988; Schoeman, 1988; Orkin, 1989; Sarakinsky, 1989) but also the as yet hidden (but hopefully extant) state documents.

The single most important indicator of the dominance of Johannesburg's service activities is reflected in the 5.9 million m² of good-quality office space found in the CBD of the city, in its suburban centres, and in its nearest municipal neighbours. In national terms that amounts to just over 1 million m² more office space, of the same quality, than occurs in the combined office buildings of the country's three other major metropolitan areas of Durban (pop. 2.2 million), Cape Town (pop. 2 million), and Pretoria (pop. 1.03 million) (Central Statistical Services, 1992; Amprops, 1994).

Up to 1970 the concentration of offices, reflecting the location of Johannesburg's tertiary services, was in the CBD. The pattern began to change noticeably from the mid-1970s onwards, as office clusters in the expanding northern suburbs and neighbouring municipalities competed for tenants. Even so, in 1993 the Johannesburg CBD alone still contained 2.7 million m^2 of the top three grades of offices. That figure amounts to 56.6 per cent of the total comparable office space in the other three metropolitan regions (i.e. not just in their CBDs) put together (Amprops, 1994).

The financial importance of the city is also reflected by the fact that it is the home of the Johannesburg Stock Exchange (JSE), the only one in South Africa. It is ranked 12th in the world on the basis of its market capitalization. The JSE is also several orders of magnitude larger than any other stock exchange in Africa (Katz, 1994, pp. 431–432; see chap. 3). As an indicator of foreign capital flows into South Africa via Johannesburg's financial institutions, it can be noted that JSE trading by foreign investors, on the basis of turnover and arbitrage, was 29.4 per cent in 1993 (Katz, 1994, p. 335). Reflecting the importance of Johannesburg as the location for major headquarters buildings is the fact that 75 per cent of the 615 firms currently listed on the JSE are located in the PWV, of which 66 per cent are in the Johannesburg Metropolitan Area (based on data extracted from Maher, 1994).

From the data given in the preceding paragraphs it should come as no surprise that the Johannesburg CBD contributes 12 per cent of South Africa's GNP. The Johannesburg Metropolitan Area consumes 9,097 GWh of electricity per annum, which is a mere 6.7 per cent of the national consumption but 5.8 per cent of the total installed (not necessarily productive) capacity of the rest of Africa (and about equal to the total annual electricity sales in Zambia or Zimbabwe) (Eskom, 1993).

Notwithstanding the glitzy wonders of Johannesburg that make it so significant an urban place in Africa, there is also a less attractive, deprived, and deeply disturbing side that remained "hidden" from many of Johannesburg's white citizens, at least until 1976. Adjacent to this, the most opulent city south of the Sahara, there are hundreds of thousands of people living in deprived communities or townships. In addition, there are tens of thousands living in informal settlements of shacks recently erected in the veld. And despite the fact that Johannesburg lies at the centre of South Africa's industrial heartland, it also lies at the centre of a region that has stagnated, and in absolute terms has actually lost ground during the endgame of the apartheid era. Political settlement in South Africa, and the advent of a government that reflects the majority of the people, has rapidly brought the plight of deprived communities to the daily attention of South Africans. The process of transformation in general, and in the province of Gauteng in particular, will depend on the successful reintegration of the formerly segregated urban components through the reallocation of resources under what is termed the Reconstruction and Development Programme (RDP) of the new government. Specific issues that emerge from the troubled past include the provision of adequate, albeit basic, municipal services such as water supply, sewerage, and garbage removal; overcoming the housing backlog; and promoting the development of commercial infrastructure and improved, affordable, and safe mass transport systems. It is towards a consideration of some of the points made above and to providing an essential historical backdrop that attention now turns.

Racial separation, segregation, and apartheid

The origins of Soweto

Although today Soweto is the best known of the black residential areas in and around Greater Johannesburg, the bulk of its "suburbs" have a much shorter history than Johannesburg itself. Fully to understand the current reconstruction motives and designs for the future, it is important to understand the manner in which black people were segregated from white residents for over a hundred years. Some background on the repeated attempts to create and maintain segregation prior to the apartheid years is also needed to explain why so many black people were concentrated in the western part of Johannesburg before the Group Areas Act was introduced in 1950. Thereafter Black people would be forced to live in the south-western townships that were then collectively known as *Vukuzenzele* (Hansard, 1953, col. 222) – a name that means "get-up-and-do-it-yourself" (Beavon and Rogerson, 1990, p. 283). Some of the essential background is provided below.

In what follows, the plight of Black labourers in the mines, who were increasingly tightly controlled and contained in compounds on the mining properties (Moroney, 1978, 1982), is not considered. Black domestic servants employed and residing in white suburban properties (see van Onselen, 1982b) are also excluded from consideration in this chapter. The focus is mainly on the Black people who were employed in the town itself and its industries. They, together with other so-called "non-white" people, were initially crowded into three small ghettos, later termed "locations," which the white officials of the emerging settlement permitted on the then periphery of the rather insalubrious western side of town from 1887 onwards. All three enclaves were known officially by derogatory racial tags (Beavon, 1982): the "Coolie Location" was for Indians who had, in the main, come via indentured labour in Natal to work and do business in the town; the "Kafir Location" was for Black people (fig. 5.3); and the "Malay Location" was set aside for Cape Coloured people, many of whom had arrived in Johannesburg as labourers in the employ of Afrikaner wagoneers.

The general site of Soweto-to-be (see fig. 5.1) was unwittingly selected in 1904 when Black people were forcibly evicted, along with Indians, from the "Coolie Location," an area that the council wanted to redevelop and integrate with the adjacent central business area (fig. 5.3) (Wentzel, 1903). The forced removals followed a 1904 outbreak of bubonic plague in the "Coolie Location" (Maud, 1938, pp. 70, 134–135). At the time, the emerging city was under the administrative control of the British (following the Boer War) and the municipal area proclaimed by them in 1903 was supposedly the largest in the world. Yet when the evictions took place the only "suitable" site that could "be found" for the Black people was a place called Klipspruit (see fig. 5.4), 19 km by road and 15 km as the crow flies to the southwest beyond the municipal boundary (Maud, 1938; Lewis, 1966). Although permits were later issued to allow some Black workers to reside temporarily closer to their places of work in central Johannesburg, no positive accommodation policy for Black people was formulated by the council (Maud, 1938; Parnell, 1991, 1993). On the contrary, slum living conditions in shacks erected in the backyards of residential, commercial, and industrial properties became the lot of tens of thousands of Black workers and their families (see, *inter alia*, Hellman, 1935; Dikobe, 1973; Koch, 1983; Parnell, 1993).

Eventually armed with clauses contained in the infamous Natives (Urban Areas) Act of 1923, the City Council began to evict slum dwellers with the intention of accommodating them in a number of segregated peripheral townships called locations. For a variety of reasons detailed elsewhere (*inter alia*, Kane-Berman, 1978; Morris, 1980, 1981; Beavon, 1982), not least the reluctance of white taxpayers to contribute towards the municipal costs of such an exercise, those attempts were less than successful, even after the council monopolized the brewing and sale of traditional African beer in order to generate increased revenues it could use for housing Black people (Proctor, 1979; Rogerson, 1986). Instead, Black people began to congregate in increasing numbers in three suburbs of Johannes-

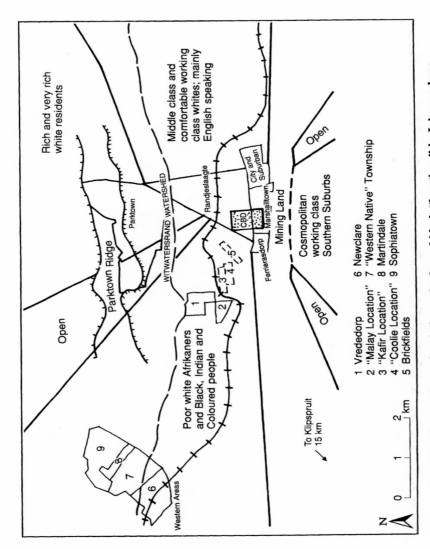

Fig. 5.3 **The positions of early key suburbs and black "locations" in Johannesburg**

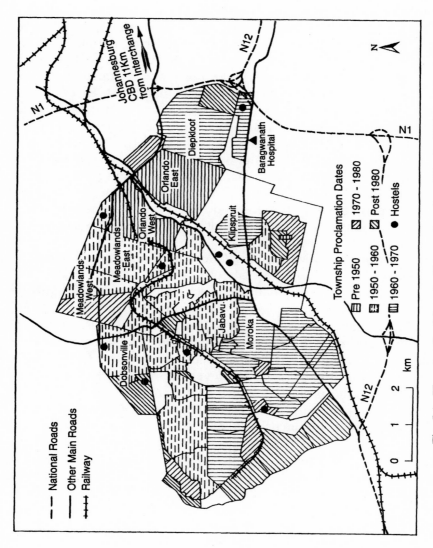

Fig. 5.4 **The growth of Soweto (Source: based on Morris, 1980)**

Legend:

National Roads
Other Main Roads
Railway

Township Proclamation Dates

Pre 1950
1950 - 1960
1960 - 1970
1970 - 1980
Post 1980
Hostels

Johannesburg CBD 11Km from Interchange

N1
N12
N12
N1

Diepkloof
Orlando East
Orlando West
Meadowlands East
Meadowlands West
Klipspruit
Jabavu
Moroka
Dobsonville
Baragwanath Hospital

N

km
0   1   2

burg, which had been eschewed by white people because, when laid out in 1902, they were adjacent to the municipal rubbish tip (Lewsen, 1953). The suburbs were Sophiatown, Martindale, and Newclare and were collectively known, together with Western Native Township (created as a "native location" on the levelled rubbish tip in 1918), as the Western Areas (SAIRR, 1953; fig. 5.3). In the suburbs of the Western Areas (excluding the "location"), Black people were entitled, through a legal quirk, to own property on a freehold basis, something denied them elsewhere by the fundamental concept built into the Natives (Urban Areas) Act, namely that Black people "should only be permitted within municipal areas insofar and for so long as their presence is demanded by the wants of the White population" (as quoted in Kane-Berman, 1978, p. 71). The Urban Areas Act was predicated on the notion that Black people would be sojourners, or temporary residents, in the urban areas (Horrell, 1978; Davenport, 1991). It was supposed that at some time in the future the Black people would be removed to the "native reserves" (later known as Bantustans and Homelands) when their services were no longer needed in the white areas.

The rapid industrialization that followed South Africa's departure from the gold standard in December 1932 (Proctor, 1979), and which was given a boost by the demand for manufactured goods to assist the Allied war effort after 1939, saw increasing demands for "cheap" Black labour that aggravated the accommodation crisis. Pushed by the central government, the City Council set up the second of the south-western townships as late as 1938 and named it Orlando (see fig. 5.4) (Morris, 1980, 1981). However, it was largely shunned by Black people, who preferred to live in the crowded inner-city slums and the vibrant Western Areas (Huddleston, 1956; Hart and Pirie, 1984) (often simply but incorrectly referred to as Sophiatown), rather than be subject to the strict regulations that governed life in the distant "locations" (Parnell, 1993). During World War II, in addition to migrants from the Transvaal, large numbers of Black people from Natal and the Orange Free State unexpectedly flocked to *e'Goli* (a popular word used by Black miners for the City of Gold). It appears that they had been attracted to the city by false rumours that the Johannesburg municipality was giving Black migrants pieces of ground on which to build their own homes. The resultant surge of Black people, soon referred to as squatters, settled "like birds in the cornfields" (Stadler, 1979) in the vicinity of Orlando. Later the squatter sites would be individually named Jabavu and Moroka (fig. 5.4) and would form parts of Soweto, so named in the 1960s after the acronym for the *south-western townships* (Pirie, 1984a). Overall it is estimated that the Black population of Johannesburg increased from a nominal 229,000 to almost 385,000 between 1939 and 1946 (Stadler, 1979).

By way of a contrast, some indication of what was happening in the white residential parts of Johannesburg is necessary. From as early as 1887 there was a distinction between what can be called the eastern and western suburbs of Johannesburg. The foreigners, or *uitlanders*, who formed the white majority in Johannesburg, had caused what they perceived as the "undesirable" people, namely the "non-whites" *and* the unskilled Afrikaners (Fourie, 1978), to be concentrated in the suburbs west of what was a white slum called Vrededorp (fig. 5.3). That action soon had a marked influence on the gross social geography of white Johannesburg as it appeared by the early 1900s (Beavon, forthcoming). Even before the Boer War the English-speaking community, from the very rich to the relatively poor, was concentrated to the east of the business district (Maud, 1938; Smith, 1971; van Onselen, 1982b). Furthermore, by 1892 the "Randlords" had begun to relocate from their south-facing view-sites of the eastern suburbs and were soon building north-facing mansions on properties that were as large as 80,000 m^2 atop the Parktown Ridge (fig. 5.3), and its east and west extensions, to the north of the town (Benjamin, 1972). That development did much to make the area north of the ridge attractive to others of the comfortable classes, who aspired to join the ranks of the rich but on properties of between 1,000 and 4,000 m^2 (fig. 5.3). And so the die was cast for residential class separation amongst the English-speaking Johannesburgers, with the more affluent opting for the central northern sector of the expanding town. To the south of the mining land, the area known as the Southern Suburbs became the home of a variety of white groups, including non-English speakers. With relatively high densities it had a distinct mining and working-class character (Smith, 1971; van Onselen 1982a,b).

Whereas there was no serious attempt to provide housing for Black people prior to 1938, there was no shortage of housing for white middle-class people and the rich. For example, when economic boom followed the departure from the gold standard and created massive overcrowding in Black accommodation, there was an immediate building boom in accommodation for whites. Some 10,400 private residential flats for white people were constructed on the northern edge of the CBD alone (City Engineer, 1967; van der Waal, 1987).

When the National Party, with its policy of apartheid, formed the government in 1948, it was determined to see the south-western townships grow. To that end there was a massive building programme that accompanied the growing number of evictions and removals of Black people from white Johannesburg. Forced removals also took place from the Western Areas, after they were declared white group areas, and their Black residents were transferred to Meadowlands (fig. 5.4). For the first time there was a significant closing of the gap between the stock of available 44 m^2 "matchbox" houses (Morris, 1980: 143) and the increasing number of Black people in Johannesburg (fig. 5.5), as well as substantial site-and-service schemes (Morris, 1980, 1981). Whereas the preceding statement might give an impres-

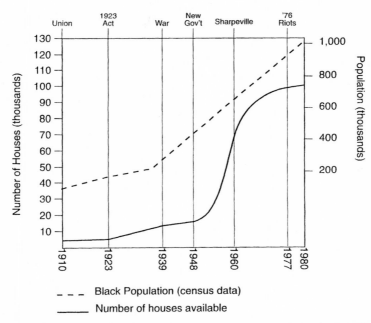

Fig. 5.5 **The Black population of Johannesburg and local authority housing provision, 1910–1980 (Source: based on Morris, 1980)**

sion of benevolence on the side of the state, that would be misleading. Rentals were charged for the sites and built accommodation, and defaulters were evicted. In 1957 the Natives (Urban Areas) Act and other repressive Acts that related to Blacks in urban areas were grouped together in the Natives (Urban Areas) Consolidation Act, which was then amended from time to time (Horrell, 1978). In terms of the provisions of this Act and its forerunner, the income-earning opportunities for self-employed Black people in the "townships" between 1923 and 1976 were severely restricted. There were only seven categories of self-employed businesses they could engage in, namely, general dealerships, "native" eating-houses, restaurants, milkshops, butcheries, greengrocers, and hawking, and then only in the townships. The numbers of businesses that would be allowed in each township were, in any event, controlled and very limited (Beavon, 1989, p. 24). Furthermore, occupation of a house in Soweto would in future be possible only if the occupier had worked continuously for one employer for 10 years. If the occupier took a job in another town, say somewhere on the Witwatersrand other than in Johannesburg, then their residence rights in Soweto could be placed in jeopardy (Hlope, 1977, p. 347; Horrell, 1978, p. 174). As such, the townships of Soweto grew by accretions and additions (see fig. 5.4), on the assumption not only that they would be temporary but also that they would be little more than crude dormitories for labour.

By the mid-1970s, when a generation of children who had been born and raised under apartheid lived in the south-western townships, the total population was estimated to be between 1 and 1.5 million (Morris, 1980, p. 35), about twice the white population of municipal Johannesburg. Occupancy of a typical "matchbox" house was put in the range of 7 (Shuenyane et al., 1977) to 14 (Johannesburg Chamber of Commerce Survey cited in Morris, 1980, p. 43) and increasingly relatives, friends, and lodgers were being accommodated in backyard shacks not dissimilar from those of the earlier slumyards. The townships of Soweto soon belied the claim by National Party politicians that apartheid was a policy of "separate but equal." Townships created after 1950 were zoned so that occupation was by specific ethnic (tribal) groups, in accordance with the apartheid ideology of divide and rule (Mashile and Pirie, 1977; Pirie, 1984b). In addition, houses in those areas were assigned seriatim and so friendship ties and income, if not class differences, typical even in working-class white areas were not catered for. The dearth of permitted self-employment opportunities and restrictive licensing meant that there was a corresponding dearth of shops and services within the townships. Consequently "illegal" or pirate dairies and butcheries operated in houses to the detriment of public health, and there were large numbers of hawkers offering foodstuffs for sale, particularly in the vicinity of transportation stopping points and termini (Beavon and Rogerson, 1990). There were only two hotels and two cinemas (Morris, 1980, p. 242). Roads were unpaved and public open space was covered by coarse veld grass if it was covered at all. There was virtually no reticulation of electric power and only 20 per cent of houses were linked to the supply system by 1976 (Morris, 1980, p. 101). Residents, therefore, not only were forced to shop in the white city but of necessity had to burn wood and coal for heating and cooking purposes. As a result, in the early mornings and evenings the whole area would be covered in thick acrid smoke. The inhospitable environment, together with poverty, and aggravated by unemployment, was reflected in the infant mortality rates, which by 1976 were 54.29 per 1,000 confinements compared with a rate of 18.09 for whites (City Health Department, 1973). Rates of malnutrition and tuberculosis were also high in Soweto. Wages were low and on average only one-third of those earned by whites (Bureau of Market Research, 1977). In addition, restricted income-earning opportunities made ownership of a motor car almost impossible. Whereas car ownership amongst whites was 1.32 vehicles per family, amongst Sowetans it was 0.2 (Bureau of Market Research, 1976). The result was that virtually all the working adults were dependent upon the slow, unreliable public transport system that had insufficient capacity to get them punctually to their places of work in what was now officially a white city.

With the all too visible and increasing differences between the comfortable and affluent lifestyles of white Johannesburg and black Soweto, and increasing resolve by organized black political groups to get rid of apartheid, it is surprising that the Soweto revolt of 1976 did not occur earlier. The uprising could have been ignited by any one of a number of privations and measures such as those cited above. When it came, the spark of revolt was dissatisfaction with Afrikaans-medium teaching in some of the schools: the first wave of confrontation in the streets on 16 June 1976 was led by schoolchildren and the first mortal casualty was Hector Petersen, a 13-year-old schoolboy (Kane-Berman, 1978).

After the 1976 revolt

Although the Soweto revolt was followed by similar upheavals in many parts of the country, prompting the government to declare a general state of emergency, those matters fall outside the focus of this chapter. What is important to note is that the uprising severely jolted the government and prodded it into a programme of urban reform, based on freedom of movement for urban workers without impairing their residence rights, as would have been the case before. Just prior to the events of 16 June 1976, the state, in response to demands from Black leaders that their people should be free to do business in the Black townships, had lifted restrictions on the variety of self-employment activities open to Blacks from 7 to a paltry 26. Following the uprising, and in an attempt to make reformist concessions while attempting to demonstrate its resolve that it would not capitulate to Black demands in general, the state increased the categories of self-employment allowed in the townships to 65, but then, realizing that such petty restrictions were pointless, it removed all of them by the end of 1977 (Beavon, 1989, 1992a). Theoretically, Black residential areas could now have the same range of businesses and services as occurred in the white suburban shopping centres and downtown. That said, however, the 44 years of severe limitations inevitably meant that Black entrepreneurs had been considerably disadvantaged in terms of developing businesses and business practices. Thus the dearth of business facilities in the townships could not be overcome overnight. Significantly, however, reform in the realm of the taxi industry was to see the extremely limited number of licensed taxis (in the form of mini-buses) rise to 1.4 per 1,000 people by 1980, and to 3.5 in 1990, resulting in more than 7,000 legal taxis operating in the township (Khosa, 1992).

More noteworthy amongst the reforms was the acceptance that Blacks residing in the urban areas of South Africa would henceforth be there legally and permanently (Hart, 1990). In the case of Soweto, plans were made to step up electrification of the suburb and improve the services. Yet at the same time the state tightened up its influx controls (Hindson, 1987) and attempted to accelerate its Bantustan programme of development by a carrot and stick approach. The proverbial carrot took the form of huge amounts of capital poured into those puppet states (Morris, 1981), in order to create jobs and provide houses in an attempt to entice Black people away from the metropoles. At the same time, the state applied the stick by cutting down on, and eventually withdrawing entirely from, the provision of funds for building houses for Black people in the urban areas. The net effect in Soweto (as in other townships) was a fall-off in housing provision and an escalation of the shortage (fig. 5.5). Alternative housing provided by the private sector proved both expensive and later problematical in terms of delivery (Hendler, 1988). In 1983 the government announced its intention to sell a large percentage of its rental stock of "matchbox" houses in Black areas to the residents. The so-called Big Sale was promoted on the basis of ownership and secure tenure (Mabin and Parnell, 1983). A year later, at the end of 1984, it was clear the sale had been a failure. The potential buyers were *inter alia* suspicious of the state's intentions, they found that loan (or mortgage bond) repayments would be higher than the rents they were already paying, they believed that their many years of "rent" payments should be discounted against the purchase price, and they had serious doubts regarding the potential future resale of township houses given the low mobility amongst township residents (Hardie and Hart, 1986).

The point that emerges from this sketch of national events is that, despite recognizing Black residents in Soweto as permanent residents of Greater Johannesburg, and despite the removal of income-earning restrictions, the fact was that very little changed. People continued to live in rented "matchboxes," and the upgrading of essential municipal services (let alone education, health, etc.) proceeded very slowly. When garbage heaped up and sewers became blocked they were not attended to as a matter of urgency. Roads remained unpaved and unlit, while public transportation was inadequate in capacity, unreliable, and expensive, so the frustrations of the populace continued to rise. Part of the ineptitude of the local authorities (originally the Johannesburg municipality, then in the 1970s the central government, and later a Black, but puppet, local authority) responsible for services in Soweto was that the township had no hope of developing a genuine tax base unless it was integrated with one of the white municipalities. Because of racial controls on investment in Black areas and the long-running restrictions on Black income-earning opportunities, there were no industries and precious little in the way of formal retail premises in the township. Certainly there were no shopping malls of the kind that popped up like mushrooms in the northern (white) suburbs from the mid-1970s onwards. There were no office parks and the rental houses were state owned. In short, there was no substantial profit-making or appreciating property base for assessment of rates to feed local authority finances. Furthermore, when political unrest broke out anew in 1985, followed once again by the proclamation of a national state of emergency (which included detention without trial, suspension of a variety of civil rights, and other draconian powers), popular protest moved up a gear and entered the arena of civil disobedience as new "civic" leaders and popular organizations of resistance emerged.

In the early 1980s the apartheid regime had attempted to gain credibility for its "separate but equal" charade by establishing Black local authorities (or BLAs) in metropolitan "locations" or "townships." Whereas the state found members of the Black population who were prepared to collaborate in the sham, popular leaders with grass-roots support were soon pushed to the forefront of opposition to the BLAs. The fact that BLAs had "inherited" economically impoverished municipal realms, devoid of retail and service businesses and industry because of apartheid regulations, meant that they were unable to provide municipal services that might have "bribed" the "electorate" into accepting their legitimacy. Instead the lack of service provision by the BLAs encouraged popular opposition. Local social movements accountable to the community emerged and were dubbed "civics." Within a short space of time there was at least one civic organization per township or per subdivision in the large townships. The leadership of the civics was overwhelmingly but not exclusively male. By contrast, the block and street committees that were the real engine-rooms of opposition to the apartheid state were fired and run mainly by women. Although born to resist the apartheid state, civics also found themselves forced to find solutions to the problems of poor municipal services, the public housing shortage, and the lack of land. They therefore linked together and joined forces with other opposition groups in the black community to find ways of dismantling apartheid. As the civics, they would later be prepared to engage in forums of discussion and planning that lay outside the formal apparatus of state administration (see below) (Coovadia, 1991; Shubane, 1991; Development and Democracy, 1994).

Inhabitants of the Black townships increasingly heeded the call of community or civic leaders and popular parties to refrain from paying rents, and any other form of taxes, to the "illegal" and repressive apparatuses of the state (Hendler, 1991). Consequently boycott of rents and payments for water, electricity, and cleansing services escalated (Swilling et al., 1991). The net results were a continued downward spiral in the level of service provision and a deteriorating living environment, which in turn prompted others to join the boycotts. These were designed to make the townships ungovernable and thereby to pressurize the National Party government to resign and transfer power to the people. Dissatisfaction, mistrust, and questions of the legitimacy of both Black (puppet) and white local authorities saw a breakdown in formal civic negotiations to the extent that a new "people-based" set of negotiating chambers and forums were established to serve as a "free" meeting place for ideas on the future. Just as an extra-parliamentary forum had been set up to negotiate an interim constitution for the country, as a precursor to holding a democratic election and the formation of a government of national unity, so a body called the Central Witwatersrand Metropolitan Chamber (hereafter, the Chamber) served a similar purpose at the local government level for the Johannesburg Metropolitan Area.

Towards an interim local government

The Chamber was the brainchild of the Soweto Civic Association, itself the popular alternative to the (puppet) Black local authority of Soweto. The Chamber was formally constituted in April 1991, following the signing of the Soweto Accord in September 1990 by five of the bodies involved in the provision of services to Greater Soweto. The parties initially involved were the Transvaal Provincial Administration, the municipal councils of Soweto, Diepmeadow, and Dobsonville (see fig. 5.4), and the Soweto People's Delegation (an organization of civics with links to the African National Congress). The agreement settled a two-year-long running dispute over poor services, rent boycotts, and unviable local authority structures. In the Accord, provision was made for the writing-off of rental arrears, the introduction of new service tariffs, the ending of the rent boycott, the establishment of joint technical committees, which would provide expertise for the Chamber, and the creation of a trust fund (or local fiscal base) known as the Greater Soweto People's Fund (Juta, 1990; Solomon, 1992; Turok, 1993).

Despite a number of crises that saw disputes about membership, the setting of interim tariffs, renewed boycotts, and sporadic outbreaks of violence in the townships, the Chamber managed by September 1994 to reach agreement not only on the formation of a Transitional Metropolitan Council (for Greater Johannesburg) but also on the realignment of the municipal boundaries of its current constituent municipalities into seven new municipal substructures (or MSSs). They were designed to serve as the base for the first democratic local authority elections in November 1995, after which the Transitional Johannesburg Metropolitan Council became the supreme local authority. In August 1995, the boundaries were again reorganized and reduced to the four MSSs that were used in the November 1995 elections (fig. 5.6). In essence the municipality of Johannesburg has been slashed and linked to formerly peripheral municipalities (see figs. 5.2 and 5.6). Parts of "old" Johannesburg are now part of the enlarged municipal areas of Randburg and Sandton, with the Black township of Alexandra being incorporated with the latter. Dobsonville (formerly part of Greater Soweto) has been amalgamated with Roodepoort. The central parts of Johannesburg, including the CBD, have been amalgamated to give rise to an enlarged "new" Soweto (or southern MSS). The manner in which the boundaries have been drawn is such that virtually every new municipal area includes a mixture of old political groupings as well as areas of "haves" and "have nots." The new boundaries mean that a significant number of depressed areas, black townships, and informal settlements now fall within and have become the responsibility of essentially white-contributing tax bases.

Only after the local elections will the black townships begin to experience by right what a local authority should provide, viz. sanitary services, electricity, piped water, roads, public transport, libraries, parks, and communal recreational services. In respect of health, housing, education, and policing, the communities will remain dependent upon the administration of the province, which in turn is dependent in large measure on the central government for its share of the state's financial resources.

The challenge for the immediate and foreseeable future is how to meld the disadvantaged and advantaged parts of the metropolitan area into a functional whole, while uplifting the underdeveloped areas but retaining the ability to draw sustainable taxes for the common fiscal base from the more developed areas. Unfortunately the task will not be easy. Despite having written off general arrears incurred up to 1990, in September 1994 local authorities were again hit by a massive boycott of rent and service payments from residents in black areas. Despite agreeing that arrears for service charges up to January 1994 would be written off, the region was again in turmoil as residents (mainly in Black, Coloured, and Indian townships) demanded very low "flat rates" for sanitary services and unlimited

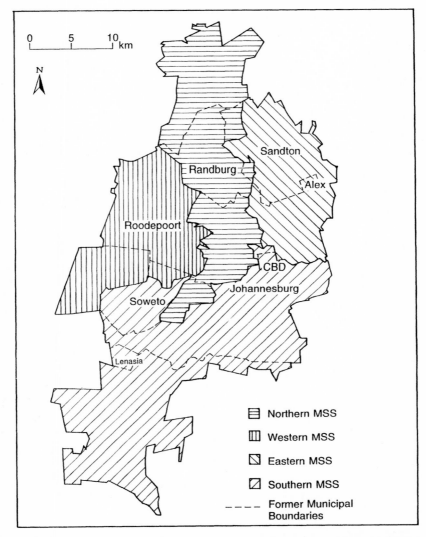

Fig. 5.6 **The new "municipal" boundaries of the Johannesburg Metropolitan Area (Source: based on Johannesburg Transitional Metropolitan Council, Map of Greater Johannesburg Metropolitan Council, August 1995)**

amounts of water and electricity regardless of the incomes of individual consumers. Furthermore there was a demand that the houses they occupy should be given to them, irrespective of whether they are rented from the state or are still mortgaged to private financial institutions. By the beginning of October 1994 communities of impoverished white residents were claiming the same concessions.

Not only will resolution of the "give me" demands be difficult but the creation of a non-racial urban texture will be slow. In the foregoing text, some indication of the spatial marginalization and the both relative and absolute differences between Soweto and former white "Johannesburg" has been given. It is now necessary to provide a little more of the contemporary detail that relates to key geographic areas and aspects of the job market in the formal sector. Thereafter it will be possible to highlight some aspects of the specific frameworks and strategies that are on the drawing-board to satisfy the political challenges that are a prerequisite to a peaceful racially integrated metropolitan area.

Stagnation and population increase: Foundation problems facing the Johannesburg Metropolitan Area

As indicated earlier, the rosy picture that can be painted of the infrastructural strengths of the PWV in general, and particularly of Johannesburg and its immediate neighbouring municipalities, is rather one sided. Over the past dozen years in particular, the dynamics of South Africa's primate metropolitan region were stifled and allowed to become contorted. On the one hand, the economy of the country, and hence the PWV region, was increasingly choked by the effect of economic sanctions, not least the refusal of foreign bankers to roll over loans. On the other hand, the state was engaged in a last desperate fling of the apartheid dice and was determined to make the Bantustans viable in the hope that this would "solve" the "problem" of too many Black people being in the white metropoles. As the effects of sanctions and a general recession bit deeper and popular resistance forces grew in strength, unemployment rose – partially as a result of lost markets and partially because businesses invested in job-cutting machines. A decade of severe droughts and the relative lack of success of the government's decentralization policy in the Bantustans saw many more Black people streaming to the cities (Urban Foundation, 1990, 1991). In the case of Johannesburg and the central Witwatersrand, the accommodation crisis, for those people then still excluded by apartheid laws from the white space, manifested itself in an increasing number of backyard shacks and shack settlements in the relatively rural area on the immediate periphery of the metropolis. By 1990 the number of people living in informal settlements in the PWV had reached 377,000. In addition there were about 1.2 million people living in some 422,000 self-built backyard shacks in the formal Black townships, together with a further 700,000 living in formal brick-and-mortar outbuildings (Urban Foundation, 1991; Beavon, 1992b). Many of the informal settlements beyond the black township boundaries were established on land that is on the periphery of the formal built-up area of the metropolis. Under the apartheid regime, that land was owned by private white people and their public bodies, including municipalities. Conflicts inevitably arose when land was illegally occupied and were resolved only when squatters were evicted or compensation was paid. One of the grounds for eviction was that shelters did not accord with the building regulations applicable to the occupied land. Since 1991 it has been possible for groups of people who legally occupy peripheral land, under whatever agreements, to erect self-help housing that is now legal under the specifications contained in the Less Formal Township Development Act promulgated in 1991 (Latsky, 1991).

Against the backdrop of the preceding remarks, it should be clear that the need for, and, since April 1994, the expectations of, acceptable formal housing for some 2 million shack and informal settlement people, representing 23 per cent of the PWV population and some 43 per cent of the region's Black population (Crankshaw, 1993), are high. Furthermore the needy expect that housing to be provided by the "new" government. Notwithstanding the fact that large tracts of derelict former mining land, still owned by mining houses, have long stood virtually empty within a short distance of the CBD of Johannesburg (see figs. 5.3 and 5.7a) and parallel with the main east–west transportation corridor of the Witwatersrand, no attempt was made by the apartheid regime, the mining houses, or the white local authorities to utilize that space in an attempt to solve at least some of the accommodation crisis. Although only minor pockets of informal housing had sprung up on the vacant land by late 1994, the possibility of a major land invasion remains.

It is to a slightly more detailed consideration of some of the matters just mentioned that attention now turns. In so doing, the setting for the consideration of the future will be completed.

Almost immediately on taking office in 1948, and certainly from 1950, the National Party, which governed South Africa continuously until the end of April 1994, conflated regional development policy and practice with the social engineering of apartheid (Rogerson, 1994a). The essence of the government's regional development was

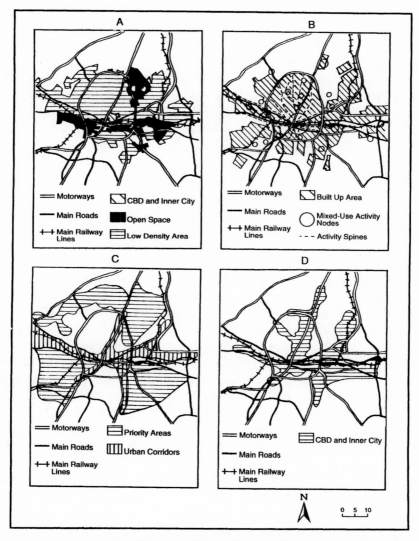

Fig. 5.7   Zones of opportunity and priority areas identified in the Interim Strategic Framework (Source: based on GAPS, 1993)

to decentralize manufacturing, and thus jobs and job opportunities, to a variety of specifically selected "growth points" situated either just on or within the borders of the Bantustans, despite the very real agglomeration economies that were offered by the PWV region in general (Rogerson, 1988; Tomlinson, 1990) and the Johannesburg Metropolitan Area in particular. Following the 1976 uprisings the state was determined to "move" its problems away from the white metropolises as soon as possible. Consequently the early 1980s saw the introduction of a more vigorous programme of regional industrial development (known as the RIDP), of which the intention was to drain industry, notably from the core of the PWV, to a host of peripheral growth points. The plan was "lubricated" by massive start-up incentives and tax breaks. The minor successes and the overall failure of the RIDP by the late 1980s are not matters for concern here, but can be followed up elsewhere (see, *inter alia*, Cobbett et al., 1985; Wellings and Black, 1986; Rogerson, 1991). More immediately relevant to the focus of this chapter is the fact that growth in formal employment in the PWV stagnated during the 1980s (Hall et al., 1993; Mabin and Hunter, 1993). Not only did the demand for labour fall some 2 per cent shy of the 4.5 per cent growth in the economically active population between 1985 and 1989 (DBSA, 1991b), but the major loss of jobs was in manufacturing. Between 1980 and 1991, it is claimed that the PWV lost some 143,400 manufacturing jobs, of which 59,000 were from the central Witwatersrand or Johannesburg Metropolitan Area (Central Witwatersrand Metropolitan Chamber, 1993, Annexure 6). The significance of these data helps to explain the surge in informal sector participants who operate not only in the Black townships but in overwhelming numbers in the central business areas of Johannesburg. In 1979/80 a survey of hawkers operating in the "defended space" of the white CBD of Johannesburg revealed a total of between 200 and 250 (Beavon and Rogerson, 1982). Recent estimates by the City Council of informal operators in Greater Johannesburg put the current number at 15,000 (Rogerson, 1993), with some 5,000 in the central city area.

The regional development policy was revised substantially in 1991 (after President de Klerk had undertaken to lead the country towards democracy). From 1991 there was a pattern of graded industrial incentives spread across the country. There are, however, no incentives on offer for industries wishing to locate in the core region of the PWV, although firms selecting sites in the immediate periphery of the core can attract a 60 per cent establishment allowance (Rogerson, 1994b). By late 1994 there had been no change in the policy by the new government. None the less, the possibilities for changes to match the state's intentions as set out in the Reconstruction and Development Programme cannot be ruled out, and that could alter the prospects for increased formal job opportunities in the Johannesburg Metropolitan Area.

In the early to mid 1980s, accommodation pressure in the Indian, Coloured, and Black townships grew considerably. At the same time, formal businesses in the CBD were increasingly aware that apartheid was entering its death throes and many city-centre firms, in disregard of then current racial laws, began to employ increasing numbers of office workers who were not white people. In 1960 there were approximately 7 whites for every 1 black employee in the CBD. In the 1970s the ratio was 2 to 1 and in 1993 it was 1 white employee to 0.85 black (Mandy, 1984; Prinsloo, 1994). The combination of accommodation pressure in black areas and employment in the city centre, together with the inadequacies of public transport to and from the peripheral "locations," prompted an increasing number of so-called "non-white" people to seek rental accommodation near their new places of work. The events of 1976, and the growing mass actions of the 1980s, had already induced a degree of white flight from the innermost parts of the city, where owners of old apartment blocks were advertising an increasing list of vacancies. When the white tenants "dried up," the landlords "decided" to admit people of other racial groups, and the process known in South Africa as "greying" commenced (Hart, 1989; Cloete, 1991).

Despite various attempts by the state to put a stop to "greying," the process of ethnic transformation in the inner-city residential areas continued. Given that they were "illegal" residents in an area reserved under apartheid legislation for white people, the poorer of the new arrivals soon fell victim to unscrupulous landlords. Rack-renting became common but, because the tenants were black, they were unable to seek legal respite, because in the eyes of the "law" they were first and foremost "illegal" residents in the "wrong group area." The net result over several years was overcrowding of inner-city apartment blocks as additional "sub-tenants" were brought in to assist those already there in meeting escalating rentals per unit. What has followed in recent years is deterioration of the inner-city apartment stock and the emergence of new "slums" populated by poor, underemployed, and unemployed black people.

The repeal of the Group Areas Acts in the early 1990s, almost four years before the general election, did little to stop the rot and improve the living conditions of the new inner-city residents, notwithstanding that access to all facilities was available to all people. By then the building stock had deteriorated to such an extent that lending institutions had implemented "red-lining," thereby in effect preventing new inner-city owner-occupiers from emerging (Crankshaw and White, 1994). Now (in 1994), although the inner-city residential areas, with 45 per cent Black residents, 20 per cent Coloured, and 14 per cent Indian (Dauskardt, 1993), more closely represent the demographic profile of the country, they have become a zone of physical blight, which in turn makes the "besieged" central business district distinctly unattractive to retail businesses. As such, many new commercial developments tend to seek premises not only in the low-density northern suburbs, but also in the distant and affluent suburbs of the "new" south, which are predominantly occupied by white people. Consequently, it can be argued, there is a current tendency to replicate a form of residual de facto segregation. Thus, as the metropolis enters a new era, it is confronted with several harsh realities that have the potential to sabotage the Reconstruction and Development Programme in the heart of Gauteng, the major province of South Africa. By way of illustration, five "problems" are highlighted here.

First is the fact that the Johannesburg Metropolitan Area lost formal jobs, in absolute and relative terms, throughout the 1980s and early 1990s at a time when ever-increasing numbers of its people are reaching job-market age. Secondly, those seeking respite in the informal sector have seen its numbers grow, and their activities on the congested pavements of the central area have prompted additional flight of formal businesses and jobs from the CBD. Thirdly, the demand for accommodation of at least a minimally acceptable standard for a growing population of homeless people on the periphery of the metropolitan area has increased. Fourthly, the opportunity of developing a stable middle-income group of apartment dwellers and owners employed in the CBD and living in the inner residential zone has been lost. And fifthly, the open space "buffer" between the former whites-only Johannesburg and Soweto remains not only a hindrance to economic integration but open and sufficiently derelict for it to be lost in an invasion of informal housing before it can be used more constructively in the redevelopment and healing process that is now under way.

As hinted at in the opening section of this chapter, the word-picture just presented is in stark contrast with the glass and glitz image of Johannesburg. Yet, notwithstanding the genuine gloom that the "picture" reflects, one of the Technical Task Groups set up by the Metropolitan Chamber believes that its analysis of the strengths and weaknesses of the Johannesburg Metropolitan Area shows a way forward towards a sustainable and better future for increasing numbers of people in the metropolitan area (GAPS, 1993). The focus now shifts to a consideration of the essence of what the Task Group charged with (urban) planning has recently put forward.

Towards spatial restructuring of the Metropolitan Area

It is not possible to present here the detailed arguments, along with the wealth of illustrative material (see GAPS, 1993), that underpins the Interim Strategic Framework (henceforth the ISF) document that currently informs those engaged in detailed negotiations associated with the transition period. Consequently what is presented below is only the essence of the ISF, based on policy guidelines placed before the Metropolitan Chamber in late 1992. Fundamental to the proposals in the ISF is the recognition that it is necessary to curb the unbridled spread of low-density physical growth that has already created a metropolitan area greater in areal extent (fig. 5.1) than that of Mexico City, probably the world's largest urban place in terms of population. The Chamber and its advisers were of the opinion that what is needed is a spatially more compact area. It should be one that can be achieved by infilling and making use of current strengths in the existing system, which include, in particular, an excellent transportation structure, a physically well-developed and well-endowed CBD, and tracts of open and derelict land both close to the core and farther afield. There is no suggestion that the ISF is a blueprint for the future. Rather it is believed that the ISF contains a logical set of arguments, coupled to an associated set of spatial considerations and implications, that should inform political leaders and their planners. At the base of the argument is the belief that ways must be found to assimilate the growing population of the area within a metropolitan urban system in such a way that the capacity for increasing the *common* wealth of all is enhanced.

More precisely, the consensus was that restructuring should aim to achieve an urban system that is predicated on a viable, sustainable, formal, *and* informal economy, that meets the immediate demands, particularly of the poor, in respect of housing and shelter, and that integrates place of living with place of work. The aim is to promote affordable access and mobility through coordinated transport services, to exploit opportunities offered by existing patterns of development, and to use social and service infrastructure to the full. It is believed that the goals of the ISF need to be coupled to strategic areas of concern (GAPS, 1993) and *inter alia* the following have been identified. Intensification, densification, and infilling of the existing urban pattern is a priority. In addition, there should be a programme of upgrading and renewal of those parts of the urban system that are under stress.

The team responsible for the ISF has identified what it styles "zones of opportunity," where opportunity can imply existing infrastructure in good order or parcels of land that have potential for development and are well located to play a key role in the restructuring process. The leading eight "zones" include the Johannesburg CBD and inner city (fig. 5.7a), activity nodes and spines (fig. 5.7b; see also the major employment zones in 5.7d), urban corridors (fig. 5.7c), low-density suburbs (fig. 5.7a), strategically located land that is currently vacant or underutilized (fig. 5.7a and 5.7c), the urban fringe, existing peripheral townships or suburbs, and the informal settlements beyond the urban fringe. To allow the ISF initiative to gather momentum as speedily and as successfully as possible, it has been suggested that it be targeted in the first phase on the priority areas just listed (fig. 5.7c).

Two important decisions since the April 1994 elections have already given momentum to aspects of what is contained in the ISF. It has now been decided that Johannesburg rather than Pretoria will be the seat and headquarters of the provincial government. The Johannesburg City Hall, located in the centre of the CBD, is currently being renovated as the provincial Capitol, and it is anticipated that a significant number of office blocks in the downtown will be taken over by provincial ministries, which should serve as a considerable boost for the hitherto waning fortunes of the CBD. In addition, the Johannesburg Metropolitan Area will receive a large slice of the central government's budgeted capital for housing through the National Reconstruction and Development Programme, full details of which are not yet available. Notwithstanding that no strategic area outside of the CBD has yet been targeted for specific upgrading, it can be anticipated that early attention will be given to integrating the newly demarcated municipal area of Soweto (see fig. 5.6) with the Johannesburg CBD and parts of Roodepoort, through developing activity spines across the vacant land separating it from the main western urban corridor and encouraging the construction of new housing on the vacant land. Similar developments are most likely to follow sooner rather than later in respect of the north-eastern sector and the new municipality of Sandton/Alexandra (figs. 5.6 and 5.7c).

Conclusion

Given its fundamental importance to the economic welfare of the country as a whole, it is important for all concerned that the process of reconstruction and development of the Johannesburg Metropolitan Area should succeed. However, political leaders will have to take care to balance proposals with how much tax revenue can be raised. In particular, care will have to be taken not to overextend those who still have a capacity to pay some more by not containing the categories of those who will be exempted from paying anything at all. The continued boycotts of rents, bond repayments, and charges for essential services by regions that contain citizens who have the vote, and also significant numbers of people who can afford to pay, is a matter for serious concern and will have to be solved very soon. Many changes to the "rules" of the "urban game," particularly planning and property tax regulations, will have to be made after the local authority elections in 1995.

What has been attempted here is to present two views of the same metropolitan place, using evidence from both the present and the past, as a base for understanding some of the current problems and strategies for dealing with them that are being devised as part of the transformation of South Africa.   ·

Notes

1. Racial terms in South Africa evolved specific historical meanings, which overlapped in part with those used in other colonies. "Black" refers to indigenous residents, who were also called Africans. Here, Black with a capital "B" is used to denote this particular group. "Coloured" refers to people of mixed race descent. Indians are people from or descended from parents who originally came from India, Pakistan, Bangladesh, and Sri Lanka. "Whites" are Caucasians, descended from people with mostly European origins. Today, and in this chapter, "African" denotes the whole population of South Africa and "black" is used to mean people other than the whites.
2. The population of Soweto has never been measured accurately. Because of the perils associated with the apartheid era, many "illegal" South African residents in Soweto evaded enumeration in the census years. Between 1989 and 1992 estimates of the population of Greater Soweto ranged between 555,443 and 3,500,000 with a mode of approximately 1,200,000 (see Mabin and Hunter, 1993).

References

Amprops. 1994. Vacancy survey of completed office buildings. Unpublished report, Anglo-American Property Services, Johannesburg.

Appelgryn, M. S. 1984. *Johannesburg: Origins and Early Management 1886–1899.* University of South Africa, Pretoria.

Beavon, K. S. O. 1982. Black townships in South Africa: *Terra incognita* for urban geographers. *South African Geographical Journal* 64: 3–20.

———— 1989. *Informal Ways: A Window on Informal Business in South Africa*. Small Business Development Corporation, Johannesburg.

———— 1992a. Some alternative scenarios for the South African city in the era of late Apartheid. In: D. Drakakis-Smith, ed., *Urban and Regional Change in Southern Africa*. Routledge, London.

———— 1992b. The post-Apartheid city: Hopes, possibilities, and harsh realities. In: D. M. Smith, ed., *The Apartheid City and Beyond*. Routledge, London, and University of Witwatersrand Press, Johannesburg.

———— Forthcoming. *Johannesburg*. World Cities Series, John Wiley, London.

Beavon, K. S. O. and C. M. Rogerson. 1982. The informal sector of the Apartheid city: The pavement people of Johannesburg. In: D. M. Smith, ed., *Living under Apartheid*. Allen & Unwin, London.

———— 1990. Temporary trading for temporary people: The making of hawking in Soweto. In: D. Drakakis-Smith, ed., *Economic Growth and Urbanization in Developing Areas*. Routledge, London.

Benjamin, A. 1972. A social history. In: A. Benjamin, C. M. Chipkin, S. Zar, and H. Aron, *Parktown 1892–1972: A Social and Pictorial History*. Studio Thirty Five, Johannesburg.

Bureau of Market Research. 1976. *Income and Expenditure Patterns of Urban Black Households in Johannesburg*. Research Report No. 50.3, Bureau of Market Research, Pretoria.

———— 1977. *Greater Johannesburg Area: Home Interview Report on Coloureds, Asians and Blacks*. Study conducted on behalf of the City Engineer's Department of the Johannesburg City Council, Bureau of Market Research, Pretoria.

Carrim, N. 1990. *Fietas: A Social History of Pageview, 1948–1988*. Save Pageview Association, Johannesburg.

CDE (Centre for Development and Enterprise). 1995. Post-Apartheid population and income trends: A new analysis. *CDE Research* 1.

Central Statistical Services. 1992. *Population Census 1991: Geographical Distribution of the Population with Review for 1970–1991*. CSS Report No. 03-01-02 1991, Central Statistical Services, Pretoria.

Central Witwatersrand Metropolitan Chamber. 1993. Report of the Economic Research Team of the Economic Development Working Group, 24 March, mimeo, Central Witwatersrand Metropolitan Chamber, Johannesburg.

City Engineer. 1967. *Central Area Johannesburg*. Report by the Forward Planning Branch, City Engineer's Department, Johannesburg City Council, Johannesburg.

City Health Department. 1973. *Medical Officer of Health Report 1969–1973*. Johannesburg City Council, Johannesburg.

Cloete, F. 1991. Greying and free settlement. In: M. Swilling, R. Humphries, and K. Shubane, eds., *Apartheid City in Transition*. Oxford University Press, Cape Town.

Cobbett, W., D. Glaser, D. Hindson, and M. Swilling. 1985. Regionalisation, federalism and the reconstruction of the South African state. *South African Labour Bulletin* 10(5): 87–116.

Coovadia, C. 1991. The role of the civic movement. In: M. Swilling, R. Humphries, and K. Shubane, eds., *Apartheid City in Transition*. Oxford University Press, Cape Town.

Crankshaw, O. 1993. Squatting, Apartheid and urbanisation on the Southern Witwatersrand. *African Affairs* 92(366): 31–52.

Crankshaw, O. and C. White. 1994. *Racial Desegregation and the Origin of Slums in Johannesburg's Inner City*. CPS Development Policy Series, Research Report No. 36, Centre for Policy Studies, Johannesburg.

Crush, J., Jeeves, A., and Yudelman, D. 1991. *South Africa's Labor Empire: A History of Black Migrancy to the Gold Mines*. Westview, San Francisco.

Dauskardt, R. 1993. Reconstructing South African cities: Contemporary strategies and processes in the urban core. *GeoJournal* 30: 9–20.

Davenport, T. R. H. 1991. Historical background of the Apartheid city to 1948. In: M. Swilling, R. Humphries, and K. Shubane, eds., *Apartheid City in Transition*. Oxford University Press, Cape Town.

DBSA (Development Bank of Southern Africa). 1991a. *A Regional Profile of the Southern African Population and its Urban and Non-Urban Distribution, 1970–1990*. Demographic Information Series No. 2, Centre for Information Analysis, Development Bank of Southern Africa, Midrand.

—— 1991b. *South Africa: An Inter-Regional Profile*. Development Bank of Southern Africa, Midrand.

Department of Regional and Land Affairs. 1992. *A Spatial Development Framework for the PWV Complex*. Government Printer, Pretoria.

Development and Democracy. 1994. Interview with Lechesa Tsenoli: President of the South African National Civics Organization. *Development and Democracy* 8: 31–35.

Dikobe, M. 1973. *The Marabi Dance*. Heinemann, London.

Eskom. 1993. *Statistical Yearbook*. Electricity Supply Commission, Megawatt Park.

Fair, T. J. D. 1977. The Witwatersrand: Structure, shape and strategy. *South African Geographer* 5: 380–389.

Fair, T. J. D. and J. G. Muller. 1981. The Johannesburg Metropolitan Area. In: M. Pacione, ed., *Urban Problems and Planning in the Developed World*. Croom Helm, London.

Fourie, J. J. 1978. Afrikaners in die Goudstad: Deel 1 1886–1924. In E. L. P. Stals, ed., *Afrikaners in die Goudstad*. Part 1. Hollandsch Afrikaansche Uitgevers Maatschappij, Cape Town.

GAPS. 1993. *An Interim Strategic Framework for the Central Witwatersrand: Document 2 Policy Approaches*. Discussion Document, Central Witwatersrand Metropolitan Chamber, Johannesburg.

Gray, E. L. and J. Gray. 1940. *Discovery of the Witwatersrand Goldfields*. Central News Agency, Johannesburg.

Gray, J. and J. A. McLachlan. 1933. A history of the introduction of the MacArthur–Forrest cyanide process to the Witwatersrand goldfields. *Journal of the Chemical Metallurgical and Mining Society of South Africa* 33: 375–395.

Hall, P., G. Saayman, D. Molatedi, and P. Kok. 1993. *A Profile of Poverty in the PWV* (2 vols.). Southern Africa Labour and Development Research Unit, University of Cape Town, Rondebosch.

Hansard. 1953. *Debates of the House of Assembly (Hansard)*, 82, Cape Times, Cape Town.

Hardie, G. J. and T. Hart. 1986. Homeownership and the "Big Sale" of state-owned housing: A view from the townships. *The Property Economist (Opinion Survey)* 5: 1–12.

Hart, D. M. and G. H. Pirie. 1984. The sight and soul of Sophiatown. *Geographical Review* 74: 38–47.

Hart, G. H. T. 1989. On grey areas. *South African Geographical Journal* 71: 81–88.

Hart, T. 1990. South Africa. In: W. van Vliet, ed., *International Handbook of Housing Policies and Practices*. Greenwood, New York.

Hellman, E. 1935. Native life in a Johannesburg slumyard. *Africa* 3: 34–62.

Hendler, P. 1988. *Urban Policy and Housing*. South African Institute of Race Relations, Johannesburg.

———— 1991. The housing crisis. In: M. Swilling, R. Humphries, and K. Shubane, eds., *Apartheid City in Transition*. Oxford University Press, Cape Town.

Hindson, D. 1987. *Pass Controls and the Urban African Proletariat*. Ravan, Johannesburg.

Hirschson, N. 1974. *The Naming of Johannesburg*. Nugget Press, Johannesburg.

Hlope, S. S. 1977. The crisis of urban living under Apartheid conditions: A socioeconomic analysis of Soweto. *Journal of Southern African Affairs* 11: 343–354.

Horrell, M. 1978. *Laws Affecting Race Relations in South Africa (to the End of 1976)*. South African Institute of Race Relations, Johannesburg.

Huddleston, T. 1956. *Naught for your Comfort*. Hardingham & Donaldson, Johannesburg.

Juta. 1990. Greater Soweto Accord. *Juta's RSC Report* 4: 23.

Kalley, J. A. 1988. *Pressure on Pretoria: Sanctions, Boycotts and the Divestment/Disinvestment Issue 1964–1988. A Select and Annotated Bibliography*. South African Institute of International Affairs, Bibliographic Series No. 17, Johannesburg.

Kane-Berman, J. 1978. *Soweto: Black Revolt, White Reaction*. Ravan Press, Johannesburg.

Katz, M. M. (chairman). 1994. *The Future Structure of the Johannesburg Stock Exchange: A Report of the Research Sub-Committee to the Johannesburg Stock Exchange Committee*. Johannesburg Stock Exchange, Johannesburg.

Khosa, M. 1992. Changing state policy and the Black taxi industry in Soweto. In: D. M. Smith, ed., *The Apartheid City and Beyond: Urbanization and Social Change in South Africa*. Routledge, London, and Witwatersrand University Press, Johannesburg.

Koch, E. 1983. "Without visible means of subsistence": Slumyard culture in Johannesburg, 1918–1940. In: B. Bozzoli, ed., *Town and Countryside in the Transvaal*. Ravan Press, Johannesburg.

Latsky, J. 1991. Developing new urban land delivery systems for the poor: Reviewing the policy of First World technicality. In: South African Institute of Town and Regional Planners, *The First World/Third World Ratio – A Recipe for Prosperity or Poverty?* National Biennial Conference Papers, South African Institute of Town and Regional Planners (Eastern Cape Branch), Port Elizabeth.

Lewis, P. R. B. 1966. A "City" within a city: The creation of Soweto. *South African Geographical Journal* 48: 45–85.

Lewsen, J. 1953. The City Council and the "Western Areas" Removal Scheme. In: South African Institute of Race Relations, *The "Western Areas" Removal Scheme: Facts and Viewpoints Presented at a Conference Convened by the S.A. Institute of Race Relations at the University of the Witwatersrand 22nd August 1953*. South African Institute of Race Relations, Johannesburg.

Lupton, M. 1992. Class struggle over the built environment in Johannesburg's Coloured Areas. In: D. M. Smith, ed., *The Apartheid City and Beyond: Urbanization and Social Change in South Africa*. Routledge, London, and Witwatersrand University Press, Johannesburg.

――― 1993a. Collective consumption and urban segregation in South Africa: The case of two Coloured suburbs in the Johannesburg Region. *Antipode* 25: 32–50.

――― 1993b. Ennerdale Newtown, South Africa: The social limits to urban design. *GeoJournal* 30: 37–44.

Mabin, A. S. and R. Hunter. 1993. Final Draft Report of the Review of Conditions and Trends Affecting Development in the PWV. PWV Forum, Johannesburg, mimeo.

Mabin, A. S. and S. Parnell. 1983. Recommodification and working-class home ownership: New directions for South African cities. *South African Geographical Journal* 65: 148–166.

McCarthy, T. S. 1986. A guide to the geology of the Johannesburg area. In: F. Mendelsohn and C. T. Potgieter, eds., *Guidebook to Sites of Geological and Mining Interest on the Central Witwatersrand*. Geological Society of South Africa in association with the South African Institute of Mining and Metallurgy, Johannesburg.

MacDonald, W. 1926. Johannesburg after forty years. In: D. Wall's Jones, ed., *Johannesburg's 40th Birthday: An Official Souvenir*. Johannesburg Publicity Association, Johannesburg.

Maher, M. G. K. (compiler). 1994. *The JSE Handbook*. Flesch Financial Publications, Johannesburg.

Mandy, N. 1984. *A City Divided*. Macmillan, Johannesburg.

Mashile, G. G. and G. H. Pirie. 1977. Aspects of housing allocation in Soweto. *South African Geographical Journal* 59: 139–149.

Maud, J. P. R. 1938. *City Government: The Johannesburg Experiment*. Clarendon Press, Oxford.

Moodie, T. D. 1994. *Going for Gold: Men, Mines, and Migration*. University of California, Berkeley, Calif.

Moon, B. P. and G. F. Dardis. 1988. Introduction. In: B. P. Moon and G. F. Dardis, eds., *The Geomorphology of Southern Africa*. Southern, Halfway House.

Moroney, S. 1978. The development of the compound as a mechanism of worker control 1900–1912. *South African Labour Bulletin* 4(3): 29–49.

――― 1982. Mine married quarters: The differential stabilisation of the Witwatersrand workforce, 1900–1920. In: S. Marks and R. Rathbone, eds., *Industrialisation and Social Change in South Africa: African Class Formation, Culture, and Consciousness, 1870–1930*. Longman, London.

Morris, P. 1980. *Soweto*. Urban Foundation, Johannesburg.

――― 1981. *A History of Black Housing in South Africa*. South Africa Foundation, Johannesburg.

Niekerk, J. van. 1995. The impact of illegal aliens on safety and security in South Africa. *ISSUP Bulletin* 7 (Institute for Strategic Studies, Pretoria).

Onselen, C. van. 1982a. *Studies in the Social and Economic History of the Witwatersrand 1886–1914*, Vol. 1, *New Babylon*. Ravan Press, Johannesburg.

――― 1982b. *Studies in the Social and Economic History of the Witwatersrand*, Vol. 2, *New Ninevah*. Ravan Press, Johannesburg.

Orkin, M., ed. 1989. *Sanctions against Apartheid*. David Philip, Cape Town, and Catholic Institute for International Relations, London.

Parnell, S. M. 1991. Sanitation, segregation and the Natives (Urban Areas) Act: African exclusion from Johannesburg's Malay Location, 1897–1925. *Journal of Historical Geography* 17: 271–288.

———— 1993. Johannesburg slums and racial segregation in South African cities, 1910–1937. Unpublished Ph.D. thesis, Department of Geography and Environmental Studies, University of the Witwatersrand, Johannesburg.

Pirie, G. H. 1984a. Letters, words, worlds: The naming of Soweto. *African Studies Journal* 43: 43–51.

———— 1984b. Ethno-linguistic zoning in South African Black townships. *Area* 16: 291–298.

Prinsloo, D. 1994. Economic and spatial trends in the Johannesburg CBD. Unpublished report, Urban Development Studies, Johannesburg.

Proctor, A. 1979. Class struggle, segregation and the city: A history of Sophiatown 1905–1940. In: B. Bozzoli, ed., *Labour, Townships and Protest*. Ravan Press, Johannesburg.

Randall, P. 1973. *From Coolie Location to Group Area*. South African Institute of Race Relations, Johannesburg.

Richardson, P. 1982. *Chinese Mine Labour in the Transvaal*. Macmillan, London.

Richardson, P. and J. J. Van-Helten. 1980. The gold mining industry in the Transvaal 1886–99. In: P. Warwick, ed., *The South African War: The Anglo-Boer War, 1899–1902*. Longman, London.

Rogerson, C. M. 1986. A strange case of beer: The state and sorghum beer manufacture in South Africa. *Area* 18: 15–24.

———— 1988. Regional development policy in South Africa. *Regional Development Dialogue* 9 (special issue): 228–255.

———— 1991. Beyond racial Fordism: Restructuring industry in the "New" South Africa. *Tijdschrift voor Economische en Sociale Geografie* 82: 355–366.

———— 1993. The PWV informal economy: Bibliography and review. Unpublished paper prepared for the PWV Economic and Development Forum, June 1993.

———— 1994a. Democracy, reconstruction, and changing local and regional economic planning in South Africa. *Regional Development Dialogue* 15(1): 102–118.

———— 1994b. South Africa: From regional planning to local development initiatives. *Geography* 79(2): 180–184.

SAIRR (South African Institute of Race Relations). 1953. *The "Western Areas" Removal Scheme: Facts and Viewpoints Presented at a Conference Convened by the S.A. Institute of Race Relations at the University of the Witwatersrand 22nd August 1953*. South African Institute of Race Relations, Johannesburg.

Sarakinsky, M. 1989. American disinvestment and unemployment. *South African Labour Bulletin* 14(1): 54–57.

Schoeman, E. (compiler). 1988. *South African Sanctions Directory 1946–1988: Actions by Governments, Banks, Churches, Trade Unions, Universities, Investment and Regional Organizations*. South African Institute of International Affairs, Bibliographic Series No. 18, Johannesburg.

Scott, P. 1951. The Witwatersrand Gold Field. *Geographical Review* 41: 561–589.

Shorten, J. R. 1970. *The Johannesburg Saga*. J. Shorten (Pty) Ltd, Johannesburg.

Shubane, K. 1991. Black local authorities: A contraption of control. In: M. Swilling, R. Humphries, and K. Shubane, eds., *Apartheid City in Transition*. Oxford University Press, Cape Town.

Shuenyane, E., S. Mashigo, C. Eyberg, B. D. Richardson, N. Buchanan, J. Pettifor, L. MacDougal, and J. D. L. Hansen. 1977. A socio-economic, health and cultural survey in Soweto. *South African Medical Journal* 51: 495–500.

Smith, A. H. 1971. *Johannesburg Street Names: A Dictionary of Street, Suburb and Other Place Names, Compiled to the End of 1968*. Juta, Johannesburg.

Solomon, D. 1992. Metropolitan Chamber. *Urban Forum* 3(1): 75–85.

Stadler, A. W. 1979. Birds in the cornfields: African squatter movements in Johannesburg, 1944–1947. *Journal of Southern African Studies* 6: 93–124.

Swilling, M., W. Cobbett, and R. Hunter. 1991. Finance, electricity costs, and the rent boycott. In: M. Swilling, R. Humphries, and K. Shubane, eds., *Apartheid City in Transition*. Oxford University Press, Cape Town.

The Star. 1987. *Like It Was: The Star 100 Years in Johannesburg*. The Star, Johannesburg.

Tomlinson, R. 1990. *Urbanization in Post-Apartheid South Africa*. Unwin Hyman, London.

Turok, I. 1993. The Metropolitan Chamber: A view from the sideline. *Urban Forum* 4(2): 69–81.

Urban Foundation. 1990. Population trends. *Policies for a New Urban Future, Urban Debate 2010*, 1, Urban Foundation, Johannesburg.

——— 1991. Informal housing, Part 1: The current situation. *Policies for a New Urban Future, Urban Debate 2000*, 10, Urban Foundation, Johannesburg.

Waal, G.-M. van der. 1987. *From Mining Camp to Metropolis: The Buildings of Johannesburg 1886–1940*. Chris van Rensburg Publications, Johannesburg.

Wellings, P. and A. Black. 1986. Industrial decentralisation in South Africa: Tool of Apartheid or spontaneous restructuring. *GeoJournal* 12: 137–149.

Wentzel, C. A. (chairman). 1903. *Report of the Johannesburg Insanitary Area Improvement Scheme Commission*. Transvaal Government, Johannesburg.

6

The challenges of growth and development in metropolitan Lagos

Josephine Olu Abiodun

Abstract

Depuis la Deuxième Guerre mondiale, Lagos a connu une croissance
démographique et spatiale phénoménale. Alors qu'elle ne comptait
que 665,000 habitants en 1963, la ville s'est élargie, absorbant des
villes et villages voisins et en 1990 l'on estimait sa population à 7.9
millions d'habitants. Mais le nombre réel d'habitants n'est pas sûr
puisqu'un recensement controversé de 1991 établissait la population
métropolitaine de Lagos à 5.3 millions. Cependant, le taux de croissance de la ville s'est ralenti, passant de 14 pour cent par an pendant
les dix premières années suivant l'indépendance en 1960 à environ
4.5 pour cent par an en 1990. De plus, quoique l'exode rural se pour-
suive, la croissance démographique de la ville est légèrement moins
importante que l'augmentation naturelle. Lagos est la plus importante des villes du Nigéria en termes d'activités secondaires, tertiaires
et, plus récemment, quaternaires. Elle est le centre d'opérations
des manufactures nigérianes et domine les activités commerciales
et financières du pays. Elle est le plus important centre national de
communications et de transports terrestres, aériens et maritimes.
Après l'amalgamation des protectorats du Nord et du Sud du Nigéria
en 1914, Lagos devint le centre de l'administration politique, puis la
capitale du pays jusqu'en 1990. Elle est au cœur de la diffusion dans
le reste du pays des innovations endogènes comme exogènes. Le

présent chapitre analyse et examine les facteurs opérationnels et la dynamique des processus de croissance et d'aménagement urbain. Divers aspects, chômage, administration et gestion politique, transports, logements et systèmes sanitaires, y sont examinés brièvement en relation avec la croissance et le développement de la ville. Après avoir pris acte du retard pris par les services par rapport à la demande, l'on recommande d'accorder plus d'attention à améliorer les capacités des administrations locales.

Introduction

Since the end of World War II urbanization in developing countries has accelerated greatly, with an increasing proportion of the urban population in each country concentrating in the large urban agglomerations. Nigeria has been no exception. Since the turn of the twentieth century, Lagos has grown phenomenally, both demographically and in spatial terms. In the first part of this chapter, the historical patterns of population and areal growth will be analysed. The second section examines the city's economy, focusing in particular on manufacturing industry and services (commerce and financial services) and on the implications of the deterioration in Nigeria's economic situation in the past 15 years or so. Changes in the political and administrative structure are then described and their implications for urban management mentioned. The problems of urban management are taken up again in an analysis of the most important elements of infrastructure and the built environment: transportation, water supply, electricity, telecommunications, environmental sanitation, and housing. The demands posed by rapid growth, attempts to deal with them, and constraints on successful approaches are examined. It is concluded that the vitality of Lagos's economy and its nodal position in the national economy and transport networks explain its large-scale and continued growth, despite the partial or complete breakdown of many basic infrastructure services and the difficulties caused by this for both economic enterprises and individual residents.

Population growth

Pre-colonial Lagos originated as a fishing and farming settlement in the seventeenth century. Owing to its physical characteristics as the only natural break for about 2,500 km along the west African coast, it became an important slave-exporting port in the eighteenth century,

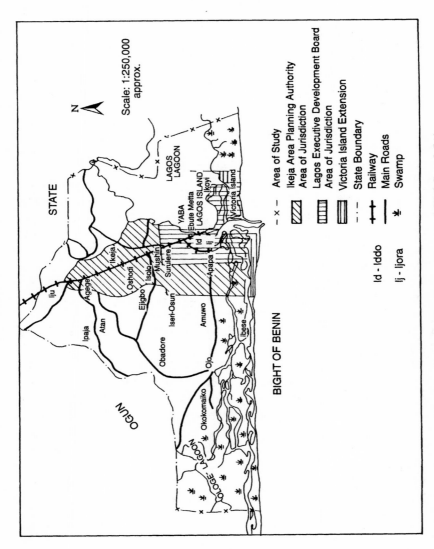

Fig. 6.1 **Metropolitan Lagos (Source: LSDPC, n.d.(b))**

194

Table 6.1 **Population of Lagos, 1911–1963**

Year of census	Area covered by the census (km^2)	Total population
1911	46.6	73,766
1921	52.3	99,690
1931	66.3	126,108
1952	69.9	272,000
1963	69.9	665,000

Source: Federal Office of Statistics, *Population Census of Nigeria*, 1952 and.1963, Lagos.

continuing, despite the abolition of the slave trade, until the mid-nineteeth century, when the British enforced the trade's termination (Mehretu, 1983). With a population of about 25,000 in 1866 (Ayeni, 1981), Lagos was one of the smaller settlements in Nigeria, the largest being Sokoto with a population of 120,000 (Mabogunje, 1968). The end of slave trading caused a temporary decline in the population of the settlement, growth of which was resumed only with its cession to the British as a colony in 1861. Earlier refugees from slavery and war in the interior, freed slaves from Brazil, and later colonial administrators and traders settled in the port, the population of which reached 40,000 by 1901 and 74,000 by 1911. By 1963 it had reached 665,000, covering 69.9 km^2 (table 6.1 and figs. 6.1 and 6.2). Today, this settlement has engulfed neighbouring towns and villages and metropolitan Lagos now encompasses about 1,068 km^2, 209 km^2 of which is covered by water and unreclaimed mangrove swamps (fig. 6.2). The provisional results of the 1991 census gave Lagos metropolis a population of 5.3 million or 93 per cent of the total population of Lagos State (table 6.2). The population is projected to reach 7.5 million by A.D. 2000. However, based on water demand, the Lagos State Water Corporation estimated a population of 7.9 million for metropolitan Lagos in 1990.[1]

It is significant to note that, between the two world wars, the growth rate of Lagos never exceeded 3.3 per cent per annum. In contrast, in the first decade after independence in 1960, metropolitan Lagos was estimated to have experienced a growth rate of 14 per cent per annum (Lagos Executive Development Board, 1971). The relative importance of natural increase and migration in the growth of Lagos to date has varied. In-depth analysis for this is hampered by a lack of accurate information, due, among other things, to boundary changes. While natural increase must have played a dominant role in

Table 6.2 **Population of Lagos State by local government area, 1991**

Local government area	Total population
Agege[a]	650,274
Badagry	118,704
Epe	99,567
Eti-Osa[a]	170,948
Ibeju-Lekki	24,825
Ikeja[a,b]	639,762
Ikorodu	181,914
Lagos Island[a]	164,352
Lagos Mainland[a,c]	869,601
Mushin[a,d]	986,847
Ojo[a]	1,011,808
Shomolu[a]	767,179
Total	5,685,781

Source: National Population Bureau, 1991 Census, provisional figures, Lagos State, Ikeja.

a. These local government areas comprise metropolitan Lagos as defined in this study. Together, they account for 5,260,771 or 93 per cent of the total 1991 population of Lagos State. The provisional figure for metropolitan Lagos has been challenged by the state government, which considers it to be an under-enumeration. School enrolment figures and water rate payments were among the facts used to argue the case at the census tribunal set up by the federal government.

b. Including Alimosho.

c. Including Surulere. The former Lagos City Council was split into two in the 1976 local government reform to give Lagos Island LGA and Lagos Mainland LGA.

d. Including Oshodi-Isolo.

the growth of the settlement up to 1950, from the decade preceding political independence to perhaps the end of the 1970s internal migration seems to have been predominant. Today, it appears that natural increase is probably more important. Again based on water demand, the Lagos State Water Corporation estimated a population growth rate of 4.5 per cent per annum for metropolitan Lagos between 1985 and 1990. Today, metropolitan Lagos is a melting pot of different ethnic groups from various states within the country, as well as expatriates from neighbouring African and other countries (Peil, 1991). The predominant ethnic groups (mainly Yoruba) are from the neighbouring states of Ogun, Oyom, Osun, Ondo, Bendel, and Kwara. Other ethnic groups that are particularly prominent in the informal sector of the economy of the city are from the eastern states such as Anambra, Imo, Cross River, and Rivers. Migrants from various parts of the northern states are also significant.

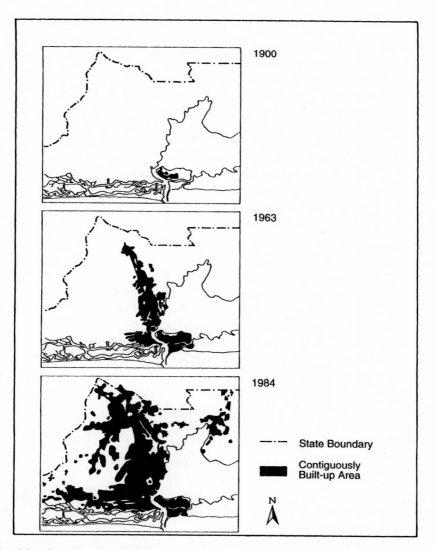

Fig. 6.2 Growth of the built-up area of metropolitan Lagos, 1900–1984 (Source: Town Planning Services, Ministry of the Environment and Physical Planning)

The absence of uncontroversial population figures makes a comparative demographic discussion of urban centres in Nigeria difficult. Nevertheless it is accepted that Lagos is now the largest city, followed by Ibadan and Kano, probably in that order. A number of factors have combined to account for the pre-eminence of Lagos metropolis in the Nigerian urban system. These include its political and admin-

197

istrative roles as Nigeria's capital and seat of administration after the amalgamation of the Northern and Southern protectorates in 1914. By the late 1950s, with the approach of political independence, Lagos grew in importance as the economic, social, commercial, political, administrative, and financial hub of Nigeria. It remained the capital after independence and, when 12 states were created in 1967, Ikeja, within the metropolis, became the seat of administration for Lagos State.

The employment generated by these functions continues to attract both domestic and international migrants to Lagos. Despite the movement of the federal capital to Abuja in 1990, metropolitan Lagos is still the main economic, social, and financial centre and the hub of national and international communications. Consequently it is the most important point for the dissemination of information and innovation throughout the country. It is also the nerve-centre of manufacturing industries and of commercial activities, with the headquarters of major national and international manufacturing, business, and financial institutions, and is unrivalled by any other urban centre in Nigeria. Metropolitan Lagos has over the decades attracted to itself important secondary, tertiary, and most recently quaternary (financial and business services) activities. In addition, it possesses the best harbour on the west coast of Africa. It became the premier seaport with the Apapa and Tin Can Island wharves. It is also the premier international airport in Nigeria, accounting for 98 per cent of international and 44 per cent of combined international and domestic air passenger movement in 1992. Moreover, being the focus of rail, road, and air transportation, Lagos has a special advantage over any other city in Nigeria in assembling raw materials and distributing finished goods, both nationwide and for export. Until 1967, the share of Lagos in Nigerian foreign trade remained at about 70 per cent. After that, it rose sharply to 90 per cent during and just after the civil war. In terms of the value of foreign trade, with 80 per cent of the total value of imports, it is still the largest Nigerian port. However, as a result of the development of the petroleum sector, its share in the total volume of exports has fallen in recent years.

The urban economy

For the whole of Lagos State, primary activities (fishing, mining and quarrying, agriculture, and forestry) accounted for less than 2 per cent of total workers in the enumerated sector in 1978, and the main formal sector employment-generating activity during the 1970s was manufacturing (Lagos State Government, 1981). Metropolitan Lagos accounted for 38 per cent of total manufacturing employment in Nigerian cities in 1976, and over 60 per cent of the total value added in manufacturing in the six major industrial centres (Enterprise Consulting Group Ltd., 1988). Commercial activities have always been very strong in the city and are carried out at both the formal and informal levels. Agriculture and fishing and distributive trade are the largest employers of people without formal education. The role of agriculture within metropolitan Lagos is, however, less than 2 per cent of the workforce, although the precise figure of employment in this sector is not available. It finds expression in market gardening and other forms of agriculture, mostly on the outskirts of the metropolis. About one-quarter of all workers are in distributive trade. Public administration accounts for another one-quarter and other services have about one-fifth of the employment in the formal sector. During the oil boom years, the multinational companies were very strong in both manufacturing and trade. However, with the downturn in the economy, the trend has been for many of them to divest their operations. Relevant figures are, however, not available. With the federal political decision-making organs and key federal ministries having moved to Abuja, industry and commerce continue to be the live wires of the economy of the metropolis and will each now be examined in more detail.

Manufacturing industries

A survey of manufacturing industry in Nigeria by the Federal Office of Statistics in 1984 (quoted in Lagos State Government, 1989) showed that 53 per cent of all manufacturing employment in Nigeria was located in Lagos State. In addition, Lagos State accounted for 62 per cent of gross industrial output and 61 per cent of the total national industrial value added. As of December 1985, 1,227 industrial establishments were identified in Lagos State, constituting more than 31 per cent of the national total (Lagos State Government, 1989). About 80 per cent of these industrial establishments and jobs are located in Lagos metropolis, illustrating continued concentration since 1976. A more recent survey of manufacturing establishments nationwide is not available.

A number of significant factors have stimulated the concentration of manufacturing activities in metropolitan Lagos. First, the presence in Lagos of the largest seaport in Nigeria offers minimum transportation costs for imported inputs from the port to the factory sites. This was particularly important from the late 1950s, when Nigeria adopted an import substitution industrialization strategy of development. Secondly, good transportation facilities linking Lagos to other parts of Nigeria are available. Thirdly, metropolitan Lagos has the largest concentration of skilled and semi-skilled manpower in Nigeria. For instance, the national survey of 1977 estimated that 40 per cent of the skilled manpower in Nigeria were employed in Lagos (quoted in Lagos State Government, 1989). Another estimate was that one in every four workers in the formal sector in Nigeria was employed in the city. Fourthly, there is a large and ready market both within the metropolis and at the national scale for the outputs of the manufacturing establishments. Fifthly, metropolitan Lagos has fairly well-developed basic infrastructural facilities to support manufacturing industries. Sixthly, Lagos has the premier national and international airport in Nigeria. Thus, it has a considerable advantage over any other centre in Nigeria in terms of communication by air. Seventhly, Lagos State has, since 1979, been participating actively in trade fairs and exhibitions. The annual International Trade Fair organized by the Lagos Chamber of Commerce and Industries attracts both national and international entrepreneurs.

When, in the late 1950s, Nigeria adopted an import substitution industrialization strategy to achieve economic development, attempts to attract industries were made by both federal and the then regional governments. Lagos, with its pre-eminent seaport, had a great advantage over any other location in Nigeria. Owing to the poor state of infrastructural facilities in the country as a whole, one of the earliest efforts aimed at promoting industrial development in an otherwise agrarian setting was the establishment of industrial estates. The first set of such estates to be established in Nigeria were in Apapa and Mushin in 1957, followed by Ikeja in 1959 (see fig. 6.1). All these are now within metropolitan Lagos. There are now 22 such industrial estates currently operating in Lagos State, of which 18 are located in metropolitan Lagos. Recently, there has been a deliberate effort to stimulate small-scale industrial enterprises. An industrial incubator project has been introduced, whereby industrial estates with basic infastructural facilities are made available to small entrepreneurs, who are given supervisory and technical advice. The pilot project for this is located in Agege (fig. 6.1).

In line with its free enterprise posture, particularly since the introduction of the Structural Adjustment Programme (SAP) in 1986, the government has concentrated its efforts on providing necessary infrastructural facilities and an environment conducive to ensuring the growth of small-, medium-, and large-scale industries rather than getting involved in actual manufacturing. Thus, although the Lagos State government has divested itself of actual manufacturing, it has set up an Investment Holding Company to manage government-owned equity shareholdings.

Nevertheless, there are problems and constraints faced by industrial establishments in metropolitan Lagos. Some of these problems are national in nature, while others are specific to the city. Among the national problems has been the impact of the SAP on the ability of manufacturers to secure the foreign exchange needed for raw materials procurement and the importation of spare parts. Owing to the inadequacy of foreign exchange to fund the Foreign Exchange Market (FEM) initiated in 1986, there was continued devaluation of the national currency, which led to escalating costs for industrialists, especially those who depend heavily on foreign inputs. Thus, the initial optimism of the government in introducing the FEM – that it would produce a realistic and sustainable market-determined exchange rate for the national currency – did not materialize. Moreover, the SAP had other elements, such as high interest rates and trade liberalization measures, all of which adversely affected the capacity utilization of local manufacturing establishments, which fell to an average of 36 per cent across all industrial sectors, as reported in December 1992 by the Manufacturers' Association of Nigeria (1993). By December 1993, it had fallen to an average of 29 per cent. Many small enterprises have closed down, while rationalization and staff layoffs are being experienced in many medium- and large-scale establishments. Between the second half of 1992 and the equivalent period in 1993, only the Food, Beverages, and Tobacco and Plastics, Rubber, and Foam products subsectors registered growing employment. The persistent economic downturn and the uncertain political climate are major contributory factors to this situation. The general insecurity of life and property in the city also tends to scare off potential investors.

A number of specific problems and constraints on manufacturing activities in metropolitan Lagos result from the performance of government parastatals responsible for providing certain basic services.

Table 6.3 **Problems of industries in metropolitan Lagos**

Service	No. of establishments reporting	% complaining of unsatisfactory service
Electricity supply	20	100
Telecommunications	20	100
Public water supply	23	91
Access roads	16	44
Drainage	16	56
Waste disposal	22	64
Security	7	86
Fire service	9	78
Public transport	20	55

Source: Enterprise Consulting Group Ltd. (1988), p. 6.20.

Most important are the National Electric Power Authority (NEPA; now known as National Electric Power plc) and Nigerian Telecommunications Ltd. (NITEL). The report of a consulting group engaged by the Lagos State government gives the principal problems for industries in metropolitan Lagos (table 6.3). Electricity, telecommunications, and water supply were almost universally considered to be inadequate and inefficient. Physical infrastructure and services are discussed in more detail below. Other problems include poor roads, drainage, and waste disposal facilities, and problems of security, fire services, and public transport. These problems find expression in the final cost of manufacturing output. For example, many establishments are forced to install generators as back-up for their electricity supply needs and to provide their own boreholes to obtain water (Lee and Anas, 1992).

Commerce and finance

Commercial activities in Lagos pre-date the manufacturing sector, because they accompanied the period of early contact with the outside world before the nineteenth century. They grew during the colonial period, as Lagos became a colony in 1860 and in 1914 the seat of the federal government of Nigeria. Lagos maintained the latter position until 1990.

The Nigerian financial system is dominated by metropolitan Lagos. Of the 50 commercial and merchant banks operating in Nigeria in

1988, about half had their head offices in Lagos. Others had branch offices in Lagos that may be considered pseudo head offices, based on the volume and value of transactions relative to other branches and the head office. All but one of the development finance institutions (i.e. the Nigerian Industrial Development Bank, the Nigerian Bank for Commerce and Industry, the Federal Savings Bank, and the Federal Mortgage Bank) have their head offices in Lagos – the only exception is the Nigerian Agricultural Bank, which is located in Kaduna. Along with the banking sector, the insurance industry in Nigeria is also dominated by metropolitan Lagos. Of the 83 insurance companies registered in Nigeria as of April 1982, 68 per cent had their head offices in Lagos, while virtually all the others had major branch offices in Lagos.

The introduction of the SAP in 1986 and the associated deregulation of the economy saw the emergence of a spate of financial establishments, including both banking and mortgage institutions and allied finance houses. Many of them were located in the metropolis. Indeed, an unprecedented growth in quaternary activities (financial and business services) occurred, with metropolitan Lagos playing the leader. As of 31 May 1994 there were 285 licensed finance companies located in the city. The activities of these finance houses have had both positive and negative impacts on the economy of Lagos and of Nigeria as a whole. With the deregulation of foreign exchange activities in 1986, most of the new finance institutions engaged primarily in foreign exchange trading. This had adverse effects on the value of the naira, which declined relative to other international currencies, stimulating inflation. Interest rates soared to unprecedented levels, sometimes exceeding 40 per cent. The new mortgage banks target the property market, financing the construction of housing and office blocks. In some areas land prices have risen by more than 120 times since 1986. This trend has found expression in soaring production costs and high costs for housing, transport, and other services. Information concerning the precise impact of the activities of these institutions on the provision of houses is, as yet, not available. However, with the re-introduction of currency regulation in January 1994, many of these mushroom financial institutions, mostly banks and mortgage finance establishments, are experiencing serious financial problems and some have collapsed. The Central Bank of Nigeria liquidated four banks in 1994. It is believed that there were 40 more distressed banks in the system as at October 1994 (*Nigerian Tribune*, 20 October 1994, p. 1).

The Nigerian capital market was founded in Lagos, with the setting up of the Lagos Stock Exchange in 1961, which thus became the first stock exchange in West Africa and the sixth in Africa. In 1978 the exchange was transformed into the Nigerian Stock Exchange, with two additional trading branches at Kaduna and Port Harcourt. About 90 per cent of the companies quoted on the Nigerian Stock Exchange have their headquarters in metropolitan Lagos, with their market capitalization running into billions of naira.

Trading activities have always been predominant in the informal sector of the metropolitan economy, although manufacturing and other services are also significant (Ayeni, 1981; Fapohunda, 1985; Peil, 1991). Trading is concentrated in but not confined to traditional markets such as Obun Eko, Ebute Ero, Egerton Square, and Faji. Many of these markets are not well serviced with piped water or refuse disposal, so, in addition, modern markets with lock-up stalls, such as Tejuoso and Alade, have been provided either by the Lagos State Development and Property Corporation (LSDPC) or by local governments. Women predominate in informal sector trading. Street trading and hawking have increased since the onset of recession. The items involved are usually meagre and often reveal a desperation on the part of the traders to eke out a living. Occasionally they are harassed off the street by law enforcement agents, but the effect is inevitably only temporary.

An adequate level of infrastructural facilities with appropriate supporting social services are a prerequisite for Lagos to sustain its leadership of the Nigerian national city system and for any meaningful programme of sustained long-term industrial and commercial development. The Lagos State government currently focuses on upgrading transportation, environmental sanitation/waste disposal, electricity and water supply services, and the provision of industrial estates (see below).

Unemployment

Unemployment continues to be one of the greatest challenges of the metropolis. It is extremely difficult to give an accurate estimate of the level of unemployment. However, the general impression is that, particularly among the young, it has increased over the years, with the downturn in the national economy and the expansion in the output of educational institutions. The earliest information on unemployment in Nigeria was the 1963 census, which gave an overall unemployment rate of 3 per cent for urban centres in Nigeria. The 1966/67 Labour Force Sample Survey (Federal Republic of Nigeria, 1972) gave an overall rate of 8 per cent for urban areas. The National Manpower Board labour force sample survey in 1974 recorded an unemployment rate of 7.2 per cent for metropolitan Lagos, while the statistical survey of Lagos State in 1976 revealed that the unemployed constituted 7.6 per cent of the labour force (Lagos State Government, 1977). About 70 per cent of the unemployed are in the age group 15–29 years. Current official figures are not available. However, it is well known that, in societies with no social security systems, open unemployment is confined to those without any means of support. The decrease in oil prices at the end of the 1970s hit Nigeria's economy hard and, particularly since the introduction of the Structural Adjustment Programme in 1986, unemployment has increased substantially, including large numbers of graduates. However, many of those affected have, as has always been the case in the past, moved into informal sector activities. An additional phenomenon that has emerged in recent years is the so-called "area boys" – unemployed, able-bodied men, possibly drug dependent, who harass other people, mostly motorists, for money in broad daylight. They operate in certain areas of the central business district on Lagos Island and may sometimes turn violent.

Protests against the adverse impacts of the SAP came to a head in rioting in 1989. As part of the SAP relief programme introduced as a result, both the federal and state governments introduced programmes targeted at unemployment. These include the National Directorate for Employment and the industrial incubator scheme in Lagos, the latter in collaboration with the United Nations Fund for Science and Technology Development. A reorientation, especially among educated young people, has also occurred, as many are now more prepared to venture into jobs hitherto passed over in preference for white-collar jobs. In addition, many are now venturing into self-employment in the informal sector. The People's Bank of Nigeria introduced a programme of rehabilitation for "area boys," including vocational training and credit. However, some are unable to cope with the discipline involved in such a programme and have returned to the streets, where they are beyond the control of the law enforcement agencies and add to the insecurity of life and property in the city.

Associated with unemployment is the issue of urban poverty. As noted earlier, the SAP has brought severe economic stress. It is now common for even those who have regular employment to engage in subsidiary economic activities. There is no doubt that the urban poor are experiencing untold levels of deprivation. The problem is of great magnitude and continues to grow. It is important that effective measures be introduced that could enable the urban poor to work, earn, and begin to overcome their deprivation. In this connection, labour-intensive approaches to infrastructure development (with international aid and technical assistance) may be explored.

Politics, administration, and management

The management of a large metropolis depends both on the formal political and administrative structures and on how these work in practice, which may be governed more by informal relationships than by formal procedures.

Politics is the lifeblood of Lagos ... Land rights, employment, industry and other sources of wealth rely on political interaction, involving patron–client relations, bribery, corruption, nepotism and/or "long-legs" (contacts). Almost everyone knows someone with a link, however tenuous, to power.... Political leadership ... operates at many levels. There is considerable interaction (some would say interference) between leaders at national, state and local levels and at least some sectors of the general public ... Chieftaincy councils, landlords' and market women's associations, trade unions and other pressure groups operate through particularist, face-to-face networks to further the goals of members and clients. These lower-level groups are particularly efficacious in local government, pressuring for building permission, exceptions to sanitary regulations, licences and tax reductions. Councillors are necessarily dispensers of patronage, and civil servants are under considerable pressure from kin, friends and neighbours to humanize the bureaucracy. Frequent investigations and even penalties for those found guilty of bribery, corruption, nepotism and so on are unlikely to change the system radically, insofar as it serves the needs of many people who would be ignored if bureaucratic norms were followed and civil probity were more widespread. (Peil, 1991, pp. 45, 65)

Metropolitan Lagos has been administered under a variety of different territorial schemes. Historically Lagos started around the Island and Mainland areas as a fishing and agricultural village and grew into a small town. When it was "ceded" to the British in 1861, it was administered as a city-state with its own separate administration. In 1866 it was included in the "West African Settlements" under a Governor-in-Chief resident in Sierra Leone, but it retained a separate legislative council and a "local" administration. Various changes followed, through its status as a separate colony, to its merger with Western Nigeria in 1951.

In 1953 a federal territory was carved out of former Western Nigeria, including the colony of Lagos, in response to two sets of problems that had emerged in 1951. First, political and administrative authority was split between two antagonistic governments – the federal government, which was dominated by the Northern Peoples' Congress, and controlled the federal territory, and the Action Group, which administered the rest of the province. This resulted in fragmented political authority, which in its turn led to a gross lack of coordination in service provision over the territorial space then constituting metropolitan Lagos. The second problem derived from the first. Owing to the much greater financial resources and administrative capacity available at the federal level, the federal territory of Lagos had a much higher degree of infrastructural development than the outer metropolitan area. Thus, there were evident contrasts in the quality of urban services available in the two areas within the metropolis.

From 1958 there was political agitation for a separate Lagos State. This was achieved in 1967. Ikeja, within the Lagos metropolis, became the capital of the new state. Since its inception, the state has been ruled by a succession of military administrators. This pattern was interrupted by only two periods of civilian administration, between 1979 and 1983 and again between 1991 and 1993. Lagos State inherited two divergent legal, administrative, and financial systems from its federal and Western Region territories. In 1967, a committee was set up "to study the existing laws applicable in the city of Lagos and the former Colony Province and to recommend laws that should apply throughout Lagos State." Following the recommendations of the committee, there was a reorganization of the local councils, because most of them were unable, even if willing, satisfactorily to promote the welfare of the communities for which they were responsible (Olowu, 1990).

Another reform took place in 1976 as a result of the federal government inspired national reform of local government. In that reform the two urban councils that exceeded 1 million in population were each split in two – thus we have Lagos Mainland and Lagos Island, as well as Mushin and Somolu. During the civilian administration of 1979–1983, 23 local governments were created within Lagos State to replace the 8 inherited. This created problems of viability, efficiency, and effectiveness. When the military administration took over again in 1983, there was a reversal to the earlier 8 local government areas. There are now 12 local government areas within the State, 8 of which are located within metropolitan Lagos (Olowu, 1990).

During the first period of military administration (1967–1979), four areas received top priority: environmental services (water, sewage, and drainage), general administration, public transportation, and education. Under the succeeding civilian administration in 1979–1983, this order was generally maintained, except that expenditure on roads and housing rose considerably and edged education into fifth position.

The problems of political control and service delivery manifested themselves once again during the brief civilian government between 1991 and 1993. Because the state government was controlled by the national Republican Convention and the local governments by the Social Democratic Party, there were allegations that the state administration was frustrating efforts at refuse clearance by not settling bills due to the Waste Management Authority, for political reasons. Whatever the truth of the matter, there is no doubt that the administration of the metropolis would be more efficiently and effectively performed if political control were the same at the different levels. During that same period (1991–1993), however, there was also a demonstration of what a dynamic local government chairman can achieve. One of them succeeded in effectively mobilizing the population in his council area for development activities, to the extent that his pace of activities outshone that of the state government.

Infrastructure, services, and housing

Transportation

Up to 1981, there was no urban transportation plan for the whole Lagos metropolitan area. What often happened was that road networks were laid out in specific areas as they became incorporated into the built-up area of the city. There are about 2,700 km of road, about 40 per cent of which are tarred, and three main bridges linking Lagos Island and the mainland. However, inadequate land was generally reserved for road networks, with the result that some houses cannot be reached by motorable roads. In many cases the provision of parking spaces for motor vehicles was virtually ignored.

The problems of providing an efficient transportation system in metropolitan Lagos are threefold. First, there are the institutional problems, which seem to constitute by far the greatest problem. At least six different public agencies are responsible for the supply of transport facilities and the provision of transport services in the metropolis. These include the Federal Ministry of Works and Planning, the Lagos State Development and Property Corporation, the Nigerian Railway Corporation, and Lagos City Transport Services. Institutional reforms to improve the capacity for transport programme development and administration are clearly needed (Federal Ministry of Transport, Aviation and Communication, 1993). The lack of co-ordination between federal, state, and local council networks results in the existence of sharp breaks in road quality and maintenance standard. Similarly, the failure of the Lagos State Development and Property Corporation to integrate development of government layouts with those of private developers has produced ineffective integration of road networks within the metropolis. The inherent physical characteristics of many areas, especially the swampy terrain, constitute a second important challenge for efficient transportation networks. This involves technical problems in providing efficient drainage networks and in building roads of a high standard. This problem can be surmounted, provided the necessary financial resources are available and contracts for the construction works are awarded on merit to capable and experienced civil engineering firms. An integrated network of underground drainage channels, though costly for the whole of the metropolitan road network, would eliminate the perennial problem of street flooding during the rainy season in the metropolis. The social problems of traffic control, traffic discipline, and the observance of traffic laws and regulations constitute the third main problem. There is generally a low standard of traffic discipline on the part of motorists. This is aggravated by the extremely low standard of traffic control at strategic four-way intersections. In addition, traffic safety measures are poor, especially with respect to cyclists and pedestrians, particularly schoolchildren.

During the oil boom period in the early 1970s, commuters who earned over 600 naira per month normally owned private means of transport, thus reducing the demand for public transport. However, the current economic situation in the country has turned many marginal car owners into public transport users. The emerging trend is that more people, irrespective of their income levels, now depend on public transport services for mobility. This trend is bound to increase, because car ownership is now beyond the reach of many workers, thus leading to rapidly expanding demand for public transport.

Estimates of transport demand in metropolitan Lagos in 1990 ranged from 7 to 10 million passenger trips daily, of which over 95 per cent were undertaken by road, primarily by car, bus, and taxi. Of these, 80–85 per cent were made by public transport. However, there has been a considerable decline in the number of vehicles available for public transport, particularly since the mid-1980s. The total vehicle fleet in Lagos State declined from 165,000 in 1984 to 100,000 in 1988. Newly registered vehicles declined from 72,000 in 1982 to 17,000 in 1986 and 10,000 in 1988. New public transport vehicles declined from 16,500 in 1983 to 1,500 in 1988 (Lagos State Government, 1990). Imported used cars and buses have partially filled the gap. In 1991, 80 per cent of the 35,000 used vehicles imported into Nigeria were concentrated in Lagos. Many of these are used to operate the unconventional, unregulated, and unregistered services called *kabu-kabu*. A survey of the *kabu-kabu* services in December 1991 recorded 3,961 such minibuses on 24 of the over 300 public transport routes in metropolitan Lagos (*The Guardian*, 11 February 1994, p. 18).

Total annual passengers carried by the Lagos State Transport Corporation have fluctuated from 90 million in 1978 to 53 million in 1983, 76 million in 1989, and possibly fewer than 60 million in 1992 (*The Guardian*, 11 February 1994, p. 18). Consequent upon the SAP riots in 1989, the federal government introduced the Mass Transit Scheme, under which buses were distributed to states to assist in both inter-urban and inter-state transportation. Lagos metropolis benefited from this. In addition, in 1991, the Lagos State government introduced new fleets of buses for metropolitan Lagos. In 1992, the state government bought 90 buses and leased them to private operators to help ease the acute transportation problem. However, the scheme appears to have been grounded owing largely to default by many beneficiaries. A Task Force has been set up to recover payments. As of June 1994, four buses had been seized by the Task Force. Other bus operations sponsored by Lagos local government, which started in 1991, have reached more than half of the Lagos State Transport Corporation's capacity. Eventually, in 1993, the Corporation was dissolved and its staff laid off owing to inefficiencies and frequent breakdown of the buses. A few local governments continue to operate their own intra-city bus services. However, the services remain grossly inadequate and private sector operators have taken advantage of the vacuum to increase their operations. The 14,000 taxis in operation carried about 1.1 million passengers in 1989. In contrast, the minibus and midi-bus operators may be carrying about 4.5 to 5 million passengers daily. They are thus the most significant means of public transport. This major adaptive service comprises mostly old, often rickety used cars and minibuses used to operate largely unregulated public transport and accounts for the bulk of the public transport service in metropolitan Lagos. They are the only means of transport available in some localities. The second adaptive service is the use of motor-cycles to carry passengers from the suburbs to the main transport interchanges or terminals. These two adaptive services have provided substantial relief to the working class and the urban poor unserved by conventional public transport.

Urban railways, even since mass transit rail passenger services were introduced in 1988 and 1990, carry fewer than 1 million passengers per year. In recognition of the acute need for commuter transportation, the Nigerian Railway Corporation, which already has a commuter service between Agege and Apapa Wharf, commissioned a commuter line from Iju to Ebute Metta on 21 April 1994 (fig. 6.1). This was the first such effort since 1965. It is claimed that the service will add 10,000 passengers per day to the commuter passenger capacity of the railway service. The most recent policy emphasis, however, is on greater use of the private sector to provide affordable public transport services (Federal Ministry of Transport, Aviation and Communication, 1993).

Apart from inadequate public transport, other problems of the road system in metropolitan Lagos include poor maintenance, and traffic congestion (Onakomaiya, 1978). Many roads within the metropolis need repairing. Potholes are often left too long before being repaired and such delays tend to increase the cost of maintenance. In addition, roads are often damaged in the process of laying water pipes and electricity cables.

Efforts made in the past to solve the perennial problems of traffic congestion have included the construction of bridges, ring roads, and expressways; restriction of access to the city centre on alternate days of vehicles with odd and even registration numbers; and the conversion of hitherto two-way roads to one-way. Although these are commendable efforts, they have not solved the problem of traffic congestion, particularly during peak periods. It was hoped that the proposed Metroline Project would have helped in reducing the congestion. However, with the cancellation and later resuscitation and drastic modification of the original project, other measures may be needed to tackle the problem. It is hoped that traffic restraint measures will be introduced in Lagos Island (Federal Ministry of Transport, Aviation and Communication, 1993). In addition, a comprehensive study of land use within Lagos Island, Ikoyi, and Victoria Island is needed, with a view to introducing policy instruments that would stimulate the relocation of certain activities to other parts of the metropolis, thereby reducing the pressure for commuter transport to the central area.

Water supply

Inadequate water supply creates a continuing headache for both private residents and entrepreneurs in metropolitan Lagos. Table 6.4 shows the installed capacity, production in September 1994, and problems of production. There are 17 waterworks in Lagos State, with a total installed capacity of 4,119.3 million gallons of water per month (MGM). In September 1994 less than half of the potential was

Table 6.4 **Monthly production of water for metropolitan Lagos, September 1994**

Name of waterworks	Designed capacity in MGM[a]	Production in MGM, September 1994	% of designed capacity	Remarks
Adiyan	2,100	1,715.05	81.67	
Iju	1,350	294.67	21.83	Irregular power supplies
Isashi	120	91.93	76.61	
Agege	72	–	–	Faulty borehole and NEPA problem
Shomolu	72	–	–	
Apapa	72	–	–	Major NEPA fault
Surulere	72	–	–	Major NEPA fault
Shasha	72	–	–	Undergoing rehabilitation
Isolo	90	24.00	26.67	Faulty clear-water pumps
Amuwo Odofin	90	–	–	
Alausa Ikeja	9.3	3.92	42.15	Production interruption owing to a burst main
Total	4,119.3	2,129.57	49.3	

Source: Lagos State Water Corporation, October 1994.
a. MGM = million gallons per month.

supplied and typically only 50–55 per cent of the water demand of the metropolis is being met. Private individuals as well as industrial and other establishments tend to supplement the piped supply by sinking boreholes or wells. In addition to the problems noted in the table, pipe breakages, inefficiency, and lack of spare parts inhibit greater output. Mini-waterworks were introduced during the period of the civilian administration between 1979 and 1983. Their capacities ranged between 2.5 million and 3 million gallons per day. They are currently not functioning properly and need upgrading. The Adiyan waterworks, the first phase of which was opened in 1991, has a capacity of 70 million gallons per day. A second phase with the same capacity is being evaluated. There are also problems of water distribution. A project assisted by the World Bank to improve the secondary and tertiary distribution network is currently being implemented. When completed, it is hoped that up to 65 per cent of the demand will be met. The state government is currently embarking on a state water supply expansion programme aimed at supplying water for all, including its rural areas, by the year 2000. There are, of course, spatial variations in the adequacy of the service. For example, the old-established neighbourhoods of Yaba and Ebute Metta, with a well-laid-out grid-iron pattern of development, are better serviced than slum neighbourhoods such as Ajegunle (fig. 6.1).

Electricity

Metropolitan Lagos accounts for about 40 per cent of the total electric power consumption in Nigeria, but inadequate and erratic power supply for industrial, commercial, and domestic demands has characterized the service provided by the National Electric Power Authority (NEPA), now renamed after commercialization as National Electric Power plc. The regular occurrence of intermittent power outages has led to nearly all industrial establishments in the metropolis acquiring their own stand-by generators (Lee and Anas, 1992). Some industrialists have claimed that, in recent times, they have had to depend on their generators and now regard NEPA as a stand-by. The ultimate consequences of this undesirable situation are low capacity utilization and higher costs of production. It was hoped that Egbin Thermal Power Station, which was commissioned in the late 1980s purposely to meet the electricity requirements of metropolitan Lagos, would improve the situation. It did for a while, until the station developed problems and could not obtain the necessary funds for spare parts. Efforts are currently being made to address the problems in collaboration with the federal government.

Telecommunications

In terms of telecommunication facilities, which could relieve the pressure on intra-urban transportation, the NITEL telephone facilities are grossly inadequate. Although metropolitan Lagos is the best serviced area in Nigeria, with most of the lines in Lagos State (which itself has 40 per cent of the national total), demand far exceeds supply and some areas are much better served than others. Although the installed capacity (155,000 connections in 1994) is yet to be exhausted (80 per cent of potential connections have been made), there are demands that cannot be met (NITEL, Lagos, October 1994). The problems include the need to replace underground cables and to expand and modernize existing external networks. A World Bank assisted programme to provide an additional 132,000 lines for metropolitan Lagos and to modernize existing lines is being pursued in three phases. Efforts to improve the efficiency of the service included the provision of digital exchanges for Lagos Island, Victoria Island, Apapa, Ikeja, and Surulere in 1992. This has considerably improved international links. However, there is still a lot to be done to ensure the availability and reliability of the service for internal communication.

Environmental sanitation

Lagos seems to have acquired the unenviable status of being one of the dirtiest cities in the world. An important element in this regard is the inability of the city management authorities to cope effectively with waste disposal. The Waste Disposal Board was established in 1977 to coordinate refuse disposal activities in Lagos State. Initially it was mandated to take charge of general environmental sanitation and the collection, disposal, and management of domestic refuse. Subsequently, it was assigned responsibility for cleaning primary and secondary drains, the collection and disposal of industrial wastes, flood relief activities, and the collection and disposal of scrap and derelict vehicles.

With the inauguration of the Board in 1978, these duties were contracted out to a firm of pollution control experts. The situation improved slightly. However, the contract was terminated in 1984 and the Waste Disposal Board assumed direct responsibility. The national environmental sanitation exercise has also made an impact on the level of cleanliness in the metropolis. On average the Waste Disposal Board collects an additional 55,000 tonnes of refuse monthly as a result of this exercise. However, the Waste Disposal Board has recently run into problems, because the vehicles and other equipment it initially acquired have broken down and need replacement. The cost of replacement has proved prohibitive because of the considerable decline in the value of the national currency. The problem of uncleared accumulated refuse has once again surfaced in various parts of the metropolis, and task forces are being set up to clear it, but it is estimated that one-third of the city has no refuse collection service (Aina et al., 1994).

The Board, now named the Lagos State Waste Management Authority, has adopted the strategy of clearing refuse at night, since traffic congestion hinders effective operation during the day. The target is to collect 5,000 tonnes of refuse daily, which is about 75 per cent of the total solid waste generated daily. Another problem that acts as a constraint on efficient operation by the Waste Management Authority is the fact that up to 60 per cent of the inhabitants of the metropolis live in inaccessible areas. It has been claimed that for each day the refuse van is unable to reach any area, it takes an additional three days to clear the backlog. A 42 ha piece of land is being developed in the outer metropolitan area as a modern landfill site capable of handling solid waste for the next 40 years.

Although the pail system of sewerage has now been eliminated and the majority of Lagos residents have access to a water-flushed toilet, the supply of water is insufficient and waste water has to be used for flushing. Treatment facilities are totally inadequate and untreated or inadequately treated effluent is discharged into the Lagoon and pollutes groundwater (Aina et al., 1994). In 1993 the World Bank approved a credit of US$63 million through the International Development Association for a Lagos Drainage and Sanitation Project. This is aimed at improving living conditions in parts of Lagos that presently suffer from regular inundation, by improving storm water drainage. It will also provide assistance to the Lagos Waste Management Authority.

Housing

One of the great challenges facing metropolitan Lagos is housing (Abiodun, 1974, 1976). The considerable gap between supply and demand has found expression in the astronomical cost of rented dwellings. Overcrowding, slums, and substandard housing are expressions of this problem. Prior to 1928, planned residential areas in Lagos were limited. They included Ikoyi, which was a reservation area for expatriates who were colonial administrators and executives of foreign firms, and had a population of 4,000, or 3 per cent of the population of the city in 1931 (fig. 6.1). Apapa, Ebute Metta, and Yaba, with a combined population of 22,000, or 17 per cent of the total, also had some element of planning, in the sense that road networks in Ebute Metta and Yaba were laid out on a grid and residential development was confined to the blocks within the road pattern. On Lagos Island, apart from the areas around the racecourse and marina, the indigenous housing was unplanned and was left to develop haphazardly, with houses built quite close together. Such overcrowded, unhealthy housing and poor environmental conditions stimulated the rapid spread of influenza epidemics and bubonic plague, which ravaged the city between 1924 and 1930. These led to the emergence, in 1928, of the pioneer planning authority in Nigeria, the Lagos Executive Development Board (LEDB), which embarked on slum clearance and the relocation of families from the Island to the Mainland at Surulere (fig. 6.1; see also Peil, 1991). Since then, the activities of planning authorities have assumed considerable importance in metropolitan Lagos.

The Ikeja Area Planning Authority (IAPA) (fig 6.1) was established in 1956 to control development in the part of the metropolis outside the then Federal Capital Territory. In 1958, the Western Nigeria Housing Corporation was created by the former Western Region government with the responsibility of providing housing finance. In 1972, the LEDB, the IAPA, and the Epe Town Planning Authority were merged to form the Lagos State Development and Property Corporation (LSDPC) to stimulate greater efficiency and eliminate delay, waste, and duplication of responsibilities in the housing sector (LSDPC, n.d. (a), (b), (c)). Table 6.5 summarizes the housing units constructed by some of these authorities. The period 1979–1983 under the Jakande administration witnessed a massive housing development programme. Nevertheless, the problem persists – mostly because of rapid population growth, but also because of the introduction of the SAP in 1986 and the threefold increase in the price of petroleum fuel in 1994. The federal government housing programme for Lagos, which was launched in 1994 under the

Table 6.5 **Planned housing schemes in metropolitan Lagos**

Housing agency	Scheme	Remarks
Lagos Executive Development Board, 1955–1975	Slum clearance of Central Lagos, 1955 to early 1960s, Olowogbowo Rehousing Scheme, Lagos Housing Scheme	1,847 families housed in Surulere. 1,337 families resettled in low-income rented houses. Sub-sidized by Ministry of Lagos Affairs
	Other housing schemes in Surulere	14,537 family units (dwellings) provided. In all, 128,800 people were provided with housing
Lagos State Development and Property Corporation (LSDPC), 1972–1979	Resettlement of slum dwellers from Central Lagos to Ogba and low-income housing in Isolo	1,000 families housed
Federal housing	Under 1975–1980 and 1981–1985 plan periods	6,000 housing units[a]
LSDPC, 1979 to date	Low-income housing Medium-income housing	16,878 housing units 1,790 housing units

Source: LSDPC (n.d.(b)).
a. Each housing unit may accommodate one or more households.

National Housing Scheme, has stalled, amongst other reasons because of the spiralling cost of building materials.

Despite the efforts of the various housing authorities, over 90 per cent of the housing in metropolitan Lagos is still provided by the private sector and individual effort. Housing has been widely seen as a secure and lucrative investment, which enhances the owner's status in the community (Barnes, 1979). Whereas access to privately owned land through customary channels or purchase has made it possible for a relatively large stock of owner-occupied housing to be built, opportunities for those excluded from these means of access to land have been limited to areas in public ownership. As a result, squatting is limited and over 60 per cent of residents are tenants, some in tenements constructed by absentee landlords, but the majority in houses occupied by landlords of modest means (Aina, 1990; Peil, 1991; Aina et al., 1994). During the 1970s it was usual for a man earning the average salary or above to build his own house, while, as profits and speculation increased, interest in providing rented rooms for the poor declined. In recent years, declining real wages and high inflation, particularly rapid increases in the prices of building materials, have resulted in workers living so close to subsistence level that they have nothing left for investment. Today only the very rich construct new housing units. In response to the slower rate of new house construction, tenancy has increased and rents have increased more than fivefold since the introduction of the SAP. High densities, overcrowding, and multi-family occupancy of dwellings have long characterized Lagos and have intensified in recent years (Ayeni, 1981; Peil, 1991).

Residential districts range from low-density areas that have been able to retain their characteristics, through medium-density districts such as Surulere and Ikeja, to substandard settlements that lack basic amenities. Some former low-density areas near the centre of the city have been penetrated by banking, commercial, and office uses, leading to a recent state government order that houses in parts of Ikoyi and Victoria Island should revert to their originally approved use. Many low-income areas were villages or peripheral settlements that have been engulfed as the city has grown. Some settlements, such as Maroko on Victoria Island, have been demolished, typically without any arrangement for resettlement, with the result that the displaced residents merely move on to already overcrowded neighbourhoods elsewhere. In addition, in response to astronomical rent increases, the rapidly increasing cost of living, and the increasing insecurity of life and property, a drift of population to villages and towns in adjacent Ogun State has been detected, increasing pressure on commuter transport links from these towns to the city.

Crucial influences on the ability of the private sector to supply sufficient housing to meet demand are access to land and the delivery of services. The inadequacy of the latter has been demonstrated above. To conclude, mechanisms for obtaining access to land will be briefly discussed. Hitherto, land for urban development could be obtained from any of the following: the Land Use and Allocation Committee based in the Governor's Office, the metropolitan development agency (the LSDPC), or indigenous landowning families and individuals. Although the Land Use Decree of 1978 vested the ownership of all undeveloped land in the state, attempts to regulate the ownership of land and transfer of rights have never been effective. Interested parties, including professionals, tend to connive to back-date transactions to make them appear to have preceded the Decree.

Currently, no more distributable land is available within Lagos metropolis through the Land Use and Allocation Committee (LSDPC, 1983). Today, land for development is obtained primarily through the private sector. Large landowners may in some cases rent land for the construction of temporary housing while they wait for its value to increase, as described by Aina (1990) for Olaleye-Iponri. Although there are examples of squatting and illegal subdivision, such cases are limited. Land rights in Lagos have historically been a route to political power and a source of wealth and conflict (Peil, 1991).

Conflicts over rights of ownership between the state and private individuals or village or family groups, or between members of families, which arise in part out of the lack of a comprehensive land register, sometimes lead to sales of the same plot to more than one buyer or to the demolition of structures by the state. For example, more than 100 well-built houses were demolished by the military state government at Aja village, about 20 km east of Victoria Island, in August 1995, despite a court order that attempted to restrain the government. Land acquired by the state in this way may benefit powerful and well-connected individuals, rather than ordinary residents. Land scarcity has become a constraint on the ability of both the public and private sectors to respond to demand for housing and accounts, in major part, for the predominance of small rental dwellings in the housing stock.

It has been claimed that, unless more vigorous actions are taken now by the relevant authorities, in concert with the inhabitants, to combat the appalling living conditions in many localities, similar to those that produced epidemics before the 1930s, metropolitan Lagos may face outbreaks of disease more devastating than ever before.

Conclusions

Undoubtedly, there has been a spectacular growth in the spatial expansion and development of metropolitan Lagos within the past three or four decades. However, the indications are that the population growth rate has slowed down in the most recent decade from an estimated 14 per cent per annum in the 1960s and early 1970s to an estimated 4.5 per cent per annum in the late 1980s. Thus migration to the metropolis is tending to contribute less to its population growth than the rate of natural increase. This trend is likely to continue as the cost of living in the city continues to rise.

Nevertheless, over the decades, metropolitan Lagos has become the pre-eminent city in the Nigerian system. Lagos functioned as the political and administrative capital of Nigeria from the time the Northern and Southern provinces of Nigeria were amalgamated in 1914, through political independence in 1960, until the federal capital moved to Abuja in 1990. During this period it acquired leadership among Nigerian cities in terms of economic and social activities, particularly in manufacturing, trade, other services, and, most recently, finance, banking, and insurance. Despite the downturn in economic activities at the national level, metropolitan Lagos is still the premier manufacturing city not only in Nigeria, but also at a regional scale, for the west coast of Africa. It is the most important seaport, both in Nigeria and on the west coast of Africa, with substantial import and export trade both nationally and internationally. Metropolitan Lagos is the most important node for telecommunications and the most accessible city in Nigeria by land, air, and sea. It has thus attracted to itself the largest concentration of multinational corporations in Nigeria. It has become not only a West African regional centre but also a focus of international interaction at continental and to some extent at the world scale.

Certain issues were identified in this study, resulting from the above developments. Among these are the problems of the liveability of the city and its sustainable growth and development, including problems of unemployment, and the emergence of an increasingly marginalized and economically pauperized group. The survival strategies of its inhabitants, especially the poor, were noted. The manageability of the metropolis and the problems associated with its governance also attracted attention. Also discussed were problems of housing, transportation, and service provision. Certain conclusions were derived from these discussions. Chief among these is the fact that, with the continued downward trend in the national economy and the more than threefold increase in the price of petroleum fuel in the mid-1990s, pauperization of the city population is expanding across the class hierarchy. It has become impossible for a salary-earner to live in the metropolis without an additional source of income.

At the same time, it seems that the responsibilities of the state to tax-paying citizens with respect to the provision of basic infrastructure are not being fulfilled. In effect, citizens are being double-taxed, as they have to provide self-reliant strategies for meeting their needs for a regular supply of drinkable water, a supply of electricity, and security services. On the other hand, it seems that governance at the local council level holds some promise for focusing attention on the needs of citizens. For instance, the brief experience of civilian administration at the local government level between 1991 and 1993 did see the emergence of certain dynamic individuals as chairmen of local government councils. These people were able, through dynamic leadership and innovative ideas, to mobilize citizens at the local level for development efforts in a manner that outshone the state administrative efforts. It seems that there is a need in the future to strengthen the local government system in terms of resources, personnel, and capacity building, to stimulate efficient and effective governance for the benefit of citizens.

Note

1. The 1963 census before independence is usually considered to be the most reliable census in Nigeria. Because of the unreliability of all subsequent censuses, due *inter alia* to the allocation of federal resources on a per capita basis to states, special efforts were made to ensure that the 1991 census was sound. However, the results are still controversial and the population of the city is still uncertain.

References

Abiodun, J. O. 1974. Urban growth and problems in Metropolitan Lagos. *Urban Studies* 11: 341–347.

——— 1976. Housing problems in Nigerian cities. *Town Planning Review* 47(4): 330–348.

Aina, T. A. 1990. *Health, Habitat and Underdevelopment in Nigeria with Special Reference to a Low Income Settlement in Metropolitan Lagos.* International Institute for Environment and Development, London.

Aina, T. A., F. E. Etta, and C. I. Obi. 1994. The search for sustainable urban development in Metropolitan Lagos, Nigeria: Prospects and problems. *Third World Planning Review* 16: 201–219.

Ayeni, B. 1981. Lagos. In: M. Pacione, ed., *Problems and Planning in Third World Cities.* Croom Helm, London, pp. 127–155.

Barnes, S. T. 1979. Migration and land acquisition: The new landowners of Lagos. *African Urban Studies* 4: 59–70.

Enterprise Consulting Group Ltd. 1988. *Industrial Inventory Survey of Lagos State. Vol. 1, Main Report.* For Lagos State Government, Lagos.

Fapohunda, O. J. 1985. *The Informal Sector of Lagos. An enquiry into urban poverty and employment.* University Press Limited, Lagos.

Federal Ministry of Transport, Aviation and Communication. 1993. *Mass Transit and Transport System. Management Programme for the Lagos Metropolitan Area.* Summary Report, Lagos.

Federal Republic of Nigeria. 1972. *Labour Force Sample Survey 1966/67*, vol. 1. Lagos.

Lagos Executive Development Board. 1971. *A Preliminary Sketch: Master Plan for Lagos*. Lagos.

LSDPC (Lagos State Development and Property Corporation). n.d.(a). *L.S.D.P.C. at a Glance*. Ikeja, Lagos.

———— n.d.(b). *50 Years of Housing and Planning Development in Metropolitan Lagos. Challenges of the Eighties*. Lagos.

———— n.d.(c). *Housing Delivery in Lagos State – Challenges of the Eighties*. Lagos.

———— 1983. LSDPC searches for land for development. *LSDPC Quarterly Magazine* 29–30(6): 8.

Lagos State Government. 1977. *Statistical Survey of Lagos State November/December 1976*. Ministry of Economic Development and Establishments, Lagos.

———— 1981. *Lagos State Regional Plan (1980–2000)*. Ministry of Economic Planning and Land Matters, Urban and Regional Planning Division, Ikeja, Lagos.

———— 1989. *Lagos State Directory of Manufacturing Companies*. Ministry of Commerce and Industry, Ikeja, Lagos.

———— 1990. *Digest of Statistics 1990*. Office of the Military Governor, Plans, Programmes and Budget Department, Statistics Division, Lagos.

Lee, K. S. and A. Anas. 1992. Costs of deficient infrastructure: The case of Nigerian manufacturing. *Urban Studies* 29(7): 1071–1092.

Mabogunje, A. L. 1968. *Urban Development in Nigeria*. University of London Press, London.

Manufacturers' Association of Nigeria. 1993. *MAN Half-Yearly Economic Review*, Lagos, App. 1.

Mehretu, A. 1983. Cities of SubSaharan Africa. In: S. D. Brunn and J. F. Williams, eds., *Cities of the World*. Harper & Row, New York, pp. 243–279.

National Manpower Board. n.d. *Report on the Labour Force Sample Survey, Lagos, Nov. 1974*, section 5.1.

Olowu, D. 1990. *Lagos State. Governance, Society and Economy*. Malthouse Press, Oxford.

Onakomaiya, S. O. 1978. Towards an efficient transport service for Metropolitan Lagos. In: P. O. Sada and J. S. Oguntoyinbo, eds., *Urbanisation Processes and Problems in Nigeria*. Ibadan University Press, Ibadan, pp. 57–62.

Peil, M. 1991. *Lagos: The City Is the People*. Belhaven Press, London.

7

Kinshasa: A reprieved mega-city?

Jean-Luc Piermay

Abstract

Deuxième agglomération d'Afrique centrale par la population, Kinshasa appartient à une sous-région qui, paradoxalement, connaît les taux de croissance urbaine les plus élevés de continent tout en étant dépourvue de tradition urbaine. Lieu d'accumulation des richesses d'un Etat prédateur, la ville a longtemps fonctionné selon une logique de redistribution. Mais la déliquescence des structures d'encadrement étatiques – et aujourd'hui leur effondrement – pose la question de l'avenir d'une mégapole qui avait toujours fondé sa croissance sur la puissance de l'Etat. Malheureusement, les données fiables manquent et le fonctionnement réel de nombreux domaines de la gestion urbaine restent inconnus. C'est pourquoi a été privilégié un exemple, celui de la gestion foncière. Il montre l'élaboration par les différents acteurs de la ville de stratégies anti-crise, le rôle réagencé de réseaux de relations, le poids dominant des petites activités et la mise au point de formes d'encadrement dans lesquelles les pouvoirs d'Etat sont mobilisés au profit des stratégies propres aux individus qui constituent ces pouvoirs. L'espace kinois en est recomposé de même que les espaces sous influence de la ville; une intense création sociale est en oeuvre. Mais l'avenir d'un organisme urbain aussi démesuré reste incertain par rapport aux capacités gestionnaires disponibles et dans le contexte d'un pays où les identités locales s'affirment et où la fragmentation commence.

Introduction

Talking about recent trends in Kinshasa's urban growth and trying to understand their causes is quite a challenge. The city, which is probably the second largest in sub-Saharan Africa in terms of population (after Lagos), is indeed poorly known at present because of the decay of its supervisory bodies and therefore the lack of reliable data. The international media have reported the crisis at its climax. In particular, the events of September 1991, marked by soldiers' extortions and plunder by those who took advantage of the situation, contributed to the destruction of part of the productive services and the wealth of knowledge accumulated on the city and the country, while revealing the state's bankruptcy. But this bankruptcy had been in the making for a long time, with services in total chaos for years and data from the census questionable.

Although it is difficult to proceed in a classical manner with the scientific analysis of such an urban set-up, understanding Kinshasa's situation is, however, crucial, because it seems to be a forerunner of what one can begin to detect elsewhere in Africa and maybe the rest of the world. How can a city of this size and deprived of supervisory bodies keep on operating? What is the future of a capital city whose growth was based on the presence of a state that has now collapsed? Is there going to be a massive urban exodus before a gigantic redistribution of the population? Can the city survive the actor that gave birth to it and maintained it despite repeated and sometimes violent reactions from peripheral regions (such as the successive revolts in the rich mining area of Shaba)? Will it be reprieved? If it is, what mechanisms can possibly replace those that have failed? These are the crucial questions that research should try to answer, a task that cannot be fully realized in this chapter, owing to the lack of data and opportunities for investigation arising out of the difficult circumstances.

A mega-city without an urban past

Kinshasa lies in a privileged position – as does Brazzaville on the other bank of the Congo/Zaire river.[1] These two capital cities – in Zaire and Congo – are situated not on the littoral as in most African coastal states but 350 km away from the sea. Rapids interspersed with falls downstream as well as a long navigable stretch upstream explain the site chosen for the cities on either side of a large becalmed part of the river (the "Pool"; see fig. 7.1). Despite this inland location, Kinshasa is actually on the periphery of the country. In the west, wedged between Angola and the Congo, the Bas-Zaire region (which

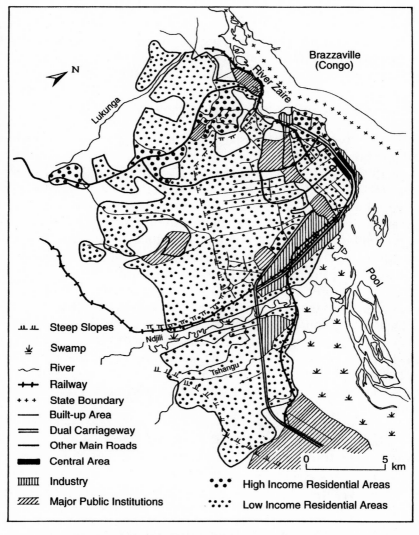

Fig. 7.1 **The urban structure of Kinshasa (Source: Pain, 1984; field surveys, 1985)**

225

comprises only 2.3 per cent of the country's territory) is the narrow outlet towards the ocean that Leopold II, the Belgian king who "created" the Congo, managed to maintain against other colonial competitors. The same Leopold II gave the city its first name (Leopoldville), which was meant to be the starting point for colonialist ventures into the heart of the continent long before it was promoted to administrative centre of the territory. That was hardly a century ago. Today Kinshasa is a mega-city, one of the conurbations that cannot be managed as a whole because of its size and the lack of supervisory capacity. It is one of the surprising paradoxes of Central Africa that a century ago there were no towns in the region and now it is one of the most urbanized parts of the continent (the urban population in Zaire was 32 per cent of the total in 1984[2]).

Recent and spectacular population growth

During the "scientific" census of 1984, Kinshasa was found to have 2,664,000 inhabitants, that is 8.7 per cent of the country's total population (30.7 million inhabitants) and 31 per cent of its urban population (INS/UNDP, 1991). Even though the census was criticized at the time, because reliable local observers felt that the capital city's population had been somewhat underestimated and was at the time nearer 3 million inhabitants, it is the last signpost we have to measure the country's population. Is it possible to establish estimates for the present? If the estimated growth rate in 1984 is extrapolated (Republic of Zaire, 1984), the lowest assumption for 1994 (5.03 per cent annual growth) is 4,335,000 and the highest (5.73 per cent) is 4,632,000 inhabitants. But what is the value of such extrapolations? To answer this question it would be necessary to have an idea of the impact on the population of the very serious crisis prevailing in the country, which affects the heart of the Zairian state and administration and therefore the capital city that is its headquarters and its symbol.

Like all the cities in Central Africa, Kinshasa is recent. There were large villages on the banks of the "Pool" before the Europeans arrived, where tradesmen plying the river lived, but the population remained small. The post set up by Leopold II's men in 1881 was of secondary importance. The city came into being when the railway line between the Pool and the Matadi sea pier was completed (1898), when the Leopoldville port was constructed to enable the development of the remarkable upstream river network, and the town was promoted to the rank of capital city of the Belgian Congo (1923). The colonial authorities were so restrictive that for a long time migrant workers were considered to be only temporary residents in the city and had to go back to their villages when their employment ended. But gradually the controls were eased and, despite racial segregation, which was fiercely maintained up to the end, the African population made the city their own, with women coming in large numbers to establish urban families. The decrease in the global sex ratio reflects these basic changes: from 200 men to 100 women in 1933, the ratio went down to 139.2 : 100 in 1955, 116.9 in 1970, and 104.1 in 1984.

The mega-city is even more recent. In 1940, there were only 50,000 inhabitants in the city, which already occupied the first rank in Central Africa in terms of population, and there were 400,000 in 1960 at the time of independence. The male population growth rate has long been spectacular, especially since the end of the 1933 crisis. Some periods featured extraordinary annual growth rates (15 per cent from 1940 to 1950, 12.6 per cent from 1950 to 1955, 10.6 per cent from 1959 to 1967), while even "lower" growth rates were considerable (1955–1959: 2.4 per cent, 1967–1976: 4.9 per cent, 1976–1984: 5.4 per cent). For 20 years now the urban population growth rate has clearly slowed down. However, city dwellers are mostly very young, with half of them below 15 years of age. Besides, not only are birth rates in Kinshasa higher than in the rest of the country (51.5 as against 48.1 per 1,000) but total fertility in the capital city too is above the national level (7.7 compared with 6.7). In this regard, Kinshasa is at the same level as the adjacent Bas-Zaire and Bandundu regions, from which most of the city's migrant workers come. Furthermore, mortality rates are clearly lower in Kinshasa (12.6 per 1,000 compared with 16.8 at the country level) thanks to its health services, despite their present sorry state. The rate of natural increase is therefore at its highest in the city (38.9 per 1,000), and this accounts for three-quarters of its total annual growth. The only possible sign of a change in the population growth pattern is the age of first marriage, which in town is 29 for men and 22.5 for women, compared with 24.9 and 20, respectively, in the country as a whole (INS/UNDP, 1991, p. 65).

Spasmodic occupation of space

Similar spasmodic progress has characterized the way the city has occupied space. Data are rather old. The city has always developed horizontally – apart from a few blocks in the centre – and the built-up area increased from 2,331 ha in 1950 to 5,512 ha in 1957 (+13.1 per cent per year), 12,863 ha in 1968 (+8 per cent per year), 17,922 ha in 1975 (+4.9 per cent per year), and 21,288 ha in 1984 (+1.9 per cent per year) (Piermay, 1993a; see also fig. 7.1).

However, this spectacular increase hides the uneven nature of the process over time. The greatest increase in area happened within a few months of the declaration of independence (1959–1960). The land occupied at this time was sufficient for the development of the city over the next 10 years or so (Pain, 1984, p. 32). The way in which space for urban development was generated explains this peculiar feature. During colonial times and up to the very end of colonialism, the so-called African districts were under very strict constraints (Africans could not own property and had to obtain a work permit to be able to reside in town), while the city's development abutted European-owned agricultural and cattle farms. The collapse of the colonial system and the civil war that followed, which ravaged the country for five years, abruptly deprived the white farmers of legal protection and allowed the de facto occupation of vast stretches of land, which was initiated by leaders of political parties, traditional leaders, and the inhabitants of neighbouring areas. Thereafter these settlements could not be challenged, because they were too massive for any return to the past to be possible, but it took a long time for houses to be built. Things therefore went from highly interventionist growth to extreme laxity. The very important building programmes of the Office des Cités Africaines (OCA, African Townships Office) in the so-called "Cités planifiées" (planned townships), which are still highly valued areas despite their increasing age, suddenly ended and were replaced by "self-production" in which an applicant for a plot is at the same time owner and "promoteur" (manager of self-built house construction). Since then the city has kept on growing and it today covers a wide area: some 28 km on its east–west axis and 19 km on its north–south axis in 1985 (fig. 7.1).

The changes in population densities clearly reflect these sudden changes in growth. However the built-up area has been growing less rapidly for some years and in particular is growing more slowly than the city's population. Whereas the average density stood at 87 inh/ha in 1950 and 92 in 1975, surveys in 1984 indicated a spectacular increase to 126. Greater distances, increasing environmental problems due to the city's encroaching on intensely erodible sandy hills (with all the consequences of their unstable nature for investment in building and the degradation of infrastructure networks), lack of roads suitable for motor vehicles in outlying areas, and the intractable problems of transport to the centre of such a vast agglomeration may have finally restricted its continuous spread and led instead to increased internal densities, although still not to vertical construction. However, the densities remain low compared with those in some West African cities. The lack of an urban tradition and the related lack of knowledge about how to manage the problems caused by proximity in limited spaces, the general aspiration for an individual plot, and the lack of experience in building upwards all help to explain this. Record densities are seen in the poorest areas adjacent to the city centre (in the "old townships" of Lingwala and Kinshasa): 300 inh/ha (fig. 7.2). On the outer edges of the agglomeration, the peripheral suburbs have much lower population densities because building is still going on. This is because Kinshasa residents like to put up permanent structures that are relatively costly and take a considerable time, usually over 10 years, especially since the crisis and its associated decrease in incomes.

The lack of an urban tradition: A paradox

The most recently urbanized region on the African continent thus became the one with the highest urbanization rates on the continent. The paradox is only superficial. A state supervisory presence was not altogether absent in the subregion prior to colonial times. But the Kongo kingdom had practically disappeared by the time Leopold II's soldiers arrived, and most of the other kingdoms were declining, weakened and disorganized first by the slave trade then by the trade in firearms. In other places, in particular in the Zaire basin, which is now the centre of the country, pre-colonial political entities were unambitious and had had only low population densities. The introduction into these weakened and poorly structured societies of all manner of colonial pressures – from the extortions by concessionary companies, to porterage duty, the harvesting or compulsory cultivation of red rubber, recruitment for roadworks and other building sites, without forgetting the appearance of little-known diseases, which frightened people away from inhabited places – destroyed the social structure of villages. In the end people turned to the cities. The turning point came after World War II when large investments created a modern economy and towns became attractive to the African populations. The country's features were deeply changed, with urban settlements acquiring a key role.

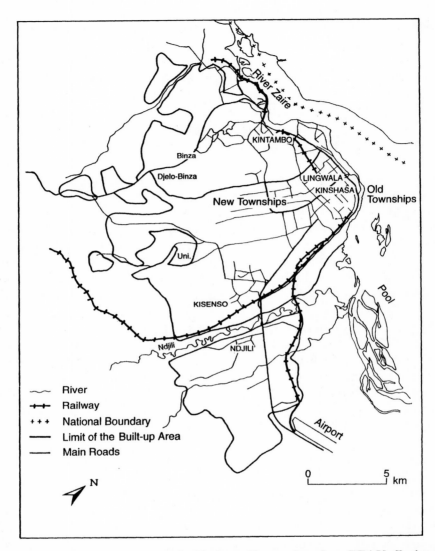

Fig. 7.2 **Urban neighbourhoods in Kinshasa (Source: based on BEAU,** *Projet de développement urbain***, Kinshasa, Polycop, 1985)**

The very collapse of colonial authority strengthened urban centres through a variety of processes that reinforced each other. During the civil war from 1960 to 1965, the rural population, which was most affected by the conflict, sought refuge in the city. Despite the fact that the growth rate slowed down after this massive migration towards the capital city, the basic trends were maintained. Coming just when world oil prices were increasing, the sudden Zaireanization measures adopted by President Mobutu in 1973 to allow Zaireans to take over formerly foreign-owned enterprises generally disrupted the Zairean economy. However, the upheaval was worst in the countryside, while the beneficiaries were chiefly city residents, who, though mainly attracted by gain, did reinvest some money in the urban areas. Based on these various processes, social networks did the rest: the city became, for modern Zairean society, *the* place to live, a place where social relations could bloom and where they could become the key to success.

But Kinshasa is also a symbol of how difficult it is to create an urban society. Each social network encompasses only a fraction of society. Outside these networks, a way of life with common rules must be created within a territory where there are many people and where the demands they make on the land are extraordinarily strong compared with those in the Central African rural areas, where the availability of vast open spaces facilitated the resolution of many conflicts. It is clear that Kinshasa never had structures adapted to such major social transformation. But its population growth rates were so high that it is doubtful whether its structures would have had the time to mature properly, even if some authority had been willing to see it through the growth process.

The mega-city, daughter of the state and social patronage

The capital city as centre for a predatory state to accumulate riches

Whereas the great crisis of 1930 led to a decrease in the urban population and post-war economic investments encouraged rapid population growth, in recent times the relation between economic growth and population growth has become blurred. There has actually been a significant de-linking of the two phenomena. Already the 1955–1959 crisis hardly influenced the population growth rate. Unlike the 1930 crisis, the civil war (1960–1965) provoked a massive influx of people who considered the city a safer place than the rural areas, where bandits were roaming and no law could be enforced. Since that time, however, the number of jobs in the formal/modern sector has steadily decreased in comparison with population figures. Whereas in 1955 the modern sector offered one job for 3.3 inhabitants, the ratio was 6.3 in 1967 and 6.1 in 1975, even though the situation is much better in Kinshasa than in the smaller towns.

However, this statement that investments do not explain the city's population growth should be put in perspective, because it is not only the growth of these investments over time that should be considered, but also the relative importance of investment in the capital city in relation to the rest of the country. In this regard Kinshasa accounted in 1971 for 50 per cent of manufactures and 49 per cent of private sector wage earnings. However, it accounted for only 20 per cent of employment and 17.4 per cent of GDP, with the first rank in this respect occupied by the Shaba province (36.2 per cent) where most of the mining industries are located (copper and cobalt).

These proportions have undergone great changes since 1960. An analysis of projects approved by the Investments Commission showed that, between 1969 and 1976, 36 per cent of national investment was in Kinshasa while Shaba province obtained only 14 per cent (Pain, 1984, p. 57). The pattern has not changed since then and the largest projects have gone to Kinshasa and its region, including major building projects and road developments (the World Trade Centre, Cité de la Voix du Zaïre, the Limete interchange), the hydropower station at Inga on the Zaire river (which is 250 km downstream of Kinshasa), the steel plant at Maluku, the national cement plant, and the creation of an industrial free zone at Inga (Willame, 1986, p. 227; see also fig. 7.3). The imbalance in wealth between the capital city and the other regions is, therefore, bound to have increased, but this process should be studied in depth. Many of these investments are in fact only white elephants generating no profits and doomed to early failure. Above all, they provide opportunities for large commissions for the local decision makers, who reinvest the money in financial markets in the capital city or invest it abroad. These funds are essentially how the city obtains most of its capital. However, they can hardly be called "investments."

The development of Inga is a good example of how the preferential treatment given to Kinshasa in terms of investment derives from a deliberate political strategy. A number of factors, such as the presence of the second-largest river in the world in terms of flow, the regularity of this flow, and the 96 m fall over 15 km of river, contribute to making Inga potentially the largest hydropower site in the world. But the building of the first power station and even more so of the second one (Inga II), which could not be justified by the immediate needs of Kinshasa itself, was politically motivated. The idea was

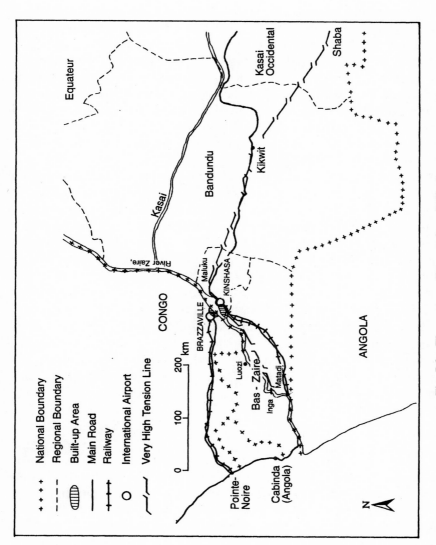

Fig. 7.3 The metropolitan region of Kinshasa

233

that Shaba province should be supplied from Inga so as to exert Kinshasa's economic hold over this unruly region. It was an enormous project, because it involved putting up an 1,800 km power line, which had to transmit at high voltage (700,000 volts) to minimize energy losses on the way. The Inga–Shaba line was completed (1972–1983) with enormous financial inputs from the state. Because it does not supply the regions in between, where consumption is not important enough to justify the building of transformers, its benefits have been limited. Electricity consumption in Shaba, declining since the beginning of the copper crisis, is hardly sufficient to justify maintaining the line in operating condition. The power station at Inga has at least enabled a major increase in Kinshasa's public lighting (Willame, 1986) and street lights are now a common feature even in the most outlying districts of the city.

A survey of money circulation and consumption in Zaire's capital city reveals even stronger contrasts. Whereas Kinshasa comprised 9 per cent of the country's total population and 31 per cent of its urban population in 1984, it accounted for 42 per cent of the building sector, nearly 40 per cent of trade, one-third of direct taxes, and one-fifth of public services (in 1970). In 1975 it consumed 72 per cent of low-voltage power and accounted for 47 per cent of water sales (Pain, 1984, p. 57). However, these data pre-date the serious crisis of governance now prevailing in the country. As for what is left at present of Kinshasa's modern sector (mainly administration, trade, port operations, and, in the industrial field, the processing of local agricultural products and of raw materials imported for local consumption), it is impossible to obtain recent data. For reasons that are easy to understand, large foreign companies are little represented in any way in Kinshasa today.

Social networks and social crisis

The relation between the accumulation of wealth and the city's population growth lies in the understanding of redistribution mechanisms. Until the crisis of the 1930s, the city was considered to be the temporary residence of male villagers, who left as soon as they lost their jobs. With the arrival of women and the constitution of urban families, the town (a colonial creation) was taken over by societies that had not known it existed a few decades before. The process worked so well that today the city is seen as the only place for social success, the place where one *must* live.

However, the city is still an uncertain place to live, so that most city dwellers maintain links with their original villages under the pretext that these will make it easier for them to leave in case of conflict. So far the city has not created many common rules, just as if the coming together of many customs from various ethnic groups has forced each group to retreat into its own identity rather than looking for solutions applicable to all city dwellers. The best example of this can be found in the laws of inheritance. The most significant legacy from a city dweller to his heirs is his house. In the rural areas around Kinshasa succession is predominantly matrilineal, with the child belonging to his mother's family and inheriting from his maternal uncle, whereas modern laws imposed by the colonial power tend to be patrilineal, with the child belonging to his father's family and inheriting from him. This is also the aspiration of the city family head, who desires his children to inherit the house he has built. However, he knows that when he dies it will be difficult to avoid conflicts between his nuclear family and the extended family of his in-laws, who will want to recover what is a very valuable item in the urban context. This explains the complicated strategies thought out by fathers to create in their lifetimes their children's pre-eminent rights over the plot on which the family lives. To achieve this and try to remedy the terrible uncertainty, they use all means at their disposal, from administrative documents to power relations or social relations.

One of the favourite strategies consists of integrating into networks of social relations, mainly ethnic relations, so that old habits are maintained in the city even amongst the most powerful citizens who want to establish for themselves a range of clients, in order to acquire power through the number of their dependants. While associations between people of the same origin maintain solidarity among their members through various family events, the manager of an enterprise, or his chief of personnel if the manager is a foreigner, will prefer to recruit among his "brothers." Therefore ties with the family remain much stronger than those with the enterprise or with the state.

However, life in the city has become harder since the mid-1970s, with a gradual deterioration in the situation up to the present. Spiralling inflation, the collapse of large enterprises (starting with Gecamine, which produced copper in Shaba province), the desperate search for income owing to the unbelievable decline in real wages, capital flight, and the so-called *"assainissement"* (purifying, meaning rationalizing) measures, i.e. the massive retrenchment of civil servants in the name of structural adjustment – these have all contributed to the declining quality of life in the city.

Some redistributive measures were maintained as long as the state had the necessary resources, but they are now jeopardized owing to the drying up of both internal and external resources. How could such redistribution be beneficial when two-thirds of households do not have high enough incomes to provide a minimum amount of food for their families?[3] In this context, a new social group has appeared, referred to as "sparrows" (children abandoned by their families and living on the streets), "fighters" (because they fight for survival), "*balados*" (petty thieves), "beggars." All these are more or less excluded from the old processes of redistribution and seek solutions in alternative practices, which in the extreme lead to plundering and ransacking (Willame, 1992, p. 226). However, the political basis of these practices and the impetus they derive from better-organized groups should not be ignored. Soldiers in the national defence forces, whether manipulated by the powers that be or of their own accord, have long been plundering civilians (Young, 1965) to make up for salaries that have always been insufficient and that are now much more so, as for all wage-earners.

There is another major factor in today's social crisis: the AIDS pandemic, which may have the highest rate of occurrence in the world in Central African cities. In 1986, it was estimated that between 5 and 8 per cent of the sexually active adult population had been in contact with the virus (Shoepf, 1991). This percentage has increased greatly since then. This high percentage, though not reaching the record level of Kigali, Rwanda, results from urban sexual practices. The city brought together groups from different cultural backgrounds while encouraging a relaxation of old restrictions. The delayed age for marriage, the increase in polygamy, and the multiple sexual partners of many individuals, married and unmarried, have facilitated the spread of the virus, so that sexual freedom has long been seen as a symptom of the crisis. Matonge, Kinshasa's red light district, remained for a long time protected from economic hardship. At first, the residents of Kinshasa refused to acknowledge the reality of the disease. They had named it the "Syndrome Imaginaire pour Décourager les Amoureux" – or Imaginary Syndrome to Discourage Lovers – based on the French abbreviation for AIDS, which is SIDA (1986–7). Though awareness later increased, little could be done about it, owing to the decay of the state and the health apparatus.

These social changes will no doubt have serious consequences for the city's population growth. There will certainly be an increase in the mortality rate, but to what extent? Will fertility rates decrease or increase to balance this? Unfortunately, we lack data and the 1984 census seems too old to be a useful reference to answer these questions. Urban population growth may stagnate, but the most deprived population groups may still consider the capital city to be a place of opportunity, where it is easier to develop strategies to combat the crisis.

Parallel authorities, on stage and behind the scenes

The powerful informal sector

The informal sector is omnipresent in Kinshasa. However, after an in-depth study in several parts of the city in 1975 and after cross-checking with data from other sources, Marc Pain, like many other researchers, refused to use the term "informal" activities, and counted 37,632 "small-scale activities" (11,782 artisanal and commercial enterprises and 25,850 itinerant businesses), employing 15,000 craftsmen and 80,000 traders, i.e. 37 per cent of city jobs (Pain, 1984, pp. 106–124). A count today would yield even more spectacular results, as state authority has dwindled and the economy collapsed.

However, the two economies should not be seen as merely co-existing, because they actually interpenetrate. Everything in Zaire indicates very strong relationships between the two, with every wage-earner acquiring a parallel income that is not only a wage supplement but often the main source of income. According to a study undertaken in Kinshasa in 1986, the proportion of income derived from wages was only 33.4 per cent for civil servants, 42.2 per cent for wage-earners, 36.8 per cent for skilled workers, 46.3 per cent for semi-skilled workers, and 46.7 per cent for unskilled workers (Houyoux et al., 1986). What is unexpected is that wages as a proportion of total income are smaller as salaries increase!

So, in relative terms and particularly in absolute terms, the wealthy are those benefiting from the informal economy. It may well offer some means of survival for the mass of urban dwellers, but mainly it increases the gaps between social groups. Indeed, small businesses need seed capital, however limited, and in particular they need social contacts and business acumen. Access to capital, to supplies whose quotas are fixed by the government, or even to some services (such as private education and health services) is obviously easier for someone in a strategic professional position or at the centre of a vast network of relations. Unofficial economic activities may therefore be perceived as an implicit advantage of wage earning, thus justifying the low levels of these wages. In a way this parallel economy appears like a tax on the whole population, a costly tax owing to the chain of intermediaries that it needs, while it does not ensure the services usually derived from normal taxes (MacGaffey, 1991, p. 175).

Rather than focusing on a census of activities, the result of which will remain uncertain because of the extent of piecework and the many enterprises that operate intermittently,[4] it would be better to observe how the informal economy – or rather the real economy, to use a term coined by Janet MacGaffey – fits into the urban system. In view of its many forms, one example will be given particular attention, because it seems to provide a perfect illustration, i.e. access to land.

The legal system of land allocation is totally unable to satisfy demand. The system was radically transformed after independence and in particular in 1973 with the Land Act 021 of 20 July. The principle was to set up a uniform procedure with a "registration certificate," a title deed to fixed property, because it was considered that only investments made in land can be privately owned and not the land itself, despite the fact that previously there were two very different procedures, one for European and the other for African areas. This system had previously existed only in the former European suburbs. However, the system never worked properly and even the conversion of old documents never took place. Thus in 1984 it was estimated that, for every 1,100 plots that were legally established, more than 11,000, i.e. 10 times more, were established outside the legal system.

The conventional mechanism for obtaining access to land since 1959, when the restrictive system set up by the colonial authorities in the African districts collapsed, gives pride of place to the Bahumbu traditional chiefs of the Kinshasa region and to their "royal" entourage. The colonial powers had hoped to exclude people in these societies from the urban areas by compensating them for the absorption of their land. However, they took advantage of the disruption that followed the civil disobedience movement of 1959 and have since retained an important role in the mechanisms by which urban growth occurs. Claiming their ancestral rights, they now mark out rough plots on a grid-iron plan with the help of so-called "surveyors," usually family members so designated for the occasion. These plots are then sold for cash to city dwellers. However, when the two parties to the deal belong to the same clan, they still resort to the traditional offering of palm wine and the sale price is adjusted in proportion to the closeness of the relationship.

This method of land disposal used by the traditional chiefs seems simple, but this is only an illusion, because the chiefs' area of jurisdiction is not easy to define. Even if things had been simple before colonization, areas were not delineated in the accurate manner necessary for a densely populated city – a tree or some other special feature in the countryside was enough. Furthermore the colonial authorities always exercised their power over chiefs by favouring those whom they could trust and dismissing those who kept on demanding their rights. At present, areas claimed by various chiefs overlap and it is impossible to know who is taking advantage of whom, that is, who is attempting to defraud the other. "Proofs" of legitimate ownership produced by various chiefs are both unreliable and varied, because they are based simultaneously on traditionally invested powers and on those conferred by the colonial authorities. In addition, the internal structure of the seller's family is often ill defined, especially when the family head is old and illiterate. Individual vested interests are then stronger and each family member may take contradictory decisions regarding the plots.

In addition, the chiefs' method does not always seem to contradict the state procedures. There are often close links between the traditional chiefs and the administration, with the chiefs' next of kin always eventually obtaining from local civil servants some official papers, which are used as proof of their right of tenure.

Acquiring a plot is a first step for any Kinshasa resident. After arriving in town and being housed for a time by a "brother," he usually becomes a tenant in one of the many peripheral high-density suburbs where overcrowding is the rule. In these areas, plots are used for rental purposes, sometimes with the centre of the plot reserved for the owner's house, which is surrounded by rows of small shacks, each housing one household; sanitary arrangements, which are extremely basic, are communal for all the inhabitants of the plot. Having acquired this urban experience for a few years and set up a network of contacts, the tenant then decides to become an "owner," even if his conception of ownership is incompatible with that of the state. This aspiring plot owner is nearly always a man, because women in Kinshasa have only limited access to urban land. According to surveys carried out in 1985,[5] only 5 per cent of plot owners were women, which was the lowest percentage in all the Central African cities surveyed. Though here, as in all of Central Africa, women are the guarantors of stable domestic life and play important roles in the retail trade, they remain "social minors" (Bayart, 1979). Perhaps a link could be made between the small number of women landowners and the weakness of urban agricultural production in Kinshasa. Even though any vacant urban land is planted at the onset of the rainy season, it is occupied only on a temporary basis. Urban agriculture, whether in the built-up or peri-urban area, cannot play more than a marginal role in feeding a city the size of Kinshasa, because of the distance it is necessary to travel to get access to the rural areas and because intensive cultivation techniques are not known.

While trying to break away from unpredictable loan sharks, Kinshasa residents also aim at social acceptance through the purchase of plots (Girard, 1993). Thereafter the building of the house will be a protracted lifetime endeavour demanding many sacrifices and all manner of tricks. Indeed, owing to the lack of clear regulations and authorities to enforce them, the new property owner must beware of all those who might threaten his purchase. These include the chief, who might try to resell the plot to a third party; the civil servant, who will try to settle there by force; the neighbour, who will try to add a few square metres to his own plot; and those who try to steal building materials. In this totally unregulated situation the weakest (or the one who seems to be the weakest) or the poorest are always more vulnerable. In the same way as purchasing a plot is a "must," building a permanent structure is a "must," and doing so without delay or at least at the same pace as the rest of the suburb is another essential.[6] However, the procurement of permanent materials such as cement, wood, and corrugated iron, and their conversion into a house by pieceworkers who will make the blocks and by a bricklayer and his team who will build, are a heavy strain on domestic incomes when most households do not earn enough for mere survival. Thus building is usually protracted and most suburbs look more like ruins than future residential areas.

Therefore actors in the urban development process are numerous, and regulatory authorities invisible. To use a Kinshasa formula, it is rule by "Article 15," by which it is meant that the advantage goes to the most resourceful, most daring, and best organized (Piermay, 1993b).

Nevertheless, the growth of the city is not merely the sum total of "spontaneous" actions, but is a real social construction, which defies the prevailing confusion in both rules and ruling authorities.

State power: From entropy to apparent collapse

The above analysis places state authorities in the back seat, an impression that is confirmed by looking at the way the administration works: dilapidated offices, massive absenteeism, very poor filing, obvious disorganization, very poor control over urban development, weak control mechanisms, and a poor capacity to adapt. This is how the urban authorities appear. Decentralization, gradually implemented since 1977, has resulted in the establishment of two levels of urban authority: the city and the zones (24 in Kinshasa), both with elected councils. But these entities have inadequate personnel and very limited financial resources, and their role, even with regard to the budget, is not clearly defined (Mbuyi, 1993, p. 185). The city's true boss is therefore the Regional Governor, a powerful political figure always chosen from among the President's favourites. It is necessary, therefore, not to be taken in by appearances. Whereas administrative structures are poorly developed and have a weak role with respect to the process of growth in the city, the members of the state apparatus play a powerful role and are ever present.

This analysis should not deal only with the main authorities of the city and the state. Studies of cadastral services in Kinshasa in 1985 demonstrated the considerable role played by surveyors working in these services. Having appropriated and divided amongst themselves the cadastral maps, which are no longer available in the offices but only in their homes, the surveyors know better than anyone not only the layout of the land but also the official procedures. They use this knowledge to further their own interests by selling their services, serving as intermediaries in land sale deals, and sometimes taking advantage of favourable circumstances. They are now feared both by the people who are threatened with expropriation and by their own superiors, against whom they can plot coups if the latter are not sufficiently docile (Piermay, 1993a). It is a truly parallel system, which operates from Kinshasa cadastral offices, and is demonstrated by the relatively constant prices for basic transactions in land and the failure of all attempts to reform the service. Thus the state's weakness does not signify that its agents are not powerful.

It is, however, obvious that, generally speaking, those who are higher in the official hierarchy have better access to opportunities for accumulation and more influence on urban growth mechanisms. Outside the political sphere there seem to be only scanty and disparate means of accumulation, as demonstrated by those many city dwellers who start building and have to save on a daily basis in order to proceed with construction. Among politicians, the main role goes to the President. Not only does his post give him privileged means of accumulation, but above all he has the power to integrate these means of accumulation into a strategy. It seems, in practice, that this strategy is of a political nature and is aimed not at increasing wealth but rather at combating the dangerous countervailing power of money by redistributing state resources in proportion to people's position in the official hierarchy. In the same way, this strategy has consisted of harnessing all alternative sources of power, whether traditional (by integrating chiefs within official honorary bodies), political (by promoting or dismissing politicians at will), scholarly, or community based (by subjugating and discouraging local initiatives). Champion of the law as well as champion in techniques of misappropriation, the President wants to present himself as the only possible recourse, the only countervailing power, in order to harness new social relations.

He has succeeded remarkably well and only the Catholic Church has maintained its resistance and counter-power, mainly because it has its own hierarchy and a head who is outside the country. Apart from the Church, the head of state's collaborators remain faithful to him in relation to their position in the official hierarchy, not excluding the possibilities of dismissal or promotion. The regime has in this way achieved remarkable staying power, as evidenced by the present impossibility of replacing it politically, even though the resource redistribution engines have all but ceased to function. Income from raw material exports and international aid has declined and the country is no longer in the strategic position it occupied during the Cold War owing to the proximity of Angola and southern Africa. But this staying power has been obtained at the expense of state entropy and has been accompanied by the decay of all the institutions and regulations necessary for governance. In general, people think that they can put their own wits to good use as well as the many possibilities for fraud offered by urban life, without being aware that the system actually deepens inequalities and splits society into innumerable contradictory micro-interests. In the final analysis, there is indeed an "individual acceptance of the crisis situation" (Willame, 1992, p. 118). As for those who cannot "cope," they are not very dangerous to the regime.

It is through these "parallel authorities" that the governance of urban areas should be viewed. In this field, as in others, the official system has failed. Any idea of overall urban planning has been abandoned, as have all projects for the improvement of infrastructure networks, because these operations would necessitate coordinated action within a coherent urban set-up. However, Kinshasa cannot be said to be without governance. It is managed by extra-ordinary stakeholders, and only by them, each one exercising some kind of control over part of the urban territory. Traditional chiefs have not relinquished all their powers – they are still in the picture when plots are subdivided and sometimes later when some members of their families are among the locally elected authorities. Some institutions and services, in particular the defence forces, have managed to maintain control over land, which was often obtained during colonial times. The same can be said of individual owners of peripheral plots, acquired more recently and vital for the city's future growth. Religious missions and various Christian churches often constitute the core around which localized development occurs.

However, the most efficient "extra-ordinary managers" are probably the intermediaries, who are numerous in Kinshasa. I have already mentioned surveyors and politicians who, thanks to their knowledge in a crucial area and their presence in social networks, are able to solve problems for their clients arising from the complexity of the urban structure. A good example is the agencies who deal in real estate and other transactions, which are often managed by civil servants taking advantage of the information that they obtain through their jobs. These specialists, who often live by solving the inevitable problems to which this unregulated urban society gives rise, are not in the least interested in attempting to minimize these problems. On the contrary, and in particular with respect to their professional activities, they may well be tempted to reinforce the problems in order to limit the number and influence of their competitors. The way in which these parallel officials manage the city is, therefore, logical from their own point of view.

This parallel system is thus based on a real functional logic that clearly favours some of the stakeholders – those who take advantage of the crisis and the deterioration of all structures to advance their own interests and guarantee themselves some kind of permanence.

"Good governance" of the city, on the other hand, would demand skills that they do not possess and means that they do not control. This conclusion should be pondered over, both by those who might try to offer simplistic solutions to the crisis in Kinshasa and by observers and authorities planning the future of other mega-cities. Paradoxically, Kinshasa may demonstrate a real state of equilibrium for a weak society within the context of laissez-faire economics at the world level.

The structuring of urban space

Towards a reconsideration of inherited plans

The colonial authorities had devised careful zoning based on racial segregation. European-reserved areas enjoyed proximity to the river and the city centre (at a time when there were no motor vehicles), whereas Africans were confined behind these residential areas beyond a so-called sanitary buffer zone, which was a manifestation of the separation between the two communities and whose permanence was ensured by the presence of large facilities, such as a golf course, zoo, and botanical gardens. Owing to the growth of the city's area, the town centre and the European suburbs have become less and less central. In addition to the "old townships," "new townships" and self-built areas (so-called "planned townships") had already been developed during colonial times and were separated from the old townships by a second sanitary buffer zone (today occupied partly by factories, but mainly by an army camp and army airport, both installations creating quite effective ruptures in the urban fabric). During the 1950s, when segregation was still strictly enforced, the first infringements of the master plan appeared, with residential suburbs built in some areas (Binza, Djelo-Binza; see fig. 7.2), as well as large developments, such as the university, on the surrounding hills far from the built-up areas, and the development of a planned estate for African wage-earners in the far eastern part of the city (Ndjili, beyond the Ndjili River).

This strict allocation of space was abandoned at independence. The civil disobedience movement initiated by the Kongo leaders against the colonial authorities was the breaking point. Land tenure and other legal shackles were jettisoned, never to be reinstated or replaced. Self-built areas submerged European farmland around the city as well as traditionally owned areas, and filled in the spaces left

244

between the town and hills, which had been partly occupied by the large developments implemented during the previous few years. The city thus spread more or less equally in all directions, despite a proposal by the urban planning office (Bureau d'Etudes et d'Aménagement Urbain, BEAU) for a master plan to direct its growth to the east. The implementation of the master plan never even started owing to lack of state resources and possibly lack of will. The powerful factors driving the city's growth, which involved so many actors, gave rise to its growth in all directions despite the considerable dangers of erosion of the sandy hills, a lack of roads accessible to motor vehicles, and questionable land tenure. It is hardly noticeable that the two surfaced roads into the city (the road to the airport and to the Bandundu region and to a lesser degree the road towards Bas-Zaire; see fig. 7.3) do contribute somewhat to the extension of the built-up area. Although the general plan is no longer respected, subdivision plans are still strictly followed. In this regard old habits have prevailed. Streets through the old neighbourhoods have been extended, sometimes in a somewhat haphazard manner up onto the hillsides, while traditional chiefs keep delineating 300–400 m^2 plots, as was always the case in the city's poor suburbs.

The peri-urban challenge

Popular thinking tends to favour urban growth. Not wishing to remain tenants forever and looking for social status through the ownership of land, citizens go searching for plots in the peripheral areas. It is a very individualistic search but not an isolated one, because solitude is not valued and is even regarded with suspicion as being linked to witchcraft. Once having found a plot and immediately made it his own, the citizen therefore wishes to be surrounded by neighbours, and the same goes for the settlement of the area some months or years later. After a protracted development period, with bouts of construction interspersed with long waiting periods, the difficult threshold to cross is when the first occupant settles in. After that the whole area is rapidly occupied.

It is interesting to analyse land tenure in the rural periphery of the city. Without necessarily being a reflection of the present state of social forces in the city, the differences between the present and what was observed in previous years indicate the way Kinshasa society has changed. The city is now mainly bordered by market gardens in the valleys or by property belonging to prominent people. Market gardeners control only small areas, which are of marginal interest for urbanization because of the level of groundwater. Cultivators are usually attached to their gardens, but are threatened by the encroachment of built-up plots and the consequent erosion, and are finally tempted to sell their land. Those who have procured property have bought it from the former European owners or from local traditional chiefs or acquired it free of charge through the Zaireanization procedures imposed in 1973. It would appear that traditional chiefs have already been evicted from land subject to speculation. It is true to say that in the past they defended themselves when buyers, whether Europeans or private companies, tried to divide up plots and sell them to city people, by claiming traditional rights that the sale could not abolish. Though this strategy should still be viable, it is unlikely to succeed if the people concerned are in high office.

The metropolitan area and its sphere of influence

Kinshasa is close to the relatively densely populated areas of the Bas-Zaire region (40 inh/km^2) west of the city. To the east, however, densities are low or very low, even at times in the Kinshasa urban area (7 inh/km^2 in the Maluku area, which covers 70 per cent of the Kinshasa region) and also in part of the neighbouring region of Bandundu (fig. 7.3).

Though Kinshasa is one of the very rare coastal African capital cities that was not built on the littoral, it is not anywhere near the centre of the national territory. The country's borders are very near the city and cut across the old Kongo kingdom: there is a border with the Congo, whose capital city can be seen on the other bank of the river, and there is a border with Angola, refugees from which were and still are in Kinshasa.[7] Owing to the proximity of these borders, and even though there is an important trade in food products to Brazzaville (which is enhanced by the difference in value between a strong CFA franc and the zaire, which has hardly any value), Kinshasa mainly exerts its influence on a limited part of the surrounding area. The sides of the road to the Bas-Zaire region have far more settlements than those of the Bandundu road, which traverses areas that are mainly desert and ecologically poor. When the powerful citizens of Kinshasa wish to acquire agricultural land, they would rather purchase large tracts towards Bas-Zaire and around the city. The land tenure legislation, which grants priority to a buyer who is able to develop the land, as well as the traditional chiefs' greed and the indifference or complicity of local authorities, enable buyers to displace many peasants, who after selling are often driven to rent the plot they used to cultivate freely before (Bulu Bobina, 1984).

Although a capital city, Kinshasa does not attract people equally from all parts of the Zairean territory. The birthplace of inhabitants enumerated in the 1984 census indicates their origins. Whereas 60.7 per cent were born in the town, 12.7 per cent and 12.8 per cent came from the Bas-Zaire and the Bandundu regions, respectively, placing these on an equal footing even though Bas-Zaire's population is probably only 54 per cent of Bandundu's. The number of inhabitants coming from outside these two regions, which constitute only 15 per cent of the country's total area, is much smaller, with more from the Equateur region (4.1 per cent), which is linked to the capital city by the river and is favoured by the powers that be, and from the Kasai Occidental region (3.2 per cent), thanks to the dynamism of its Luba population (INS/UNDP, 1991). Therefore there is still a vast population pool from which the city can draw future migrants if the country maintains its present configuration.

The regions from which Kinshasa obtains its material supplies are more or less the same, including Bandundu, Bas-Zaire, and Equateur during the dry season. Freight is carried by dilapidated trucks, ancient whaling boats, small boats, and even bicycles for shorter distances. These are now complemented by small traders travelling on foot, called "*par colis*" ("by small parcel"), who use any means of transport available. They leave the city with manufactured items for sale or barter and come back laden with food products (Tillens, 1991). Kinshasa's supplies depend on the informal sector and on many small enterprises that have limited funds for investment. The same goes for Zairean food products, which are sold to the neighbouring city of Brazzaville by Zairean traders wishing to obtain CFA francs. Despite this lively trade, the food produced by peasants is not distributed properly. It is estimated that only half of the commercial food production from the Luozi area, though only 250 km away from Kinshasa and ideally situated near the Congo border (fig. 7.3), is actually sold (Mkwala-ma, 1991). The formal sector, though it may not actually deserve this name, more easily controls trade through the port of Matadi and Ndjili international airport.

The regions from which potential migrants look to Kinshasa are those where people speak Lingala (the language spoken along the river upstream of the city) and Kikongo (spoken in Bas-Zaire and Bandundu), the two "national" languages used in Kinshasa. On the other hand, regions using Tshiluba (Kasai) and Swahili (the east and south of the country), the other two national languages, do not send many migrants to the capital city. But Kinshasa's influence goes beyond this. Its role as a capital city is essential for President Mobutu, who has never forgotten the first secession of the rich Shaba province and has deliberately favoured the convergence on Kinshasa of all trade to the detriment of the economic development of the outlying areas. In this regard the most spectacular and absurd development was to make Shaba depend on power from the Kinshasa area. But Kinshasa is also a major cultural centre thanks to the attraction of bands from Matonge and the other neighbourhoods, who popularized rumba in the whole of Central Africa and thereby gave some measure of prestige to the Lingala language in neighbouring countries.

Conclusion: Whither Kinshasa?

Despite its number of inhabitants and recent growth rate, the question of the continuation of Kinshasa in the future arises. The crisis of the Zairean state is such that its very survival is in doubt, thus posing a crucial dilemma for a city whose expansion was based on that of the state.

The erosion of state power has made other collective bodies that have emerged through various initiatives more visible. Despite the total failure of periodic official attempts to mobilize labour for collective projects (called *salongo*), the state did not take kindly to any initiatives taken outside its authority. These were for a long time in practice the monopoly of the Catholic and Protestant churches, which set up structures often complementary to those of the state, whether colonial or post-colonial, and benefited from direct contacts with powerful Western charitable organizations. In the suburbs, parish authorities are still vital on all social fronts, including the health field. In the crisis situation, religious people have maintained a moral stature that has enabled some of them to play a major role even in the 1992 National Conference. But for some time now, other types of initiative have bloomed, of which the intervention of businessmen in local projects and the many private and local church-run universities are the most striking examples. Today in Zaire, the sum total of these isolated initiatives adds up to a dynamic city.

In this way competition is generated between "neglected" and "supported" towns. A few years ago only Mbuji-Mayi, the administrative capital of the Kasai Occidental region, was really "supported" by businessmen enriched by illegal trade in diamonds and united in their feeling of belonging to the Luba "nation." Since then this example has been taken up in various provincial towns by other regional or ethnic groups, including some of those residing in Kinshasa. What will then be the lot of Kinshasa now that the state, which was its mainstay, is bankrupt and external funds have all but dried up? Will the city of Kinshasa also be "supported" by its citizens? But how many Zaireans actually consider themselves to be "from Kinshasa"? It is true that habits and permanent features should be taken into account: new citizens establish themselves in the city by buying a plot. But the example of Brazzaville, with an agglomeration of peoples similar to that in Kinshasa and similar land practices, should be food for thought. During the urban conflicts of 1992/93 in the Congolese capital city, did we not see many evictions of plot owners whose identity was not to the taste of the local mafias? Thus, the Zairean urban network may still be subject to change. New cities could still be created and the relative size of the present urban centres could change.[8] In a country where vast tracts of land are unoccupied and where people mainly live in outlying areas far from the capital city, other big towns may develop and – why not? – turn into mega-cities. Will Kinshasa, when the crisis is over, resume a role commensurate with its size? In a country that has to be reconstructed (Piermay et al., 1991), is not a new pattern of urbanization in the making?

Notes

1. Still referred to as "Congo" on the northern bank, the river was renamed "Zaire" on the southern bank at the same time as the country itself, because of the ethnic connotation of the old name, derived from the "Kongo," a large group of people living on the Atlantic Coast.
2. Any town of more than 15,000 inhabitants is considered to be an urban area.
3. In 1986, 57 per cent of the total household budget was devoted to food (Houyoux et al., 1986).
4. These intermittent businesses (*entreprises conjoncturelles*) are linked to others. The networks of contacts lie dormant most of the time, but are activated when an order is placed (Delis et al., 1986).
5. Surveys carried out by the author in Kinshasa, Mbuji-Mayi, and Kisangani, Zaire; Bangui, Central African Republic; Brazzaville, Congo; and Libreville, Gabon.
6. The same goes for Brazzaville, on the other bank of the Congo/Zaire river, but not for other Central African cities.
7. Because of the civil war, which has divided the country, 15 per cent of Kinshasa's population in 1975 were Angolans. However, they appeared to comprise scarcely more than 2 per cent of foreigners in 1984; these data are very questionable.

8. Mbuji-Mayi, which was the third Zairean city in terms of population, is certainly the successor to the small mining centre of Bakwanga. But it acquired its present role when the Luba people returned to their land of origin between 1959 and 1962, increasing its population sevenfold in the course of this brief period. It has today become the second-largest city in the country in population terms.

References

Bayart, J.-F. 1979. *L'Etat au Cameroun*. Presses de la Fondation Nationale des Sciences Politiques, Paris.

Bulu Bobina, B. 1984. Le problème des terres cultivables en milieu rural. Cas de la Zone de Kasangulu. *Zaïre-Afrique* 189: 539–552.

Delis, Ph., C. Girard, and R. de Maximy. 1986. Une entreprise "buloki": Flair et conjoncture dans le BTP de Kinshasa. Colloque international "MTEC 86," Paris.

Girard, C. 1993. Costruzione e crasione fondiaria. *Storia Urbana* 63: 153–165.

Houyoux, J., N. Kinavwuidi, and O. Okita. 1986. *Budgets des ménages, Kinshasa, 1986*. Département du Plan-BEAU, Kinshasa.

INS/UNDP (Institut National de la Statistique and United Nations Development Programme). 1991. Zaïre: Un aperçu démographique. Résultats du recensement scientifique de la population en 1984. *Zaïre-Afrique* 255: 227–261.

MacGaffey, J., ed. 1991. *The Real Economy of Zaire*. James Currey, London.

Mbuyi, K. 1993. Problèmes de la gestion urbaine, de l'infrastructure et de l'approvisionnement en nourriture. In: R. Stren and R. R. White, eds., *Villes Africaines en Crise: Gérer la Croissance Urbaine au Sud du Sahara*. L'Harmattan, Paris (originally published in English in R. E. Stren and R. R. White, eds., *African Cities in Crisis: Managing Rapid Urban Growth*. Westview, Boulder, Colo., pp. 148–175).

Mkwala-ma, M. ye B. 1991. The trade in food crops, manufactured goods and mineral products in the frontier zone of Luozi, Lower-Zaire. In: J. MacGaffey, ed., *The Real Economy of Zaire*. James Currey, London, pp. 97–123.

Pain, M. 1984. *Kinshasa, la ville et la cité*. Editions de l'ORSTOM, Collection Mémoires 105, Paris.

Piermay, J.-L. 1993a. *Citadins et quête du sol dans les villes de l'Afrique centrale*. L'Harmattan, Paris.

———— 1993b. L'article 15, ou le Zaïre à la recherche d'articulations de rechange. *Travaux de l'Institut de Géographie de Reims* 83–84: 99–107.

Piermay, J. L. et al. 1991. Zaïre: Un pays à reconstruire. *Politique africaine* 41.

Republic of Zaire. 1984. *Combien sommes-nous? Recensement scientifique de la Population (1 juillet 1984), résultats provisoires*. Institut National de la Statistique, Secrétariat National du Recensement, Kinshasa.

Shoepf, B. G. 1991. Political economy, sex and cultural logics: A view from Zaire. *African Urban Quarterly* 6(1/2): 94–106.

Tillens, E. 1991. Nourrir Kinshasa. Une analyse du système d'approvisionnement en produits vivriers. Katholieke Universiteit Leuven, Centrum voor Landbouweconomisch Onderzoek Ontwikkelingslanden, Leuven (quoted by Willame, 1992, pp. 104–105).

Willame, J.-C. 1986. *Zaïre: L'épopé d'Inga. Chronique d'une prédation industrielle.* L'Harmattan, Collection Villes et Entreprises, Paris.

———— 1992. *L'automne d'un despotisme. Pouvoir, argent et obéissance dans le Zaïre des années quatre-vingt.* Karthala, Collection Les Afriques, Paris.

Young, C. 1965. *The Problems of the Congo: Decolonization and Independence.* Princeton University Press, Princeton, N.J.

8

Abidjan: From the public making of a modern city to urban management of a metropolis

Alain Dubresson

Abstract

Regroupant aujourd'hui plus de 2.5 millions d'habitants, la métropole abidjanaise a été précocement insérée dans la division internationale du travail. Ville-relais du système colonial, localisée en bordure de l'Océan Atlantique et bénéficiant d'un remarquable site portuaire, Abidjan doit son fulgurant essor démographique à la vigoureuse croissance économique impulsée, durant trente ans, par l'économie de plantation, le modèle agro-exportateur ivoirien et les investissements étrangers. L'édification d'un appareil d'Etat puissant et centralisé a renforcé en permanence le poids de la capitale économique, dont les industries et les services sont articulés au système-monde. Le projet urbain moderniste, indissociable des choix politiques fondamentaux de croissance dans la dépendance, confère à Abidjan une structure unique en Afrique de l'ouest. Le volontarisme public, la planification, la tentation de l'urbanisme intégral ont abouti à la mise en place de remarquables infrastructures de transport et d'un imposant dispositif de maîtrise du sol et de production de logement: à la veille de la récession économique le parc immobilier public regroupait plus de 22 pour cent des citadins. A cet "endroit" du modèle s'oppose cependant un "envers," constitué par les cours communes, forme d'habitat rassemblant toujours la majorité des Abidjanais.

252

Depuis le début des années 80, la crise du modèle agro-exportateur, la raréfaction des ressources financières de l'Etat, les impasses
des options urbanistiques et le ralentissement de l'élan démographique ont eu des conséquences considérables sur la dynamique de la
ville. Le temps n'est plus aux grands investissements publics mais à la
gestion privatisée des services, à la décentralisation et au développement local, nouveaux fétichismes maniés par la Banque Mondiale,
devenue le principal interlocuteur de l'Etat, et les organisations non-
gouvernementales. Des trois types d'acteurs principaux, l'Etat et les
sociétés concessionnaires de services publics, les 10 communes de
plein exercice, la "Ville d'Abidjan," entité supra-communale, c'est
cette dernière qui a été mise hors-jeu de la gestion urbaine. La
décentralisation a des aspects positifs, mais les pouvoirs municipaux
ne maîtrisent pas les mécanismes producteurs d'inégalités dans l'ensemble de la ville de sorte que, faute de poser clairement la question
des modes et des échelles d'arbitrage et de péréquation, et finalement
de la nature des pouvoirs, les écarts entre les communes les plus
riches et les plus défavorisées se sont accrus. Par son intérêt et surtout par ses limites, l'expérience abidjanaise montre que l'efficacité
du gouvernement de la ville pour le plus grand nombre des citadins
repose sur la nécessaire articulation entre la richesse des dispositifs
locaux et les ressources d'un système plus global d'encadrement.

Introduction

With probably more than 2.5 million inhabitants in 1994 (there were
1,934,000 at the 1988 census and the annual growth rate between
1984 and 1988 was 4.2 per cent), Abidjan is the second- or third-
largest West African city after Lagos, and perhaps Ibadan, and has all
the characteristics of a metropolis. The city hosts more than one-fifth
of Côte d'Ivoire's total population, who came in successive waves of
migration from every region of the country, as well as from neighbouring states. It is both an inheritance from the colonial past and an
economic centre, which has been dynamized by basic development
opportunities based on integration into the global market. These
opportunities, which have influenced both the settlement's dynamics
and the concentration of economic activities, have had a considerable
impact on the urban structure and organization. The circumstances
and the results are unique in West Africa.

Abidjan comprises at present 10 communes (districts) with a total area of 57,735 ha, of which 8,991 ha are lagoons (AUA, 1989), while 17,000 had been urbanized one way or another by 1988. Often referred to as "the pearl of the lagoons," Abidjan is the outcome of a modernist project financed by the vigorous economic growth of the 1960s and 1970s. Recession, a slower population growth rate in the 1980s and 1990s, the financial crisis of the state, which was the main investment player, and the dead end of a far too selective modernization process have changed the urban set-up. The time for large state spending is no more. It has given way to the privatization of services, meant to attract productive investments; to decentralization; and to local development – the latest fetishes of the World Bank and non-governmental organizations (NGOs). Does this mean that the providers of public and centralized services should cease from being necessary stakeholders; or that integrated planning and urban development, which offer some measure of equality and fairness, should be rejected because they cannot be the responsibility of local players and district authorities, particularly in the case of a metropolis?

The Abidjan conurbation

From colonial stopover to economic centre

Inherited from the colonial past: Early involvement in the international division of labour
To understand the Abidjan phenomenon, this gathering of people, investments, capital, and assets, it is necessary to recall, however briefly, its colonial past, because the emergence of this urban area is linked to the forging of a tool in the colonial system of exchange, as a means to subordinate the colonial periphery to the needs of the colonial power (Antoine et al., 1987). It derives from the search for a healthy site where Europeans could be safe from the yellow fever and malaria that decimated them, haunting the colonial administration and justifying a "hygienistic" urbanization pattern, which has had a durable imprint on the urban structure.

In 1934, when Abidjan, whose first housing estates dated back to 1903 and 1904, was promoted to be the capital city of the Côte d'Ivoire instead of Grand-Bassam and Bingerville, it was still a modest coastal town, with 17,000 inhabitants, fewer than in Bouaké. The transfer of the capital, decided in 1920, signified the triumph of the administration over the mercenary aspirations of the merchants. By concentrating political and economic leadership, Abidjan became the core from which "civilization" could shine and colonial development could be promoted.

The capital city's functions were clearly defined: it was the apex of the administration's pyramid, the stopover point from which tropical products were exported to France and manufactured goods imported, safe from the customs barriers set up by the empire. The choice of the site, therefore, was not only based on its salubriousness, but also proceeded from the search for the best site for emerging trade, enabling transhipment between the railways serving the interior and a deep-water harbour, which served as an axis for external relations (Rougerie, 1950). Having been systematically explored since 1897, the Abidjan "lagoon complex" (Haeringer, 1977; see fig. 8.1) was considered highly appropriate for the construction of a harbour, offering vast possibilities for development. A large lagoon of about 800 ha at Ebrie, west of the island of Petit-Bassam, and in some places as much as 10 m deep was protected from the breaking ocean rollers by a sandy offshore bar, so narrow it was easy to break through. Not far from the shore lies an ocean deep, called Trou-sans-Fond, into which the sands from the coastal drift could be swept, preventing the gradual blockage of the channel to be built between the lagoon and the ocean. In addition, it was desirable that the railway line should cross the southern forests by the shortest route and Abidjan was very well situated near the pre-forest savannah of the "V Baoulé," thus reducing the distance through the forest that the railway had to traverse to approximately 150 km.

The maritime area thus selected was bordered to the north by a 30 m high plateau of sedimentary rock, cut by deep bays, where most slopes and soils provided ample space for easy building, and where the colonial authorities had no problem forcibly resetting the indigenous rural Ebrie population.

The work on the railway line started in 1904, as well as the first excavations for the channel. But whereas the railway line progressed smoothly, reaching Dimbokro in 1910, Bouaké in 1912, Ferkessé-dougou in 1926, and Bobo-Dioulasso in 1934, the building of the first channel, badly sited, was a failure. By 1910 Abidjan was still without a harbour, and although a wharf was commissioned in 1927 at Port-Bouët, with a direct link to the railway station, the city did not enjoy a decisive advantage over its rival, Grand-Bassam. It was only in 1950, after the opening of the Vridi channel, that the work on the harbour could start. Abidjan was then dynamized by rapid colonial

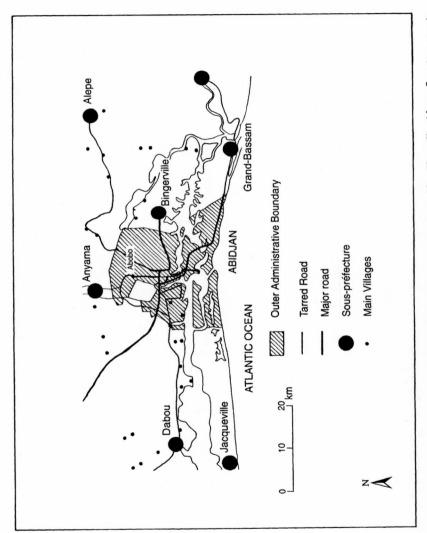

Fig. 8.1 The "lagoon" complex of Abidjan (Source: based on Aka Kouadio Akou, Les transports collectifs à Abidjan, Ph.D. dissertation, Université de Paris X Nanterre, Nanterre, 1989)

development, with the building of tracks and roads, the fast expansion of trade following exploitation of the forest, and, above all, village-level production of coffee and cocoa. The headquarters and warehouses of the big import–export firms were set up in the town, which, now linked by the railway line to Ouagadougou and with a vast road network converging towards the harbour, became the hub for foreign trade. Extensive urban development, the construction of the harbour and its activities, the cumulative impact of the growth of services, and the first factories set up with French capital contributed to create a wage sector that attracted a massive influx of local and foreign workers. By 1960, the population had increased 2.7-fold in 10 years and Abidjan, with 180,000 inhabitants, saw its built-up area progressing rapidly outside the old colonial town boundaries (fig. 8.2).

Abidjan: Accelerated dynamism-dependent growth
Abidjan's pre-eminent status and the modern urban project chosen for the town cannot be separated from the fundamental characteristics of the agricultural export model of the Côte d'Ivoire in the 1960s. By giving priority to increased involvement in the global market and export-oriented agriculture, and by opening up to overseas personnel and technicians as well as to foreign capital, while favouring state intervention, Abidjan's potential for production and services was strengthened. Thus in 1975 the city accounted for 40 per cent of the country's gross capital formation, 50 per cent of household consumption of finished products, 90 per cent of value added from so-called modern trade, 80 per cent of value added from the tertiary sector, and 67 per cent of value added from manufactures. All the surveys carried out at the end of the 1970s recorded a high level of urban economic activity (in 1978, 437,500 people, i.e. 59 per cent of the adult population, were employed, including 89 per cent of men and 36 per cent of women). The high proportion of workers in waged employment (60 per cent of the economically active population in 1978) was unique in Côte d'Ivoire. By 1984, when government was blaming the broader economic climate rather than domestic crisis for the country's poor economic performance, Abidjan's structure remained characterized predominantly by so-called "modern" activities, which accounted for 58 per cent of urban jobs. Public administration, services, and trade accounted for 67 per cent of wage-earning jobs and 74 per cent of wage income, whereas manufacturing and construction accounted for 32 per cent of formal employment. The pre-eminence of the tertiary sector and the relative importance

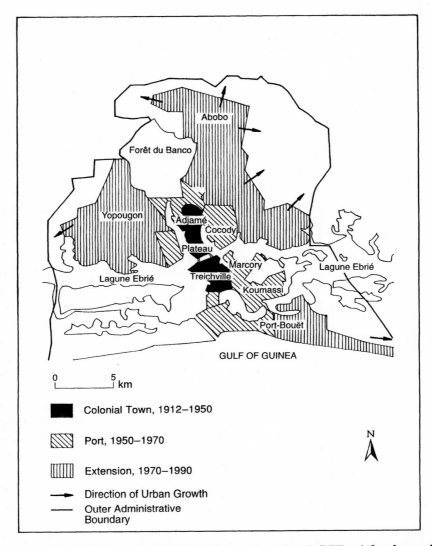

Fig. 8.2 **The spatial growth of Abidjan (Source: based on DCGTx, *Atlas des modes d'occupation des sols, état 1989*, AUA, Abidjan, 1992)**

of industrial establishments were due to the role given to Abidjan in the process of dependent growth (Fauré and Médard, 1982).

The first player in this process was the state. "What the Côte-d'Ivoire will not and should not experience, for its own good, is local capitalism. The only capitalism we must build is State capitalism," stated President Félix Houphouët-Boigny in his policy speech of 3

January 1961 at the National Assembly. At the time of independence, the state was thought to be the only local agent capable of immediate, large-scale, economic action to ensure the desired accelerated growth. Deliberate public intervention meant both a consolidation of government power and accumulation in part by or through the state, which organized the reception of foreign capital, was responsible for economic planning, and promoted the transfer of surpluses from agriculture to infrastructure and industry. The setting up of a powerful and centralized state apparatus permanently strengthened Abidjan's decision-making capacities, because ministries were still located there in 1995, while the transfer of the political and administrative functions of the capital city to Yamoussoukro in 1983 remains symbolic. The operations of an interventionist administration, as well as those of the banking system and public investment, were considerable driving forces (between 1970 and 1978 public investment made up 8–13 per cent of GDP). These, together with the centralization of decision-making powers, consolidated Abidjan's central position linked to its harbour and facilitated local and foreign investment in the city. Planned to serve as a focus for growth, the capital city has enjoyed enormous support from the state, which from 1970 to 1980 spent two-thirds of all public funds for local development (infrastructure) there (i.e. 547,000 million CFA francs[1] (1980), as against 205,000 million for the towns of the interior and 68,000 million for Yamoussoukro).

In his pursuit of "economic diplomacy" towards Europe and North America, President Félix Houphouët-Boigny used his charisma to help diversify the foreign partners of the newly born state. Up until 1967, the Caisse centrale de coopération économique (CCCE) and the United States Agency for International Development (USAID) were its two main financial partners in development activities, but from 1968 onwards the country obtained loans from Italy, Germany, and Canada, as well as assistance from the World Bank, the European Development Bank, and the African Development Bank. When economic growth was at its fastest, between 1973 and 1977, multinational banks became the Côte d'Ivoire's main partners, with external funds financing 60 per cent of public spending; integrated into the global economy, Abidjan was established as the focus for the transfer of international flows of finance.

The permanent consolidation of the city's infrastructure and facilities, the creation of new industrial–port areas, and the institution of a favourable tax environment (Investment Code and Tariff Code) stimulated private foreign investment. The continuous general economic growth (7 per cent per annum from 1960 to 1978) and the real though unequal redistribution of monetary resources in the country (household consumption increased by 3.79 per cent per annum from 1960 to 1978 while population grew at more than 4 per cent) guaranteed an exceptional degree of political and economic stability and were essential for foreign stakeholders. The spectacular expansion of coffee and cocoa plantations in the southern forests, the development of large government, parastatal, and private plantations in the north (for sugarcane production) and the south (for oil palm, hevea, and pineapple), and the expansion of cotton production in the Sudanese savannah produced raw materials for agro-industries, supported national demand for manufactures, and strengthened Abidjan's hold on the whole country.

Enhanced by remarkable efforts to provide the country with a communication infrastructure, this hold also derives from the city's enlarged food supply, because local agriculture is geared to feed it. Urbanization has not radically changed people's eating habits, or driven them to a Western lifestyle (Requier-Desjardins, 1985; Dubresson, 1989) and even members of the élite express their national identity by eating early yams. Local products such as cassava, yam, plantains, and rice have remained staple foods for urban dwellers, who have adopted new consumer products (beverages, milk, butter, stock cubes, vinegar) without abandoning their former diet. In 1988, urban consumption was 158,000 tons of rice, 27,500 tons of maize, 102,400 tons of cassava, 52,600 tons of yam, and 135,000 tons of plantain, all mainly brought in from distant districts outside the Abidjan region. This preservation of traditional diets has led to serious changes in the rural areas, where food crops became cash crops to supply the urban markets (Chaléard, 1994). Because of its size and cosmopolitan nature and the variety of cultural groups living there, Abidjan is the country's largest market, accounting for one-third of the national demand for food products coming from all over the country and further, from Burkina-Faso and Mali.

Despite the new port in San Pedro, it is Abidjan harbour (with an average turnover of 10 million tons) that handles 90 per cent of exports of agricultural products, whether raw materials or processed, and the imports of capital goods and inputs for manufactures and building (fig. 8.3). Foreign private capital, invested mainly in import–export trade and import substitution industries, is concentrated in Abidjan, whose industrial structure, based mainly on agro-industries, chemicals, and metal processing for final consumption, has been developing steadily since 1983. In that year, 24 countries were represented in Côte d'Ivoire's industrial capital stocks (France 19.9 per cent, Switzerland 3.5 per cent, Lebanon and the United Kingdom 2.3 per cent each, United States 1.7 per cent). There were only a few multinationals (Nestlé, Union Carbide, and oil companies), but whereas local private and state stakeholders were major owners of fixed assets, foreign capital controlled 41 per cent of production and more than 53 per cent of value added (Dubresson, 1989).

Through the cumulative growth of services, trade, and industry, in 1980 Abidjan accounted for approximately 50 per cent of the country's GDP and the per capita product was 682,000 CFA francs, 2.7 times higher than that of the country as a whole. Diversification of foreign capital, Abidjan's dominance over the whole country, and penetration of West African Economic Community markets have transformed Abidjan into an economic metropolis, as demonstrated by its stock exchange and the fact that 45 per cent of the built-up land is used for amenities or economic activities (fig. 8.3).

Crisis in the agricultural export model: A city in recession
Since the beginning of the 1980s, however, all the macroeconomic indicators have thrown doubt on the Côte d'Ivoire agricultural exports model. Income from the exports of coffee and cocoa, for which the country is, respectively, third and first world producer, has plummeted (293.5 million CFA francs in 1992 compared with 747 million in 1985), and total exports have decreased (728.6 million CFA francs in 1992 compared with 1,240.4 million in 1975), while GDP, which stagnated (in constant terms) for some time, has decreased continuously since 1987. According to the World Bank, the balance of payments deficit grew from US$73 million to US$1,614 million between 1970 and 1991 and total foreign debt stood at US$19,146 million in 1993, i.e. more than 224 per cent of the GNP. Although opening to the world enhanced Abidjan's growth, the city is now suffering from the full force of the crisis of the model on which Côte d'Ivoire's economy was based.

Subjected to structural adjustment, the state was forced to review its whole strategy (Contamin and Fauré, 1990; Fauré, 1992). The closing of 18 parastatals and the restructuring of public companies have led to the loss of some 11,000 jobs, many of them in Abidjan. Civil service recruitment has been frozen and, following the 1991

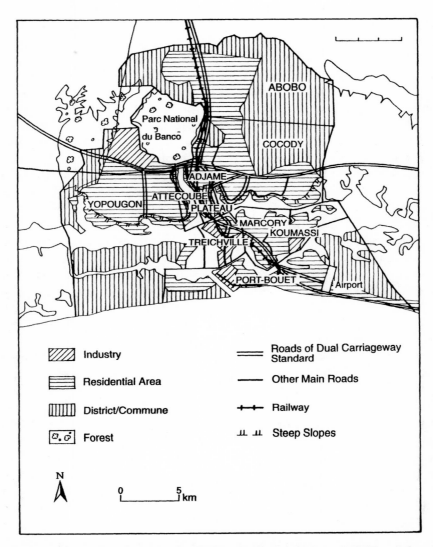

Fig. 8.3 **The urban structure of Abidjan (Source: based on DCGTx, *Atlas des modes d'occupation des sols, état 1989*, AUA, Abidjan, 1992)**

census of personnel, thousands of daily workers were retrenched. Further to the loss of jobs in the state and parastatal sector, building and public works have collapsed and industrial production has decreased; from 1983 to 1993, over 15,000 jobs were lost in manufacturing, more than half of them in Abidjan.

During these 10 years, the employment market was so transformed that, in contrast with previous prosperous times, it is the so-called "informal" sectors of crafts, services, and small-scale trade that have assumed a dominant role. Up to 1978, although the gap between Abidjan's annual population growth rate of more than 10 per cent on average and the creation of modern jobs at 7 per cent per year resulted in the existence of an economic sector to accommodate those excluded from modern wage earning, informal employment had remained a minority sector in the city. It accounted for 40 per cent of total jobs in 1978, according to the Enquête budget–consommation (EBC), of which 32 per cent were self-employed people and small business owners, 7 per cent apprentices, and 2 per cent domestic workers. In 1980, there were 383,000 jobs in the formal/modern sector and 330,000 in the informal sector (de Miras, 1982). By 1988, according to the census, the economic activity rate had gone down to 42 per cent (compared with 59 per cent in 1978) and 58 per cent of those jobs were in the informal sector, within which the proportion of self-employed had grown from 32 to 41 per cent in 10 years. All data confirm this increase in crafts and small trade: according to the Direction et contrôle des grands travaux (DCGTx), in 1988, small businesses, street markets, and house-to-house sales accounted for 63 per cent of employment.

Are such activities a solution to the crisis? There is no indication to that effect, rather the contrary. Most of the literature available (de Miras, 1982; Oudin, 1985; Lootvoet, 1988; Dubresson, 1989) shows that the dynamism of crafts and small-scale trade depends largely on demand from the wage sector. The financial survival of craftsmen and small business usually depends on wage earnings, even if their seed capital rarely comes from such earnings. Most workshops and small shops rarely make sufficient surplus to function beyond simple reproduction levels, without real accumulation. Besides, production is not as well represented as services and trade, and those producers who do make a surplus scarcely ever reinvest it in production to increase the value of their fixed assets. Small-scale trade obviously enables young people excluded from the formal sector to become apprentices and gives many women access to money income, but it would be an illusion to believe that the informal sector can efficiently replace the formal sector and promote an accumulation process sufficient for a city with more than 2.5 million inhabitants.

Table 8.1 **Population growth in Abidjan, 1955-1991**

Year	Population	Annual rate of growth (%)
1955	127,585[b]	7.1
1960[a]	180,000	11.1
1963[a]	246,650	12.1
1970[a]	550,000	11.6
1975	951,216	10.1
1978	1,269,071	5.9
1980[a]	1,422,000	3.8
1984[a]	1,653,000	3.9
1988	1,934,342[c]	5.7
1991[a]	2,280,385	

Sources: Le Pape et al. (1992); DCGTx for 1991.
a. Estimated.
b. Revised figure – M. Le Pape, Historiens d'Abidjan, *Chroniques du Sud* 10, 1993, pp. 6–15.
c. Revised figure produced by Statistical Office.

The development model in which extensive accumulation was based on plantations and state regulation of economic redistribution, of which Abidjan was such a dramatic example, has run its course. Once a formidable integrative machine, the "pearl of the lagoons" has today become a city of excluded people, with 15.7 per cent of its total economically active population and 22.4 per cent of its Ivoirian population unemployed in 1988.

From the focus of migration to decreasing population growth

Thirty years of rapid population growth
Abidjan had only 17,000 inhabitants in 1934 but witnessed a dramatic population growth after the Vridi channel was opened: 65,000 inhabitants in 1950, more than 125,000 in 1955, 950,000 in 1975, nearly 2 million in 1988 (table 8.1). From independence to the end of the 1980s, the annual rate of population growth remained at about 10 per cent and the city's population doubled approximately every seven years. As the natural population growth was little more than 3 per cent, the engine of growth came from migration: in 1978, only 35 per cent of the inhabitants had been born in the town, and these were mainly children; among the 15–59-year age groups only 1 in 10 had been born in Abidjan. Even in 1988, 59 per cent of residents had been born out of town.

Table 8.2 **The composition of Abidjan's population, 1955–1988**

Year	Ivoirians		Other Africans		Non-Africans	
	No.	%	No.	%	No.	%
1955	59,300	49.4	52,625	43.8	8,126	6.8
1975	560,659	58.9	365,307	38.4	25,250	2.7
1978	784,322	61.8	436,304	34.4	48,445	3.8
1988*a*	1,202,565	62.3	704,392	36.5	22,122	1.2

Sources: Le Pape et al. (1992); 1975 census (RGP) and Antoine et al. (1987); 1988 census (RGPH).
a. Breakdown not available for revised total given in table 8.1.

Migrants from all parts of the country, but also from other West African countries, outnumbered the indigenous Ebrie people, who comprised 37 per cent of the city's inhabitants in 1936, 7 per cent in 1955, and only 2 per cent in 1988. The relative importance of different migration streams from outside the country has long been very important. Up to the end of the 1930s, better-educated Senegalese and Dahomey citizens were employed as clerks, workers, and craftsmen, making up a middle-class élite. Migrants from Upper Volta and the Sudan (Mali) were employed on large colonial development projects and the influx increased during the 1950s. The people coming to Abidjan thus came from a vast catchment area, including neighbouring states such as Upper Volta, the Sudan (Mali), the Gold Coast (Ghana), and Guinea, as well as distant countries such as Nigeria. In 1955, 44 per cent of the total city population were Africans from outside the country, while locals were a minority (table 8.2).

Since the 1960s, the non-indigenous population has steadily decreased (41 per cent in 1975, 38 per cent in 1988; table 8.2), but it has left a durable impact on the city's urban and social history. The arrival of many non-Africans, mostly French and Lebanese (over 8,000 in 1955, more than 48,000 in 1978), with considerable purchasing power stimulated the high-cost land and property market, and the growing demand from African in-migrants spurred on the rapid development of rental accommodation, which in turn was the engine for the local small-scale private sector building industry. This was also stimulated by the massive influx of local people flocking to the capital city after independence. All the main cultural groups of the Côte d'Ivoire are represented in Abidjan, and the hierarchy dividing Akan, Krou, Northern Mandé, Southern Mandé, and so-called Vol-

Table 8.3   **The African population in Abidjan, 1955–1988 (% of total population)**

Cultural group	1955	1975	1988
Akan	27.2	29.6	29.2
Krou	10.4	13.0	12.4
North Mandé	6.0	7.4	10.2
South Mandé	4.0	4.4	4.8
Voltaic[a]	1.8	3.6	4.7
Other Ivoirians	0.0	0.9	0.9
Non-Ivoirian Africans	43.8	38.4	36.5

Source: Antoine et al. (1987) and RGPH, 1988.
a. Term describing groups from the north of Côte d'Ivoire.

taic groups has hardly changed since 1955 (table 8.3). These migrants, who came in through various family, village, or regional networks (Gibbal, 1974), originated mainly from other towns to which they had migrated or where they were born. They were extremely mobile: 272,000 people arrived in Abidjan in 1978/79, but 192,000 people left town. These regular movements represent one of the features of the intensive traffic of people and goods between the rural and urban areas of the country (Chaléard and Dubresson, 1989). As a result, city people's practices, lives, and beliefs always reflect their town and village background. For many migrants, Abidjan is more than just an employment market, it is the site for putting into practice strategies to maintain or subvert village order; a refuge to express independence, in particular for the ever-increasing number of women who head households; and a battleground for individuals or groups engaged in political conflicts originating in their respective regions. In this vast intermixing, every family, clan, or village is or has been linked to the capital city, from where recession is now affecting all national chains of relationships.

Slower growth and city life in crisis
The annual population growth rate, which averaged 10–12 per cent per annum between 1960 and 1978, fell in the 1980s to 4–6 per cent per annum (table 8.1). Abidjan's population growth rate is now lower than that in middle-sized towns; the foreign non-African population is smaller than in 1975 (22,122 in 1988, 25,250 in 1975) but incorporating an underestimation of the number of Lebanese, whose actual number is unknown; and migration has slowed. The last phenomenon

can be attributed to the decline of the formal waged sector, which has exacerbated labour market segmentation, increased competition for the few remaining jobs, and upset the social pyramid by generating downward socio-economic mobility.

In order to remain in the city during the recession, people must first be able to demonstrate their capacity to live there, which is possible for those who are "aligned" with a job but whose restricted buying power has led them to adopt crisis management practices, thus generating spatial mobility. These practices are meant to increase money income while decreasing domestic expenses. Income is generated by subletting parts of houses, by supplementary activities in crafts and small-scale trade, and by renegotiating marriage contracts to reallocate incomes from husbands' and wives' work to prevent a downgrading of households, particularly in relation to schooling. Decreases in domestic expenses are accomplished by changing residence, and sometimes the type of accommodation, with many locals moving to temporary housing quarters, sometimes to communal types of houses built from wood, where rents are lower. Economies are also achieved by decreasing the size of households, with children being sent back to attend primary school in the villages from which families had come, or even sent to secondary schools in other towns where it is less costly; by "inviting" relatives to go out to work or find alternative accommodation; and by sending wives, small children, or other inactive household members back to their villages of origin. These population transfers, as illustrated in the literature (Faussey-Domalain and Vimard, 1991), are dependent on the wage-earners' ages and their status in the extended family, both of which influence the scope for decreasing the size of a household (Vidal and Le Pape, 1986).

Those who lose a paid job have to move into something new or leave the city. However, there is nothing to prove that the majority of indigenous people actually return to their original villages, because the land question has become more and more controversial and the state-engineered programmes to send young school drop-outs back to the land have yielded only poor results (Affou Yapi, 1990). It appeared from the 1988 census that towns with 20,000–40,000 inhabitants were growing rapidly, and small urban centres kept on growing through the 1980s. Thus a new urban configuration is appearing, with small and medium-sized towns welcoming back "locals" and others excluded from the Abidjan employment market, as will perhaps be confirmed by the 1993 migration study, whose results were still not known in 1995. Many foreigners are leaving, in particular those from Burkina-Faso who were adversely affected by the disappearance of large public projects and the decrease in domestic workers' positions owing to the departure of European expatriates. Abidjan's fertility rate has remained rather high (6.41 in 1980/81 according to the Enquête ivoirienne de fécondité and 4.74 in 1988 according to the census), but population growth rates are no longer supplemented by massive arrivals, so that the city is not growing at the rate envisaged by its planning authorities in the 1970s. In 1992 it was estimated that, at constant rates of fertility and migration, Abidjan should have 3.3 million inhabitants in 2003, 5.9 million in 2018, and 8.9 million in 2028 (INS, 1992).

An unequal society marked by reductions in people's status

In 1987, 37 per cent of Abidjan households earned 80 per cent of total income and 40 per cent of African households earned less than 7 per cent of money incomes (see also table 8.4). Upward social mobility, legitimized only through political capacity bestowed by the President (Cohen, 1974), gave the city a unique status until 1980. The "high and mighty" in the President's entourage, senior executives, and those who distinguished themselves by their professional excellence, their dominant position, and their integration in the ruling classes had for a long time conferred a privileged status on the city, the focus of investment and accumulation, before fighting each other at the regional level following decentralization (Jaglin and Dubresson, 1993). Belonging to the powers that be, achieving élite status, and becoming a member of the ruling class could then be achieved only in Abidjan, where the élite's inherited practices, style of life, knowledge, and contacts (Vidal, 1991) facilitated an "eruption of investments of distinction" (Le Pape et al., 1992, p. 8). However, the dwindling of financial resources exacerbated struggles for state funds, monopolized until then by the powerful. The opening up of a new political scene by the decentralization reforms changed the élite's renewal processes. Still, whether in Abidjan or in other urban areas, the powerful have, in the final analysis, maintained or even increased their social distance not only from the poor but also from the middle classes, who have been the main victims of social downgrading.

White-collar workers and technicians in the state sector, the parastatals, industry, and what is generally called the modern tertiary

Table 8.4 **Household income distribution in Abidjan, 1963–1988 (current CFA francs except 1963)**

	1963 SEMA (in 1977 CFA francs)		1978 EBC pre-survey[a]		1985 USAID survey		1988 DCGTx household survey	
	Monthly income categories ('000)	% of households	Monthly income categories ('000)	% of households	Monthly income categories ('000)	% of households	Monthly income categories ('000)	% of households
	0–20	12.8	0–20	7.4	0–35	3.0	0–40	16.2
	20–50	48.8	20–50	42.3	35–100	41.9	40–80	36.5
	50–100	26.8	50–100	31.4	100–200	31.5	80–160	28.2
	100–200	10.4	100–200	14.7	200–500	18.0	160–250	9.3
	>200	1.3	>200	4.2	>500	5.6	250–500	5.7
							>500	4.1
Average household income (CFA francs)	54,500		69,300		177,800		125,800	
Median household income (CFA francs)	42,000		48,500		108,500		78,400	
Minimum wage (CFA francs/month)			24.912		33.274[b]		33.274[b]	
Consumer price index for African households in Abidjan (1960 = 100)	110.6		347.4		610.3		770.4	

Source: DCGTx, 1989.

a. African population only.
b. Since 1982 for 173.3 hours/month.

sector, as well as the upper fringe of commerce and crafts – the "middle classes" – are a non-homogeneous stratum that is difficult to quantify. In 1978, qualified wage-earners in the tertiary sector, African entrepreneurs, and "modern" businessmen accounted for 11 per cent of the total population. With all qualified wage-earners, the "middle classes" accounted for 50,600 households, or 345,000 people, i.e. 27 per cent of Abidjan's population (Manou-Savina et al., 1985). If their class characteristics (petty bourgeoisie?) may be questioned, their urban practices testify to the existence of a group that could be assimilated neither in the state bourgeoisie nor in the popular masses and whose elements endeavoured to assure, defend, or legitimize their position in the city, in particular their access to subsidized public housing. These dwellings, officially meant for economically deprived people, were taken over by the middle classes, who also benefited from the state's policy on administrative leases, land, and credit concessions.

This dependent relationship, based on the transfer of capital to a minority, was destroyed by the state's financial crisis. The urban economic foundation upon which the middle classes had depended for their accumulation strategy slowly disintegrated. Social downgrading prevails as much in the subsidized public housing that is now up for sale as in the communal courtyard quarters. Obviously, not everyone has been affected in the same way. Middle or big businesses have benefited from the enlarged market created by supplying the city with food products from the whole country (Chaléard, 1994). Civil servants and technical personnel who have kept their jobs and have been able to buy state houses or gain access to urban land outside the official market keep up their building endeavours and offer for rent new types of partially or totally individualized housing (Soumahoro, 1993). Nevertheless, social decline has affected most groups at "the top of the bottom" and "the bottom of the top," as people refer to the middle class. Their conditions of life continue to be uncertain and their mutual help mechanisms, however strong they may have been (Vidal, 1992), are unable to cushion the crisis. Although some trends that existed previously have been maintained even during the recession, i.e. the increasing importance of women, a strong feeling of belonging to the city, and the maintenance of active relations between Abidjan and the rest of the world, within and outside the country (Le Pape, 1992), there is now a real crisis in the political–economic mechanism of urban integration, and pauperization affects a large number of urban dwellers (table 8.4 and Marie, 1995).

From integrated town planning to district management

The modern city project

Attempting integrated town planning (Haeringer, 1985): The "right" side of town

At the time of independence, the new government had to take up the challenge of the quantity and quality of inherited structures, which were not suited to developments that, according to its statements, were supposed to address the needs of all social strata. It then adopted a resolutely modern project with the aim of eradicating all the "slums" (illegal shanties and insalubrious courtyard houses) within 10 years and building a city for all nationals of the Côte d'Ivoire. The town planning policy thus initiated was an integral part of the development strategy, with its theme of modernization, which was systematically propagated by all government officers, the President himself advocating a bold social policy. Therefore, the liberal choice made at independence was not to be equated with laissez-faire; it was backed by voluntaristic action to control the whole city building process.

In contrast with towns ruled by local chiefs, the building of Abidjan city was driven by planning goals that had been a constant feature of all governments' urban policies since 1926, when the first town development plan was mooted. Successive plans since independence – SETAP Plan, 1960; AURA Development Plan, 1969; 1/50,000 Structural Diagram, 1967; Town Master Plan, 1972; Town Development Plans since 1976 – have permitted control over the distribution of main activities along the industrial–harbour axis; assisted the provision of infrastructure, in particular a noteworthy inter-urban road network; and defined those housing developments initiated by the state.

Indeed, government ensured total control over land (Ley, 1972) by appropriating all so-called vacant land, a process fraught with problems owing to customary land rights which had to be cancelled after violent clashes with the Ebrie people, who finally obtained compensation in cash and plots for the land they had lost (Yapi Diahou, 1981). This state land was then subdivided into plots, developed for building, and transferred either through grants or as private property, depending on the wishes and means of the recipients.

The state made property rights dependent on proper standards of development so as to control, at least in theory, where and how the city would expand and also to have an impressive means of promoting so-called "modern" housing at its disposal. Modernization could be understood only with reference to a scale of values: at the bottom were those houses surrounding a courtyard, where several households shared a plot, a bathroom, and a kitchen; at the top were spacious houses with gardens, tokens of social success. State intervention came in between. The public sector was to build suitably serviced government houses as a first step towards modernization, as well as a way to ensure social stability by redistributing, through this subsidized housing, some of the fruit of the country's growth.

Between 1960 and 1975, the government set up an impressive machine that benefited Abidjan first and foremost: a subsidized public housing building mechanism, by means of a state company (Société de gestion et de financement de l'habitat – SOGEFIHA, 1963) and a parastatal company (Société ivoirienne de construction et de gestion immobilière – SICOGI, 1959); a financing mechanism, first with the Office de soutien à l'habitat économique (OSHE, 1968), a state department under the Ministry of Finance to manage budget allocations, then with the Banque nationale d'épargne et de crédit (BNEC), a state company created in 1975 and which merged with the OSHE in 1977, responsible for the management of a Housing Fund; and an urban development mechanism – the Société d'équipement des terrains urbains (SETU), which is a state company responsible for the provision of roads and other infrastructure to land allocated for low-cost housing projects (table 8.5).

At the same time, existing districts with state housing estates built before independence or with unbuilt areas were renovated. Land was gradually divided into plots with roads and sometimes other infrastructure, or re-structured by brutally removing squatters and destroying their shacks. Basic housing estates on the outskirts of the city were built in compensation and to alleviate the conflicts that followed the bulldozing of some 20 per cent of existing houses between 1969 and 1973. The basic and supposedly provisional and temporary nature of these areas showed that in Abidjan, in contrast to other towns, they were not meant to ensure modernization, which, until 1971, was to be based on subsidized public housing.

Considerable efforts were made. In 1963, housing societies controlled some 6,000 housing units, in which 10 per cent of households lived. In 1971, government housing accounted for some 12,000 units,

Table 8.5 Occupancy by type of housing in Abidjan, 1963–1988

Type of housing	1963 Population ('000)	%	1973 Population ('000)	%	1977 Population ('000)	%	1979 Population ('000)	%	1988 Population ('000)	%
High-income private housing	15.3	5.9	51.9	6.5	85.9	7.5	116.8	8.4	89.1	4.2
Subsidized public housing	42.3	16.4	161.4	20.5	249.7	21.7	307.8	22.1	499.4	23.8
Communal courtyards	163.7	63.3	414.0	52.5	641.3	55.7	757.3	54.3	1,226.3	58.4
Spontaneous shacks	37.3	14.4	161.7	20.5	174.5	15.1	211.8	15.2	285.3	13.6
Total	258.6	100.0	789.0	100.0	1,151.4	100.0	1,393.7	100.0	2,100.1	100.0

Source: Ph. A. B. Zanou, Projet d'étude sur l'insertion en milieu urbain de Côte d'Ivoire, Abidjan, Centre ORSTOM de Petit-Bassam, *Bulletin du GIDIS* 8: 19–35.

273

housing 20 per cent of the population; between 1971 and 1977, 5,000 housing units were built per year and by 1979, when the recession started, more than 22 per cent of urban dwellers lived in subsidized public housing. Budget allocations were witness to this state commitment: from 1973 to 1977, 46 per cent of investment in the building of housing went to state housing, and 60 per cent of the cost of low-cost housing was subsidized. However, the creation of SETU at the beginning of the 1970s indicated that ready-made housing was no longer seen as the only solution. By then, an intensive land policy aimed at making building land available complemented the house-building programme: from 1974 to 1981, the SETU developed 1,545 ha and 11,000 building plots.

Despite these vast programmes, which gave the city a structure and features unique in West Africa (apart from new cities such as Yamoussoukro and Abuja), by 1985 this public sector urban model could house only one-fifth of the city's inhabitants and in 1988 58.4 per cent of Abidjan residents still lived around communal courtyards, legally or otherwise. Spatial growth was indeed brought under control and illegal housing, permanent or temporary, occupied only 932 ha, compared with 6,600 ha of legal housing, in 1984, i.e. 12 per cent of the built-up residential area (23 per cent in 1963). In 1988, so-called modern housing (private houses and blocks of flats) occupied 47 per cent of residential land. However, access of the masses to modern housing was still a problem and not only because of the discrepancy between state funds for housing and the massive influx of migrants.

A city of tenants living around courtyards: The reverse of the modern model

By facilitating middle-class access to modern housing and urban land, by enabling them to get rich from rents, legally or illegally, the state redistribution practices led to a diversion of social housing. A detailed analysis of its distribution made during the first 10 years after independence shows how the ruling classes acquired a new urban political base by making the middle classes their clients, and how the adoption of sophisticated and costly building standards contributed to the exclusion of self-employed workers, craftsmen, and small traders, so that the official model could meet the demands of only a privileged few.

A city of tenants, with only 15 per cent of household heads owning their accommodation in 1985 and 19 per cent in 1988, Abidjan has remained a city of courtyards. This type of housing results from three forms of land acquisition: a legal one by the purchase of a plot from the authorities, and two illegal ones – buying a plot in an estate developed by a customary landowner or settling on insalubrious *non œdificandi* land or vacant land reserved for other uses in the urban plan. Legal courtyard dwellings were set up by the authorities prior to independence. Some are parts of reception areas created after 1960 and others belong to old unsubdivided or illegally subdivided districts that were later redeveloped. Legally or illegally, land is often rapidly occupied and dwellings are constructed with minimum investment – simple dirt tracks and basic plot demarcation without any services, giving rise to discontinuities in the urban fabric.

A courtyard is a differentiated space with a built-up part, using permanent materials or wood, comprising living quarters and out-buildings (bathroom, kitchen), and an open part, the actual courtyard, usually in the middle of the plot. Each house is composed of adjacent rooms of approximately 10 m², each living unit comprising one room (bed-sitter), two rooms (bedroom and sitting room), or, most rarely, three rooms. Kitchens are small cubbyholes, while bathrooms are used collectively by all residents. Some plots include craft workshops or small traders' shops and the open courtyard serves as a meeting place, a playground for children, and a space for domestic chores. Built without state help, mainly for rent, most of the courtyards accommodate several families and various ethnic groups, enabling the mixing of the city's population and cultures. They are structured on the basis of a rental strategy.

Most of the courtyard buildings, whether legal or illegal, are permanent structures (40 per cent of the residential area in 1988). Most are built of cement breeze-blocks with corrugated iron roofs, though scarcely ever by the occupier and his family. The owner is not the builder either; building is usually entrusted to pieceworkers, artisans who negotiate their conditions of work and their payment with the plot owner. Big businessmen, many civil servants, and other private landlords are able to ensure a fast and continuous building process, with highly variable completion periods. In the illegal areas that have not yet been divided into plots, and where some isolated permanent or "banco" (clay) structures can be spotted, most of the dwellings are built of wood, with roofs of salvaged corrugated iron, plant material, plastic sheeting, or cardboard. During the 1980s, craftsmen started producing prefabricated panels ("cut and nail") for rapid assembly. These so-called "spontaneous" dwellings, inherently temporary and illegal, housed 14 per cent of the total population in 1963, 21 per cent in 1973, and 14 per cent in 1988. They were restricted and even partly destroyed, but their area increased between 1984 and 1987, from 750 to 1,053 ha (+41 per cent), and in 1990 the AUA counted 68 such areas in all the city's districts, except the Plateau (Yapi Diahou, 1994; see fig. 8.3).

The concept of building, of permanent or wooden structures, goes hand in hand with letting, so that owners try to build as much as possible to increase their rental income. Buildings therefore progress horizontally, plots becoming ever more densely occupied and some courtyards reduced to a corridor, then vertically, an additional floor being added on one side, while the courtyard is maintained. High-density housing and high-density population are interlinked and gross density in some central districts reaches as much as 500 inh/ha, with maximums of 700 in non-subdivided areas. Overcrowding and lack of privacy are the main features of the courtyard dwellings, as well as a general lack of services. Some old central areas have a few streets, some of them surfaced, a partial drainage system with open gutters, as well as water and electricity in most streets. The plot may be connected to services without the dwellings being directly connected: often a tap in the courtyard is used by all the tenants. Alternatively, in the absence of a distribution network, water has to be bought from official or unofficial sources. Areas subdivided into plots during the 1960s have no sewerage system and suffer from severely deficient infrastructure: 1 shower for 20 residents in Abobo-gare, 1 toilet for 20 residents in Attécoubé in 1985 (Antoine et al., 1987). In most cases, sewerage is individual: cesspools or septic tanks, which are emptied more or less regularly. This increases the risk of epidemics in these temporary dwellings, which are ignored by public services and where infant and child mortality rates are sometimes higher than in the rural areas.

Whether legal or illegal, courtyard dwellings do not satisfy modern standards as defined by the authorities, even if permanent concrete block buildings provide a measure of modernization and actual slums house only 14 per cent of the population. But the replacement of courtyard housing with well-serviced individual houses, which should have been the second step on the way to modernization, never happened, though some new forms of courtyard dwellings have appeared, with adjacent individualized dwellings (Soumahoro, 1993).

The problem of maintaining the courtyards is all the more crucial because changes in urban policies, with the state abandoning house-building in favour of improving services and management, have placed courtyards at the heart of recent projects supported by the World Bank since 1981.

Changes in the 1980s: Time for "urban management"

Since the beginning of the 1980s, the dramatic drying up of state funds has generated a change in urban planning. As early as 1975–1979, warning signs of today's problems led to the gradual end of social housing programmes. The principle of free housing for some civil servants was reconsidered, while the closing down of state companies, the review of higher civil servants' salaries, and the higher cost of credit aggravated the impact of recession. Many more social categories are therefore affected by problems of housing (including land tenure, housing proper, and services) and modernization, with the lower middle class relegated to the level of the excluded masses. The state, while addressing the exclusion of the most downtrodden, must also consider the problems faced by its clients, former beneficiaries of modernist policies. The changes in its urbanization policy therefore also derive from internal pressures, which may endanger in the long term the stability of a regime anxious to preserve its alliance with the urban middle classes who have been affected by the crisis.

However, it would be wrong to attribute policy changes to recession only. Some actions were taken before state funds started dwindling, in particular the administrative reform that gave new power to local authorities as the main managers of the cities. The law on district (commune) administration, passed in 1980, was first conceived at the end of the 1970s, when coffee and cocoa revenues were still high. Contrary to most decentralization processes in Africa, which appear to have followed the economic crisis, Côte d'Ivoire's reforms came earlier. As a local reaction to internal tensions, decentralization created opportunities for popular politics (Labazée, 1993), and offered positions to senior civil servants who could no longer be accommodated in the overstaffed central administration. In the same way as other democratization measures, decentralization seems to have proceeded from a renewal of the apparatus for socio-political regulation.

Changes also resulted from external pressure, such as World Bank recommendations in the field of urban development, within the general framework of structural adjustment policies that were adopted by the bankrupt state to solicit financial assistance. The World Bank, which appeared on the Côte d'Ivoire scene in 1974, has repeatedly criticized the government housing and subdivision policies, in particular the high standards for services and their impact on costs, as well as the terms and conditions of allocating and financing plots and houses, which had already been argued against by the French aid agency in order to justify withdrawing funds for low-cost housing. The various city development plans, which have increased functional and social segregation, are considered to have worsened transport problems and deepened the inequalities between central and peripheral areas, while grandiose prestige projects are also denounced. The World Bank's "recommendations" are based on the following principles: enabling low-income population groups to gain access to ownership; easing building standards and improving the land tenure system; co-opting private enterprises by entrusting them with house-building; ending the demolition of existing private dwellings; engaging non-citizens in housing projects; obtaining payment from the beneficiaries through proper pricing policies and using the resources available from local taxes; and, finally, prioritizing needs, starting by providing sanitation and a clean water supply in the most deprived districts.

Following protracted and difficult negotiations, the World Bank finally managed to impose its views. The mainstays of state intervention – BNEC, BCET, SOGEFIHA, and SETU – have disappeared; state housing has been sold and the government is putting pressure on the SICOGI for it to adopt a similar privatization policy. Great efforts are being made to facilitate the access of tenants to ownership. Flats and houses belonging to the SOGEFIHA, which was wound up in 1986, were sold either by SOGEFIHA-liquidation (in the case of houses bought on instalments) or by the Direction des ventes immobilières (DVI) of the DCGTx (for individual rented dwellings) at prices discounted by 48 per cent compared with market prices. Those who were renting or buying on instalments and who could pay cash when the sale offer was made got an additional 25 per cent discount; those who undertook to pay within two years obtained a 10–15 per cent rebate. The SICOGI offered its tenants an average reduction of 44 per cent on market prices and set up a case-by-case system of instalment purchase, sometimes over more than 10 years, based on amounts negotiated so that buyers would not need bank loans, on which interest rates are very high.

This process benefited higher-income tenants who had been clients of the former system and lived in, or more often sublet, rented houses: by increasing their real property they have consolidated their social status. In contrast, low wage-earners found it more difficult to respond and most of them today are among the 25 or 30 per cent of people who have "reserved" housing but who cannot pay, or have difficulty in paying, their instalments. The situation is even worse for those tenants whose salaries have been cut or who have lost their jobs because of the crisis. The former cannot purchase their dwellings and often offer them for sale, before expulsion orders arrive, to wealthier people who may have been former absentee tenants building up their real estate property thanks to privatization. This kind of parallel so-called "amicable" settlement goes against the official social nature of the sales operations, but it benefits all concerned, as was indicated in the country's main daily newspaper:

the real estate agency which gets the real sales price of the dwelling, the former tenant who obtains money from a buyer for a house he did not build himself and the latter who now owns a house which was not meant for him and which he will never occupy. (*Fraternité-matin*, 22 November 1992, p. 11)

The unemployed are in a very difficult position and, although some have formed associations that enjoy special treatment (easy long-term payment conditions based on their unemployment benefits), most of them did not manage to keep their accommodation after unemployment benefits were cut from 75,000 to 50,000 CFA francs in 1992. Generally, only those whose payments were not up to date at the time of the sales offer have been officially evicted, while the SOGEFIHA-liquidation as well as the DVI have been rather flexible, in particular with subtenants and illegal tenants, to whom they sometimes offered accommodation. However, a measure of social discrimination actually favoured the best-off categories.

Development of building land has been entrusted to the DCGTx, a strong agency created in 1978 and attached to the President's Office in 1981, and the main instrument for the implementation of government policies. The Atelier d'urbanisme d'Abidjan (AUA) was integrated with it in 1985 and since 1987 the DVI has functioned as an implementing agency, distributing plots in accordance with the Third Urban Development Project (UDP3). Finally, the World Bank has become the state's main partner. It financed 41.4 per cent of UDP3 (1987–1992), while USAID financed 2.8 per cent, the state 20.5 per cent, the beneficiaries 34.8 per cent, and private international players 0.5 per cent. Urban management has replaced house construction and even public investment in the dominant discourse as well as in practice.

What does "governance" mean?

Stratification of powers: How the city was thrown out of the game
Abidjan comes under the jurisdiction of three types of actor: the state
and its public service agencies; the "city of Abidjan," an intermediate
body above the districts; and the 10 district (commune) authorities
created in 1978 (fig. 8.3). Good governance, the international donors'
latest creed for improving urban productivity and thus ensuring the
city's efficiency (Venard, 1993), entails a search for complementarities between actors, their scope for action, and their fields of jurisdiction. However, the state and its centralized public service agencies
have retained their main powers, while the city's power has been
reduced to what the district authorities are willing to tolerate (Attahi,
1989, 1991). The City Council comprises the mayor, elected from
amongst the mayors of the 10 districts, these 10 mayors, and 50
councillors (5 per district) elected by the district councils from
amongst their members. Understandably, local representatives are
fiercely protective of the powers of their districts, which they want to
shield from possible interference by the city, whose jurisdiction is
indeed not very important in terms of existing regulations. Actually,
apart from refuse collection and street lighting, practically no basic
services (water, power, sanitation, transport) are the city's responsibility and it is unable to coordinate sectoral actions by government
ministries and concessionary agencies. Thus, most important services
are still managed by central agencies, while districts try to promote
local development by levying taxes as authorized by the legislation on
decentralization.

New approaches to land management to recover costs
As a first component of the UDP3 on housing, 750 ha were to be
developed with 18,500 plots for a unit cost of 640,000 CFA francs
(1986), i.e. 16 per cent of the estimated demand for 1987–1992. Four
types of plots were to be developed: those with basic sanitation (250
m^2, clean water from a supply point, no electricity) for households
with incomes of less than 70,000 CFA francs; plots for households
with incomes of 70,000–100,000 CFA francs (as above, plus electricity); plots for households with incomes of 100,000–180,000 CFA
francs (300 m^2, lined stormwater drains, underground links to the
water and electricity network); and plots for households with incomes
of more than 180,000 CFA francs (450 and 600 m^2 plots, surfaced
streets, sewage disposal). The two districts where these developments

were to take place were Abobo and Cocody, thus confirming the long-planned social stratification of Abidjan. Applicants were selected according to their means, while an internal balancing mechanism was intended to ensure that those who bought high-quality plots partly financed the poorly serviced plots for the low-income groups. As far as building is concerned, the better-off buyers were to obtain credit from formal sector housing finance institutions (CAA/CDMH), while the others were permitted to build their own dwellings. By 1992, low-income plots had not yet been developed and, in the final analysis, these "ready to occupy" plot operations have once more benefited the middle classes (Yapi Diahou, 1994), the Norwegian–Ivoirian privately owned joint venture company, semi-private companies (SICOGI, GFCI), as well as the savings associations and small owners who control more than 10,000 new dwellings. Private players have indeed replaced the state, but the clients are the same – low-income population groups are still excluded from the modernization process.

The renovation of courtyard districts: Profiting the owners
Renovation – advocated by the World Bank but argued against by the country's rulers, who refused the proposed lowering of standards for a long time, and resisted by many small private owners worried about their rental income – started only in 1981, although the idea had already been included in the first UDP adopted in 1976. Full servicing of existing districts (with clean water, electricity, sanitation), new road networks, collective services, and land regularization affected only the legally recognized districts, whereas temporary settlements were left out. In Abobo, Adjamé-Fraternité, Bromakoté, and Port-Bouët II, the first developments financed with World Bank assistance (60 per cent of primary networks) and USAID help (30 per cent of secondary networks) have clearly improved the level of services but the networks thus set up are often underutilized, because many owners are discouraged by the technical option (individual connections) and its cost. Further, most of the residents were tenants, who had to suffer rent increases as owners passed on the cost of connections and operations once the plots were linked to the networks. Thus many tenants were forced to leave, but absentee landlords came to settle, taking advantage of land regularization which gave them permanent tenure. At the end of the day, the main beneficiaries of this renovation were the owners, a minority who mostly collect rents (Manou-Savina, 1986).

Services management: Time for privatization

The donors' management beliefs are often accompanied by some reservations as to the value of large-scale investments. However, the transport plan in the first UDP advocated the improvement of the already well-developed urban road network (improvements of streets, completion of the highway between Cocody and the Banco plateau, a traffic plan for the Plateau; fig. 8.3). Similarly the 1975–1978 urban water and sanitation plan (2.5 million CFA francs) financed by the Fonds national d'assainissement (40 per cent) and the World Bank (60 per cent) has enabled the installation of the first stage of a substantial sanitation network (including the main sewer from Abobo to the Cocody bay) and a special sanitation programme (1977–1982, 10 million CFA francs) to improve drainage on the Petit-Bassam island by building a canal at Koumassi. Nevertheless, the lagoon waters are heavily polluted by chemical and organic materials, and are threatened with eutrophication (de-oxygenization) (Guiral, 1984). Above all, it is the privatization of marketed services to which attention is drawn. This is nothing new, as clean water distribution was entrusted to a private company, the Société de distribution d'eau de la Côte d'Ivoire (SODECI), as far back as independence through a concessionary contract. SODECI's share capital belonged in part to the Société pour l'aménagement urbain et rural (SAUR, Bouygues group, 46 per cent shares) and in part to some 900 local shareholders (45 per cent), the remainder belonging to the Fonds commun de placement (5 per cent), the state (3 per cent), and private French shareholders (1 per cent). Supplied through a network of boreholes mainly located to the north of the lagoon to exploit the edge of the Continental groundwater layer (Saint-Vil, 1983), 86 per cent of households have access to clean water according to the 1988 census (by direct connection to dwellings, taps on plots, or nearby private water supply points), while others supply themselves from wells and/or from itinerant or sedentary sellers. Water management has remained centralized (in 1988, 65 per cent of the SODECI's turnover came from Abidjan) with the government determining tariffs (for households and industrial users) upon submission by the SODECI, whose jurisdiction goes from supply to billing.

In 1990, the Compagnie ivoirienne d'électricité (a subsidiary of SAUR-Afrique, 65 per cent, and EDF International, 35 per cent) obtained a 15-year concessionary contract for the management of the power network (electricity production, supply, and distribution, and management of assets), while the infrastructure still belonged to the

EECI, a parastatal company that was until then the sole actor, but from then on dealt only with investments for renovation and expansion. Supplied by the power station of Vridi, which is intended to use gas from deposits off the shores of Jacqueville when they are exploited, and is essentially powered by the Côte d'Ivoire dams (Ayamé I and II, Kossou, Taabo) and to a smaller extent from Ghana (Akosombo), the city's consumption accounted for 59 per cent of national consumption in 1986 (Attahi, 1991). In 1988, 67 per cent of Abidjan households used electric light.

Therefore, neither the city nor the districts have any control over the expansion and management of the centralized water and power networks, which depend on negotiations between government and the concessionary companies. In view of the technical requirements, in particular in terms of personnel, it is unlikely that the local authorities could take over these services in the near future. But this lack of control over the planning and development of building plots has some advantages. Legislation on decentralization empowers the districts to initiate new plot developments, but in Abidjan the DCGTx assumes this task. In other cities, it is difficult to provide plots with water and power because the concessionary companies, whose interests and expansion programmes do not necessarily coincide with those of the local authorities, initiate projects only in those areas where existing settlement guarantees that they will recover their costs. In the Abidjan metropolis, the DCGTx has no problem in initiating land development with integrated services because all decision-making bodies are at hand.

The city and the districts do not, either, control the main public transport system, the Société de transports abidjanais (SOTRA), whose buses and ferries in 1981 provided for 63 per cent of all commuters (52 per cent using buses only). During the 1970s, vast investment in public transport services changed trip patterns to the detriment of individual cars and metered taxis (which provided 52 per cent of trips in 1974), while privately owned minibuses (*gbakas*) were relegated to the outskirts. However, the changes in public service fares owing to structural adjustment measures and the financial problems of the SOTRA led in the 1980s to a retreat of the centralized network in favour of private minibuses and illicit taxis (*woro-woro*), which in 1994 had come back into the very heart of the city. Because the city allocates operating permits and levies taxes on privately owned public transport, it could seize this opportunity, in these times of public service reductions, to establish its authority over activities that are essential to the functioning of the city and that have thus far been contested by private owners and the state. Is this desirable? As in the cases of water and electricity, there is nothing to guarantee that substituting the city, in its present form, for centralized concessionary companies, which ensure unified tariffs in all districts and manage their networks city-wide without having to try to maintain a delicate balance between the interests of 10 districts, would be an improvement for city dwellers.

Room to manœuvre for the 10 districts

The 1980 administrative reform defined the conditions for the transfer of jurisdiction to the district authorities, as local legal entities that are financially autonomous under the Ministry of Home Affairs and are managed by a municipal council elected by universal suffrage. These transfers were completed in several fields: education (preschools and primary schools, teachers' housing, school canteens, and facilities attached to state schools), health and hygiene (training, animal and other product controls), and local cultural and social facilities. The districts are responsible for household refuse collection, management of water supply points as well as parks and gardens, and a network of streets classified in 1984 as falling under local authorities.

To fulfil these obligations, they have three sources of funds: a state subsidy given as a global operating endowment; taxes levied at national level and returned in part to the districts; and local taxes. Unable to forecast the state subsidy, which is in principle computed by the ministry in relation to population, and because the local return on national taxes has been systematically curtailed (100 per cent of main licences in 1980 as against 35 per cent in 1992), mayors can look only for means to increase local taxes in order to establish services to replenish local finances as fast as possible. All possibilities have been considered, from a systematic census of economic activities to the improvement of local methods of levying taxes. Owing to the unequal distribution of the most lucrative services (such as the large marketplaces), of economic activities, and of local taxes, there are great disparities between the resources, and hence the investment capacities, of the 10 districts, with no system of adjustment among them (table 8.6).

For investment purposes, the municipal councils can borrow from a local authorities' fund set up with 71 per cent financing from the World Bank and 29 per cent from the state. The fund was meant to

Table 8.6 **Budgets of the 10 districts (communes) of Abidjan in 1990**

Commune	Population, 1988	Budget, 1990 (CFA francs '000)	Revenue budget (CFA francs/person)	Capital budget (CFA francs/person)
Plateau	11,647	2,213,876	164,200	25,633
Treichville	110,040	2,163,537	16,026	3,635
Marcory	146,098	1,495,000	8,147	2,085
Port-Bouët	168,725	1,496,000	7,099	1,767
Adjamé	199,720	1,475,381	7,387	1,607
Cocody	128,756	969,471	5,038	2,494
Koumassi	229,963	731,787	2,420	744
Yopougon	374,524	711,844	1,298	602
Abobo	401,211	734,524	1,405	4,262
Attécoubé	163,658	230,415	1,148	260

Source: Saint-Vil, J., *Tableau de bord communal*, Abidjan, DCGTx, 1991.

finance, first and foremost, district servicing projects that could bring in rapid returns (markets, bus stations) and that cost from 10 million to 190 million CFA francs. Districts can also look for foreign partners and have established many links with European and North American local authorities. Local development and the ideology of "near is beautiful" – "old wine in new bottles" according to Stren (1991) – are the new fetishes (Jaglin and Dubresson, 1993) and provide a means, for some actors, to circumvent the state, which they do not consider to be qualified to promote urban development.

Among the main results are new market-places (such as those at Treichville and Marcory), which are vital elements in daily life (the AUA counted 78 markets with more than 50 stands in 1987/88) and return a high level of local taxes. Their management, the subject of alliances and conflicts between big business and local authorities, is a primary financial and political stake.

Forgotten by the urban development projects, the residents of temporary dwelling areas are looking to the local authorities to serve as intermediaries in order to solve infrastructure and land tenure problems. Subdivision into plots, felt to imply a promise of later services, is their main demand, all the more because the universal ballot and multi-party system since 1990 enable them to negotiate with their votes. Caught between the state urban policy, whose principles are beyond them, and the demands of their voting constituencies, mayors are looking for negotiated middle-of-the-way solutions. Some, following initiatives by their constituencies, have ensured that former illegal dwellings are transformed into legal plots (the Zoé Bruno neighbourhood in the Koumassi district) or provided with services (the Zimbabwe quarter in the Port-Bouët district). Not all councils adopt the same position in their bargaining with the state. Settlements in temporary neighbourhoods vary greatly from one district to another and some mayors' passivity is not only due to weaknesses in the legislation on decentralization or the DCGTx's power in the field of land development. It also derives from their ambiguity towards foreign residents' rights to live in the city. Do they have a right to acquire land, and do they ask for it? Political stakes are not identical in every district and the "struggle for recognition of the *fait accompli*" (Yapi Diahou, 1994) has not had the same outcome everywhere.

A positive side to decentralization lies in the numerous local development projects, which are supposedly better adapted to people's needs. Investments shared jointly by residents and district councils have thus made it possible to improve infrastructure and nearby services (schools, clinics, public baths, professional training centres), but this kind of sharing is restricted, partly owing to the limited financial and technical capacities of both residents and district council personnel. Also, because they are usually limited to one-off actions, they are scarcely ever complemented by management and maintenance follow-up. Actions at district level are efficient only if complementary actions are initiated at other levels. An attempt to entrust young Abobo residents with primary household refuse collection failed owing to poor connections with the centralized refuse collection networks. Finally, the exercise of delegated powers, as in the case of Port-Bouët, where the district council plays a catalytic role in private and community initiatives, does not necessarily ensure that projects are better adapted to local conditions and often reveals strong tensions that were previously hidden or arbitrated by the central powers.

Conclusion: Local management and the city's survival

The population growth rate of the Abidjan metropolis decreased during the 1980s, but the annual increment remains high: 110,000 to 130,000 inhabitants if the 1988 rate has remained steady. The government's statements, which focus on management of existing infrastructure and services (whose importance nobody denies), are fraught with ambiguity and, while searching for efficient management, one should not forget the necessary investments and the no less necessary hierarchy that needs to be established with respect to actors and the scope of their interventions.

From this angle, even though decentralization is useful to generate local initiatives and improve access to resources for residents, it is also dangerous in that it has created and increased social and economic inequalities between the 10 districts of the city, whose financial bases are very different (table 8.6). These disparities proceed from the districts' differing urban inheritance, between Plateau and Abobo or Koumassi, for instance; from a different distribution of assets among communities and ethnic groups; from variations in the property tax base; and from varying degrees of efficiency of local authorities in taking local initiatives. The city authority cannot control this mechanism, which is unfair and which is difficult to regulate through the dispersed decision-making bodies. Redistribution, through the design and monitoring of balancing mechanisms, would imply a voluntaristic public commitment to remedy these inequalities. Those who initiated decentralization were aware of this and created a body above the districts, the city, which could contribute, with the state, to implementing remedial action so that all citizens enjoy the same rights.

For the time being, the reverse is happening. The two richest districts, Plateau and Treichville, have the biggest investment budget per inhabitant and the gap is large: in 1990 district investment per inhabitant was nearly 43 times higher in the Plateau, which was already well provided for, than in Yopougon, 14 times higher in Treichville than in Attécoubé; in 1987, the per capita capital budget was 60 times higher in Plateau than in Attécoubé, but in 1990 it was 99 times more. Whereas the centralized concessionary companies in charge of water and electricity are maintaining equal tariffs, the most impoverished residents of the poorer districts, such as Attécoubé and Yopougon, do not benefit from these low levels of local investment.

Indeed, the creation of districts has generated competition in a pluralist electoral framework and many mayors have shown their political acumen when the new relations between the state and the districts enhanced "authoritarian decompression" (Bourmaud and Quantin, 1991) and facilitated the emergence of democratic practices. However, efficiency in the management of the city for the majority of its residents depends on the interdependence between strong local mechanisms and the resources of the central system of government. Only the state can reconcile the necessary public control of long-term

287

urban planning to create conditions for all to enjoy their rights in the city and the often contradictory and antagonistic short-term aspirations of its inhabitants. If the questions relating to the modes of and scope for arbitration, and in the final analysis to the nature of power (starting with state power), are not clearly formulated, decentralization and management objectives will not generate the type of democratic engineering stated in the law and by the stakeholders. Thus, the Abidjan experience is interesting, though limited, and can serve as a reference and an example to those in charge of Africa's mega-cities.

Note

1. 1 French franc = 50 CFA francs.

Glossary of abbreviations

AUA	Atelier d'urbanisme d'Abidjan	Abidjan Urban Planning Office
AURA	Agence d'urbanisme de la région d'Abidjan	Abidjan Provincial Planning Office
BCET	Bureau central d'études techniques	Central Office for Technical Studies
BNEC	Banque nationale d'épargne et de crédit	National Savings and Credit Bank
CAA	Caisse autonome d'amortissement	Autonomous Redemption Fund
CCCE	Caisse centrale de coopération économique (devenue CFD, Caisse française pour le développement)	Central Economic Cooperation Fund, later CFD, French Development Fund
CDMH	Compte de mobilisation pour l'habitat	Building Account
CIE	Compagnie ivoirienne d'électricité	Ivory Coast power company
DCGTx	Direction et contrôle des grands travaux	Public Works Inspection Department
EBC	Enquête budget–consommation	Survey on income and consumption
EDF	Electricité de France	French power company
EECI	Energie électrique de Côte d'Ivoire	Ivory Coast power company
EIF	Enquête ivoirienne de fécondité	Survey on fertility

FNA	Fonds national d'assainissement	National Sanitation Fund
GFCI	Groupement foncier de Côte d'Ivoire	Real Estate Office
INS	Institut National de Statistique, Abidjan	National Standards Bureau
OSHE	Office de soutien à l'habitat économique	Low-Cost Housing Support Department
RGPH	Recensement général de la population et de l'habitat	National Census
SAUR	Société pour l'aménagement urbain et rural	Urban and Rural Development Company
SEMA	Société d'Economie et de Mathématiques Appliquées	Economics and Applied Mathematics Society
SETAP	Société pour les études techniques d'aménagement planifié	Planned development engineering agency
SETU	Société d'équipement des terrains urbains	Urban Land Development Company
SICOGI	Société ivoirienne de construction et de gestion immobilière	Ivorian Building and Real Estate Company
SODECI	Société de distribution d'eau de la Côte-d'Ivoire	Water Distribution Company
SOGEFIHA	Société de gestion et de financement de l'habitat	Housing Finance and Management Company
SOTRA	Société de transports abidjanais	Abidjan Transport Company

Bibliography

Affou Yapi, S. 1990. *La relève paysanne en Côte-d'Ivoire. Etudes d'expériences vivrières*. Karthala–ORSTOM, Paris.

Antoine, P., A. Dubresson, and A. Manoù-Savina. 1987. *Abidjan côté cours. Pour comprendre la question de l'habitat*. Karthala, Paris.

Attahi, K. 1989. Côte d'Ivoire: An evaluation of urban management reforms. In: R. Stren and R. R. White, eds., *African Cities in Crisis: Managing Rapid Urban Growth*. Westview, Boulder, Colo., pp. 112–146.

———— 1991. Planning and management in large cities: A case study of Abidjan, Côte-d'Ivoire. In: UNCHS, ed., *Metropolitan Planning and Management in the Developing World: Abidjan and Quito*. United Nations Centre for Human Settlements (Habitat), Nairobi, pp. 31–82.

AUA (Atelier d'urbanisme d'Abidjan). 1989. *Abidjan, Atlas des modes d'occupation des sols (MOS)*. AUA–DCGTx, Abidjan.

Bonnassieux, A. 1987. *L'autre Abidjan. Chronique d'un quartier oublié*. INADES, Karthala, Paris.

Bourmaud, D. and P. Quantin, eds. 1991. Les chemins de la démocratie. *Politique Africaine* 43: 4.

Chaléard, J.-L. 1994. Temps des villes, temps des vivres. L'essor du vivrier marchand en Côte-d'Ivoire. Ph.D. dissertation, Université de Paris X, Nanterre.

Chaléard, J.-L. and A. Dubresson. 1989. Un pied dedans, un pied dehors: à propos du rural et de l'urbain en Côte d'Ivoire. In: B. Antheaume et al., eds., *Tropiques, lieux et liens*. ORSTOM, Paris, pp. 277–290.

Cohen, M. A. 1974. *Urban Policy and Political Conflict in Africa. A Study of the Ivory Coast*. University Press of Chicago, Chicago.

Contamin, B. and Y.-A. Fauré. 1990. *La bataille des entreprises publiques en Côte-d'Ivoire. L'histoire d'un ajustement interne*. ORSTOM–Karthala, Paris.

Direction de la statistique et de la comptabilité nationale. 1991. *Séminaire national de présentation des résultats du recensement général de la population et de l'habitat*. Abidjan.

Dubresson, A. 1989. *Villes et industries en Côte d'Ivoire. Pour une géographie de l'accumulation urbaine*. Karthala, Paris.

Fauré, Y.-A. 1992. Le quatrième plan d'ajustement structurel de la Côte-d'Ivoire: de la technique économique à l'économie politique. *Canadian Journal of Development Studies* 13(3): 411–431.

Fauré, Y.-A. and J. F. Médard, eds. 1982. *Etat et bourgeoisie en Côte-d'Ivoire*. Karthala, Paris.

Faussey-Domalain, C. and P. Vimard. 1991. Agriculture de rente et démographie dans le sud-est ivorien. Une économie villageoise assistée en milieu forestier péri-urbain. *Tiers-Monde* 32(125): 93–114.

Gibbal, J.-M. 1974. *Citadins et villageois dans la ville africaine. L'exemple d'Abidjan*. Maspéro, RUG, Paris, Grenoble.

Guiral, D. 1984. Devenir de la matière organique particulaire dans un milieu eutrophe tropical (baie de Biétry, lagune Ebrié, Côte-d'Ivoire). *Revue d'Hydrobiologie tropicale* 17(3): 191–206.

Haeringer, P. 1969. Structures foncières et création urbaine à Abidjan. *Cahiers d'études africaines* 5(34): 211–270.

––––––– 1977. Abidjan 1976. Occupation de l'espace urbain et péri-urbain. In: *Atlas de Côte-d'Ivoire*. Ministère de Plan–ORSTOM–IGT, Abidjan.

––––––– 1985. Vingt-cinq ans de politique urbaine à Abidjan ou la tentation de l'urbanisme intégral. *Politique Africaine* 17: 20–40.

INS (Institut National de la Statistique). 1992. *Séminaire national sur les perspectives démographiques de la Côte-d'Ivoire, document de base*. 18–20 November, Abidjan.

Jaglin, S. and A. Dubresson, eds. 1993. *Pouvoirs et cités d'Afrique noire. Décentralisations en questions*. Karthala, Paris.

Labazée, P. 1993. Les dynamiques du champ de pouvoir en pays kiembara: alliances et conflits entre autorité locale et appareil d'Etat. In: S. Jaglin and A. Dubresson, eds., *Pouvoirs et cités d'Afrique noire. Décentralisations en questions*. Karthala, Paris, pp. 219–243.

Le Pape, M. 1992. Avant la récession et maintenant: des tendances sociologiques. Communication à la table ronde du GIDIS-CI Crises et ajustement structurel: les dimensions sociales et culturelles, 31 November – 2 December, Bingerville.

Le Pape, M., C. Vidal, and A. Yapi Diahou. 1992. *Abidjan: du cosmopolitanisme à la mondialisation*. ASP CNRS–ORSTOM, Paris.

Ley, L.-A. 1972. *Le régime domanial et foncier et le développement économique de la Côte-d'Ivoire*. Librairie générale de droit et de jurisprudence, Paris.

Lootvoet, B. 1988. *L'artisanat et le petit commerce dans l'économie ivoirienne. Eléments pour une analyse à partir de l'étude de quatre villes de l'intérieur (Agboville, Bouaké, Dimbokro, Katiola)*. ORSTOM, Collection Etudes et thèses, Paris.

Malhomme, F. 1986. *Abidjan, quelles ressources pour quelle croissance?* Mairie d'Abidjan, Abidjan.

Manou-Savina, A. 1985. Politiques et pratiques urbaines à Abidjan. Ph.D. dissertation, Université de Paris I, Paris.

———— 1986. Modalités d'accession à la terre urbaine à la périphérie d'Abidjan. Port-Bouët II, pari gagné? In: B. Crousse, E. Le Bris, and E. Le Roy, eds., *Espaces disputés en Afrique noire. Pratiques foncières locales*. Karthala, Paris, pp. 51–71.

Manou-Savina, A., P. Antoine, A. Dubresson, and A. Yapi Diahou. 1985. Les "en-hauts des en-bas", "les en-bas des en-hauts". Classes moyennes et urbanisation à Abidjan. *Tiers Monde* 26(101): 55–68.

Marie, A. 1995. "Y a pas l'argent"; l'endetté insolvable et le créancier floué, deux figures complémentaires de la pauvreté abidjanaise. *Tiers Monde* 142: 1303–1324.

Miras, C. de. 1982. L'entrepreneur ivoirien, ou une bourgeoisie privée de son état. In: Y.-A. Fauré and J.-F. Médard, eds., *Etat et bourgeoisie en Côte-d'Ivoire*. Karthala, Paris, pp. 181–230.

Oudin, X. 1985. Les activités non structurées et l'emploi en Côte-d'Ivoire. Définition et mesure. Ph.D. dissertation, Université de Rennes, Rennes.

Requier-Desjardins, D. 1985. Urbanisation et évolution des modèles alimentaires. L'exemple de la Côte-d'Ivoire. In: N. Bricas et al., eds., *Nourrir les villes en Afrique sub-saharienne*. L'Harmattan, Paris, pp. 161–178.

Rougerie, G. 1950. Le port d'Abidjan. Le problème des débouchés maritimes de la Côte-d'Ivoire. Sa solution lagunaire. *Bulletin de l'IFAN* 12(3): 751–837.

Saint-Vil, J. 1983. L'eau chez soi et l'eau au coin de la rue. Les systèmes de distribution de l'eau à Abidjan. In: P. Haeringer, ed., *Abidjan au coin de la rue*. Cahiers ORSTOM, série Sciences Humaines, 19(4): 471–489.

Soumahoro, C. 1993. Evolutions spatiales, dynamiques dans le cadre de l'habitat locatif populaire. *Chroniques du Sud* (no. Abidjan 1903–1993, recherches et projets), 10: 112–121.

Stren, R. 1991. Old wine in new bottles? An overview of Africa's urban problems and the "urban management" approach to dealing with them. *Environment and Urbanization* 3(1): 9–22.

Venard, J.-L. 1993. Bailleurs de fonds et développement local. In: S. Jaglin and A. Dubresson, eds., *Pouvoirs et cités d'Afrique noire. Décentralisations en questions*. Karthala, Paris, pp. 19–34.

Vidal, C. 1991. *Sociologie des passions (Côte-d'Ivoire, Rwanda)*. Karthala, Paris.

———— 1992. Les rhétoriques de la "solidarité africaine". Communication à la table ronde du GIDIS-CI Crises et ajustement structurel: les dimensions sociales et culturelles, 31 November – 2 December, Bingerville.

Vidal, C. and M. Le Pape. 1986. *Pratiques de crise et conditions sociales à Abidjan, 1979–1985*. ORSTOM, Petit Bassam, CNRS, Abidjan.

Yapi Diahou, A. 1981. Etude de l'urbanisation de la périphérie d'Abidjan. L'urbanisation de Yopougon. Ph.D. dissertation, Université de Toulouse – Le Mirail, Toulouse.

———— 1994. Les politiques urbaines en Côte-d'Ivoire et leurs impacts sur l'habitat non planifié précaire. L'exemple de l'agglomération d'Abidjan. Ph.D. dissertation, Université de Paris VIII, Paris.

9

Nairobi: National capital and regional hub

R. A. Obudho

Abstract

Etablie par les colons anglais à l'intérieur du Kenya au cœur du réseau ferroviaire est-africain, puis comme capitale du Kenya, Nairobi compte aujourd'hui environ 1.5 millions d'habitants. Bien que le Kenya soit indépendant depuis 1963, nombre des caractéristiques spatiales et institutionnelles de Nairobi portent encore la marque de la ségrégation raciale de l'époque coloniale et les autorités locales sont structurées sur le modèle britannique. Capitale d'un pays colonial, Nairobi a une population comptant plus de 40 per cent d'Européens et d'Indiens jusqu'à l'indépendance, chiffres qui ont probablement diminué depuis en termes relatifs mais pas en termes absolus. Dans les années suivant l'indépendance, le Kenya essaye de s'industrialiser et le secteur de l'emploi formel augmente rapidement avec une multiplication des emplois de fonctionnaires. Mais depuis de nombreuses années, la création d'emplois salariés ne suit par le rythme de la croissance de la force de travail, tendance encore exacerbée par les crises économiques et les réformes d'ajustement structurel des années 80 et 90. Dans l'impossibilité de travailler dans le secteur formel, nombreux sont ceux et celles qui se consacrent aux activités du secteur informel, y compris les manufactures, le commerce et les services. Certaines de ces entreprises ont des profits respectables, mais pour la plupart d'entre elles, il s'agit simplement

de survivre, de gagner au mieux de quoi subsister. La pauvreté citadine, dont témoigne le nombre croissant d'enfants des rues, a dram-
atiquement augmenté ces quinze dernières années. Nairobi a tour à
tour été administrée par un Conseil élu et par une Commission dés-
ignée à cet effet. La situation politique volatile est liée à des rivalités
de classes et d'ethnies et à un marché immobilier fortement com-
mercialisé. La propriété est le plus souvent privée, tenue en propriété
perpétuelle et libre ou louée par l'État. Par conséquent, obtenir un
terrain est difficile pour toute personne n'ayant pas accès aux voies
officielles, qu'elle manque de ressources financières, qu'elle soit arri-
vée en ville au mauvais moment ou qu'elle ne dispose pas d'appuis
bien placés. C'est pourquoi la majeure partie de la population s'est
installée vaille que vaille sur des terrains de propriété incertaine,
manquant de services et le plus souvent surpeuplés. Nombre de rési-
dents de ces établissements et autres logements "à loyers modérés"
n'occupent qu'une seule pièce. La centralisation du pouvoir, l'insuffisance des revenus locaux, la mauvaise récupération des coûts,
la capacité limitée des administrations locales, la croissance démographique rapide, l'urbanisation sauvage et l'adoption de normes
inutilement élevées, tout a contribué à l'insuffisance des logements et
des infrastructures par rapport aux besoins et à de graves inégalités
entre les groupes sociaux. Les problèmes écologiques et sanitaires
s'aggravant en même temps que les insuffisances des infrastructures,
la pauvreté est en augmentation, et les administrations locales et
centrales ne peuvent réagir de façon efficace. Il faudrait mieux admi-
nistrer la croissance urbaine, améliorer la gestion financière et insti-
tutionnelle, mettre en place des programmes plus efficaces de promotion de la construction de logements et de services, appuyer le
secteur informel et adopter des politiques et programmes écologiques
plus systématiques.

Introduction

Urbanization in Kenya has a long history in the coastal region but a
short history in the interior parts of the country (Obudho, 1982, 1983,
1992, and 1994). The pattern that exists today predominantly reflects
the development of British colonization rather than traditional
African settlement patterns. The proportion of the population living
in urban areas has increased from 8 per cent at independence in 1963
to 20 per cent in 1995. In 1948, there were 17 urban centres with
an aggregate population of 176,000, of which 83 per cent was con-

centrated in Nairobi and Mombasa. By the 1962 population census, the number of urban centres had doubled to 34 and their population had increased to 671,000. In 1979, the overall proportion living in urban areas had risen to 9.9 per cent, with Nairobi accounting for 36 per cent of the total. The 1979 census indicated 90 urban centres with a total urban population of 2.3 million, which increased to 3.7 million in 1989. The 1989 population results indicate that 18 per cent of the population resided in urban areas. A total of 139 urban centres were reported, of which Nairobi was still the largest, with a similar proportion of the total (36 per cent) as in 1979. The current profile of the city of Nairobi has, in turn, been shaped by geographical, historical, and contemporary forces.[1]

I shall first describe Nairobi's location, historical development, and population growth. The system of land tenure and administration, which has influenced the pattern of urban development, will then be outlined, followed by aspects of the city's economy and socio-political structure. Next, the provision of urban services will be analysed, with particular reference to housing, water, solid waste disposal, transportation, and recreation. Following a discussion of environmental and health problems, the final section will suggest appropriate strategies for the future development of the city.

Site and situation

Nairobi is situated at the south-eastern end of the agricultural heartland of Kenya and most of its energy and food requirements can be obtained within a short distance of the city. The immediate environment of Nairobi consists of the productive highland area extending northwards and westwards to embrace the rich farming lands of the Rift Valley. Within a radius of about 10 km from the central business district (CBD), vegetables, fruit, herbs, flowers, and fuelwood are produced. Beyond this zone and in the suburbs, commercial ranching is carried out for the production of milk and meat, to be consumed by Nairobi residents. In addition to the upland agriculture, there is also active, although illegal, cultivation within the city limits (Freeman, 1991; Lado, 1990).

The settlement's administrative boundaries were extended as its population increased from 8,000 in 1901 to 118,579 by 1948 (figs. 9.1 and 9.2). At the time of independence in 1963 the population had grown to an estimated 350,000, although much of the growth was due to the major boundary extension, which increased the urban admin-

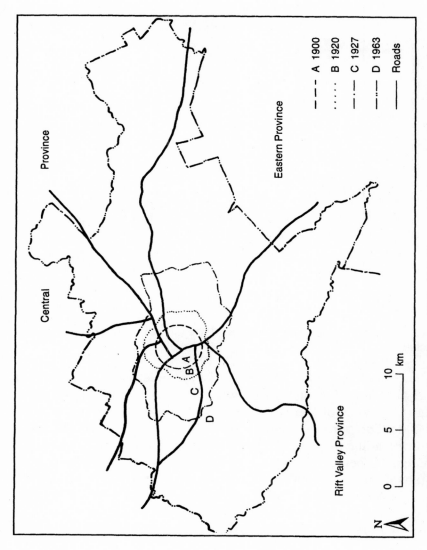

Fig. 9.1 **Nairobi: Boundary changes, 1900–1963 (Source: Obudho and Aduwo, 1992, p. 53)**

Province

Central

Eastern Province

Rift Valley Province

A 1900
B 1920
C 1927
D 1963
Roads

0   5   10
km

N

295

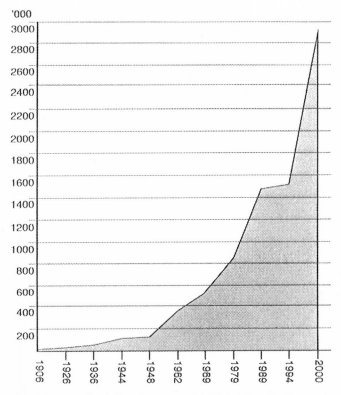

Fig. 9.2   **Nairobi's population growth, 1906–2000 (Source: See table 9.1. Projection by author)**

istrative area to 690 km². The city's 1994 population was estimated to be 1.5 million and its current growth rate to be about 5 per cent per annum (Republic of Kenya, 1994), with a population of between 2.8 and 4.0 million persons expected by the year 2010. Nairobi is likely to continue leading in terms of absolute population size, although its rate of increase is below the average urban population growth rate, which is estimated to be 7.7 per cent per annum for Kenya as a whole. Continued growth of the city has been taking place in the face of renewed strategies towards decentralized planning, which focus on the promotion of small and intermediate urban centres (Obudho, 1992).

Historical background

The site of Nairobi was chosen by the Kenya Uganda Railway (KUR) authorities because it offered a suitable stopping place between

Mombasa and Kisumu; adequate water supply from the nearby Nairobi and Mbagathi rivers; ample level land for railway tracks and sidings; elevated cooler ground to the west suitable for residential purposes; and apparently deserted land offering freedom for land appropriation. Another primary consideration for the selection of the site was that the place was free from tropical diseases, especially malaria. The new settlement was named after the Maasai name *Enkare Nairobi*, which means "a place of cold waters," although there was no permanent African settlement since the place was grazing land and a livestock watering point. In 1896, a small transport depot was established at the site to keep provisions for oxen and mules (White et al., 1948, p. 10). The railhead reached the site in June 1899 and by July it had become the KUR headquarters (Boedecker, 1936; White et al., 1948; Foran, 1950, p. 220; Hallman, 1967, pp. 14–28; Hake, 1977, p. 20; Obudho and Aduwo, 1992). By the end of 1899 the Government of Kenya (GOK) had selected a site on the high ground on the northern side of the Nairobi River and away from the railway station to be the administrative headquarters (Morgan, 1968; see fig. 9.3). In 1900, the Nairobi Municipal Community (NMC) regulations were published by the GOK and these defined the urban centre as "the area within a radius of one and a half miles from the offices of the sub-commissioner of the Ukambani Province" (Morgan, 1976, p. 100; see fig. 9.1). A small number of settlers had begun settling in the urban centre by then and, with the construction of the KUR on the move, it became essential to designate a mid-way site where a well-equipped maintenance depot could be built. The then Engineer stated that:

Nairobi has with great judgement, been selected as the site for the principal workshops. It is about 5,500 m above the sea level, which ensures a comparatively salubrious climate; there is ample space of level ground for all sorts of requirements, and excellent sites for the quarters of officers and subordinates. On the higher ground there is a fairly good supply of water but reservoirs and tanks will have to be constructed. (Walmsey, 1957, p. 18)

Once the KUR authorities had made the decision to locate a depot in Nairobi, spatial patterns around it and the railway station emerged. Europeans established their homes on the hill to the west, away from Asians and Africans (fig. 9.3), soon leading to exclusive European residential settlements. Meanwhile, Asian employees who had been discharged from KUR employment established shops not far from the railway station, an area that came to be known as the Indian

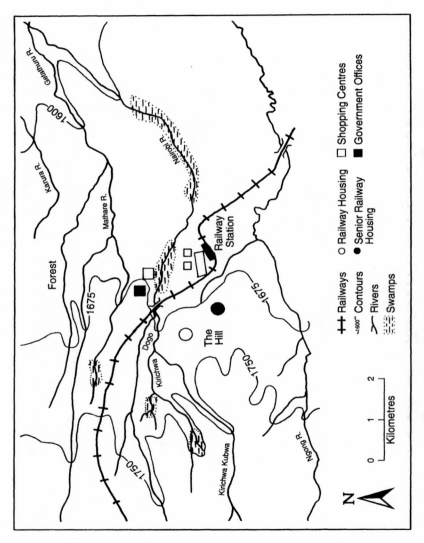

Fig. 9.3 **Nairobi circa 1900 (Source: White et al, 1948, p. 11)**

Bazaar. The Asian buildings were used both for business and as living quarters by a few Africans who worked for the KUR, while others lived in employee housing and shanty villages to the east (White et al., 1948). By 1906 the original KUR depot and camp had grown into an urban centre of over 10,000 people and definite land-use zones had appeared, though these had not been planned, with the Europeans mainly occupying the cooler westlands, the Indians in the north, and the African workers mainly concentrated on the periphery (fig. 9.4). With the completion of the KUR and the influx of more non-African settlers, the settlement expanded rapidly. By 1909 much of its internal structure, especially the road network in the CBD, was already established.

In 1919, the Nairobi Municipal Community was replaced by Nairobi City Council (NCC). At the same time the boundary was extended to include peri-urban settlements (Cloix, 1950, pp. 23–24). The boundary was again extended in 1927 to cover 30 square miles (White et al., 1948; see fig. 9.1). From 1928 to the time of independence of Kenya in 1963, this boundary remained the same, with only minor additions and excisions taking place. By 1950, permanent residential zones had already been demarcated, very much along the lines first established in the early years of the century. In 1963, the boundary of Nairobi was further extended and remains the same today (fig. 9.1). Expansion was expected to take place within this area, mainly on the 20 square miles of black cotton soil and ranching land to the east of the early settlement (Ferraro, 1978).

Population growth and dynamics

The population of Nairobi grew from 10,512 in 1906 to 118,976 in 1948 (table 9.1). By 1962, it had a population of 266,795 people. Between the 1948 and 1962 censuses, the population grew at an average rate of 5.9 per cent per annum, compared with 7.6 per cent in the previous 12-year period. The African and Asian population grew hand in hand with the total population until 1960, with the former making up just under 60 per cent and the latter one-third of the total (table 9.2) (Obudho and Muganzi, 1991). A decline in the number of Europeans and Asians resulted from emigration following independence (Tiwari, 1972 and 1979) and these groups formed only 4 per cent and 14 per cent, respectively, of the city's population in 1969, falling to 1 per cent and 4 per cent, respectively, in 1989.

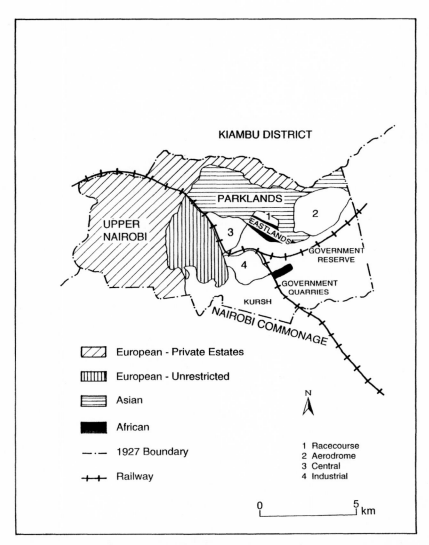

KIAMBU DISTRICT

PARKLANDS

UPPER NAIROBI

EASTLANDS

1

2

3

GOVERNMENT RESERVE

4

GOVERNMENT QUARRIES

KURSH

NAIROBI COMMONAGE

▨	European - Private Estates
⦀	European - Unrestricted
⬓	Asian
■	African
—·—	1927 Boundary
┼┼┼	Railway

N

1 Racecourse
2 Aerodrome
3 Central
4 Industrial

0   5 km

Fig. 9.4 The segregation of residential areas in Nairobi, 1909 (Source: Mazingira Institute, 1993, p. 2)

A feature of the post-independence period has been the movement of people from the rural areas to Nairobi. The main sources of short-distance migrants are the districts of Central Province, while long-distance migrants come from the Eastern, Western, and Nyanza Provinces. The 1989 census put the city's population at 1.3 million, 80 per cent of whom are accommodated on 20 per cent of the land.

Table 9.1   **Nairobi: Population for selected years, 1906–1994**

Year	Area (ha)	Population	% increase p.a.
1906	1,813	10,512	4.4
1928	2,537	29,864	17.1
1931	2,537	47,944	} 6.5
1936	2,537	49,606	
1944	2,537	108,900	
1948	2,537	118,976	2.2
1962	2,537	266,795	5.9
1969	68,945	509,286	9.8
1979	68,945	827,775	5.1
1989	68,945	1,324,570	4.8
1994[a]	68,945	1,690,000	5.0[a]

Sources: East African Statistical Department (1986), Republic of Kenya (1966, 1971, 1981, 1994).
a. Estimated.

Table 9.2   **Nairobi: Population by race for selected years, 1906–1989**

Year	Africans No.	%	Europeans No.	%	Asians No.	%	Total No.	%
1906	6,351	60.4	579	5.5	3,582	34.1	10,512	100.0
1928	19,112	64.0	1,492	5.0	9,260	31.1	29,864	100.0
1931	26,761	55.8	5,195	10.8	15,988	33.4	47,944	100.0
1936	27,700	55.8	5,357	10.8	16,549	33.4	49,606	100.0
1948	66,336	55.8	10,830	9.1	41,810	35.1	118,976	100.0
1962	157,865	59.2	21,476	8.0	87,454	32.8	266,795	100.0
1969	421,079	82.6	19,185	3.8	69,022	13.6	509,286	100.0
1979	768,032	92.8	19,050	2.3	40,693	4.9	827,775	100.0
1989	1,260,149	95.1	15,822	1.2	48,599	3.7	1,324,570	100.0

Sources: East African Statistical Department (1986), Republic of Kenya (1966, 1971, 1981, 1994).

Population is heavily concentrated in a number of inner-city wards, in some of which, such as Pumwani and Maringo, densities are extremely high (over 26,000 people per km^2; see fig. 9.5). Alternative projections to 2010 range from 2.8 to 4 million (Mazingira Institute, 1993; Obudho and Aduwo, 1992, p. 57) and it is estimated that 550,000 families will need to be sheltered by the year 2000 (Republic of Kenya, 1993). This increase has and will continue to exert a lot of demands on the environment unless adequate measures are taken.

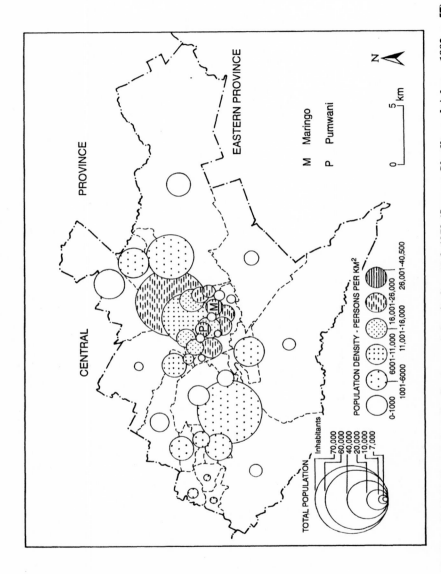

Fig. 9.5 **Nairobi: Population distribution and density by ward, 1979 (Source: Obudho and Aduwo, 1992, p. 57)**

Table 9.3 **Nairobi: Sex ratios, 1948–1989**

Year	Male	Female	Sex ratio
1948	94,755	24,221	391.2
1962	190,606	76,189	250.2
1969	303,219	206,067	147.1
1979	479,448	348,327	137.6
1989	752,597	571,973	131.6

Source: East African Statistical Department (1986), Republic of Kenya (1966, 1971, 1981, 1994).

Table 9.4 **Nairobi: Primacy index, 1948–1989**

Urban centre	1948	1962	1969	1979	1989
Nairobi's population	118,976	266,795	509,286	827,775	1,324,570
Four next-largest urban centres	121,163	260,887	345,042	637,145	934,706
Primacy index: Nairobi as % of four next-largest urban centres	98%	102%	148%	130%	142%

Source: East African Statistical Department (1986), Republic of Kenya (1966, 1971, 1981, 1994).

The population of Nairobi is predominantly male. In 1962, there were over twice as many adult males as females, so that the sex ratio (including children) was 250 males to 100 females but with striking differences among racial groups. Although the numbers of women and men have become somewhat more even since then (table 9.3), the continued predominance of men in Nairobi can be attributed to the fact that the majority of rural–urban migrants are men.

Nairobi's primacy in Kenya's urban settlement size distribution has increased rapidly since independence, as expressed by a four-city index (table 9.4), which shows that the city's population as a percentage of the population of the four largest centres increased from 98 per cent in 1948 to 142 per cent in 1989, even though its proportion of the total urban population fell from 42 per cent to 36 per cent as the growth rate of smaller urban centres increased (Obudho, 1993a). Nairobi's primacy has been sustained by the economies of agglomeration offered to enterprises by locating in the city (Obudho and Aduwo, 1992), despite the attempts of the GOK to deconcentrate urbanization and facilitate more balanced spatial development. Some programmes have aimed at reducing migration to Nairobi through such instruments as tax incentives, limitations on investment, and demolition of slum and squatter settlements. The last policy was designed to force residents to resettle in rural areas. The GOK also promoted regional centres by extending support services to them, improving infrastructure, and strengthening the linkages between these centres and Nairobi. Integrated rural development programmes were implemented to provide agricultural inputs and social services, increase infrastructural investments, and improve agricultural productivity and incomes. These policies and programmes failed to affect population distribution significantly and Nairobi has continued to grow rapidly. The reasons for the insignificant impact of these policies vary, depending upon the economic and political context. Two reasons, however, seem to be the most common. First, the objectives of spatial strategies were not adequately reflected in GOK sectoral decisions, which shaped public and private investments. Thus, the programmes were insufficient to offset market forces that overwhelmingly favour concentration of social and economic activities in large urban centres. Rapid growth of Nairobi since the 1950s has been associated with several negative consequences: an increasing incidence of urban poverty, inadequate access to housing and such basic services as primary health care and water supply, the proliferation of slums and squatter settlements, and urban environmental degradation, among others. In an attempt to tackle these problems and improve the distribution of population within the city region, so-called accommodationist policies and programmes attempted to improve urban housing and services and deconcentrate the growth of Nairobi by promoting dormitory and satellite urban centres around it (Obudho and Aduwo, 1992).

Land tenure, use, ownership, and management

Nairobi was born out of colonial policy to build the KUR. Before the railway line could be laid, legal decisions had to be made regarding the ownership of the land covered by it. The British government anticipated land-title disputes, because its experiences in India and other places had demonstrated that speculators could take advantage of the need for land and thereby increase the cost of constructing the railway. In addition, possible future conflicts between the indigenous peoples and the British had to be guarded against. The British authority assumed the power to obtain any land without regard to indigenous territorial claims, particularly along the whole route covered by the railway. The land was taken over by the Crown, which had the responsibility of subdividing it. Land-use patterns became well defined, reflecting the commercial and residential segregational policies pursued by the colony. By 1902, the reservation of areas for European settlement had been adopted and all of the western part of Nairobi was allocated for Europeans (fig. 9.4). This explains why the western and northern parts of the city are still in the hands of private individuals. There were also policies to segregate land allocation in the commercial areas. However, these efforts failed because the European businessmen needed Asian and African customers if they were to continue in business.

Much of Nairobi's land, including the CBD, is publicly owned and leased to private owners, usually for 99 years (Ondiege, 1989). GOK leasehold covers most of the legalized residential areas, and corporate ownership of land in these areas has become increasingly widespread. Freehold land is privately owned either by individuals or by groups of individuals and can be put on the market for sale without limits to the period of ownership. This covers a small portion of Nairobi's land, being found in the western and north-western suburbs in areas such as Dagoretti, Mwimuto, Runda, and Gigiri (fig. 9.6). It also covers part of the Kahawa area in the north. Overall, over half of the city's area was estimated to be in private ownership in 1993 (Karuga, 1993, p. 22). A number of the larger illegal residential areas are found in these freehold zones (Ondiege, 1989; see fig. 9.7).

GOK land forms the second-largest portion of Nairobi (40 per cent in 1993). This includes Nairobi National Park and other major parks and forest areas, airports, Kenyatta and Nairobi universities, and Kamiti prison. The NCC owns 5 per cent of the total, mostly in the east (Karuga, 1993, p. 22). However, in practice, the public sector has very little direct control over land available for development (Macoloo and Maina, 1994). Between 1911 and 1914 Asians were allowed to acquire control of areas to the north-east of the town centre (including Eastleigh), which were at the time located outside the urban boundary. In 1920 the boundary was adjusted to incorporate land that had been alienated by the GOK for residential purposes. The new boundary showed the line between the GOK's land and the private estates that had been alienated as homesteads.

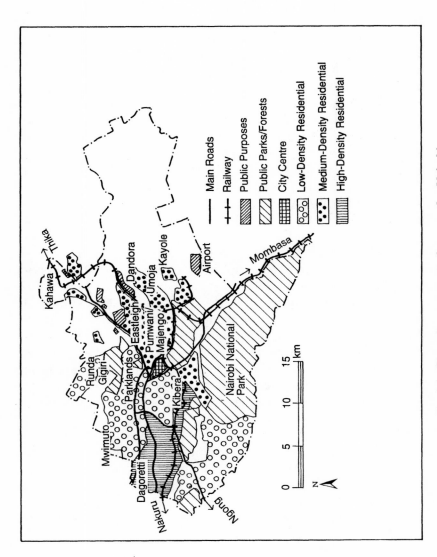

Fig. 9.6 **The urban structure of present-day Nairobi**

Main Roads
Railway
Public Purposes
Public Parks/Forests
City Centre
Low-Density Residential
Medium-Density Residential
High-Density Residential

Kahawa
Thika
Dandora
Umoja
Kayole
Airport
Mombasa
Eastleigh
Pumwani/
Majengo
Runda
Gigiri
Parklands
Kibera
Nairobi National
Park
Mwimuto
Dagoretti
Nakuru
Ngong

N

0   5   10   15
km

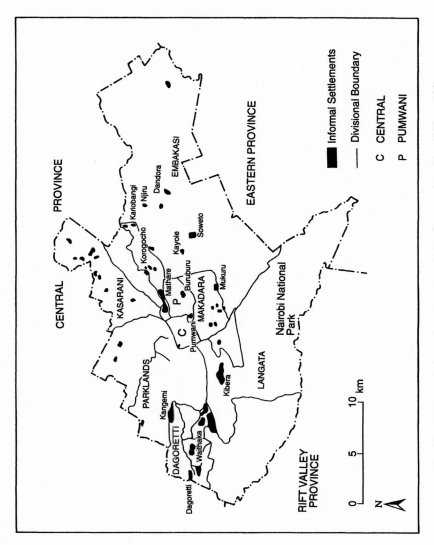

Fig. 9.7 **Nairobi: Informal settlements, 1992 (Source: Obudho, 1992, p. 100)**

Land and property prices in Nairobi reflect the quality of residential neighbourhoods. This pattern has largely developed from the colonial land segregation policies, hence land that was allocated to non-Africans in the western part of Nairobi is highly valued. The pattern has also been affected by the density of people residing in various areas, with high-density areas showing low prices. The CBD has the highest land prices, because of its intensive commercial use. The industrial areas (light industries) also have high land values. Whereas land in the CBD might, in 1994, have a value of KSh10 million per acre, its price in the light industries area was KSh1 million per acre. The prime residential areas are generally located in the western part of Nairobi, although parts of the northern section of the city have equally high land values. The eastern and northern parts of Nairobi generally have lower land prices. The eastern part of the city is generally flat land with black cotton soils, which are less attractive to residential development than the cooler, hilly areas in the west.

Access to land in Nairobi is controlled by legislation governing its use, allocation, and management. The land-use planning framework has been provided by the Nairobi Urban Study Group's report of 1973 (NCC, 1973). However, the process of land allocation is fraught with corruption and disregard for regulations and planning standards. Both the general public and private agencies ignore the regulations and this has led to irregular developments. Developers, for instance, have put up high-rise blocks and extensions in areas where such developments are prohibited by law. Slums and squatter settlements have also developed, and subdivision is occurring outside the boundary (Obudho and Aduwo, 1989; see fig. 9.7). The NCC is endowed with extensive development control powers but these have not been effectively enforced. As a result, current zoning patterns no longer protect the quality of life and the resulting environment is costly to maintain and service (Karuga, 1993). Publicly owned land has also been allocated to private individuals, who have erected illegal structures, leading to a shortage of land for public developments. The repossession of such land has met with political resistance, as the individuals allocated such land have called on their patrons for support. The Nairobi City Convention held in 1993 recommended a special task force to deal with land use and allocation procedures to help ensure that planned developments follow the legal guidelines (Karuga, 1993).

Political economy

Employment

Of people in Nairobi aged between 15 and 50, 63 per cent are economically active (Mazingira, 1993, p. 5). Since independence, there has been considerable growth in wage employment in the modern sector. Access to formal sector employment improved considerably in Nairobi, whereas it worsened in the rest of the urban centres in Kenya, with the result that Nairobi dominates urban formal sector employment. Nevertheless, the growth of jobs has not kept pace with that of the labour force. In 1992, formal wage employment in Nairobi was 376,200 persons (73 per cent of those working). However, there has been a decline in wage employment in the public sector in Kenya owing to the restructuring and privatization programme introduced in 1990. Wage employment in Nairobi includes the following: in 1992 66,600 of Nairobi's labour force were in manufacturing industry; 36,300 in building and construction; 47,300 in trade, restaurants, and hotels; 41,300 in finance, insurance, real estate, and business services; while community, social, and personal services employed 136,800 people (Republic of Kenya, 1993, p. 55).

The livelihood of most dwellers in Nairobi comes from regular wage employment and, although it is likely that the proportion in formal sector employment is decreasing, estimates of the size of the informal sector vary. The 1992 Economic Survey, for example, showed that there were 141,877 persons engaged in the informal sector (an apparent 27 per cent increase over 1991). The high rate of growth is a consequence of increased demand for goods and services (Republic of Kenya, 1993), although the informal sector also acts as a safety-valve. The activities in this sector range from painting, carpentry, shoe making, driving, and domestic service to petty trading and hawking of various food commodities. Informal income-generating activities can perhaps best be thought of as the unregulated and unprotected production of goods and provision of services by those with relatively little capital. Earnings from many informal sector activities in Nairobi compare favourably with those from urban unskilled or rural agricultural wage employment. The formal and informal sectors are generally thought to be symbiotic, with the vitality of the informal sector depending upon the wages and demand generated by formal sector (House, 1978).

The most important way in which women generate income in the informal sector is through the marketing of farm and marine products, as well as of imported manufactured goods. The first category is comprised of women engaged in trade at either retail or wholesale level, mostly in the low-income zones. Some sell in large quantities and regulate the major supplies to urban areas. The majority engage in retail trade in small kiosks that sell consumables. Others are engaged in distributing sisal products such as ropes for making "*kiondos*," a type of local basket. The second category comprises urban women who sell a wide variety of goods ranging from food and jewellery to imported new and old shoes and clothing. They sell hair products and engage in hair styling. These women are to be found in the medium-income zones in Nairobi (Mwatha, 1988).

The informal sector contributes significantly to Nairobi's economy and has strong backward linkages with commercial and public enterprises. The creation of employment opportunities in this sector is not necessarily dependent upon direct public expenditure and commitment of public investment in advance. The other advantages of the informal sector are that it uses simple technology appropriate to the resource base of the communities and that it produces jobs at lower costs. Despite the growth of this sector, unemployment is particularly widespread among young urban dwellers and women.

Poverty

Poverty in Nairobi is as old as the city itself. A growing portion of residents could be termed "poor." Currently the population is categorized into low-, middle-, and high-income groups. In 1983, 60 per cent earned less than KSh2,300 per month, 20 per cent earned between KSh2,300 and 3,700 per month, and the remaining 20 per cent had a monthly income of over KSh3,700. Those who earned less than KSh2,300 accounted for only 24 per cent of the total income in the city, whereas those in the next income group accounted for 21 per cent, and the last group for 56 per cent of total income (Syagga and Kiamba, 1988). The low-income group is comprised of drivers, watchmen, clerks, and typists, among others, in formal sector employment. Those in the informal sector include street hawkers, metal artisans, shoe shiners, construction workers, and street cleaners. Households in this group spent more than 56 per cent of their income on food in 1983 (Mazingira, 1993, p. 7). They walk to their places of work because they cannot afford bus fares every day. On average, households in this group spent 14 per cent of their income on rent in informal sector housing, in comparison with 20 per cent and 17 per cent for the middle- and high-income groups respectively.

Under the Structural Adjustment Programmes (SAPs), inflation in Kenya went up significantly from 15.8 per cent in 1990 to 19.6 per cent in 1991 and 27.5 per cent in 1992 (Republic of Kenya, 1993). The first quarter of 1993 was marked by a general increase in consumer prices. As a result, the month-on-month rate of inflation in Kenya was recorded at 32.4 per cent in January 1993, rising to 41.9 per cent in February 1993 (Republic of Kenya, 1993, p. 4). Among the factors contributing to the inflationary pressures were price decontrol, the withholding of foreign donor aid to Kenya, the use of foreign exchange certificates in importing goods and services, increases in administered prices, devaluation of the Kenyan shilling, and rapid monetary expansion (Republic of Kenya, 1993). The low-income group has been the most seriously affected by the inflationary trends since 1990. In addition, a substantial number of middle-income households have been pushed into the low-income category. According to the revised Nairobi consumer price indices, the cost of living for all income groups has more than doubled from its 1987 level.

Street children

A major consequence of urbanization and poverty is the existence of "street children" (Ayako, 1994; Aptekar et al., 1994). In Nairobi, the term "parking boys" is used to refer to such children, being derived from one of their most common activities, which is directing motorists to available parking spaces along the crowded kerbs during peak hours. The children guard the cars until the drivers return. Their tips depend on the generosity of the drivers. The problem of street children is increasing in Nairobi. It is illegal to mistreat dependent children and it is also illegal to assault, neglect, or abandon children. Parents who do so are liable to arrest, but in most cases the authorities merely arrest children for loitering or wandering aimlessly and put them in foster homes. One of the major reasons for the increase in the number of street children in Nairobi is the stark poverty that drives parents to neglect, ignore, and finally abandon their children; a good number of children are left to fend for themselves when their parents are arrested and sent to jail; some parents leave their children to drift aimlessly without proper adult supervision and there is said to be a breakdown of family life as a result of the urbanization process.

The problem of street childen in Nairobi is serious and needs to be thought about carefully by the GOK, individuals, and non-governmental organizations (NGOs). It is important to devise lasting solutions. One method of improving the welfare of street children is by allocating land to their parents, many of whom are landless women. However, generally it is not good enough to have street children from Nairobi resettled in a rural area since they are not part of that community. While trying to improve the well-being of the children, their sense of dignity and pride must be maintained. In most cases an educational approach will be most fruitful. Rehabilitation centres for street children providing education, literacy, and vocational training should be located in their neighbourhoods, where the children can identify with the community's aspirations. The street children must be encouraged to be independent so that they do not rely on other people or on free donations. It should be remembered that many street children have survived on their own. Unless this trend is changed, the majority of street children in Nairobi will also be parents of street children, in which case we are building a culture of poverty.

The structure and system of government

The Nairobi City Council (NCC) is supervised by the central government through the Ministry of Local Government. The NCC performs mandatory functions such as provision of public health and primary educational facilities, maintenance and repair of urban roads, and burial of destitutes, as well as permissive functions, which include administrative activities, sewerage and drainage, water supply, collection of garbage, markets, and social welfare services. The relationship between the central government and the NCC is an advisory one, with the Minister of Local Government having veto powers. The day-to-day operations of the NCC are carried out by the mayor and his elected councillors. There are also nominated councillors who are co-opted onto the NCC. Politics has had a lot of impact on the delivery of services to urban dwellers. At independence in 1963, Nairobi was a fully fledged urban centre run by an elected council. However, the council was dissolved in 1983 and replaced by a Nairobi City Commission. For nine years, Nairobi was run by various appointed commissioners. In 1992, the City Council was reconstituted and it is now run by an elected mayor and councillors who are members of different political parties. The politics of Nairobi is currently dominated by opposition parties. Whether elected or appointed, the local government has failed to cope adequately with the growth of the city. The problems can, *inter alia*, be attributed to a lack of resources, bureaucratic lethargy, corruption and indiscipline, lack of clear lines of authority, and disregard of public opinion.

Ethnicity and racial groups

Nairobi is comprised of a variety of ethnic communities, with considerable diversity of language, organizational systems, historical experience, and ways of life (Werlin, 1974). The non-African communities in Nairobi also have distinct organizational and cultural systems. The colonial GOK set up administrative units to coincide with ethnic units, with Africans employed as civil servants usually in their own ethnic area. In each section of Kenya, the British set up native courts, using the customary laws prevailing in the area and giving local chiefs or elders executive as well as judicial powers. This meant that those who moved into new areas were generally considered ethnic strangers and, as such, prevented or discouraged from acquiring property and in other ways discriminated against. The location of schools, urban centres, and commercial undertakings was such as to benefit some ethnic groups more than others. This type of approach still prevails in Nairobi to a more limited extent.

In addition, the colonial government consciously or unconsciously used one ethnic group against another. For example, the British recruited Kamba, Kipsigis, and Kalenjin ethnic groups for army and police work against the Kikuyu, whom the British saw as the primary threat to colonial rule. Through the denial of opportunities for trans-ethnic politics and the discouragement for many years of African nationalist parties, political organizations, and newspapers, the British left the way open for ethnic parties and associations. Likewise, with the belated introduction of extensive African legislative representation through popular elections, local politics with an ethnic orientation prevailed. Since there were few experienced African administrators, judges, politicians, and military or police officers, there was a dearth of respected Africans who could mediate inter-ethnic disputes or could handle problems that generated inter-ethnic conflict. Moreover, most Africans lacked the integrative experience of formal education, including the learning of a common language, the forming of multi-ethnic friendships, and the development of ethnically cross-cutting associations.

At independence, the Kenya African National Union (KANU) came to be increasingly dominated by Kikuyu and Luo. As such, it could hardly mediate inter-ethnic disputes. Likewise, because the struggle for political power was so intense, elections could not be used to resolve inter-ethnic conflict peacefully. At the same time, the legislature, bureaucracy, judiciary, army, and police were no longer considered ethnically neutral.

Although inter-ethnic tension had always existed in Nairobi, the manifestations became more serious with independence. There was overwhelming evidence of ethnic discrimination. Conflict arose from the fact that, because of ethnic prejudice, certain groups seemed to be getting ahead faster than others. Tension between the Luo and the Kikuyu was the most obvious. Ethnic favouritism in job allocations was undoubtedly the greatest source of animosity in view of the existing urban poverty and unemployment. Management of urban services in Nairobi has been worsened by inter-racial and inter-ethnic conflict originating to a large extent in the colonial period. This, of course, adversely affects the attainment of the cooperative relationship necessary for successful decentralization and management of urban services. What intensifies social conflict in Nairobi is the existence of a large group of poor people alongside a wealthy minority. Amid poverty and unemployment, great pressure is put on those in power to distribute jobs and favours to members of their own ethnic group. As this happens, there is an intensified resentment of ethnic favouritism on the part of the politically disadvantaged. Political party affiliation is currently playing a determining role in the appointments to local government and even civil service positions.

Distrust resulting from party affiliations and such appointments is dysfunctional in a number of ways; for example, the various political party groupings into which the NCC members and employees are divided do not trust one another and those associated with the NCC are distrustful of those associated with central government. This impedes the communication process necessary for administrative efficiency and results in the inordinate prolongation of committee meetings, upon which the functioning of the NCC depends. Chief officers sabotage decisions of councillors and the mayor, and vice versa. In this way, technical decisions or advice of the officers come to be viewed as politically motivated. Such conflicts have affected the policy-making process, reduced the operational effectiveness of the NCC, and reduced its ability to provide services to residents (Karuga, 1993). The non-Africans, such as Asians and Europeans, however, have kept away from politics by spending most of their time in business. But because they control wealth they also exercise some influence over Nairobi politics.

The provision of urban services

The provision of basic urban services has not kept pace with the rapid growth of the city. The vast majority of the urban poor do not have access to such services, which are inadequate and not properly maintained. Whereas the urban population has doubled in size during the past decade, infrastructural development has proceeded far more slowly. The result has been an ever-widening gap between the need for and the supply of essential services. Revenue is collected primarily from property taxes (80 per cent in 1986/87), and also from fees (4 per cent), rents (15 per cent), and other sources, but is not adequate to finance urban services (Mazingira Institute, 1993, p. 10). Revenue sources have been depleted as a result of the central government abolition of the Graduated Personal Tax. Although a Local Service Charge Tax was introduced in 1988, because of corruption, mismanagement, and cross-indebtedness between the central government and the NCC between 1973 and 1988 the NCC is still running a serious financial deficit.

Urban sprawl is associated with a rapidly deteriorating quality of life, with particularly adverse impacts on the urban poor who have the poorest access to the existing facilities. Mostly affected are housing, water supply, sewerage, and transport. Access to infrastructure has been dependent on income levels rather than population density, with higher standards of provision in high-income areas than in high-density, low-income areas.

Housing

Racial segregation was promoted by the early European settlers and this resulted essentially in ethnic tripartition of Nairobi, with the Europeans overwhelmingly inhabiting the north-western and western areas of high rents and land values, and the Asians predominating in the north-eastern parts, while Africans were relegated to the densely populated areas to the east and south. This residential segregation has been reduced since the attainment of independence and the exodus of the European and Asian population, although ethnic partition has not been completely eradicated. Thus, three distinct sections can still be recognized today in Nairobi. There is the high-income residential region to the north and west of the CBD formerly devoted exclusively to the European residents, but which now accommodates a few affluent Africans and Asians. The second discrete section of Nairobi is Eastlands, where the predominantly African working class resides. The third distinct area is the Parklands–Eastleigh area, which houses the majority of the Asian population.

The colonial rulers regarded Africans as temporary sojourners in Nairobi and thus made little provision for their accommodation. It was thought that the provision of extensive public housing would encourage an excessive influx of Africans into the city, resulting in increasing criminal activities and disease. Inadequate provision of housing led to the emergence of squatter settlements during this period (Obudho and Aduwo, 1989, pp. 17–29). Colonial efforts to curb such settlement by demolition did not succeed, because most of the residents continued to construct houses elsewhere. Housing stress zones in Nairobi are, therefore, not new. They date back to the first decade of the twentieth century when the city was still in its infancy. The emergence of many more such settlements has been a function of the relatively high rate of demographic growth in Nairobi during the post-war decades, coupled with a growing shortage of conventional housing and related infrastructural facilities. After the lifting of the Mau Mau Emergency in 1960 and independence in 1963, there was a large influx of people into the city. Nairobi developed a reputation for a good standard of living and, therefore, attracted in-migrants from around the nation. An acute housing shortage developed. Homeless people resorted to squatting on unoccupied land or renting land from private owners and building houses. Tiny shacks proliferated on empty land throughout the city. Over time, the use of permanent building materials and the development of rooms for rent became widespread. These housing areas are characterized by: overcrowding and high densities; small one- and two-room dwelling units; poor sanitation and lack of other communal facilities; lack of adequate support infrastructure; buildings in poor structural condition and constructed of temporary and semi-permanent materials; and a high degree of tenure insecurity. In Nairobi the main zones of poor housing are in the Dagoretti, Langata (Kibera), Kasarani, and Makadara divisions (fig. 9.7). Informal settlements occupy 6 per cent of the residential area but house 55 per cent of the city's population, a total of 750,000 people (Alder, 1994).

As noted above, the result of inadequate formal sector housing provision has been the development of informal settlements (Ross, 1973; Hake, 1977; Memon, 1982; Kabagambe and Moughtin, 1983; Obudho and Aduwo, 1989; Obudho, 1992, pp. 102–103). There are at least four different types of such development in Nairobi, with some overlap between types: semi-permanent rural; semi-permanent urban; temporary urban; and temporary and semi-permanent infill. The first two groups account for the oldest areas and the largest number of people. A distinction is made between uncontrolled urban and rural areas in the city to underline the difference between traditional rural housing and newer urban settlements, whose population is committed to developing its own brand of urban life. The households in these informal areas have poor access to communal and infrastructural services such as water, sanitation, and solid waste disposal, and are thus exposed to ill-health and disease. Frequent demolitions of temporary dwellings destroy the lives and housing of Nairobi's poor. The shelter problem is intensified by the exorbitantly high rents for single rooms.

Housing development problems in Nairobi are a result of high rates of urban growth; a lag in the development of the urban infrastructure that supports housing development; the low purchasing power of the majority of urban households; and a lack of appropriate building standards owing to restrictive building by-laws. Constraints on the improvement and supply of housing in Nairobi include the limited supply of serviced land; rapid growth of unserviced peri-urban settlements in urban centres such as Githurai, Ngong, Machakos, and Kikuyu; and serious restrictions on access to formal housing finance, because of the strict lending criteria of financial institutions. Nairobi is suffering from a shortage of cheap and affordable housing. The public and formal sectors do not build enough houses to cater for the need arising from the increase in population. About 25,000 housing units are required annually (fig. 9.8) but the public and private sectors together have built, at most, 3,000 "standard" housing units per annum in recent years.

The NCC policy is to formulate and adopt realistic and performance-oriented building standards, especially in the area of low-cost

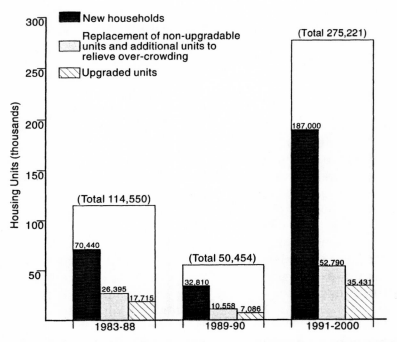

Fig. 9.8   **Nairobi: Housing needs, 1983–2000 (Source: Mazingira Institute, 1993, p. 8)**

housing. In publicly constructed houses, the housing standards are usually followed. Formal private housing schemes also observe the prescribed building standards. However, in private housing, especially in informal settlements but also in middle-income housing areas, standards are not adhered to. The issue of standards is closely linked to affordability. The requirement for standards that are comparatively high has often led those who cannot afford such houses to resort to units that are substandard, but the penalties for not building according to the standards are not enforced. The first phase of the Dandora site and service scheme, for instance (see below), failed to conform with health regulations. At the policy level, attitudes and approaches to building standards seem to be changing. This has been demonstrated by the Council's use of cheap building materials designed by the University of Nairobi. In addition, the NCC has not tried to interfere with the housing upgrading activities of the Undugu Society of Kenya. At the central government level, there is a consensus that the building regulations should be revised.

Approaches to the housing problem

Until the 1970s the typical response of the NCC and the wider public sector was to provide conventional housing either for rental or for sale. This approach had little impact on housing need, because the dwellings provided were invariably not affordable by low-income groups. Moreover, the subsidies that underlay public housing were, on the whole, both inefficient and inequitable. Many tenants occupy prime properties rented out by the NCC at rents far below the market rates (Karuga, 1993). Starting in the mid-1970s, the NCC received substantial support from foreign donors and was able to focus its attention more on the shelter needs of lower-income groups. A second generation of housing projects thus emerged, largely taking the form of sites and services and core housing.

The first of these was the Dandora community development project to the east of the city, implemented between 1975 and 1978 and financed jointly by the World Bank and GOK. It consisted of 6,000 serviced plots of 100–160 m^2 each, with individual water and sewer connections, access to roads, security lighting, and refuse collection services. The project included community facilities such as primary schools, health centres, multi-purpose community centres, and market stalls. The beneficiaries were intended to be poor households, but, although some low-income families were allocated plots, many allottees were not in the lowest income group, many plots had absentee landlords, and many residents were tenants (UNCHS, 1987; Lee-Smith and Memon, 1988; Syagga and Kiamba, 1988).

The second urban project, also financed by the World Bank, comprised 14,409 serviced plots and some upgrading. It, however, covered other urban centres in Kenya as well as Nairobi. The third urban project, comprising 25,000 serviced plots and squatter upgrading programmes, also sponsored by the World Bank, covered small and intermediate urban centres in Kenya, excluding Nairobi. In all these programmes, the element of improving informal settlements was very small. This is possibly because, in the eyes of the political élite, administrators, and professionals, upgrading is not attractive for political display.

The other low-cost shelter schemes implemented in Nairobi were: Umoja Phase I, comprising 2,400 units, financed by USAID, and completed in 1976; and Umoja Phase II project, also funded by a loan from USAID and completed in 1991. It was decided to provide condominiums instead of housing units on individual plots. Umoja Phase

II, which started in 1985, consisted of 4,406 condominium units. Five to six people share communal facilities, and each allottee is provided with a room and an option to build another. The element of subsidy was, however, tremendously reduced and each allottee paid for 96.3 per cent of the development cost, with the NCC being responsible for only off-site infrastructure and land. However, affordability of housing schemes in Nairobi has been limited by excessively high building and construction standards, the application of rigid restrictions on the use of houses for commercial and informal sector activities, and limitations imposed on the way in which loans could be used. Recent developments of flats in Majengo, Pumwani, and Kibera by the National Housing Corporation have been advertised at a cost that is unaffordable by the low-income groups for whom they were meant.

Various housing for sale schemes have also been started in Nairobi. These include the Kayole North Mortgage Housing Scheme located in the northern sector of Kayole, which is being developed by the Kenya Building Society Ltd., a wholly owned subsidiary of the Housing Finance Company of Kenya. The scheme was intended for the medium-income group, but rapid inflation led to final sale prices above those affordable by the target group. The private sector thus builds houses that are for the middle- and upper-income classes.

Water resources

An estimated 89 per cent of Nairobi's population is supplied with water through house connections, communal watering points, and water kiosks. The remaining 11 per cent obtain their water supplies from boreholes. The major health problems related to inadequate water supply and sanitation are centred on the poor urban areas. None of these areas has an adequate water supply. Informal settlements are entirely dependent on public water kiosks. Thus residents restrict their water purchases to levels that are barely adequate. The city has a growing problem of water supply which has its roots in the original choice of the site. Nairobi was not originally planned to be a large conurbation and the available water resource was sufficient only for a smaller population. To meet the growing demand, water has to be pumped from locations outside the city. However, apart from occasional water shortages, especially during the dry seasons, the basic problem has been one of distribution. Annual expenditure on water and sewerage declined dramatically in real terms between 1981 and 1987 – capital expenditure by 91 per cent and expenditure on maintenance by 68 per cent (Mazingira Institute, 1993, p. 10) – and the situation has not shown any significant improvement since then.

Sewerage systems

The sewage produced in urban areas consists of waste water, industrial effluent, and storm water, which may enter sewers through faulty or damaged manholes. The inadequate capacity of existing treatment plants results in the disposal of untreated sewage into Nairobi River and other small streams. This poses a health hazard to users of such streams. Approximately 58 per cent of Nairobi's population is served by the existing waterborne sewerage system, which suffers from a number of problems, including poor maintenance, illegal connections, use of toilets for the disposal of garbage, and deliberate blocking of sewage pipes for irrigation. The remainder of the population is served by septic tanks, conservation tanks, or pit latrines, which contribute to the pollution of groundwater and of piped water owing to seepage into pipes when the pressure is low. There are no foul or storm water connections to the sewerage systems in the slum and squatter areas. Instead, filthy uncared for pit latrines are used. The sanitation problems are compounded by densities in some housing areas that are higher than those for which the sewerage system was originally planned, and the location of some informal housing in areas unsuitable for residential use.

Solid waste disposal

The collection and disposal of solid wastes in Nairobi has become increasingly infrequent. It is estimated that, in 1994, 800–1,000 tonnes of refuse were generated per day, out of which fewer than 200 tonnes were collected. The NCC has the responsibility of collecting and disposing of solid wastes. However, lack of resources, especially vehicles, and the general apathy of residents have led to uncollected waste piling up in several parts of the city. Some private companies now operate, and privatizing waste collection has been considered as a possible remedial measure, but has not yet been adopted as official policy. As Nairobi grows and the volume of refuse increases, the NCC should promote reclamation, re-use, and recycling of materials as a way of reducing the problems. Such activities could create employment for a section of the population as well as being a source of raw materials.

Transportation

One of the earliest problems that Nairobi faced during this period was that of traffic. It has been argued that in 1928 Nairobi was in fact the most motor-ridden urban centre in the world in proportion to its non-African population (Aduwo, 1990). Parking and speeding became major problems that were often discussed by the authorities. From 1929 a programme to tarmac all roads in the CBD was carried out. The relatively large numbers of cars contributed to the thinning out of the western side of Nairobi, which by 1962 had a population density as low as 6.1 people per acre, compared with the African residential zone in the east with 125.9 people per acre during the same period (Hake, 1977, p. 24). Meanwhile, a public bus service was inaugurated following an agreement with United Transport International (Aduwo, 1990). The result of this agreement was the establishment of the Kenya Bus Service (KBS), which was given the exclusive franchise of carrying fare-paying passengers in and around Nairobi. During this time the demand for public transport was low, consisting mainly of European and Asian expatriates and a growing number of African workers.

Today transport in Nairobi can be split into five components: private vehicles, buses, *matatus*, commuter trains, and taxis. Private vehicles are almost exclusively reserved for the middle- and upper-income groups because of the high cost of purchase and maintenance. The KBS, which has over 300 buses, operates commuter transportation mainly oriented towards the eastern part of Nairobi where low-income people live. Although the fares are quite low they are still high for the majority of residents. It was hoped that the Nyayo Bus Services launched by the GOK in 1986 would ease the commuter problem in the city, but 90 per cent of its buses are not functioning owing to gross mismanagement and lack of spare parts. The *matatu* is an African invention. Originally private taxis, they offer regular services with better frequencies than the bus service, thus providing a relatively quick means of transportation to the CBD and increasing the accessibility of many of the outlying areas (Aduwo, 1990; Obudho, 1993b, pp. 91–109). Recently, commuter trains were introduced by the Kenya Railway to help ease transportation to the suburbs and this service has been well received despite the high fares (Aduwo, 1990; Obudho 1993b, pp. 91–109). Taxis have little impact on the mass transportation systems in Nairobi, because they have primarily geared themselves to tourists (Ndegea, 1995). Despite all these urban transportation systems, the majority of trips are still undertaken using non-motorized forms of transport, even over long distances.

The inherited transport patterns, together with the additional travel generated mainly by an increased population, exerted demands on the urban form and its infrastructure that they were ill equipped to meet. A major problem here has been the centralization of the civil service, commerce, and other service activities in the CBD and industrial area, where it is estimated that over 75 per cent of commuters are employed. Much of the employment in wholesale and retail trade, restaurants and hotels, transport and communications, finance, insurance, real estate, and business services is located within the CBD. The CBD has for a long time been subjected to numerous traffic problems, which are exacerbated by a lack of space in its vicinity. The post-independence period also witnessed a relaxation (not by design) of traffic regulations, parking restrictions, and land-use control. Hence within a few years after independence much of the formal land-use urban pattern of the original settlement structure was eroded. Since 1970, the city has expanded tremendously and a new population distribution pattern has emerged. Even more important is the fact that a large percentage of low-income users of public transport now live further away from the CBD. Expansion of the city to the east, south, and north has not been matched by an expansion in transport facilities and services. The annual rate of growth of daily passenger journeys is currently estimated to be almost 6 per cent (table 9.5). A clear manifestation of the unmet demand for public transport services is the daily stampede and jostling at most of the city's transport terminals, especially during the rush hours, and the overflowing number of passengers transported by the existing modes of public transport. Nairobi's transportation problems are due to neglect of maintenance, inadequate investment, poor management of traffic systems, breakdown of road discipline, and failure to develop an adequate policy and planning framework.

Recreation and leisure

The aesthetic and recreational environment has received little attention from planners in Nairobi. Industrial and commercial enterprises

Table 9.5   **Nairobi: Public transport demand, 1985, 1990, and 2000**

Year	Passenger journeys per day ('000)	Growth rate per annum (%)
1985	676	5.82
1990	873	
2000[a]	1,393	5.95

Source: Obudho (1993b), p. 97.
a. Estimate.

have so far received attention at its expense. Urban parks and gardens have been usurped for the development of commercial buildings. The few that remain are not cared for and continue to be threatened by commercial development. Currently there are only six major open spaces: Uhuru/Central parks, Jamhuri and City parks, one arboretum, and two forest areas. In addition, there are several public playing fields and sports centres and a number of privately owned parks in various parts of the city. Nairobi also contains the renowned Nairobi National Park and the affiliated Wild Animal Orphanage. The dramatic growth of the city in size, numbers, and complexity has had profound impacts on its open spaces. The impact is manifested basically in the form of overcrowding in some recreational areas such as Uhuru Park, Jevanjee Gardens, and other neighbourhood parks; the conversion of existing open spaces to other development purposes, for example the "Uhuru Park saga" where the government wanted to take part of the park for an office complex; open spaces being turned into open-air markets; and illegal usage of these spaces for agriculture and squatter settlements. The importance of open spaces for recreation and environmental protection is given low priority in the development and spatial planning of Nairobi. New neighbourhoods are constructed without open spaces or playgrounds.

Environmental and health problems

Urban environmental problems are as old as Nairobi itself. They occur because of rapid population growth, poor planning, scarcity of capital resources, industrial growth, and poverty. In addition to the environmental problems related to water supply, sewage disposal, and solid waste management, a range of pollution and health problems will be discussed in this section.

Atmospheric, water, noise, and odour pollution

The main sources of atmospheric pollution are vehicles and industries. Vehicles emit fumes that contain carbon monoxide, nitrogen oxide, and sulphur dioxide. Lead and smoke are particulate matter produced by vehicles. Although the penal code is particular about emissions by motor vehicles, nothing so far has been done to reduce the level of air pollution in Nairobi. Industrial establishments, most of which are located in proximity to the residential estates of low-income earners, also contribute to air pollution. In 1992, measurements of the concentration of suspended particulate matter revealed the highest concentrations in the industrial area (252 μg/m^3). Other areas of the city had levels less than a third of this (80 and 83 μg/m^3 in Buruburu and Woodley areas, respectively).

Surface water pollution in Nairobi has also reached an alarming level. The main surface water sources are the Nairobi and Ngong rivers. Clean when they enter the city, by the time they pass through it, they have collected all sorts of refuse, industrial effluent, and effluent from sewage works.

Noise pollution is on the increase, mainly from motor vehicles, locomotives, motor cycles, aircraft, industries, and construction sites. It may lead to health problems such as high blood pressure, mental illness, loss of hearing, fatigue, and irritability.

Odour pollution arises from industrial activities such as food processing and chemicals production, as well as urban farming. The unpleasant odours are caused by industries that use sulphur and nitrogen components, ammonia, hydrogen sulphide, and phosphorus, among others. As Nairobi industrializes, the problem of odour pollution, which causes adverse physical reactions including nausea and loss of sleep, as well as reduction in the enjoyment of external and internal environments, will increase.

Health problems

More than half of Nairobi's residents are crowded into unplanned or inadequately serviced settlements, living and working in unhealthy environmental conditions. Residents, especially children, in these areas are frequently ill with diarrhoea and intestinal parasites, colds, influenza, and skin infections. All these illnesses are related to poor environmental hygiene, which in turn is a consequence of poverty, overcrowding, and neglect of the urban poor, and is exacerbated by the high densities in some of the areas, such as Pumwani (42,633 inh/km^2), Mathare (33,470 inh/km^2), and Kariobangi (33,195 inh/km^2) (Republic of Kenya, 1994). The problems particularly affect women and place an unfair burden on them because of their low incomes and their responsibilities for child care, fetching water and domestic fuel, and providing food for their families.

The AIDS epidemic in Kenya has been on the increase particularly in the major urban centres (Obudho, 1995). According to the Kenya National Aids Control programme, Nairobi had a total of 2,542 cases by 1991, of whom 1,664 were men. In 1994, 250,000 urban AIDS cases were reported (National Aids Control Programme, 1994), of which two-thirds were in urban centres such as Mombasa, Kisumu, and Nairobi. The rates and patterns of increase in AIDS and HIV cases suggest that it has urban origins in Kenya. Urban centres are the gateway to cross-border international migration. Nairobi attracts a substantial number of international migrants as well as migrant labourers, prostitutes, and sexually active adults. Since about 90 per cent of HIV is transmitted through sexual relationships, the link between urbanization and sexual mobility, especially commercial sex, means that Nairobi's population is very susceptible (Konde-Lule, 1991). In Nairobi, the suspected risk factors for HIV and AIDS include living or working in the city without a permanent spouse, having a large number of heterosexual partners, using unsterilized syringes, and receiving infected blood transfusions. However, sexual relationships account for the largest number of transmissions. It appears that urbanization has led to a decline in sexual relations within the family circle, with commercial sex being on the increase. Sexual networks have broadened and there is a lot of overlapping, making people extremely susceptible to disease. Although prostitution is illegal in Kenya, commercial sex workers are found in bars, in lodging houses, and even in the streets. For many people, increased access to cash promotes sexual mobility because there are more opportunities and society is more permissive (Konde-Lule, 1991). However, to counteract this, Nairobi also provides better opportunities for the dissemination of information related to the preventive measures that individuals should take: the National Aids Control Programme has its headquarters in the city; and people in urban areas are usually better educated and have easier access to medical services and mass communication facilities than their rural counterparts. Nairobi may, therefore, be seen as a source of contracting

STDs, HIV, and AIDS, while at the same time providing channels through which to educate residents about preventive measures (Obudho, 1995).

Urban development programmes, policies, and strategies

The problems associated with the development of Nairobi call for gearing urban development programmes, policies, and strategies to achieve sustainable growth. The planning of Nairobi was done on an ad hoc basis until 1926, when the first plan was prepared. In 1948, a Nairobi Master Plan was completed (White et al., 1948). Since the introduction of the 1948 plan, the city boundary has been extended, its population has grown beyond that projected, and a post-colonial government with a new political orientation has come to power. The Nairobi Metropolitan Growth Strategy was formulated in 1973, but it has never been implemented. Because of the lack of a clear planning strategy, the city has experienced an unplanned, haphazard pattern of development, leading to settlements containing incongruous mixtures of activities, an overconcentration of employment in the CBD and industrial area, resulting in traffic congestion and environmental pollution, and rapid growth of informal settlements. Coordinated and focused urban and regional policy strategies for the city region are lacking. In addition, there tends to be too much emphasis on the provision of services and too little on involving the people and their resources in the planning and development process.

The overriding objective of urban development must be to contribute productively to urban, regional, national, and spatial development. Attention should be focused on the role that Nairobi could and should play in supporting development in the essentially rural agricultural economy of Kenya. It is worth noting that urban residents have benefited from the "urban bias" in investment and employment creation. Hence, reducing or eliminating this bias will be politically difficult, especially because the urban élite control political power. There is a need for a series of specific operational objectives that should comprise the building blocks for achievement of a long-term urban planning strategy for the city. City planning must provide a series of policies and a spatial framework to guide social and economic activities, coordinate and integrate development activities, and mobilize the involvement of residents in the planning and development process. The planning of Nairobi, despite past planning mistakes, should take into account and protect various racial and ethnic community interests, be cost-effective, be sensitive to the environment, and be consistent with broad regional and national urbanization policies. Owing to the severe shortages of trained staff, fiscal resources, and administrative capacity, major programme objectives clearly cannot be achieved in the short term. Instead, incremental improvements are needed on various fronts.

Because policies and programmes to control rural–urban migration and redistribution of population have not been successful, there is an increasing recognition that the growth of Nairobi is inevitable and that the solutions to the city's problems depend heavily on their effective management. The main issues faced by Nairobi are gaining greater control over the urban growth process; improving its financial and institutional structure and management; providing shelter, basic urban services, and infrastructure; strengthening the role of the informal sector; and formulating environmental policies and programmes.

Gaining control over unmanageable urban growth

In order to reduce the attractiveness of Nairobi to migrants and increase equity in national resources, the present level of national subsidies to the city needs to be reduced. This will require a review of the present system of pricing of services to recover an increasing share of the cost (see also below).

Both to encourage economic diversification and to avoid further urban sprawl, planning for the city region should pay more attention to the development of satellite urban centres including Machakos, Ongata, Rongai, Ngong, and Kikuyu. Neglected in the past, these centres have an important role in agricultural processing, marketing, storage, and distribution. Their prosperity depends on the availability of markets in Nairobi and the city's ability to supply them with goods and services such as agricultural equipment and repair services.

Land use in Nairobi was basically a reflection of the British colonial land-use patterns, which were determined by race. Although the legacy of these earlier patterns is seen in the segregation of residential areas by income, land uses have become mixed and poorly planned, because planning norms and standards have been ignored in land allocations and development control has been ineffective. Improved land-use planning is needed, to anticipate problems and plan for them in advance rather than reacting to crisis, to produce an environmentally sound and healthy urban environment, and to ensure that public needs are satisfied.

Improving the management of the financial and institutional structure

The resources to support urban development in Nairobi have been supplied by both local and central government, but those available from the latter in particular have been insufficient to deal with worsening urban problems. International agencies or donors have been of substantial assistance especially by providing financial support and/or equipment to the NCC. At least 14 international agencies have sponsored projects in Nairobi since independence, including the World Bank, USAID, the Friedrich Naumann Foundation, the Canadian International Development Agency, the Chandaria Foundation, the Deutsche Gesellschaft für Technische Zusammenarbeit, and eight UN agencies. In addition, friendly countries, including the United Kingdom, Germany, the Nordic countries, Italy, the United States, and Belgium, have provided loans and grants. The projects that have been funded include housing, roads, refuse collection vehicles, fire fighting equipment, water supply and sewerage, public health, education, the informal sector, and social service projects. Housing and water supply, in particular, have received enormous funding from the World Bank and USAID. The delivery of services has, however, not improved significantly despite this financial assistance. This may be attributed to inappropriate programmes and conditions imposed by the donors, corruption during the implementation stage, and apathy on the part of NCC officials.

Improvements to revenue generation are needed, initially by increasing the proportion of service costs recovered from users wherever possible in order to reduce subsidies and eliminate financial constraints on extending delivery. The present system, whereby services reach a small proportion of the urban population and many of these are not obliged to pay, is unsustainable. In addition, measures are needed to ensure that higher-income residents are not subsidized and that service provision is extended to currently unserviced or inadequately serviced low-income areas. Alternative means of generating increased revenue, such as increasing the yield from existing taxes and fees, bidding for a larger share of national taxes from central government, and mobilizing resources from the private large- and small-scale sectors and NGOs, need to be investigated.

However, political support and administrative capacity are crucial in implementing resource mobilization policy. Increased revenue generation is unlikely to succeed without greater decentralization of power to the city government and political support at both central and local levels in order to surmount pressures from vested interests. Further obstacles include a severe shortage of trained personnel in the local authority, particularly accounts and finance managers, low staff morale because of low wages and limited career opportunities, and ineffective monitoring and evaluation systems.

Thus public sector institutions in the city need to be strengthened. In particular the Nairobi City Council should be given greater financial autonomy, its responsibilities defined more clearly, staff development supported, adequate staff and finance provided for planning functions, and the urban information system improved. Given the financial and institutional weaknesses of the city government, however, it is imperative that programmes be designed that stimulate greater community participation in the financing and delivery of services (see below).

Providing shelter, basic urban services, and infrastructure

Policy and programme responses to deficiencies in shelter, services, and infrastructure have been disjointed and ad hoc. The access of the urban poor in particular to shelter and services has been constrained by high land prices, lack of access to credit, inadequate opportunities for participating in the planning and implementation of shelter projects, inadequate cost recovery, high and inflexible building codes and standards, and the high cost of building materials. More appropriate standards for infrastructure provision and housing construction are needed, in addition to measures to reduce other constraints and provide services more cheaply. The efficiency of relevant institutions needs to be improved, and private sector provision, the use of community-based organizations and NGOs, and self-help programmes encouraged.

Strengthening the role of the informal sector

The informal sector significantly contributes to Nairobi's economy, generates a large volume of employment, and has strong backward linkages with commercial and public enterprises. It provides a variety of goods and services, a greater part of which enter into the "consumption basket" of individual households. Although large-scale public sector investment is probably not needed, appropriate support to the sector might include improved infrastructure, credit, and training.

Formulating environmental policies and programmes

There are major gaps in policy with respect to environmental protection and management. In addition, institutional weaknesses inhibit the enforcement of controls that do exist and the realization of the potential for enlisting the participation of residents in solving environmental problems. Environmental policies and action programmes need to be formulated in accordance with the call emerging from the 1992 UN Conference on Environment and Development for local Agenda 21s to be prepared. These must deal, *inter alia*, with solid waste management, pollution control, and the conservation of natural resources (including forests, flora, and fauna) and must involve a wide range of interests, including public sector institutions, private enterprises, and residents.

Conclusion

There has been heightened public awareness of the need for the Nairobi City Council to take decisive measures to improve conditions in the city. The requirement for a clearly formulated urban policy thus arises precisely because of the importance of ensuring an appropriate perspective for urban and regional development. In view of the economic crisis, declining agricultural productivity, and scarce capital investment and management resources, the city should strive for "affordable decentralization." In doing this, the following policy options should be considered: ensuring that sufficient investment is made in Nairobi to maintain its overall contribution to national economic growth, but at the same time reducing the subsidies that encourage development of the city; emphasizing investment in other growth centres; and investing in the inter-urban transport and communications network, which is essential to link up the city with other urban centres of major economic potential (Van Huyck, 1988, p. 201). At the regional level, development should be encouraged in satellite centres to reduce unplanned sprawl. Within the city, efforts should be made to decentralize activities out of the CBD, to improve environmental conditions at the city and neighbourhood levels, and to support economic activities. Reforms to financial and institutional struc-tures and procedures will be needed to achieve these policy goals.

Note

1. For an account of Nairobi's development and characteristics set within a wider framework of relationships between African cities and the world economy, see Simon (1992).

References

Aduwo, G. O. 1990. Productivity, efficiency and quality of source of the matatu mode of public transportation in Nairobi, Kenya: A geographical analysis. Unpublished M.A. thesis, University of Nairobi, Geography Department.

Alder, G. 1994. Tackling poverty in Nairobi's informal settlements: Developing an institutional strategy. Paper presented to the CROP Workshop on Urban Poverty, 7–9 October, Bergen.

Aptekar, L. et al. 1994. Street children in Nairobi, Kenya. *African Urban Quarterly* 9(3/4): 365–374.

Ayako, A. B. 1994. Financing street children programmes in Kenya. *African Urban Quarterly* 9(3/4): 340–353.

Boedecker, E. 1936. *Early History of Nairobi Township*. Macmillan, Nairobi.

Cloix, L. 1950. City status for Nairobi. *Commonwealth Survey* 43(12): 23–24.

East African Statistical Department. 1986. *African Population of Kenya Colony and Protectorate: Geographical and Tribal Population Census, 1948*. East African Community, Nairobi.

Ferraro, G. P. 1978. Nairobi: Overview of an East African City. *African Urban Studies* 3: 1–13.

Foran, R. 1950. Rise of Nairobi: From campsite to city – phase in the history of Kenya's capital which is soon to receive a Royal Charter. *The Crown Colonist* 20, March.

Freeman, D. 1991. *A City of Farmers: Informal Urban Agriculture in Open Spaces of Nairobi, Kenya*. McGill University Press, Toronto.

Hake, A. 1977. *African Metropolis: Nairobi's Self-Help City*. Chatto & Windus, London.

Hallman, D. M. 1967. The city of Nairobi. In: W. T. W. Morgan, ed., *Nairobi: City and Region*. Oxford University Press, Nairobi.

House, W. J. 1978. *Nairobi's Informal Sector: A Reservoir of Dynamic Entrepreneurs or a Residual Pool of Surplus Labour?* University of Nairobi Working Paper No. 347, Institute of Development Studies, Nairobi.

Kabagambe, D. and C. Moughtin. 1983. Housing the urban poor: A case study in Nairobi. *Third World Planning Review* 5(3): 227–248.

Karuga, J. G., ed. 1993. *Actions Towards a Better Nairobi: Report and Recommendations of the Nairobi City Convention*. Nairobi City Council, Nairobi.

Konde-Lule, J. K. 1991. The effects of urbanization on the spread of AIDS in Africa. *African Urban Quarterly* 6(1/2): 13–18.

Lado, C. 1990. Informal urban agriculture in Nairobi, Kenya. *Land Use Policy* 7: 257–266.

Lee-Smith, D. and P. A. Memon. 1988. Institution development for delivery of low-income housing: An evaluation of the Dandora community development project in Nairobi. *Third World Planning Review* 10(3): 217–238.

Macoloo, G. C. and B. C. Maina. 1994. *Urban Land Management: Regularization Policies and Local Development in Africa and the Arab States: A Kenya Case Study.* University of Nairobi, Nairobi.

Mazingira Institute. 1993. The information presented on various aspects of the city of Nairobi in graphs, charts and maps. Paper presented to Nairobi City Convention, 27–29 July, Charter Hall, Nairobi, Kenya.

Memon, P. A. 1982. The growth of low-income settlements: Planning response in the peri-urban zone of Nairobi. *Third World Planning Review* 4: 145–158.

Morgan, W. T. W. 1968. The location of Nairobi. In: H. Berger, ed., *Ostafrikanische Studien.* Freidrich-Alexander Universität, Nuremberg.

———— 1976. *Nairobi: City and Region.* Oxford University Press, Nairobi.

Mwatha, R. G. 1988. Women business entrepreneurs in urban informal sector. Paper presented to the First International Conference on Urban Growth and Spatial Planning of Nairobi, Nairobi, Kenya.

National Aids Control Programme. 1994. *AIDS in Kenya: Background, Projections, Impact and Intervention.* National AIDS Control Programme, Nairobi.

NCC (Nairobi City Council). 1973. *Nairobi Metropolitan Growth Strategy, Volumes I and II.* Nairobi.

Ndegea, S. 1995. The role and potential of the taxi mode of urban transport in the city of Nairobi, Kenya: A geographical analysis. Unpublished M.A. thesis, University of Nairobi.

Obudho, R. A. 1979. Urban primacy index in Kenya. In: R. A. Obudho and D. R. F. Taylor, eds., *The Spatial Structure of Development: A Study of Kenya.* Westview Press, Boulder, Colo.

———— 1982. *Urbanization in Kenya: Bottom–up Approach to Development Planning.* University Press of America, Washington, D.C.

———— 1983. *Urbanization and Development Planning in Kenya.* Kenya Literature Bureau, Nairobi.

———— 1992. Urban and rural settlement in Kenya. *Regional Development Dialogue* 13(4): 86–117.

———— 1993a. The role of small and intermediate urban centres in economic recovery and regional development in Kenya. Paper presented to the Research Workshop on the Role of Small Urban Centres in Economic Recovery and Regional Development in Africa, 1–7 December, Nyeri, Kenya.

———— 1993b. Urban public transport in Nairobi, Kenya. In: D. Plat, ed., *Transports en Afrique Sub-Saharienne.* Laboratoire d'Economie de Transport, Lyon, pp. 91–112.

———— 1994. Kenya. In: J. D. Tarver, ed., *Urbanization in Africa: A Handbook.* Greenwood Press, Westport, Conn., pp. 198–212.

———— 1995. STDs, HIVs, AIDS and urbanization in Kenya. *Journal of Health Sciences* 2(1): 27–38.

Obudho, R. A. and G. O. Aduwo. 1989. Slums and squatter settlements in urban centres of Kenya: Towards a planning strategy. *Netherlands Journal of Housing and Environmental Research* 4(1): 17–29.

———— 1992. The nature of the urbanization process and urbanism in the city of Nairobi, Kenya. *African Urban Quarterly* 7(1/2): 50–62.

Obudho, R. A. and Z. Muganzi. 1991. Population growth and urban change: A case study of Nairobi, Kenya. In: M. Bannon et al., eds., *Urbanization and Urban Development: Recent Trends in a Global Context*. University College, Dublin, pp. 108–120.

Ondiege, P. O. 1989. *Urban Land and Residential Market Analysis in Kenya*. Urban Management Programme, UNCHS (Habitat), Nairobi.

Republic of Kenya. 1966. *Kenya Population Census, 1962*. Government Printer, Nairobi.

———— 1971. *Kenya Population Census, 1969. Vol. II. Urban Population*. Government Printer, Nairobi.

———— 1981. *Kenya Population Census, 1979. Vol. I Tribes. Vol. II Urban Population*. Government Printer, Nairobi.

———— 1993. *Economic Survey 1992*. Government Printer, Nairobi.

———— 1994. *Population Census 1989: Volumes I and II*. Government Printer, Nairobi.

Ross, M. H. 1973. *The Political Integration of Urban Squatters*. Northwestern University Press, Evanston, Ill.

Simon, D. 1992. *Cities, Capital and Development: African Cities in the World Economy*. Belhaven Press, London.

Syagga, P. M. and J. M. Kiamba. 1988. Housing the urban poor. Paper presented to the First International Conference on Urban Growth and Spatial Planning of Nairobi. Nairobi, Kenya.

Tiwari, R. C. 1972. Some aspects of the social geography of Nairobi, Kenya. *African Urban Notes* 6(1): 36–61.

———— 1979. A comparative analysis of the functional structure of Central Business Districts in East Africa. In: R. A. Obudho and D. R. F. Taylor, eds., *The Spatial Structure of Development: A Study of Kenya*. Westview Press, Boulder, Colo., pp. 110–124.

UNCHS. 1987. *Case Study of Sites and Services Schemes in Kenya: Lessons from Dandora and Thika*. United Nations Centre for Human Settlements, Nairobi.

Van Huyck, A. 1988. The primate city: A friend or foe to national development? *African Urban Quarterly* 3(3/4): 197–203.

Walmsley, R. W. 1957. *Nairobi. The Geography of a New City*. Eagle Press, Kampala.

Werlin, H. H. 1974. *Governing an African City: A Study of Nairobi*. Africana, New York.

White L. W. T., L. Silberman, and P. R. Anderson. 1948. *Nairobi: Master Plan for a Colonial Capital. A Report Prepared for the Municipality of Nairobi*. HMSO, London.

Part III
The dynamics of city development

10

Globalization or informalization? African urban economies in the 1990s

Christian M. Rogerson

Abstract

La persistance de la crise économique africaine, en particulier en matière d'insuffisance de l'emploi et de pauvreté massive, se manifeste dans la situation des grandes villes du continent. Ce chapitre a pour objectif de faire ressortir les nouvelles tendances des économies urbaines africaines dans les années 90. L'on a choisi d'évaluer l'impact respectif de la *mondialisation* et de la *marginalisation*, processus indissociables structurant l'aspect et la situation de l'économie urbaine. La discussion se présente dans trois sections. L'on étudie d'abord la signification et la ramification de la mondialisation en termes de disparition des emploi du secteur moderne ou formel dans les grandes villes d'Afrique. L'on examine ensuite le progrès de la *marginalisation*, à savoir la progression massive du secteur informel dans pratiquement toutes les villes africaines. La troisième section est axée sur une facette particulière de la *marginalisation* qui est en train de transformer de façon spectaculaire le paysage des principales villes africaines: le développement de l'agriculture urbaine. La conclusion met l'accent sur la nécessité d'assurer en Afrique une "gestion urbaine" qui abandonne la réglementation et le contrôle du développement au profit d'une promotion active du développement économique urbain local.

Introduction

In the 1990s assessments on the state of African economies make dismal reading. It is now apparent that most of the development scenarios in the 1980s severely underestimated the length and the extent of the structural adjustment, and its ramifications for employment and unemployment, particularly in the continent's large cities. The optimistic scenarios for the 1990s had been premised on a much earlier recovery of international commodity prices and a speedier response of and support from national and international investors. Beyond these failures, another unexpected setback to economic upturn was the reappearance of East European countries as strong competitors for the already diminishing flows of external resources to the continent. Overall, available evidence reveals that the anticipated upturn in growth and employment failed to materialize across most of Africa and that the long-term prospects for economic recovery, especially in sub-Saharan Africa, "are most sobering and disturbing" (ILO–JASPA, 1992, p. 5). Africa is now the only global region where, during the next decade, the economic situation is expected to deteriorate, with "significant increases in the proportion of the population under poverty" (ILO–JASPA, 1992, p. viii). Accordingly, it is argued that the question of unemployment and its impact on poverty "still remains, perhaps, the number one social problem facing many African countries" (ILO–JASPA, 1992, p. 1).

The persistent economic crisis in Africa, particularly as regards weak employment growth and mass poverty, is manifest most visibly in the condition of the continent's large cities. The objective in this chapter is to tease out emerging trends in the state of Africa's urban economies in the 1990s. This task will be approached in terms of assessing the respective impacts of *globalization* and *informalization* as interwoven processes shaping the complexion and condition of city economies. Three major sections of discussion are presented. First, the meaning and ramifications of globalization in terms of the demise of modern or formal sector employment in Africa's large cities will be reviewed. Against this background, in the second section the focus turns to examine the advance of informalization and of the massive extension of the informal economy throughout most of urban Africa. The third section centres on a particular facet of informalization that is dramatically altering the landscape of major African cities, namely the advance of urban cultivation. Lastly, the concluding comments draw attention to certain urban policy initiatives that might offer signposts for a way forward from the current economic dilemma of Africa's large cities. Although source material and examples will be cited from all parts of Africa, the discussion is biased towards the experience of the urban areas of eastern, central, and southern Africa.

Globalization and the demise of urban formal economies

As explored in chapters 2 and 3, the phenomenon known as globalization – the progressive integration of various parts of the world into a global economy and global finance system – has attracted considerable debate over the past decade (Dieleman and Hamnett, 1994). For some writers, notably Castells (1992), the forging of a global economy is an intoxicating and momentous process, one of the major structural features of the contemporary age. The global economy is viewed as one:

that works as a unit on real time on a planetary scale. It is an economy where capital flows, labour markets, commodity markets, information, raw materials, management and organization are internationalized and fully interdependent throughout the planet, although in an asymmetrical form, characterized by the uneven integration to the global system of different areas of the planet. (Castells, 1992, p. 5)

Most observers agree that, in the current phase of globalization, "a new structure of global competition has arisen" as a result of the appearance of "global" markets and "global" production complexes (Thrift, 1994, p. 368). Although many factors contribute to the making of this new structure of competition, particular importance is attached to new innovations in technology, such as micro-electronics, telecommunications, or materials science, which exert a profound impact on refashioning world production systems. Key elements in globalization have been the growth of transnational production and the increasing openness of and interdependence among national economies. Alongside new globalized production strategies "there has been a parallel integration of financial markets which, together with a vastly improved global telecommunications and transportation infrastructure, has increased global economic integration in general" (Doohan, 1994, p. 26).

Such changes have profound impacts at the level of both national and urban economies and for individual enterprises. At the level of national and urban economies, the major impact has been an intensification of international and local competition for markets and investments. Increasingly, rates of growth of GDP and of employment hinge on an economy's ability to compete successfully within the new system of globalized production. At the level of the enterprise, the effects have been to stress the importance of adopting new process technologies, of new flexible systems of work organization, and of shifting towards flexible rather than Fordist mass production systems. Recent processes of globalization have given rise to new geographies, with the global economy described as a "space of flows" (Castells, 1989) or a necklace of localized production agglomerations strung out around the world (Storper, 1992). As noted by Rakodi in this volume (chap. 2), a central place in the organization, coordination, and control of the new global economy is accorded to sets of global or world cities. In addition to managing a new international division of labour in manufacturing, these cities are key hubs for the control and coordination of global finance and producer services. Because world city status brings with it considerable economic benefits in terms of the development of new, dynamic, high-income growth sectors of the economy, "global city status is something to be coveted, defended and fought over" (Dieleman and Hamnett, 1994, p. 358).

What are the implications for Africa and its cities of recent globalization trends and of the new competition? In many respects the changes associated with globalization are disturbing. None the less, it is clearly better for national and urban economies to be affected by them than to be left out. For all its negative side-effects, exposure to "the new competition" seems to be increasingly essential for augmented growth, efficiency, and sustained job creation (Storper, 1992; Doohan, 1994). Despite some notable African efforts at place marketing for industrial investment (fig. 10.1), most of Africa has been "left out" of the globalization processes now taking place. With notable exceptions, such as parts of North Africa and Mauritius (Rogerson, 1993a), the so-called new international division of labour, characterized by export-processing manufacturing, has bypassed the major part of the continent. Participation in the globalized production system was determined partly by location and geopolitical significance, partly by the existence of a strong, repressive, and reliable state apparatus, and partly by the existence of a technological and human resource infrastructure (Schmitz, 1984). In Africa the preconditions were not established for national and urban economies to compete successfully in the new growth sectors of the global econ-

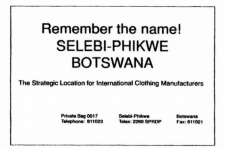

Fig. 10.1   **Place marketing in Africa**

omy; overall, Africa has lacked the infrastructure, human resource base, and the capacity for state intervention that the experience of the newly industrializing countries shows are so essential to capture new growth opportunities.

Looking to the prospects for flexible production, it is evident that in certain parts of the developing world the shift to flexibility may generate renewed growth opportunities for both import substitution and export-oriented production (Pedersen et al., 1994; Rogerson, 1994a). Kaplinsky (1991, p. 33) points out that flexible production "is

341

inherently descaling at the plant level in many sectors, and this holds open new possibilities for renewed import substituting industrialization." Moreover, additional opportunities for new manufacturing growth are raised by the possibility of fashioning production to take account of product specialization. This capacity to "niche" output to the specific conditions of individual markets opens the prospect of evolving appropriate products for developing world markets and the development of niche products (Kaplinsky, 1991, p. 34). Nevertheless, the prospects for evolving export-oriented flexible production are recognized as highly uneven because key changes in the transition to flexible production are of an organizational nature and thus human resource intensive, a situation that creates particular problems in much of Africa. For example, in Zimbabwe it was concluded that a fully fledged scenario of flexible specialization is "not on the agenda" (Rasmussen and Sverisson, 1994, p. 30). Overall it has been suggested that the greatest future potential for evolving post-Fordist production forms lies in Mexico and the Caribbean, North Africa, and the economies of the Association of South East Asian Nations, with the weakest overall prospects in sub-Saharan Africa (Kaplinsky, 1991, p. 34), with the possible exception of a democratic South Africa (Rogerson, 1994a).

As Simon and Rakodi both argue (chaps. 2 and 3), central to Africa's progressive peripheralization and current economic crisis is the fact that the continent has been largely unable to transcend its traditional functions in the world economy of raw material supplier and a captive market for imported manufactured goods. Put simply, globalization processes have been "stalled" in Africa, with corresponding severe consequences for its urban economies. In terms of manufacturing investment, as Rakodi notes, large foreign enterprises have shunned the continent, particularly since 1980, creating a situation that for many African countries the major sources for outside investment derive from international development agencies rather than private capital investment. Accordingly, Africa is the only large and populous continent without a true newly industrializing country, "seemingly another reason for its marginality to global circuits of commercial, industrial and financial capital" (Simon, 1993, p. 7), despite some progress in state and external investment in industry in North African countries between the 1950s and the 1970s. Much attention (and hope) currently centres on the prospects over the next decade for a post-apartheid democratic South Africa to emerge on the global stage and attain the status of a true newly industrializing country. Indeed, the city of Johannesburg is targeting its urban economic development strategy for the next decade to an ambitious goal of attaining "world city" status (Rogerson, 1994b; Rogerson and Rogerson, 1994). Elements of that strategy will involve building up the financial and producer services sector, attracting the offices of international organizations, and developing a cultural strategy to "image" the city better to foreign investors. In this respect, over the next decade, Johannesburg will increasingly be in the business of competing with Nairobi, currently the only other sub-Saharan African city that assumes a supranational role in the sphere of information flows, international agencies, and financial transactions (Simon, 1992, 1993).

The stalled process of globalization in Africa underpins the emasculated character of the formal economy in the majority of the continent's cities. In most countries of sub-Saharan Africa, regular urban wage employment opportunities constitute only a small fraction of total employment, typically between 5 and 10 per cent (ILO, 1992). For the period of the early 1980s, ILO studies disclose that regular urban employment fell in many countries (down 33.6 per cent in the Central African Republic in 1980–1986 and down 27 per cent in the Gambia between 1979 and 1986) and elsewhere failed to match the growth of the non-agricultural labour force (van Ginneken, 1988, p. 17). For example, in Windhoek, Namibia, the most recent data point to employment growth in the formal sector running at "probably less than 1 per cent" (Frayne, 1992, p. 7). The slow-down in modern sector employment in recent years is essentially attributed "to the fact that the public sector – as the engine of employment growth – has become increasingly unable to sustain the high rates of labour absorption of the 1970s and early 1980s" (ILO–JASPA, 1992, p. 47).

The impact of structural adjustment, which created shortages of imported materials, reduced investment, and led to declining effective demand, has meant that urban-based manufacturing has suffered particularly badly (ILO, 1987, p. 92; Gilbert, 1994). Although large-scale manufacturing enterprises have created an impressive volume of jobs in the newly industrialized countries of Asia and Latin America, they have generated only a relatively small number of employment opportunities in urban Africa (Rondinelli and Kasarda, 1993, p. 105). Indeed, as described by Beavon in chapter 5, the downturn in large-scale manufacturing has affected even the most dynamic industrial agglomeration in Africa, the Pretoria–

Witwatersrand–Vereeniging region – South Africa's economic heartland. Underpinning this downturn has been a complex of factors including a decline in mining, cut-backs in military production, and the consequences of excessive decentralization programmes that encouraged the outflow of labour-intensive production activities, most notably of much of the region's clothing and textiles manufacturers (Rogerson and Rogerson, 1994; Rogerson, 1995a), rather than structural adjustment.

In some countries, such as Tanzania, private sector formal employment has been stagnant ever since the mid-1960s, producing a situation that "public sector employment is *the* most important source of formal employment," especially in cities (Therkildsen, 1991, p. 252). In Luanda, employment in "public service and state enterprises absorbed almost half of the working population" (Aguilar and Zejan, 1994, p. 348). In Kenya, where it was estimated that the public sector accounted for 50 per cent of employment, job growth in this sector hovered around 4 per cent in the early 1980s, accelerating to 4.7 per cent per year in 1987/88 (Moser et al., 1993, p. 40). Nevertheless, under adjustment programmes, civil service reform has meant that public sector employment has no longer expanded rapidly and been able to serve in part as a welfare system during periods of economic downturn (ILO–JASPA, 1992, p. 48). Instead, public sector reform in several African countries has precipitated substantial layoffs, particularly in the lower echelons (Fapohunda, 1991; ILO–JASPA, 1992). A wave of public sector retrenchments took place in the 1980s and has continued into the 1990s (see table 10.1) effecting a downturn in urban jobs in particular. Women appear to have been most affected by the retrenchments and restructuring of the civil service because they tend to concentrate in the lower end of the occupational hierarchy (ILO–JASPA, 1992). Alongside this general faltering in public sector driven urbanization across Africa (Therkildsen, 1991), there has been a sharp fall in modern sector wages in urban areas, especially once again among civil servants (ILO, 1992, p. 39; ILO–JASPA, 1992; Hodd, 1993). For example, in Mozambique "probably no family in an urban context is able to survive on the income derived from one of the 400,000 formal sector jobs" (Assuncao, 1993, p. 32). The impact of these trends on employment is noted by Dubresson in Abidjan (chap. 8), Obudho in Nairobi (chap. 9) and, complicated by the transfer of the capital to Abuja and the role of oil prices, Abiodun in Lagos (chap. 6).

With public sector retrenchments accompanied by a declining

Table 10.1 **Public sector retrenchments in selected African countries, 1980s and 1990s**

Country	Period	Numbers retrenched	% of total period public sector employment
Nigeria	1984–1988	156,550	20
Kenya	1992–1997	149,000	30
Zimbabwe	1990/91–1994/95	123,000	25
Ethiopia	1992–1995	80,000	15
Tanzania	1992/93–1994/95	80,000	30
Uganda	1991–1994	80,000	26
Ghana	1987–1991	49,873	15
Cameroun	1985/86–1991/92	47,639	20
Guinea	1986–1991	40,000	20
Côte d'Ivoire	1983–1990	15,000	15
Togo	1983–1985	5,000	10
Gambia	1985–1986	n.a.	17

Source: based on ILO–JASPA (1992), p. 55.

absorptive capacity of the (private sector) formal economy, levels of open unemployment have escalated across urban Africa. During the 1980s few urban areas of sub-Saharan Africa escaped major increases in joblessness; current estimates are of unemployment levels in the range of 20 per cent, which, it is projected, "could exceed 30% in most cities in sub-Saharan Africa by the year 2000" (ILO–JASPA, 1992, p. 29; see also Dubresson, chap. 8). Even South African cities are part of this continental trend, with open unemployment in Port Elizabeth climbing to an estimated 25 per cent in 1991 owing to restructuring and a severe shake-out in the city's manufacturing sector (Rogerson, 1995b). The ILO (1994a, p. 24) records increasing open unemployment in African urban areas and notes that a "worrying aspect is that unemployment is creeping up the education ladder, with even university graduates now being affected." The worst levels of unemployment, however, are among the urban youth, who are said to constitute 60–75 per cent of the unemployed though they account for only one-third of the labour force (ILO–JASPA, 1992, p. 16). Typically, in urban Kenya the most affected age group for unemployment comprises those aged 20–29, who represent 65 per cent of all those reported as unemployed (House et al., 1993, p. 1212). Abiodun (chap. 6) notes that at least 70 per cent of the unemployed in Lagos State are aged between 15 and 29.

The consequences of stalled globalization on the formal economies of Africa's cities have therefore been devastating. Adjustment and economic restructuring have produced major changes in urban economies and the urban labour market since 1980 (van Ginneken, 1988; ILO, 1994a). The security, if not the stability, of regular wage employment has declined and as a result the distinctions between employment conditions in the formal and informal economies of cities have become progressively blurred. With the erosion or slow growth of the formal economy, large numbers of people have moved into either self-employment or casual wage employment or have to supplement formal sector wages with income generated from informal sector activity. This has produced the widely noted phenomenon of the informalization of the urban economy in Africa (Stren, 1992a, p. 542).

The informalization of the African city

In almost all the cities of sub-Saharan Africa (with the exception of certain South African cities) the majority of the urban workforce are currently engaged in a highly differentiated range of small-scale, micro-enterprise or informal activities such as hawking, scavenging, informal construction, small-scale production, or the provision of a host of low-cost services, including public transport activities. The diversity of informal economic life across the continent is evident from examining a cross-section of research studies from all parts of the continent (see, for example, Olowolaiyemo, 1979; Oyeneye, 1980; Fowler, 1981; Jourdain, 1982; Abdel-Fadil, 1983; Lachaud, 1984; Schamp, 1984; Aboagye, 1986; Hofmann, 1986; Antony, 1989; Maldonado, 1989; ILO, 1991; Mutizwa-Mangiza, 1993; Tevera, 1993, 1994; Yankson, 1995; Rogerson, 1996).

Informal economic enterprises – those defined as small-scale, mostly family-operated or individual activities that are not legally registered and usually do not provide their workers with social security or legal protection – absorb at least half of the workforce in many large African cities (Rondinelli and Kasarda, 1993, p. 106). The most recently available data produced by ILO–JASPA (1992, p. 29) reveal that, for sub-Saharan Africa, the informal economy currently engages 63 per cent of the total urban labour force. Moreover, the informal economy is still on an upward growth trajectory as regards labour absorption (Doohan, 1994, p. 25). Evidence from urban Zambia suggests that during the 1980s the size of the informal economy "more than trebled in six years" (Peters-Berries, 1993a, p. 3). The ILO estimates that during the 1990s the informal economy will be "generating some 93 per cent of all additional jobs in urban Africa" (ILO, 1992, p. 39; Maldonado, 1993, p. 245). Such findings underscore the conclusion that the small-scale, micro-enterprise or informal economy currently represents the most rapidly expanding employment segment of the contemporary African urban economy (ILO–JASPA, 1992, p. 29; Stren, 1992a, p. 542). That said, it must be acknowledged that in certain parts of the continent, particularly in the urban areas of west and north Africa, the informal economy is not a new phenomenon; rather, there is evidence that the economies of many pre-colonial cities in west and north Africa have been "informal" for centuries (see, for example, Peil, 1979; Diemer and van der Laan, 1981; Findlay and Paddison, 1986).

The small-scale or micro-enterprise economy in urban Africa exhibits considerable differentiation. In South African research a useful conceptual distinction is made between two categories of informal enterprise (Rogerson, 1996). First are *survivalist enterprises*, which represent a set of activities undertaken by people unable to secure regular wage employment or access to an economic sector of their choice. Generally speaking, the incomes generated from these enterprises, the majority of which tend to be run by women, usually fall short of even a minimum income standard and involve little capital investment, virtually no skills training, and only constrained opportunities for expansion into a viable business. Overall, poverty and the desperate attempt to survive are the prime defining features of these enterprises. Second is the category of *growth enterprises*, which are very small businesses, often involving only the owner, some family members, and at most one to four paid employees. These enterprises usually lack all the trappings of formality, in terms of business licences, formal premises, operating permits, and accounting procedures, and most have only a limited capital base as well as rudimentary business skills among their operators. None the less, many growth enterprises have the potential to develop and flourish into larger formal small-scale business enterprises.

In most cities, including many of those studied in part II of this volume, the pattern is overwhelmingly of a small-scale and informal economy weighted towards trade-related activities (on Angola see Assuncao, 1993; on Botswana see Karim-Sesay, 1995; on Namibia see Frohlich and Frayne, 1991; on Zambia see Peters-Berries, 1993a; on South Africa see Rogerson, 1992a, 1996; see also in this volume

Abiodun on Lagos and Piermay on Kinshasa). Typically, a 1988/89 survey in Dakar disclosed that 72 per cent of enterprises were in commercial trading activities (ILO, 1992, p. 39). In the urban areas of southern and eastern Africa a sectoral breakdown of micro-enterprise discloses that the share of trading enterprises is at least 50 per cent in Swaziland, more than 60 per cent in Botswana and Malawi, and reaches almost 70 per cent in the cities of Kenya and South Africa (Liedholm and Mead, 1993, p. 9). A converse pattern appears for manufacturing micro-enterprise, ranging from 17 per cent in South Africa and Botswana, to 35 per cent in Lesotho, to 65 per cent in Zimbabwe, mostly engaged in the production of textiles and garments (Liedholm and Mead, 1993, p. 8). Although the structure of Zimbabwe's urban small-scale economy distinguishes it from most other African countries, recent evidence suggests that one impact of structural adjustment has been to change "the structure of the [expanding] urban informal sector from predominantly manufacturing to more trading activities" (Peters-Berries, 1993b, p. 8).

Participation in the small-scale enterprise economy does not mean that most of the workforce is self-employed. Recent ILO (1992, pp. 39–40) research shows that often a considerable proportion of the workforce, almost two-thirds in the case of Abidjan, work for wages rather than profit (see also chap. 8). However, it is clear that the vast majority of micro-enterprises employ only limited numbers of workers. In their seven-country comparative investigation of micro-enterprises in urban areas of southern and eastern Africa, Liedholm and Mead (1993, p. 12) demonstrate that consistently over 90 per cent of enterprises engage fewer than five workers and the largest share (normally at least 50 per cent in most countries) is made up of one-person enterprises. What these data suggest is that the growth recently recorded in the small-scale sector of African cities is occurring primarily through the replication of informal businesses, a pattern of involution rather than evolution, which would result in an increase in the number of employees. Manning and Mashigo (1993, p. 16) write of a process of "growth through replication, or 'extensive' growth rather than growth through 'intensification' or capital/skill/ technology upgrading" as typical of most urban micro-enterprise.

Finally, one other effect of the increased importance of the informal and small-scale economy in African cities is that more women are now working. Consistently, women emerge as the major proprietors of micro-enterprise in urban Africa (Liedholm and Mead, 1993, p. 14; Aguilar and Zejan, 1994, p. 349; Karim-Sesay, 1995). Thus, for example, in Kenya between 1977/78 and 1986 women's participation in the urban workforce rose from 39 to 56 per cent, accounted for largely by their prominence in informal work (ILO, 1992; House et al., 1993; see also chap. 9). Several studies draw attention to the existence of marked gender divisions of labour within the urban small-scale economy of Africa. In urban areas of Lesotho, women cluster in businesses that are "an extension of domestic chores (such as selling food items) and a spatial and temporal extension of traditional activities (such as beer brewing)" (ILO, 1994b, p. 33). Likewise, a clear sexual division of labour surfaces in urban Zambia and Angola, with women predominating in petty trade whereas men are mostly found in activities surrounding manufacturing, construction, or repair services (Peters-Berries, 1993a, p. 3; Aguilar and Zejan, 1994, p. 349). For Windhoek, Frohlich and Frayne (1991, p. 8) observed marked sexual divisions of labour in trading activities, with fruit, giblet soup, offal, and vetkoek sold mainly by women, "whereas all other groceries, clothes, wood and luxury goods were sold by men almost exclusively." In South Africa, women cluster in trade, food preparation, dressmaking, and child-care activities (Liedholm and McPherson, 1991; Rogerson, 1994c). Moreover, research discloses the disproportionate number of women relegated to the lower end of the informal economy in terms of profitability and long-term development potential. Businesses run by women in urban South Africa, for example, were more likely to be a source of supplementary household income than were those run by male proprietors (Riley, 1994). An important finding is that women earn less than men in the informal economy, because the most profitable and fastest-growing small-scale businesses are dominated by male entrepreneurs (Friedman and Hambridge, 1991; Riley, 1994).

In seeking to explain the recent widespread surge of activity in the micro-enterprise economy across urban Africa, two major sets of issues must be discussed. The first concerns the demise of the formal economy, the mushrooming of survivalist enterprise, and a linked decline in the profitability of certain formerly promising spheres of informal work. The second relates to the increasing "informalization" of formal enterprise, which is associated with an expansion of subcontracting and outwork in a number of economic sectors. It is important to monitor the balance between these two trends in terms of assessing the long-term developmental implications of informalization processes in urban Africa.

The key explanatory factor for the proliferation of small-scale and informal economic enterprise is undoubtedly the progressive emasculation of the formal economy. This can be linked back in turn to the nature of stalled globalization, producing a mosaic of unevenness in the global economy. The implications of structural adjustment have further exacerbated the contraction of the formal economy. Clearly, informal work is not a refuge for newly arrived migrants to African cities, because many participants are long-term urban residents. Falling real wages in the formal economy forced many employed workers to search for a supplementary income source in the informal economy, as has been richly documented for Kampala (Bigsten and Kayizzi-Mugerwa, 1992), Maputo (Assuncao, 1993), and Kinshasa (Piermay, chap. 7). The withering of the formal economy (including both public and private sector components) gave rise, however, to a renewed impetus for an outflow of skilled labour into the small-enterprise economy (Fapohunda, 1991, p. 28). Retrenchments in the public sector affect not only civil servants but also skilled technicians made redundant owing to restructuring or closure of public sector enterprises. Because the informal economy "has become an important means of survival for this group of workers," this raises the prospect of technological upgrading of the small-scale economy (Tesfachew, 1992, p. 26). For example, Tesfachew notes that Structural Adjustment Programmes in Nigeria induced informal sector enterprises to increase their intake of apprentices, thereby furnishing new skills. Nevertheless, the impact on the small enterprise sector of wide-scale retrenchments and/or closure of formal enterprise may not always be positive (Tesfachew, 1992). In many cases a flood of new entrants into the informal economy can engender a situation of "overtrading" and a consequent decline in incomes earned and working conditions in such activities (Mhone, 1995). For instance, Dawson (1990, p. 11) observed of the Ghanaian experience: "While a steady flow of skilled labour into small firms acted to inject new skills and ideas into the sector, the avalanche of new entrants which followed on from the implementation of the retrenchment process – which saw 20 per cent of the total salaried labour force retrenched by the end of 1989 – had an altogether more negative impact." In urban Zimbabwe, there is alarming evidence that many areas of informal services and production, particularly those activities dominated by women, are now saturated and cannot absorb any more labour (Kanji, 1995, p. 46).

In urban South Africa the demise of the formal economy is, to a large degree, responsible for the surge in the number of survivalist enterprises in already "overtraded" income niches such as spazas (informal retail businesses) and hawker operations (see Rogerson, 1991a, 1994c, 1996) and for falling levels of profitability in activities such as the operation of taxis or shebeening, which formerly exhibited signs of expansion and seeming long-term growth potential. Recent work shows that in both these particular spheres of small-scale enterprise, a rash of new business entries has been associated with a deepening crisis of declining returns for entrepreneurs and worsened working conditions for employees (Khosa, 1993).

Overall, it must be emphasized that the combined impacts on the small-scale enterprise economy of recession in the formal economy and of structural adjustment measures are both varied and potentially contradictory. One set of consequences, noted above, has been the flood of survivalist enterprises in urban activities such as hawking, trading, or transport services, as occurred in Ghana, Zambia, Zimbabwe, or South Africa (see Tesfachew, 1992; Peters-Berries, 1993a,b; Rogerson, 1994b; Kanji, 1995; Mhone, 1995). By contrast, in Côte d'Ivoire "the informal sector appears to have been protected or shielded from the unfavourable trends in the world economy" (ILO, 1987, p. 93). Here the recession has reinforced or strengthened the comparative advantage of the urban small-scale economy by the transference of a large share of the demand for modern sector goods to informal enterprise (ILO, 1987). What appears to have occurred in urban Côte d'Ivoire is a process of informalization that has shifted the locus of production activity away from formal to informal establishments (Moser et al., 1993, p. 43). The evidence is less clear, but seemingly "a similar shift is said to have occurred in Kenya" (Moser et al., 1993, p. 28). Nevertheless, Dubresson (chap. 8) is far from convinced that the small-scale enterprise sector can replace the formal sector and promote an accumulation process sufficient to sustain Abidjan's economic vitality.

A second key theme in the expansion of the African urban small-scale and informal economy relates not to the demise of the formal economy as such but to growing linkages between formal and informal enterprise. Informalization is the process by which formal factory jobs are increasingly displaced by jobs in unregistered plants and home-working. The advantages of contracting out work to informal producers are the circumvention of labour regulations and the lowering of labour costs. A strengthening trend has been noted towards the so-called "informalization of formal enterprise," which refers to situations in which larger business enterprises seek to bypass regulations covering employment protection and labour security by establishing or linking their production to small, informal ancillary enterprises on terms that make those who work within the latter particularly vulnerable to exploitation (Rogerson, 1991b, 1994a). Nevertheless, whereas subcontracting of production activities is a widespread phenomenon in Latin America and parts of Asia (Rogerson, 1994a), its occurrence is less common in urban Africa "owing to the lower levels of industrialization, and the lower levels of skills and quality in African informal sectors" (Meagher and Yunusa, 1991, p. 3). Evidence is available of limited amounts of industrial subcontracting between formal and informal micro-enterprise taking place variously in the cities of South Africa (Rogerson, 1994b, 1995c) and Côte d'Ivoire (Moser et al., 1993). More prevalent than production subcontracting is subcontracting by formal sector commercial firms to informal traders in order to take advantage of lower overheads and the wider markets available within the informal economy (Meagher and Yunusa, 1991).

It has been argued by some observers that the "predominance of trade-based linkages and survival strategies in African informal sector expansion suggests a low potential for the emergence of a productive dynamic informal sector, particularly under conditions of economic crisis and structural adjustment" (Meagher and Yunusa, 1991, p. 3). The international experience of "informal economies of growth" points to the conclusion that a dynamic informal economy of "growth enterprises" cannot be created simply by legislative programmes for deregulation; rather, what will be required is state support in the areas of credit, technical training, and human resource development, together with coherent interventions to support a transition of informal enterprise beyond merely the production of low-quality consumer goods into other spheres of production (Rogerson, 1991b,c, 1995c). An important focus for nurturing the group of "growth enterprises" is the adoption, assimilation, and upgrading of technology (Maldonado, 1989; Maldonado and Sethuraman, 1992). In addition, ILO research cautions that "in formulating policies towards the informal sector, policy-makers (in Africa) need to give more attention to the macro policy environment rather than focussing exclusively on projects targeted at specific groups of enterprises" (Tesfachew, 1992, p. 29). Conditions for fostering an "informal economy of growth" as opposed to an "informal economy of bare survival" are rarely evident if one reviews the patterns of state intervention as regards the micro-enterprise economy. The picture that emerges overwhelmingly across Africa is of a weak implementation capacity and limited attempts, if any, to nourish a flourishing small-scale enterprise economy linked to large-scale enterprise in a mutually supportive manner (see Assuncao, 1993; Peters-Berries, 1993a,b,c). To cite two recent assessments of Kenyan state policies towards the informal economy, Macharia (1992, p. 235) argues that the state in Kenya has supported the informal sector "only half-heartedly, despite public statements and policy publications"; likewise, another study concluded that the government "speaks strongly in support of the urban self-employed, but practical support has been limited and uneven" (House et al., 1993, p. 1218). Moreover, although official documents assert the importance of informal and small enterprise development, "program development and implementation have frequently lagged behind and occasionally contradicted stated policy" (House et al., 1993, p. 1218). The situation of the urban informal economy in contemporary Zambia typifies much of the rest of the continent: the micro-entrepreneur "has to struggle with an extensive underwood of inhibitive regulations, hostile local authorities and lack of support facilities" (Peters-Berries, 1993a, p. 11).

A final set of issues concerning inter-enterprise relationships relates to the assertion of Schmitz (1990, 1992) that the encouragement of flexible specialization and of sectoral clusters of small and medium-sized firms is potentially an important means for boosting competitiveness and collective efficiency in urban African industrial development. The notion of flexible specialization relates back to "the new competition" in the global economy, which is based on an entrepreneurial firm, often located in an industrial district (van Dijk, 1993a,b; Pedersen et al., 1994). A major premise is that the capacity for growth of small enterprises cannot be achieved individually; instead it depends on the efficiency and flexibility made possible by geographical clustering and by a division of labour between enterprises. As Dawson (1992, p. 34) avers, the degree to which "small firms are capable of dynamic and innovative endogenous growth is seen as being primarily dependent on clustering." In turn, this "opens up efficiency and flexibility gains which individual producers can rarely attain" (Schmitz, 1992, pp. 64–65). Recent important research points to the possible emergence in the developing world of local areas of "collective efficiency" within sectoral agglomerations of small-scale industrial enterprises, including parts of urban Africa (Schmitz, 1990; Dawson, 1992; van Dijk, 1993a,b; Nadvi, 1994; Pedersen et al., 1994).

The developmental possibilities of further promoting this form of flexible specialization, small-firm industrial development in Africa have been raised by several writers (Aeroe, 1992; Rasmussen, 1992a,b; Rasmussen et al., 1992; Rogerson, 1994a). Policy interventions to foster inter-firm cooperation should consider the lessons of international experience, which point to the potential for encouraging dynamic growth based on cooperative networks of small firms and micro-enterprise. In dynamizing sectoral agglomerations of micro-enterprise, an important "enabling" role falls to local urban authorities. Although the major models for advocating this type of urban economic development are drawn from the successful small-firm industrial districts of Italy and Denmark (Pyke, 1993), the relevance of the "industrial cluster" model to the developing world context has been convincingly shown in a series of important works (Schmitz, 1990, 1992; Schmitz and Musyck, 1993; Nadvi, 1994; Nadvi and Schmitz, 1994). Undoubtedly, the extent to which this small-firm industrial development model can be successfully fostered will be vital to the trajectory of African urban economies in the 1990s. In particular, the fostering of small-firm industrial districts could make the informalization of African urban economies a positive base for long-term urban efficiency.

Finally, beyond policy interventions directed towards an informal economy of growth, government decision makers in urban Africa must formulate a set of strategic programmes to furnish an appropriate environment for the operations of survivalist informal enterprise. Several studies have offered packages for enhancing livelihoods in this informal economy of survival, which is often dominated by communities of hawkers and garbage pickers, or an array of home-based enterprises (Rogerson, 1991c; Tevera, 1993, 1994).

Urban cultivation

One key facet of informalization, widely present in African cities, is the expansion of "urban cultivation," which takes place through the proliferation of agricultural micro-enterprise (Stren, 1992a). As Drakakis-Smith (1994) points out, urban agriculture is extensive in much of Africa partially as a consequence of the limitations imposed on the development of an "informal economy of growth" or on the operations and livelihoods of survivalist enterprise. In policy circles a re-thinking is occurring on the role of urban agriculture in Africa and of its potential contribution to feeding the cities as a broader element of sustainable economic development (Rogerson, 1992b, 1993b; Mbiba, 1995). Indeed, Wekwete (1992, p. 131) is emphatic that "urban farming has become a critical variable in sustainability."

Although "urban agriculture" is a new concept in African development policy and planning, it must be acknowledged that the cultivation of "food crops within the overall boundaries of towns and cities is not new," although in the 1960s and 1970s it was forgotten or largely ignored by researchers and local policy makers (Rakodi, 1988a, p. 495). With the impact of economic recession, the effects of Structural Adjustment Programmes, and the crises of the 1980s and 1990s, the cultivation of food crops in public and private open spaces is now both more widespread and economically significant in many African urban areas (Sanyal, 1985; Tricaud, 1987; Drakakis-Smith, 1991, 1994; Lee, 1993a,b,c). At certain periods of the year, especially the seasonal rainfall peak, "many urban centres are transformed by armies of 'urban farmers' tilling the open spaces to produce flourishing vegetable gardens and fields of grains and fruit" (Lado, 1990, p. 257). It was revealed from surveys conducted in the late 1980s in Kenya, Egypt, Mali, and Tanzania that poor urban households spent around 60 per cent – and in some cases as much as 89 per cent – of their incomes on food (Mougeot, 1993a, p. 1). Moreover, price surveys disclosed that city dwellers paid 10–30 per cent more for their food than rural inhabitants did (Mougeot, 1993a). Accordingly, the "push" of worsening food insecurity underpins much of the burgeoning of agricultural micro-enterprises on the African city-scape, particularly since the late 1970s.

In contemporary Africa, urban cultivation is a widespread activity that is becoming a permanent part of the landscape in most large cities. In spatial terms the two main areas of cultivation are in home gardens (on-plot cultivation) or at the urban periphery (off-plot cultivation) (Drakakis-Smith, 1994; Mbiba, 1994). The most dramatic manifestation of self-production of food is, perhaps, the practice of keeping livestock fed on domestic refuse on the rooftops of buildings in Cairo; for the early 1980s, it was noted that Egypt's capital city had at least 80,000 households raising animals at home (Khouri-Dagher, 1986, p. 41). By the 1990s it could be observed by Freeman (1991, p. 2) that "urban agriculture is both prevalent and economically significant" across Africa. Likewise, another researcher describes urban farming as "a ubiquitous, complex and dynamic feature of the urban and socio-economic landscape in Africa" (Lachance, 1993, p. 8). During the era of late apartheid the spread of urban cultivation practices began to extend to the cities of South Africa (Rogerson, 1993c). Accelerating city growth after the removal of influx control measures, escalating levels of food inflation, and the reduced absorptive capacity of a sanctions-weakened formal economy together triggered the appearance of cultivation on vacant land fringing the formal African townships and especially around the country's mushrooming informal shack settlements (Rogerson, 1993c; May and Rogerson, 1995).

For the early 1980s Guyer (1987, p. 13) estimates between 10 and 25 per cent of the total urban population in Africa "may be involved in some sort of agriculture." Recent evidence suggests that overall participation rates may be considerably higher. For example, it was pointed out that in Kenya and Tanzania "two out of three urban families are engaged in farming" (Smit and Nasr, 1992, p. 142). In Tanzania, "every open space, utility service reserve, road, valley or garden in the towns has been taken up for planting of all sorts of seasonal and permanent crops, ranging from vegetables, maize, bananas, to fruit trees" (Mosha, 1991, p. 84). The rapid pace of growth in urban cultivation is evidenced particularly by data from Dar es Salaam, where in 1980 44 per cent of low-income earners had farms but by 1987 "70 per cent of heads of households engaged in some farming or husbandry" (Mougeot, 1993b, p. 3).

The widespread expansion in farming as both a part-time and a full-time occupation for African urban households has been tracked in several investigations. Broadly speaking, Sanyal (1986, p. 22) asserts that "insufficient income is a primary cause for the practice of urban cultivation" in Africa. Urban research in East and Central Africa suggests that the invasion of cities by subsistence cultivation is symptomatic of economic collapse in urban Zaire (Ngub'usim and Streiffeler, 1982; Streiffeler, 1987), Uganda (Amis, 1992; Bibangambah, 1992), and Tanzania (Mlozi et al., 1992). Kinshasa was described recently as "a giant garden plot – by every roadside, on traffic islands and roundabouts, cassava leaves sprout in lovingly tended rows" (*The Economist*, 1994, p. 59). Household survival in Uganda depends on multiple income sources, including urban farming (Amis, 1992, p. 6; Lee, 1993b, p. 10); in Kampala, where besides the city centre "most empty spaces are covered by perennial crops," it is observed that "one gets the feeling that the rural sector is overtaking the city instead of the reverse" (Bigsten and Kayizzi-Mugerwa, 1992, p. 1436). Even in Nairobi there is a considerable body of evidence to confirm that informal urban cultivation of open space is markedly on the increase in this so-termed "city of farmers" (Lado, 1990; Freeman, 1991). It has been remarked that "there are few areas of the city of Nairobi where the activities of urban farmers cannot be observed" (Freeman, 1991, p. 2). A similar march of urban cultivation has been noted in West Africa (Tricaud, 1987; Lachance, 1993). On the outskirts of Lagos, "the putrid jungles bordering the highways into the city have fallen under cultivation" by part-time farmers, including Nigeria's professional classes (Mustapha, 1991, p. 13). Gefu (1992) argues that the escalation in part-time farming in urban Nigeria represents a survival strategy for many urban wage-earners to supplement declining real wages in the wake of structural adjustment measures. Economic crisis and structural adjustment in Nigeria fostered the development of multiple modes of social livelihood, and many public servants moonlight as part-time urban cultivators (Mustapha, 1991, p. 13). Likewise, with a declining formal economy in Tanzania, the inability of households to live on a single income source has precipitated an expansion in urban farming (Mosha, 1991).

In southern African cities the phenomenon of urban agriculture has been widely documented. Lesotho's capital, Maseru, exhibits a diverse range of agricultural pursuits, with dairy cows, maize production, sheep- and pig-rearing, and vegetable and fruit production all being "prominent and conspicuous activities" (Mbiba, 1994, p. 192). Around metropolitan Durban in South Africa it was disclosed that 25 per cent of households were cultivating a garden for subsistence food production (May and Rogerson, 1995). In Harare, home gardens act as a vital source of subsistence food production for the city's poorest populations (Drakakis-Smith and Kivell, 1990; Drakakis-Smith, 1992a). Since the mid-1970s a substantial extension of informal "off-plot" cultivation has taken place in the shallow valleys occupying this city's periphery (Mazambani, 1982, 1986; Mbiba, 1994). Significantly, the expansion of cultivation in the urban periphery of Harare has been at the expense of the destruction of woodlands used for fuelwood (Mazambani, 1986). Thus, paradoxically, "increasing amounts of the food grown in the peri-urban area is [sic] being sold either through the petty-commodity market (as cooked or fresh food) or to government marketing agencies in order to obtain cash for the purposes of purchasing commercially marketed fuelwood or kerosene" (Drakakis-Smith, n.d., p. 9).

Despite a "spectacular expansion" observed in peri-urban agriculture in Harare (Drakakis-Smith, n.d., p. 8), urban cultivation reaches its most striking extent in the case of the "garden city" of Lusaka. In Zambia's capital city, nearly 60 per cent of low-income households are estimated as cultivating food gardens (Sanyal, 1985, 1986). The pace of expansion of urban agriculture in Lusaka has been so extensive that the city has been described as "the world capital of urban cultivation" (Sanyal, 1986, p. 7). In the words of Sanyal:

It was February and Lusaka looked abundant. The rainy season was just over and bright yellow sunlight touched the edges of dark green maize plants which had sprung up all over the city. There were maize plants outside the Lusaka International Airport, standing in contrast to the purple bougainvillea which had been carefully planted by the Department of Public Works to welcome the dignatories of an International Conference. Maize plants grew all along the edges of the Great East Road – the thoroughfare connecting the airport, the university, the National Assembly building and the central business district. Even outside the boundary walls of the elegantly designed Hotel Intercontinental, maize grew in abundance.

The abundance of maize plants was not only confined to the "official areas" of Lusaka. Hidden from the main thoroughfares of Great East Road and Great North Road, the squatter communities ... looked lush and green with only small mud houses reminding one of habitation. There was maize in front of the mud houses and around the periphery of the communities: there were large banana trees around the rickety structures of pit latrines. Pumpkin leaves covered low fences that separated unfriendly neighbors; and tomatoes and ground nuts grew in front of the houses where women sat together washing dishes and lighting fires. (Sanyal, 1986, pp. 1–2)

The advance of urban cultivation and its growing significance throughout African cities has occurred much to the surprise and embarrassment of proponents of modernization, ranging from city officials to international aid donors (Sanyal, 1985). Contrary to popular opinion, this process of the "ruralization" of African cities is not the consequence of mass rural–urban migration. Sanyal (1987, p. 198) interprets the post-1980 upsurge of cultivation by the urban poor in Africa as an innovative response from below to the decline of formal urban economies; this response "reduces their vulnerability to the fluctuations of fortune that currently beset the economies of developing countries' cities." The findings of research on urban farmers in Nairobi and Lusaka demonstrate clearly that "urban cultivation is not practised exclusively or even primarily by recent migrants" (Sanyal, 1985, p. 18). Instead, the majority of farmers originate from poor households that are fully entrenched in the urban economy. More than 60 per cent of Lusaka's farmers had been in the city for more than five years before embarking on plot gardens and nearly 45 per cent for more than 10 years (Mougeot, 1993b, p. 4). A profile of urban cultivators in Kenya shows that "average length of urban farmers' residence was 20.4 years, 85% had resided in the city for at least five years, 57.5% had been living there for 15 years or more, while 15% had dwelt there for more than 40 years" (Lado, 1990, p. 262). Cultivation taking place in Harare is primarily conducted by low-income families who grow food crops for domestic consumption and sale (Mazambani, 1982, 1986; Drakakis-Smith, 1992a; Mbiba, 1994, 1995). In Nairobi, the vast majority of cultivated plots "are creations of the very poor, and represent a major source of subsistence for the urban underclasses" (Freeman, 1991, p. 87). Research on urban cultivation in Kenya, Zambia, and Zimbabwe underscores the vital role of women as major food producers (Rakodi, 1988a,b; Lado, 1990; Stren, 1992a; Mbiba, 1994, 1995). In particular, Stren (1991) records the findings of a study in which the majority of women urban farmers in Kenya said they would starve or suffer considerably without urban agriculture. In Lusaka, farming is a particularly important survival activity for groups of low-income women with limited schooling or marketable skills in the formal economy (Rakodi, 1985, 1988a,b).

Although for much of Africa the produce and revenues of urban agriculture constitute a much-needed source of income and nutrition for the urban poor, especially for the growing numbers of female-headed households, it must be acknowledged that "in some cities much of the food produced is not grown by the poor" (Drakakis-Smith, 1992b, p. 47). The participation of middle-income households in urban food production has been a notable finding of research undertaken in Nigeria (Gefu, 1992), Mozambique (Sheldon, 1991), and South Africa (May and Rogerson, 1995). Indeed, in Durban, participation in cultivation was evenly spread among seven different kinds of household, with the smallest proportions of farmers drawn from the poorest and the wealthiest groups of households (May and Rogerson, 1995). This situation suggests that the "ability of a household to produce food is inevitably a function of its control over basic inputs such as land, labour and capital, together with some influence with the urban authorities which usually have the power to prevent if they wish, much of this activity" (Drakakis-Smith, 1993, p. 205). Such findings underscore the complexities of urban farming in Africa (Drakakis-Smith, 1992b, p. 49). None the less, they do not support the proposition that urban agriculture in Africa is merely a last resort for the poor in urban areas, albeit subsistence food production admittedly does represent one important survival niche adopted by the most vulnerable urban households.

Across urban Africa, official reactions to urban cultivation have varied across space and time but have tended to be inhibitive rather than accommodative (Drakakis-Smith, 1993, 1994; Rogerson, 1993b; Mbiba, 1994, 1995). The advance of urban cultivation has occurred often in the face of negative actions by African local authorities. Despite its widespread occurrence for subsistence consumption, urban food and livestock production "is usually not appreciated by urban authorities and certainly not planned for and supported" (Lee-Smith and Trujillo, 1992, p. 79). Moreover, as Lee-Smith and Stren (1991, p. 33) observe, "neither land-use planning nor urban management are traditionally geared to coping with urban food production." Repressive attitudes towards urban agriculture appear to be particularly common in the former colonial-settler regions of east, central, and southern Africa. For example, urban authorities in Kenya perceive informal cultivation as part of the broader embarrassment of the informal sector, a blot on the city landscape, "a continuous but unwelcome reminder that programmes for development and efforts to project an aura of modernity and progress have not reached very far below the surface" (Freeman, 1991, p. 44). State repression in Lusaka took the form of destroying plants on the grounds that urban cultivation was a "health hazard" linked to an increased incidence of malaria (Sanyal, 1986, 1987). None the less, by the 1980s, as national indebtedness increased, a reversal in policy attitudes took place, with the Zambian state shifting to a position of urging people to grow their own vegetables and cereals. In Zimbabwe, urban managers consider uncontrolled cultivation to be "trivial or a nuisance," and periodic repressive measures are enacted to destroy crops (Mbiba, 1994, p. 200).

Benign neglect of urban farming is a common official stance in much of Africa; typically, regulations in Uganda ban cultivation in the city but in practice most farming in the cities is widely tolerated (Lee, 1993b, p. 11). Only in Mozambique, Zaire, Malawi, and Nigeria are there signs that official authorities have come out tentatively in favour of urban farming, introducing enabling measures to enhance the prospects for cultivation (UNCHS, 1991, p. 23; Assuncao, 1993, p. 35; Lachance, 1993, p. 8). A negative policy environment towards urban cultivation is regrettable, given that ecologically sustainable urbanization in Africa will be impossible without the activities and

contributions of urban farming towards resource recycling, food production, and job creation (Rogerson, 1992b; Smit and Nasr, 1992;
Wekwete, 1992; Drakakis-Smith, 1994). Nevertheless, important recent research on the environmental effects of uncontrolled urban
cultivation in Harare points to the need for policy formulation to
minimize the effects of variously a changing hydrological regime, soil
loss, chemical pollution, and vegetative change (Bowyer-Bower and
Tengbeh, 1995).

Concluding remarks

It has been argued in this chapter that the economies of large African
cities can be interpreted to a large extent as a product of the simultaneous unfolding and impact of processes of globalization and
informalization. These processes are producing a complex set of policy challenges that demand urgent attention at all levels of government. Nevertheless, it must be acknowledged that in the current
context of global restructuring, economic development increasingly
has become a localized phenomenon (Storper, 1992; Ettlinger, 1994).
This points to potentially new and important roles for the local governments of Africa's large cities in confronting the economic challenges of the next decade.

As emphasized within the body of writings on "urban management," the conventional roles assumed by African city governments
(and more particularly by urban managers) have centred around
issues of prevention and control of development rather than the
active promotion of economic development (see Stren, 1992b, 1993;
Wekwete, chap. 15 in this volume). In the 1990s there is an urgent
need for a redirection of urban management programmes "to provide
the necessary framework in which urban economic development can
take place, and to facilitate the provision of opportunities for the
widest range of income generating activities" (Devas, 1989, pp. 5–6).
Indeed, throughout urban Africa one essential future task for urban
management is taking up the challenge of promoting local urban
economic development and of attracting new investment to cities
rather than acting to prevent such development (see Devas and
Rakodi, 1993). Currently, however, there are only a small number
of functioning initiatives for local economic development in urban
Africa. By far the most advanced initiatives for planning local
urban economic development exist in South Africa's largest cities –
Johannesburg, Durban, and Cape Town. These have involved coher-

ent sets of strategic interventions designed to improve the general economic performance of these cities as well as to enhance income opportunities for the urban poor (for details, see Rogerson, 1994b,d, 1995d). During the 1990s, the lessons of these ongoing South African initiatives may provide important pointers for other large African cities in tackling the policy challenges posed by "stalled globalization" and the march of informalization.

References

Abdel-Fadil, M. 1983. *Informal Sector Employment in Egypt.* International Labour Office, Geneva.

Aboagye, A. A. 1986. *Informal Sector in Mogadishu: An Analysis of a Survey.* ILO/ Jobs and Skills Programme for Africa, Addis Ababa.

Aeroe, A. 1992. *Rethinking Industrialization – From a National to a Local Perspective: A Case Study of the Industrialization Process in Tanzania with Particular Emphasis on the Construction Industry.* Project Paper 92.3, Centre for Development Research, Copenhagen.

Aguilar, R. and M. Zejan. 1994. Income distribution and the labour market in Angola. *Development Southern Africa* 11: 341–350.

Amis, P. 1992. Sustainable urban development and agriculture in Uganda. Paper 15 presented at the International Workshop on Planning for Sustainable Urban Development: Cities and Natural Resource Systems in Developing Countries, 13–17 July, Cardiff.

Antony, E. 1989. Can the traditional crafts in Moroccan towns be assigned to the informal sector: The example of the mat weavers of Sale. *Applied Geography and Development* 33(2): 93–108.

Assuncao, P. 1993. *Government Policies and the Urban Informal Sector in Sub-Saharan Africa: A Comparative Study on Kenya, Tanzania, Mozambique and Angola.* WEP 2-19/WP.64, International Labour Office, Geneva.

Bibangambah, J. R. 1992. Macro-level constraints and the growth of the informal sector in Uganda. In: J. Baker and P. O. Pederson, eds., *The Rural–Urban Interface in Africa: Expansion and Adaptation.* Scandinavian Institute of African Studies, Uppsala, pp. 303–313.

Bigsten, A. and S. Kayizzi-Mugerwa. 1992. Adaption and distress in the urban economy: A study of Kampala households. *World Development* 20: 1423–1441.

Bowyer-Bower, T. A. S. and G. Tengbeh. 1995. The environmental implications of (illegal) urban agriculture in Harare, Zimbabwe. Working Paper No. 4 of ODA Research Project R5946 presented at the Workshop on the Environmental, Social and Economic Impacts of (Illegal) Urban Agriculture in Harare, Zimbabwe, 3–31 August, University of Zimbabwe.

Castells, M. 1989. *The Informational City.* Blackwell, Oxford.

——— 1992. *European Cities, the International Society, and the Global Economy.* Centre for Metropolitan Research, University of Amsterdam.

Dawson, J. 1990. The impact of structural adjustment on the small enterprise sector: A comparison of the Ghanaian and Tanzanian experience. Unpublished paper prepared for the Conference on Small and Micro-scale Enterprise Promotion, 30 September – 2 October, the Hague, the Netherlands.

―――― 1992. The relevance of the flexible specialisation paradigm for small-scale industrial restructuring in Ghana. *Bulletin, Institute of Development Studies* 23(3): 34–38.

Devas, N. 1989. *New Directions for Urban Planning and Management, Institute of Local Government Studies.* Development Administration Group, Papers in the Administration of Development No. 34, University of Birmingham, Birmingham.

Devas, N. and C. Rakodi, eds. 1993. *Managing Fast Growing Cities: New Approaches to Urban Planning and Management in the Developing World.* Longman, London.

Dieleman, F. M. and C. Hamnett. 1994. Globalisation, regulation and the urban system: Editors' introduction to the special issue. *Urban Studies* 31: 357–364.

Diemer, G. and E. C. W. van der Laan. 1981. The informal sector in historical perspective: The case of Tunis. *Cultures et Développement* 13: 161–172.

Dijk, M. P. van. 1993a. Industrial districts and urban economic development. *Third World Planning Review* 15: 175–186.

―――― 1993b. Small enterprises and the process of globalization and regional integration. *Small Enterprise Development* 4(3): 4–13.

Doohan, J. 1994. The jobless horizon: Unsettling prospects. *World of Work* 8: 24–27.

Drakakis-Smith, D. n.d. *The City Region: Basic Demands on the Urban Environs.* Discussion Paper, Centre of Urban Studies and Urban Planning, University of Hong Kong.

―――― 1991. Urban food distribution in Asia and Africa. *Geographical Journal* 157: 51–61.

―――― 1992a. Strategies for meeting basic food needs in Harare. In: J. Baker and P. O. Pederson, eds., *The Rural–Urban Interface in Africa: Expansion and Adaptation.* Scandinavian Institute of African Studies, Uppsala, pp. 258–283.

―――― 1992b. And the cupboard was bare: Food security and food policy for the urban poor. *Geographical Journal of Zimbabwe* 23: 38–58.

―――― 1993. Food security and food policy for the urban poor. In: J. Dahl, D. Drakakis-Smith, and A. Narman, eds., *Land, Food and Basic Needs in Developing Countries.* Department of Human and Economic Geography, University of Gothenburg, Gothenburg, pp. 197–212.

―――― 1994. Food systems and the poor in Harare under conditions of structural adjustment. *Geografiska Annaler* 76B: 3–20.

Drakakis-Smith, D. and P. T. Kivell. 1990. Urban food distribution and consumption: The case of Harare. In: A. M. Findlay, R. Paddison, and J. A. Dawson, eds., *Retailing Environments in Developing Countries.* Routledge, London, pp. 156–180.

Economist, The. 1994. The Zairean art of muddling through. 17 December.

Ettlinger, N. 1994. The localization of development in a comparative perspective. *Economic Geography* 70: 144–166.

Fapohunda, O. J. 1991. *Retrenchment and Redeployment in the Public Sector of the Nigerian Economy.* WEP 2-43/WP.51, International Labour Office, Geneva.

Findlay, A. M. and R. Paddison. 1986. Planning the Arab city: The cases of Tunis and Rabat. *Progress in Planning* 26(1): 1–82.

Fowler, D. A. 1981. The informal sector in Freetown: Opportunities for self-employment. In: S. V. Sethuraman, ed., *The Urban Informal Sector in Developing*

Countries: Employment, Poverty and Environment. International Labour Office, Geneva, pp. 51–69.

Frayne, B. 1992. Urbanisation in Post-Independence Windhoek. Research Report No. 6, Namibian Institute for Social and Economic Research, Windhoek.

Freeman, D. B. 1991. A City of Farmers: Informal Urban Agriculture in the Open Spaces of Nairobi, Kenya. McGill University Press, Montreal and Kingston.

Friedman, M. and M. Hambridge. 1991. The informal sector, gender and development. In: E. Preston-Whyte and C. Rogerson, eds., South Africa's Informal Economy. Oxford University Press, Cape Town, pp. 161–180.

Frohlich, C. and B. Frayne. 1991. Hawking: An "Informal" Sector Activity in Katutura, Windhoek. Discussion Paper No. 7, Namibian Institute of Social and Economic Research, Windhoek.

Gefu, J. O. 1992. Part-time farming as an urban survival strategy: A Nigerian case study. In: J. Baker and P. O. Pederson, eds., The Rural–Urban Interface in Africa: Expansion and Adaptation. Scandinavian Institute of African Studies, Uppsala, pp. 295–302.

Gilbert, A. 1994. Third world cities: Poverty, employment, gender roles and the environment during a time of restructuring. Urban Studies 31: 605–633.

Ginneken, W. van. 1988. Employment and labour incomes: A cross-country analysis (1971–86). In: W. van Ginneken, ed., Trends in Employment and Labour Incomes. International Labour Office, Geneva, pp. 1–31.

Guyer, J. I. 1987. Introduction. In: J. I. Guyer, ed., Feeding African Cities: Studies in Regional Social History. Manchester University Press, Manchester, pp. 1–54.

Hodd, M. 1993. Employment Planning within the Context of Economic Reforms: A Tanzanian Case Study. WEP 2-46/WP.44, International Labour Office, Geneva.

Hofmann, M. 1986. The informal sector in an intermediate city: A case in Egypt. Economic Development and Cultural Change 34: 263–277.

House, W. J., G. K. Ikiara, and D. McCormick. 1993. Urban self-employment in Kenya: Panacea or viable strategy? World Development 21: 1205–1223.

ILO. 1987. Sub-Saharan Africa. In: ILO, World Recession and Global Interdependence: Effects on Employment, Poverty and Policy Formation in Developing Countries. International Labour Office, Geneva, pp. 75–98.

——— 1991. The Urban Informal Sector in Africa in Retrospect and Prospect: An Annotated Bibliography. International Labour Bibliography No. 10, International Labour Office, Geneva.

——— 1992. World Labour Report 1992. International Labour Office, Geneva.

——— 1994a. World Labour Report 1994. International Labour Office, Geneva.

——— 1994b. Promoting Gender Equality in Employment in Lesotho: An Agenda for Action. Interdepartmental Project on Equality for Women in Employment, International Labour Office, Geneva.

ILO–JASPA. 1992. African Employment Report 1992. Jobs and Skills Programme for Africa, International Labour Organization, Addis Ababa.

Jourdain, R. M. 1982. Development planning and the informal sector: A case study of automobile repair shops in four cities of tropical Africa. Unpublished M.A. dissertation, University of British Columbia, Vancouver.

Kanji, N. 1995. Gender, poverty and economic adjustment in Harare, Zimbabwe. Environment and Urbanization 7: 37–55.

Kaplinsky, R. 1991. Direct foreign investment in third world manufacturing: Is the future an extension of the past? *Bulletin, Institute of Development Studies* 22(2): 29–35.

Karim-Sesay, P. A. N. 1995. The non-spatial and spatial character of the informal sector in Gaborone (Botswana). Unpublished B.A. (Soc.Sci.) dissertation, Department of Environmental Science, University of Botswana.

Khosa, M. M. 1993. Transport and the "taxi mafia" in South Africa. *The Urban Age* 2(1): 8–9.

Khouri-Dagher, N. 1986. *Food and Energy in Cairo: Provisioning the Poor*. Research Report No. 18, Food–Energy Nexus Programme, the United Nations University, Paris.

Lachance, A. 1993. A plot of one's own in West African cities. *IDRC Reports* 21(3): 8–9.

Lachaud, J. P. 1984. Les activités informelles et l'emploi à Bangui (République Centrafricaine): Analyse et stratégie de développement. *Canadian Journal of African Studies* 18: 291–317.

Lado, C. 1990. Informal urban agriculture in Nairobi, Kenya: Problem or resource in development and land use planning? *Land Use Policy* 7: 257–266.

Lee, M. 1993a. Recognizing Ethiopia's urban farmers. *IDRC Reports* 21(3): 12–13.

——— 1993b. Farming logic in Kampala. *IDRC Reports* 21(3): 10–11.

——— 1993c. Breaking new ground in Dar es Salaam. *IDRC Reports* 21(3): 14–15.

Lee-Smith, D. and Stren, R. 1991. New perspectives on African urban management. *Environment and Urbanization* 3: 23–36.

Lee-Smith, D. and C. H. Trujillo. 1992. The struggle to legitimize subsistence: Women and sustainable development. *Environment and Urbanization* 4: 77–84.

Liedholm, C. and D. Mead. 1993. *The Structure and Growth of Microenterprises in Southern and Eastern Africa: Evidence from Recent Surveys*. GEMINI Working Paper No. 36, Bethesda, Md.

Liedholm, C. and M. A. McPherson. 1991. *Small Scale Enterprises in Mamelodi and Kwazakhele Townships, South Africa: Survey Findings*. GEMINI Technical Report No. 16, Bethesda, Md.

Macharia, K. 1992. Slum clearance and the informal economy in Nairobi. *Journal of Modern African Studies* 30: 221–236.

Maldonado, C. 1989. The underdogs of the urban economy join forces: Results of an ILO programme in Mali, Rwanda and Togo. *International Labour Review* 128: 65–84.

——— 1993. Building networks: An experiment in support to small urban producers in Benin. *International Labour Review* 132: 245–264.

Maldonado, C. and S. V. Sethuraman, eds. 1992. *Technological Capability in the Informal Sector: Metal Manufacturing in Developing Countries*. International Labour Office, Geneva.

Manning, C. and P. Mashigo. 1993. Manufacturing in micro-enterprises in South Africa. Unpublished report submitted to the Industrial Strategy Project, University of Cape Town.

May, J. and C. M. Rogerson. 1995. Poverty and sustainable cities in South Africa: The role of urban cultivation. *Habitat International* 19: 165–181.

Mazambani, D. 1982. Peri-urban cultivation within Greater Harare. *Zimbabwe Science News* 16: 134–138.

———— 1986. Aspects of peri-urban cultivation and deforestation around Harare, Zimbabwe. In: G. J. Williams and A. P. Wood, eds., *Geographical Perspectives on Development in Southern Africa*. Commonwealth Geographical Bureau, James Cook University of North Queensland, Townsville, pp. 189–197.

Mbiba, B. 1994. Institutional responses to uncontrolled urban cultivation in Harare: Prohibitive or accommodative? *Environment and Urbanization* 6: 188–202.

———— 1995. *Urban Agriculture in Zimbabwe: Implications for Urban Management and Poverty*. Avebury, Aldershot.

Meagher, K. and M.-B. Yunusa. 1991. *Limits to Labour Absorption: Conceptual and Historical Background to Adjustment in Nigeria's Urban Informal Sector*. Discussion Paper No. 28, United Nations Research Institute for Social Development, Geneva.

Mhone, G. C. Z. 1995. *The Impact of Structural Adjustment on the Urban Informal Sector in Zimbabwe*. Issues in Development Discussion Paper No. 2, International Labour Office, Geneva.

Mlozi, M. R. S., I. J. Lupanga, and Z. S. K. Mvena. 1992. Urban agriculture as a survival strategy in Tanzania. In: J. Baker and P. O. Pederson, eds., *The Rural–Urban Interface in Africa: Expansion and Adaptation*. Scandinavian Institute of African Studies, Uppsala, pp. 284–294.

Moser, C. O. N., A. J. Herbert, and R. E. Makonnen. 1993. *Urban Poverty in the Context of Structural Adjustment: Recent Evidence and Policy Responses*. Discussion Paper TWU DP #4, Urban Development Division, World Bank, Washington D.C.

Mosha, A. C. 1991. Urban farming practices in Tanzania. *Review of Rural and Urban Planning in Southern and Eastern Africa* 1: 83–92.

Mougeot, L. 1993a. Urban food self-reliance: Significance and challenges. Unpublished mimeographed report, International Development Research Centre, Ottawa.

———— 1993b. Urban food self-reliance: Significance and prospects. *IDRC Reports* 21(3): 2–5.

Mustapha, A. R. 1991. *Structural Adjustment and Multiple Modes of Social Livelihood in Nigeria*. Discussion Paper No. 26, United Nations Research Institute for Social Development, Geneva.

Mutizwa-Mangiza, N. D. 1993. Urban informal transport policy: The case of emergency taxis in Harare. In: L. M. Zinyama, D. S. Tevera, and S. D. Cumming, eds., *Harare: The Growth and Problems of the City*. University of Zimbabwe, Harare, pp. 97–108.

Nadvi, K. 1994. Industrial district experiences in developing countries. In: UNCTAD, *Technological Dynamism in Industrial Districts: An Alternative Approach to Industrialization in Developing Countries*. UNCTAD/ITD/TEC 11, United Nations, Geneva, pp. 191–255.

Nadvi, K. and H. Schmitz. 1994. *Industrial Clusters in Less Developed Countries: Review of Experiences and Research Agendas*. Discussion Paper No. 339, Institute of Development Studies, University of Sussex, Brighton.

Ngub'usim, M. N. and F. Streiffeler. 1982. Productive work for low-income families in an urban environment: An experience in Zaire. *Ideas and Action* 149: 3–9.

Olowolaiyemo, M. 1979. *Urban Petty Producers in Nigeria and Programmes for*

Assisting Them. Monograph No. 3, Centre for Development Studies, University College of Swansea.

Oyeneye, O. Y. 1980. Apprentices in the informal sector of Nigeria. *Labour, Capital and Society* 13(2): 69–79.

Pedersen, P. O., A. Sverrisson, and M. P. van Dijk, eds. 1994. *Flexible Specialization: The Dynamics of Small-Scale Industries in the South.* Intermediate Technology Publications, London.

Peil, M. 1979. West African urban craftsmen. *Journal of Developing Areas* 14: 3–22.

Peters-Berries, C. 1993a. *The Urban Informal Sector and Structural Adjustment in Zambia.* WEP 2-19/WP.62, International Labour Office, Geneva.

—— 1993b. *The Urban Informal Sector in Zimbabwe: From Insignificance to the Employer of the Last Resort.* WEP 2-19/WP.61, International Labour Office, Geneva.

—— 1993c. *Putting Development Policies into Practice: The Problems of Implementing Policy Reforms in Africa.* WEP 2-19/WP.63, International Labour Office, Geneva.

Pyke, F. 1993. *Industrial Development through Small-Firm Cooperation.* International Labour Office, Geneva.

Rakodi, C. 1985. Self-reliance or survival?: Food production in African cities with particular reference to Zambia. *African Urban Studies* 21: 53–63.

—— 1988a. Urban agriculture: Research questions and Zambian evidence. *Journal of Modern African Studies* 26: 495–515.

—— 1988b. Urban agriculture in Lusaka, Zambia. In: I. Dankelman and J. Davidson, comp., *Women and Environment in the Third World: Alliance for the Future.* Earthscan, London, pp. 108–110.

Rasmussen, J. 1992a. *The Local Entrepreneurial Milieu: Enterprise Networks in Small Zimbabwean Towns.* Research Report No. 79, Department of Geography, Roskilde University, Copenhagen.

—— 1992b. The small enterprise environment in Zimbabwe: Growing in the shadow of large enterprises. *Bulletin, Institute of Development Studies* 23(3): 21–27.

Rasmussen, J. and A. Sverisson. 1994. *Flexible Specialisation, Technology and Employment in Zimbabwe.* WEP 2-22/WP.241, International Labour Office, Geneva.

Rasmussen, J., H. Schmitz, and M. P. van Dijk. 1992. Introduction: Exploring a new approach to small-scale industry. *Bulletin, Institute of Development Studies* 23(3): 2–7.

Riley, T. 1994. *Characteristics of and Constraints Facing Black Businesses in South Africa: Survey Results.* Informal Discussion Paper on South Africa No. 5, World Bank, Washington D.C.

Rogerson, C. M. 1991a. Home-based enterprises of the urban poor: The case of spazas. In: E. Preston-Whyte and C. Rogerson, eds., *South Africa's Informal Economy.* Oxford University Press, Cape Town, pp. 336–344.

—— 1991b. Deregulation, subcontracting and the "(in)formalization" of small-scale manufacturing. In: E. Preston-Whyte and C. Rogerson, eds., *South Africa's Informal Economy.* Oxford University Press, Cape Town, pp. 365–385.

—— 1991c. Policies for South Africa's urban informal economy: Lessons from the international experience. In: E. Preston-Whyte and C. Rogerson, eds., *South Africa's Informal Economy*. Oxford University Press, Cape Town, pp. 207–222.

———— 1992a. The absorptive capacity of the informal sector in the South African city. In: D. M. Smith, ed., *The Apartheid City and Beyond: Urbanization and Social Change in South Africa*. Routledge, London, pp. 161–171.

———— 1992b. Feeding Africa's cities: The role and potential for urban agriculture. *Africa Insight* 22: 229–234.

———— 1993a. Export-processing industrialization in Mauritius: The lessons of success. *Development Southern Africa* 10: 177–197.

———— 1993b. Urban agriculture in South Africa: Policy issues from the international experience. *Development Southern Africa* 10: 33–44.

———— 1993c. Urban agriculture in South Africa: Scope, issues and potential. *Geo-Journal* 30: 21–28.

———— 1994a. Flexible production in the developing world: The case of South Africa. *Geoforum* 25: 1–17.

———— 1994b. Johannesburg's initiatives for local economic development. Unpublished report for the Urban Foundation, Johannesburg.

———— 1994c. South Africa's micro-enterprise economy: A policy-focused review. In: R. Hirschowitz, M. Orkin, C. M. Rogerson, and D. Smith, eds., *Micro-Enterprise Development in South Africa*. European Union, Pretoria, pp. 14–37.

———— 1994d. Democracy, reconstruction and changing local and regional economic development planning in South Africa. *Regional Development Dialogue* 15(1): 101–118.

———— 1995a. South Africa's economic heartland: Crisis, decline or restructuring? *Africa Insight* 25(4): 241–247.

———— 1995b. The employment challenge in a democratic South Africa. In: A. Lemon, ed., *The Geography of Change in South Africa*. John Wiley, Chichester, pp. 169–194.

———— 1995c. Looking to the Pacific Rim: Production subcontracting and small-scale industry in South Africa. *International Small Business Journal* 13(3): 65–79.

———— 1995d. Reconstruction and contemporary local authority initiatives for local economic development in South Africa. Paper prepared for the Conference on Reconstruction and Development in Southern Africa, 22 September, Royal Holloway, University of London, Egham.

———— 1996. Urban poverty and the informal economy in South Africa's economic heartland. *Environment and Urbanization* 6(1): 167–181.

Rogerson, C. M. and J. M. Rogerson. 1994. The central Witwatersrand: A metropolitan region in distress? Unpublished report for the Urban Foundation, Johannesburg.

Rondinelli, D. A. and J. D. Kasarda. 1993. Job creation needs in third world cities. In: J. D. Kasarda and A. M. Parnell, eds., *Third World Cities: Problems, Policies, and Prospects*. Sage, London, pp. 92–119.

Sanyal, B. 1985. Urban agriculture: Who cultivates and why? A case-study of Lusaka, Zambia. *Food and Nutrition Bulletin* 7(3): 15–24.

———— 1986. *Urban Cultivation in East Africa*. Research Report No. 14, Food–Energy Nexus Programme, the United Nations University, Paris.

———— 1987. Urban cultivation amidst modernization: How should we interpret it? *Journal of Planning Education and Research* 6: 197–207.

Schamp, E. 1984. The economic situation of private small garages in Bamenda. *Revue de Géographie du Cameroun* 4(2): 1–6.

Schmitz, H. 1984. Industrialisation strategies in less developed countries: Some lessons of historical experience. *Journal of Development Studies* 21: 1–21.

——— 1990. Small firms and flexible specialisation in developing countries. *Labour and Society* 15: 257–285.

——— 1992. On the clustering of small firms. *Bulletin, Institute of Development Studies* 23(3): 64–69.

Schmitz, H. and B. Musyck. 1993. *Industrial Districts in Europe: Policy Lessons for Developing Countries?* Discussion Paper No. 324, Institute of Development Studies, University of Sussex, Brighton.

Sheldon, K. 1991. *Farming in the City: Urban Women and Agricultural Work in Mozambique.* Centre for the Study of Women, University of California, Los Angeles.

Simon, D. 1992. *Cities, Capital and Development: African Cities in the World Economy.* Belhaven, London.

——— 1993. *The World City Hypothesis: Reflections from the Periphery.* Research Paper No. 7, Centre for Developing Areas Research, Department of Geography, Royal Holloway, University of London, Egham.

Smit, J. and J. Nasr. 1992. Urban agriculture for sustainable cities: Using wastes and idle land and water bodies as resources. *Environment and Urbanization* 4(2): 141–152.

Storper, M. 1992. The limits to globalisation: Technology districts and international trade. *Economic Geography* 68: 60–93.

Streiffeler, F. 1987. Improving urban agriculture in Africa: A social perspective. *Food and Nutrition Bulletin* 9(2): 8–13.

Stren, R. 1991. Helping African cities. *Public Administration and Development* 11: 275–279.

——— 1992a. African urban research since the late 1980s: Responses to poverty and urban growth. *Urban Studies* 29: 533–555.

——— 1992b. Large cities in the third world. In: UNCHS (Habitat), *Metropolitan Planning and Management in the Developing World: Abidjan and Quito.* United Nations Centre for Human Settlements, Nairobi, pp. 1–30.

——— 1993. "Urban management" in development assistance: An elusive concept. *Cities* 10: 125–138.

Tesfachew, T. 1992. *Government Policies and the Urban Informal Sector in Africa.* WEP 2-19/WP.59, International Labour Office, Geneva.

Tevera, D. S. 1993. Waste recycling as a livelihood in the informal sector: The case of Harare's Teviotdale dump scavengers. In: L. M. Zinyama, D. S. Tevera, and S. D. Cumming, eds., *Harare: The Growth and Problems of the City.* University of Zimbabwe, Harare, pp. 83–96.

——— 1994. Dump scavenging in Gaborone, Botswana: Anachronism or refuge occupation of the poor? *Geografiska Annaler* 76B: 21–32.

Therkildsen, O. 1991. Public sector driven urbanization in Tanzania. *African Urban Quarterly* 6: 252–256.

Thrift, N. 1994. Globalisation, regulation, urbanisation: The case of the Netherlands. *Urban Studies* 31: 365–380.

Tricaud, P.-M. 1987. *Urban Agriculture in Ibadan and Freetown.* Research Report No. 23, Food–Energy Nexus Programme, United Nations University, Paris.

UNCHS. 1991. *Global Strategy for Shelter to the Year 2000*. United Nations Centre for Human Settlements, Nairobi.

Wekwete, K. H. 1992. Africa. In: R. Stren, R. White, and J. Whitney, eds., *Sustainable Cities: Urbanization and the Environment in International Perspective*. Westview, Boulder, Colo., pp. 105–140.

Yankson, P. W. K. 1995. Employment issues in the urbanisation process in Ghana. Paper presented at the Conference organized by the United Nations University on Human Settlement in the Changing Global Political and Economic Processes, 25–27 August, Helsinki, Finland.

11

Residential property markets in African cities

Carole Rakodi

Abstract

Ce chapitre porte sur le fonctionnement des marchés immobiliers et la façon dont ils sont modelés par les relations politiques et sociales entre les parties concernées, plutôt que par les caractéristiques physiques de l'environnement construit résultant. L'on y examine attentivement la disponibilité des terres indispensables du fait de la rapidité de la croissance des villes et des besoins de terres où bâtir des logements. Avant même l'époque coloniale, les régimes d'occupation des sols commençaient d'évoluer compte tenu des situations nouvelles. Mais la nécessité d'évoluer se fit plus pressante avec l'impulsion du colonialisme et la croissance urbaine rapide qui suivit les indépendances. Les régimes d'occupation de terres importés de diverses parties d'Europe ont coexisté tant bien que mal avec les systèmes autochtones d'administration des terres. Avec l'augmentation des pressions, ces derniers se sont commercialisés de plus en plus tout en posant des problèmes, là où ils subsistent, pour les responsables de la gestion urbaine. Les tentatives de répondre aux besoins de nouveaux logements en offrant de vastes terrains répartis en lots et en y pourvoyant des services sont restées insuffisantes. Près de la moitié des pays de l'Afrique subsaharienne ont nationalisé les terres et/ou remplacé la propriété foncière perpétuelle et libre par la tenure à bail, mais sans obtenir les résultats souhaités. Malgré d'apparentes "réformes" il n'y a eu que peu de changements apportés aux règles et procédures de l'époque coloniale. En pratique, la majeure partie de la demande de terre à bâtir dans les villes est satisfaite illégalement, soit avec des installations de squatters soit, de plus en plus, avec des lotissements illicites. Les terres et d'autres composantes nécessaires à la construction de logements sont assemblées en combinaisons variables par divers ensembles d'acteurs. Dans la plupart des villes d'Afrique, la construction de logements publics n'a jamais satisfait qu'une petite proportion des besoins et la majorité des maisons, dans les secteurs formels et informels, sont construites par des particuliers, la construction autogérée ayant depuis longtemps remplacé la construction auto-assistée. En plus des difficultés que rencontrent de plus en plus les propriétaires prospectifs à obtenir des terres, la construction des logements est aussi handicapée par l'absence de crédit et l'insuffisance des matériaux de construction. L'accès à la propriété immobilière étant devenu toujours plus difficile dans de nombreuses villes, la location est de plus en plus courante. Les transactions immobilières dans les zones bâties, l'évolution et le fonctionnement mêmes du système immobilier, les échanges de logements et l'aménagement des centres villes font que même une zone déjà urbanisée n'est pas statique mais dynamique. Les opinions varient quant à la meilleure façon pour les pouvoirs publics de surmonter les problèmes d'occupation, d'enregistrement et d'administration des sols; certaines sont incompatibles ou prêtent à controverses. Les recommandations suivantes sont avancées: favoriser la propriété individuelle, (re)-privatiser les terres, régulariser et enregistrer les occupations illicites, réformer les normes et les procédures et prendre des mesures pour surmonter les autres obstacles à la construction de logements.

Introduction

The urban built environment is the outcome of a series of transactions in land and property, together with a process of construction. Deals in property are not merely economic transactions, but are shaped by political and social relations between the parties involved, and it is on these market processes that this chapter will focus rather than on the resulting physical patterns of land use and building. Attention will be paid both to the land development process by which rural land is urbanized and to transactions in land and property within cities. The state, both central and local, has had an important role in urban development, both as a direct actor and as a result of attempts to guide and regulate the process. The outcomes over time of these attempts to intervene through the instruments of land and housing policy will be assessed.

The first and largest part of the chapter will focus on evolving systems of land supply for urban development. Because the current situation is characterized by the coexistence of different modes of supply originating at different stages in the development of cities, the historical origins of these systems will be examined, as well as their more recent evolution. Pre-colonial land tenure, the impact of colonialism, changes to indigenous land allocation systems since independence, the impact of attempted reforms based on nationalization of land, and the illegal supply of privately owned land will be discussed in turn. This extensive consideration of land supply is justified by rapid urban growth rates and the primary importance of land in the production of shelter. The assembly of land together with other components, in varying combinations and by varying sets of actors, to produce housing is the subject of the second main section. The pattern of urban development and the housing stock that are produced by the urbanization of agricultural land and the construction of dwellings are, however, not static. The third section will outline property markets within built-up areas: rental tenure, exchange of land and houses, and inner-city renewal. In conclusion, some of the policy and management implications of evolving land and property markets and development processes will be briefly explored. Contrasts between cities in different parts of the continent will be illustrated and explained, but restrictions on space preclude full recognition of the variety of urban conditions or detailed qualification of the broad trends and characteristics identified.

The supply of land for urban development

Pre-colonial land tenure

In most of sub-Saharan Africa and despite considerable variations, it is safe to say that pre-colonial land tenure was based on the concept that ownership of land was vested in a community (tribe, clan, lineage, family), the head of which held it in trust and administered it on behalf of the group's ancestors, its currently living members, and its members yet to be born. All adult members of the community had rights to use the land, although these use rights varied with status, gender, etc. The head of the group had the right and responsibility to allocate unused land and arbitrate in disputes, and the usufruct rights were inheritable. Variations in the system arose from political structures, types of agriculture, rules of succession, and so on. The spread of Islam, in which private individual ownership of land is part of *sharia* law, led to modifications in indigenous tenures, for example in northern Nigeria, the Sudan, and coastal Kenya. The land system in Mombasa, for example, where "freehold" land can be leased to a tenant who pays a goodwill fee (*kilemba*) for the right to build and an annual rent, differs from the rest of Kenya. As a result, whereas in Nairobi 23 per cent of dwellings are in "shanties" and only 14 per cent in rooming (Swahili) houses, in Mombasa the proportions are 5 per cent and 66 per cent, respectively (Ondiege, 1989). In Morocco, several types of ownership are established in *sharia* law, for example *habous*, *melk*, and *guich* (Ameur, 1995).

In urban settlements that existed before colonialism, rights in land were held by the indigenous occupants, originating with the king or paramount chief, who held the absolute rights in the land in trust, and descending to individuals via intermediate groups (Bruce, 1988). Each member of a rural community had a claim to as much land as he (usually) could farm or, in urban areas, as was his due, depending on seniority. There were a variety of secondary tenures, such as sharecropping or women's rights in their husband's land. Land allocated to an individual and his (or occasionally, in matrilineal societies, her) descendants under such usufruct tenure would be forfeit only if not productively used. Rights of occupancy might be subject to the payment of tribute or the rendering of other services (Acquaye and Asiama, 1986). Arrangements for accommodating non-members of the group existed in rural areas, for example tenancy, but prior approval of the group (typically the chief and elders) was needed (Bruce, 1988). Land was not, therefore, private property; control over and access to land were inextricably linked to socio-political relationships and land was not just a physical entity, but had symbolic or spiritual significance as the embodiment of a link between the generations (Aquaye and Asiama, 1986; Frishman, 1988; van Westen, 1990).

The indigenous system was adapted for use in urban areas. It provided access to urban land for group members of widely varying economic status, a means of administering the allocation and occupation of land, and a deterrent to the entry of land into the open market. Typically, family "compounds" accommodated (in a patrilineal society) a man, his wife/wives, their children, and his adult sons and their families (Mabogunje, 1993). However, claims to land were unequal between and within families, with the more powerful and/or wealthy being more likely to have their claims granted (Bruce, 1988). Commonly, urban administration was the responsibility of a traditional ruler, and cities were divided into quarters under the jurisdiction of sub-rulers with administrative roles including land allocation (Mabogunje, 1993). Arrangements evolved to deal with non-indigenes, for example traders and other migrants. In northern Nigeria, areas for northern Islamic non-indigenes (*Tudun Wada*) and southern migrants (*Sabon Gari*) were allocated (O'Connor, 1983). Elsewhere, non-indigenous in-migrants were dealt with on an individual basis and greater ethnic mixing occurred as a result. Traditionally, a token payment of "drinks money" was made to the chief or other person responsible for land allocation. Land was not regarded as a commodity and this payment was not a "price" related to the value of the land. However, in places, for example Kano, land had become scarce before the end of the nineteenth century and its allocation without charge had been replaced by sales (Frishman, 1988).

Indigenous tenure was, therefore, evolving to deal with new developments even before the advent of colonial administration. However, pressures for change intensified firstly with the imposition of colonial rule and subsequently with the increased rates of population growth that have succeeded independence. These changes in circumstances and the way in which urban land supply has adapted to them will be examined in turn.

The impact of colonialism on urban land

The impact on settlement patterns and processes of urban development varied, as has been described in chapter 2, with the identity and purposes of the colonizing power and the nature of the existing political economy on which external rule was imposed. In much of coastal West Africa, strong existing states and peasant agriculture that could produce the crops of interest to colonial traders gave rise to the British system of indirect rule and French colonization of Senegal. French administration was established by military conquest in much of the interior. It was accepted that existing urban settlements would remain, and many flourished as colonial trade and communications were extended, although others were bypassed. The urban residence of their African populations was accepted and existing modes of administration and tenure were allowed to continue, although they were modified by the needs of the colonial administration for land for its own administrative and trade functions and personnel.

Land around the urban centre or in a parallel European settlement was appropriated and declared Crown or state land. In the settler and labour reserve colonies of east, central, and southern Africa, where few substantial urban settlements existed, and where indigenous inhabitants were dispossessed of large areas of rural land and confined to reserves, urban settlements were established on state-controlled land. Land titling was introduced for this land, which was alienated to individuals under freehold or leasehold tenure. Legislation based on that which had evolved in Europe was enacted and thus varied between colonial powers, but the procedures for survey and registration were typically cumbersome and land was generally taxed for local revenue. Large areas of land were sold at low prices to European (and sometimes Asian) immigrants, especially in the settler colonies of Kenya, Zimbabwe, South Africa, Angola, and Mozambique, and much remained vacant for years. Such land entered into a land market, transactions in which reflected the economic fortunes of both the colonial power and its colony. Periods of economic prosperity and immigration, for example after World War II, were marked by price increases, new development, and further subdivision, often on a highly speculative basis. In periods of political uncertainty and economic depression, especially in the run-up to independence, prices were typically depressed and the property market stagnant, for example in Zambia and Zimbabwe (Van den Berg, 1984; Rakodi, 1995).

In the early years of colonial administration, Africans were not, generally, permitted to own land where they did not already do so in established settlements. However, in the settlements of ex-slaves, settlers were allocated freehold plots on arrival, for example in Togo and Liberia (O'Connor, 1983; Mabogunje, 1993). Occasionally the imported tenure system was adapted to local practice. For example, in northern Nigeria a leasehold system was adopted as being closest to the indigenous form of tenure (O'Connor, 1983). Elsewhere, intermediate levels of rights were introduced that gave Africans use of land for house construction but not ownership. In the French colonies, three basic procedures were instituted (Durand-Lasserve, 1993):

- *le permis d'occuper* (occupation permit), which gave use rights for a limited period, with no provision for conversion into a higher-level right;
- *le permis d'habiter* (permission to live), which was conditional on the builder satisfying minimum regulations, revocable at any time by the state and neither inheritable nor saleable;
- *la concession foncière urbaine* (land concession). These were plots made available on a provisional basis following public land sub-division, which could be made definitive when the plot was developed in conformity with the relevant regulations, the property had been valued, and the formalities completed.

In the labour reserve colonies, control over the workforce was enforced by a variety of mechanisms, including prohibiting urban home ownership to ensure that migrants returned to their villages on completion of their contracts or retirement. In countries such as Zambia, therefore, only rented housing was provided, both for African workers (by employers or government) and for colonial administrators. In the settler economies, especially South Africa, whites and other immigrants took up permanent residence, and thus ownership of land and property was crucial to their prosperity and maintenance of control, whereas the indigenous labour force was mostly forced to rent (as described by Beavon for Johannesburg in chap. 5).

Where indigenous tenure in urban areas survived the imposition of colonial rule, it was sometimes drastically modified. In Uganda, for example, large areas of land were allocated by agreement with the British as virtual freehold in square mile units (*mailo*) to the Kabaka and the chiefs. Most farmers and urban residents were, therefore, tenants on this land, which could be inherited but not sold (Barrows and Roth, 1990; see also Gayiiya and Walaga, 1995). Even where such transformation did not occur, indigenous tenure systems continued to evolve as a result of changes stemming from colonial rule. In Nigeria, for example, the British co-opted certain chiefs (usually the paramount chief) through whom to exercise indirect rule, thereby eroding the role of other chiefs who had perhaps had important roles in urban administration or land allocation (Bruce, 1988; Mabogunje, 1993). Financial transactions increasingly supplanted social transactions in both rural areas (for example tenancy arrangements) and urban centres. In Kano, there was evidence of a land market, which progressively excluded low-income residents, in the 1940s (Frishman, 1988).

At independence, therefore, African countries inherited a "dual" system of land supply, in which European notions of tenure, systems of land administration, and policies that embodied colonial aims and social relations coexisted uneasily with indigenous tenure and land administration that reflected the social and political relations of tribal society. Neither had been static: European urban policies had been modified as the revenue implications of earlier policies were realized and difficulties experienced in their implementation, for example to permit urban land ownership by Africans even in some of the settler societies; the structure of tribal society had changed under colonial rule, with effects on both administrative systems and approaches to urban land, in which family interests were becoming relatively more important. The main changes brought by independence were a determination to give Africans access to economic opportunities, education, and property and the ending of such influx control as existed, leading to more rapid rural–urban migration and urban population growth. However, as will be seen in the next section, much of the inherited urban land-supply system continued virtually unchanged until the 1970s.

Post-independence urban land development

In recent decades the indigenous tenure system has come under increasing pressure. In many West African cities, for example in Ghana and Nigeria, strong group or family attachment to land has been retained since pre-colonial times, inhibiting individual sales. However, unwillingness to sell also poses obstacles to the acquisition of land for public purposes and to redevelopment of old and poor-quality inner-city housing; as well as giving rise to many disputes over claims and failure to secure contributions to funding for infrastructure installation. Often rights are not clearly defined, overlapping rights exist, and "contracts" are unenforceable (Durand-Lasserve, 1993). As a result, transaction costs are high, and the residual risk of other claims coming to light following a sale decreases the value of the land and deters investment. In the area covered by the Traditional Council in Kumasi, Ghana, for example, the rights of the paramount stool chief (the *Asantahene*) and 55 sub-stool chiefs, each with sub-sub-stools and families, have produced a very unclear set of claims to land and complex procedures for acquisition. These have given rise to extensive disputes and litigation, with an outstanding backlog of 16,000 cases in the High Court (Asiama, 1989, 1995; Acquaye and Associates, 1989).

Long-term vesting of land in families has both reduced the control of chiefs and given rise to a tenure form that is more accurately described as "customary freehold" (Mabogunje, 1993) than usufruct. Accommodation in the family houses that are built on such land means that rent-free (or low-rent) accommodation is available to poorer members of kin groups (Korboe, 1992). One- and two-storey compound houses eventually containing as many as 80 rooms accommodate three-quarters of households in Accra, of which 65 per cent live rent free (Malpezzi et al., 1990; Tipple and Willis, 1991; Korboe, 1994). Because the rent control legislation (see below) allows tenants to be evicted if a dwelling is needed for a family member, and because of declining real incomes and the return of Ghanaians working in other countries, the proportion of households living rent free in family houses has increased (Korboe, 1992). As better-off households move out to avoid increasing responsibility for maintenance and other housing-related costs, the condition of the houses deteriorates, while sale for redevelopment is opposed by those who benefit from the cheap housing provided, and who are able to justify such opposition by appealing to the inalienable status of family land. In Nigeria likewise, customary tenure has prevented non-indigenes from achieving house ownership in cities such as Calabar and Akure, and housing built on land held under this form of tenure, especially in inner-city areas, is old and deteriorated, leading to the concentration of low-income residents in the centre of cities (Sule, 1994). As in rural areas, the solution often advocated is an individualization and privatization of tenure in order to encourage redevelopment (Barrows and Roth, 1990).

Not only are group claims to land being supplanted by family rights, but within families an individualization of rights is occurring. Obtaining access to urban land by purchase rather than grant or inheritance is regarded as an achievement, offering the possibility of founding a segmentary lineage (Barnes, 1979) or passing the property on to a man's wife and children rather than his traditional successors (Dickerman, 1988). However, the situation is complex: although the increasing prevalence of individual sales may give women with independent means a chance to purchase property and individualization of ownership may increase the rights of widows and divorcees, individualization of tenure in the names of men may represent a narrowing of rights to family land, and recourse to traditional rules of succession on the death of a property owner may disadvantage women (Dickerman, 1988; CASS, 1991).

Because transactions in land held under indigenous tenure have been either unrecognized or only partly recognized by both colonial and post-independence governments, legislation governing the exchange process has often not been enacted. One of the clauses such legislation might contain is provision either for the profits from land sales to be taxed or for sellers to be obliged to service the land in advance of sales. In Ghana, for example, levels of service provision to land disposed of by stool chiefs, as well as areas occupied under customary tenure arrangements, are inadequate. As a result, infrastructure standards and land prices are lower in the central area than in the surrounding middle- and upper-income residential areas subdivided under formal systems of tenure (Asiama, 1989; Acquaye and Associates, 1989).

The increasing problems caused by the undocumented nature of land rights and transactions are underscored by the increasing commercialization of indigenous tenure as urban pressures intensify. Evidence has accumulated of traditional payments approximating more closely to "prices" and of landholders selling land without the consent of their kin. This seems to be occurring both within pre-colonial settlements and on the outskirts of cities throughout the continent where peripheral land is held under "communal" tenure arrangements (Amis, 1990). In the area of communal tenure north of Lusaka, there was no evidence of payments being made to chiefs until the late 1970s, when reports began to emerge of rental being paid for land reclaimed from farms by the chief or headmen and of payments to the chief for consenting to the issue of statutory leases for individual plots (Van den Berg, 1984). Kironde and Rugaiganisa (1995) assert that there has been a market in land under customary tenure on the periphery of Dar es Salaam for decades. Wellings (1988) quotes similar evidence of chiefs in peri-urban areas in Lesotho terminating land rights, ostensibly to prevent overcrowding but in practice to sell plots. The subdivision and sale of land held under "communal" tenure have provided opportunities for the entry of brokers. In Burkina Faso, the traditional authorities sold land for urban development between 1960 and 1984, despite 1960 legislation that did not recognize their tenure rights (Bagre et al., 1995). In Bamako, Mali, since the late 1960s, traditional leaders have made the initial allocations of land in subdivisions, but, when these develop further, the leaders lose control over land and the remaining free land tends to be appropriated by middlemen, who act as inter-mediaries for rental housing developed by outside investors (van Westen, 1990). In Abidjan, customary owners of peripheral land have sold it to intermediaries for illegal subdivision since the 1950s, retaining some of the land for themselves (Dubresson and Yapi-Diahou, 1988; see also chap. 8 in this volume). Similar processes are described in Kinshasa and Douala (Canel and Girard, 1988) and on land belonging to the Lebou villagers of Cap-Vert (Navarro, 1988).

Although the traditional payment was seen as an expression of thanks, it increasingly approximates a price, albeit one in which the economics of the transaction are moderated by socio-political con-siderations. In Kumasi in the past, because the payment was not officially the cost of a lease, there was no incentive to lease a small plot, and most were about 1,000 m²; Ashanti chiefs made land avail-able almost free to their subjects, and, on the basis of slightly higher payments, to other Ashantis, but charged considerably more to non-Ashantis. By the 1970s, although they offered discounts to their own subjects, they did not significantly tax non-Ashantis. Asabere (1981a) recognizes that the socio-political objectives of chiefs were satisfied by the granting of subsidized land to indigenes, but criticizes the practice, on the basis of very limited evidence, for encouraging in-efficient utilization of land by Ashantis while repelling proposed investment by non-Ashantis from Kumasi to other places. Korboe (1994), on the other hand, considers the high densities produced by family land and housing to represent efficient space utilization, and Tipple and Owusu (1994) suggest that, as payments come more closely to approximate prices, the potential for leasing smaller plots is increasing. In Accra, however, the overall constraints on availability of stool land have led to shortages of subsidized plots, queues, and litigation (Asabere, 1981b; Asiama, 1995). In Conakry, Durand-Lasserve concludes that there are several prices depending on the tenure status of land sold by indigenous landholders, in particular related to the prospects of regularization. As a result, although prices are obscured by a "facade of customary procedures" (Durand-Lasserve, 1994, p. 59), he asserts that the market is in practice quite efficient.

Access to land through customary tenure procedures did in the past enable low-income urban residents to obtain access to land for house construction without resorting to illegal occupation. As a result, squatting has been less extensive than in other parts of the world (see below), and the major problem faced by urban residents has been inadequate provision of infrastructure rather than access to land. However, the increasingly commercialized process by which land held under indigenous tenure is disposed of, the markets that are developing in such land, and the processes of house production with which they are associated mean that the traditional responsibilities of community leaders are giving way to profit-making, opportunities are being provided for brokers with purely commercial aims, and the process of illegal subdivision and house production on this land is increasingly resembling that on land held under forms of individual tenure. Before examining the characteristics of the latter, the attempts of post-independence governments to intervene in land supply will be examined.

Urban land "reforms" and their consequences

In the years immediately after independence in many countries, the expansion of civil services and diplomatic corps, in some cases success in attracting foreign investment, and later the expansion of the indigenous bourgeoisie gave rise to increased demand for housing at the middle- and upper-income end of the market. In the ex-colonies that had been administered by expatriate civil servants, such as Zambia, the majority lived in subsidized rental housing. Undeveloped housing finance institutions, a construction sector with limited capacity, and the expectation of indigenous employees that such provision would continue led to continued reliance on employers to provide housing and only belated development of any volume of private sector formal housing. In Zambia, for example, it was not until demand from the new indigenous élite increased in the late 1960s (following independence in 1964) that prices of land started to rise again (Van den Berg, 1984). In the settler colonies, such as South Africa and Zimbabwe, in contrast, the European (and Asian) population had invested in property both for their own occupation and as an investment. A development sector and, in some cases, housing finance institutions had evolved to meet their needs, while indigenous successors in formal sector wage employment perceived the advantages of home ownership and did not expect employers to meet their needs.

Price trends in the formal residential and commercial sectors have reflected general economic conditions, although they vary geographically within cities and between sub-markets. In Nairobi, for example, Ondiege (1989) and Macoloo (1994) agree that real land prices increased between 1979 and 1982, fell during the years of drought and economic crisis between 1982 and 1986, and subsequently rose rapidly as economic growth picked up with the help of a boom in coffee prices. Within cities, status, location, and especially infrastructure give rise to price variations, as Obudho describes for Nairobi (chap. 9), while price levels and trends may also vary between tenures. Rising rents and prices and evidence of speculation in land, as well as the increasing difficulties governments were experiencing in fulfilling their independence promises to improve the quality of life for the African majority, led in the 1970s to a number of attempts at reform. These were related in one way or another to land in public ownership.

Part of the state land inherited at independence was used for public purposes. As the supply of appropriately located state land was exhausted, many countries attempted to strengthen their capacity to expropriate land in communal or individual ownership, their success depending largely on the level of compensation payable. State land was also available for subdivision for private sector house construction, potentially for all income groups. Government held the responsibility, under a variety of pieces of legislation and administrative agencies, for subdivision, survey, title registration, allocation, development and building control, and taxation. Generally, the legal basis for the sale of land to private developers or upper-income households was different from that for the provision of public housing or serviced plots to lower-income households. Invariably, however, the procedures were complex and time consuming and made more so by a lack of human, technical, and financial resources. In Gabon, for example, registration of title takes 6–24 months, while in Cameroon it takes 15–18 months in easy cases, and 2–7 years is not uncommon (Mabogunje, 1993). Cities attempted to maintain high planning standards and control over development, in part because of the political clout of high-income residents seeking to ensure their access to high-quality residential environments. However, bottlenecks in the process of survey and registration resulted in a shortfall of supply, so such land started to command a premium. Access was gradually restricted to the wealthy and well connected.

Sometimes, large stocks of publicly owned land and rapid subdivision resulted in a relatively well-planned process of urban development. In Côte d'Ivoire, for example, 11,000 building plots were made available between 1974 and 1981. This continued an earlier pattern by which, since the 1930s, the state had allocated plots on which allottees built courtyard houses; 85 per cent of Abidjan's households were accommodated in such houses as tenants. In 1984, 88 per cent of the city's area had been legally subdivided, although many plots were undeveloped (Dubresson and Yapi-Diahou, 1988, and chap. 8 in this volume). Still, by 1990, only a quarter of Abidjan households were living in unauthorized housing, 79 per cent were tenants, and the median rent was only 13 per cent of the median household income of renters (UNCHS/World Bank, 1993). In Conakry between 1963 and 1985, one-third of the extensions to the city's area were in public subdivision schemes (Durand-Lasserve, 1994). In the 1960s in Egypt, the construction sector and land development were nationalized and extensive sales of serviced land to public concessionary companies whose profits were limited by law, together with large-scale public sector house construction for rent, accommodated a large proportion of middle- and lower-income households (El Kadi, 1990; see also chap. 4 on Cairo in this volume). Elsewhere, large amounts of public sector land were used for sites and services schemes. In Malawi, for example, the allocation of state land to low-income residents kept pace with demand until the mid-1970s (Pennant, 1990).

However, sustaining such large-scale subdivision of state land was problematic in the face of diminishing supplies of land in public ownership and changing economic circumstances that either made land and property development more profitable or reduced the revenue available to finance infrastructure installation and land administration. Even in Zimbabwe, where government capacity is greater than in many other countries, slow land delivery for low-income housing has resulted in failure to fulfil targets, let alone needs (Rakodi with Withers, 1993; Musandu-Nyamayaro, 1994). Attempts by international agencies to finance sites and services schemes in the 1970s and 1980s were rarely successful in supplying sufficiently large quantities of affordable plots to reduce their attractiveness to households outside the intended target groups. Nor did they succeed in developing in-country capacity to formulate and implement appropriate land, planning, and construction sector policies (Rakodi, 1991). The supply of formal sector plots by either public or private subdividers is, therefore, generally restricted. As a result, the allottees or purchasers are either those with social and political influence, bureaucratic connections, and access to financial resources, or those who can trade a promise of political support for land allocation.

About half the countries in sub-Saharan Africa have nationalized land and converted freehold into leasehold tenure, mostly in the 1970s or at independence, although Burkina Faso and Côte d'Ivoire had done so in 1960 and Algeria in 1962 (Bagre et al., 1995; Ajavon et al., 1995; Boumedine, 1995). They included a few that believed they were carrying on the principles underlying traditional African communal tenure practices, colonies in which customary tenure had never been recognized, some that hoped to increase efficiency in the allocation of land for public and other uses, some that pursued the reforms for ideological reasons, and some that saw them as part of a wider programme of collectivization of production (Mabogunje, 1993; see also Simon, 1992).

In Tanzania, for example, land was nationalized in 1967 and rental buildings (mostly owned by Asians) in 1972. Since 1974 land has been leased through a process of administrative allocation, and property cannot, in theory, be transferred or mortgaged without government consent. In practice, the fees payable have been much less than the market price of the land and costs of infrastructure would have been, with the result that service provision has lagged behind subdivision and many plots have remained undeveloped (Kombe, 1994). In Zambia similarly, freehold was converted to leasehold, land declared to have no value, and transactions in property made subject to government approval at prices reflecting only the value of unexhausted improvements. The elimination of land prices, it was suggested, encouraged extravagant use, while delays in issuing leases created the need and opportunities for "oiling the wheels" in the relevant agencies.

The 1978 Land Use Decree in Nigeria aimed at introducing a uniform system of land administration, making land available to government for its needs, increasing equity, and curbing speculation. In practice, the nationalization of undeveloped land above a 0.5 ha ceiling in urban areas gave rise to resistance; the establishment of Land Use and Allocation Committees at state level to issue certificates of occupancy has provided scope for inefficiency, delay, and corruption; inconsistencies in the legislation have facilitated evasion; administrative requirements have favoured civil servants and businessmen with wealth and connections; inadequate mapping has inhibited implementation and enforcement; and land has become increasingly concentrated in the hands of the privileged. The reform has improved government access to land but has not replaced customary allocation systems or achieved its other aims (Okpala, 1982;

Dickerman, 1988; Okolocha, 1993; see also Abiodun on land problems in Lagos, chap. 6 in this volume).

In Ethiopia, it was estimated that in the early 1970s 5 per cent of Addis Ababa's population owned 95 per cent of the privately owned land. The revolutionary government placed a ceiling of 0.5 ha on urban land, limited each family to one house, and prohibited the sale of this property; the remaining land and property were nationalized (O'Connor, 1983; Wendt et al., 1990; Mabogunje, 1993). Rents fell by up to a half for nationalized dwellings but maintenance responsibilities were shifted onto the public sector. Houses with low rents were managed by neighbourhood associations (*Kebele*), which retained 15 per cent of the revenue. However, the low levels of the rents resulted in inadequate maintenance. Private house construction was discouraged by the prohibition of speculative house construction and private renting, while sales were deterred by limits imposed by government on the prices charged. Subdivision of state land was increasingly insufficient to keep pace with demand, and illegal occupation, as well as transfers for a price, proliferated. The decree was eventually revoked in 1990 and leasehold tenure re-established, although sale of leaseholds had not commenced by 1995, resulting in an explosion of peripheral illegal settlement (Assefa, 1994; Galaup et al., 1995). In Uganda, the *mailo* land granted to the Buganda at the beginning of the twentieth century was nationalized, but the land information system was poor and much of the development that took place was illegal.

Because of declarations that land had no value or of administrative price setting that failed to keep pace with market prices, land subdivided and sold by the private sector was commonly subsidized, at least on the surface (Asiama, 1989). This, together with the shortfall of supply, increased its attractiveness to developers and the incentives for corruption (Simon, 1992). In practice, the official fees often did not equal the payment made for land, which should be taken to include bribes at the going rate, whether officially or illegally subdivided plots are being considered. The dividing line between these land markets is becoming increasingly blurred: the systems coexist and are closely related in both economic and political terms, as illustrated by Durand-Lasserve's (1994) account of how land prices are arrived at in Conakry. While price trends are related to wider economic and political conditions, in charging bribes for procedures to register an illegal plot, officials expect an amount equal to a proportion of the resale price of the plot. The "price" for an illegally subdivided plot is thus comprised of its market price, together with registration fees and bribes, and generally totals 70–80 per cent of the price at which registered and legally subdivided plots in public subdivisions resell. Durand-Lasserve quotes similar findings from other francophone West African countries.

Despite the ostensible "reforms" to land policy, the basic colonial rules and procedures have not been changed. Instead, states have used them to benefit their own clients, despite the lip-service paid to widening access to land and home ownership by means of public programmes and land nationalization. In some cases, for example Algeria and Burkina Faso, re-privatization of land has occurred (Boumedine, 1995; Bagre et al., 1995). Two other forms of informal land and housing supply remain to be considered: squatting and illegal subdivision of individually or state-owned land.

Illegal land supply

In colonial economies based on migrant wage labour, as has been noted, the government tried to limit the urban population to that needed to fill unskilled and semi-skilled wage jobs in the formal employment sector. No housing was provided for urban residents not in formal wage employment and in practice the supply of housing for wage-earners in the formal sector lagged behind demand, even before independence. Residents providing informal sector services or reluctant or unable to return to their villages were unable to gain access to public or employer rental housing. Where areas of indigenous tenure abutted the urban area, such residents were able to rent or even buy a plot or a house from a holder of customary tenure rights. Where undeveloped land was in public or private ownership under European tenure, this option did not exist. In some instances, European landowners allowed employees or retired workers to settle on their land, or permitted huts to be built on payment of a monthly rental. Around Lusaka, these owners soon lost control over the land, especially after independence, when it became politically unacceptable for them to charge rent. Legally, the existing and new residents on such land, on land with absentee European owners, and on state land became squatters. Further settlement occurred, sometimes incrementally, occasionally (for example in South Africa) by invasion, but more often by means of an adapted indigenous tenure allocation system.

Thus, in Lusaka in the 1960s and 1970s, the political party organization in a squatter area issued permission to occupy land owned by the state or absentee European owners, and even in some areas subdivided plots. Failure to understand the nature of private individual tenure meant that such house builders regarded the process of land settlement as an exercise of their familiar rights to usufruct tenure of unutilized land, whereas urban administrators regarded it as illegal and periodically attempted demolition. Interestingly, in the upgrading programmes of the 1970s, regularization was based on an occupancy licence that gave existing house owners use rights for 30 years. In the pressured situation of Nairobi, councillors, ward representatives, and members of the national legislature intervene in the semitraditional allocation system in squatter areas, to advocate community interests, represent formal sector interests, or mediate between the community and the bureaucracy. Alternatively, they may use their position to obtain access to land, often by initiating land companies or cooperatives, which have bought out many of the original owners (Lee-Smith, 1990; Yahya, 1990). Achieving access to land for the urban poor is thus a source of varying levels of cash income and political support.

As cities have grown, pressure on land has increased, and prices have risen, the scope for squatting has been reduced. In cities where indigenous tenure was predominant it was never widespread; elsewhere the proportion of existing land settlement that is squatting has been reduced by regularization and upgrading, and the proportion of new land occupation that is squatting has declined. Whereas in the late 1970s 12–25 per cent of the population of Egyptian cities, for example, lived in self-built houses on publicly owned land, squatting has become less important than illegal subdivision in the supply of new land. Squatting is now confined to the poorest, who occupy cemeteries, roofs, etc. (Soliman, 1988; El Kadi, 1988; see also chap. 4 in this volume).

Illegal subdivision has overtaken all other means of residential land supply in volume in many African cities. On private land, it is the subdivision and sometimes the sale and the construction that are unauthorized rather than the rights of the landholder. Illegal subdivision of state land, often by public officials, also occurs. In both cases the prospects for regularization vary over time and between cities – from almost certain to unlikely.

In Cairo between 1970 and 1981, 84 per cent of all housing units were produced informally, over half by adding additional floors to existing buildings and the remainder by illegal subdivision of private or government-owned desert land (UNDIESA, 1990; Metwally et al., 1995). As described by Yousry and Aboul Atta in chapter 4 in this volume, the interventionist housing policies of the 1960s were abandoned in favour of an extreme form of economic liberalism in 1973, leading to an explosion of investment in property, fuelled by remittances from migrants in the Middle East. Local development companies moved from the production of middle-income rental housing to the production of high-income housing and commercial development within the built-up area. Peasant owners of urban fringe land responded to the massive increase in demand by selling or subdividing their land. Such sales were not illegal, although the change of use from agricultural to urban use and the construction were (Steinberg, 1990). The opportunities available encouraged the evolution of subdivision and development companies able to develop and market on behalf of owners with insufficient capital. Other owners financed the process by building incrementally using rental income, or by securing key money from a prospective tenant with remittances to invest. Typically, walk-up blocks were constructed, especially along the main roads. Some developers were fined, but demolitions rarely occurred and eventually infrastructure was installed and several suburbs have been regularized. Many of the developer–entrepreneurs have created roles for themselves as local notables, using the indebtedness to them of land purchasers to gain political support and access to political position, and then using this position to obtain infrastructure connections. Analysts suggest that, despite the loss of agricultural land, which the state deplores, the satisfaction of popular demands by illegal subdivision and construction and the means of social control implicit in patronage relations between developers and residents have ensured state toleration of the activity (El Kadi, 1988, 1990; Pickvance, 1988). The massive surplus of capital available as a result of oil price increases and Middle Eastern demand for labour fuelled both extensive redevelopment, favouring large-scale capital and resulting in considerable oversupply of high-cost apartments, and profitable urban extension, which provides opportunities for smaller-scale capital, peasants, and international migrants. Although the process has slowed down more recently, companies offering a range of relevant services have continued to flourish (El Kadi, 1990). Although the government has now adopted a regularization policy, the approach is non-participatory, gives no scope for retaining land for infrastructure provision, and has given rise to fears that areas will become overdeveloped, leading to environmental deterioration (Metwally et al., 1995).

In Tunis, public *habous* (*waqf*) and French-owned land was nationalized on independence in 1956 and much of the agricultural land transferred to individuals in 1970. Because of land shortage within the urban boundary and the inability of the majority to afford the ready-built public housing being produced, one-third of the new housing in the later 1970s occurred in illegal subdivisions undertaken by both owners and agricultural tenants on state land. The whole process is less elaborate and sophisticated than in Cairo: information on land for sale circulates informally, no brokers are involved, and purchasers undertake building themselves. However, notaries work with subdividers to produce statements that land is vacant, as a basis for registering their ownership and to give purchasers the appearance of legality. The lack of infrastructure makes the land affordable to middle- and low-income groups, while subdividers, as in Cairo, use the indebtedness of purchasers buying land by instalments to achieve political office, which is in turn used to strengthen their position by obtaining infrastructure (Chabbi, 1988; Stambouli, 1990). Since the 1970s, many of these settlements have been regularized and upgraded (Chabbi, 1995).

Although the process of illegal subdivision was delayed in Fès, Morocco, by the availability of cheap rented housing in the inner city, some peripheral development is now occurring. As prices have increased and areas have been regularized and upgraded with World Bank assistance during the 1980s, the poor have gradually been excluded and driven back into the *medina*, further increasing its physical deterioration (Escallier, 1994).

Much of Nairobi's recent peripheral expansion has been on illegally subdivided privately and state-owned land, resulting in a dearth of land in public ownership for legal subdivision. The sale of undeveloped plots in sites and services schemes by officials also occurs. A Bill is currently before parliament to regularize illegal allocations of state land (Maina and Macoloo, 1995). In places, officials even took it upon themselves to allocate state-owned land where they were not authorized to do so, for example in Korogocho in Nairobi (Lee-Smith, 1990). The unofficial control exercised by state employees over land allocation in Kinshasa is described by Piermay in chapter 7 in this volume.

This extended account of the processes by which land is made available for residential development has drawn attention to a number of features that characterize cities continent wide, although to varying extents depending on the impact of colonization on indigenous tenure and social organization, subsequent economic conditions, and state policies. The informalization of land subdivision and development in the face of rapid urban growth and limited state capacity and the commercialization of formerly non-commercial processes are both widespread, although there has been little *official* adaptation of land policy and legislation to either. Inextricably linked to the supply of undeveloped land are the processes of house production and transactions in property within the built-up area. Both have been referred to in passing, but will now be discussed specifically.

The production of housing

Because the precondition for house construction is access to land, most attention has been devoted to this issue. Land is, however, only part of the residential package – the provision of infrastructure is closely associated with subdivision of land and has a major influence on land prices. In this respect, publicly initiated provision has lagged far behind needs, not least because of the failure of government to recognize and register various forms of land occupancy as a basis for property taxation (Durand-Lasserve and Tribillon, 1995). This section, is, however, concerned with the production of the shelter itself.

Despite urban housing policies since independence that have stressed the responsibility of governments and local authorities to meet the housing needs of the poor, state production of housing (even in partnership with individual households, as, for example, in sites and services schemes) has only ever met a small proportion of the need. In Nairobi, for example, between 1976 and 1987 only one-tenth of the increased numbers of residents were accommodated in publicly initiated housing projects, half in sites and services schemes (Ondiege, 1989). In Cairo, public sector housing also accounted for only about 10 per cent of total house production between 1960 and 1983 (Soliman, 1988; El Kadi, 1988). As Yousry and Aboul Atta note in chapter 4 of this volume, many of the public housing units constructed in new settlements outside the city were unaffordable despite subsidies, and they remain unoccupied (see also Metwally et al., 1995). In both cases, the proportion of total house production initiated by the public sector has declined over time and the dwellings or serviced plots made available have not been affordable by the lowest income groups. At the other end of the continuum has been Zimbabwe, where there is little squatting and illegal subdivision, and almost all low-cost dwellings have been developed in serviced plot areas in recent years (Rakodi with Withers, 1993).

Whether in the serviced plot schemes that have typified more recent public housing programmes, in areas of illegal subdivision, or in areas with tenure based on indigenous systems of land allocation, the majority of houses in both the formal and informal sectors have been built on an individual rather than mass produced or speculative basis. Some medium- or large-scale formal sector industrialized production has occurred, typically of public sector or employer housing or of private sector housing for rent or sale. In most middle- and upper-income housing areas, houses and walk-up apartments are commissioned by developers or their owners for occupation or rental from small and medium master builders. In the middle- and lower-income areas where subdivision and construction are unauthorized, housing may be commissioned from small formal sector and artisanal builders. Wherever there is de facto security of tenure, construction takes place by means of labour-only contracts and is generally incremental. The predominance of informal construction and the need for gradual construction are necessitated partly by the lack of credit for house construction, because of both the lack of title and the under-developed nature of the housing finance sector. These together account for the low ratio of total value of mortgages in 1989 to total formal and informal investment in housing, which was, for example, 25 per cent in Rabat, 20 per cent in Tunis, 12 per cent in Nairobi, 8 per cent in Abidjan, and 3 per cent in Dar es Salaam (UNCHS/World Bank, 1993).

Although sometimes the use of artisanal builders is supplemented by household labour, self-help (*autoconstruction*) has long been replaced by self-managed construction (*autopromotion*) (Coquery, 1990). Quite apart from gaining access to land, accumulating savings, the assembly of building materials, and the selection of a builder take urban knowledge and are, today, more rarely embarked upon by recent migrants than in the 1950s and 1960s when land, traditional construction skills, mud for bricks, and even thatch for roofs were relatively easily available. Today, only the makeshift dwellings of some squatter areas, temporary shelters used during the early stages of house construction, and backyard shacks are built by self-help and even these, in places, may be assembled from prefabricated components.

Although access to land is the single most important component in housing production, lack of capacity in the housing finance, construction, and building materials production sectors is in many African cities a constraint on house production. However, mechanisms to assist individual households to save enough to buy land or a house or to start construction have developed to alleviate the first constraint, including instalment purchases and saving via rotating credit associations. In Enugu, Nigeria, for example, recent data show that 78 per cent of the housing stock has been owner built, that three-quarters of the buildings contain tenants (and 23 per cent are wholly let), but that only 35 per cent of builders had had access to formal institutional credit. Almost all these had combined a bank loan with informal sources, including personal savings, rotating credit associations, social clubs, and inherited money (Osondu and Middleton, 1994). There seems little point increasing the capacity of housing finance institutions until a wider range and greater quantity of housing is eligible for formal sector credit. Lack of capacity in the formal construction and building materials production sectors in many African countries is caused primarily by lack of foreign exchange and skills. However, when building regulations are relaxed, as they are in most informally produced housing, it is clear that the small-scale sector has considerable capacity and is often more adaptable in times of economic crisis than are formal sector firms (Coquery, 1990). The liberalization of import controls on components for high-cost buildings, the lack of policy attention to the development of indigenous construction and building materials construction sectors, as well as the retention of inappropriate building regulations can hinder house production, as illustrated by the continued dependence of many countries on imported building materials even for housing (for example, 37 per cent by value in Nairobi, 45 per cent in Dakar, 35 per cent in Abidjan, and 25 per cent in several other cities; UNCHS/ World Bank, 1993).

This section has focused on the production of housing. For the majority of urban residents in most African cities, house ownership is aspired to. This includes both for own occupation and for the generation of rental income. However, such an aspiration is by no means universal, either between or within cities. In parts of Africa, urban residents maintain strong ties with their home communities, often leaving their families behind to farm and directing their savings into remittances for both consumption purposes and investment in land, cattle, or housing. Although less commonly than in colonial times, many urban residents intend to retire to their home areas and prefer to rent in town, for example in Ghana (Korboe, 1994) or Kenya (Andreasen, 1987). An intention to retire elsewhere does not, of course, deter every resident from becoming an urban house owner, because the appreciating value of a house is seen as both a good investment and something to pass on to his or her children (Dickerman, 1988). Single people, newly formed households, and very poor households, as well as those living apart from spouses and children, may not aspire to ownership either because they prefer the limited responsibilities of rental housing or because they have insufficient resources to embark on house construction or purchase. However, for many poor households, especially those headed by women, access to home ownership forms an important part of their survival strategies if it can be achieved, because it potentially provides a secure source of shelter and income from renting. Rental housing markets will be further discussed in the next section.

House purchase or construction depend, however, not just on aspirations but also on opportunity. Even in areas of customary tenure, not all achieve owner-occupation. Peil's study of West African cities found that owner-occupiers were typically men aged 50 or more, especially those who were self-employed, and that ownership was often the result of a long process of planning, organizing, and saving (Peil with Sada, 1984). Barnes (1979), in an earlier study of Mushin in Lagos, found that, despite the attractions of ownership in terms of economic returns and social status, fewer than one in five of migrants succeeded in acquiring urban property. In areas of public land, access depends on political and bureaucratic connections, as well as luck (when sites and services schemes, for example, are massively oversubscribed) and economic status (often the ability to pay bribes in addition to proof of a regular income). The proportion of urban residents who achieve home ownership varies widely, from around two-thirds in Tunis, Johannesburg, Ibadan, and Dakar to under half in Algiers, Rabat, and Harare, one-third in Lilongwe and Cairo, little more than a quarter in Dar es Salaam, Nairobi, and Accra, and only one-fifth in Abidjan (UNCHS/World Bank, 1993).

Property markets in developed areas

In addition to the development of rental housing markets, which will be discussed first, changes in social structure, economic conditions, and the circumstances of individual households result in transactions in both undeveloped land and developed property, which may change patterns of access to land and housing, modify land uses, and provide opportunities for investment to different fractions of capital. Exchange of plots and houses and redevelopment will be briefly considered below.

Where access to land and house ownership is limited, the majority become tenants. In many West African cities, for example in the eight towns studied by Peil in Ghana, the Gambia, and Nigeria in the 1970s, rents were modest (10–25 per cent of average male incomes), although demands for key money or several months' rent in advance were becoming increasingly common (Peil, 1981). Extensive renting has also emerged in areas of public housing, including municipal housing (for example in Zimbabwean towns and cities in the 1960s and 1970s) and sites and services schemes. In Nairobi by 1983 over 90 per cent of owners in Umoja I were renting out rooms and 85 per cent in Dandora (Kiamba, 1992). Renting also emerges quite early in the development of squatter and other illegal housing areas. Consolidation or upgrading in such areas often result in rent increases, even though rents may still remain more affordable to lower-income people than in areas of legal land tenure (Ondiege, 1989). Even in circumstances where the supply of land is relatively good, a substantial proportion of households may choose or be forced to rent. In Malawi, for example, 80 per cent of plots in the Traditional Housing Areas (serviced plot schemes) had tenants by 1980, while 68 per cent of the THA and 38 per cent of the total urban population were tenants (Pennant, 1990). Returns on the construction of additional rooms for rent in such areas are considerable (Lee-Smith, 1990), and letting out additional rooms may be an important element in household coping strategies in times of economic hardship. In most parts of Africa only a small minority of women are property owners and potential landlords, despite the paucity of wage employment and other income-earning opportunities open to them. However, in Gaborone, Botswana, 83 per cent of landlords are women, although almost half of these have husbands who are absent, typically working in South Africa. Although more dependent on rental income, women household heads let fewer rooms at lower rents than male landlords, because of their disadvantaged access to capital for construction (Datta, 1995).

Rent levels are affected by the location and quality of accommodation, supply in relation to demand, and general economic conditions. Rents may increase in real terms as a result of shortfalls in supply, but they may also fall over time. In Nairobi between 1980 and 1992, for example, Amis (1996) claims that rents in informal housing areas halved in real terms, as did the minimum wage, while average wages declined by one-third. The proportion of income that tenant households devoted to rent (15–20 per cent) and occupancy levels remained relatively constant, so the fall, he suggests, is explained by a combination of increased poverty (and thus what the market will bear) and an increase in supply, facilitated by state withdrawal from interference in informal housing production.

Rents may also be depressed by government-imposed rent control or rent freezes. Although a large number of countries in Africa have rent control legislation (often introduced by the colonial powers), in relatively few is it effectively enforced. It has had perhaps the most widespread effect in Cairo, where rents are set at market levels for new tenancies but then frozen, deterring mobility in the housing stock and leading to unnecessarily long journeys to work (World Bank, 1988). Initial market rents and the key money demanded by landlords to offset the subsequent decline in real rents make access to new leases costly and discriminatory against new tenants (Wikan, 1990). Thus, whereas controlled rents are just under 40 per cent of market rent levels, total payments come to nearer 70 per cent of market rents (see also Metwally et al., 1995). In Ghana, rent control has been in force since the 1940s and rent levels are periodically set for different types of property. Rents are low, accounting for 2 per cent on average of income in Kumasi in 1986 (Malpezzi et al., 1990) and 6 per cent in Accra in 1989 (UNCHS/World Bank, 1993). A variety of means of evading rent control have developed, including key money, demanding that tenants finance the construction of the room they wish to rent, and declining to let vacant rooms (Korboe, 1994). Thus rents do not, for many tenants, reflect real housing costs. Low rents can be attributed only partly to rent control legislation and, although they have contributed to low rates of new construction, increasing costs and difficulty in obtaining land and building materials have also played a role.

In Zimbabwe, rent control is only partially enforceable. It is ineffective in low-income areas of rented rooms and backyard shacks. In middle- and upper-income areas it has led to the sale of previously rented dwellings and the cessation of construction of flats for rent. Average rent increases were depressed in the 1980s, but varied between blocks owned by large landlords or employers, in which rent control was enforced, and flats let by individual owners, where, because of the shortage, tenants felt unable to appeal to the Rent Tribunal (Rakodi with Withers, 1993). In Nigeria, rent control has been unenforceable, with the result that in Benin City, for example, where 65 per cent of households are tenants and 13 per cent live rent free in family houses, rents constitute 15–29 per cent of income, the proportion increasing with decreasing income (Ozo, 1990). Nigeria is fairly typical: in the majority of cities rent control legislation is unenforceable and should be reconsidered, although there is a continued need to provide legislative protection for tenants against summary eviction and harassment.

It has generally been accepted that plots and houses sold to middle- and upper-income households will enter the private market. At independence, this, together with the indigenization of senior public sector posts, enabled indigenous residents to penetrate residential areas previously reserved for Europeans. However, penetration did not occur at the same rate in all residential areas: higher costs in more exclusive areas deterred house purchase, while settler groups such as Asian owners in Nairobi were sometimes less likely to sell (Kimani, 1972). The dynamics of these submarkets have not been examined in any detail in most cities. In Mbezi public subdivision in Dar es Salaam, three-quarters of plots have remained undeveloped, largely because of the failure to provide infrastructure, and an active informal land market has developed (Kombe, 1994). In Ismailia, Egypt, the sale prices of serviced plots, which were originally subsidized, increased in real terms, allowing sellers to realize windfall profits (Davidson, 1990).

Increasingly, serviced plots for "low-income" households are allocated freehold or on long leases, often with no or limited (and unenforceable) restrictions on resale. In some cases, inappropriate location of a scheme, failure to develop, or default on loan repayments may force allottees to sell. Elsewhere, if the plots have been subsidized, allottees soon realize that the considerable profit available on resale provides an incentive for queue-jumping in the initial allocation process, or selling out and realizing the full market value of the property and any self-help labour inputs. Whether or not allottees do sell depends on the relative returns from renting out rooms and from sale, as well as other motives for owning. If allottees are forced to sell and so do not realize the full market value, the buyer benefits from part or all of the subsidy, whereas sale at market value provides a windfall profit to the allottee (Pickvance, 1988). In Zimbabwe, sales are constrained by the lack of alternative housing, appreciation of the value of home ownership, and residual local authority controls. As a result, prices are several times the cost of construction on a newly serviced plot. The shortfall of plots and medium-cost houses attracts cash buyers who are, on average, higher income than the original allottees and include a larger proportion of absentee landlords (Teedon, 1990; Rakodi with Withers, 1993).

Similar sales occur in squatter and other unauthorized areas. In Zambia in the 1970s, a substantial minority of owner households had bought their houses, usually from the original builder. In Msimbazi in Dar es Salaam, the original occupants of plots on low-lying land allocated for agricultural use were subdividing and selling. Written agreements of sale were witnessed by an elder or relatives and the local political leader (Kombe, 1994; see also Kironde and Rugaiganisa, 1995).

Because of the maintenance burden of public sector rental housing, widespread aspirations to ownership, and the ideological backing given to ownership by international agencies and governments alike in the 1970s and 1980s, many public sector housing organizations have more recently embarked on programmes of sale. In Ghana, houses were discounted by a standard 20 per cent, eliminating the need for a down payment before issue of a mortgage (Derkyi, 1994). In South Africa, resistance to government attempts to sell to tenants inhibited take-up, but in Zimbabwe generous discounts enabled tenant purchase for payments identical to previous rent levels and most local authority houses are currently being rented-to-buy (Rakodi with Withers, 1993). Although the cost-saving rationale may be legitimate, wider issues are rarely considered. These include the effects on tenants who cannot afford or do not wish to buy, the effects on mobility, and the results (especially if no constraints are imposed on resale) of the entry of public sector housing into the open market.

In all cases, the sale of public houses or houses on publicly initiated schemes, as well as encouraging the displacement of lower- by higher-income households, provides investment opportunities for absentee landlords. In many areas, landlords live locally, have similar socio-economic characteristics to their tenants, and own only between one and three properties (Aina, 1990; Ozo, 1990; Lee-Smith, 1990). Elsewhere, even within the same city, large-scale landlordism has also developed (Amis, 1984). However, inadequate information is available to detail the conditions under which large-scale landlordism emerges and whether petty landlordism invariably evolves into capitalist landlordism (Simon, 1992).

Trends in property markets in inner-city areas vary over time and between cities. Distinctions can be drawn between "modern" central business districts, "ancient" city centres (the *medinas* of North African settlements), and the surrounding inner-city areas. In some inner-city areas, constraints on sale inhibit investment in maintenance and redevelopment, resulting in poor physical environments, out-migration of upper-income groups, and a predominance of poor-quality residential use. Elsewhere, commercial and handicrafts activities (and increasingly business as well as consumer services) have been attracted to inner-city bazaar areas in greater volumes (Troin, 1993). Despite the clear attraction of *medina* areas for both certain categories of residents and (especially) business enterprises, and their historical significance, neither occupiers nor authorities attach much importance to conservation, except in a few cases where tourism is significant. Even then, regeneration may be confined to street frontages (Troin, 1993). In Fès, Morocco, for example, the departure of merchants for Casablanca made available a substantial supply of rental tenement housing in the *medina*. Increasing pressure for commercial use and overcrowding then led to an increase in peripheral illegal subdivision. However, increased demand for middle-income housing and regularization and upgrading of the suburban areas later excluded the poor, who moved back into the old town, accelerating the process of physical deterioration (Escallier, 1994). In Kariakoo, adjacent to the CBD in Dar es Salaam, since the early 1980s resistance to the sale of plots to the government because of inadequate levels of compensation has given way to commercial deals, mostly with Tanzanians of Arab and Indian origin, and redevelopment for higher-density commercial and residential development, often part-financed by capital contributed by international migrants (Kombe, 1994). In Woodstock, a residential area near the centre of Cape Town, which resisted segregation under South Africa's Group Areas Act, mixed-race gentrification occurred even before the segregationist legislation was repealed and has continued since (Garside, 1993). Beavon describes recent changes in the inner-city housing market of Johannesburg in chapter 5 in this volume.

The conversion of inner-city housing to commercial uses and redevelopment at higher densities typify CBDs and their surrounding areas. Investment booms, Bond (1991) asserts, follow over-accumulation in other sectors, which results in surplus manufacturing capital seeking speculative opportunities in property and driving up prices. He identifies investment booms, followed by slumps, in central area property markets in Harare and Johannesburg that can be explained in this way. Very little information is available on property markets in the central areas of African cities. Simon (1992) believes, largely on the basis of evidence from Nairobi, that, because no African city plays a role as a global financial centre and because, in some countries, of restrictions on foreign investment and property ownership, multinational capital has not been attracted to investment in property. However, foreign companies, governments, and financial institutions in search of offices to rent have attracted domestic capital at the expense of investment in industry, agriculture, and residential property, driving up prices. Such properties, often designed by expatriate architects, built by foreign contractors, and using a substantial proportion of imported components, resemble office blocks, hotels, and banks in cities worldwide. The role of the state in CBD commercial property markets has not been studied, although it is likely to be more than regulatory.

Conclusion

To conclude, the implications of some of the characteristics of and trends in urban property markets for future land management policies will be explored. African cities are almost invariably characterized by the coexistence of two or more systems of land supply: indigenous tenure, illegal modes, capitalist markets, and bureaucratic allocation procedures. These overlap, vary in their characteristics and interactions, and produce confused, complex patterns of land supply (Simon, 1992). Modified forms of indigenous tenure dominate only in some West African cities, but are important in many others, and have become increasingly commercialized in recent years. True squatting is generally limited and access to both privately and publicly owned undeveloped land has also become more commercialized. Commercialization of access has been paralleled by an increasing prevalence of illegal development (Simon, 1992) – over half the urban housing stock in Tanzania and Kenya (Amis, 1996; Kombe, 1994). This reflects the inability of formal urban management mechanisms, planning procedures, and housing supply to keep pace with rapidly increasing demand. It also expresses, as did indigenous and colonial tenure systems, contemporary social relations, including the relationships between residents seeking shelter, entrepreneurs seeking opportunities for profit, political forces, and the apparatus of the state, which is concerned with implementing outdated and ineffective land policy and laws.

It seems evident that the trends identified in this chapter will continue and intensify. They raise, above all, questions about the nature of appropriate public sector responses. The problems are only too obvious (Simon, 1992; Durand-Lasserve, 1993; Mabogunje, 1993):

- different systems of rights and practices, with different degrees of legitimacy and compatibility, leading to complexity and conflict;
- information on land (including mapping) that is poor, scattered, discontinuous, and opaque;
- administrative responsibility that is scattered and overcentralized, leading to poor coordination;
- policy that is incoherent and ambivalent;
- legislation that is fragmented, outdated, and only partially enforceable;
- failure to register many types of land occupancy, reducing the ability to raise revenue from property taxation.

Two views as to the best way forward can be detected.

One suggests that indigenous tenure is inefficient, encouraging wasteful use of land, discouraging infrastructure installation and improvement or redevelopment of deteriorated buildings, and complicating land administration systems. As in rural areas, it is advocated that formal individual title should be universalized, to increase eligibility for credit, encourage investment, and simplify administration. The evidence as to whether individualization of rural tenure has produced the expected increases in production is mixed. On balance, analysts suggest that it has increased inequality in access to land and credit (because the supply of credit has not increased), narrowed rights to land while improving security of tenure for some, and failed to create a well-functioning land market because customary law continues to determine sales and succession (Reyna and Downs, 1988; Fleuret, 1988; Shipton, 1988). Barrows and Roth (1990) conclude that rural tenure registration may have positive net social benefits when new economic opportunities also occur, including the potential for utilizing new farming technology previously prevented by tenure patterns, but that without such increases in markets, prices, credit, etc. no increase in production occurs.

Similarities with urban land markets are obvious: individualization of tenure discriminates in favour of those who succeed, via claiming group rights or exploiting their wealth or connections, in achieving land and house ownership, while it excludes those who previously benefited from family claims or non-commercialized access via squatting. Investment in improvement and redevelopment will occur only if capital is available and the proceeds will be widely distributed only if owners of small plots can get access to such capital. The majority of urban residents are already tenants and do not stand to benefit from individualization of tenure – indeed, if it is accompanied by increased enforcement of planning and building standards, the supply of rooms may be adversely affected, driving up rents. Lack of administrative capacity will inhibit any attempts to issue full legal titles to land universally, restricting benefits to those who can jump the queue. Nevertheless, the problems caused by unregistered tenure (conflict, opportunities for fraudulent sales, and loss of revenue) and unplanned development (loss of agricultural land, settlement of hazardous sites, and increased costs of infrastructure installation) cannot be denied.

A similar set of arguments to those used to advocate individualization of group tenure rights is used with respect to nationalized land. Because bureaucratic allocation processes have evidently failed, land, it is argued, should be denationalized. Simon (1992) suggests that such a move would probably encourage international capital to move into property because the rate of return in this sphere exceeds that in directly productive sectors. Whether or not such an influx is prevented by legislation prohibiting foreign ownership of property, denationalization combined with the issue of legal title is likely, just as is individualization of communal tenure, to be largely regressive. It has echoes of the blind faith in market forces that, reflected undiscriminatingly in policy conditionality, has caused such problems for African countries undergoing structural adjustment.

The alternative view is that the ability of the state to tackle urban problems depends above all on the financial resources available to it. Ability to subdivide and service land will increase its legitimacy, especially of local government, in turn enabling it to embark on improving its regulatory activities. The priority then is to improve revenue generation from land. Durand-Lasserve (1993) advocates the establishment of simple fiscal land registers (cadastres) based on the occupier of land, and including both regular and irregular development, as a first stage. Benin's experience with the establishment of land registers and Burkina Faso's with new techniques for plot subdivision and allocation as well as the introduction of property tax are promising (Oloudé, 1995; Bagre et al., 1995). Although control of the process should be retained by the public sector, private sector organizations can be used in many of the operations involved. At a later stage, such a cadastre could evolve into a multi-purpose one, including registration of title and not merely occupancy. Mabogunje (1993) calls for working with the traditional administrative structure as it has evolved today into, for example, a mixture of chiefs and neighbourhood organizations in west African cities, or neighbourhood councils focused on mosques in Khartoum. Neighbourhood organizations should, he argues, be integrated into urban local government and be used to help in establishing and administering a fiscal cadastre. Other analysts, while not advocating the abolition of indigenous tenure in urban areas, suggest that its operation can be improved by simplifying procedures, improving documentation, and imposing requirements for infrastructure installation (Asiama, 1989). Measures to deter speculation and ensure the sale and subdivision of land ripe for development are also seen as urgent in many cities, although appropriate measures may be facilitative (e.g. land readjustment) rather than penal (e.g. higher taxes) (Acquaye and Asiama, 1986; Rakodi with Withers, 1993). This second approach is based on minimal interference with either bureaucratic procedures or market processes, at least initially. It recognizes that incremental improvements to existing systems of land supply are both more realistic and safer than radical changes, especially given the political and administrative difficulties of reform, where ethnic and class conflict over property is prevalent (Simon, 1992).

Experiences of regularization demonstrate that it must be handled with care. Regularization that results in major disruption to existing houses and employs bureaucratic and cumbersome procedures and attempts to register full legal titles, as in Benin's earlier experience (Oloudé, 1995) and Cameroun's attempts to regularize and upgrade Nylon in Douala (Kanga et al., 1995), is undesirable. Although some re-planning may be needed, disruption should be minimized, participation encouraged, and procedures kept simple (for example, Botswana issues Temporary Occupancy Permits, which are converted to Certificates of Rights when the area is gazetted). Infrastructure provision may signal de facto regularization, even while progress with legal regularization is delayed by its complexity, as in the Côte d'Ivoire (Ajavon et al., 1995). Arrangements for cost recovery are also often problematic.

It is very clear that the house construction sector has considerable capacity to produce large numbers of dwellings, even without state backing. There are, however, constraints on housing supply other than land, and, for the supply of dwellings of an appropriate standard and cost to keep pace with need, attention is needed in most places to the supply of building materials and credit and to revisions to planning and building regulations, while in some places support to the construction sector is needed to ensure small firms in particular can get access to working capital, skilled labour, and equipment. In addition, measures to extend infrastructure and improve service delivery must be planned, if not implemented, by the public sector, both to most existing areas (whether illegally occupied or not) and to guide future patterns of land subdivision and occupation. Even here, Guinea's experience in Conakry with a joint public–private development company responsible for implementation shows that informal subdivision is likely to overtake the formal process once minimal infrastructure is installed, making cost recovery difficult (Bourdon, 1995).

The overriding importance of land in the process of urban development has been reflected in the attention paid to it in this chapter. However, housing and other property are produced by the assembly of a variety of components, the supply of none of which should be considered in isolation either from each other or from the political, social, and economic context.

References

Acquaye, E. and S. O. Asiama. 1986. Land policies for housing development for low-income groups in Africa. *Land Development Studies* 3: 127–143.

Acquaye, E. and Associates. 1989. *Study of Institutional/Legal Problems Associated with Land Delivery in Accra*. Report to the Government of Ghana, UNDP, and the UN Centre for Human Settlements, Kumasi.

Aina, T. A. 1990. Petty landlords and poor tenants in a low-income settlement in metropolitan Lagos, Nigeria. In: P. Amis and P. Lloyd, eds., *Housing Africa's Urban Poor*. Manchester University Press, Manchester, pp. 87–102.

Ajavon, A., P.-C. Kobo, and C. Nado. 1995. Côte d'Ivoire. In: A. Durand-Lasserve, R. Pajoni, and J.-F. Tribillon, eds., *Urban Land Management, Regularisation Policies and Local Development in Africa and the Arab States: Summaries of the Case Studies*. GDR Interurba–CNRS and Association Internationale des Techniciens, Experts et Chercheurs, Paris, for the World Bank/UNCHS/UNDP Urban Management Programme, pp. 43–46.

Ameur, M. 1995. Morocco. In: A. Durand-Lasserve, R. Pajoni, and J.-F. Tribillon, eds., *Urban Land Management, Regularisation Policies and Local Development in Africa and the Arab States: Summaries of the Case Studies*. GDR Interurba–CNRS and Association Internationale des Techniciens, Experts et Chercheurs, Paris, for the World Bank/UNCHS/UNDP Urban Management Programme, pp. 9–11.

Amis, P. 1984. Squatters or tenants: The commercialization of unauthorised housing in Nairobi. *World Development* 12(1): 87–96.

—— 1990. Key themes in contemporary African urbanisation. In: P. Amis and P. Lloyd, eds., *Housing Africa's Urban Poor*. Manchester University Press, Manchester, pp. 1–34.

—— 1996. Long run trends in Nairobi's informal housing market. *Third World Planning Review* 18(3): 271–285.

Andreasen, J. 1987. *Rented Rooms and Rural Relations: Housing in Thika, Kenya 1969–1985*. Royal Danish Academy of Fine Arts, Copenhagen.

Asabere, P. K. 1981a. The price of urban land in a chiefdom: Empirical evidence on a traditional African city, Kumasi. *Journal of Regional Science* 21: 529–539.

—— 1981b. The determinants of land values in an African city: The case of Accra, Ghana. *Land Economics* 57(3): 385–397.

Asiama, S. O. 1989. *Land Management in Kumasi, Ghana*. Report to the World Bank, Kumasi.

—— 1995. Ghana. In: A. Durand-Lasserve, R. Pajoni, and J.-F. Tribillon, eds., *Urban Land Management, Regularisation Policies and Local Development in Africa and the Arab States: Summaries of the Case Studies*. GDR Interurba–CNRS and Association Internationale des Techniciens, Experts et Chercheurs, Paris, for the World Bank/UNCHS/UNDP Urban Management Programme, pp. 67–69.

Assefa, T. 1994. Source of housing finance for the urban poor in Ethiopia. Paper presented to the European Network for Housing Research 2nd Symposium, "Housing for the Urban Poor," Birmingham.

Bagre, A. S., D. Belemsagha, D. Guiebo, and G. Kibtonre. 1995. Burkina Faso. In: A. Durand-Lasserve, R. Pajoni, and J.-F. Tribillon, eds., *Urban Land Management, Regularisation Policies and Local Development in Africa and the Arab States: Summaries of the Case Studies*. GDR Interurba–CNRS and Association Internationale des Techniciens, Experts et Chercheurs, Paris, for the World Bank/UNCHS/UNDP Urban Management Programme, pp. 29–36.

Barnes, S. T. 1979. Migration and land acquisition: The new landowners of Lagos. *African Urban Studies* 4: 59–70.

Barrows, R. and M. Roth. 1990. Land tenure and investment in African agriculture: Theory and evidence. *Journal of Modern African Studies* 28(2): 265–297.

Bond, P. 1991. Geopolitics, international finance and national capital accumulation: Zimbabwe in the 1980s and 1990s. *Tidschrift voor Economische en Sociale Geografie* 82(5): 325–337.

Boumedine, R. S. 1995. Algeria. In: A. Durand-Lasserve, R. Pajoni, and J.-F. Tribillon, eds., *Urban Land Management, Regularisation Policies and Local Development in Africa and the Arab States: Summaries of the Case Studies*. GDR Interurba–CNRS and Association Internationale des Techniciens, Experts et Chercheurs, Paris, for the World Bank/UNCHS/UNDP Urban Management Programme, pp. 1–2.

Bourdon, D. 1995. Guinea. In: A. Durand-Lasserve, R. Pajoni, and J.-F. Tribillon, eds., *Urban Land Management, Regularisation Policies and Local Development in Africa and the Arab States: Summaries of the Case Studies*. GDR Interurba–CNRS and Association Internationale des Techniciens, Experts et Chercheurs, Paris, for the World Bank/UNCHS/UNDP Urban Management Programme, pp. 47–50.

Bruce, J. W. 1988. A perspective on indigenous land tenure systems and land concentration. In: R. E. Downs and S. P. Reyna, eds., *Land and Society in Contemporary Africa*. University of New England Press, Hanover, NH, pp. 23–52.

Canel, P. and C. Girard. 1988. Un paradigme a l'épreuve des faits: l' "autoconstruction" en ville Africaine. *Revue Tiers Monde* 29(116): 1121–1133.

CASS (Centre for African Settlement Studies and Development). 1991. *Women in Urban Land Development in Africa: Case Studies from Nigeria and Ghana*. Report to the UN Centre for Human Settlements, Ibadan.

Chabbi, M. 1988. The pirate subdeveloper: A new form of land developer in Tunis. *International Journal of Urban and Regional Research* 12(1): 1–7.

——— 1995. Tunisia. In: A. Durand-Lasserve, R. Pajoni, and J.-F. Tribillon, eds., *Urban Land Management, Regularisation Policies and Local Development in Africa and the Arab States: Summaries of the Case Studies*. GDR Interurba–CNRS and Association Internationale des Techniciens, Experts et Chercheurs, Paris, for the World Bank/UNCHS/UNDP Urban Management Programme, pp. 13–17.

Coquery, M. 1990. Autopromotion de l'habitat et modes de production du cadre bati: l'apport de recherches récentes en Afrique noire francophone. In P. Amis and P. Lloyd, eds., *Housing Africa's Urban Poor*. Manchester University Press, Manchester, pp. 55–71.

Datta, K. 1995. Strategies for urban survival? Women landlords in Gaborone, Botswana. *Habitat International* 19(1): 1–12.

Davidson, F. 1990. Lessons from implementation: The impact of an active land management policy on integrated land development in Ismailia, Egypt. In P. Baross and J. van der Linden, eds., *The Transformation of Land Supply Systems in Third World Cities*. Avebury, Aldershot, pp. 277–294.

Derkyi, E. 1994. Providing affordable and sustainable housing loans to lower income earners: Ghana's experience. Paper presented to the European Network for Housing Research 2nd Symposium, "Housing for the Urban Poor," Birmingham.

Dickerman, C. 1988. Urban land concentration. In: R. E. Downs and S. P. Reyna, eds., *Land and Society in Contemporary Africa*. University of New England Press, Hanover, NH, pp. 76–90.

Dubresson, A. and A. Yapi-Diahou. 1988. L'état, "le bas", les cours: exclusion sociale et petite production immobilière à Abidjan (Côte-d'Ivoire). *Revue Tiers Monde* 29(116): 1083–1100.

Durand-Lasserve, A. 1993. *Conditions de mise en place des systèmes d'information foncière dans les villes d'Afrique sud-Saharienne francophone*. UMP 8, World Bank, Washington D.C.

——— 1994. Researching the relationship between economic liberalization and changes to land markets and land prices: The case of Conakry, Guinea, 1985–91. In: G. Jones and P. M. Ward, eds., *Methodology for Land and Housing Market Analysis*. UCL Press, London, pp. 55–69.

Durand-Lasserve, A. and J.-F. Tribillon. 1995. Suggestions for debate. Paper presented to the World Bank/UNCHS/UNDP Urban Management Programme Seminar on Urban Land Management, Regularization Policies and Local Development in Africa and the Arab States, Abidjan.

El Kadi, G. 1988. Market mechanisms and spontaneous urbanization in Egypt: The Cairo case. *International Journal of Urban and Regional Research* 12(1): 22–37.

——— 1990. L'articulation des deux circuits de la gestion foncière en Egypte: le case du Caire. In P. Amis and P. Lloyd, eds., *Housing Africa's Urban Poor*. Manchester University Press, Manchester, pp. 103–122.

Escallier, R. 1994. Morocco. In J. D. Tarver, ed., *Urbanization in Africa: A Handbook*. Greenwood, Westport, Conn., pp. 246–261.

Fleuret, A. 1988. Some consequences of tenure and agrarian reform in Taita, Kenya. In R. E. Downs and S. P. Reyna, eds., *Land and Society in Contemporary Africa*. University of New England Press, Hanover, NH, pp. 136–158.

Frishman, A. 1988. The rise of squatting in Kano, Nigeria. In R. A. Obudho and C. C. Mhlanga, eds., *Slum and Squatter Settlements in Sub-Saharan Africa: Toward a Planning Strategy*. Praeger, New York.

Galaup, A., Z. Lakew, and T. Tigabu. 1995. Ethiopia. In: A. Durand-Lasserve, R. Pajoni, and J.-F. Tribillon, eds., *Urban Land Management, Regularisation Policies and Local Development in Africa and the Arab States: Summaries of the Case Studies*. GDR Interurba–CNRS and Association Internationale des Techniciens, Experts et Chercheurs, Paris, for the World Bank/UNCHS/UNDP Urban Management Programme, pp. 63–65.

Garside, J. 1993. Inner city gentrification in South Africa: The case of Woodstock, Cape Town. *GeoJournal* 30(1): 29–35.

Gayiiya, E. N. and W. M. Walaga. 1995. Uganda. In: A. Durand-Lasserve, R. Pajoni, and J.-F. Tribillon, eds., *Urban Land Management, Regularisation Policies and Local Development in Africa and the Arab States: Summaries of the Case Studies*. GDR Interurba–CNRS and Association Internationale des Techniciens, Experts et Chercheurs, Paris, for the World Bank/UNCHS/UNDP Urban Management Programme, pp. 85–88.

Kanga, M., A. Logone, and J. Yango. 1995. Cameroun. In: A. Durand-Lasserve, R. Pajoni, and J.-F. Tribillon, eds., *Urban Land Management, Regularisation Policies and Local Development in Africa and the Arab States: Summaries of the Case Studies*. GDR Interurba–CNRS and Association Internationale des Techniciens, Experts et Chercheurs, Paris, for the World Bank/UNCHS/UNDP Urban Management Programme, pp. 37–42.

Kiamba, M. 1992. Regeneration of low-income housing and squatter settlement areas in Nairobi, Kenya. In: L. Kilmartin and H. Singh, eds., *Housing in the Third World: Analyses and Solutions*. Concept, New Delhi, pp. 231–250.

Kimani, S. M. 1972. The structure of land ownership in Nairobi. *Canadian Journal of African Studies* 6: 379–402.

Kironde, J. M. L. and D. A. Rugaiganisa. 1995. Tanzania. In: A. Durand-Lasserve, R. Pajoni, and J.-F. Tribillon, eds., *Urban Land Management, Regularisation Policies and Local Development in Africa and the Arab States: Summaries of the Case Studies*. GDR Interurba–CNRS and Association Internationale des Techniciens, Experts et Chercheurs, Paris, for the World Bank/UNCHS/UNDP Urban Management Programme, pp. 81–83.

Kombe, J. W. M. 1994. The demise of public urban land management and the emergence of informal land markets in Tanzania: A case of Dar-es-Salaam city. *Habitat International* 18(1): 23–43.

Korboe, D. 1992. Family-houses in Ghanaian cities: To be or not to be? *Urban Studies* 29(7): 1159–1172.

——— 1994. A policy-sensitive analysis of low-income urban housing in Ghana.

Paper presented to the European Network for Housing Research 2nd Symposium, "Housing for the Urban Poor," Birmingham.

Lee-Smith, D. 1990. Squatter landlords in Nairobi: A case study of Korogocho. In P. Amis and P. Lloyd, eds., *Housing Africa's Urban Poor*. Manchester University Press, Manchester, pp. 175–188.

Mabogunje, A. L. 1993. *Perspective on Urban Land and Urban Management Policies in Sub-Saharan Africa*. World Bank Technical Paper 196, Washington D.C.

Macoloo, C. 1994. Land price changes and residential development in Kenya: What future for the urban poor? Paper presented to the European Network for Housing Research 2nd Symposium, "Housing for the Urban Poor," Birmingham.

Maina, B. C. and C. Macoloo. 1995. Kenya. In A. Durand-Lasserve, R. Pajoni, and J.-F. Tribillon, eds., *Urban Land Management, Regularisation Policies and Local Development in Africa and the Arab States: Summaries of the Case Studies*. GDR Interurba–CNRS and Association Internationale des Techniciens, Experts et Chercheurs, Paris, for the World Bank/UNCHS/UNDP Urban Management Programme, pp. 71–73.

Malpezzi, S., A. G. Tipple, and K. G. Willis. 1990. *Costs and Benefits of Rent Control: A Case Study in Kumasi, Ghana*. World Bank DP 74, Washington D.C.

Metwally, M. with M. El Bahran, M. Madcouly, and M. Khairy. 1995. Egypt. In: A. Durand-Lasserve, R. Pajoni, and J.-F. Tribillon, eds., *Urban Land Management, Regularisation Policies and Local Development in Africa and the Arab States: Summaries of the Case Studies*. GDR Interurba–CNRS and Association Internationale des Techniciens, Experts et Chercheurs, Paris, for the World Bank/ UNCHS/UNDP Urban Management Programme, pp. 3–7.

Musandu-Nyamayaro, O. 1994. Procedural impediments to the low income housing land delivery process in cities of Zimbabwe: A case study of Harare. Paper presented to the European Network for Housing Research 2nd Symposium, "Housing for the Urban Poor," Birmingham.

Navarro, R. 1988. Irrégularité urbaine et invention de la ville Africaine au Cap-Vert (Sénégal). *Revue Tiers Monde* 29(116): 1101–1119.

O'Connor, A. 1983. *The African City*. Hutchinson, London.

Okolocha, C. F. 1993. The evolution of a land policy. In: R. W. Taylor, ed., *Urban Development in Nigeria*. Avebury, Aldershot, pp. 189–195.

Okpala, D. C. I. 1982. The Nigerian land-use decree revisited. *Habitat International* 6(5/6): 573–584.

Oloudé, B. 1995. Benin. In: A. Durand-Lasserve, R. Pajoni, and J.-F. Tribillon, eds., *Urban Land Management, Regularisation Policies and Local Development in Africa and the Arab States: Summaries of the Case Studies*. GDR Interurba–CNRS and Association Internationale des Techniciens, Experts et Chercheurs, Paris, for the World Bank/UNCHS/UNDP Urban Management Programme, pp. 23–26.

Ondiege, P. 1989. *Urban Land and Residential Market Analysis in Kenya*. Report for UNDP, UN Centre for Human Settlements and World Bank, Nairobi.

Osondu, I. N. and A. Middleton. 1994. Informal housing finance in Nigeria. Paper presented to the European Network for Housing Research 2nd Symposium, "Housing for the Urban Poor," Birmingham.

Ozo, A. O. 1990. The private rented housing sector and public policies in developing countries: The example of Nigeria. *Third World Planning Review* 12(3): 261–279.

Peil, M. 1981. *Cities and Suburbs: Urban Life in West Africa*. Africana Publishing Co., New York.

Peil, M. with P. O. Sada. 1984. *African Urban Society*. Wiley, Chichester.

Pennant, T. 1990. The growth of small-scale renting in low-income urban housing in Malawi. In: P. Amis and P. Lloyd, eds., *Housing Africa's Urban Poor*. Manchester University Press, Manchester, pp. 189–203.

Pickvance, C. 1988. Introduction: Land and housing development in Middle Eastern and North African cities. *International Journal of Urban and Regional Research* 12(1): 1–7.

Rakodi, C. 1991. Developing institutional capacity to meet the housing needs of the urban poor: Experience in Kenya, Tanzania and Zambia. *Cities* 8(3): 228–243.

——— 1995. From a settler history to an African present: Housing markets in Harare, Zimbabwe. *Society and Space* 13(1): 91–115.

Rakodi, C. with P. Withers. 1993. *Land, Housing and Urban Development in Zimbabwe: Markets and Policy in Harare and Gweru*. Occasional Paper in Planning Research, Department of City and Regional Planning, University of Wales, Cardiff.

Reyna, S. P. and R. E. Downs. 1988. Introduction. In: R. E. Downs and S. P. Reyna, eds., *Land and Society in Contemporary Africa*. University of New England Press, Hanover, NH, pp. 1–22.

Shipton, P. 1988. The Kenyan land tenure reform: Misunderstandings in the public creation of private property. In R. E. Downs and S. P. Reyna, eds., *Land and Society in Contemporary Africa*. University of New England Press, Hanover, NH, pp. 91–135.

Simon, D. 1992. *Cities, Capital and Development: African Cities in the World Economy*. Belhaven Press, London.

Soliman, A. 1988. Housing the urban poor in Egypt: A critique of present policies. *International Journal of Urban and Regional Research* 12(1): 65–86.

Stambouli, F. 1990. Tunis: crise de logement et réhabilitation urbaine. In: P. Amis and P. Lloyd, eds., *Housing Africa's Urban Poor*. Manchester University Press, Manchester, pp. 141–156.

Steinberg, F. 1990. Cairo: Informal land development and the challenge for the future. In: P. Baross and J. van der Linden, eds., *The Transformation of Land Supply Systems in Third World Cities*. Avebury, Aldershot, pp. 111–132.

Sule, R. A. O. 1994. Land as a constraint on urban housing development. In R. W. Taylor, ed., *Urban Development in Nigeria*. Avebury, Aldershot, pp. 196–203.

Teedon, P. 1990. Contradictions and dilemmas in the provision of low-income housing: The case of Harare. In P. Amis and P. Lloyd, eds., *Housing Africa's Urban Poor*. Manchester University Press, Manchester, pp. 227–238.

Tipple, A. G. and S. E. Owusu. 1994. *Transformations in Kumasi, Ghana, as a Housing Supply Mechanism*. Centre for Architectural Research and Development Overseas WP2, Newcastle upon Tyne.

Tipple, A. G. and K. G. Willis. 1991. Tenure choice in a West African city. *Third World Planning Review* 13(1): 27–45.

Troin, J.-F. 1993. Urbanization and development: The role of the *Medina* in the Maghreb. In H. Amirahmadi and S. El-Shakhs, eds., *Urban Development in the Muslim World*. Rutgers University Centre for Urban Policy Research, New Brunswick, NJ, pp. 94–107.

UNCHS (United Nations Centre for Human Settlements)/World Bank. 1993. *The Housing Indicators Program, Volume II: Indicator Tables*. UNCHS/World Bank, Nairobi and Washington.

UNDIESA (UN Department for International Economic and Social Affairs). 1990. *Population Growth and Policies in Mega-cities: Cairo*. UNDIESA, Population Policy Paper No. 13, New York.

Van den Berg, L. 1984. *Anticipating Urban Growth in Africa: Land Use and Land Values in the Rurban Fringe of Lusaka*. Zambia Geographical Association Occasional Study No. 13, Lusaka.

Wellings, P. A. 1988. The squatters of Lesotho: A case of mistaken identity. In R. A. Obudho and C. C. Mhlanga, eds., *Slum and Squatter Settlements in Sub-Saharan Africa: Toward a Planning Strategy*. Praeger, New York, pp. 261–280.

Wendt, S., S. Wahning, K. Mathéy, and M. Scaramella. 1990. Ethiopia. In: K. Mathéy, ed., *Housing Policy in the Socialist Third World*. Mansell, London.

Westen, A. C. M. van. 1990. Land supply for low-income housing. Bamako, Mali: Its evolution and performance. In: P. Baross and J. van der Linden, eds., *The Transformation of Land Supply Systems in Third World Cities*. Avebury, Aldershot, pp. 83–110.

Wikan, U. 1990. Changing housing strategies and patterns among the Cairo poor, 1950–1985. In: P. Amis and P. Lloyd, eds., *Housing Africa's Urban Poor*. Manchester University Press, Manchester, pp. 123–140.

World Bank. 1988. Weighing the benefits of rent control. *Urban Edge* 12(7): 1–6.

Yahya, S. S. 1990. Residential land markets in Kenya. In: P. Amis and P. Lloyd, eds., *Housing Africa's Urban Poor*. Manchester University Press, Manchester, pp. 157–174.

12

The state and civil society: Politics, government, and social organization in African cities

Tade Akin Aina

Abstract

Ce chapitre est une tentative d'examen concret et détaillé des relations entre l'État et la société civile dans les villes d'Afrique. Les divers concepts sur lesquels repose l'analyse y sont d'abord expliqués, en soulignant la nécessité de comprendre la nature des pouvoirs centraux et locaux et en appelant l'attention sur la (ré)-émergence de la société civile, cette sphère d'interaction sociale englobant la famille, la vie associative, les mouvements sociaux et les formes de communications publiques à l'oeuvre dans le secteur qui s'organise en dehors de l'État et du marché. Le concept d'urbanisme s'entend des relations entre l'État et la société civile et l'on recommande d'aborder la gestion urbaine de manière globale. L'on a mis l'accent sur les évenements et processus des premières phases d'aménagement et de construction puis de crise de la période post-coloniale pour examiner trois catégories de relations entre État et société: coopération et soutien; opposition; indifférence et neutralité. Suit une analyse d'ensemble des relations entre État et communauté, État et éléments de la société civile, État et autorités locales. Il en ressort que les relations entre État et communauté se sont caractérisées simultanément par des processus d'adaptation et d'incorporation, d'abandon, d'exploitation et de répression pour se détériorer au fur et à mesure que la classe politique dominante cherchait à consolider sa mainmise sur le pouvoir central. La société civile qui avait joué un rôle crucial dans la marche vers l'indépendance est passée au second plan lorsque l'État a pris la direction du processus de développement. Mais il y a eu ces derniers temps une résurgence des luttes sociales, surtout dans les zones urbaines mais pas seulement au sujet des problèmes des villes. Deux formes d'organisations sociales sont présentées plus en détail, les associations féminines et les organisations non gouvernementales, avec un examen en profondeur de l'évolution contradictoire de leurs relations avec l'État. L'on étudie ensuite ce qu'implique pour la gestion urbaine les conflits et la concurrence entre le pouvoir central et les autorités locales. Le chapitre conclut que s'il reste encore beaucoup à faire pour assurer une répartition équitable des ressources entre les différents groupes et structures des zones urbaines africaines, les relations entre État et société ont évolué, passant d'une forte centralisation et concentration à plus de décentralisation et de participation. Mais le devenir de cette évolution ne sera déterminé que par les luttes en cours au sein même de ces villes.

Introduction

Since around the end of the 1980s, remarkable events, unprecedented since the massive nationalist politics of constitutional decolonization, have been sweeping through sub-Saharan Africa, forcing changes in political arrangements and leading to the emergence of multi-partyism and political pluralism, a new emphasis on the importance of human rights, dialogue between political opponents, and the liberalization of the erstwhile post-colonial polities (Hyden and Bratton, 1992; Mamdani and Wamba-dia-Wamba, 1995). These transformations are changing the language and content of national politics and polities and creating new forms of collective social confidence expressed in bolder modes of demand making and renewed struggle for engagement and participation. Like the waves of nationalist protests of the 1940s and 1950s, the origin and centre of these protests and movements are urban based.

This emerging politics is concerned with larger national governance issues, such as constitution making, multi-partyism, representative democracy, and human rights, rather than with immediate urban management issues such as access to shelter and provision of services. However in Africa, with the predominance of primate cities (O'Connor, 1983; Simon, 1992), national politics, except in a few cases, is urban derived, urban based, and urban driven. Thus this politics, in its organization, style, and constituencies, is primarily urban politics even though it is perhaps geared first towards resolving some of the dominant contradictions of national political economies (Ake, 1989). The struggles that are creating these changes are being carried on by broad coalitions of market women, workers, the urban poor, students, professional associations, women's groups, young people, business groups, religious organizations, etc. It is the range and waves of these actions in the very diverse arena that constitutes urban Africa that have led some to proclaim that so-called civil society is emerging in Africa.

In this chapter, I examine the implications of these political phenomena for state–society relations in urban Africa. My point is that the African crisis in general and the urban crisis in particular have had tremendous implications for emergent political arrangements and consciousness. For whatever it is worth, a new watershed with respect to definitions of the nature of state–society relations and the very substance of politics in Africa has been crossed. It is also argued here that, although the most dominant manifestations of the new politics are concerned with larger issues of governance and people's rights, these are only beginnings. Issues grounded in the more locally specific realm of urban politics are already beginning to emerge, and decentralized structures, institutions, and practices are evolving in response (Kanyinga et al., 1994).

This is inevitable, because Africa's urban crisis (Stren and White, 1989), that is the crisis of urban development and management, expressed in terms of increasing poverty and deprivation, structural inequality in access to strategic resources, and the collapse of services and institutions, cannot be reduced to a mere technocratic or managerial question. It is important to reiterate here that state–society relations, even in cities, are not only concerned with urban management, even though this is important. The struggle for the city goes beyond access to land and the provision of services, to embrace social relationships and people's livelihoods and all that these imply socially and economically. In its very constitution, the urban crisis is a political crisis. It must be understood from within the larger domain of politics and power relations that define the process of control, allocation, and distribution of societal resources and the very organization and structuring of production and social relations. For urban Africa, this has both an external global element in terms of its location in the hierarchical global economy, as discussed in chapters 2 and 3 (and see Aina, 1993a), and an internal element in terms of the history, culture, and political economy of specific settlements and regions.

It is the latter that this paper attempts to explore, through an examination of the dynamics and structure of state–civil society relations in urban Africa. Given the complexity of the questions subsumed under this broad theme, my focus here is on the intertwining of two elements, that is, how these relations can contribute to the emergence of a sustainable, equitable, and participatory urban management process in Africa and the linkages of this process to democratization. It is in these larger questions that the more specific questions of access to land, sustainable livelihoods, and basic services are grounded. Unfortunately, a paper such as this cannot take in many of the elements of these questions. It can recognize only their wide range and diverse nature, suggesting questions that deeper and wider conceptual and empirical work might take up.

In examining state–society relations in African cities, two sobering points should guide our analysis. The first is recognition of the simultaneous collapse of state structures and disintegration of social order in the crisis-ridden cities of African countries such as Somalia, Liberia, and Rwanda. This underlines in the harshest tones the vulnerability of some of our "political orders." The second is that, in observing and understanding the organizations and movements of ordinary people, intellectuals need to show greater empathy and restraint in their desire to project their anxieties and "revolutionary optimism" onto the day-to-day struggles of the urban poor. Indeed their organizations

are not only agencies for massive structural transformation for the poor but sites and instruments of the process of "learning by doing". A place and point where lessons in autonomy, empowerment, popular participation and democratic struggles are learnt, internalized and disseminated into the community of the poor ... Here they are transformed and recreated into the cultural equipment and weapons for individual and collective development and liberation. (Aina, 1990a, p. 4)

The rest of this paper is structured into four parts. I commence with a clarification of some of the key notions, namely the state, civil society, urban politics, and urban management. I then proceed to an examination of contemporary urban development, looking at both the context of the crisis and what impact it has had on the urbanization process. The third and fourth parts of this paper examine the interplay between the state and civil society in terms of what is identified as the major question of African urban politics, namely the struggle for access to and control of resources. These issues are discussed around the two broad axes of state–society relations and central–local state relations. They interrogate the manner and process of struggle for basic needs and sustainable livelihoods by different urban interest groups and categories and what different interpretations and practices of urban management imply for them. The third part offers a preliminary typology of state–civil society relations and how these change or operate in a contradictory manner depending on the specific configuration of the articulation of interests and balance of social forces. The implications of the tensions in central–local government relations are briefly discussed before the conclusion examines the substance of the urban challenge in terms of trends in state–society relations, and the options with regard to the development of urban governance that is equitable, productive, and sustainable.

Clarifying the key notions

Some of the notions we are concerned with here are complex. They have been discussed in an extensive literature that cuts across the boundaries of disciplines and paradigms, and disagreements are common. My concern here is briefly to specify how they are understood in this chapter.

The state

This is perhaps one of the most important ideas in the understanding of contemporary human politics and governance. Conceptualizations of the state have been defined not only by the specific historical forms it has taken but also by epistemological and methodological issues and differing ideological positions that colour the implicit and explicit elements embodied in the notion. Rakodi (1986a, p. 426), in an attempt to grapple with the state in an urban context in Africa, identifies four broad ways of theorizing it that illustrate these differing ideological and methodological perspectives. Also of importance to our understanding of the African context is the need to periodize the state in terms of its changing forms and the changes in social relations and politics that these involve (Doornbos, 1990). Shorthand formulations of the peripheral capitalist state conceptualize it as an "institution of social and economic reproduction" and as "the site of class interactions and struggles," conceptions that assist us in seeing different patterns not only of state–economy relations but also of state–society relations. It must be pointed out that the state in Africa, even though it can be categorized as peripheral, underdeveloped, and capitalist, does not have a single form of expression. A variety of forms and subcategories have emerged, determined by the specific history of the society under consideration. It is this complex expression that explains the multiple and often contradictory forms that state–society relations can take in any African social formation. Claude Ake (1989, p. 44) attempts to capture this when he points out that:

[the state] is a specific modality of class domination ... in which the system of institutional mechanisms of class domination are [*sic*] differentiated from the ruling-class and appears as an objective force standing alongside society. The essential feature of the state form of domination is that the system of institutional mechanisms of domination is autonomized and becomes largely independent of social classes including the hegemonic social class ... the state really is ... a contradiction of interests, of powers and of social forces. The dominant social forces struggle to maintain their domination and the subordinate social forces struggle against their subordination and related disabilities. This is the context in which public policies including development strategies are made.

The class character of the state raises the question of the interests represented and the implications for politics, public policy, and action. Apart from the conventional expression of the interests of dominant classes and their fractions, the very nature of the state and class formation in the African context allows the interplay and coming to the fore of interests and social forces not clearly located in the relations of production. Some of these interests are at the ideological and identity levels and are expressed as ethnic, racial, or religious interests. Others are those of strategic groups located within the state apparatus, either military or bureaucratic. Thus there are specific instances when the state is dominated by racial interests, as in the Afrikaner example of apartheid South Africa, or by religious interests, as in the case of the Sudan. However, these interests are often linked with class domination, as expressed through the representations and actions of dominant classes and their fractions. There is also a need to distinguish between the state as a locale for the expression of class domination and the state apparatus, including agents of state domination, such as the police, the military, etc. These are part of the state, serve the state, but do not by themselves constitute the state.

At a different level of territorial concern is the "local state," which locates the institutions and agents of the state at a different spatial and administrative/political level. A troubled notion, the conceptual ambiguity embodied in it, centring on the extent to which the local state is autonomous from rather than merely an agent of the central state, has led not only to criticism but in some cases to outright rejection (Duncan and Godwin, 1982; Bryne, 1982). However, the notion opens up further space for the discussion of decentralization and participation in urban politics and management (Rakodi, 1986a; Mabogunje, 1990a). In spite of the difficulties, the concept of an urban local state contributes to the understanding and evaluation of institutions and agents grounded in closer proximity to the concrete activities and lives of the variety of urban actors.

Civil society

Unlike society, which sociologists broadly agree is the field of structured social relations and action, notions of civil society are as varied and contested as those of the state. More recent use of the notion has tended to veil its pluralistic ideological and philosophical origins. In their concern with civil society as "bourgeois" or liberal democratic society, or as the outcome of market-dominated economic development, they fail to see that this represents only one perspective (Bayart, 1989; Cohen and Arato, 1990; Gellner, 1991; Fatton, 1992).[1] The concern with civil society has essentially been Eurocentric, and recent attempts at applying the concept in the African context have remained either ethnocentric or insufficiently rigorous and historically sensitive in their analysis.[2] Mahmood Mamdani (1995a,b) and Abdel Kader Zghal (1995), in recognition of the limitations of these analyses, have recently offered a more Africa-relevant and non-Eurocentric application of the concept to contemporary Africa.

Mamdani (1995a, p. 3), in an introduction to a recent book on social movements and democracy in Africa, asks:

What is civil society? Does it exist or is it emerging? Is it confined to the "modern sphere", whose organizations are predicated on a differentiation between the political and the social, the social and the economic? Or does it include the "traditional" sphere where the organization of life process proceeds on the basis of a diffusion, and not differentiation, between the economic, the social and the political? Is the problem solved by making a distinction between "modern civil society", and "traditional civil society" ... Or is it thereby simply shelved? On the other hand, does the notion of a "civil society" as a modern construct lead at best to a one-eyed vision of social and political processes?

The response to this questioning leads to a rejection of not only the conventional and simplistic state–civil society dichotomy and the prescriptive modernization perspective that characterized development theory in the 1970s, but also both the romanticization and the denial of civil society in Africa. It links the concept politically with the notion and practice of social movements, in terms of their contribution to democratic politics, the defence of people's rights and livelihoods, popular participation, and empowerment. It is also recognized that neither society nor civil society must be idealized or conceived of as a homogeneous entity with consensual political direction. Rather plurality, polarization, contradictions, and conflict of interests are all aspects of the existence of civil society. Furthermore, the relationship of civil society to the democratization process is not at all times progressive. Indeed there are often strong conservative trends.

Civil society in this context refers to the sphere of social interaction that comprises the intimate sphere (family), associational life, social movements, and forms of public communication operating in the arena of the organized non-state, non-market sector with origins in both the modern and traditional bases of society (Cohen and Arato, 1990). It is not synonymous with or inchoately distinguished from society at large but is a differentiated dimension of society with distinctive political functions (Harbeson, 1992). It is important to point out that the notion of "associational life" extends beyond secular or modern voluntary associations and includes associations defined on more particularistic and at times primordial identities such as race, kinship, ethnicity, and religion. Civil society, of course, interacts with both the market and non-marketized elements of the economy and the state in the pursuit of its constituents' interests. Although Zghal (1995) has argued for the inclusion of unorganized and spontaneous protests in civil society, there is a need to exercise caution, because sustained and patterned existence seems to be important in the relevance of this arena to political life.

Urban politics

Since the relationship between the state and civil society operates essentially in the political domain, the notion of urban politics deserves examination here. Let us begin first with politics, which is

418

the struggle for control of the means whereby power is used to affect any organizational context, be it national societies, voluntary associations, or economic institutions. Politics is essentially the struggle for the control of power relations, whether institutionalized or not.

Politics in Africa can be characterized as containing not only undemocratic and non-participatory processes but also centralized, authoritarian, and at times archaic structures inherited from the colonial era and most unsuited to the conditions and needs of expanding populations, limited human resources, and contemporary demand for human and civic rights. This problem with political structures manifests itself clearly in the sluggishness, lack of faith in, and conflict between the different levels of the political system, such as between the central and local authorities or the judiciary and the executive. Although it is hard to generalize about "African politics," certain common, although not necessarily desirable, elements have emerged (Ake, 1989; Fatton, 1992). As I have observed elsewhere:

Africa's politics is currently characterized by fragile but authoritarian and over-extended state formations with weak roots in civil society. These are controlled by an insecure, non-hegemonic political elite who are dependent on the state for accumulation and who utilize both corruption and patronage as media of bargaining, negotiation and legitimation. Furthermore, a central element in their search for security and stability is dependence on external, often western, support to counter the main oppositional forces ranged against them on the domestic front. As part of their search for security, rulers utilize repression and non- and anti-democratic means to retain power without showing any concern for the human and democratic rights of their citizens, which they flagrantly breach. These rulers often adopt a political style that divides their citizens along ethnic, economic, religious and even racial lines, fuelling costly diversions which keep their nations off the track of development. ... All of this makes participation in African politics a highly precarious, yet significantly profitable venture for a dominant few, while at the same time it imposes limitations on effective democratization and popular participation. It further reinforces the tendency towards the concentration and centralization of power and personal rule, and the de-politicization and departicipation of the majority ... This kind of political situation leaves open only the option of violence in the form of coups, urban riots, insurrectionary struggles, etc. as effective means of participation and expression for a marginalized majority or political aspirants. Recent examples from Liberia, Benin Republic, Togo, Cameroon and Zaire amply demonstrate these dynamics. (Aina, 1993a, pp. 13–14)

As was pointed out at the beginning of this paper, given the nature of African cities and their central role in politics, economics, and culture as "theatres of accumulation," sites of domination, and the locus of cultural life, national politics tends to be defined and expressed mainly in the dominant city and by the most powerful interests within it (Simon, 1992). For instance, most of the recent political struggles for democratization and protests against economic decline have emerged from the cities and towns (Bratton and van de Walle, 1992; Mamdani and Wamba-dia-Wamba, 1995). It is this larger context and practice of politics that defines urban politics in sub-Saharan Africa. In recent times, there have been some attempts to posit an overwhelming defining character for African politics in terms of either corruption or personal rule (see, for example, Post and Vickers, 1974; Joseph, 1987; Sandbrook, 1993; Bayart, 1993). The main problem with these analyses is their lack of recognition of the complexity of politics in general and African politics in particular. Given the significance of factors such as religion, ethnicity, and neo-colonial relations, corruption and personal rule do not constitute complete explanations of African politics. Of course, these two elements matter, but they are often determined and driven by historical conditions and structural processes that allow them to predominate, as a result of the weakening and dissolution of other social institutions and countervailing forces. In terms of its main components, "urban" politics has been described as embracing both "the politics of want, of basic services, of minimum security of life and property" and the "politics of clan and tribe" (Sivaramakrishnan, 1994, p. 11).

Urban management

Increasingly the urban crisis in Africa is being tackled by what has been called the "urban management" approach. In terms of how this is being promoted and used by leading international agencies such as the World Bank, it refers to a body of techniques, rules, and practices for the planning and organization of modern urban settlements. In essence it is a professionalized approach to the management of these settlements. According to Stren (1991, p. 10), it encompasses at least four important elements: (i) a concern to situate urban development projects in the context of city-wide and institutional considerations; (ii) a concern to pay more attention to sources of local finance for more decentralized municipal government; (iii) a concern to devise alternative means of organizing and financing urban services such as water supply, public transport, electricity, sanitary services, and waste disposal; and (iv) a concern to seek and promote local community and participatory sources of support for urban services and infrastructure.

Rakodi has already subjected some of these ideas to critical review in chapter 2. From the point of view of our concern with state–society relations, the approach also has a number of problems, a major one being that it is too "state centred" (Lee-Smith and Stren, 1991). Apart from this, it is also too narrow, formalized, and technocratic, relying mainly on a body of professional knowledge and inputs from trained urban managers. Even though it seeks to incorporate so-called participatory methods, it is still too top–down and needs to incorporate the non-formalized but extensive "urban management" techniques and strategies of popular urban groups. That is, it needs to respect and incorporate the wide range of human practices and actions utilized by the poorer sectors and communities of African cities in providing themselves with urban services. As Lee-Smith and Stren (1991) have pointed out, the "urban management" approach misunderstands or neglects the informal sector, the question of gender, and community participation. For urban management to be relevant, it must incorporate aspects of popular knowledge and technology. It must thus seek to be less technocratic or managerialist and more participatory and popular.

Post-colonial urban development in Africa: Context, patterns, and problems

It is important to note that state–society relations in urban Africa are neither fixed nor unchanging. They are to a great extent determined by the wider historical, political, and economic context. They must therefore be situated historically. This requires that we attempt a periodization of both urban development and the evolution of state–society relations. Perhaps the most interesting point of historical delimitation, which affected most of the societies and nation-states of Africa, was the experience of colonization, which had implications for structures and processes in politics, society, the economy, and the urbanization process. At the broadest level, therefore, encompassing the political economy, the urbanization process, and state–society relations, we can identify distinctive colonial and post-colonial periods for most of Africa.

Here, we need not delay ourselves with the colonial period if our focus is on the contemporary dynamics. In addition, the colonial experience has received a tremendous amount of attention in the literature (see, for example, O'Connor, 1983; Coquery-Vidrovitch, 1991). As noted earlier in this volume, especially by Rakodi in chapter 2, in the post-colonial period some definite trends in economies, politics, and the urban development process can be identified. These consist of two distinct but in some respects overlapping phases. The first can be broadly called the *"early post-colonial period"* or the *"Development and Building Phase."* Recognizable for most countries in the continent, it occurred roughly within the first 10 years of independence for many countries in sub-Saharan Africa, i.e. from the late 1950s to the mid-1970s. The second clearly identifiable phase is what I will term the *"crisis phase,"* which began to emerge from the mid-1970s and became more evident in the 1980s and early 1990s.

Although ascribing dates to these phases gives a false impression of uniformity, they do assist in identifying landmarks meant to denote specific processes and structural changes. The processes and timing differ between the states of north Africa, most of sub-Saharan Africa, and southern Africa, particularly the Republic of South Africa. Islamic, Arabic, and to some extent Mediterranean influences in north Africa and settler colonialism and the politics, social relations, and urban planning of racial segregation and apartheid in southern Africa define urban characteristics and experiences in these regions and distinguish them from sub-Saharan Africa. In addition, the "politics of identity," in terms of religious fundamentalism and race, has come to define the social dimensions of these regions and their cities to a greater extent than elswhere in Africa (Smith, 1992; El-Kenz, 1991; Farah, 1994; Tayeb, 1994; Zghal and Krichen, 1995; Parnell and Mabin, 1995; Rogerson, 1995; Abouhani, 1996). However, there are also many similarities, such as the experience of settler-colonization and liberation struggle in Algeria, Mozambique, Zimbabwe, Namibia, and South Africa; the strategies of consolidation adopted by the post-colonial ruling groups; and the structural crises of the post-colonial era. In addition, throughout Africa, social relations have remained fundamentally the relations of inequality and domination, although the details of differentiation and responses to it vary between countries. Using the periodization given above, we can identify two definite patterns and phases applicable to the understanding not only of post-colonial urbanization, as explored in chapter 2, but also of state–society relations and central–local government relations.

The early post-colonial period, or the development and building phase

The early post-colonial phase coincided with the attainment of independence by mainly the sub-Saharan African states and the attendant optimism, confidence, and limited economic growth, albeit over a short period. Commencing from a relatively low level of urbanization, the early phase involved extensive physical and political expansion and construction (Vaidyanathan, 1992). As Richard Stren (1991, p. 16) has put it: "The 1960s and early 1970s were for most African countries a period of construction of an elaborate central state structure." They were also a period for the construction of new physical signs of nationhood, including infrastructure and prestigious airports, ports, military bases, and massive white elephant projects. Development plans contained massive allocations for these purposes.

Describing the context in a discussion of central–local government relations, Stren (1991, p. 16) points out that:

the consolidation of power by an aggressive nationalist party, the establishment of one-party (or military) government, the restriction of civil politics outside the direct control of the state, the setting up of mechanisms for central economic planning, the growth of a vast array of state administrative structures and parastatal bodies, and the emphasis on a highly personal form of presidential rule in many countries all reinforced the tendency towards centralization.

As for the economy, this was in fact a phase of increasing affluence for the more privileged strata as they achieved élite status and positions. The early phase of post-colonial urbanization was thus predominantly geared to the expansion of colonial physical and social space to incorporate new indigenous interests and needs and thereby spreading the "fruits of independence" to privileged and other groups with the capacity to stake claims to these, as shown in the accounts of cities such as Abidjan, Nairobi, and Lagos in this volume.[3] But there were real limits to physical and social incorporation in the context of finite resources, particularly in a situation of rapid population growth, and especially where structural inequality is paramount. As a result, existing urban problems of poverty and inequality, unemployment, pressure on resources, deterioration of services and infrastructure, and the weakening of social and spatial order and control were exacerbated. Things began to get worse as the mid-1970s approached.

The crisis phase in post-colonial urbanization

As discussed especially in chapter 2, from around the middle of the 1970s, most African nations entered a phase of long-drawn-out economic decline, accompanied in certain areas by drought, famine, severe ecological degradation, political instability, conflict, indebtedness, and the imposition of Structural Adjustment Programmes (SAPs). Economic decline and the debt crisis constituted the most critical elements of this problem-ridden era, and stabilization and SAPs their expected antidote (Culpeper, 1987; Mkandawire, 1991; Oxfam, 1993; Adepoju, 1993; Mkandawire and Olukoshi, 1994).[4]

With respect to urban life, an important element of the philosophy of the economic reforms was their explicit anti-urban bias (see also chap. 13 in this volume). The reform packages were geared towards uplifting the rural and agricultural sectors and reducing the extent to which their resources are supposedly drained by the so-called exploitative and parasitic urban sector. The adjustment programmes were thus meant to affect cities and their residents adversely. As observed by a senior World Bank official, the response of hard-headed macroeconomists to the pain felt by urban areas is that: "This is what adjustment is meant to be. It means reduction of real wages and urban subsidies in the interest of restoring macro-economic balances and meeting external debt obligations" (Cohen, 1990, p. 50). That this unsentimental treatment caused pain for urban areas was undeniable and recognized by the World Bank itself, the leading physician (World Bank, 1991). Taking a closer look at specific contexts, Jacob Songsore and Gordon McGranahan (1993) have provided some preliminary documentation of the relationships between the economic crisis, structural adjustment, and poverty in the Greater Accra Metropolitan Area of Ghana, while the case-studies of Nairobi, Lagos, and Abidjan in this volume, in particular, examine the impacts of structural adjustment in these cities.

On the implications of the economic crisis for urban management, the collective work edited by Stren and White (1989) clearly depicts the crisis situation that African cities have been thrown into with regard to urban management. The volume traces the decline in urban resources over the critical years of the 1980s and shows how the problem of diminishing resources was compounded by "rapid population increase in the cities so that per capita levels of urban expenditure on services and infrastructures have fallen dramatically" (Stren, 1991, p. 14). The collapse of services therefore became the major element used to characterize the condition of urban centres in the mid-1980s and in many cases up till now. These well-known features include traffic congestion, floods, bad roads, blocked drains, overflowing and open sewers, erratic electricity and water supply, failing telephone systems, and mounting vermin-infested rubbish heaps. While the health and environmental hazards multiplied, health facilities, starved of essential resources and supplies and/or suffering from prolonged industrial action by dissatisfied personnel, failed to cope (Hardoy et al., 1992; McGranahan et al., 1993; Aina et al., 1994).

The basis of law and order was also increasingly eroded as economic pressures mounted while ill-motivated and underpaid security agents either could not cope or were too vulnerable in terms of their material needs. The war against crime was often lost before it began, as, for example, in some parts of Nigeria, where criminals were better equipped with raincoats, torchlights, vehicles, and weapons than the police who were meant to prevent crime. To offer themselves some protection in their homes and settlements, communities organized vigilante groups and community watches, for example in the form of the famous *Sungusungu* of east Africa. These often administered instant justice by lynching suspected criminals. Although undesirable, this represents an expression of "self-help" organizing in response to difficult conditions.

Thus "self-help" in urban areas moved gradually from the "community development" efforts of the colonial and early post-colonial periods, which were often externally stimulated and directed by bureaucrats, to self-help (more as an autonomous, self-protective response based on real needs and pressures) in the provision of services such as waste disposal, drain clearing, and crime fighting. Where self-help (i.e. service provision not geared towards profit) was not well developed, or could not take off, small commercial enterprises emerged in waste disposal, education, dispensing medicine, etc. These included efforts such as petty waste disposal units with wheel barrows and baskets, water vending from buckets carried on heads and shoulders, and "lessons" teachers instructing groups of children in backyards or front sheds. Wherever the state failed or was absent and the formal private sector would not go or imposed user charges that were too high, the urban poor organized to fill the gap either through collective non-profit responses or through small enterprises that charged affordable fees and provided appropriate services. This provided the state and the international financial institutions with further ammunition in their drive to encourage privatization and commercialization of urban services. The poor were already paying anyway! Formal privatization of public sector service delivery and "appropriate pricing" followed.

But the hardships, along with the corruption and insensitivity of rulers and the wave of political liberalization worldwide, generated new consciousness. Even the middle classes, hard hit by economic hardships, began to organize, both within their professional associations and in newly established human rights groups, to protest against hardship, corruption, insensitivity, and resistance to change. For people who organized in their settlements for self-help or in professional associations and workplaces for better working conditions, and who had to deal with hardship and the arrogance of outmoded and often senile power on a daily basis, the leap to protest and resistance was a short one. All it needed in many cities was another increase in fuel, rice, or flour prices, or a leader rescinding on a previous agreement to hold elections or allow open opposition (examples are referred to in the chapters in this volume on Lagos and Cairo; see also Abouhani, 1996). With this, a new era of state–civil society relations emerged, which we will now examine.

State–society relations in urban Africa

The terrain of state–society relations obviously extends beyond that of civil society as strictly defined at the beginning of this paper. It includes sub-domains, which have been called political society, economic society, and the community (Cohen and Arato, 1990). Given that our investigation here is focused on cities and urban problems, it is only proper that the domain of the community as an identifiable field of social interaction and bonding be included. And indeed, in terms of urban politics, state–community relations tend to be important. Also, struggles over issues related to what was earlier called the "politics of want" tend to be organized and initiated from community and neighbourhood levels. Neighbourhood and community organizations are therefore important elements of urban settlements' politics. Under the broad state–society relations rubric, we shall therefore be looking at both state–civil society relations and state–community relations.

But, first, what general patterns do state–society relations take? Scholars concerned with analysis of the shifting nature of state–society relations have offered a wide range of more or less specific characterizations (see, for example, Ngunyi and Gathiaka, 1993).

Their attempts have often been based on their understanding of the character of the modern state *vis-à-vis* society, particularly the peripheral capitalist state. In recent times, these characterizations have offered new labels rather than new explanatory insights.[5] The key element of state–society relations is that the state is in constant and changing interaction with the various elements of society at any given time. This interaction depends on the balance of social forces involved in the institutional and class interactional nature of the state, but the state, in relation to them and to fulfil its functions, "seeks to dominate them, regulate their activities and set the rules by which conflict between them can be resolved" (Ngunyi and Gathiaka, 1993, p. 29).

Taking this as a major defining element, state–society relations can be classified in the broadest sense as threefold:

(1) cooperative/supportive;
(2) oppositional;
(3) neutral/indifferent.

These broad classes do not carry any evaluative connotation. They can be either positive or negative depending on the specific outcomes for democracy and/or sustainable and equitable urban management. Under *cooperative/supportive relations* we can have promotive, integrative, and co-optative interactions between the state and the institutions of society. Under *oppositional relations* we can include hostile, repressive, adversarial, extractive, competitive, and exploitative interaction, while the class of *neutral and indifferent interactions* includes deliberate or unconscious neglect, ignorance, or inadequate knowledge about the other party or sheer lack of capacity to do anything with or for the other party. Having specified the broad classes of state–society relations, the rest of this section will be devoted to an analysis of these broad patterns in post-colonial urban Africa, within the scope of the two earlier defined periods. For greater focus, the relations will be examined as they relate more clearly to (a) urban management questions, i.e. access to tenure, basic services, infrastructure, and livelihoods; and (b) larger democratic/social justice issues such as struggles for democratization and human rights or resistance to economic hardship.

State–community relations

Urban communities are by no means homogeneous entities. Within and between them, differentiation occurs along hierarchical and unequal lines of class, gender, race, and ethnicity. They therefore have multiple relations with the modern state depending on their composition or general characterization, for example as low-income communities and/or as illegal areas said to be predominantly inhabited by low-status aliens, women, and in-migrants. Perhaps the most obvious defining characteristics are those of poverty and class. Low-income communities are often distinct in form, organization, and composition from those of the middle and upper classes. State–community relations, therefore, often follow the structured inequality of the larger political economy.

Given the alien origin of the colonial state in Africa, state–community relations were inherited in the main in terms of legislation, town planning and building norms and rules, differential access to services and infrastructure, attitudes and policies, and legislation that reflected the specific form and needs of the colonial venture (Mabogunje, 1968; Home, 1983; Rakodi, 1986b). In many ways these relationships were unequal, alien, exploitative, extractive, and separatist. Colonial urbanization developed separate settlements for the colonialists, the foreign traders (Asians and Levantines), the different races, the immigrant and indigenous workers, and the natives of the environs of the city.

During the immediate post-independence period, some excluded groups were incorporated, mainly the élite groups and certain privileged communities. With the nation-building and development project, communities and community organizations were also mobilized and admonished to support and work with the state in attaining development. This was the era of self-help groups built along ethno-regional, gender, settlement, and other similar lines. In West Africa, voluntary associations operating as "Home Town Unions" and "Town Development Associations" with predominantly self-help and community development objectives linked urban and rural communities. The same applied in East Africa, with the "Harambee" movements of Kenya as an illustration (Barkan et al., 1991; Seppälä, 1992a).

Although there is a need to distinguish between urban-based, urban interest organizations and urban-based, rural interest organizations, both of these often organize under the broad category of Town Development Associations, which are more prevalent in West Africa. The Town Development Associations are more than likely to be based in the particular town that is their subject of concern, whereas the Home Town Unions, although often urban based, tend to refer to another settlement. These are quite often associations of migrants concerned with the development of their own places of origin ("home towns"), which could be rural or urban. Quite often, however, the concerns and strategies of these associations and unions are the same, i.e. provision of some basic services or facilities through self-financing, engaging in other wider fund-raising activities, or lobbying politicians and governments to provide these.

In terms of larger political issues, these organizations concerned themselves with struggling for resources to be allocated to their home towns, villages, or neighbourhoods. Communities and individuals built linkages with strong political barons through whom they could command resources, and protested against injustices at the level of the communal or collective denial of resources or rights to them by the state (Mabogunje, 1990b). These linkages, again a predominantly West African phenomenon, are amply documented in the case of Mushin, a suburb of Lagos, by Sandra Barnes. They take many forms and often operate as "interlocking dyadic ties" (Barnes, 1986, p. 213), with hierarchical structures in which a neighbourhood or local community or a whole town is linked to a strategic political or bureaucratic personality, either directly as his or her constituency, or through contacts established by a traditional chief, religious leader (*malam* or *marabout*), or minor politician. The strategic figure intercedes regularly with central or local government to ensure favourable consideration for the allocation of resources, such as basic services, employment-creating establishments, or even police stations, and plays a major role in ensuring that faults and breakdowns such as burst water mains or blown electricity transformers are promptly repaired.

Thus state–community relations contain different dimensions of the three broad elements stated above, with the result that they are often unclear and contradictory. As summarized by a local study of state–urban community relations in Lagos:

the post-colonial state is often felt and seen by the poor through the operations and manifestations of its laws, institutions, various apparatus and their personnel. All of these ... often appear as alien, hostile and at times indifferent to the real activities and existence of ordinary people. They appear to the residents ... as agencies that tax and levy them, that force them in some cases to carry out unpaid public works, that evict them from their land, demolish their homes and work places, and impose on them rules and regulations on which they were never consulted. On the other hand, these same institutions that harass them, provide amenities and services to the more privileged settlements of the elites ... The urban poor therefore hold an ambivalent attitude to the state. It is obviously a source of great power capable of doing both good and evil. It can give a lot as much as it can destroy a lot. It can provide roads, jobs, schools, water and hospitals just as it can detain, demolish, harass and evict. (Aina, 1990b, pp. 70–71)

There have thus been simultaneous processes of accommodation and incorporation, indifference and neglect, exploitation and repression.

As post-colonial politics became consolidated, centralized, and monolithic, the main objective of the dominant political classes was to control all institutions and entities outside the state. However, the decline of the economy and the crisis came at the same time as the intensification of personal rule and reduced political accountability. Opposition began to grow, as well as repression. Increasingly, cases of human rights violations in settlement issues, such as mass evictions and demolition of the properties of the poor, occurred all over Africa, in places like Kenya, Senegal, Egypt, and Nigeria (Audefroy, 1994). These were often done with inadequate or no resettlement. Relations between state and urban communities deteriorated further, oscillating between oppositional or hostile and systematic indifference and deliberate neglect. Thus members of deprived urban communities have often constituted the foot soldiers of urban protests and riots against economic hardships, political oppression, etc. that are initiated by more organized groups in civil society, such as students, labour, market women, and professional associations.

State–civil society relations

Contemporary civil society in Africa consists of a large body of associations and civil institutions, most of which are modern, even though they take on traditional forms and symbols. They are mainly urban based and include labour unions, Christian and Islamic religious associations, ethnic associations, women's organizations, professional associations, employers' and occupational bodies, student and youth groups, cooperatives/mutual help associations, special interest groups such as human rights organizations, and a new range of non-governmental organizations (NGOs) such as community and neighbourhood groups and philanthropic and welfare associations. In terms of historical development, this wide range of associations and civil institutions can be broadly grouped into the conventional older groups (trade unions, community organizations, self-help groups, ethnic associations, women's organizations, professional bodies, religious groups) and the new groups, including some NGOs and human rights groups. It is the latter, with their new styles, global linkages, and heavily publicized advocacy, that have prompted the much-trumpeted "rediscovery" or "emergence" of civil society. In reality, civil society has long existed in Africa but became dormant or stifled, reverting to hidden and less obvious forms of resistance and struggles during the early post-colonial phase of neo-colonial élite consolidation and centralization. Indeed, what has occurred from the late 1980s on, with large numbers of political protests and massive coalitions for multi-partyism and democratization, is similar to the ferment of the 1950s and 1960s, when nationalist coalitions struggled to attain independence and constitutional decolonization (Ngunyi and Gathiaka, 1993).

Like that experience, contemporary civil society is urban based but not necessarily restricted to urban issues. Its effectiveness today is more or less tied up with the nature of the issues with which it is concerned; thus wider social justice or democratization issues have broader constituencies and tend to have a larger impact than narrower, spatially specific urban management issues, although their struggles may not be less intense. This larger impact has been seen particularly in recent times in the struggle for democratization and multi-partyism in a wide range of countries, such as Togo, Benin Republic, Kenya, Mali, Zambia, Malawi, and Tanzania. Concerned with broader struggles against monolithic state structures, dictatorships, and economic hardship, these associations, along with older movements such as labour and women's organizations, have formed broad-based coalitions that have led to changes in government or greater democratization of national politics. Other determinants of the effectiveness of activities of civil associations include the role of leaders, their linkages with both the grass roots and the élite, the extent of the threat they pose to established interests, their links with effective power blocs both locally and internationally, and their capacity to manage and sustain protests. Although the claims of the World Bank and international organizations that they support pluralism and participation are often challenged, solidarity and funds from international NGOs are generally welcomed.

For the rest of this section, we intend to examine the relationships between the state and women's organizations and the state and NGOs, as illustrations of our arguments. Each set of organizations illustrates one of the two broad components of civil society, i.e. the conventional older component exemplified by women's organizations and the advocacy type illustrated by the new NGOs. Consideration of these organizations and their relationships with the state will contribute to a better understanding of both the state and politics in general, and urban politics in particular.

Women's organizations

Right from the pre-colonial era, women's associations have existed as distinct and autonomous units for organizing social relations, productive work, and even ritual and religion. In fact, Ifi Amadiume (1995), in a reinterpretation of power relations, classified traditional African women's organizations as *anti-power* movements, that is, groups engaged in struggles not to gain power but simply to defend and maintain their autonomy. Predominantly a response to patriarchal domination, women's organizations are a necessary part of social organization, without which societies cannot function.

With colonization, they continued to play important roles in both the urban and rural areas. In fact women had added to their traditional roles in households the new roles that emerged with the colonial economy. These roles, which often imposed additional burdens of support for spouses and families incorporated into the colonial economy in disadvantaged ways, also included new forms of subordination, embodied not only in pre-capitalist patriarchal relations but also in those of European capitalist patriarchy. In response to the wide variety of new roles in production and distribution, etc., women's organizations such as market women's associations, farmers' groups, and hawkers' associations emerged. Although these organizations were essentially economic in their aims, they often played political, social (convivial, supportive, and mutual benefit), self-help, and development roles (Stamp, 1986). In fact, during the anti-colonial struggles, there were several instances (such as the Aba Women's Riot in Eastern Nigeria in the 1920s and the labour unrest amongst Kikuyu women in Kenya) of a contribution of radical protest to these struggles (Priestly, 1986; Awe, 1992). In other cases, women contributed material support to nationalist parties. They were therefore unambiguously part of the struggles for independence, if not visibly so.

However during the early part of the post-colonial period, that is, the development or building phase, the activities and roles of women's organizations were defined as essentially supportive of and cooperative with the state in the nation-building process, and in different parts of the continent their autonomy was attacked. In an attempt at explaining the process of demobilization of civil society in the post-colonial period, Ngunyi and Gathiaka (1993, pp. 31–32) identified three major elements that applied in the Kenyan case. These were:

(a) the beginning of a gravitation towards a "maximum leader" and the disintegration of the "nationalist coalition";
(b) the emergence of factional patronage networks; and
(c) "the enfeeblement of certain institutions of civil society as actors on the ... political stage."

These same processes have been identified for women's organizations in Tanzania alongside the important fact of the systematic exclusion of women from the formal political and economic spheres.

Aili Mari Tripp (1992a) has traced the changes that occurred in the activities of urban voluntary associations in Tanzania between the colonial era and the early post-independence period. She shows how these vibrant and useful associations were systematically suppressed in an effort by the dominant political party and the state to ensure centralization and control:

The government and party expanded their monopoly control of social relations by gradually centralizing party activities, by abolishing local governments in 1972, and by absorbing, eliminating or curtailing key independent organizations, creating new ones and preventing others from being formed ... The crowding out of interest group activity was part of a trend of party and government expansion that saw these institutions increasingly encroach into new political, economic and social spaces. (Tripp, 1992a, p. 230)

This process embraced both formal women's organizations and other types of civil institutions. At the same time, as ordinary people saw that avenues for participation in formal associations were being blocked, they began to form informal, small-scale community and special interest organizations. These proliferated all over African cities around this period, because they more clearly served the needs of ordinary people for participation.

The main dimensions of state–women's organizations relations were essentially those of co-optation and domination or of neglect and indifference. The large, formal, broad-based national or sectoral women's associations were the target of co-optation and domination and were forced into supplementing and supporting the "development" and other goals of national parties and governments. The informal associations, which covered a wide range of needs such as "mutual help," burials, childbirth, rotating credit, and disaster relief, were systematically neglected by the state.

However, just as the economic crisis and the reform programmes forced limits on state–community relations, this was also the case with civil associations and institutions. With the intensification of the economic burden and its own fiscal crisis, the state neglected and abandoned its function of providing services for collective consumption and also could not effectively guarantee law and order all over its territory. In response, people had to provide ways and means of meeting societal needs through their organizations. As Tripp (1992a, p. 235) has pointed out:

Where the state's attempts to exert monopolistic control over society and the economy exceeded state capacity to regulate social relations and allocate resources effectively, people's own organizational structures often emerged to fulfil a variety of societal needs. The state's growing inability to guarantee adequate police protection, ensure that wages bore some relation to the cost of living, and provide basic social and public services led people to form their own organizations to cope with the difficulties they faced.

In urban Africa, women were part of these responses and initiatives, both autonomously and along with men. They emerged among the leaders of new urban welfare organizations, responding to flooding or the AIDs pandemic, contributing to providing and maintaining health and educational facilities, and becoming involved in a variety of other activities (Tripp, 1992b).

A response to both the emergence of global support and the proliferation of independent and active (if small) women's organizations was the attempt to reorganize and incorporate them into the state domain through what Amina Mama has called "femocracy" – that is, state-directed feminism operated via the first ladies (wives of African presidents and heads of state). With the dual intention of cornering the increasing international funding for women's organizations and directing efforts away from protests, femocracy emerged in the 1980s as an alternative mode of organizing the relations between the state and women's organizations (Mama, 1994). It was, however, vulnerable, because it was sustainable only as long as there were resources to nurture it, and as long as the male head of state kept his hold on power against coups and electoral changes, or had a wife or wives who could operate the femocracy.

The state–NGO relations

Although there had been a wide range of non-governmental efforts and organizations in the humanitarian, relief, and welfare sectors prior to the 1980s, NGOs as we know them today are really a product of the African crisis and the responses it occasioned. Although, in common-sense terms, NGO would refer to any organization not owned or created by government and operating in the social and development sector, it has become acceptable to think of NGOs as the more formalized, registered non-governmental, non-profit organizations created primarily to serve developmental or altruistic objectives. In terms of size, scope, origins, history, and focus, a wide range of NGOs can be identified in any given African country today (Seppälä, 1992b; Kanyinga, 1993; Kiondo, 1993; Sandbrook and Halfani, 1993). Firm boundaries between them in terms of organization and functions do not always exist. Moreover, they have evolved, changed focus, and undergone major organizational transformations over time. An attempt to summarize the broad non-governmental sector in Nigeria led to the following:

They consist of a wide variety of civil associations and development activities operating on different levels. The first tier, which tends to be highly formalized and large-scale, includes international agencies and donor organizations. The second tier, emerging gradually in Nigeria, includes large formal indigenous organizations, foundations, and civil associations that are national in composition and staffed by a few professional people. This second tier overlaps with the national branches or offshoots of global groups such as the Red Cross/Red Crescent, Boys' Scouts, and Rotary. The third tier consists of Town and Regional Development Associations, voluntary groups based on membership subscriptions and donations but oriented exclusively to their own local problems. At the bottom are community-based organizations of small villages and parts of towns. They are grassroots organizations, a category which also includes small-scale neighbourhood groups, special interest groups such as women's organizations, occupational and trade groups, and guilds. Finally, religious associations or societies formed from churches or mosques occupy an ambiguous position, operating across local, regional and national levels. (Aina, 1993b, p. 141)

It is this complexity and variety of the constituents of the NGO sector that has created such a nightmare for analysts attempting a classification. Some have resolved the problem by emphasizing formalization, scale, range of resources available, and origin to generate two categories, namely NGOs and popular or grass-roots organizations. These two broad classes have also been linked to approaches that distinguish between top–down and bottom–up origins. A similar attempt at making sense of this sector classifies NGOs into membership organizations and predominantly service-oriented organizations run by a few professional staff. What is important here is not the organizational analysis of NGOs but rather their importance in the developmental and political lives of African cities and towns. It is this that actively brings them into a set of relations with the state.

Using our earlier periodization, the early post-colonial period was not as active a period as more recent times for NGOs. Then they were mainly welfare, philanthrophic, and relief organizations and religious groups, predominantly with origins in the West, such as the Boy Scouts, the Red Cross, and the Young Men's Christian Association (YMCA). These provided civic and religious training for young people, offered charitable and welfare services, and were involved in disaster relief. Their indigenous counterparts were often religious associations, and ethnic and mutual aid organizations. In terms of relationships with the state, these were mainly cooperative and supportive (i.e. helping with civic training and duties) or purely neutral and indifferent. The state, using inherited colonial practices, did not tax, monitor, or control these organizations. NGOs, in turn, neither bothered much with nor criticized the state. Their various welfare operations occurred in both urban and rural locations. For the centralizing state these NGOs were generally neither a threat nor a problem. However, with the second phase of post-colonial development, namely the crisis period, external and internal factors combined to change the nature, focus, methods, and concerns of NGOs.

In his study of the Kenyan experience, Kanyinga (1993) has effectively captured these elements. The external factors comprise: (i) the growth of northern NGOs with interests in Africa and in development issues; (ii) the change in the agenda of the donors; and (iii) the globalization of human rights and democratic struggles. The first two elements, namely the growth of northern NGOs and changes in the agenda of donor agencies, are closely related to the African crisis. The massive ecological and political crises of the 1970s in the Sahel and the Horn of Africa, resulting in famines and starvation, led to a regeneration of the international relief industry with Africa as a focus. Also many northern NGOs began to go beyond relief to the root causes of the problems they had to tackle, that is, development.

They therefore began to focus on development, poverty alleviation, and projects of social transformation. The change in the agenda of the donor agencies was mainly led by the international financial institutions directed by the World Bank, in terms of economic reforms that emphasized market and non-state-centred strategies. NGOs and other private interests, therefore, began to receive direct international approval and support. The liberalization of economies also implied the withdrawal of the state from the social sector. The element of the globalization of the democratization and human rights questions was partly related to the African crisis and partly related to the democratic transitions in Eastern Europe, the old Soviet Union, and large parts of Latin America. Human rights issues and NGOs, which later received their formal stamp of approval at the UN Conference on Human Rights in Vienna in 1993, became central players in the global agenda. Their African counterparts became important elements in the struggle against post-colonial centralization and monolithic political structures.

The internal reasons for the growth of NGOs are also directly related to the African crisis; this generated a fiscal and capacity crisis for the state, which could no longer provide basic social services. At the beginning, international NGOs, in what Fowler (1992) has called the "internationalization of social welfare," involved themselves in combating poverty and direct community development projects. But the difficulties of the terrain, their lack of familiarity with it, cultural and political sensitivity, and sheer capacity difficulties led to their adopting an intermediary role – supporting grass-roots organizations and community groups and stimulating and/or reinforcing indigenous NGOs.

With all these, a boom in the number and activities of NGOs in the late 1980s and 1990s occurred. These were of all types, including specialized human settlements and environmental groups such as the Mazingira Institute and Green Belt Movement in Kenya, ENDA in Senegal, and the Nigerian Environmental Study Action Team in Nigeria (Aina, 1993b). Relations with the state varied and were often contradictory for the formalized human settlements groups. Development work, research, and policy advocacy were their central functions. Given the increasing scale of poverty and the social devastation occasioned by the crisis and governmental insensitivity and corruption, merely researching and documenting the issues was often considered subversive. But project implementation often needed their cooperation with central and local governments and this necessitated contact and collaboration. On larger human rights and democracy questions – as with human settlements rights issues, particularly the eviction and demolition of the settlements of the poor – state–NGO relations were oppositional. In fact, such NGOs risked being pro-scribed and having their officers sacked, detained, and harassed. This has been the case with human rights groups, journalists, and lawyers in Nigeria, Egypt, Côte d'Ivoire, Ghana, Zambia, Kenya, the Sudan, Togo, etc. More generally, the state, recognizing the strength of the global contacts and constituencies of the NGOs and their partial autonomy, has sought to control their expansion, operations, and funding. Resistance to this has cut across Africa and has been supported by international organizations and other bodies. NGOs therefore operate in a situation of fragile autonomy that the govern-ment is anxious to pounce on at the slightest pretext – particularly that of financial accountability. This particular aspect of state–NGO relations remains in a state of precarious balance all over Africa and is a possible entry point by governments for controlling NGOs. Another strategy is the creation by governments of their own NGOs favourable to state positions in specific sectors such as the envi-ronment and, as noted above, women's movements. These new phenomena have been aptly christened by observers as GONGOs (government-owned NGOs).

Central–local government relations

Apart from their centrality to the institutional framework for urban management, central–local government relations also embody some of the elements of democratization, participation, and accountability to constituencies posed by the larger questions of state–society and state–community relations discussed above. The literature contains extensive information on the problems related to central–local rela-tions in both their specific and Africa-wide dimensions (Stren and White, 1989; Lee-Smith and Stren, 1991; Grest, 1995). Again, as Stren (1991) has pointed out, the movement towards centralization in the early post-colonial period stimulated the gradual erosion of the autonomy of local authorities in all parts of Africa irrespective of the constitutional system, be it unitary or federal. Examining the history of the two traditions of local administration dominant in Africa – the francophone and the anglophone – Stren (1989) points out that, in spite of the differences in colonial history, in which there were sig-nificantly more centralizing traits in the French system, post-colonial

African regimes have consistently pursued central domination.[6] In some cases, particularly anglophone countries such as Nigeria, periods of high centralization and ineffective local government have been followed by attempts to redress the balance through decentralization. This does not mean that African politicians and statesmen did not recognize the virtues of decentralization and "local democracy," but there have been wide gaps between proclamations and actions, and at times attempts at effecting large-scale decentralization goals have produced ridiculous outcomes, such as the case of Tanzania, when decentralization replaced both rural and urban local governments with regional and district committees that were dominated by central government officials (Kanyinga et al., 1994).

With the emergence of the crisis of the mid-1970s, the problems of centralization and concentration of resources, functions, and power worsened, leading to the virtual collapse of urban management in many countries, most dramatically in Zaire (see chap. 7 in this volume). As has been amply documented in the different case-studies in Stren and White (1989), the arguments for decentralization and increased participation of micro-units, apart from being political arguments, are also efficiency arguments. The decentralizing ethos increasingly pushed by international agencies such as the World Bank led to a strong need to reconsider issues of more effective decentralization and local participation. In addition, the trend towards increasing democratization often manifest in the introduction of electoral and multi-party politics at the local level created new openings for some local participation and accountability.

Central–local relations therefore oscillated between dominant–supportive patterns in which the central government was the senior and stronger partner in the early post-colonial phase, to the oppositional–competitive patterns of the crisis era in which decentralization opened up political competition and challenges to the central state. The points of tension now occur at many levels. In terms of the hierarchy of government, local governments tend to be constitutionally disadvantaged. Most national constitutions give residual powers to the local level in legislative matters and therefore reduce their capacity to deal with even local issues of revenue and administration once these are defined as national in scope. Thus most local authorities are restricted from dealing adequately with the management of resources such as land.

The struggle for autonomy in central–local relations has also been complicated by the fact of political pluralism. Many African countries have been persuaded to hold local government elections, e.g. Nigeria, Côte d'Ivoire, Uganda, Kenya, Tanzania, and Senegal. In those contexts where the parties controlling local authorities have been different from those at the centre, the tension and conflict have been tremendous. For example, in Lagos State, Nigeria, in 1992, a great degree of tension occurred between the elected chairman of the Lagos Island local government and the elected governor of Lagos State, who were from different political parties. This tension contributed to limiting the dynamism and effectiveness of the local government chairman, whose success would have proved to be a formidable threat to the incumbent governor's chances of re-election. Even in cases where the political party has been the same, there have been reports of conflict between local authorities and their overseeing central ministries, generally the Ministry of Local Government in anglophone Africa and that of the Interior in francophone Africa. In particular, central government is prone to regard local authorities as inept and corrupt, leading to a situation in which, when more effective services are required, parallel centrally based institutions and parastatals are set up, further undermining the confidence and capacity of local authorities.

These conflicts and the inherent competition between central and local authorities have had far-reaching implications for urban management, particularly the administration of services, resource allocation, and local participation. Institutional and behavioural arrangements for managing this tension and operating what Sanyal (1994) has called "cooperative autonomy" are a priority. Indeed, over the past few years, a new local level of politics and active decentralization is emerging in Africa, which is giving a new dimension to issues of participation and local accountability but nevertheless has not avoided the tensions and competition discussed above (Kanyinga et al., 1994).

Conclusions   State–society relations: The urban challenge

In this chapter, an attempt has been made to document the trends and patterns of state–society relations in urban Africa. Some time was spent clarifying concepts, so that the rather complex issues of urban politics and the way they are differently understood were elucidated. The role of external and internal factors in the expression and resolution of some of the major issues and questions of concern has also been examined. Options and directions for state–society relations must emerge from the concrete struggles and efforts of collective and individual political actors with different vested interests, goals, and ideals. However, one thing is clear from the discussion, and this is that since the 1980s the patterns of state–society relations have started to undergo serious changes, with the emergence of more fundamental questioning of the principle of state domination by important actors in both national and global civil society. This has been accompanied by an increase and fundamental change in the pattern of collective demand making. Social justice and equity questions now confront not only larger issues but the more mundane questions of urban management and administration of services. Local and popular participation, accountability to stakeholders, sustainability, ownership by end-users, and equitable resource allocation are all components of the demand making. Although the responses to these demands must be long term and large scale, they also have the potential to contribute immediately to efficiency, effectiveness, and collective well-being as perceived by the subjects of policy and administration. This is the major urban challenge.

Notes

1. An interesting related dimension of the concept of civil society is its globalization both in practice and as an idea (Lipschutz, 1992).
2. However, there has been an interesting application in the context of South Africa, where the concern is with the transition to a pluralistic democracy and uneasiness about an ANC-dominated state. In the debate, the notion has had a wide range of use, from the banal and literal-meaning level to more theoretical debates between the neo-conservative, Marxist, and critical perspectives. See, for instance, Fine (1992), Simone and Pieterse (1993), Gouws (1993).
3. My reading of the situation in the Republic of South Africa in the mid-1990s does not significantly controvert the similarity of this experience there. The African National Congress alliance's Reconstruction and Development Programme is in essence about the incorporation of excluded social groups, except for the fact of a more popular base. So also is the ongoing debate about economic restructuring in South Africa (see Nolan, 1995).
4. For accounts of the social effects of structural adjustment in Nigeria, see Aina (1989) and, in Tunisia, Hammouda (1995).
5. The 1980s literature was filled with this stereotyping and characterization, particularly by North American Africanists, who seemed to be engaged in a struggle over who could find the most sensational label for the African state.
6. The lusophone tradition is documented by Grest (1995).

References

Abouhani, A., ed. 1996. *Urbanisation et mouvements sociaux au Maroc*. CODESRIA Books, Dakar.

Adepoju, A., ed. 1993. *The Impact of Structural Adjustment on the Population of Africa*. UNFPA, Heinemann, and James Curry, London.

Aina, T. A. 1989. The Nigerian crisis and the middle class. *Vierteljahresberichte Journal of the Frederich-Ebert-Stiftung* 116(June): 173–180.

——— 1990a. Understanding the role of community organizations in environmental and urban contexts. *Environment and Urbanization* 2(1): 3–6.

——— 1990b. *Health, Habitat and Underdevelopment in Nigeria*. International Institute for Environment and Development (IIED), Human Settlements Programme, London.

——— 1993a. Development theory and Africa's lost decade: Critical reflections on Africa's crisis. In: M. von Troil, ed., *Changing Paradigms in Development – South East and West: A Meeting of Minds in Africa*. Scandinavian Institute of African Studies, Uppsala.

——— 1993b. Empowering environmental NGOs: The experience of the Nigerian Environmental Study Action Team (NEST). In: R. Sandbrook and M. Halfani, eds., *Empowering People: Building Community, Civil Association and Legality in Africa*. Centre for Urban and Community Studies, University of Toronto.

Aina, T. A., F. E. Etta, and C. I. Obi. 1994. The search for sustainable urban development in Metropolitan Lagos, Nigeria. *Third World Planning Review* 16(2): 201–219.

Ake, C. 1989. How politics underdevelops Africa. In: J. Ihonvbere, ed., *The Political Economy of Crisis and Underdevelopment in Africa: Selected Works of Claude Ake*. JAD Publishers, Lagos.

Amadiume, I. 1995. Gender, political systems and social movements: A West African experience. In: R. Sandbrook and M. Halfani, eds., *Empowering People: Building Community, Civil Association and Legality in Africa*. Centre for Urban and Community Studies, University of Toronto, pp. 35–68.

Audefroy, J. 1994. Evictions trends worldwide – and the role of local authorities in implementing the right to housing. *Environment and Urbanization* 6(1): 8–20.

Awe, B., ed. 1992. *Nigerian Women in Historical Perspective*. Sankore/Bookcraft, Ibadan, Nigeria.

Barkan, J. D., M. L. McNulty, and M. A. O. Ayeni. 1991. "Hometown" voluntary associations, local development and the emergence of civil society in Western Nigeria. *Journal of Modern African Studies* 29(3): 457–480.

Barnes, S. 1986. *Patrons and Power: Creating a Political Community in Metropolitan Lagos*. Manchester University Press, Manchester.

Bayart, J.-F. 1989. Civil society in Africa. In: P. Chabal, ed., *Political Domination in Africa*. Cambridge University Press, Cambridge.

——— 1993. *The State in Africa: the Politics of the Belly*. Longman, London and New York.

Bratton M. and N. van de Walle. 1992. Towards governance in Africa: Popular demands and state responses. In: G. Hyden and M. Bratton, eds., *Governance and Politics in Africa*. Lynne Rienner, Boulder, Colo.

Bryne, D. 1982. Class and the local state. *International Journal of Urban and Regional Research* 6(1): 61–82.

Cohen, J. L. and A. Arato. 1990. *Civil Society and Political Theory*. MIT Press, Cambridge, Mass.

Cohen, M. A. 1990. Macroeconomic adjustment and the city. *Cities* 7(1): 49–59.

Coquery-Vidrovitch, C. 1991. The process of urbanization in Africa (From the origins to the beginning of independence). *African Studies Review* 34(1): 1–98.

Culpeper, R. 1987. *Forced Adjustment: The Export Collapse in Sub-Saharan Africa.* North–South Institute, Ottawa, Canada.

Doornbos, M. 1990. The African state in academic debate: Retrospect and prospect. *Journal of Modern African Studies* 28(2): 179–198.

Duncan, S. S. and M. Godwin. 1982. The local state and restructuring social relations: Theory and practice. *International Journal of Urban and Regional Research* 6(2): 157–185.

El-Kenz, A., ed. 1991. *Algeria: The Challenge of Modernity.* CODESRIA Books, Dakar.

Farah, N. 1994. Civil society and freedom of research. In: M. Mamdani and M. Diouf, eds., *Academic Freedom in Africa.* CODESRIA Books, Dakar.

Fatton, R., Jr. 1992. *Predatory Rule: State and Civil Society in Africa.* Lynne Rienner Publishers, Boulder, Colo., and London.

Fine, R. 1992. Civil society theory and the politics of transition in South Africa. *Review of African Political Economy* 55: 71–83.

Fowler, A. 1992. Distant obligations: Speculations on NGO funding and the global market. *Review of African Political Economy* 55: 9–29.

Gellner, E. 1991. Civil society in historical context. *International Social Science Journal* 129: 415–510.

Gouws, A. 1993. Political tolerance and civil society: The case of South Africa. *Politikon: The South African Journal of Political Studies* 20(1): 15–31.

Grest, J. 1995. Urban management, local government reform and the democratization process in Mozambique: Maputo City, 1975–1990. *Journal of Southern African Studies* 21(1): 147–164.

Hammouda, H. B. 1995. *Tunisie: Adjustement et difficulté de l'insertion internationale.* Forums du Tiers Monde, Editions l'Harmattan, Paris.

Harbeson, J. W. 1992. Civil society and state reformation in Africa. Paper presented to the International Conference on Civil Society in Africa, 5–10 January, Jerusalem, mimeo.

Hardoy, J. E., D. Mitlin, and D. Satterthwaite. 1992. *Environmental Problems in Third World Cities.* Earthscan, London.

Home, R. K. 1983. Town planning, segregation and indirect rule in colonial Nigeria. *Third World Planning Review* 5(2): 165–176.

Hyden, G. and M. Bratton, eds. 1992. *Governance and Politics in Africa.* Lynne Rienner, Boulder, Colo.

Joseph, R. A. 1987. *Democracy and Prebendal Politics in Nigeria: The Rise and Fall of the Second Republic.* Cambridge University Press, Cambridge.

Kanyinga, K. 1993. The social political context of the growth of non-governmental organizations in Kenya. In: P. Gibbon, ed., *Social Change and Economic Reform in Africa.* Scandinavian Institute of African Studies, Uppsala, pp. 52–77.

Kanyinga, K., A. S. Z. Kiondo, and P. Tidemand. 1994. Introduction: The new local-level politics in East Africa. In: P. Gibbon, ed., *The New Local Level Politics in East Africa: Studies on Uganda, Tanzania and Kenya.* Scandinavian Institute of African Studies Research Report No. 95, Uppsala, pp. 11–21.

Kiondo, A. S. Z. 1993. Structural adjustment and non-governmental organizations in Tanzania: A case study. In: P. Gibbon, ed., *Social Change and Economic Reform in Africa*. Scandinavian Institute of African Studies, Uppsala.

Lee-Smith, D. and R. E. Stren. 1991. New perspectives in African urban management. *Environment and Urbanization* 3(1): 23–26.

Lipschutz, R. D. 1992. Reconstructing world politics: The emergence of global civil society. *Millenium: Journal of International Studies* 21(3): 389–420.

Mabogunje, A. L. 1968. *Urbanization in Nigeria*. Africana Press, New York.

—— 1990a. Urban planning and the post-colonial state in Africa: A research overview. *African Studies Review* 33(2): 121–203.

—— 1990b. The organization of urban communities in Nigeria. *International Social Science Journal* 125: 335–367.

McGranahan, G., D. Mitlin, and D. Satterthwaite, eds. 1993. Health and well-being in cities. *Environment and Urbanization* 5(2): 3–185.

Mama, A. 1994. "Feminism or Femocracy?" State feminism and democratization in Nigeria. *Africa Development* 20(1): 37–58.

Mamdani, M. 1995a. Introduction. In: M. Mamdani and E. Wamba-dia-Wamba, eds., *African Studies in Social Movements and Democracy*. CODESRIA Books, Dakar.

—— 1995b. A critique of the state and civil society paradigm in Africanist studies. In: M. Mamdani and E. Wamba-dia-Wamba, eds., *African Studies in Social Movements and Democracy*. CODESRIA Books, Dakar.

Mamdani, M. and E. Wamba-dia-Wamba, eds. 1995. *African Studies in Social Movements and Democracy*. CODESRIA Books, Dakar.

Mkandawire, T. 1991. Crisis and adjustment in sub-Saharan Africa. In: D. Ghai, ed., *The IMF and the South: Its Social Impact of Crisis and Adjustment*. Zed Press, London.

Mkandawire, T. and A. Olukoshi, eds. 1994. *Between Liberalization and Repression: The Politics of Adjustment in Africa*. CODESRIA Books, Dakar.

Ngunyi, M. G. and K. Gathiaka. 1993. State–civil institutions relations in Kenya in the 1980s. In: P. Gibbon, ed., *Social Change and Economic Reform in Africa*. Scandinavian Institute of African Studies, Uppsala, pp. 28–52.

Nolan, B. 1995. Poverty, inequality and reconstruction in South Africa. *Development Policy Review* 13(2): 150–171.

O'Connor, A. 1983. *The African City*. Hutchinson, London.

Oxfam. 1993. *Africa: Make or Break: Action for Recovery*. Oxfam, Oxford.

Parnell, S. and A. Mabin. 1995. Rethinking urban South Africa. *Journal of Southern African Studies* 21(1): 39–61.

Post, K. and M. Vickers. 1974. *Structure and Conflicts in Nigeria, 1960–1965*. University of Wisconsin Press, Madison.

Priestly, C. A. 1986. Labour unrest among Kikuyu women in colonial Kenya. In: C. Robertson and I. Berger, eds., *Women and Class in Africa*. Africana Publishing House, New York and London, pp. 255–273.

Rakodi, C. 1986a. State and class in Africa: A case for extending analyses of the form and functions of the national state to the urban local state. *Society and Space* 4: 419–446.

—— 1986b. Colonial urban policy and planning in Northern Rhodesia and its legacy. *Third World Planning Review* 8(3): 193–217.

Rogerson, C. 1995. Forgotten places, abandoned places: Migration research issues in South Africa. In: J. Baker and T. A. Aina, eds., *The Migration Experience in Africa*. Nordiska Afrikainstitutet, Uppsala.

Sandbrook, R. 1993. *The Politics of Africa's Economic Recovery*. Cambridge University Press, Cambridge.

Sandbrook, R. and M. Halfani, eds. 1993. *Empowering People: Building Community, Civil Association and Legality in Africa*. Centre for Urban and Community Studies, University of Toronto.

Sanyal, B. 1994. *Cooperative Autonomy: The Dialectic of State–NGOs Relationship in Developing Countries*. International Institute for Labour Studies, Research Series 100, Geneva.

Seppälä, P. 1992a. The dialectics of control and local initiative: The case of the Harambee Movement in Kenya. In: P. Seppälä, ed., *Civil Society in the Making: People's Organizations and Politics in the Third World*. Institute of Development Studies Report B26/1992, University of Helsinki, pp. 86–96.

——— ed. 1992b. *Civil Society in the Making: People's Organizations and Politics in the Third World*. Institute of Development Studies Report B26/1992, University of Helsinki.

Simon, D. 1992. *Cities, Capital and Development: African Cities in the World Economy*. Belhaven Press, London.

Simone, A. M. and E. Pieterse. 1993. Civil societies in an international Africa. *Social Dynamics* 19(2): 41–49.

Sivaramakrishnan, K. C. 1994. Is urban politics unique? *Urban Age* 2(2): 10–12.

Smith, D. M., ed. 1992. *The Apartheid City and Beyond: Urbanization and Social Change in South Africa*. Routledge, London.

Songsore, J. and G. McGranahan. 1993. Structural adjustment, the urban poor and environmental management in the Greater Accra Metropolitan Area (GAMA). Stockholm Environment Institute, Ghana, mimeo.

Stamp, P. 1986. Kikuyu women's self-help groups. In: C. Robertson and I. Berger, eds., *Women and Class in Africa*. Africana Publishing House, New York and London, pp. 27–46.

Stren, R. E. 1989. Urban local government in Africa. In: R. E. Stren and R. R. White, eds., *African Cities in Crisis: Managing Rapid Urban Growth*. Westview, Boulder, Colo., pp. 20–36.

——— 1991. Old wine in new bottles? An overview of Africa's urban problems and the urban management approach to dealing with them. *Environment and Urbanization* 3(1): 9–22.

Stren, R. E. and R. R. White, eds. 1989. *African Cities in Crisis: Managing Rapid Urban Growth*. Westview, Boulder, Colo.

Tayeb, C. 1994. Les mouvements islamistes contemporaines au Maghreb: triomphe ou fin de l'Islam? *Afrika Zamani*, new series no. 2: 81–99 (CODESRIA publications, Dakar).

Tripp, A. M. 1992a. Local organizations, participation and the state in urban Tanzania. In: G. Hyden and M. Bratton, eds., *Governance and Politics in Africa*. Lynne Rienner, Boulder, Colo., pp. 221–242.

——— 1992b. Gender and the transformation of civil society in contemporary Tanzania. Paper presented to the International Conference on Civil Society in Africa, 5–10 January, Jerusalem, mimeo.

Vaidyanathan, K. E. 1992. Population trends, issues and implications. *African Development Review* 4(2): 1–32.

World Bank. 1991. *Urban Policy and Economic Development: An Agenda for the 1990s*. Washington, D.C.

Zghal, A. K. 1995. The "bread riot" and the crisis of the one-party system in Tunisia. In: M. Mamdani and E. Wamba-dia-Wamba, eds., *African Studies in Social Movements and Democracy*. CODESRIA Books, Dakar.

Zghal, A. K. and Z. Krichen. 1995. The Islamic fundamentalist movement in Tunisia, 1970–1990: History and language. In: M. Mamdani and E. Wamba-dia-Wamba, eds., *African Studies in Social Movements and Democracy*. CODESRIA Books, Dakar.

13

Urban lives: Adopting new strategies and adapting rural links

Deborah Potts

Abstract

Ce chapitre porte sur la façon dont la vie des citadins a été affectée par les graves difficultés caractéristiques des économies de la plupart des pays d'Afrique depuis la fin des années 70. Le tableau détaillé de la chute drastique des salaires réels révèle la crise de consommation qui en a résulté dans de nombreux ménages, dont les revenus ne suffisent même plus à leur assurer le minimum vital, et encore moins aux autres dépenses essentielles que sont le logement ou le transport. Les politiques d'ajustement structurel, sapant délibérément les conditions économiques des populations urbaines, ont terriblement exacerbé les difficultés des citadins les plus pauvres. Il semble que ce choix de viser les citadins, partant de la conviction qu'ils étaient nettement privilégiés par rapport aux habitants des zones rurales, ait été bien souvent mal fondé, notamment parce que la différence entre les revenus des populations urbaines et rurales s'était déjà amoindrie vers la fin des années 70. La détérioration des services a aussi érodé les prétendus avantages de la vie citadine. L'éthique de récupération des coûts prônée par les institutions financières internationales n'a probablement pas grand chose à offrir aux citadins pauvres en termes d'amélioration des services. Confrontés à cette situation, les citadins ont adopté toutes sortes de stratégies, adaptant la nature des liaisons villes–campagnes qui ont toujours constitué un élément significatif de la nature du processus d'urbanisation en Afrique. Il y a eu notamment un changement dans la nature des migrations, le rythme de la croissance urbaine de certains pays révélant de nettes diminutions en raison d'un déclin net de l'exode rural. D'autres stratégies ont consisté à de nouveaux transferts des zones rurales aux zone urbaines, des modifications dans la composition des ménages, une pléthore de solutions informelles pour répondre aux besoins de services, une augmentation spectaculaire des activités du secteur informel et/ou des occupations secondaires, et de l'agriculture urbaine et un changement dans l'alimentation des ménages. Nombre de ces stratégies ont eu des conséquences fâcheuses pour les citadins mais elles se sont avérées indispensables pour leur permettre de survivre à la crise.

Introduction

Until fairly recently it was often assumed that people resident in urban areas in African countries were generally fairly well off compared with their rural counterparts. Their incomes were reckoned to exceed those generated in rural economic activities, and the rural:urban income gap was regarded (correctly) as the main cause of rapid urbanization, which was largely fuelled by rural–urban migration. Income, however, was not the only advantage that the urban populace was deemed to have: access to superior services, such as piped water, schools, and clinics, was an important element of their higher living standards. Another significant factor was that African governments tended to subsidize urban food prices. This is not to say that urban poverty was not recognized or studied, or that urban life was considered to be easy; access to housing and formal employment was evidently a problem by the 1970s, for example. Nevertheless, belief in the existence of a privileged urban population, created and sustained by unwarranted and inefficient urban bias in African government policies, has made the urban sector one of the major targets of the structural adjustment policies that have affected most African countries since 1980 (for example, Rakodi, chap. 2 in this volume). The economic analysis and thinking that have influenced such policies (e.g. World Bank, 1981; Bates, 1981) put a good deal of the blame for Africa's economic woes on "urban bias," which is argued to have led to major inefficiencies in resource allocation.

As noted by Rogerson in chapter 10 of this volume and in several of the city case-studies in this volume, the reductions in government expenditure on salaries and services have hit urban areas very hard, since they are inevitably centres for service and administrative provision. Specific efforts to reduce the advantages of the so-called urban "labour aristocracy" (which was perceived to have been created by massive subsidies from resources transferred from rural production) have also dramatically reduced living standards: these include the ending of food subsidies and the ending of urban wage protection (e.g. the abolition of minimum wages, or the freezing of wages during periods of rampant inflation).

The main aim of this chapter is to examine the nature of contemporary urban life in African cities, with an emphasis on the poverty that characterizes the experience for the majority. As part of this analysis it will be shown that the savagery of the anti-urban policies that Structural Adjustment Programmes have insisted on has largely been misplaced, since by the time of their implementation the presumed privileges of urban residents had already largely disappeared. The policies of the 1980s and 1990s have therefore drastically, and sometimes tragically, increased the hardships of urban residents, most of whom were already poor and vulnerable.

This chapter will also discuss the strategies that urban residents have adopted and adapted to cope with impoverishment and the increasing administrative and financial incapacity of urban governments. An important theme will be the importance of rural–urban links, and changing patterns of migration. African urban residents have long maintained strong social and economic links with their rural "home" areas, although the nature of those links has varied over time, as the nature of migration streams has adapted to changing economic and political circumstances, and from country to country with variations in factors such as colonial policy, urban history, and land tenure and land availability. The recent era of severe economic decline and structural adjustment has seen such linkages assume a new and vital significance.

Trends in urban poverty: Life for the new urban poor in African cities

Most residents of African cities today are poor by any standards. Accurate city-wide data on income distribution are rare, but there have been many surveys, particularly during the period of structural adjustment, that show quite clearly how urban incomes have been devastated and explore the ramifications of this for household welfare, including health and nutrition. In many cases the levels of income reported are so low that it is hard to see how households can feed themselves, let alone cover other necessary costs, such as housing and transport to work, or vital welfare expenditure on health, education, or clothing. Significantly there is now much evidence that average rural incomes frequently exceed the incomes available from most formal wage work in the cities (e.g. Jamal and Weeks, 1993).

The boost to urban living standards that used to derive from superior access to affordable public services compared with rural areas has also very significantly diminished in many cities. Cuts in health and education expenditure mean that schools and clinics are increasingly overstretched; sometimes they are quite unable to cope with the demand and the private alternatives are unaffordable for the urban poor. The crucial area of housing has also suffered. Although the need for low-income housing was never satisfied in the 1960s and 1970s, the adoption of more realistic approaches to this sector in the 1970s had led to some improvements: many city administrations ceased arbitrary demolition of unplanned settlements, and "squatter" upgrading programmes went some way to providing basic services in some of these settlements and enhancing security of tenure. The site and service approach also helped the poor to some degree, although the hoped-for benefits were often reduced by stubborn insistence on overly high building and service standards and downward raiding by higher-income groups, which squeezed out many of the intended beneficiaries (e.g. Amis and Lloyd, 1990; Stren, 1990; Potts with Mutambirwa, 1991). During the 1980s, however, public housing programmes often languished or ceased altogether, owing to lack of finance. Examples include Côte d'Ivoire, Nigeria, and Tanzania (Stren, 1989; Dubresson, chap. 8 in this volume). Most new housing is therefore unplanned, unserviced, and unsubsidized – as in the rural areas.

Although there had been real increases in formal sector wages for urban workers in many countries in the 1960s, there is some debate about how much benefit, in terms of disposable income for non-essential items, this meant for workers. In eastern and southern Africa it had been colonial policy to discourage or ban family migration to towns, and wages were largely set to cover the basic needs of a "single" male labourer. Jamal and Weeks (1993) show that the rises in incomes in the 1960s were mainly necessary adjustments to make some allowance for urban workers' *family* consumption needs – and did not necessarily mean that wage-workers could afford improvements in their standard of living, since the extra income was absorbed in meeting the basic needs of family members. The in-migration of women and children was certainly one of the most significant changes in the post-independence era (O'Connor, 1983; Potts and Mutambirwa, 1990). It was evidenced by a normalization of city population pyramids away from the colonial pattern of a heavy bias towards working-age men, more normal sex ratios (which for many cities are now at or near the national average), and a resultant rise in the rate of urban natural increase, so that most urban growth is now derived from this component rather than net in-migration.

Jamal and Weeks' analysis is in opposition to the view, accepted by many academics and policy makers in the 1970s and 1980s, of African wage-workers as a "labour aristocracy," which was successfully defending its privileges through organized activity such as trade unions. In their analysis, the reductions in urban income, which they show often began in the 1970s as economic conditions deteriorated, reduced urban residents who were already far from well-off to real poverty. Thus the devastation of urban living standards wrought by structural adjustment policies served *further* to immiserize most urban households, rather than to reduce a privileged lifestyle. Amis (1989), on the other hand, believes that really significant gains did accrue to the African urban labour force in the 1960s, and that their labour aristocracy status in that decade has some validity, but he concurs with Jamal and Weeks that these gains were soon dissipated in the 1970s.

The combined impact of the debt crisis and structural adjustment policies reduced urban workers to astonishing levels of poverty, evidence of which, as incomes from *wages* slipped completely out of line with the minimum required to keep a family (or in many cases even an individual) fed, let alone sheltered and clothed, abounds in the literature. The most comprehensive analysis of the fall in urban incomes during the 1970s and 1980s is provided in Jamal and Weeks' (1993) book: *Africa Misunderstood*, which is tellingly subtitled "Whatever happened to the rural–urban gap?" A selection of their data for different African countries, supplemented by some other sources, is presented in table 13.1.

As a consequence of the massive falls in most urban incomes, sometimes combined with improvements in rural incomes accruing from better agricultural prices,[1] the "new" urban poor of Africa[2] are often poorer than rural households in crude income terms. In fact the measurement of the rural:urban income gap is notoriously difficult,

Table 13.1 **Indices of real minimum wages for selected African countries**

Country					Index^a (date)		
Uganda	29 (1957)	100 (1972)				6 (1980)	10 (1990)
Zambia	56 (1960)	128 (1970)				83 (1985)	
Tanzania	100 (1957)	206 (1972)					37 (1989)
Ghana		100 (1970)	149 (1974)			18 (1984)	34^b (1986)
Nigeria						100 (1981)	10 (1990)
Egypt^c				100 (1974)		119 (1981)	72 (1986)

Sources: compiled from data in Jamal and Weeks (1993), Gefu (1992), Jeffries (1992), Zaytoun (1991).
a. Indices are not comparable across countries.
b. This small recovery in Ghanaian minimum wages was subsequently dissipated when they fell again by 45 per cent in real terms between 1988 and 1990, for which a 30 per cent rise in 1990 only partly made up (Jeffries, 1992).
c. The Egyptian index is for real wages in the government employment sector only.

since in both sectors so much of household income is irregular and non-monetized. The surrogates often used are average rural household income and average or minimum urban wages.[3] The reversal of the income gap has been clearly documented for Nigeria, Sierra Leone, Uganda, and Tanzania. For Nigeria, Jamal and Weeks (1993) calculate that the ratio of unskilled wages to average rural household incomes was already 1:1 by 1978/79 (*before structural adjustment*), and Collier (1988) states that by 1984/85 the urban self-employed had lower incomes than rural households, since the average real incomes of the former fell twice as fast as those of the latter from 1980/81 to 1984/85. In Sierra Leone, average non-agricultural wages were estimated to be 72 per cent lower than average rural household incomes in 1985/86 (Jamal and Weeks, 1993), a situation supported by Riley's (1988, p. 7) contention that by 1986 the urban poor of that country were "a deprived group with fewer income or equivalent earning opportunities than the rural poor." In Uganda, the average farmer's income was 30 per cent higher than the average income of an urban minimum wage-earner in 1984 (Jamal and Weeks, 1993). In this case, the calculation is of particular note, because the urban income estimate *has* taken into account earnings from other non-wage sources – in fact *80 per cent* of the wage-earner's income is assumed to come from other sources. For Tanzania the rural:urban income gap reduced from about 1:3 in the mid-1970s, to 1:1.4 by 1980 (Mtatifikolo, 1992), and by 1982 average smallholder income was 21 per cent more than the minimum urban wage in that year (Jamal and Weeks, 1993).[4] In Lesotho, the 1986/87 household budget survey designated 24–27 per cent of urban households as "poor," compared with only 7–11 per cent of rural households (Sembajwe and Makatsjane, 1992).[5]

The fact that urban poverty may now surpass rural poverty is of particular significance to any study of the nature of urbanization in Africa. First, it is a particularly telling indicator of the levels of poverty urban households must bear, and it is important to remember that in some ways they are even more vulnerable than farmers, because their most basic need, food, is much more endangered by household income fluctuations. The significance of food self-sufficiency for rural households in comparisons of urban and rural livelihoods is particularly emphasized by Jamal and Weeks.[6] Secondly, it is vitally important that policy makers recognize this, now longstanding, situation so that urban poverty can be tackled and further deliberate reductions in living standards prevented. That this is necessary is indicated by Amis and Rakodi (1994, p. 632), who point out that in sub-Saharan Africa "a view that urban areas are well off and that all the poverty is rural has proved remarkably robust." Thirdly, the nature of the rural–urban income gap is, in theory, the most important factor influencing rural–urban migration, and hence urban growth rates. Despite some assertions in the literature that economic recession in Africa has not led to reduced migration and urban growth (e.g. see World Bank, 1981; Jamal and Weeks, 1993; Gilbert, 1993), there is in fact mounting evidence that migration patterns in Africa *have* adapted to the deterioration of urban incomes, in line with theoretical expectations (see Potts, 1995). These important adaptations will be addressed in greater detail later in this chapter.

The wages:food gap and urban nutrition

For millions of urban families throughout Africa the economic circumstances described above have had seriously negative consequences for their ability to feed themselves adequately. Many surveys emphasize urban poverty in the 1980s and 1990s by calculating how much food typical wages can buy, and a range of illustrative data are set out below. It is important to note that, were these data to tell the whole story, obviously there would be mass famines in African cities; since this is not the case, equally obviously urban households have adopted coping strategies and these will be discussed in the next section. However urban diets *have* suffered tremendously, and not just in terms of protein intake, but often even in terms of calories, so that people are not just malnourished but undernourished. There is abundant evidence that urban households have substituted cheaper foods for preferred foods (e.g. cutting out bread and eating more staples such as maize); have cut down on or virtually ended the addition of high-protein items such as meat, milk, or fish; and have cut out some daily meals altogether. Furthermore, because proper preparation of traditional foods is often quite time consuming (which is one of the reasons why convenient bread became so popular in many parts of urban Africa), and women's time for domestic duties has been very hard hit by many of the adaptations made necessary by urban economic decline, there is also evidence that the form in which food is being consumed is changing (e.g. cold rather than hot, semi- rather than finely processed[7]), which usually means it is less nutritious. As always, it is the health and welfare of the most vulnerable members of the household, such as small children, that are most affected by adverse dietary changes. Given that most families would not introduce such drastic changes in their diets except as a last resort, it is obvious that urban families have already forgone vital expenditure in other areas such as clothing, education, and housing.

The fact that the measurement of urban living standards requires consideration of expenditure on much more than food is highlighted by Tripp's Tanzanian data, from which she estimates that, if other basic costs are included, the average monthly income in the late 1980s would cover an urban household of six for only *three days* (Tripp, 1990). Another East African example comes from Kenya, where 30 per cent of urban wage-earners could not buy the minimum amount of calories needed for a family of five by 1988 (Jamal and Weeks, 1993). Steep food price rises in Zambian towns combined with drastic falls in real wages to bring about a nutrition crisis in the 1980s. A survey of 100 households from different townships in Lusaka, the capital city, found that "as prices rose, poor families stopped buying meat, chicken, fish and bread. They also cut back on vegetables and even on mealie meal. *Most families reduced from two to one meal per day* in order to save money" (Mulenga, 1991; emphasis added). According to an Oxfam report, this had had adverse health effects, particularly for children (Clarke and Allison, 1989). Increases in child malnutrition in urban Zambia in the late 1980s are also reported in Jespersen (1990, p. 44), and by the 1990s infant mortality rates were rising and life expectancy was falling (*Financial Times*, 1994).[8] In the Malawian cities of Blantyre and Lilongwe, low-income households were spending nearly two-thirds of their incomes on food in 1987/88, compared with about one-quarter in 1980 (Chilowa and Roe, 1990; Roe and Chilowa, 1990). The situation in Angola was even more extreme: although it too has had a (self-imposed) form of structural adjustment, the main cause of dire urban poverty here is the civil war, which started again, after a short respite, in late 1992 and which drove huge numbers of rural people into the towns. In Luanda, refugees have built shelters on any available space – former market gardens, factory land, city parks, and even the municipal rubbish dump. The minimum monthly wage in 1994 was sufficient to purchase only 5 loaves of bread or 10 buckets of clean water (*Observer*, 1994). In Zaire, urban living standards also fell dramatically in the 1970s and 1980s, and Mbuyi (1989) reports that many inhabitants of the capital, Kinshasa, state that they now take only one main meal a day (see also Piermay, chap. 7 in this volume).

West African examples include Sierra Leone, where by 1988 the *average* monthly urban wage covered only a week's food for a family of four (Jamal and Weeks, 1993). Supporting evidence for the gross insufficiency of Sierra Leonean urban incomes at this time is found in Riley (1988). Drawing on UNICEF data and his own estimates of the sort of diet that urban families had been reduced to by 1987 (a diet of significantly less nutritional and calorific value than that common in pre-structural adjustment times), he calculates that the minimum wage could cover the cost of only 10 meals a month in the capital, Freetown. He suggests that this must have had adverse consequences for infant mortality rates and malnutrition, a contention supported by a UNICEF study in 1989 (Jespersen, 1990). Another example is Ghana: Jeffries (1992) estimates that an urban resident on the minimum wage in 1990 could just about *feed* him- or herself, although no other necessary expenditure could be covered, or the subsistence needs of any dependants.[9] Similar evidence of urban deprivation is found for Nigeria, West Africa's most populous state, which has by far the most urban centres in the region. Peil (1991) estimates that the minimum wage in 1989 would have bought a total of half a tin of local rice, one tin of garri (dried cassava), one tin of powdered milk, a litre of groundnut oil, two small loaves of bread, and six eggs. She also points out that many employees in small firms would receive less than this minimum wage, as would many of the self-employed; this of course is also true of all the other countries so far cited. The economic situation has worsened since then in Nigeria, with major currency devaluation and price rises in 1994 making the lives of the urban poor even harder (E. Blunt, personal communication, 1994; and see Abiodun's description of Lagos in chap. 6 in this volume).

Of course the impact of economic decline and structural adjustment policies has not been uniform across Africa, or even across the urban hierarchy within any one country. As a broad generalization it is the countries of tropical sub-Saharan Africa that have experienced the most extreme falls in urban living standards, and in some of these drought and/or wars have been even more important macro-influences on processes of urbanization and migration. The countries at the southern tip of the continent – South Africa, Namibia, Botswana, Lesotho, and Swaziland – have so far escaped the imposition of drastic austerity and liberalization programmes. In North African countries, structural adjustment policies have been implemented since the 1980s, with predictable consequences for the urban poor, but it appears that the impact on urban livelihoods has not been as extreme as in sub-Saharan Africa, presumably because their economies were and are less weak than those of most sub-Saharan states. In Egypt, for example, serious falls in real wages have mainly occurred in the government, rather than private, sector (see table 13.1). In the private sector, wages had often strengthened during the 1980s, and the agricultural wages index increased from 100 in 1975 to 215 by 1986 (Zaytoun, 1991). However, strong pressure from the IMF in 1990 led to steep price rises for staple foods, with rice prices rising 50 per cent (Niblock, 1993). Strong political protests from the urban population against increasing poverty appear to have been more common in North African countries (although sub-Saharan Africa has also experienced food riots), and this aspect of urban lives is well represented in the regional literature (e.g. Seddon, 1989, 1993; Denoeux, 1993).

The ideology of economic "liberalization" and cost recovery and urban living standards

The gap between food costs and urban wages has arisen not only because wages have fallen in real terms but also because there have been significant price rises for food items. This has largely been caused by the liberalization of the food trade, in line with IMF conditionality, so that food prices are no longer fixed by government decree, and previous government subsidies that reduced the price to the buyer have been removed. In Tanzania, for example, the food trade was liberalized in 1984; between 1982/83 and 1987/88

456

real consumer prices for both maize and rice rose roughly fivefold (Maliyamkono and Bagachwa, 1990, table 3.6). Fixed prices for many products had often meant that parallel markets developed as demand outstripped supply, and urban families sometimes had to resort to these much higher-priced products. Inflexible and unrealistic fixed pricing, which led to serious shortages, was undoubtedly a disbenefit for the urban poor. In urban Tanzania and Zambia in the early 1980s some food and many other products were virtually unobtainable except on the parallel market (Maliyamkono and Bagachwa, 1990; Mulenga, 1991; Rakodi, 1994a), although subsidized maize meal was usually readily available in Zambia. Full liberalization of the food trade according to the IMF ideology that prices should be set by supply and demand, that marketing should be privatized, and that there should be full recovery of the costs incurred in marketing food to urban areas has obviously, however, contributed to the income problems faced by the "new" urban poor.

The idea that cost recovery and privatization will provide *better* services in urban areas is also encouraged or forced upon urban authorities by the international financial institutions. By the 1980s the situation with regard to services such as water supply, sewerage, electricity, public transport, and rubbish removal was disastrous in most urban areas (Stren and White, 1989). The debt crisis meant that foreign exchange shortages and general financial restrictions were faced by nearly all service suppliers. As a result, newly developing areas of the city (whether planned or unplanned) could often not be publicly serviced at all, and in the older urban areas existing infra-structure could not be maintained. In all sectors the common story was that there was not enough equipment, or supplies of inputs, or vehicles, or what was available was not functioning for lack of spare parts. Privatization and/or cost-recovery strategies in a liberalized economic environment are argued by the World Bank to be the answer. Although this could lead to some service improvements, the bland assumption that the poor will benefit too is often misplaced (see also Aina, chap. 12 in this volume, for a critique of this approach to urban services). A common pro-privatization argument is that residents in unplanned settlements often pay more for their water (per unit) than the wealthy with piped supplies – and would therefore be happy to pay for an efficiently run unsubsidized water supply to their settlement. However, the poor cannot avoid consuming water, and the logic of generalizing from the case of water provision to other services is deeply flawed. There *has* been significant recourse to the private sector for services (e.g. septic tank emptying, rubbish collection) by the urban wealthy for some time (Stren and White, 1989), but at a considerable cost premium. Since the poor can rarely afford services now, it is usually untenable that a more expensive service, albeit one that functions, is going to help in any way.

In terms of living standards, the introduction of cost-recovery systems in education and health has even greater implications. Most African governments subsidized these services to a significant degree, and much higher charges are usually now being made. This is putting further pressure on the budgets of the urban poor, who now often have to withdraw their children from school and delay going to clinics, or not obtain medical help at all. In Harare, the capital city of Zimbabwe, user costs for education and health have increased dramatically since the Economic Structural Adjustment Programme (ESAP) was instituted in 1990. People in low-income residential areas are finding the extra costs a difficult burden (Kanji, 1993), and my research in 1994 found that recent migrants to the city often mentioned the problems caused by price rises for health and education first when discussing the impact of ESAP (Potts with Mutambirwa, forthcoming). Maternity services, for example, now cost so much that hospital deliveries have declined and the maternal death rate has soared.

In comparison with many other African nations, however, the situation in Harare is still favourable, even for the urban poor. In others, state health and education services have virtually collapsed. Thus in 1994 in Luanda in Angola it was difficult to educate a child outside the private sector, where one month's fees are roughly double the minimum wage (*Observer*, 1994). In Ouagadougou, Burkina Faso, peri-urban areas in the early 1980s had virtually no services of any kind. Mass mobilization of the residents from 1983 by revolutionary committees brought about significant improvements in educational facilities in particular, which were built "privately" and eventually staffed by government teachers (Jaglin, 1994). However, levies had to be paid to the committees for the new schools, representing an additional "tax" burden for those least able to afford it.

Although most new housing for the urban poor today is completely or virtually unplanned, and therefore largely unserviced, government financial constraints and the cost-recovery ethos mean that planned sites are now so minimally serviced that the difference between planned and unplanned housing in physical environmental terms is not very marked. This has been true of many site and service schemes in South Africa (Potts, 1994). In Tanzania, planned sites and services programmes in the 1980s were provided with no infrastructure, not even water or unsurfaced roads.

The incapacity of African urban government to maintain infrastructure and services has been a major contributor to the declining living standards of the urban poor. Although the wealthier sections of the population have not by any means escaped the problems, the poor are more vulnerable and have fewer options. In the context of Nigeria, Uduku (1994, p. 75) has recently argued that "the commercialization drive and possible deregulation [in social infrastructure provision] ... that is currently being pursued is unlikely to benefit the average city dweller," since current levels of poverty are such that most people could not be serviced at a profit and will thus not be serviced at all. Similar fears for the poor about this approach to services have been voiced by Stren (1990) and Gilbert (1992). The picture so far painted of life in urban areas has been one of increasing hardship and real impoverishment. Most people are now very poor, and were they to rely on formal wages and public sector infrastructure they would not be able to survive. The impossibility of staying alive on typical urban wages in Africa has been dubbed the "wages puzzle" by Jamal and Weeks (1993). That people do survive is testimony to their ingenuity, determination, and sheer hard work – a host of coping strategies have developed. It is to these strategies that this chapter now turns.

Household survival strategies

The urban poor have adopted a number of strategies[10] in their attempts to manage the changes in their economic circumstances. Two major coping strategies have now been well documented. The first involves an increase in informal sector activity, with previously non-earning household members entering the petty commodity sector, as well as wage-earners taking on supplementary cash-earning activities (see, for example, Tripp, 1989; Jespersen, 1990; Roe and Chilowa, 1990; Maliyamkono and Bagachwa, 1990; Bibangambah, 1992; Bigsten and Kayizzi-Mugerwa, 1992; Kanji, 1993; Adepoju, 1993; Rogerson, chap. 10 in this volume; Piermay, chap. 7 in this volume; and, for a general review of evidence for such strategies in third world cities, including Africa, Gilbert, 1994). The second strategy involves the development of food-growing by urban households on any available patch of arable land within and around the urban area (e.g. Sanyal, 1985; Mulenga, 1991; Gefu, 1992; Holm, 1992; Mlozi et al., 1992; Mbiba, 1994; Drakakis-Smith et al., 1995; Rogerson, chap. 10 in this volume). New ways of accessing services or of adapting to their absence are other types of coping strategies. Many of these strategies have fairly specific gender implications and may bring the poor into conflict with urban authorities. A final and very important survival strategy involves the strengthening and adaptation of the rural–urban linkages that have always been such an important part of urbanization processes in sub-Saharan Africa (Potts and Mutambirwa, 1990). The following sections consider these issues in more detail, beginning with the nature of rural linkages and adaptations in migration patterns.

Vital rural linkages: Continuity and change

There is a long tradition of academic interest in the nature of linkages between rural and urban areas in Africa. One aspect of this interest has been a fascination with the degree of commitment urban residents have to their urban life and lifestyle and the urban milieu generally, and how best to analyse and categorize those who maintain strong rural ties (e.g. Epstein, 1958, 1961, 1967; Mitchell, 1959, 1966, 1987; Gluckman, 1960, 1961; Mayer, 1961, 1962, 1964; Gugler, 1971, 1991; Stopforth, 1972, 1977; Moller, 1973; Gutkind, 1974; Gugler and Flanagan, 1978; O'Connor, 1983; Potts and Mutambirwa, 1990; Mabin, 1990; Andreasen, 1990). Research on related topics has included surveys of urban residents' social and political affiliations and their attitudes toward urban living. It is usually assumed that of great significance for understanding and gauging commitment to town are the incidence and degree of maintenance of rural links, such as rural land, a rural house, family ties, and rural–urban and urban–rural economic transfers, and that the ultimate "proof" of weak urban roots is a stated intention to return to a rural lifestyle at some point in the future.

The focus of much such research tends, for obvious reasons, to be on people who were originally rural–urban migrants. For many African urban settlements such migrants made up most of the population until about the 1970s. One reason was the colonial practice in much of Africa of considering towns as European areas. A range of policies "encouraged" African workers to come to town as "single" male migrants, rather than as families, and *not* to settle down permanently. Of critical significance in facilitating circular migration was the nature of land tenure: for most of sub-Saharan Africa this was communal and the vast majority of the population had rights to land through their lineage or marriage, which migration to town did not abrogate. In South Africa, Namibia, and Southern Rhodesia, these policies were formalized, and racist influx controls on permanent African residence were institutionalized. Even there such policies were never fully effective, and elsewhere their implementation varied over time. Inevitably a stabilized urban-born component of city populations developed. Nevertheless, patterns of circular migration, whereby in-migrants eventually returned "home," were firmly established. After independence, a shift towards more family migration occurred, and it became more common for migrants to stay in town for longer periods of time, perhaps for their working lives, and many settled permanently. In the 1960s, migrants still dominated urban populations, especially since the rate of migration increased significantly throughout the continent. However, the fact that more women were now present inevitably meant that natural increase was becoming more significant, and by the 1970s there was often a rough balance in urban growth rates between net in-migration and internally generated population increase.

In the literature, particularly amongst the earlier social observers, negative connotations were often associated with African rural–urban migrants who retained strong rural links. There was a feeling that they were somehow socially and politically unformed or chaotic, and that their position implied a rejection of the urban milieu and a degree of mental stress (Gutkind, 1974). Certainly their situation made them hard to define in standard anthropological, sociological, or political economy categories, as reflected in the common assertion that they were not "fully urbanized," with its implication that they were, in some way, not "complete." Such attitudes are quite misplaced; as will be seen, the strength and nature of African urban–rural linkages vary over time as macro-political and economic conditions change, and such links represent vital safety-valves and welfare options for urban people who are very vulnerable to economic fluctuations in the absence of state welfare systems (Potts and Mutambirwa, 1990). The nature of the linkages is thus not a given, and neither are their implications. The anxieties about where migrants' affiliations lay were questioned early on by Gluckman (1961, p. 69) in his famous assertion: "an African townsman is a townsman, an African miner is a miner." Gutkind (1974) went further in criticizing the conception that migrants are not deeply involved in town life and what he felt was an overemphasis on the problems migrants faced in adapting to towns. Although acknowledging that such adaptations were not always easy, he stated that they were "not generally the central problem for the migrant. What matters is the availability of housing, work, and adequate wages" (Gutkind, 1974, p. 53).

In concert with Gutkind it is now more generally recognized that *most* migrants to town have a fairly realistic idea of what faces them, because information flows and visits between rural and urban areas are well established. Gutkind's reformulation of the implications of migrancy and rural–urban links even asserted that the latter, which were absolutely vital to the migrant, could *increase* migrants' commitment to town. He argued that:

The degree of contact the African urbanite maintains with his [*sic*] home community does not involve him in less participation in the life of the town but, frequently, in deeper and more persistent involvement. Visits to a rural home, or other regular links, are usually a reflection of a fairly high degree of commitment to an urban-based wage economy or to the perception by the migrant that life in town provides him with the potential of some degree of upward economic and social mobility which, if realised, in turn increases his stature in the rural community. Thus rural (traditional) influences rather than making a migrant less of an urbanite might actually involve him more deeply in the urban milieu. (Gutkind, 1974, pp. 31–32)

Although the importance of status considerations cannot be ignored, it would be hard to maintain that this interpretation of rural–urban linkages is of most relevance to understanding today's links. Instead, as will be shown, it is vital economic considerations that currently dominate.

It is now firmly established that economic considerations are the primary cause of rural–urban migration (e.g. Mitchell, 1959; Gugler, 1969; Caldwell, 1969; Todaro, 1969, 1971; O'Connor, 1983; Potts and Mutambirwa, 1990). When the rural:urban income gap was strongly in favour of urban areas in the 1960s and early 1970s in most African countries, the advantage of moving to town was fairly obvious. Although rising levels of urban unemployment (measured in "formal" terms) in the 1970s somewhat affected this economic advantage, continued rapid urban growth was generally explained in terms of a generalized "Todaro" model whereby migrants assessed their lifetime's earning potential in urban versus rural areas.[11] Other important factors in rural–urban migration were the better health and education facilities available in town. It has also been shown that migrancy is a selective process, being particularly prevalent amongst younger working-age men and those with a better education. However there has been a significant increase in female migration since independence, with the move towards more family migration being an important factor. There are of course regional variations in these patterns; Ethiopia, for example, has always had a preponderance of female rural–urban migration (O'Connor, 1983), and this was also noted for Zaire in the early 1970s (Mbuyi, 1989). The causes of the high incidence of female migration in these countries are not clear, although in Ethiopia they presumably have something to do with the notably different history of land tenure in that country compared with most of sub-Saharan Africa.

The shift to longer periods of migration or permanent migration by the 1970s did not mean that full "stabilization" had occurred – that all migrants brought their families and intended to remain permanently. The persistence of male and circular migration,[12] and of the implicit rural–urban linkages, has been somewhat contrary to certain theoretical expectations, which foresaw a greater degree of stabilization as economic development occurred, policies "encouraging" return migration came to an end, and modernization weakened social ties to villages. An assumption that this was a one-way process has been quite strong. In fact it is now clear that return migration and rural–urban linkages have strengthened in many countries since, and sometimes during, the 1970s. Such processes are well exemplified by Zambia, and the implications of such changes and their relationship to the model of eventual stabilization have been debated between Macmillan (1993) and Ferguson (1990, 1994).

By the 1980s, the idea that economic advantage was fostering rapid rural–urban migration no longer made much sense, particularly for those sub-Saharan African cities where the gap between formal earnings and even the most frugal expenditure on food was so evident. Yet the urban growth reported for most countries appeared to show rates that suggested continued significant net in-migration. These reported rates were usually derived from World Bank or United Nations published data, and have been endlessly regurgitated in the mainstream literature on third world or African urbanization (e.g. see Gilbert, 1992; Jamal and Weeks, 1993). Thus it was common in the 1980s for Africa to be characterized as the continent with the lowest levels of urbanization but the highest urban growth rates. Given that the majority of the population of so many African towns and cities experienced a massive decline in their living standards at this time, it seemed increasingly puzzling that urban growth rates, and rural–urban migration, were not felt to have been much affected by the squeeze on urban incomes and employment.

In reality, urban growth rates *have* fallen, sometimes quite dramatically for certain towns, in a number of African countries. The tendency to assume that very rapid growth has persisted in Africa derives, as noted by earlier contributors to this volume, from the uncritical use of outdated projections (see Piermay, chap. 7 in this volume, for a useful discussion of the problems and dangers of assuming that past growth rates for Kinshasa are in any way a useful guide to current growth). Careful analysis of recent census data (unfortunately available for only a handful of countries) suggests a very different scenario, and demonstrates not only that rural–urban linkages persist, but also that they have undergone specific and logical adaptations in response to urban economic decline. Three main types of change have occurred in rural–urban linkages and migration processes: adaptations in household composition; increases in rural–urban transfers; and declining in-migration and increased out-migration.

Household composition

As discussed above, there has been a major trend towards more family[13] migration, in the case of married people, since the colonial period, although young single people are naturally still an important component of rural–urban flows. That many people should want to live in family units is scarcely surprising; this is after all a social norm in most societies worldwide. Nevertheless, some countervailing factors have continued to operate, so that for some migrants, and in some areas, the disadvantages of bringing all immediate family members to town outweigh the advantages. For example, where land is in short supply a migrant might decide that continued rights to communal land might have to be guaranteed by leaving an actively cultivating spouse behind. This is a complex issue and its significance varies geographically. There is no clear-cut evidence of a relationship between rural population pressure and the composition of migrant flows; many other factors such as lineage status, relationships with authorities involved with land, or the amount of family land may also affect the decision. Despite creeping commercialization of land in some parts of Africa, the perception that rural–urban migrants have a strong birthright to land is still very strong, as is the feeling that it will be honoured. Gugler (1991) has shown that migrants in Enugu, Nigeria, are still convinced that they will be able to return home and farm after decades in town, and the strength of rural–urban land ties in Nigeria has also been demonstrated by Andrae (1992). In Zimbabwe, where land is in very short supply, Potts and Mutambirwa (1990) found that three-quarters of migrants by the 1980s were choosing to bring their spouses and children to town with them, but also that roughly one-third of migrants definitely intended not to stay permanently in town – and the vast majority of these expected to return to farming in the future. However, Potts and Mutambirwa also identified complex visiting patterns to rural areas, particularly involving wives, which allowed much of the land held by those migrants who still had land assets to be cultivated. Van Donge (1990) does, however, pinpoint land shortage in a specific region of Tanzania (Mgeta division in the Uluguru mountains south of Morogoro) as a prime reason for Waluguru migrants wanting to establish themselves permanently in Dar es Salaam.

Other reasons for leaving family members behind in rural areas are lack of income to support them and lack of housing (Potts and Mutambirwa, 1990). Although overcrowding in urban dwellings is virtually ubiquitous, and very high proportions of poor urban households can afford to occupy only one room (O'Connor, 1983; Potts with Mutambirwa, 1991; Tipple, 1994; Amis and Lloyd, 1990), for some inadequate accommodation may be a factor in determining migrant household composition. In Thika, Kenya, for example, Andreasen (1990) has documented such appalling poverty, insecurity, and inadequate housing for some migrants that family life would be quite impossible. Undoubtedly the decline in real incomes that urban residents have suffered since the 1970s may have encouraged the tendency to leave some people behind or to send some "home." This is particularly reinforced by urban households' desperate need for food: people at "home" can grow food, some of which can supplement urban sources, as noted for Uganda by Jamal and Weeks (1993) and for Zambia by Mulenga (1991). On the other hand, a rather different adaptation has been noted in Harare, where in some households where female spouses *usually* spent most of their time in the rural areas the women were now spending more time in town "in order to save on transport costs for either spouse to visit each other but also, for women to try and earn hard cash in town," although the women were still expected to maintain rural food output as well (Kanji and Jazdowska, 1993, p. 21).

Another aspect of changing household composition involves children. Declining urban educational facilities combined with their increased expense may encourage parents to return children to rural areas where schools are cheaper (e.g. see Dubresson on Abidjan, chap. 8 in this volume). Nelson (1987) has also documented the strategy of fostering urban children in rural areas in Kenya in order to reduce urban expenditure. Additionally, there is evidence of more children attempting to earn money and an increase in the number of children living on the streets, as described by Obudho for Nairobi (chap. 9 in this volume).

Adaptations in rural–urban and urban–rural transfers
Transfers of goods and cash between urban and rural households have always been a vital part of African migration processes (O'Connor, 1983), but the dominant flow has tended to be of cash remittances to rural dependants. In many societies these have been fundamental to the survival of rural households, particularly in southern Africa where unequal land division between black and white and influx controls rendered many rural households virtually destitute. However there is evidence of significant shifts in the nature of such transfers.

It appears that far more food is now being brought in from rural areas, which of course greatly enhances urban residents' vested interests in maintaining their social and economic rural links. These transfers can rely on surpluses generated by existing rural kin or on urban residents returning in the rainy season to cultivate, which they would probably not choose to do if they could afford urban food prices or could gain access to sufficient land *in* town to grow food. On the other hand, there is some evidence that remittances to rural areas are declining as urban households find it harder to spare any money. This was true of urban households in Harare (Kanji, 1993) and in Lilongwe and Blantyre (Chilowa and Roe, 1990). In the latter cities in 1988/89 only 17 per cent of households remitted to rural areas during a three-month period.

Migrants no more and escaping the city?
It has already been asserted in the introduction to this section on rural–urban linkages that, despite a prevalent view to the contrary, African urbanization rates have fallen in response to the economic crisis (Potts, 1994). This is due mainly to two factors: rates of in-migration have declined, and rates of "return" migration have tended

to increase; thus net in-migration has often fallen significantly. These are of course quite rational responses, in line with what one might expect given the narrowing or reversal of the rural:urban income gap.

A range of census data on urbanization for selected African countries is presented in table 13.2, with comparisons with World Bank estimates. The choice of countries has been very largely determined by the availability of census data for relevant periods; unfortunately very few countries meet even this simple criterion, and in some cases (e.g. Sierra Leone) the data were deemed too unreliable to be worth analysing. Although it is acknowledged (see also chaps. 2 and 3 in this volume) that African census data should be treated with some caution, it is contended that the evidence of a significant slackening in the rate of population increase in a number of cities in a *range* of countries, *combined* with the fact that those countries that have suffered the worst urban crises have recorded the greatest fall in urbanization rates, suggests that a real trend is being identified.

Ghana was one of the first countries to suffer serious economic decline, and it is evident from table 13.2 (see also chap. 3) that it also experienced very limited urbanization during its second post-independence intercensal period of 1970–1984. Accra's growth, which had generally been thought to be very high, was only 20 per cent higher than national population growth rates (compared with more than double between 1960 and 1970). It is difficult to know what natural increase rates are in most African cities, but it is here assumed that they are not very different from national rates. This is because, although there does tend to be lower *fertility* in African urban areas, death rates are lower and birth rates are often higher[14] because they are boosted by the more youthful composition of the urban areas, with a higher proportion of people being in child-bearing age groups. Unbalanced sex ratios used to reduce urban births, but by the 1970s sex ratios in many major cities were often about parity. On this basis, therefore, it is argued that the Ghana census data in table 13.2 show that net rural–urban migration slowed very significantly. Indeed, for Kumasi and Sekondi-Takoradi, the second and third cities, this period must have seen a net out-migration of urban people to rural areas.

It is also clear that Uganda experienced significant reverse migration from major towns in the 1970s, and even the capital city did not grow much faster than the national population. The 1980s, however, saw a return to net in-migration and higher urban growth rates.

Table 13.2 **Comparisons of average annual growth rates of national, urban, and selected city populations for selected African countries, 1960s–1990s (census data and other estimates)**[a]

Country/urban area	1960s	1970s	1980s	1990–>
Ghana				
National population	$2.4^{(60-70)}$	$2.6^{(70-84)}$		
Total urban: census	4.8	3.2		
WB estimate			$4.2^{(80-88)}$	
Accra	5.4	3.15		
Kumasi	4.4	2.2		
Sekondi-Takoradi	2.7	0.3		
Tema	15.6	4.6		
Nigeria				
Lagos[b]		$12.5^{(63-74)}$	$6.6^{(74-88)}$	
Tanzania				
National population		$3.3^{(67-78)}$	$2.8^{(78-88)}$	
Total urban: census		11.4	10.7	
WB estimate		$11.7^{(65-80)}$	$11.6^{(80-88)}$	
Dar es Salaam		9.7	4.8	
Mwanza		11.1	4.5	
Tanga		4.9	2.9	
Mbeya		17.9	5.5	
Morogoro		8.5	6.6	
Arusha		5.0	6.4	
Moshi		6.2	6.3	
Tabora		11.2	3.2	
Dodoma		6.2	6.2	
Iringa		9.2	4.0	
Mtwara		8.2	4.7	
Kigoma		8.0	4.0	
Data for selected regions[c]				
Regional HQs (35,000–175,000)			*5.6*	
Intermediate towns (10,000–34,999)			*7.0*	
Small towns (5,500–9,999)			*6.4*	
Uganda				
National population		$2.8^{(69-80)}$		$2.5^{(80-91)}$
Total urban: WB estimate		$4.7^{(65-80)}$	$5.1^{(80-88)}$	
Kampala		3.0	4.9	
Jinja		−0.6	3.4	
Mbale		1.6	6.1	
Masaka		7.6	5.0	
Entebbe		0.0	6.6	
Fort Portal		11.7	1.9	
Tororo		0.4	−	

Table 13.2 **(cont.)**

Country/urban area	1960s	1970s	1980s	1990->
Zambia				
National population	$2.5^{(63-69)}$	$3.0^{(69-80)}$	$3.2^{(80-90)}$	
Total urban: census	8.9	5.8	3.7	
WB estimate		$7.2^{(65-80)}$	$6.7^{(80-88)}$	
Lusaka	13.8	6.5	6.1	
Ndola	9.5	4.0	4.0	
Kitwe	8.4	2.6	2.4	
Chingola	9.6	2.1	2.5	
Kabwe	6.3	6.6	2.0	
Mufulira	5.0	2.1	1.2	
Luanshya	4.2	1.3	2.8	

Sources: Ghana census data – Ghana, *1984 Census Provisional Results*, Accra, 1984; Tanzanian census data – United Republic of Tanzania, Bureau of Statistics, President's Office, Planning Commission, *1988 Population Census: National profile, basic demographic and economic characteristics*, Dar es Salaam, 1992, *Population Census: Regional profile: Dar es Salaam*, Dar es Salaam, 1992, and other regional profiles; Barke and Sowden (1992), table 2; Holm (1992), table 1; Uganda census data – Republic of Uganda, *Report on the 1980 Population Census: Volume 1: Provisional results by administrative area*, Census Office, Kampala, 1982; and Republic of Uganda, Statistics Department, *Final Results of 1991 Population and Housing Census (Prerelease)*, Kampala, 1992; Zambia census data – Republic of Zambia, Central Statistical Office, *1990 Census of Population, Housing and Agriculture: Preliminary report*, Lusaka, December 1990; World Bank data – *1991 World Development Report*, cited in Jamal and Weeks (1993).

a. Intercensal periods indicated by superscript on national population growth rates (e.g. 60–70 = 1960–1970). Estimates of growth rates are in italics, with periods indicated in superscript.
b. Estimates taken from Peil (1991), p. 19.
c. "Cleaned" census data from Holm (1992), table 1.

For Zambia a similar picture emerges of significantly reduced urban growth by the 1970s, and the level of urbanization increased a mere 2 per cent from 40 per cent in 1980 to 42 per cent in 1990. Although the capital city, Lusaka, has maintained a high growth rate, experiencing significant net in-migration for the whole post-independence period, the Copperbelt towns have tended to grow more slowly than the national population since the 1960s; in fact their experience could be typified as counter-urbanization. Their reduced growth accords with Zambia's economic decline, which began in the early 1970s with the usual exigencies of a debt crisis, exacerbated by a dramatic collapse in copper prices and expensive transport problems caused by regional political instability and its principled opposition to white majority rule in neighbouring countries. The reductions in growth in many Zambian cities are obvious from table 13.2.

The situation in Tanzania is much less clear cut than in Uganda and Zambia, for, although there is clear evidence of a reduction in the growth rate of Dar es Salaam and many other individual cities in the 1980s compared with the 1960s and most of the 1970s, the census data indicate that net in-migration is still contributing significantly to growth in most urban areas (see also chap. 3). Table 13.2 shows that for Tanzania there *has* been a fall in the rate of urban growth, at least for the major centres including the capital city, but there is no evidence of net out-migration, as in some other countries. There are, however, a number of problems in interpreting the census data for Tanzania.[15] It is unclear how the census defined and enumerated the *total* urban population. The growth rates of the major urban areas shown in table 13.2, however, suggest a lower overall growth rate than 10.7 per cent. Holm has managed to manipulate the census data to establish realistic growth rates for some other urban size categories for five specific regions: Iringa, Kilimanjaro, Arusha, Morogoro, and Mbeya, which are also shown in table 13.2. Although high (between 5.6 and 7.0 per cent), these still do not suggest a national rate of urbanization of over 10 per cent per year. It may be that the establishment of *ujamaa* nucleated villages in the 1970s led to the reclassification of very large numbers of new settlements as "urban" by 1988, explaining this seeming anomaly. Holm's study indicates that the scope for successful urban agriculture in intermediate and small towns in Tanzania may mitigate the downward pressure on rural–urban migration exerted by the impact of recession on wages and food prices. This helps to explain how the pressures for returning to rural areas are moderated in the specific context of these smaller towns, and points to the importance of detailed case-study material for interpreting census data, as well as the need to be aware that adaptations to economic decline may vary across the urban hierarchy. In Nigeria, for example, further dramatic declines in urban living standards in 1994 are reported to have encouraged Lagos residents to consider moving to second-order cities where the cost of living might be cheaper, or to return to home areas (Abiodun, personal communication, 1994). Thus reductions in the growth of large cities might in some cases be balanced by somewhat enhanced growth in some smaller centres.

Even in Zimbabwe, which experienced rapid urban growth in the 1980s (although lower than that projected), the new economic policies of the 1990s, which follow IMF prescriptions very closely, may be having a dampening effect on rural–urban migration. Research on recent migrants to Harare in 1994, for example, indicates that they almost universally perceive the impact of current economic policies to be far worse in urban than in rural areas (Potts with Mutambirwa, forthcoming).

In the light of the above discussion, it is clear that rates of rural–urban migration have often been lower than projected. In a number of settlements in various countries, it is also evident that there has actually been net out-migration. Such "return" migration has in fact been reported in a variety of sources, although it is usually in passing and rarely are any data produced to support the contention. Examples include Nigeria, where Collier (1988, p. 778) states that the relative decline in urban incomes between 1980 and 1985 led to a reversal of net migration to towns, with many return migrants *cutting short* their migrant careers (see also Mosley, 1992).

In Uganda, Jamal and Weeks (1993) accept that urban residents have migrated to rural areas as one coping strategy, despite their belief that, in general, rural–urban migration has not abated. They state that: "wage-earner households re-established their links with the countryside, reversing the labour force stabilisation process of the 1960s.... Unlike in other African countries, urban migration actually slowed down or even changed its net flow up to 1985" (Jamal and Weeks, 1993, p. 39). Urban–rural migration in Uganda is also noted by Bigsten and Kayizzi-Mugerwa (1992, p. 1425), who state that reverse migration was "quite substantial" in the 1970s and early 1980s.

For Zambia, increased rates of return migration as urban economic conditions deteriorated in the 1980s have been noted by a number of analysts (Ferguson, 1990; Purbrick, 1990; Mulenga, 1991; Macmillan, 1993; Rakodi, 1994a). Pottier (1988) had earlier signalled that rural–urban migration patterns were changing in his anthropological study *Migrants No More*. Purbrick (1990, pp. 145–146) notes that changes were already occurring in the 1970s:

[The 1980 census] indicated a significant increase of urban–rural migration. Urban–rural migrants were identified as urban-born people with links in the rural areas, dependents of rural–urban migrants and retiring or unemployed migrants. The migration of urban-born people to the rural areas was a fundamental departure from trends in the colonial period and the first years of independence. It indicated that urban distress had mounted throughout the 1970's and 1980's. Increasingly people were looking to the rural areas for a viable survival strategy ... the long-term nature of the 1970's economic decline has meant that a return to the land is the only option for many in the Copperbelt.

471

On the basis of surveys conducted on the Copperbelt in the mid-1980s, Ferguson (1990) argues that unemployed and retired urban-dwellers were increasingly adopting strategies that involved them returning to rural "homes." Records from one mine indicated that 90 per cent of ex-miners intended to return "home," even if they had never actually lived there.

Access to land is a key variable in determining the extent to which urban–rural migration can operate as a successful coping strategy. This will vary not only between countries but also between different groups of residents within any one city, because they will be drawn from or associated with regions with differing land resources and allocation processes. In addition, there may be variations in the ease of access to land according to length of stay in the city and how successfully the urban-dweller has maintained his or her links with the "home" village. Female-headed households will frequently be much less able to "return" because their access to rural land is generally far more constrained than a man's (and may be the reason why they left for town in the first place).

The significance of land tenure in affecting return migration processes is emphasized by Andrae (1992), who studied textile workers in the Nigerian towns of Kano and Kaduna. They were living with their wives and children in town, but many expected to have to go (reluctantly) to "home" rural areas if they were made redundant, where 70 per cent had access to adequate land. Andrae also emphasizes that commercialization of land would very much affect return migration. Freehold title to land is now the norm for parts of Kenya, for example, and here Andrae believes that the "high level of commercialisation of land ownership has closed this escape route for large sections of the urban working class" (1992, p. 219). The very severe land shortages that characterize the rural sector of a country such as Egypt also constrain such options for the urban poor (see chap. 4 in this volume).

Further evidence of urban–rural migration comes from Ghana and Tanzania. In Ghana, Jeffries (1992) reports that many redundant public sector employees invested in farming, because the drastic narrowing of the rural:urban income gap made cash-cropping appear more advantageous than for many years. The census data for Ghana (see above) suggest that reductions in net migration have been occurring over a considerable period for some centres. For Tanzania, work by von Troil (1992) suggests that here return migration is perhaps a phenomenon of the 1990s rather than the 1980s. In a paper that mainly focuses on the causes and effects of *rural–urban* migration in 1984/85, she indicates that by 1990, after structural adjustment had been operating for some time, there had been some changes in urban survival strategies, specifically including a return to the village. Thus the increasing gap between wages and food costs, together with improved farm prices, meant that "many of the young men who had left earlier to try their luck in towns had been persuaded to return and take up farming" (von Troil, 1992, p. 235).

In this volume, Piermay's analysis of contemporary Kinshasa (chap. 7) also considers whether that city has experienced a decrease in population, owing to the remarkable severity (even by sub-Saharan African standards) of Zaire's political and economic climate. Dubresson (chap. 8 in this volume) notes that migration to Abidjan had slowed by the end of the 1980s. Many of the migration and rural linkage strategies discussed here have apparently been adopted in that city, and in the case of Côte d'Ivoire there is some evidence that "return" migration is boosting the growth of smaller towns, at the expense of Abidjan, possibly because land is easier to obtain. Remarkably, Yousry and Aboul Atta (chap. 4 in this volume) report that, in Egypt, rural population growth rates have exceeded urban rates for the past few years, although this appears to be due to spill-over effects just beyond urban boundaries.

Significant adaptations have therefore occurred in the nature of rural–urban and urban–rural migration in Africa. These changes have often not been recognized by the World Bank or IMF or even some academic observers, although they often began before structural adjustment policies were imposed. Given that "migration and migrants are a sensitive barometer of the totality of change taking place" (Gutkind, 1974, p. 54), this has serious implications. The IMF policies towards urban areas are partly predicated on the assumption that these areas are privileged and that continued rapid growth indicates the persistence of urban bias in government policies; yet the evidence is that the supposed privileged starting point had long been eroded and that urban growth was greatly exaggerated.

It should be noted that generalizations about migration trends for the whole of Africa will rarely be valid for all countries. Factors affecting the sorts of adaptations detailed above include the severity and timing of economic decline and the nature and timing of structural adjustment. As noted by Simon in chapter 3, the impact of war and/or drought is another vital variable, because these tend to increase rural–urban migration dramatically,[16] overwhelming the negative impact of structural adjustment policies. On the other hand, the wars in Somalia and Rwanda have led to an emptying of urban centres, and it is as yet too early to know what will happen in these countries if, and when, political stability is re-established. As emphasized by Aina in chapter 12 in this volume, some countries in Africa have experienced a "simultaneous collapse of state structures and the disintegration of social order." In such circumstances the impact on urban processes is bound to be locally specific. A number of factors related to land have also been discussed above. These include the availability of rural land for migrants; the commercialization of land; and the nature of urban settlement patterns and land tenure and its implications for access to land for housing and agriculture. Of critical significance as well is the nature of government policy towards the rural sector.

Having detailed the importance of rural–urban linkages and their changing nature, this chapter now turns to consideration of strategies adopted by those who must, or choose to, stay in town.

Informal sector and second jobs

The informal sector is not a new phenomenon in African cities. Its importance for urban employment was highlighted in the 1970s (see O'Connor, 1983), and its more recent growth is detailed in this volume in chapter 10 by Rogerson (see also chap. 6 on Lagos by Abiodun). The huge number of jobs created in this sector often involve self-employment and include a wide range of activities from food vending, shoe shining, and hair braiding, to repair and maintenance services, "illegal" transport services, and small-scale metal fabrication. Because open unemployment is difficult to maintain for long periods of time in the African urban context, in the absence of any institutionalized welfare systems, the jobs developed in the informal sector, albeit usually low paid, have played a central role in accommodating rapid labour force growth.

There is no doubt that the informal sector has become even more important in the era of debt crisis and structural adjustment because of the massive and precipitate decline in formal wages and the significant absolute fall in formal sector jobs in many African cities since the 1980s (see Rogerson, chap. 10 in this volume). Large-scale redundancies have resulted largely from structural adjustment policies: in the public sector, donor conditionality often insists on contracting the civil service payroll in order to cut budget deficits, and, in the private sector, trade liberalization has made many previously protected enterprises uncompetitive, while reductions in demand (e.g. for new clothes) owing to increasing poverty have forced others to close or retrench.

Prior to the introduction of trade liberalization policies, controls on foreign exchange, imports, and prices of many domestically produced products created illegal job opportunities in parallel markets. Thousands of urban residents became involved in trading scarce goods at prices well above the official price, and this was another important coping strategy in the late 1970s and much of the 1980s (see, for example, Maliyamkono and Bagachwa, 1990, for Tanzania; and McGaffey, 1991, and Piermay, chap. 7 in this volume, for Zaire). This trade was often very lucrative, and many formal sector workers ameliorated their impossible "wages puzzle" because they had access to officially priced goods (or stole them) and sold them at the "market-determined" price. Thus, in Kampala at the end of the 1980s, the explanation for how people got enough money to survive was "each eats from his place of work," meaning illicit trade or *"magendo"* (Mutasa, 1989).

Trade liberalization and currency devaluation in many African countries have now significantly reduced the opportunities in parallel markets. However, many formal sector workers retain their jobs, even though it might seem that they would be better off concentrating on their informal sector activities. There are a number of reasons for this: keeping a foot in the door of the formal sector may be a good idea in case the economy picks up; the job may give the worker access to important, wealthier individuals; and many jobs give access to services that may be difficult to obtain "on the outside." This gives workers the opportunity to sell access to the service to others (e.g. telephones) or to use it to further a second, informal sector job (Maliyamkono and Bagachwa, 1990).

The rate of growth in the informal sector increased in the 1980s as the formal economy declined. For example, research in Dar es Salaam by Tripp in 1987/88 found that 64 per cent of surveyed informal enterprises had begun in the previous five years, compared with only 15 per cent in the five years before that (Tripp, 1988, cited in Maliyamkono and Bagachwa, 1990). A separate survey of the informal sector in Dar es Salaam and Arusha confirmed this trend: four-fifths and three-quarters, respectively, of the informal sector activities sampled had been established between 1980 and 1987 (Maliyamkono and Bagachwa, 1990).[17] Furthermore, Tripp found evidence that the low level of formal wages was increasingly driving workers out of the formal and into the informal sector (including full-time urban agriculture): only 30 per cent of respondents who had transferred between sectors had done so during the pre-crisis period of the 1970s, whereas 70 per cent had moved after 1980.

That the necessity of taking on second jobs is not confined to the poorest is also evident from Tanzania. The ratio between the take-home pay of a worker on the minimum wage and a top salary-earner fell from 1:19 in 1962 to 1:6 by 1985. Between 1980 and 1985, top-level public sector employees' earnings fell 66 per cent in real terms. By 1987 it was estimated that most senior executives in large parastatals could cover the necessary costs of maintaining their family in town for only two weeks of the month. Thus top-level "moon-lighting" became necessary. Amongst poorer urban workers the second-job syndrome was rife: a survey in 1985/86 of poor, lower-middle-income and middle-income wage-workers in Dar found that 54 per cent had secondary activities (Maliyamkono and Bagachwa, 1990). Another survey of Dar household heads in 1986/87, in which only 17 per cent of respondents were in a low-income bracket and 56 per cent were owner-occupiers, found that 72 per cent had supplementary incomes. Furthermore, half the households had more than one person working, and 70 per cent of these jobs were in the informal sector (Kulaba, 1989).

A rather different form of second-job strategy is to send a household member abroad and use their remittances as a supplement to urban incomes. El Sammani et al. (1989) have documented the increasing importance of this strategy for poor households in unplanned areas in Khartoum during the 1980s. In 1985, remittance contributions from workers who had migrated to Arab countries were vital to maintaining urban families, making up 67 per cent, 71 per cent, and 100 per cent of household budgets in three different neighbourhoods, respectively. Such remittances are also vital to an understanding of the urban economy in Somalia (Jamal and Weeks, 1993). As an *urban* strategy this option seems to be largely confined to north-eastern African countries with access to Arab job markets, including Egypt (see chap. 4 in this volume).

Growing your own food: The expansion of urban agriculture

Food looms large in the household budgets of the urban poor, and came to dominate budgets in the 1980s. Strategies for reducing the impact of food purchases on meagre cash resources involve obtaining food from sources other than the market. As already seen, rural linkages play an important part in this, but growing one's own food within the urban area (or just outside the boundary), on plots sufficiently accessible to allow the "farmer" to remain an urban resident, has played a major part in survival strategies. The scale of the operation ranges from intensive cultivation of garden plots around one's home (a common enough practice before the onset of serious economic decline), to small plots of staple food crops on undeveloped urban land or peri-urban land, to quite large-scale, formal sector enterprises on the urban periphery. Not only crops but livestock raising may be involved.

As with the informal sector, urban agriculture was part of the African urban scene before the onset of serious economic decline. The difference today is that far more households are involved, far more land is involved, and the role of the food produced is much more critical to household survival. Writing in the mid-1970s, Gutkind (1974, p. 71) commented that the urban population was dependent on food supplies from the rural areas, and "few urban Africans are able or willing to grow their food needs." Shortly after this, the situation was to change quite markedly – the remarkable expansion of urban agriculture in more recent years is documented in this volume by Rogerson (chap. 10). This section therefore focuses on identifying some factors that influence the extent to which urban agriculture can contribute to household coping strategies in the different types of cities and regions in Africa.

One factor is the density of settlement within the city. Very densely settled cities, with closely packed plots even in unplanned areas and very little open space (e.g. Cairo, some South African conurbations, the older areas of Lagos), clearly do not offer much chance for the poor to grow food. A second factor is the size of the city, especially if densely settled. In large cities, access to land on the edges of the city is more difficult for many residents because of the sheer distances involved. Piermay (chap. 7 in this volume) identifies this as a factor hindering the development of urban agriculture within Kinshasa, for instance. Thirdly, there is the issue of land tenure, both within and on the periphery of the urban area. If land is held on a freehold or leasehold basis and the land market and registration are functioning (e.g. Harare, most South African cities), then illegal farming on vacant land may receive short shrift and the farmers be driven off. A fourth factor is the attitude of city authorities and local politicians: if they are unsympathetic to the needs of the poor and unresponsive to democratic demands, then again urban agriculture may be vulnerable.

In fact, in many African towns and cities the conditions for urban agriculture are quite positive. Small, spread-out settlements with many open areas are typical of much of Africa's urban network, giving relatively easy access to cultivable land. Even many of the larger cities incorporate areas that are not densely settled, and of course, by Asian or Latin American standards, even most African capitals are still fairly small. Access to land within the city boundaries may be through traditional routes, even when there are, officially, formal and bureaucratic procedures (e.g. Kinshasa – see Mbuyi, 1989; Piermay, chap. 7, and Rakodi, chap. 11, in this volume). This may be because the official system is simply too corrupt or overloaded to function. City land may largely be under the control of one ethnic group, giving it priority and security in obtaining plots for urban agriculture. Thus a marked increase in growing food within Kampala's boundaries was particularly a Baganda phenomenon, because they had control over the land and many in-migrants found it difficult to get access to it (Jamal and Weeks, 1993). Land just outside the city boundaries, and quite easily accessible in many towns, is very often under communal tenure. Depending on the density of the rural population, it may be quite simple to obtain permission to use a plot for cultivation at low cost. As Rogerson notes in chapter 10, city planners are rarely keen on unplanned land use. However, local party officials may be far more prepared to lobby for the rights of constituents to use land for food, which greatly increases the security felt by urban farmers. This has been noted by Kulaba (1989) for urban Tanzania, where urban agriculture was encouraged by the ruling party after a 1974 nationwide drought and food shortage, and for urban Zambia when Kaunda's UNIP party was in power (Mulenga, 1991). Urban agriculture not only provides food for cultivating families but may also be a source of supplementary income when surpluses are sold. In this way this strategy contributes to the informal sector coping mechanisms already discussed.

Servicing and shelter strategies

The collapse of urban services in African cities has been thoroughly documented in Stren and White (1989), and further case-study material is provided in Touré and Fadayomi (1992). In most urban areas, particularly in anglophone countries, urban service infrastructure such as urban transport, electricity, water, and sewerage was run by parastatals. Health and education were primarily government functions. The causes of deteriorating urban services and the effects of structural adjustment policies on the service and welfare sectors have been discussed above. Here the scale of the problem will be illustrated with some selected examples, and the types of service adaptations that have emerged to fill the service "gap" discussed.

Many of the unplanned housing areas that have been built since the beginning of the 1980s will have had virtually no services of any type installed – even squatter upgrading programmes, which were quite successful in the late 1970s and early 1980s in a number of countries (e.g. Zambia, Tanzania), are too much for many governments' current austerity programmes. Thus there may be not much difference between the *service* environment of unplanned areas in Abidjan, Dakar, Kinshasa, or Dar es Salaam and that of rural villages.

In 1980 it was estimated that nearly one-half of poor urban households had no services of any kind (e.g. water, electricity, sanitation, refuse disposal) in Côte d'Ivoire's towns; and a mere 7.5 per cent had collective electricity connections (Touré et al., 1992). Water supplies in Côte d'Ivoire's urban areas are provided by a private company, SODECI. According to the World Bank (1983, cited in Stren, 1989, p. 41) this is an efficient supplier because it operates on a full cost-recovery basis and can charge low rates for smaller users, so the poor can afford water connections. Unfortunately this flies directly in the face of the evidence: between 1977 and 1983 the levels of water connections in Abidjan fell from 57 per cent to 47 per cent of the population. This was because the growing population was mainly settling in unplanned settlements, where the level of connections was, "in principle," zero. Instead, water is provided by vendors at about five times the unit price paid by those with connections. During the 1970s, as described by Dubresson in chapter 8 in this volume, there was far more state-planned low-income housing, and the state in fact subsidized water connections to homes in poorer areas. The dramatic fall-off in connections in the 1980s reflected the shortage of government funds available to continue this programme (Stren, 1989). It is evident from Abidjan that a purely cost-recovery, market approach to water supplies cannot help the urban poor.

The capital city of the Central African Republic, Bangui, has no public highway maintenance or garbage collection system at all. Most of the more recent peripheral settlements have virtually no services of any kind, and water supply and electricity networks meet only 20 per cent of demand (Faustin and Takam, 1992). Similarly the southern peripheral extensions of Kinshasa, which have housed most recent population growth, have few services and no electricity (Mbuyi, 1989). In Khartoum, conditions are even worse: many of the new squatter areas do not even have pit latrines (El Sammani et al., 1989). A 1986/87 survey of Tanzanian socio-economic and housing conditions found that in Dar es Salaam there was an average of 15 people per house, and 89 per cent of houses had unimproved pit latrines as their sole sanitation, of which 21 per cent overflowed during the rains. Only 17 per cent of the household heads of these dwelling units (which also housed large numbers of tenant families) were regarded as low income (Kulaba, 1989). The cost of lack of public transport services is also a problem for the urban poor.

The response to the shortage or absence of public or large-scale private provision of services often involves self-provision, usually on an individual but sometimes on a collective basis. In terms of shelter, many of the poor erect houses in unplanned areas and build some sort of latrine. Very often some sort of title to the land may be obtained from a local chief or local family, although its legality is sometimes questionable (Mbuyi, 1989; Tipple, 1994). Many more poor households are then housed in such dwellings as tenants – for the house-owner, who often lives on the premises, this may represent a desperately needed extra source of income. One response to the urban economic crisis has been to adapt existing housing to accommodate tenants by converting kitchens to bedrooms, or covering courtyards to provide an extra room, and adding outhouses, as, for example, in Abidjan in the 1980s (Stren, 1989). Various forms of outhouses for rental occupation on formal, planned low-income housing plots are very common in southern African countries such as Malawi, Zimbabwe, and South Africa, where they are often known as "backyard shacks" (e.g. see Beavon on Johannesburg, chap. 5 in this volume). Despite the lamentations of urban planning authorities, it is now relatively rare for people to be evicted, given the absence of any alternative. Collective political action at a local level often wards off any such threats; local MPs or councillors may find their entire constituency consists of people in unplanned housing. Thus in Dar es Salaam, or in most South African cities, the issue of removing informal settlements is usually too politically hot for administrations to contemplate. However in Harare, Zimbabwe, squatters are never allowed to remain in any one place for long, and the incidence of unplanned settlements is still very minor, involving hundreds, rather than hundreds of thousands, of people, as in most other African cities (Potts with Mutambirwa, 1991). Recent reports of evictions also come from Dakar, Senegal (Sy et al., 1992), and Khartoum, where the ability to organize politically is a key factor in preventing settlement demolition (El Sammani et al., 1989).

As indicated by the Harare example, demand for housing cannot always be met by "unplanned" solutions within the city. Strong free-hold land markets, high land prices, and high-density occupation are factors that will mitigate against such solutions. In these circumstances, alternative solutions may operate. In Cairo, for example, there has been significant "decentralization" to agricultural land outside the urban boundary. Very high land prices in the city (partly driven up by flows of remittances from temporary migrants to Middle Eastern countries – Yousry and Aboul Atta, chap. 4 in this volume) have driven many people out to become commuters. Strictly speaking it is illegal to build housing on the agriculturally valuable delta land, but the sheer demand for accommodation has overwhelmed planning controls there (El Shakhs, personal communication, 1994). According to Abiodun (chap. 6 in this volume), land scarcity within Lagos metropolis has also driven up prices there to a remarkable degree, and illegal land occupation is now limited because land development controls are being enforced.

Illegal hook-ups to electricity may be one strategy for obtaining power, but so many of the residential areas occupied by the poor have no nearby power sources that this is a much less common strategy than in Latin America or Asia. In many African cities, private minibuses and taxis have become a vital part of the transport system – for example, *matatus* in Nairobi, *dala-dalas* in Dar es Salaam (Lee-Smith, 1989; Kulaba, 1989), emergency taxis in Harare, or "Zola Budds" in South African cities. The urban authorities were very often initially reluctant to allow these facilities, but the incapacity of public provision made them necessary, as in Tanzania, where they were permitted after 1983 (Stren, 1989). However, they always cost more than the public buses and are frequently unaffordable to many of the poor. Very early starts and a long walk to work are thus the usual "strategy." The private taxis also often have a notoriously dangerous reputation because they are driven fast in order to increase narrow profit margins or driver commissions – the South African Zola Budds are so-called because of their speedy driving.

A service that it is hard for the poor to provide for themselves is water. In some areas, digging wells is possible, although rarely feasible for every house. Once an area is established, the authorities find it hard not to provide at least some standpipes. However, the adequacy of this solution varies enormously between settlements and depends on the distribution and number of standpipes in relation to the geography and population of the settlement and on the reliability of the water supply. Where there are few water points and/or they are far away, many people have to rely on private water vendors because the time and energy involved in collecting and queuing for water are not feasible. However, as previously discussed, water thus purchased is often expensive in relation to public supplies (see, for example, Stren, 1989, on water supplies in Dar es Salaam, Abidjan, and Nouakchott in Mauritania; El Sammani et al., 1989, on Khartoum; Mbuyi, 1989, on Kinshasa; Jaglin, 1994, on Ouagadougou).

Refuse collection for the poor is rarely provided. Periodic town clean-ups encouraged by government exhortations sometimes occur, as in Tanzania and Nigeria. Recycling waste is common, adding to informal income-generating activities.

For many wealthier households throughout Africa the solution to the service crisis is the private sector, and private refuse collection, septic tank emptying, electricity generators, and even, on occasions and for the rich, telecommunications are all well established (Stren, 1989; Uduku, 1994). A significant increase in the provision of private educational facilities has also occurred as government provision has deteriorated (e.g. Uduku, 1994), but the costs involved may put this option beyond the reach of the poor. Community self-help projects to provide schools are often popular, however, reflecting the great demand for education. Such community projects are very common in Khartoum, for example (El Sammani et al., 1989), and in Ouagadougou water sales at public taps enabled revolutionary committees to finance schools and dispensaries (Jaglin, 1994).

Urban people have, therefore, adopted a range of strategies to meet those service shortages that have the highest priorities. However, it must be said that these are rarely very satisfactory; in particular, many of the practices have negative health implications. Poor sanitation is a major issue (Potts, 1994); expensive and distant water discourages water consumption, with negative hygiene implications; walking to work may adversely affect already undernourished workers; and unregulated transport is often dangerous, as are illegal electricity connections.

Gender issues: The increasing burden on women's time and energy

Many of the problems faced by the urban poor and the strategies discussed above imply significant extra burdens, in terms of people working both harder and for longer hours. The burden of extra work is usually unevenly distributed amongst household members, and the impact on women has often been even more serious than it has been on men. The expansion of informal sector activities has tended to involve more women than men. If a woman was not working for cash before, then she usually worked full time on domestic duties. Thus new income-generating work is in addition to those duties, which have always involved looking after household reproduction – obtaining food and water, cooking, cleaning, washing clothes, and looking after children, the elderly, and the sick. When parallel markets are at their most active, even obtaining food can be virtually a full-time job. The problems of obtaining water have clearly worsened for many households; again, any extra time or energy expended will usually be a woman's. Even where food is now more available, the huge increase in prices means that it is women whose ingenuity is stretched and who bear most of the stress of trying to feed their families adequately. Many cannot succeed, and evidence worldwide shows that in these circumstances it is usually women rather than men who forgo food in order to feed their children. If household budgets preclude or discourage visits to clinics, then any extra burden of caring for the sick falls on women. Thus, even without having to take on extra cash-earning activities, the impact of economic decline and Structural Adjustment Programmes on women would have been very serious. This is the context in which so many have had to take on informal sector work. In addition, urban agriculture is often (although not always, especially if livestock are involved) largely a woman's responsibility.

In Dar es Salaam in the late 1980s, Tripp (1990) found that 66 per cent of women were in self-employment, and 78 per cent had begun these jobs in the previous five years. By comparison, O'Connor (1983, table 11) cites data for Dar that showed only 23 per cent of women self-employed in 1967. In Gweru, a secondary town in Zimbabwe, Rakodi (1994b) reports a significant increase in the involvement of women in informal sector jobs between 1991 and 1993, with 63 per cent of surveyed adult women earning by 1993. In Harare, Kanji and Jazdowska (1993) have also documented the greater burdens of structural adjustment in Zimbabwe for women than for men and state that almost all their women respondents felt that the burden was unequally distributed, mainly because of their primary concern for household consumption and welfare.

A much vaunted "solution" to many of the problems facing the urban poor is that community self-help projects should be encouraged, in order to "empower" people and improve their environment. Undoubtedly these projects are usually very valuable, and may indeed be the best short-term means of overcoming acute service problems, but they often assume that women have spare time. It is quite likely in fact that such activities impose an extra, and damaging, drain on women's time (see Muthwa, 1994, for a discussion of these issues for women in Soweto, Johannesburg).

Children also suffer: in some cases they have to be withdrawn from school, and many are involved in informal sector activities themselves. They are particularly vulnerable if diets are inadequate; the most vulnerable are those who need weaning foods, and the time involved in preparing these may mean that women use less suitable preparations, with serious health consequences for their children. This has been noted in urban Zambia, for example (Jespersen, 1990).

Conclusion

This chapter has focused on the nature of contemporary life for residents in African urban centres. Policy and management aspects of recent urbanization have been briefly discussed where they provide the necessary context for understanding why people's lifestyles have changed. It has been shown that drastic falls in urban incomes, which frequently pre-dated structural adjustment policies but have been further exacerbated by them, are the main reason residents are adopting and adapting new strategies to cope with the challenges of urban living. The deterioration of existing infrastructure plus the lack of new services in more recently developed parts of the cities add to the challenges facing the urban poor. Quite often, even the wealthier sections of the population have been adversely affected, although their options tend to be greater and their coping strategies less "survivalist" in orientation.

It is clear that residents have suffered greatly as national and urban economic conditions have declined. The urban sector has been a particular target for reduced expenditure under the policies favoured by the international financial institutions. In some countries, the impact on the urban areas could have been famine had the urban population not found new sources of income and food outside the formal sector economy. Although their survival is a testament to the ingenuity and determination of urban residents, it must be noted that many of the "strategies" that have been discussed in this chapter are not without serious costs and drawbacks for those involved. The time and energy implications of engaging in secondary, usually informal sector, jobs can be very serious. Where family members are forced into the job market for the first time, this may often be at the expense of other vital activities such as education and child care. In addition, people are frequently working harder in the context of a qualitative and/or quantitative decline in their food consumption. Many of the strategies adopted can bring residents into conflict with the authorities, although the sheer scale of the problems facing the administration often means that it is unable to do much to prevent the people's "solutions." However, even ad hoc harassment and threats create a climate of insecurity that adds to the burdens of the poor.

The crisis has not only generated changes in the way people conduct their lives within the city. As has been shown, an important element of urban adaptations relates to the urbanization process itself – and there is increasingly widespread evidence of reductions in urban growth rates, reflecting falling rates of net in-migration from rural areas. These result from some combination of fewer people moving to town in the first place (mainly, it is argued here, because the rural:urban income gap has narrowed in many countries) and an enhanced rate of return migration from urban areas to villages. Although return migration has always been important, the recent evidence suggests that, in some countries at least, migrants are shortening their period of residence in urban areas below the norms established in the 1960s and 1970s. Both of these migration processes accord with theories that ascribe economic rationality to migrants. A variety of other rural–urban linkages have also adapted to the new economic circumstances of Africa's urban centres, including increased rural–urban resource transfers.

Generalizing about urban life and responses to urban economic decline for the whole of Africa is, of course, very difficult. There will always be countries, or specific cities or towns, that have quite different experiences from the broad trends identified in this chapter. Of great significance to the nature of the urban challenge in any one country is its general economic performance in the past 20 years and its room for manoeuvre *vis-à-vis* the international financial institutions and their policy formulations. Thus countries at both the southern and northern tips of the continent have so far avoided the extreme reductions in urban incomes and services that have characterized many tropical sub-Saharan countries. This means not only that their urban populations have had less need to adopt drastic strategies but also that there are fewer changes in the broad trends of urbanization in these countries. Thus there can be no doubt that rapid rural–urban migration has been the norm in South Africa during the 1980s and 1990s as political circumstances changed, the crisis in the African rural economy deepened, and influx controls were finally removed. Countries with particularly favourable resource endowments, such as Gabon, are also unlikely to mirror the urban trends of more economically vulnerable sub-Saharan African states. Shock factors such as drought and war can also overwhelm other economic processes. In some cases these may increase urban growth rates and hinder rural–urban linkages, although many of the internal urban strategies such as informal housing, informal jobs, and urban agriculture may be highly developed in such circumstances.

A further issue is the lack of reliable data on urban populations and mobility patterns in most African countries. Although it is contended here that a tendency to rely on outdated projections has created a misleading picture of recent trends in urbanization for many African countries, it must be conceded that for many countries it is not possible to ascertain whether, or to what extent, migration patterns and urbanization processes have adapted in the ways suggested here. For this reason, case-study material plays an important part in building up a picture of the urban experience for many African countries.

There are also important variations in the extent to which certain adaptations can be efficacious in reducing the adverse impacts of declining urban incomes for different subgroups of the urban population. There are obvious differences between the strategies suited to the poor compared with the wealthy. There are also important gender variations. Important variables affecting rural–urban linkages, and in particular the ability to "escape" the city and return "home," are land availability and the nature of land tenure. Many people in African cities have no viable access to rural land, and thus this option is not open to them. They include many female-headed households and longstanding international migrants (e.g. Malawians and Mozambicans in Zimbabwean urban areas). Such groups might be categorized as being "trapped" in urban areas and may experience absolute destitution. The fact that a host of adaptations has occurred in African urban areas to meet the challenges of economic decline should not, therefore, be allowed to hide the fact that new policies and directions are desperately needed to alleviate the real suffering that many of the urban poor are experiencing.

Notes

1. One of the usual recommendations of structural adjustment is for governments to increase prices for crops and to liberalize marketing arrangements. However, analysis of specific country experiences shows that often seemingly significant price rises are rapidly eroded by inflation, so that farmers' gains in real terms are short lived. This, for example, was true of Malawian maize prices in the 1980s. Furthermore, the ending of farmers' subsidies (particularly on fertilizer) may negate crop price rises, and liberalization of agricultural trade has often not helped farmers, because the capacity of private traders to fill the technical, transport, and capital investment gaps left by marketing boards has often been grossly overestimated. Thus arrangements for marketing the 1993/94 maize crop in Zambia were chaotic, and disastrous for the farmers.
2. The term "the *new* African urban poor" was used for a series of workshops held at the School of Oriental and African Studies, University of London, in the late 1980s, which focused on the emergence of a new stratum of poor in African cities faced with the effects of national economic decline and Structural Adjustment Programmes.
3. These surrogates are not ideal as measurements of the income gap perceived by potential rural–urban migrants. For example, migrants are frequently young people, perhaps single or recently married with a young child, and they are unlikely to command the average rural household income at this stage in their domestic life cycle. Furthermore, urban households are usually smaller than rural households, which increases the per capita urban household income *ceteris paribus*. Also, using urban average or minimum wages as the income for the whole household assumes that multi-member migrant households expect only one member to earn any income, which is unrealistic in contemporary Africa.
4. These estimates, reported by Mtatifikolo (1992), are based on ILO and Ministry of Agriculture reports. This author also cites an ILO report (ILO, 1982) that estimated that real farm incomes in Tanzania had increased by 8.5 per cent between 1969 and 1980, whereas average wages had fallen 47.6 per cent over the same period, and that average farm incomes already exceeded the minimum wage by 20 per cent in 1980, two years earlier than Jamal and Weeks' estimate of the same gap.
5. To be designated poor meant to have less than 86 maloti (about US$40) per "consumption unit" and to lack selected assets. In Lesotho an important factor in this differential between urban and rural areas was that rural households were twice as likely as those in Maseru (the capital and only large urban centre) to have at least one migrant worker working in South Africa. Remittances from migrants are crucial to the Lesotho economy at both the national and household level.
6. The benefit of this factor of course varies hugely between African countries; in some, such as Tanzania, Zambia, or Ghana, many rural households can be largely food self-sufficient (barring drought), whereas in others, such as Malawi, Lesotho, and South Africa, land shortages mean that many rural households must purchase large proportions of their annual food requirements.
7. Some semi-processed foods may be more nutritious than finely processed (e.g. maize) – but some staples do require lengthy cooking and/or processing to be really palatable, a very important issue for the nutrition of small children in particular.

8. Although AIDS-related deaths will have made some contribution to the deteriorating urban health situation in Zambia, there can be no doubt that urban poverty was a major factor. The harshness of the impact of structural adjustment policies on urban Zambia could be ameliorated if international financial institutions were less greedy. As noted by the *Financial Times* (1994, p. 11), donors refuse to "address an anomaly in Zambia's external debt obligations which require a country following economic reform to the letter to maintain a net outflow to the International Monetary Fund of $100m a year."

9. It is worth pointing out that Ghana is supposed to be an important success story for the IMF, and by 1990 it had followed its economic reform programme closely for some years. Yet, as Jeffries (1992, p. 207) says, "it is ... clear, however, the majority of urban inhabitants in the lower income groups have experienced very little, if any, improvement in their real incomes, and that some – it is unclear how many – are probably worse off than they were six or seven years ago."

10. A "strategy" implies some alteration in an individual's or household's (usually economic) behaviour, in order to lessen the adverse impact of, for example, declining incomes or deteriorating infrastructure or services. A strategy may be a long-term planned response to circumstances (e.g. embarking upon urban agriculture) that yields generally positive benefits. However, many strategies may be more "survivalist" and ad hoc, with more negative connotations for the household. Examples would include not obtaining medical help because of the cost, or cutting down on food consumption.

11. With reference to Kinshasa's rapid growth in the 1960s and into the 1970s while formal employment rates fell, Piermay (chap. 7 in this volume) has argued that this indicates a "clear de-linking" of the relation between economic growth and population growth. However this conclusion is not really supportable; and his own analysis demonstrates that at that time Kinshasa's economic and infrastructural development was sufficiently positive, relative to most of the rest of the country, to account for rapid net in-migration.

12. An example of the significance of urban–rural migration is found in chapter 8 in this volume on Abidjan, by Dubresson. In-migration to Abidjan in 1978/79 totalled 272,000 but net in-migration was only 26 per cent of that figure (i.e. 80,000), because 192,000 people also left the town in that year.

13. The term "family" includes people related to each other. In this context it primarily concerns conjugal family units, i.e. husband and wife and their children. Very often, co-residing family units in Africa will include other relatives (e.g. grandparents, grandchildren), but it is the redressing of the most socially disruptive aspect of colonial migration patterns (the division of spouses and of men from their children) that is of particular significance in the post-independence period. The term "household" is often defined as a group of co-residing people who habitually eat together. In the context of urban households with strong rural links, this is not really satisfactory, because some members may spend significant amounts of time in rural areas (e.g. cultivating or in rural schools). Such households may have a considerably more fluid composition than the classic definition – and membership would require consideration of where they spend most of the year and of their own perceptions of their primary household affiliation.

14. Higher rates of natural increase in urban compared with rural areas are, however, reported for Côte d'Ivoire for 1978/79 (3.7 per cent compared with 3.1 per cent; Touré et al., 1992), the Congo (Mokima et al., 1992), the Central African Republic (Faustin and Takam, 1992), and Kinshasa, where not only birth rates but also *fertility* exceed the rural rates (Piermay, chap. 7 in this volume).

15. In a number of cases, for example Mbeya and Mwanza, where the reported 1967–1978 growth rates for individual towns are particularly high, the growth was partly due to boundary changes that incorporated large numbers of rural people. I am indebted to Tony O'Connor for this information. In addition, for most of the smaller centres, it is not possible to make meaningful comparisons between the population in 1978 and 1988 "as a result of

irregularities in defining urban, rural and mixed categories for the ... censuses" (Holm, 1992, p. 240).

16. Examples include Angola, Mozambique (wars), Mauritania (drought), and the Sudan (war and drought). See also Piermay (chap. 7 in this volume) for the impact of the 1960–1965 civil war in Zaire on urbanization there.

17. Surveys of this kind are likely to find more recently opened enterprises, given that some begun in previous periods will have closed down by the time of the survey. However, even if this is taken into account, it is obvious that the urban informal sector expanded more rapidly in the 1980s.

References

Adepoju, A., ed. 1993. *The Impact of Structural Adjustment on the Population of Africa: Implications for Education, Health and Employment.* James Currey in association with United Nations Population Fund, London.

Amis, P. 1989. African development and urban change: What policy makers need to know. *Development Policy Review* 7: 375–391.

Amis, P. and P. Lloyd, eds. 1990. *Housing Africa's Urban Poor.* Manchester University Press, Manchester.

Amis, P. and C. Rakodi. 1994. Urban poverty: Issues for research and policy. *Journal of International Development* 6(5): 627–634.

Andrae, G. 1992. Urban workers as farmers: Agro-links of Nigerian textile workers in the crisis of the 1980s. In: J. Baker and P. O. Pedersen, eds., *The Rural–Urban Interface in Africa: Expansion and Adaptation.* Seminar Proceedings No. 27, Scandinavian Institute of African Studies, Uppsala.

Andreasen, J. 1990. Urban–rural linkages and their impact on urban housing in Kenya. In: J. Baker, ed., *Small Town Africa: Studies in Rural–Urban Interaction.* Seminar Proceedings No. 23, Scandinavian Institute of African Studies, Uppsala.

Barke, M. and C. Sowden. 1992. Population change in Tanzania 1978–88: A preliminary analysis. *Scottish Geographical Magazine* 108(1): 9–16.

Bates, R. 1981. *Markets and States in Tropical Africa: The Political Basis of Agricultural Policies.* University of California Press, Berkeley.

Bibangambah, J. 1992. Macro-level constraints and the growth of the informal sector in Uganda. In: J. Baker and P. O. Pedersen, eds., *The Rural–Urban Interface in Africa: Expansion and Adaptation.* Seminar Proceedings No. 27, Scandinavian Institute of African Studies, Uppsala.

Bigsten, A. and S. Kayizzi-Mugerwa. 1992. Adaption and distress in the urban economy: A study of Kampala households. *World Development* 20(10): 1423–1441.

Caldwell, J. 1969. *African Rural–Urban Migration: The Movement to Ghana's Towns.* C. Hurst, London.

Chilowa, W. and G. Roe. 1990. Expenditure patterns and nutritional status of low income urban households in Malawi. In: G. Roe, ed., *Workshop on the Effects of the Structural Adjustment Programme in Malawi. Volume 2: Papers Presented.* Centre for Social Research, University of Malawi, Zomba.

Clarke, J. and C. Allison. 1989. *Zambia: Debt and Poverty.* Oxfam, Oxford.

Collier, P. 1988. Oil shocks and food security in Nigeria. *International Labour Review* 127(6): 761–782.

Denoeux, G. 1993. *Urban Unrest in the Middle East: A Comparative Study of Informal Networks in Egypt, Iran and Lebanon.* State University of New York Press, Albany, NY.

Donge, Jan Kees van. 1990. Waluguru traders in Dar es Salaam: An analysis of social construction of economic life. Paper presented to the People in African Cities panel, African Studies Association Conference, Birmingham.

Drakakis-Smith, D., T. Bowyer-Bower, and D. Tevera. 1995. Urban poverty and urban agriculture in Harare: An overview of the linkages. *Habitat International* 19(2): 183–193.

El Sammani, M. O., M. O. El Hadi Abu Sin, M. Talha, B. M. El Hassan, and I. Haywood. 1989. Management problems of Greater Khartoum. In: R. E. Stren and R. R. White, eds., *African Cities in Crisis: Managing Rapid Urban Growth.* Westview Press, Boulder, Colo.

Epstein, A. L. 1958. *Politics in an African Urban Community.* Manchester University Press, Manchester.

——— 1961. The network of urban social organization. *Rhodes–Livingstone Journal* 29: 29–62.

——— 1967. Urbanization and social change in Africa. *Current Anthropology* 8: 275–295.

Faustin, M. and M. Takam. 1992. Interactions between development policies and population dynamics in a landlocked country: The Central African Republic. In: M. Touré and T. O. Fadayomi, eds., *Migrations, Development and Urbanization Policies in Sub-Saharan Africa.* CODESRIA, Dakar.

Ferguson, J. 1990. Mobile workers, modernist narratives: A critique of the historiography of transition on the Zambian Copperbelt. *Journal of Southern African Studies* 16(3): 385–412 (Part I) and 16(4): 603–621 (Part II).

——— 1994. Modernist narratives, conventional wisdoms, and colonial liberalism: Reply to a straw man. *Journal of Southern African Studies* 20(4): 633–640.

Financial Times. 1994. *Financial Times Survey: Zambia.* London, 24 October.

Gefu, J. O. 1992. Part-time farming as an urban survival strategy: A Nigerian case study. In: J. Baker and P. O. Pedersen, eds., *The Rural–Urban Interface in Africa: Expansion and Adaptation.* Seminar Proceedings No. 27, Scandinavian Institute of African Studies, Uppsala.

Gilbert, A. 1992. Third world cities: Housing, infrastructure and servicing. *Urban Studies* 29: 435–460.

——— 1993. Third world cities: The changing national settlement system. *Urban Studies* 30(4/5): 721–740.

——— 1994. Third world cities: Poverty, employment, gender roles and the environment during a time of restructuring. *Urban Studies* 31(4/5): 605–633.

Gluckman, M. 1960. Tribalism in modern British Central Africa. *Cahiers d'Etudes Africaines* 1: 55–70.

——— 1961. Anthropological problems arising from the African industrial revolution. In: A. W. Southall, ed., *Social Change in Modern Africa.* Oxford University Press, London.

Gugler, J. 1969. On the theory of rural–urban migration: The case of sub-Saharan Africa. In: J. A. Jackson, ed., *Migration.* Cambridge University Press, Cambridge.

―――― 1971. Life in a dual system: Eastern Nigerians in town. *Cahiers d'Etudes Africaines* 11: 400–421.

―――― 1991. Life in a dual system revisited: Urban rural ties in Enugu, Nigeria, 1961–87. *World Development* 19: 399–409.

Gugler, J. and W. Flanagan. 1978. *Urbanization and Social Change in West Africa.* Cambridge University Press, Cambridge.

Gutkind, P. C. 1974. *Urban Anthropology: Perspectives on Third World Urbanization and Urbanism.* Van Gorcum, Assen.

Holm, M. 1992. Survival strategies of migrants to Makambako – An intermediate town in Tanzania. In: J. Baker and P. O. Pedersen, eds., *The Rural–Urban Interface in Africa: Expansion and Adaptation.* Seminar Proceedings No. 27, Scandinavian Institute of African Studies, Uppsala.

ILO (International Labour Organization). 1982. *Basic Needs in Danger: A Basic Needs Oriented Development Strategy for Tanzania.* JASPA/ILO, Addis Ababa.

Jaglin, S. 1994. Why mobilize town dwellers? Joint management in Ouagadougou (1983–1990). *Environment and Urbanization* 6(2): 111–132.

Jamal, V. and J. Weeks. 1993. *Africa Misunderstood: Or Whatever Happened to the Rural–Urban Gap?* Macmillan, London.

Jeffries, R. 1992. Urban popular attitudes towards the economic recovery programme and the PDNC government in Ghana. *African Affairs* 91: 207–226.

Jespersen, E. 1990. Household responses to the impact of the economic crisis on social services. In: G. Roe, ed., *Workshop on the Effects of the Structural Adjustment Programme in Malawi. Volume 2: Papers Presented.* Centre for Social Research, University of Malawi, Zomba.

Kanji, N. 1993. Gender and structural adjustment policies: A case study of Harare, Zimbabwe. Unpublished Ph.D. thesis, University of London.

Kanji, N. and N. Jazdowska. 1993. Structural adjustment and the implications for low-income urban women in Zimbabwe. *Review of African Political Economy* 56: 11–26.

Kulaba, S. 1989. Local government and the management of urban services in Tanzania. In: R. E. Stren and R. R. White, eds., *African Cities in Crisis: Managing Rapid Urban Growth.* Westview Press, Boulder, Colo.

Lee-Smith, D. 1989. Urban management in Nairobi: A case study of the *matatu* mode of public transport. In: R. E. Stren and R. R. White, eds., *African Cities in Crisis: Managing Rapid Urban Growth.* Westview Press, Boulder, Colo.

Mabin, A. 1990. Limits of urban transition models in understanding South African urbanization. *Development Southern Africa* 7(3): 311–322.

McGaffey, J. 1991. *The Real Economy of Zaire: The Contribution of Smuggling and Other Unofficial Activities to National Wealth.* James Currey, London.

Macmillan, H. 1993. The historiography of transition on the Zambian Copperbelt – Another view. *Journal of Southern African Studies* 19(4): 681–712.

Maliyamkono, T. and M. Bagachwa. 1990. *The Second Economy of Tanzania.* James Currey, London.

Mayer, P. 1961. *Townsmen or Tribesmen: Conservatism and the Process of Urbanization in a South African City.* Oxford University Press, Cape Town.

―――― 1962. Migrancy and the study of Africans in town. *American Anthropologist* 64: 576–592.

———— 1964. Labour migrancy and the social network. In: J. F. Holleman et al., eds., *Problems of Transition.* Natal University Press, Durban.

Mbiba, B. 1994. Institutional responses to uncontrolled urban cultivation in Harare: Prohibitive or accommodative? *Environment and Urbanization* 6(1): 188–202.

Mbuyi, K. 1989. Kinshasa: Problems of land management, infrastructure and food supply. In: R. E. Stren and R. R. White, eds., *African Cities in Crisis: Managing Rapid Urban Growth.* Westview Press, Boulder, Colo.

Mitchell, J. C. 1959. Labour migration in Africa south of the Sahara: The cause of labour migration. *Bulletin of the Inter-African Labour Institute* 6: 12–46.

———— 1966. Theoretical orientations in African urban studies: Methodological approaches. In: M. Banton, ed., *The Social Anthropology of Complex Societies.* Tavistock, London.

———— 1987. *Cities, Society and Social Perception: A Central African Perspective.* Clarendon Press, Oxford.

Mlozi, M. et al. 1992. Urban agriculture as a survival strategy in Tanzania. In: J. Baker and P. O. Pedersen, eds., *The Rural–Urban Interface in Africa: Expansion and Adaptation.* Seminar Proceedings No. 27, Scandinavian Institute of African Studies, Uppsala.

Mokima, J., C. Mayoukou, and M. N. Dinga. 1992. Effects of development policies in a sparsely populated country: The Congo. In: M. Touré and T. O. Fadayomi, eds., *Migrations, Development and Urbanization Policies in Sub-Saharan Africa.* CODESRIA, Dakar.

Moller, V. 1973. Some aspects of mobility patterns of urban Africans in Salisbury. *Proceedings of Rhodesian Geographical Association* 7: 22–32.

Mosley, P. 1992. Nigeria's economy and structural adjustment. *African Affairs* 91(361): 227–240.

Mtatifikolo, F. P. 1992. Population dynamics and socioeconomic development in Tanzania. In: M. Touré and T. O. Fadayomi, eds., *Migrations, Development and Urbanization Policies in Sub-Saharan Africa.* CODESRIA, Dakar.

Mulenga, M. 1991. Peri-urban farming: A study of the agriculture under pressure of urban growth in Lusaka, Zambia. Unpublished Ph.D. thesis, King's College, London.

Mutasa, A. 1989. And they survive: "Each eats from one's place of work." *Africa Events* May: 11.

Muthwa, S. W. 1994. Female household headship and household survival in Soweto. *Journal of Gender Studies* 3(2): 165–175.

Nelson, N. 1987. Rural–urban child fostering in Kenya. In: J. Eades, ed., *Migrants, Workers and the Social Order.* Tavistock, London.

Niblock, T. 1993. International and domestic factors in the economic liberalization process in Arab countries. In: T. Niblock and E. Murphy, eds., *Economic and Political Liberalization in the Middle East.* British Academic Press, London.

Observer. 1994. Survival of the blitzed in hidden African Dresden. London, 13 November.

O'Connor, A. M. 1983. *The African City.* London, Hutchinson.

Peil, M. 1991. *Lagos: The City Is the People.* G. K. Hall, London.

Pottier, J. 1988. *Migrants No More: Settlement and Survival in Mambwe Villages, Zambia.* Manchester University Press, Manchester.

Potts, D. 1994. Urban environmental controls and low-income housing in southern

Africa. In: H. Main, ed., *Environment and Housing in Third World Cities.* Belhaven Press, London.

—— 1995. Shall we go home? Increasing urban poverty in African cities and migration processes. *Geographical Journal* 161(3): 245–264.

Potts, D. and C. C. Mutambirwa. 1990. Rural–urban linkages in contemporary Harare: Why migrants need their land. *Journal of Southern African Studies* 16(4): 676–698.

Potts, D. with C. C. Mutambirwa. 1991. Low-income housing in Harare: Overcrowding and commodification. *Third World Planning Review* 13(1): 1–26.

—— Forthcoming. "Basics are now a luxury": Perceptions of ESAP's impact on rural and urban areas in Zimbabwe. *African Affairs.*

Purbrick, C. R. 1990. Migrant labour in Zambia: Understanding the rural–urban and regional divides. Unpublished M.Phil. thesis, University of Liverpool.

Rakodi, C. 1994a. Zambia. In: J. Tarver, ed., *Urbanization in Africa: A Handbook.* Greenwood Press, Westport, Conn.

—— 1994b. Urban poverty in Zimbabwe: Post-independence efforts, household strategies and the short-term impact of structural adjustment. *Journal of International Development* 6(5): 655–663.

Riley, S. 1988. Structural adjustment and the new urban poor: The case of Freetown. Paper presented at the Workshop on the New Urban Poor in Africa, School of Oriental and African Studies, London.

Roe, G. and W. Chilowa 1990. A profile of low income urban households in Malawi: Results from a baseline survey. In: G. Roe, ed., *Workshop on the Effects of the Structural Adjustment Programme in Malawi. Volume 2: Papers Presented.* Centre for Social Research, University of Malawi, Zomba.

Sanyal, B. 1985. Urban agriculture: Who cultivates and why? A case study of Lusaka, Zambia. *Food and Nutrition Bulletin* 7(3): 234–242.

Seddon, D. 1989. Popular protest and political opposition in Tunisia, Morocco and Sudan 1984–85. In: K. Brown et al., eds., *Urban Crises and Social Movements in the Middle East.* Editions L'Harmattan, Paris.

—— 1993. Austerity protests in response to economic liberalization in the Middle East. In: T. Niblock and E. Murphy, eds., *Economic and Political Liberalization in the Middle East.* British Academic Press, London.

Sembajwe, I. and T. Makatsjane. 1992. Migration and rural crisis in a labour reserve economy: Lesotho. In: M. Touré and T. O. Fadayomi, eds., *Migrations, Development and Urbanization Policies in Sub-Saharan Africa.* CODESRIA, Dakar.

Southall, A. 1961. Introductory summary. In: A. Southall, ed., *Social Change in Modern Africa.* Oxford University Press, London.

—— 1966. The concept of elites and their formation in Uganda. In: P. C. Lloyd, ed., *The New Elites of Tropical Africa.* Oxford University Press, London.

Stopforth, P. 1972. *Two Aspects of Social Change: Highfield African Township, Salisbury.* Occasional Paper No. 7, Department of Sociology, University of Rhodesia, Salisbury.

—— 1977. Local impediments to social change among urban Africans. *Zambezia* 5(1): 31–40.

Stren, R. E. 1989. The administration of urban services. In: R. E. Stren and R. R. White, eds., *African Cities in Crisis: Managing Rapid Urban Growth.* Westview Press, Boulder, Colo.

———— 1990. Urban housing in Africa: The changing role of government policy. In: P. Amis and P. Lloyd, eds., *Housing Africa's Urban Poor*. Manchester University Press, Manchester.

Stren, R. E. and R. R. White, eds., 1989. *African Cities in Crisis: Managing Rapid Urban Growth*. Westview Press, Boulder, Colo.

Sy, M., A. Ba, and N. Ndlaye. 1992. Demographic implications of development policies in the Sahel: The case of Senegal. In: M. Touré and T. O. Fadayomi, eds., *Migrations, Development and Urbanization Policies in Sub-Saharan Africa*. CODESRIA, Dakar.

Tipple, A. 1994. The need for new urban housing in sub-Saharan Africa: Problem or opportunity. *African Affairs* 93(373): 587–608.

Todaro, M. P. 1969. A model of labor migration and urban unemployment in less developed countries. *American Economic Review* 59: 138–148.

———— 1971. Income expectations, rural–urban migration and employment in Africa. *International Labour Review* 104: 387–413.

Touré, M. and T. O. Fadayomi, eds. 1992. *Migrations, Development and Urbanization Policies in Sub-Saharan Africa*. CODESRIA, Dakar.

Touré, M., S. Ouattara, and E. Annan-Yao. 1992. Population dynamics and development strategies in the Ivory Coast. In: M. Touré and T. O. Fadayomi, eds., *Migrations, Development and Urbanization Policies in Sub-Saharan Africa*. CODESRIA, Dakar, pp. 7–50.

Tripp, A. M. 1988. Defending the right to subsist: The state vs. the urban informal economy in Tanzania. Paper presented to the African Studies Asssociation Annual Meeting, 28–31 October, Chicago.

———— 1989. Women and the changing urban household economy in Tanzania. *Journal of Modern African Studies* 27(4): 234–256.

———— 1990. The informal economy, labour and the state in Tanzania. *Comparative Politics* 22(3): 253–264.

Troil, M. von. 1992. Looking for a better life in town: The case of Tanzania. In: J. Baker and P. O. Pedersen, eds., *The Rural–Urban Interface in Africa: Expansion and Adaptation*. Seminar Proceedings No. 27, Scandinavian Institute of African Studies, Uppsala.

Uduku, N. O. 1994. Promoting community based approaches to social infrastructure provision in urban areas in Nigeria. *Environment and Urbanization* 6(2): 57–78.

World Bank. 1981. *Accelerated Development in Sub-Saharan Africa: An Agenda for Action*. World Bank, Washington D.C.

———— 1983. *World Development Report*. Oxford University Press, New York.

Zaytoun, M. 1991. Earnings and the cost of living: An analysis of recent developments in the Egyptian economy. In: H. Handoussa and G. Potter, eds., *Employment and Structural Adjustment in Egypt in the 1990s*. The American University in Cairo Press, Cairo.

Part IV
Rising to the challenge

14

Towards appropriate urban development policy in emerging mega-cities in Africa

Salah El-Shakhs

Abstract

Si l'avenir des grandes villes africaines est incertain, il est sûr qu'elles vont continuer d'occuper une place dominante dans la hiérarchie nationale des établissements humains et que la croissance démographique va se poursuivre, même si elle ne se maintiendra probablement pas au même niveau que par le passé ni à celui actuellement prévu. Les principales questions qui se posent en termes de développement et de gouvernement sont notamment la surcharge des services, les problèmes socio-économiques, la détérioration de l'environnement, la demande sans cesse croissante de terres, d'infrastructures et de logements, les faiblesses de l'administration et les insuffisances de la planification. Les tentatives de surmonter les problèmes des grandes concentrations en décentralisant des industries ou au moyen d'initiatives communautaires financées par les pouvoirs publics n'ont réussi que très partiellement. D'autres initiatives ont mieux abouti, notamment les mesures de planification et de gestion des métropoles, le soutien aux autorités locales autonomes, le programme d'urbanisation durable des agences internationales, les partenariats entre collectivités locales et les organisations non-gouvernementales, les initiatives d'aménagement de quartiers et autres actions écologiques locales. Il faudrait trouver à l'avenir des réponses plus souples, fondées sur la participation, co-ordonnées et dépendant le moins possible de la capacité du secteur public, en déléguant suffisamment de pouvoir aux administrations locales et en favorisant la croissance urbaine le long de couloirs d'interaction intense, comme au sein des mégapoles, en freinant l'expansion horizontale contiguë de la ville, en articulant sa structure spatiale interne et en restructurant les aménagements périphériques. Planification et administration devraient donc être réorganisées pour assurer la coordination au niveau des régions en même temps que seraient consolidées l'autonomie, l'initiative et l'identité locales hors du centre ville.

Introduction

This chapter considers the future of major metropolitan areas in Africa (large or mega-cities) and discusses policies and planning strategies appropriate for facing the challenges of their urban growth and development. Depending on the definitions and boundaries being used, three or four of the six principal African metropolitan areas being dealt with in this book (Cairo, Lagos, the Johannesburg metropolitan region, and Kinshasa) are or will be bona fide mega-cities according to the UN population criterion by the year 2010. The other two (Abidjan and Nairobi), though smaller, are principal cities in their systems, exhibit the same enormity of development issues, and are important players in the world system.

Concerns about the future of these large or mega-cities in Africa are unique in many respects. First, perhaps with the exception of Cairo (which, as shown by Yousry and Aboul Atta in chap. 4 in this volume, dates back to the seventh century and arguably even before), these cities are generally young and represent new frontiers of urban development in their systems. Secondly, they are expected to grow rapidly for some time to come. They are in the midst of urbanization processes that are in their early stages and have a long way to go. After all, Africa is one of the fastest-growing regions in the world in terms of both total population and urbanization. Africa's urban population has been projected to increase by over 200 million (or to more than double) between 1980 and 2000 (Rondinelli, 1988). Thirdly, they embody the major tribal, ethnic, and regional diversities that characterize their political systems. Finally, they emerged under world colonialism and settler regimes, exhibit common experiences in political and civil development, and share burdens and hopes that are inex-

498

tricably linked to Africa's unique position within the world economic and political system.

Having said that, however, it would be a gross mistake to assume that these cities are not historically, culturally, and developmentally unique, as has been made abundantly clear in the previous chapters. For example, Cairo owes its origin to the Arabs and continues to be a major player in the Middle East; Lagos has recently lost the function of national administrative capital; Johannesburg is just beginning the transition from apartheid; Nairobi and Abidjan are home to major UN institutions; and Kinshasa is still reeling from the effects of major civil conflicts. My discussion, therefore, while dealing with general patterns, processes, and policy directions, will necessarily leave out many city-specific issues and recommendations, some of which are mentioned in the city chapters. The fact that these could not be dealt with in this general discussion, however, does not make them any less important.

The future of mega-cities

The thought that some mega-cities might be expected to grow, according to current UN projections (UN, 1993), to well over 22 million by 2010 has become a nightmare for both policy makers and planners. In absolute numbers, the large cities of the less developed countries (LDCs) are expected to house a population, by the year 2000, that is roughly equivalent to the LDCs' total 1980 urban population (0.96 compared with 1.01 billion), and more than the 1980 combined total urban population of the more developed countries (0.80 billion). Among this group, mega-cities (those with 8 million or more population) are projected to show the greatest growth by the year 2000 (218 per cent increase compared with 174 per cent for large cities of 1 million or more population as a whole). Africa's patterns of large- and mega-city growth are no exceptions.[1] According to the United Nations (1993), Lagos is expected to have a population of 21.1 million by the year 2010, Cairo 13.4 million, and Kinshasa 7.9 million.

The nature of primacy

With the exception of Cairo, the mega-cities of Africa may not be considered primate on the basis of population alone. However, their dominant positions within their urban systems become clearly evident, as indicated in the previous chapters, when one considers their shares of the formal socio-economic activities (such as industry, finance, international trade, communications, transportation, social infrastructure, and so on), their privileged quality of life (in such areas as personal income, education, levels of services, and amenities among others), or their shares of decision-making power and political control in their systems (Rondinelli, 1988). Such dominant positions have inadvertently been bolstered further by the introduction of Structural Adjustment Programmes (SAPs), because of the relatively superior competitive advantage of these cities.

Their development to dominant political and economic positions may be explained in terms of economic processes that, at least in part, can be related to developments in the world economic and political system (Gilbert and Gugler, 1992). They acquired major industrial and commercial activities and a large proliferating informal sector, which continue to make them attractive destinations. Their real or perceived employment opportunities and superior quality of life continue to lure rural migrants and migrants from small urban places. These cities support very large informal sectors of small-scale enterprises, particularly in the commercial and trade sectors, which attract migrants. Typically one-third (Abidjan) to one-half (Nairobi) of the labour force is engaged in small-scale commercial activities (Rondinelli, 1988, and chaps. 8 and 9 in this volume). Informal housing markets often constitute a major source of their housing supply (nearly half in the case of Cairo; see chaps. 4 and 11 in this volume).

Such increasing concentration and dominance, however, are inevitably accompanied by mounting problems, diseconomies, and disparities. The resulting dissatisfactions as well as opportunities spurred efforts by both the private sector and governments towards decentralization and counter-primacy measures. These took a variety of forms, ranging from administrative decentralization and strengthening local governments to radical measures such as the building of a new capital in Nigeria or the new desert cities in Egypt. As these processes pick up momentum, the real or perceived advantages of primate cities may tend to become less and less compelling, and smaller and medium-sized cities may become more and more attractive to migrants and to capital.

Uncertain futures: Where are they heading?

A recent article on mega-cities (Linden, 1993) remarks that, four decades ago, cities such as Mexico City and Cairo were relatively attractive places to live, with little traffic along their spacious, cleanly swept boulevards. Now that their populations have quadrupled and their quality of life greatly degenerated (they are held to be the first and second most polluted capitals in the world), their in-migration rates have declined, although people continue to flock to smaller cities. This trend suggests that living conditions in mega-cities can eventually become intolerable. Given the various scenarios of decentralization in response to a combination of market forces and governmental actions, it becomes questionable whether future population growth projections of mega-cities will in fact materialize. Most developing countries perceive the spatial distribution of their population and the resulting primate city patterns as unacceptable, and many governments have attempted to change such patterns through indirect national policies or explicit spatial development strategies.

Recent evidence indicates that at some point in their development, after initial periods of very rapid growth, mega-cities slow down considerably in their population growth rates. Although their populations may continue to increase in absolute terms, they grow at rates lower than those of other intermediate and smaller cities in their systems. Cairo, Calcutta, Mexico City, Buenos Aires, São Paulo, and Seoul, among others, are already experiencing such processes, as have mega-cities in advanced countries before them (Renaud, 1981; Richardson, 1989). The United Nations, in fact, has had to revise its large-city population projections downwards at least three times over the past two decades.

Among the cities studied in this book, both Kinshasa and Abidjan have slowed down considerably over the past three decades from population growth rates of over 10 per cent to nearly half as much, despite major differences in their development planning, management, and quality of life. Abidjan's growth rate is currently smaller than that of small and medium-sized cities in the Côte d'Ivoire. Cities with 20,000–40,000 population are growing vigorously by receiving in-migrants from their regions, as well as children, the aged, and the unemployed who out-migrate from Abidjan (see chap. 8 in this volume). Similarly, Cairo's population growth rate declined from 4.14 per cent in 1960 to about 3.45 per cent by 1986, and its share of national industrial employment declined from 48.0 per cent in 1976 to 35.0 per cent by 1988 (see also chap. 4 in this volume).

If such trends continue, the processes and problems of concentration at both national and regional levels may eventually give way to the reverse processes and problems of deconcentration and dispersion. This is clearly contingent on active governmental efforts as well as the market processes that tend to spread development outside the mega-cities. In fact, deconcentration within the core regions (largest metropolitan or mega-city regions) would likely precede and signal the onset of a wider process of decentralization within their national urban systems (El-Shakhs, 1992).

The fact remains that no one can be certain exactly how big African mega-cities are now, or how rapidly they are expanding or going to expand in the future. However, mega-cities in the LDCs in general, and in Africa in particular, will likely continue to grow rapidly in the foreseeable future. In the process, such growth expands the city's influence and functions over a much wider region, including other cities and rural settlements and a frequently uncontrolled and unplanned periphery. This requires a redefinition of the nature and structure of future mega-cities. Current administrative and political boundaries and definitions of mega-cities in effect lose their meaning. It is equally clear that the pressures, demands, and challenges facing urban governments and planners in mega-cities, as well as their capacity to respond to them, are in large part determined by national and international forces and pressures beyond their control.

Basic issues of development and governance

The cities dealt with here, although unique, share certain problems in common. These include problems brought about by rapid population growth and spatial expansion, by overconcentration of national activities, by duality or indeed multiplicity of their social and spatial structures, and by extreme disparities. In addition, mega-city governments are faced with major additional demands brought about by virtue of these cities' positions and roles within their national urban systems and global urban networks. At the same time, mega-city governments often do not have the authority, power, or resources to deal effectively with these demands. Inefficient revenue collection practices and limitations imposed by highly centralized national governments on revenue raising strain the municipal governments' ability to keep up with urban service needs (Rondinelli, 1988). The result is an ever-widening gap between the supply of and demand for jobs as well as services and utilities, and shortages in urban land and housing, particularly for the urban poor.

Systems overload

Inevitably, rapid expansion brings with it major pressures on service and utility systems. It not only calls for a quantitative increase in supplies but, beyond a certain size, may also call for a change in the type, organization, and nature of the systems themselves. This often requires capital and technologies beyond the capacity of local governments. This is particularly true in the areas of mass transit, communications, and utilities. Rapid growth also brings pressures on the administrative and institutional ability to plan for, and control, development. It defies the governments' ability to respond in a timely fashion, because planning and development of major infrastructure projects are by their very nature time-consuming processes. In face of the rapid pace of change, many improvements become either inadequate or obsolete by the time they are finished.

Thus governments invariably end up playing a costly catch-up game. Cairo's estimated 14 million people are currently being served by infrastructure planned for 4 million at best. Effective mass transit systems that were proposed for Cairo and for Lagos in the 1950s and 1960s were finally only partially introduced in the 1980s, at several multiples of their originally estimated costs and compounded construction problems. In Lagos, the authorities cannot cope with the supply of basic household amenities such as water and electricity (Ayeni, 1981). Often, industries have to rely on inefficient and costly private generators because of the unreliable and unstable supply of electric power, thus increasing the final cost of their output. These problems have been further exacerbated by the impacts of the Structural Adjustment Programme (SAP) introduced in 1986 (see chap. 6 in this volume).

Economic and social problems in Africa's mega-cities also result in serious environmental damage and degradation. This is one of the most alarming and uncomfortable problems of metropolitan Lagos, according to Ayeni (1981, p. 137), "because it can be seen almost everywhere." The efforts of the Waste Disposal Board, created in 1978, quickly ran into the twin obstacles of inadequate equipment, which is costly to maintain, and the relative inaccessibility of almost 60 per cent of the inhabitants of the metropolis to such refuse collection equipment. In Cairo, toxic fumes make it difficult to breathe the air along certain sections of the Autostrada because of rubbish burning. Most mega-cities also have an adverse impact on their rivers, seriously threatening water supplies; for example, the Tjiliwung in Jakarta, the Han in Seoul, the Psig in Manila, and the Hooghly in Calcutta, among others, all receive large amounts of industrial and human waste (Kasarda and Rondinelli, 1990), and the Nile River is no exception.

Mega-cities are also experiencing explosive increases in demands for shelter and physical and social infrastructure and in urban land costs. Cairo's housing needs for a 20-year period (1980–2000) were estimated at 3.6 million units. The cost of land in certain favourable locations (for example the Nile front) has increased 2,000-fold over the past two decades, and consequently housing costs have sky-rocketed. Unacceptable densities and unmanageable patterns of growth often result in overcrowded housing, insanitary conditions, extremely long and cumbersome journeys to work, loss of agricultural land and of open space, and haphazard peripheral development, among others.

Integration and disintegration

Paradoxically, as mega-cities grow and consolidate their power and functional unity (as the premier socio-economic and political entities within their systems), administrative weaknesses and fragmentation within their government systems and among their subdivisions begin to intensify. Kinshasa provides a classic example of a fragmented metropolis that was never really united (see chap. 7 in this volume). Glaring dysfunctions, disparities, and inequalities among these cities' constituent communities have also tended to increase in recent years, as discussed by Aina in chapter 12 in this volume. The traditional political and administrative arrangements, which might have been appropriate for the smaller colonial cities they once were, clearly do not fit the more complex new phenomena of rapid expansion and post-colonial political adjustments.

It appears that, when African cities grew, they not only developed major diseconomies of urbanization but also became the loci for intensifying social and political problems within their societies. Not the least of these are deterioration in order and control, unemployment, urban poverty, squatters, and homelessness. It is estimated that 21 per cent of Cairo's population falls within the two lowest income categories of the "poor" and the "destitute," both of which are below acceptable poverty levels (Ibrahim, 1982). In South Africa, as described by Beavon for Johannesburg in chapter 5 in this volume, apartheid historically split functionally homogeneous urban areas into separate administrative jurisdictions on the basis of race. The resulting extreme disparities in income and expenditure, and in the level and quality of services, are likely to persist for some time in the future. In African cities, class has replaced race as the mechanism for segregation and maintenance of inequality (Gilbert and Gugler, 1992; Saff, 1994) and this is likely to happen in the cities of South Africa too.

Ineffective planning and/or governance

It is not surprising that mega-cities frequently receive a disproportionate share of government attention and planning activities. It is not clear, however, that such planning processes take full account of: (a) the socio-economic and political context within which planning activities occur, (b) the capacity of the state bureaucracies to plan and implement, or (c) the uncertainties and dynamics of the long-range processes of restructuring within regions and urban settlement systems (Rakodi, 1992; El-Shakhs, 1992).

As the previous chapters make clear, existing urban planning structures and processes in Africa are generally inadequate to deal with the scale of the urban problems confronting mega-cities. Part of this has to do with shortages of adequate fiscal resources and trained urban planners, and rigid, unresponsive bureaucratic planning delivery systems. In Kinshasa, as Piermay shows (chap. 7), the state apparatus and the city's managerial structures have all but collapsed. In Lagos, the Lagos State government has taken over many of the functions of local governments because of their inability to satisfy such basic needs as water supply and waste disposal (Onibokun and Agbola, 1994). The Langata community started the Green Belt tree planting and environmental clean-up movement in Nairobi because of the city authority's inability to undertake such functions (M'Rabu et al., 1990).

Existing planning processes are often adapted from models developed outside of Africa. This leads to over-complex planning processes, driven in a top–down manner by the state planning bureaucracy. Thus plans are developed with little or no local input or consultation. Further, even if these models were in themselves adequate as planning exercises, their implementation is generally beyond the resources and delivery capacity of the existing planning structures. Governments' ability to enforce rules and regulations is generally very weak in Africa, particularly when they relate to unrealistic standards or activities that go against the grain of market forces (Richardson, 1980). Plans are often not respected even by those government bureaucrats and politicians who approved them in the first place (El-Shakhs, 1994). In addition, projects are frequently abandoned or radically changed before they are given a chance to mature. Much of the problem lies in the often undemocratic nature of the state itself. This leads to favouritism, nepotism, biased allocation of resources, distorted priorities, and stifling of local initiative and innovation.

This is compounded by the lack of objective and reliable statistics and projections. In Lagos, for example, as Abiodun notes in chapter 6, there has not been a reliable headcount since 1963 because the census is too politicized (see also Onibokun, 1989). Chaotic conditions and the collapse of the state in Zaire make it impossible to find any dependable data since 1984. Similarly, in the mid-1960s, the Greater Cairo Planning Commission's 25-year population projections were dismissed by political leaders as exaggerated and politically inflammatory, and therefore could not be used as a basis for planning and infrastructure development (El-Shakhs, 1971). Such projections were partly based on the assumption that the government was unable to take effective measures towards decentralization, and proved to be close to target 25 years later. Finally, exogenous factors, including climatic variability (drought), oil price fluctuations, fluctuations in the world economy, and external pressures to cut services and urban subsidies, have also contributed to the severity of urban problems, particularly in mega-cities (White, 1989).

Innovative solutions: What seems to work?

Major demographic and spatial shifts in population and economic activities are likely to continue indefinitely to shape and reshape our cities and our urban systems. An effective response thus requires a better understanding of these long-range shifts, of market forces and activity, and of the capacity to influence them through public policy. An essential aspect of such policies is a continuous national effort to equalize the levels and burdens of social welfare and of urban services and amenities. This would pave the way for flexible and timely responses to change, hasten the processes of spatial and social transition, and avoid going against the tide by reinforcing the status quo.

For instance, policies of continuing to overbuild and concentrate activities and improvements in mega-cities, within their currently defined boundaries and particularly in their centres, is a short-range response to the systematic overload on their infrastructure and supply of productive employment. It is not surprising that mega-cities, because of what they are, frequently receive a disproportionate share of government attention, resources, and planning activities. Such a shortsighted and biased response creates rigidities that would inhibit decentralization processes. This in turn would hinder moves towards localization and wider participation in the region and democratization nationally.

Governments in LDCs have generally been dissatisfied with the trends and consequences of concentration and have sought to address these issues. A number of efforts have been attempted, including industrial decentralization, privatization, and community self-help programmes, among others. Their success, however, seems to have been very limited (White, 1989). Several reasons have been given for this outcome, among them:

(a) Government's direct involvement or interference in local and community initiatives, which become looked upon as government programmes that are to be forcefully obeyed, ignored, or met with apathy as irrelevant. For example, the Monthly Environmental Sanitation exercise in Lagos (introduced in 1983 and re-emphasized recently), where residents are to have three hours of released time on the last Saturday of each month to clean up their neighbourhoods thoroughly, turned out to be no more than an excuse for some extra free time (Onibokun and Agbola, 1994).

(b) Contradictions between government policies, some of which aim at decentralization of population and activities, while others simultaneously reinforce the concentration of economic and political power at the centre. For example, Sadat City (part of the New Desert Cities programme in Egypt) suffered from such contradictions, when the Ministry of Development and New Communities, which promoted and built the city to absorb some of the national capital functions, spearheaded by the ministry itself, opted to stay in Cairo instead. The city was thus perceived as a dumping ground for those not important or powerful enough to stay in the capital, a reaction that has adversely affected the New Desert Cities programme (El-Shakhs, 1994).

Some examples of successful initiatives

Networking for metropolitan planning and development

Urban management has to be intergovernmental in nature, and metropolitan regions are often plagued with fragmentation. Networking between the proliferating number of existing organizations and institutions is important for providing information flows between activity clusters. Networking should also include non-governmental organizations (NGOs) and volunteer groups. This proves to be less threatening to existing agencies and institutions and may stand a better chance of influencing or guiding development than their replacement. Examples from Asia as well as Africa can be illuminating. The experiences of Calcutta's Metropolitan Planning Organization and of the Greater Cairo Planning Commission provide good examples of such initiatives.

For years, the Calcutta metropolitan region was plagued with factionalism, fragmentation, and conflicts of interest among various levels of administration. There was no legal or administrative recognition of a growing metro area of some 6 million people until the creation of the Calcutta Metropolitan Planning Organization (CMPO) in 1961. It was set up by the state government, in reaction to a major health crisis in the wake of the 1958 cholera epidemic, to prepare a master plan for water supply and drainage and to recommend measures for the economic and physical regeneration of the metropolis (Sivaramakrishnan and Green, 1986). The Ford Foundation, the United Nations Development Programme (UNDP), and the World Health Organization provided help and international experts to the CMPO, which quickly grew to a staff of 600 and produced the Basic Development Plan by 1966. In addition to a set of immediate specific projects, the plan aimed at directing future population growth, strengthening development planning and implementation, and mobilizing finance and local government more effectively. Eventually, the Calcutta Metropolitan Development Authority (CMDA) was created in 1970 and undertook a large number of successful urban improvement projects with financial help from the World Bank.

Cairo's experience, on the other hand, started as a totally local initiative proposed by Egyptian planners without outside help at the time. The idea of creating a truly metropolitan organization, the Greater Cairo Planning Higher Committee (GCPC), was suggested to the prime minister of Egypt in 1965 by a group of local planners (including myself) in the Ministry of Housing (El-Shakhs, 1971). The GCPC was established by a presidential decree. It had a planning staff to assist its policy-making body, which was composed of most members of the cabinet, several university professors, and the three governors of Cairo, Giza, and Qalyubia, and was headed by the prime minister. The Committee's mandate was to integrate the planning function and coordinate implementation among all administrative units and at different levels within the Greater Cairo Region, which was to be defined by the Committee as a first order of business. This body was assisted by a planning organization (the Greater Cairo Planning Commission referred to above) that undertook the necessary research and made planning and policy recommendations for immediate as well as long-range strategic development. The Committee was given the power of review over all major projects in the region and produced a set of development policies and a preliminary long-range development plan, before its work was interrupted by the 1967 war with Israel. Although the GCPC was subsequently changed in character and absorbed into the national General Organization for Physical Planning (GOPP), policies articulated during its short-lived existence had a significant impact on the development of Greater Cairo after 1966, particularly in the areas of decentralization, new towns, infrastructure, and transportation systems.

Local autonomy and popular initiatives

Some examples from Zimbabwe and Tanzania, however limited, go to show what local urban autonomy can achieve within the African context. Local urban government in Zimbabwe has enjoyed a relatively high degree of autonomy in both organizational and financial terms. As a result, the local capacity to raise revenues and the ability to provide necessary urban services in a city such as Bulawayo have been found to be quite high. The municipal government depends almost entirely on its own resources, is run by an elected city council, has authority to hire and fire staff, who are relatively well paid, and works with residents' associations in the low-income areas. The city has been able to maintain not only a high level of services but also a "stable and productive work force" (Mutizwa-Mangiza, 1991, p. 375).

Experiences outside cities can also be indicative of the potentials of popular initiatives. Efforts to expand secondary education in the Kilimanjaro region of Tanzania, for example, led to the re-creation of local government in the form of committees, initially formed by prominent individuals and eventually formalized by elected membership. The committees displayed many of the characteristics of an autonomous local government. They raised funds, negotiated with the national government, and collected taxes. Although this experience was limited to a single clear goal (a school), it is indicative of the capacity for organization and institution building were local initiatives to be freed from overly centralized bureaucracies (Samoff, 1989).

"Sustainable Cities" programme experience
The "Sustainable Cities" programme (SCP), as a coordinating and participatory approach to managing cities, has been adopted by Dar es Salaam since 1992, as one of the 11 cities included in that global initiative of the UN Centre for Human Settlements, the UNDP, and the World Bank. Although it is still too early for this experience to be fully evaluated, the process of its application has resulted in some notable achievements (Halla, 1994). Among these is the completion of an environmental profile of the city documenting information about the dominant issues. This was followed by consultation meetings, with wide participation from the public, private, and popular sectors, covering basic issues and priorities. Small working groups of interested citizens were formed to formulate and execute action plans in response to those issues. Thus action plans and strategies involve local groups and individuals in identifying their needs and developmental goals. This in itself is an important step towards achieving sustainable development (Tacconi and Tisdall, 1993). It helped focus discussion on improvement of basic urban services, infrastructure, and environment, including solid waste management. One result of the SCP is that the Dar es Salaam Metropolitan Development Authority (DMDA) is expected to continue to coordinate the city's development through such participatory processes.

Local community/NGO partnerships for development
A good example of a community/NGO alliance is Cairo's Zabbaleen Environmental and Development Programme (Mega-Cities Project

and EQI, 1994). The Zabbaleen is an Upper Egyptian Coptic in-migrant community of garbage collectors who have traditionally gathered, sorted, and recycled a substantial part of the city's waste (see chap. 4 in this volume). As the city grew and the amount of garbage multiplied (over 6,000 tons per day), the solid waste crisis pushed the traditional collection system beyond its limits and overwhelmed the Zabbaleen's capacity to provide this service. The Zabbaleen system was considered obsolete and their livelihood was threatened when the government outlawed the use of donkey carts on Cairo's streets, and instead introduced mechanization to the municipal sanitation force, which shared certain tasks in the waste collection system. The community was squatting in squalid conditions on the marginal slopes of the Mokattam Hills near the centre of the city, where garbage heaps were to be found everywhere and sorted refuse covered the roadways. They had no services, no utilities, no schooling, little income, and deplorable environmental and health conditions, with no sewerage system, not a single telephone, and no means of transporting emergency patients to the hospital.

In 1981 the Zabbaleen Environmental and Development Programme was launched as a combined initiative of a local collective (Gameya), an NGO, the local Coptic Church, and a group of Egyptian international environmentalists, with initial funding from the Ford Foundation. Over the next five years, a series of community development initiatives were introduced, which included area upgrading and infrastructure extension, internal clean-up, health care, small industries, waste collection route extensions, mechanization, a composting plant, a veterinary centre, credit groups, and women-headed household projects. These were made possible through credit, cost recovery, and increased local income, which resulted from an expanded, more efficient waste collection system, increased land values, and micro-enterprises. Additional funding from a variety of sources helped consolidate the programme's successes. The results to date have largely been positive. In addition to improved environmental and living conditions in the community, greater literacy, an improved public image, and higher incomes, it led to the institution of a sustainable low-cost waste management system for Greater Cairo. The system was expanded to cover high-, middle-, and low-income neighbourhoods and spawned several recycling, conversion, and commercial activities that diversified the local economy and provided additional employment. This experience of engaging the informal sector in rendering an important service under a formal arrangement with the local authorities is being emulated elsewhere in Egypt (Mega-Cities Project and EQI, 1994).

Neighbourhood upgrading

Neighbourhood upgrading programmes, on the other hand, have recently become a favourite target for international support by such organizations as the World Bank and the United States Agency for International Development. There are numerous examples around the world, ranging from Ismailia's "Sustainable City" low-income housing development programmes in Egypt, to the Kampung Improvement Programmes, which have helped provide essential services to about half of Jakarta's population (Karamoy and Dias, 1986; Devas, 1993, p. 82). The greening programme at Bidara Cina in Jakarta, which aimed at upgrading the quality of the environment through a community–government partnership, also raised people's incomes through the planting of vegetables and other economically viable plants. The "Pueblo unido" (or "united people") in the Il Molino squatter settlement in Mexico City incorporated several innovations into their community, including housing modules prefabricated from local materials and above-ground rubber piping of sewage to a filtering and drying basin to produce water for aquaculture and fertilizer (Mega-Cities Project, 1993).

Self-reliance and environmental clean-up

The awakening of self-reliance in poor communities following the destructive earthquakes of 1991 in Cairo and 1985 in Mexico City is not an isolated incident but a global phenomenon. Emergency responses to shelter and health needs, as well as assistance in rebuilding the shattered communities, typify local initiatives, with or without assistance from NGOs, governments, and international agencies. Examples of successful sanitation and environmental clean-up projects in large cities are many. These include: the Zabbaleen project in Cairo mentioned earlier; waste paper recycling in Nairobi; the Green Exchange Programme in Curitiba, Brazil, where residents of certain inaccessible areas take their garbage to designated sites for pick-up in exchange for bags of surplus vegetables; the Magic Eyes programme in Bangkok, where street rubbish was reduced by 85 per cent by "encouraging children to hum a jingle about sloppiness when they see their parents litter" (Linden, 1993, p. 32); the reforestation of favelas in Rio de Janeiro, where the planting of fruit trees and vegetables on the hillsides has prevented erosion and provided jobs and nutrition; and the pilot project for a self-installed sewerage system in the Orangi district in Karachi, where some 70 per cent of the area has been connected (Linden, 1993).

Appropriate approaches for the future

Planning for the future development of mega-cities in Africa is fraught with tremendous uncertainties, an extremely rapid pace of change, and the seeming inability of governments and the formal sector to cope with such change. Adequate responses would, therefore, have to be based on promoting:
• flexibility, adaptability, and speed of response;
• democratization, participation, and the harnessing of local community initiatives;
• system-wide coordination and cooperation;
• privatization and greater reliance on the informal sector.
Training more planners and increasing budgets may be essential, but they are only a small part of any effective approach to urban planning in Africa's largest cities. If planning is to be made more relevant to the lives of the bulk of the urban population, new responsive and consultative processes that do not promise more than can be delivered will have to be developed. Many of the current problems of overconcentration in cities and failure of planning responses lie in the excessively centralized and often undemocratic nature of the state.

Without democratization of the state itself, it is hard to envisage truly responsive planning and development processes that can be sustained, particularly at the local level through community-based organizations, a view with which Aina would concur (chap. 12 in this volume). The commitment to a genuine process of democratization of urban government through devolution of political power and control of local financial resources, however, will not come easy. It will require extraordinary political will and intense pressure from local business interests, non-governmental organizations, and citizens' alliances. Crises in the delivery of urban functions and the general degradation of the quality of life, with increased population pressures in face of bankrupt urban management, might help bring that about.

The 1990s' debate, therefore, is no longer about "whether there should be more or less government intervention but about the nature of government, the type of governance" (Shoshkes, 1994, p. 24). Administrative and spatial restructuring efforts, at both the national and the mega-city levels, should aim at strengthening local initiatives and facilitating grass-roots responses to change. Restructuring mega-cities in a sustainable manner in order to improve community live-ability has "serious implications for urban form, for the material basis of urban life, and for community social relationships that must be expressed as practical measures in planning" (Rees, 1991, p. 17). Such measures would focus on the efficient use of urban space and reducing energy consumption. Restructuring also requires a set of consistent governance and planning policies, the aim of which would be to articulate and redefine the structure of the urban system and of mega-cities in terms of an integrated system of interdependent, largely autonomous communities with identifiable activity centres and population settlements.

Strategies for such restructuring can be based on one of two general premises: (1) centralized manipulation of the economic basis of development and control of factor movements by legal and administrative means and regulations; or (2) empowering people to do things for themselves and creation of the social, psychological, and political environment for sustainable development through decentralization of decision-making power and local control over development (El-Shakhs, 1982a). The first has figured prominently in most national planning experiences to date, with no or very limited success. On the other hand, experience shows that the effects of strategies such as regionalization of budgets, decentralization of administrative functions, and revenue sharing with a measure of local autonomy can produce positive results, particularly in LDCs with large public sectors and government employment. Thus an effective and sustainable framework for the management of urban development in Africa's largest cities requires actions at both national and local levels.

At the level of the national urban system, development strategies should aim to promote nascent democracy movements and strengthen local governments, to target certain strategically located intermediate urban centres for development, and to guide the inevitable spontaneous development of urban regions along corridors of potentially intense urban interaction between major cities.

At the mega-city level, planning effort should aim at containing the uncontrolled horizontal spatial expansion of central cities, articulating their internal structure into identifiable local communities with viable business subcentres, empowering peripheral communities to restructure themselves into viable, spatially identifiable settlements, and promoting area-wide differentiation of functions and specialization of settlements.

Spatial restructuring of mega-cities: At the level of the national settlement system

Genuine devolution of political power and decentralization of government and amenities

Decentralization and greater citizen participation are effective only if they are accompanied by greater local autonomy and home rule. There is a danger that, without genuine autonomy and transfer of control, decentralization may simply mean allocation of responsibilities to local levels of administration, the net impact of which would in effect be to strengthen the presence of central government (Batley, 1993; Shoshkes, 1994). Similarly, citizen participation without empowerment could simply lead to the transfer of added burdens and responsibilities and not of economic and political power to local groups. Thus, localities should acquire control over much of their resources, be given taxing powers, and retain a good portion of their taxes, fees, and other locally generated income.

Members of the local élite, politicians, and entrepreneurs need to have a sense of "place" and feel that they have a future in their communities. "A sense of place is an asset in which people are willing to invest and from which they gain returns" (Fainstein and Markusen, 1993, p. 1465). They need the assurances and the certainty that they have a stake, and that if they develop a political and/or economic base locally it will pay off for them and their children after them. This is particularly important in Africa where different local areas are identified with specific ethnic groups. Aspirations for regional and national stature can thus be realized through local involvement rather than by physically migrating to capital cities. Such development of local élites and a local power base will help not only in local economic development but also in the development of the social infrastructure and amenities necessary to retain and attract population (El-Shakhs, 1982b).

Promoting growth in intermediate urban centres and along corridors of intense interaction

Interregional decentralization efforts, which would promote growth in smaller and intermediate cities and regional centres, would clearly go a long way towards solving the problems of overconcentration in mega-cities. Such a process, however, is often difficult to achieve in the face of rapid urban growth in the early stages, and may create other problems, e.g. the tragic consumption of agricultural land by urban land uses in Egypt. Additionally this is often a slow process and not very attractive to migrants intent on trying their luck in the largest cities.

Thus, policies for the development of mega-city regions should give particular attention to the growth potential along intense transportation corridors linking them to other major cities, both within the national urban settlement system and between countries. A close look at the growth patterns of large cities would show that such potential may have already generated major growth areas (e.g. the Cairo–Alexandria and the Lagos–Ibadan corridors) and created significant urbanization economies extending considerable distances out of such cities, particularly at the transportation centres in between. Experience indicates that the development of such urban regions is inevitable and is in fact under way in many less developed countries. Independent settlements located along major corridors of interaction provide attractive alternatives for both basic and service industries, as well as for migrants, and thus constitute rational choices for incremental decentralization moves out of the mega-city. They also enhance the potential for development of intermediate cities and regional centres within the national settlement system.

Spatial restructuring within the mega-city region

Policies to contain the horizontal expansion of central cities
One short-sighted response to the rapid growth of mega-cities has been to allow a process of continuous incremental vertical and horizontal expansion of the main built-up area. This has been the case in Cairo, whose area has more than tripled over the past 30 years, and in Lagos where it probably more than doubled between 1985 and 1994 (Onibokun and Agbola, 1994; see also chaps. 4 and 6 in this volume). The patterns of settlement expansion in the six cities studied in this book, to a greater or lesser extent, show such contiguity. Whether planned or not, such contiguous development offers a course of least resistance. It is relatively easily accessible to existing utility and service systems, which are frequently overextended. Such horizontal peripheral expansion often extends outside urban administrative jurisdictions and their planning and building controls and regulations. The consequences of such development policies and patterns are many: (1) unplanned rigid and long-lasting built environments with little or no limits or safeguards dictated by the natural

environment, sustainability, or human scale; (2) extreme overloads on utility and transportation systems with frequent breakdowns, which threaten the health and safety of the population; (3) jobs/housing locational imbalances, thus decreasing accessibility to jobs, amenities, and open space; and (4) increased levels of congestion and concentrations of urban environmental pollution.

An alternative development process should attempt spatially to separate new urban development by green belts or reserves of open land, and create independent communities as an approach to expanding the urban land market. This approach would distinguish these communities from the core built-up area of the central city and reduce their dependence on its utilities and service systems. At the same time as they are given separate physical and administrative (governmental) identities, they should be made easily accessible to, and identifiable with, the mega-city itself. This would extend the glamour and mystique of the mega-city to them and thus increase their attractiveness to population and economic activities and their viability as growth alternatives. Such examples existed in the development of Heliopolis and Maadi (and more recently 6 October) outside Cairo and Ikeja outside Lagos. Unwittingly, however, horizontal expansion of the central city and lax or inappropriate land-use controls allowed developments in the interstices between them and the main built-up areas.

Thus a multi-nucleated regional development pattern requires a two-pronged strategy of increasing the supply of accessible urban land in planned locations, on the one hand, and tightening land development and preservation controls on the other. The first requires the expansion of convenient, inexpensive, and energy-conserving mass transit links to outlying development centres. Such links should be designed to leapfrog (by limiting access) intermediate areas where development is to be discouraged or halted, for example agricultural areas or open space. Land development and control concepts such as regional zoning, manipulating accessibility through the provision of roads and utilities, designation of priority zones for development, green belts, land banking or pooling on the outskirts of central cities, acquisition of development rights, transfer of development rights, or outright public acquisition of existing and/or potential urban land provide examples of the many tools that may be used to enforce such policies. There are, moreover, many examples of successful applications around the world. Perhaps the most common is the use of roads and utilities to guide development, in Curitiba and

São Paulo among others (and to determine land values, as is being attempted in Jakarta). Other experiences include green belts in Delhi and Seoul, the capturing of the improvement increment in land values to finance planned developments in Taiwan and Ismailia, and new town developments (Sivaramakrishnan and Green, 1986; Yeung and McGee, 1986; Devas, 1993).

Processes to articulate the internal structure of central cities
The sense of community within central cities themselves is often compromised or weakened by development pressures. The lack of identifiable boundaries or areas of transition, the loss of open and civic space, the general tendency toward more central control of local services, and the concentration of business and cultural activities and amenities in the city centre are all detrimental to local identity, sense of space, and pride. The usually rich heritage of diverse communities tends to disappear. Also, needless burdens are added to transportation systems as a result of the increased dependence on the city centre. Transportation projects frequently respond to and reinforce such centrality.

Development and planning policies should be designed in a way that would help identify established communities and community centres within mega-cities, through a bottom–up participatory approach, and strengthen them through land-use, transportation, and redevelopment assistance plans (for example, this was recommended in the 1970 preliminary strategic plan for Greater Cairo and elaborated as the "homogeneous sectors" in the 1983 development plan; see chap. 4). Decentralization of business, cultural, and governmental activities into secondary business subcentres can help reduce extreme centrality and create a more balanced poly-nucleated pattern of viable communities. The boundaries of communities can be sharpened, for instance by redevelopment of the often marginal uses and transitional areas at the edges.

Such spatial restructuring could be accomplished through urban land policies. For instance, public ownership or acquisition of land through eminent domain, where feasible, provides one approach. Land-pooling and readjustment schemes where appropriate could provide another approach (South Korea, Taiwan). In this case the owners of a given site get smaller but better-serviced parcels at least as valuable and better planned, and the local government gets a portion of the land to sell for cost recovery or use for services. If well

518

planned as intensive-use readjustments, such redevelopment processes could enable the creation of buffer zones, passive open spaces, or right of ways for major high-speed roads or limited-access highways. While improving accessibility to the identified communities and their business centres, such roads could also act as defining barriers or edges between them. The spatial definition and articulation of a system or hierarchy of communities and neighbourhoods can go hand in hand with moves toward governmental decentralization and local self-reliance.

Restructuring peripheral developments
Regional development policies should anticipate and prepare for eventual deconcentration or "counter-urbanization" within the mega-city region. Such processes are already occurring in most large metropolitan regions, including Cairo, Lagos, Abidjan, and Johannesburg. Unregulated spontaneous dispersal can be costly as well as wasteful in its indiscriminate use of valuable land resources. Proper planning, especially during stages of rapid mega-city growth, would help spark a step-wise process of decentralization and reduce growth pressures on the central city. It can promote the development of a hierarchy of regional intermediate and small urban centres. This could include new towns and expanded towns, which prove more successful when they are developed as integral parts of mega-city subsystems (e.g. new towns in the Cairo region such as 6 October, compared with independent new cities elsewhere such as Sadat City; El-Shakhs, 1994). In addition, the use of approaches such as priority development zones and industrial estates to focus and synchronize development efforts within large regions provides added valuable experience in this context.

Spontaneous peripheral settlements and squatters should be recognized and stabilized as elements of any peripheral restructuring. Such communities should be integrated into the envisioned settlement pattern and activity subcentres. Their inclusion in itself would help stabilize as well as control land uses in such settlements. In the process, spatial relocation may be inevitable, but should be kept to a minimum in order to reduce social and economic costs. Land-pooling and readjustment schemes in the periphery could prove to be of major utility for upgrading and servicing these developments, as well as allowing for redevelopment of infrastructure and open space.

Specialization and functional differentiation of settlements

Functional specialization within national urban settlement systems is nothing new. Although all cities provide basic urban services, locational or historical factors tend to differentiate them and endow them with major distinguishing functions. Thus many cities develop special roles as ports, industrial agglomerations, resort areas, educational centres, religious meccas, administrative capitals, and so on. Problems of overconcentration are often exacerbated when all or most of these functions reside in one mega-city, e.g. Lagos (particularly prior to the move of the capital to Abuja) and Cairo (with the exception of the port functions in Alexandria and the Suez Canal cities). The degree of urban primacy is often very low or absent when these functions are distributed among several national centres (e.g. the United States, Sweden, Italy, India, Saudi Arabia, South Africa, the United Arab Emirates, and others).

The same rationale exists, and may be easier to achieve, within mega-city regions. The high degree of unity, interdependence, and self-reliance within such regions allows for a significant degree of diversity and specialization among their constituent settlements. Major economic, cultural, entertainment, business, and governmental functions tend to agglomerate individually within specific locations in and around mega-cities. This trend of spatial differentiation of major functions and specialization of settlements could become an important approach in the planning for deconcentration of mega-cities. Such an approach would help redefine the functions of the main centre and of secondary centres, provide room for expansion and often badly needed open space within the primary centre (e.g. moving several of the national government agencies from the city centre to Nasr City in Cairo in the 1950s and 1960s), separate major noncompatible uses, and deconcentrate congestion and environmental pollution.

Implications for governance and planning

Current approaches to urban planning and management have to be realistic about the expectations and potentials of urban development, the limitations on the capacity of the institutions involved, and the need for flexibility in planning and incrementality in implementation. This requires the expansion and reorganization of planning and administrative functions to provide area-wide coordination, yet to strengthen local autonomy, initiative, and identity both within and outside the central city. There needs to be a greater reliance on the private sector for a substantial part of metropolitan services and a shift towards greater local participation and community self-help through volunteer efforts (Sivaramakrishnan and Green, 1986).

Promoting local autonomy and initiative within area-wide coordination
The first step in facing the challenge of mega-city growth is to establish meaningful and workable mechanisms for region-wide planning and coordination and control of development. These should articulate a division of authority and responsibility that maximizes local participation while preserving integration at a regional scale. Such mechanisms and institutions, be they jurisdictional or networks, should be flexible enough so that their authority and its boundary can be frequently adjusted to fit the phenomena.[2] Local initiative and control at the small scale of towns and districts would enhance chances for self-reliance and sustainability for many urban functions and make it feasible to attract qualified personnel. This would reduce the burden on the mega-city government and thus enable it to cope with the increasingly complex regional functions such as transportation, communications, utilities, public safety, and protection of the environment. In order to be effective, local administrations must have a say in or control of capital investment, priorities, and local resources. Only a strong local official (a mayor or manager) with powers to deliver can cut deals with private enterprises and community groups in a relevant, timely, and responsive manner at the local level.

Promoting participation and self-reliance
The future salvation of mega-cities has to rely in large measure on "the vibrancy, dedication, creativity and ambition of the poor who inhabit these cities in improving their lot" (Onibokun and Agbola, 1994, p. 3). In face of the increasing complexity of mega-city systems and of dwindling municipal revenues, community-initiated self-help programmes become key to any improvement. Governments should thus pursue a more community-based approach to development by integrating local initiatives and voluntary associations into their plans. Incorporating traditional groups in the planning process would also serve as a stabilizing influence during periods of fundamental change (Kooperman, 1987). Such approaches would force governments to re-evaluate their own centralized bureaucratic structures, mobilize local groups, and reorient the decision-making process to

make it more responsive to people's needs. Certainly democratization of the planning process, and of the state itself, would go a long way towards this end.

These moves towards greater participation at community levels, however, call for more, not less, coordination and integration at higher levels of government. The increasing complexities of large cities seem to shift more importance and burdens from city government to both lower (local neighbourhood or district) and higher (regional or national) levels. While unification of area-wide jurisdictions leads to better coordination, strengthening of lower tiers makes genuine popular participation possible. This articulation of authority also tends to place more importance on people's capacity and ingenuity to do things for themselves. In this respect, governments should recognize the importance and potential of the informal sector (Lee-Smith, 1989).

Integrating the planning and administration of development
Creating networks within and between existing organizations and institutions would facilitate information flows and enhance coordination throughout the process, including: research and analysis of metropolitan systems, formulation of goals and objectives, evaluation and choice among feasible alternative policies and strategies, implementation, and monitoring and feedback. Such experiences, as experimented with in the Greater Cairo Planning Commission, exist in a variety of forms in major Asian mega-cities (e.g. Tokyo's federal government, the city-states of Singapore and Hong Kong, and the Metro Manila Management Coordination Board) and are instructive in this respect. They provide an alternative and support to the more rigid traditional hierarchical command structure (Sivaramakrishnan and Green, 1986). The unique advantage of networks is that they can easily cross lines and levels of authority, include internal and external institutions, link formal and informal organizations, and shrink or expand their boundaries as needed in response to changes within the metropolitan system.

Conclusion

A multi-level cooperative administrative approach to urban management and planning, based on democratization and participation and focused on greater local initiative and control, would provide a flexible strategy that would be responsive and adaptable to future uncertainties. Instead of reinforcing the status quo, it would better anticipate and facilitate the likely long-range changes and minimize their adverse impacts. Combined with promoting a poly-nucleated approach to the spatial restructuring of mega-cities, it would help organize urban regions along manageable and humane dimensions, were they destined to continue their unabated growth for long periods in the future. Such approaches would, at the same time, promote a more socially and environmentally sustainable development process. They would empower people to do things for themselves, increase their participation in decisions that affect their lives, encourage local identity and self-reliance, and increase popular participation in the provision of urban services and in the planning process. They would provide an effective framework and incentives for the generation of growth and its distribution at local levels. They would also help preserve human scale and access to nature. The efficient use of urban land and of energy resources through a better-balanced distribution of population and systems of settlements would go a long way towards protecting the environment, preserving natural capital, and creating liveable communities.

Major international funding and technical assistance organizations such as the World Bank, traditionally accustomed to funding giant projects, have increasingly come to recognize the importance of supporting small community-based projects and the virtues of fostering citizen participation as important elements in local planning and sustainable development. There is also an emerging emphasis on the role of non-governmental organizations or private voluntary organizations in the planning, management, and finance of development at all levels. If freed from government intervention, the proliferating numbers of NGOs (for example, there are at least 60 in Nigeria) and their close association with urban residents can, in addition to supporting community-based initiatives, play an important role in the area of networking and information flows for region and metropolitan area-wide planning.

The continuous exchange of ideas and experiences among mega-cities' governments and planners worldwide is another promising and important area of action at the international level. Such exchanges have already begun under a variety of rubrics: the United Nations Population Fund's large-city mayors' conferences, the Mega-City Project based in New York, the World Bank's Sustainable Development annual conferences, and the organization "Metropolis" based in Paris, among others. Regional African city associations may also play an important role in encouraging indigenous research and experimentation and in sharing successful experiences in the planning and management of large and mega-cities.

Acknowledgements

The author acknowledges the help with the translation and research for this chapter ably provided by Catherine C. Galley, Hassan Hegab, Melissa Mandoz, Grant Saff, and Apana Subaiya, all graduate students in Urban Planning and Policy Development at Rutgers University.

Notes

1. The absence of reliable census figures for most African countries and the lack of knowledge of urban growth rates during the years of recession have been referred to in many earlier chapters and discussed especially by Simon (chap. 3) and Potts (chap. 13). In this context, projections should be regarded with considerable scepticism and are used here only for indicative purposes.
2. This has been possible in terms of formal municipal boundaries in Turkey, Zimbabwe, and Kenya, where municipalities can legally and politically expand their boundaries to incorporate their immediate environs and peri-urban periphery. Frequent and major extensions took place in Kenya in the 1970s and 1980s. In Turkey, not only did municipal boundaries expand to service unplanned settlements, but a "powerful upper tier metropolitan authority has been created for the larger conurbations" (Davey, 1993, p. 156).

References

Ayeni, B. 1981. Lagos. In M. Pacione, ed., *Problems and Planning in Third World Cities.* St. Martin's Press, New York.

Batley, R. 1993. Political control of urban planning and management. In: N. Devas and C. Rakodi, eds., *Managing Fast Growing Cities: New Approaches to Urban Planning and Management.* Longman, London, pp. 176–206.

Davey, K. 1993. The institutional framework for planning and the role of local government. In: N. Devas and C. Rakodi, eds., *Managing Fast Growing Cities: New Approaches to Urban Planning and Management.* Longman, London, pp. 153–175.

Devas, N. 1993. Evolving approaches. In: N. Devas, and C. Rakodi, eds., *Managing Fast Growing Cities: New Approaches to Urban Planning and Management.* Longman, London, pp. 63–101.

El-Shakhs, S. 1971. National factors in the development of Cairo. *Town Planning Review* 42(3): 233–249.

———— 1982a. National and regional issues and policies in facing the challenges of the urban future. In: P. Hauser, R. Gardner, A. Laquian, and S. El-Shakhs, eds., *Population and the Urban Future.* SUNY Press, Albany, NY, pp. 103–180.

———— 1982b. Regional development and national integration in the Third World. In: N. Fainstein and S. Fainstein, *Urban Policy under Capitalism.* Sage, Beverly Hills, Calif., pp. 137–158.

———— 1992. The future of mega-cities: Planning implications for a more sustainable development. In: B. Hamm et al., eds., *Sustainable Development and the Future of Cities*. Universität Trier Press, Trier, Germany.

———— 1994. Sadat City, Egypt and the role of new town planning in the developing world. *Journal of Architectural and Planning Research* 11(3): 239–259.

Fainstein, S. and A. Markusen. 1993. The urban policy challenge: Integrating across social and economic development policy. *North Carolina Law Review* June: 1463–1486.

Gilbert, A. and J. Gugler. 1992. *Cities, Poverty and Development: Urbanization in the Third World*. Oxford University Press, New York.

Halla, F. 1994. A coordinating and participatory approach to managing cities. *Habitat International* 18(3): 19–31.

Ibrahim, S. E. 1982. Social mobility and income distribution in Egypt, 1952–1977. In: G. Abdel-Khalek and R. Tignor, eds., *The Political Economy of Income Distribution in Egypt*. Holmes & Meier, New York.

Karamoy, A. and G. Dias. 1986. Delivery of urban services in kampungs in Jakarta and Ujung Pandang. In: Y. M. Yeung and T. G. McGee, eds., *Community Participation in Delivering Urban Services in Asia*. International Development Research Center, Ottawa.

Kasarda, J. D. and D. A. Rondinelli. 1990. Mega-cities, the environment, and private enterprise: Toward ecologically sustainable urbanization. *Environmental Impact Assessment Review* 10: 393–404.

Kooperman, L. 1987. African urban planning and redevelopment. *Journal of African Studies* 14(1): 12–16.

Lee-Smith, D. 1989. Urban management in Nairobi: A case study of the *matatu* mode of public transport. In: R. E. Stren and R. R. White, eds., *African Cities in Crisis*. Westview Press, Boulder, Colo.

Linden, E. 1993. Mega-cities. *Time Magazine* 141(2), 11 January.

Mega-Cities Project. 1993. Mega-cities and the innovative technology: An assessment of experience. Unpublished paper, Mega-Cities Project, New York.

Mega-Cities Project & EQI (Environment Quality International). 1994. Zabbaleen environmental and development program: Cairo. Unpublished case-study, Mega-Cities Project, New York.

M'Rabu, E. J., A. Musyoki, P. W. Muiruri, and S. K. Wambugu. c.1990. The green belt: A grassroots environmental movement, Nairobi. Unpublished case-study, Mega-Cities Project, New York.

Mutizwa-Mangiza, N. D. 1991. The organization and management of urban local authorities in Zimbabwe: A case study of Bulawayo. *Town Planning Review* 13(4): 357–380.

Onibokun, A. G. 1989. Urban growth and urban management in Nigeria. In: R. E. Stren and R. R. White, eds., *African Cities in Crisis: Managing Rapid Urban Growth*. Westview Press, Boulder, Colo., pp. 68–111.

Onibokun, A. G. and T. Agbola. 1994. Megacities, urban environmental problems and community based initiatives. Unpublished paper, Mega-Cities Project, New York.

Rakodi, C. 1992. Some issues in urban development and planning in Tanzania, Zambia, and Zimbabwe. In: D. Drakakis-Smith, ed., *Urban and Regional Change in Southern Africa*. Routledge, London, pp. 121–146.

Rees, W. E. 1991. Sustainable communities: Planning for the 21st century. *Plan Canada* 313 (May): 15–25.

Renaud, B. 1981. *National Urbanization Policy in Developing Countries*. Oxford University Press, New York.

Richardson, H. 1980. Polarization reversal in developing countries. *Regional Science Association Papers* 45: 67–85.

—— 1989. The big bad city: Mega-city myth? *Third World Planning Review* 11: 355–372.

Rondinelli, D. A. 1988. Giant and secondary city growth in Africa. In: M. Dogan and J. Kasarda, eds., *A World of Giant Cities, The Metropolis Era: Volume 1*. Sage, Beverly Hills, Calif.

Saff, G. 1994. The changing face of the South African city: From urban apartheid to the deracialization of space. *International Journal of Urban and Regional Research* 18(3): 377–391.

Samoff, J. 1989. Popular initiatives and local government in Tanzania. *Journal of Developing Areas* 24(1): 1–18.

Shoshkes, E. 1994. Toward a political ecology of urban redevelopment: A theoretical framework for studying the impact of global restructuring on urban form. Unpublished paper, Department of Urban Planning, Rutgers University, New Brunswick, N.J.

Sivaramakrishnan, K. G. and L. Green. 1986. *Metropolitan Management: The Asian Experience*. Oxford University Press, New York.

Tacconi, L. and C. Tisdall. 1993. Holistic sustainable development: Implications for planning processes, foreign aid and support for research. *Third World Planning Review* 15(4): 411–428.

UN (United Nations). 1993. *World Urbanization Prospects: The 1992 Revision*. United Nations, New York.

White, R. R. 1989. The influence of environmental and economic factors on the urban crisis. In: R. E. Stren and R. R. White, eds., *African Cities in Crisis*. Westview Press, Boulder, Colo.

Yeung, Y. M. and T. G. McGee, eds. 1986. *Community Participation in Delivering Urban Services in Asia*. International Development Research Center, Ottawa.

15

Urban management: The recent experience

Kadmiel H. Wekwete

Abstract

Les caractéristiques des mesures administratives et politiques de l'administration des villes durant la période post-coloniale sont relevées dans le cadre d'un examen d'ensemble de l'évolution de la gestion urbaine. Quelles qu'aient été les différences entre les divers héritages coloniaux, l'administration des villes étaient habituellement confiée aux autorités locales, malgré l'importance du contrôle exercé par le gouvernement central, en particulier dans les pays francophones, les municipalités dépendant plus ou moins des transferts de fonds du gouvernement central. Cette méthode de gestion mettait fortement l'accent sur la planification physique et l'aménagement d'infrastructures et confiait un rôle important au secteur public, tandis que les autres acteurs du développement urbain ne participaient pas activement au processus. On sait l'échec de cette méthode, tout particulièrement à la suite des changements politiques et de la dégradation économique survenus dans le milieu des années 70. Suite à cet échec, dans le cadre de leurs politiques de restructuration économique, la plupart des pays d'Afrique ont tenté de réduire l'intervention de l'État en même temps que les dépenses publiques et de ressusciter le secteur privé. L'on suggère qu'un nouveau modèle d'urbanisme est en train d'apparaître dans le cadre duquel divers acteurs – organisations non gouvernementales, communauté et secteur privé – participent de plus en plus activement au processus de prise de décision et à l'apport de services. Toutefois, ces changements sont le plus souvent imposés de l'extérieur, la décentralisation des responsabilités ne s'est pas accompagnée d'un apport suffisant de ressources, il n'existe pas de mécanismes qui incorporent les ONG dans la prise de décision au niveau des municipalités et l'on ne dispose que de peu d'informations quant à l'impact de la participation accrue du secteur privé dans l'apport des services. Il ressort des quelques exemples disponibles qu'un modèle impliquant en même temps les secteurs public et privé est en train d'apparaître, avec des ONG sans cesse plus nombreuses intervenant parmi les populations à faible revenu, le programme d'urbanisation durable du Centre des Nations Unies pour les Établissements Humains (HABITAT) et la mise en place de mécanismes de consultation pour décider des priorités. Toutefois, il n'existe pas suffisamment d'analyses rigoureuses des résultats de ces initiatives pour permettre d'en tirer des conclusions précises, que ce soit au sujet de la mesure dans laquelle cette nouvelle méthode est en train de remplacer l'ancien modèle sectoriel, fondé sur le secteur public, hiérarchisé de haut en bas ou quant à la question de savoir si ce nouveau modèle orienté sur l'action, autorisé par le secteur public, décentralisé, à vocation socio-économique, a des chances de surmonter de façon plus efficace les problèmes de la croissance urbaine.

Introduction

The elusiveness of urban management as a concept has been widely acknowledged (Stren, 1993; Mattingley, 1994). Indeed, Stren observes that the concept is strongly lacking in content and that it is largely an analysed abstraction. This is in spite of the significant interest in urban management that has been generated at local and international levels, as represented particularly in the World Bank, UN Centre for Human Settlements (UNCHS), and UN Development Programme (UNDP) Urban Management Programme of 1986–1999. The key question still remains: What is urban management? What are the objects to be managed and what is the operational reality of that management?

In Africa, urban management refers to the political and administrative structures of cities and the major challenges that they face to provide both social and physical infrastructure services. These include managing urban economic resources, particularly land and the assets of the built environment, creating employment, and attracting investment in order to improve the quality and quantity of goods and services available (Clarke, 1991). Enumerating the challenges and aims, however, does not necessarily specify how urban management can achieve all these different goals.

The traditional view associates urban management primarily with municipal and central government. This is a largely supply-driven model, whereby the state and its agencies have the statutory responsibilities for management. The provision of services and their maintenance are therefore viewed as rights that citizens expect, partly as a result of the taxes they pay and partly because of the political legitimacy that they give to both the state and local authorities. Indeed, in many countries in sub-Saharan Africa, there are local government statutes or decrees that define local responsibilities and also articulate centre–local relationships.

A more recent view of management articulates a broader governance view that brings to the fore the role that civil society plays and expands the range of stakeholders to include private sector agencies, non-governmental organizations (NGOs), community-based organizations (CBOs), and a variety of interest groups (Mabogunje, 1990). Urban management within the broader governance perspective has to be more participative, broader in outlook, more transparent, and less bureaucratic. Although there are no significant changes in what is being managed, the range and scope of actors significantly increase.

Urban management has been influenced by other forces at work, particularly the globalization of the world economy. The importance of globalization and global restructuring of the world economy has been discussed earlier in this volume by Rakodi (chap. 2), Simon (chap. 3), Rogerson (chap. 10), and others. Rapid advances in information technology and the liberalization of the international capitalist regime have significantly reduced the barriers of territorial borders, and have, in particular, reinforced the position of cities and towns as significant points of exchange and interaction. This transformation has been linked to the "regimes of accumulation" thesis, which highlights major changes in labour markets and consumption patterns, particularly the deregulation of markets. The organization of production has shifted away from the Fordist principles that shaped the industrial revolution of the Western world, with the systems now becoming more technologically driven, flexible, and decentralized. Globally, cities are more interlinked and have to be competitive in a global sense to attract capital. Older cities have to compete with new centres of production, and more and more have less of a manufacturing base as their economies become more service oriented.

At local and national levels, a major trend has been the shift from centralized government systems to more decentralized ones (Mawhood, 1983/1993). The international structural adjustment process, together with the end of the Cold War, has reinforced the idea of the market and placed less and less emphasis on state intervention. Decentralization and local government have been emphasized in many countries and this has significantly improved the visibility of municipal and city governments.

Although, as emphasized by Rakodi, Simon, and others in this volume, Africa has been relatively marginalized by recent globalization processes, it has nevertheless been influenced by the major global trends and has also made some adaptations. Structural economic adjustment has been a major trend in all African countries, and this has involved devaluations of currencies, major restructuring of the public sector, and in many cases increased poverty and unemployment (see, especially, chap. 13 in this volume). The positive scenario is that this is temporary and will be followed by growth in the economy. In most countries, however, structural adjustment policies have generally ignored urban areas and the local institutions that must manage them. Indeed, structural adjustment has been hailed as a possible solution to the problems of urban bias, as the terms of trade shift in favour of the productive rural areas (Becker et al., 1994; see also chaps. 3 and 13 in this volume).

The major trend in most towns and cities has been that of an increasing crisis in terms of failure to provide services and to attract new investment. Calls have been made for improved urban management and building up capacities at local and national levels. Some commentators have viewed urban management as a new paradigm, representing a shift from master plans to a much more dynamic process of managing urban economies (see also chap. 14 in this volume). There is no substantive evidence that such a new paradigm has emerged to date, because urban management has continued to operate within the framework of a traditional sectoral, public sector management model. Urban management has continued to be viewed in terms of addressing problems of land, environment, infrastructure, poverty, and finance, which are the traditional domains of city and town management. A typical municipal/city government operates on the basis of departments (e.g. Health, Town Planning, Engineering), which have responsibility for providing and maintaining services.

These departments are usually linked to the operations of those central government ministries with responsibility for managing cities. Indeed all these models are top–down, sectoral, and based on a link-pin system for the organization of the state apparatus.

The objective of this chapter is to highlight the urban management experience in Africa in the 1980s and 1990s. Given the major challenge of rapid urbanization, the chapter will examine the challenges and highlight some of the key experiences. Significant interest has been generated in this subject since the publication of an edited volume by Richard Stren and Rodney White (1989) on African cities in crisis. This volume captured some very interesting case-studies across Africa, particularly highlighting the growing deficiency in services and the inability of traditional management systems to provide the answers. An important question to ask is: Are any new models emerging from the experiences both of the large cities reviewed in this book and of others, and how are they shaping the management systems?

Conceptual framework for urban management in Africa

The management of towns and cities in Africa is part and parcel of the public sector management system of government inherited from the colonial era. Towns and cities operate through elected and appointed local government representatives, who have the political and administrative mandates to provide and manage social and physical infrastructure services. The powers of local governments are provided by central government (state/federal governments) and within the model there are variations in terms of the nature of local government structures and centre–local relationships.

In both francophone and anglophone Africa, the responsibility for managing towns and cities revolves around land management and related built environment services. The local authorities aim to determine planning permission for all development and, together with central government, to provide and manage services. Other responsibilities are defined by the enabling statutes and are translated into the work of both political and technical–bureaucratic committees. This is the nature of the inherited municipal management model, although it is far removed from actual practice in many African cities today.

Urban management responsibility in African cities straddles urban physical planning, urban administration, and social services provision.

This represents several areas of responsibility, which form the basis for the key administrative departments. The main stakeholders in urban management include central government, local government, non-governmental agencies, private sector business, urban households, and the various segments of civil society. These groups have interests in the way towns and cities are managed and create a dynamic environment of both competing and complementary interests. Traditionally, local government represents the public interest, and in particular the management of externalities created as a result of the operations of the different interest groups. Like central government, local government aims to ensure that public interest is maintained and regulates activities to ensure free and fair competition. The intention is to provide a restraint on the operation of markets to serve private interests, and to ensure the protection of all interest groups in society. In terms of management objectives, the aims of government differ significantly from private sector corporate objectives, which usually have a focus on profit maximization, although in the end there is convergence in terms of a need for efficiency and effective management.

Although current development thinking tries to separate markets and politics, it is clear that in urban management they are linked and mutually dependent. Urban management addresses key public goods that are prerequisites for markets to function – various dimensions of law and order, property rights, and enforcement of contracts through planning permits. Of particular importance is providing the physical skeleton and circulatory systems that are essential to the functioning of urban economies, because they allow goods and services to move to the market.

The objects to be managed vary significantly by country and city, depending on the powers of the local government system. Table 15.1 shows the range of local responsibility, ranging from primary responsibility to no responsibility at all. In all cases the role of central government is important, so that, even where the municipality has primary responsibility, central government sectoral ministries or agencies still play a key role, particularly in terms of project funding and providing expertise. In table 15.1 there is significant commonality in the area of general urban services provision and physical planning. There is also general agreement that the local authorities are the main actors in terms of municipal management. They assume this primary responsibility because they directly provide services and usually levy charges for what they can provide. The crisis in most

Table 15.1 Local responsibility for services in selected African cities

Function	Harare (Zimbabwe)	Francistown (Botswana)	Nairobi (Kenya)	Lusaka (Zambia)	Lagos (Nigeria)	Kinshasa (Zaire)
Public utilities						
Water supply	P	P	P	P	S	N
Sewerage and drainage	P	P	P	P	S	N
Electricity	S	P	N	N	N	N
Telephone	N	P	N	N	N	N
Social services						
Primary education	S	S	P	N	P	N
Health	S	S	P	S	S	S
Social welfare	P	N	S	S	N	S
Housing	P	S	P	P	N	N
Transportation						
Highways and roads	P	P	P	P	P	P
Street lighting	P	P	P	P	P	P
Mass transportation	S	N	N	N	S	N
General urban services						
Refuse collection	P	P	P	P	P	P
Parks and recreation	P	P	P	P	P	P
Markets and abattoirs	P	P	P	P	P	P
Cemeteries	P	P	P	P	P	P
Fire protection	P	P	P	P	P	P
Law enforcement	S	N	N	N	N	N
Planning and engineering services	P	P	P	P	P	S

Source: based on Bahl and Linn (1992) and Wekwete (1992).
P = primary responsibility
S = secondary responsibility
N = no responsibility

African cities is the failure to provide services, particularly as most urban areas have expanded without formal planning. The new spontaneous and squatter areas are not covered by formal services, despite accommodating as many as 60 per cent of urban residents. This is a problem of both management capacity and increasing poverty, because most of the new migrants do not have formal jobs and have limited incomes (see also chap. 13).

Within the areas already provided with services there is a maintenance crisis – potholes in the roads, broken water pipes, lack of garbage collection services, and a general lack of investment in infrastructure. The per capita levels of investment in infrastructure have declined to zero in the past decade for most major cities. There are no new highways, street lighting, refuse collection trucks, or markets. Cities such as Nairobi, as already discussed by Obudho in chapter 9, are experiencing major decay in terms of infrastructure. The source of this problem is government policy that has not allowed significant resource flows to towns and cities, and has not provided local autonomy for revenue generation.

Another important local responsibility that has significantly emerged is that of social services. This has been the result of the rapid urban growth, civil disorder, lack of employment, and the refugee crisis faced in many countries. Municipal/city governments have been called on greatly to expand the horizon of their management responsibilities to include a significant component of social services delivery. There is a call that they should address a variety of social problems that emanate from lack of employment and growing social disintegration in urban areas (UNCHS/UNDP/World Bank, 1995).

In defining local responsibility, it is crucial to factor in centre–local relationships because they determine overall resource allocation and determine the limits of powers that local authorities enjoy. The tradition in both francophone and anglophone countries is that, although local authorities have been given a whole range of responsibilities, this is not always matched with the resources they are granted. The mismatch is particularly severe because of the rapid growth of urban areas and the attendant demand for services. In most African cities the major services have been neglected or abandoned because of the failure to transfer resources from the centre.

In terms of the capacity to generate local revenues, many urban local authorities are severely hampered because they are responsible for highly inelastic taxes and have poor means for local collection. The overall median of local taxes as a percentage of total local expenditure was 46 per cent for a sample of developing countries before 1979 and 39 per cent after 1979. Table 15.2 shows a sample of towns and cities in sub-Saharan Africa and the significance of local tax revenues in local expenditures. Data are very patchy in most African countries and so a major exercise is under way to strengthen the gathering of baseline data at local levels (UNCHS/UNDP/World Bank, 1995). This is an important dimension of the extent of local authority in local economic decision-making. In most African cities the contribution of local revenues is very limited and therefore they have to depend on transfers from central government for their development budgets. This dependence has been growing as the range of responsibilities has increased. In table 15.2 it is clear that after 1979 there was a significant decline in local tax revenues. This is the result of both poor management capacity and a lack of new taxable investments.

To be able to construct a meaningful model for urban manage-ment, two issues have to be identified: first, responsibility and, sec-ondly, the objects to be managed. In recent years the responsibilities of local government have grown significantly as cities have grown and their range of interests increased. Of importance in African cities is the role that local and international NGOs increasingly play in the development of urban services. There is also growing participation by the private sector. The definition of responsibility therefore requires a clear delineation of what the different actors do and the matrix of management responsibility. The local government statutes usually stipulate what municipalities and metropolitan governments should do, but in practice they fail to articulate the roles of the different actors in urban management. In terms of micro-level support to households

Table 15.2 **Local taxes as a percentage of total local expenditure in selected Afri-can cities**

City/town	Before and incl. 1979	After 1979
Francistown (Botswana)	46.8	33.5
Nairobi (Kenya)	–	34.1
Lagos (Nigeria)	50.9	42.8
Tunis (Tunisia)	36.8	24.7
Kinshasa (Zaire)	25.4	–
Lusaka (Zambia)	39.3	–

Source: Bahl and Linn (1992).

and individuals, NGOs and CBOs have been very active in interventions to strengthen health, education, and credit, as well as strengthening decentralization in decision-making, particularly in low-income urban areas (see also El-Shakhs' discussion of these issues in chap. 14 of this volume). Part of re-emergent civil society (see chap. 12 in this volume), they have mobilized poor urban communities on a location basis and provided them with support to improve their livelihoods. One of the major new dimensions of urban management is therefore the increased involvement of new management actors. Urban households have become much more involved in the process of management, sometimes out of sheer necessity and sometimes through the active involvement of CBOs and NGOs. There are many varieties of community-based organizations, including social and cultural groups, religious groups, and other more specific task-related groups.

Although the private sector has always been the economic engine of city economies, it has never been formally incorporated as part of the management system. The traditional model of management has always been driven by public sector investment programming, and one of its key objectives has been to create favourable conditions for private capital investment. As long as public funds were invested in essential infrastructure, the private sector role was seen in terms of paying taxes and other service charges for the services rendered. With the growing inability of the public sector to provide services, private firms have began to provide their own services (private electricity generators, private maintenance of service roads, private garbage collection). This involvement has been out of need, although it is now formalized as public–private partnerships in urban management. Another source of the collaboration has been through increased subcontracting of services traditionally carried out by municipalities.

In developing a conceptual model for urban management there is a need to capture some of these dynamics and also to include all the key political, economic, and social variables. The major transformations are occurring at all levels, thus making the management matrix complex and multidimensional. Table 15.3 depicts the traditional urban management model, with a clear sectoral public sector orientation and an emphasis on physical planning and infrastucture provision. In this model, local and especially central government are the dominant actors, with non-governmental organizations and international assistance playing a limited role in social sector provision

Table 15.3 **The traditional urban management model**

Actors	Responsibilities (management variables)
Central government	Political and administrative control of local governments Provision of grants and loans for all major utility provisions Development control and land administration Infrastructure development and management Preparation and approval of master plans
Local governments	Directly elected or appointed representatives constituting a decision-making body (local government)
Municipalities Metropolitan governments	Direct provision of social and physical infrastructure Maintenance of services and utilities Development control; preparation of master and local plans
Non-governmental sector	Local-level interventions Social services provision Housing – site and service schemes and upgrading Refugees and rehabilitation

and other emergency relief, perhaps accounting for one-fifth of all management activity.

This is the model that was inherited at independence and prevailed in the first two decades of post-colonial development. Politically the local authorities were elected or appointed bodies with defined jurisdictions. These ranged from relatively high levels of devolved authority (Zimbabwe, South Africa, Kenya) to the much more circumscribed powers found in francophone cities. The level of development of civic culture varied significantly but in most cases, because central authority was a dominant feature of the development paradigm, this tended to hamper local autonomy. In the economic and social spheres, municipal and city governments raised their own local revenue through local taxes and charges, but these were adequate to cover only basic maintenance and recurrent costs. The major portion of local resources was provided by central government in the form of grants and loans. This became even more significant in the 1970s when most countries in sub-Saharan Africa adopted one-party models that politically and economically centralized decision-making. The powers of municipalities and city governments were severely curtailed, and in Tanzania urban local government was actually abolished after the 1967 Arusha declaration. Where local governments were retained, they became part of a hierarchical model of state devolution of political and administrative authority.

Table 15.4 **The emerging public–private sector model of urban management**

Actors	Responsibilities (management variables)
Central government	Political and administrative control of local governments Limited provision of grants and loans Emphasis more on coordination
Local governments	Formally more decentralized Provision and maintenance of basic services Development control; preparation of coordination plans Limited direct provision of services
Non-governmental and private sector	Increased local-level interventions (food for work; upgrading) Social services provision Focus on poverty; informal activities; credit Rehabilitation and refugees

Urban management thinking has been significantly shaped by trends in the broader development debates, where there is a de-emphasis on state intervention and much more faith put on market forces. This rethinking means that the roles of both the state and local governments have been changed. In table 15.4, the emerging public–private sector model of management is depicted, with a reduced role for the central state consistent with the macroeconomic Structural Adjustment Programmes prevailing in many African countries since the early 1980s. Inadequate resources at the central government level affected the levels of grants and loans that could be provided to local authorities. Politically and administratively, less control has been exerted over local governments, and there is a stronger directive to strengthen their autonomy.

The range of actors involved in urban management has grown significantly and there is an emphasis on local-level interventions by NGOs and CBOs. Indeed there has been an abandonment of master plans in favour of more flexible and incremental planning. This is reflected in a range of coordination-type plans that municipalities and cities are advocating. Attention has shifted away from a predominant central government/municipality involvement to the new actors, including local non-governmental agencies, international non-governmental agencies, and private sector business. There is less of a focus on blueprint land-use planning and public sector investment planning and more on coordination planning, where the municipality plays the role of enabler. One could argue that the public–private model is based on the enabling doctrine, according to which government provides an environment conducive to maximum participation by different actors, and that the agenda for management has shifted more to social issues as opposed to traditional physical planning. In all cases the enabling agenda has been more human oriented, focusing on the living standards of urban households, with more attention paid to the informal sector, poverty reduction, access to justice, and broader governance questions.

This public–private sector management model has been largely sustained by external support and resources, particularly from NGOs and bilateral donors, because most cities have limited resources and their revenue bases have not expanded. Indeed, although decentralization of responsibility might have formally increased, there are still very severe constraints on making it function. In theory, the de-emphasis on central public sector planning should strengthen local-level operations, but in practice in many African countries central governments are granting maximum autonomy to local government without adding any extra resources. The dependence of local authorities on central government is being replaced by dependence on donors, which could have adverse long-term consequences for the overall national development process. Thus three sets of relationships must be recognized, critically examined, and re-formed if the shift towards a new form of urban management is to make progress and achieve its aims.

First, as discussed earlier in this volume, urban growth is occurring within economic and political circumstances that are relatively unstable and without sustained economic growth. The shift from model I to model II is therefore not entirely organic, in that, like the institutions and laws that underpin the management structures, it is largely externally induced. The consequences of the Structural Adjustment Programmes are all pervasive and have particularly influenced the development model adopted, from one dominated by the state apparatus to one now largely left to market forces. For many countries and cities the change has not been out of choice but as a direct or indirect result of policy conditionality imposed by the influential Bretton Woods institutions (the IMF and World Bank), which have exerted a significant influence in shaping macroeconomic policies and in turn influence the policies of bilateral donors.

Secondly, although the focus of municipal and city government has always been at local government level, this is very dependent on centre–local relationships. Only in a few countries (e.g. Namibia) is local government enshrined in the constitution. In most cases local government is created by central government and therefore receives its powers and responsibilities from the enabling statutes or decrees. This situation continues to prevail even where there has been a significant shift to a public–private sector model of management. The issue of local government autonomy remains a major factor in the resolution of the nature and character of urban management. Recently, countries such as Zambia, Uganda, and Ghana, under the impetus of the Structural Adjustment Programmes, have proclaimed a significant degree of autonomy for local government. This is a positive approach, allowing for the consolidation of local decision-making powers and may promote meaningful public–private sector development at local levels, if economic growth is achieved.

Thirdly, although the role of NGOs and CBOs has been acknowledged, in most cases there are no formal structures at municipal levels to incorporate them in ongoing decision-making processes. In only very limited cases are non-governmental organizations formally involved in decision-making. They usually get involved in specific local-level interventions that municipalities may view as ad hoc and short lived. There is also a major problem of coordination, which has been experienced in cities such as Lusaka, Nairobi, and Freetown. The role that NGOs are playing is significant. They are responsible for the majority of improvements in low-income settlements. What is lacking are formal relationships, which need to be established between elected local governments and NGOs and CBOs, so that the former can become more demand responsive and the latter better coordinated.

Finally, another important trend has been the debate on public–private partnerships focusing on the profit-making private sector. An increasing role for the private sector has been projected, in terms of franchising, contracting out, leasing, etc. Several major conferences have been held in sub-Saharan Africa (the most recent a Mayors' Colloquium held in Accra in November 1995) to discuss the prospects for strengthening private sector involvement. Some interesting experiences are emerging in the provision of utilities where the private sector is playing a dominant role. There is a need for further research to document the experiences and to map out the changes occurring.

In synthesizing the shift from the traditional urban management model to the public–private sector model it is important to factor in a range of specific country socio-economic and political variables and to track their influence in the process. This can be achieved only through detailed case-studies. In this chapter, only limited evidence will be cited to demonstrate the changes that have occurred or are occurring. It is important to re-emphasize that there are major differences between countries, particularly in relation to differences in size and level of urbanization, which influence both the scale and nature of the problems and appropriate institutional frameworks.

Reviewing experience

The most effective way of addressing the experience with the changes that have occurred in urban management is to use a common time-scale and to chart the changes through it. In the process, the experiences of different cities can be mirrored together. The case-studies in this volume go a long way to achieving that purpose and therefore this particular review will be synthetic, highlighting what are considered to be the major trends.

As noted by Rakodi in chapter 2, at independence in the late 1950s and early 1960s the level of urbanization was very low. In most countries, fewer than 20 per cent of their population were living and working in urban areas. In spite of that, towns and cities still accounted for a substantial portion of total economic activity. Over half of Africa's gross domestic product (GDP) is generated in urban centres and it has been estimated that 75 per cent of industrial activity is urban based and up to 50 per cent of all services. Even when agricultural production is dominant, urban centres are still responsible for providing essential inputs and specialized services, whether produced locally or imported. During the colonial and immediate post-colonial eras the management of towns and cities followed what have been described as the "anglophone" and "francophone" models of government (Alderfer, 1964). These were typical traditional municipal management models, where service provision and maintenance were very much centred on the city hall. In most countries, rural to urban migration was a controlled phenomenon (particularly in southern and eastern Africa), resulting in relatively well-planned and functional urban centres. The image of towns as places of "European settlement" prevailed, and the patterns and processes of governance reflected this. Management was centred on the physical fabric of urban areas, and usually physical planning and provision of services were a prerequisite for development.

In all the countries, it is crucial to understand the colonial legacy and how it shaped the philosophies and ideologies of planning and managing cities. Colonial urbanization implanted new settlements in what were primarily agrarian societies, and the new settlements were completely packaged to reflect the needs of colonial administrators, traders, and settlers. This brought in new value systems, which shaped both the physical and social spaces created in urban areas, as shown by Anyumba (1995) for Kisumu. The new post-colonial administrators adopted the colonial inheritance but were immediately confronted by the major contradictions it presented. These "islands" of economic activity had to be transformed so that they could benefit the needs of the majority of the population, who were still largely rural. The urban areas set high standards for development, and so one of the legacies of colonial Africa has been the maintenance of standards. Until the 1973 oil shocks, most of the major urban centres managed to maintain their social and physical infrastructures fairly well, and, indeed, as highlighted by Becker et al. (1994), most African countries experienced rapid employment growth, with manufacturing employment growth rates of over 10 per cent per year. However, after 1975 there was slower growth and by 1985 patterns of negative growth began to prevail in most countries. This had a major effect on private investment in urban areas, and infrastructure investment declined to zero.

Besides the changes in economic performance, African countries underwent major political changes. Most significant was the almost universal adoption of one-party systems of government and the emergence of military forms of government as a result of coups in the 1960s and 1970s. This had major consequences for local government in both rural and urban areas, and the impact was more significant for the established municipal and city governments.

The first consequence was the loss of the relative autonomy of local governments, as representation became largely a reflection of the one-party structures or military government appointees. Very limited decision-making capacity was left at local level. This applied to all the major countries that had attained independence in the late 1950s and early 1960s – for example, Ghana, Nigeria, Zambia, Tanzania, and Uganda. In the case of Ghana and Nigeria, the military took over, signalling the end of elected national and local governments. In Zambia and Tanzania, the adoption of one-party systems seriously weakened the local government systems. In Uganda, there was growing political instability, which eventually resulted in a military dictatorship. The new governmental structures in all these situations resulted in a growing centralization of political and administrative powers. In francophone countries, which already had a tradition of centralized government, the post-independence adoption of one-party systems reinforced the situation.

The second consequence, closely linked to the first, was the growing management and administrative paralysis at city and municipal government levels. The usurping of all decision-making powers by central government created a major problem in terms of the traditional roles that city local governments had played. The lack of effective municipal governments meant a serious lack of attention to urban problems. There was no political constituency to articulate problems of infrastructure development and maintenance at city government levels. The people who were made mayors and chief executives of urban local authorities had neither the experience nor the competence to deal with urban affairs. In most cases they were simply party or military appointees with no specific urban interests. This represented a major departure from the tradition of civic leaders and aldermen, which was based on a culture of civic interest. In this tradition, towns and cities were managed by those with an interest in the basic activities of the urban economy.

Decentralization of decision-making under one-party systems was largely focused on de-concentrating central government authority to the lowest levels. This authority was in the form of the party, government ministries, and the public sector investment framework. The decentralization did not recognize specific urban interests, which were treated equally with rural district interests. In many cities this distorted land information systems, disrupted the formalization of property rights (Kinshasa, Zaire; Dar es Salaam, Tanzania), and instituted high-level corruption in the functioning of the urban economy, particularly with respect to land allocation (see also chap. 11 in this volume). Even within cities such as Nairobi, functioning in a highly capitalized environment, central government interests and interference distorted normal market functions, making land access largely a political issue.

By 1980, evidence from most major African cities clearly reflected the strain on services, lack of maintenance of infrastructure, and virtual collapse of the traditional municipal model of government. This was the result of political interference, demographic pressure, lack of investment, and poor management. Politically and economically, towns and cities were viewed as part of a chain leading up to central government. There was a clear formal exclusion of other development actors in the process. The lack of autonomy in decision-making meant that local revenue collection was neglected or even abandoned at city level. There was no effective management of human resources and so key personnel left or became redundant. This is a major problem in most African cities today, where there is no cadre of managers with competence and a vision to manage the cities. Salaries are very low and so motivation is non-existent. This is, however, not unique to municipalities, because it affects the whole public sector.

Recent case-studies have highlighted problems of rapid, uncontrolled, and unplanned urbanization: acute shortages of housing and basic shelter; lack of employment; and a high incidence of crime and violence (Stren and White, 1989; Amis and Lloyd, 1990). In Kinshasa, Zaire, Mbuyi (1989) forcefully concluded that "the law of the strongest prevails and the anarchy of Kinshasa's land systems benefits heavy capitalist speculation" (see also Piermay, chap. 7 in this volume). In most cases the management systems have been run down and are riddled with corruption. These problems have been highlighted for Nairobi, Kampala, Addis Ababa, Lusaka, Dakar, and Khartoum (Stren and White, 1989) and for the cities considered in this volume. The problem is not only a lack of resources but a lack of vision. This vision should normally be embedded in both the political and administrative structures, which must be robust enough to respond to the dynamic changes in urban economies.

In response to the well-documented deficiencies and collapse of management systems at city and municipal levels, a variety of non-traditional public sector approaches have been adopted. Most have been supported and funded by external non-governmental organizations and bilateral donors. Initially the focus of most of these agencies was on rural development, but since the 1980s there have been dramatic changes in terms of support to the urban sector. In the late 1970s and early 1980s new approaches emerged in the shelter/housing sector, largely sponsored by the World Bank (for example Dakar, Lusaka, Nairobi), advocating a site and services approach, aided self-help, and a variety of other enabling strategies. This was a recognition of the problems of delivering complete housing units and the high standards that made the outputs unaffordable. There was a call for more community involvement in management processes and a more incremental approach to urban development. In terms of overall urban management, this important shift was an acknowledgement of the role that households play in the development process, and of the city as a dynamic entity with processes occurring at different times and scales.

However, such innovations were not fully incorporated in the political and administrative structures of cities, which in most cases continued to collapse. The new projects created management structures that sometimes duplicated existing municipal structures. The new structures were externally funded and usually managed by expatriates. The end result was that they became unsustainable when the project life expired (for example, in Lusaka and in Dandora in Nairobi). It was not possible to replicate them because the local conditions were never fully recognized in project management. The projects remained outside innovations, with their own structures and direct funding. This has continued to be a major problem with donor-funded projects, in that instead of reforming existing institutions they have usually created new ones linked specifically to project funds.

In the 1980s and 1990s, as also discussed by Aina in chapter 12, there has been a major flourishing of NGOs and CBOs and they have become accepted as part of the urban management scene. In Nairobi, Kenya, for example, there are at least 20 NGOs and CBOs operating at various levels and locations within the city. Their focus is very diverse, but their main thrust is to support urban households in improving their livelihoods. Support has been given to the *jua-kali* (informal) sector, which includes skills training, improving access to credit, and marketing of *jua-kali* products. There has also been a strong focus on poverty-reduction programmes at local neighbourhood level, e.g. Action Aid programmes in Korogocho, Nairobi, and Undugu Society programmes, which are city wide. In some cases, interventions by the non-governmental sector have been carried out in conjunction with the city and central government management systems. There are also several cases where external agencies have provided direct support to localities in conjunction with the local authorities. This has been typical when emergency action is required, e.g. support to refugees and displaced people. This has happened in Tanzania and in Zaire after the Rwandan tragedy. It has also been experienced in peacetime conditions in Lusaka, Zambia, where the World Food Programme has provided support for food-for-work programmes in the spontaneous and squatter areas.

There have been a variety of interventions in other cities sponsored by bilateral donor aid, external NGOs, and multilateral programmes. In all cases the intervention is a direct function of the collapse or non-functionality of the public sector management model. As cities fail to provide water supply, to remove garbage, to provide basic infrastructure, to provide shelter and housing, space has been created for the participation of the non-governmental sector, and new forms of cooperation have emerged in addressing the problems of urban low-income residents. Like the rural sector in the 1960s and 1970s, there are now a significant number of new management actors operating in towns and cities. This has been positive, but there are still major problems of developing integrated management approaches to avoid duplication and disjointed project implementation.

Although no distinct new paradigm of management has emerged, there is no doubt that both central and local governments have recognized the role and importance of the non-governmental sector in urban management. There are several areas where NGOs and CBOs clearly have advantages over the traditional city management models. These include community mobilization in poor and disadvantaged areas, social support at local levels, and the provision of services that are affordable and have adaptable standards. However, it is clear that, if they operate in a political and/or administrative vacuum, major problems arise in terms of ad hoc approaches, donor-driven orientation, and generally a lack of sustainability.

Promising initiatives

More recently, new approaches have been proposed to strengthen the urban management capacities of municipalities. One example is the UNCHS (Habitat) Sustainable Cities Programme (SCP; see also chap. 14 in this volume), whose key objective has been to strengthen the planning and management capacities of urban governments. The programme uses environmental issues as an entry point in trying to strengthen the capacities and abilities of municipalities and encourage broad-based and effective public participation. The approach is largely procedural. The four key steps recommended are:
- identifying priority urban environmental issues and involving the stakeholders;
- formulating urban environmental action plans;
- capacity-building and institutionalizing environmental management strategies and routines;
- formulating and implementing environmental action plans (UNCHS, 1995).

The approach is being implemented in several cities globally, and in most cases it is too early to draw any definite conclusions. In Africa the approach has been adopted in Dar es Salaam, Ibadan, and Accra, with Dar es Salaam as the oldest project (started in 1991/92).

The other major global initiative is the Urban Management Programme, which was launched in 1986, to strengthen the technical and management capacity of countries with respect to urban development. Policy papers have been prepared for the key sectors (land, environment, finance, infrastructure, and poverty) and used in city and country consultations. There is no doubt of the importance of the programme in raising global awareness of urban issues and providing a framework for dissemination of best practices. Like the Sustainable Cities Programme, the focus has been on cities and improving their management performance. Although the annual programme evaluations have been positive, a major criticism has been the scattered nature of the programme and particularly its lack of focus at regional level.

In spite of these initiatives, African cities continue to lack management systems to deal with the challenges of urban development. Most of the global initiatives concentrate on technocratic and procedural issues and fail to address key political and other social dimensions. They have also tended to lack a strong grounding in economic issues, and therefore have hardly addressed critical issues such as the Structural Adjustment Programmes that many countries have been grappling with. Issues such as decentralization have been highlighted without a clear understanding and knowledge of the political dynamics. Therefore hope lies more in the small changes and initiatives that are occurring at local municipal and city levels. Some of these, which could be positive indicators for the future, are reported in anecdotal form in the succeeding paragraphs.

In Johannesburg, South Africa, the city council has been relatively innovative in terms of improving the economic opportunities of the small business and informal sectors, even before the end of apartheid. In the city centre, the planning authority has tried to accommodate informal vendors, thus improving their employment and income opportunities. There is also a much stronger economic orientation in city management in Johannesburg and other South African cities than in other African countries, and this has, *inter alia*, promoted a more efficient development control system geared to catering for the needs of developers. However, as Beavon has emphasized (chap. 5 in this volume), the legacy of apartheid remains strong and will be difficult to overcome in spite of the non-racial political structures being established. The new local government system that was established in 1995 will require significant resources and good management to address the legacy of segregated cities effectively.

In Harare, Zimbabwe, although there have been no major new management innovations, some successes have been recorded since 1980 in adapting the colonial city to the broader needs of the African population. In housing, although major shortages exist, the policy of selling municipal houses to sitting tenants has been successful in empowering African householders, who have become more permanent urban residents and small landlords in many cases. The city has also retained a capacity to generate local revenues and to maintain its infrastructure (Wekwete, 1992). However, there are growing problems of providing services for the increasing numbers of school leavers and those retrenched as a result of the intensified Structural Adjustment Programme since 1990, and of sustaining service provision in a situation of increased economic stress.

In Lusaka, Zambia, the new movement for multi-party democracy reinstated democratic local government in 1991. However, because of years of decay, not much change has occurred and the municipalities still need to be overhauled. There is still too much administrative control in spite of the autonomy enshrined in the Local Government Act. Lusaka offers a good laboratory in terms of the role of private, non-profit actors who have claimed space in the management matrix. Several bilateral aid agencies have set up projects in Lusaka's unplanned compounds, focusing on upgrading and providing social services. The major crisis is the lack of strategic decision-making, which is crucial for major infrastructure investments to improve the performance of the city as a whole (UNCHS, 1993a). The experience of the city shows that the restoration of local democracy requires civic education both amongst citizens and amongst those elected to public office: in 1995 all the elected councillors were suspended and some departmental directors suspended or transferred.

In Dar es Salaam, Tanzania, the city has suffered major infrastructure decay since the mid-1960s and has grown spontaneously without a municipal management system. Central government has a major influence in decision-making through the ministries and parastatals. In 1992, the Sustainable Dar es Salaam project began, with the objective of strengthening management capacity and improving the participation of key stakeholders. The project has set up working groups to deal with the priority areas identified in the environmental profile. This has stimulated significant activity and attracted central government attention to the urban management needs of the city. However, the project has not yet addressed the structural problems that the city faces. These include central–local relationships, particularly the administrative and financial questions. Both these dimensions are still dominated by the central government, and there are few resources for the city to operate with. The major innovation of the project has been the strengthening of a participatory system of management and a forging of public–private sector partnerships. These, however, will not be sustainable unless the management structure is overhauled and the city is able to generate its own local revenues (Mabogunje et al., 1990).

As discussed by Obudho in chapter 9 in this volume, in Nairobi, Kenya, the city has declined from being a vibrant capital of East Africa to one bogged down by lack of basic services. The decay has been explained in terms of corruption at "City Hall," too much central government interference, and the rapid informal development of the city. The then mayor of Nairobi opened the Nairobi City Convention (July 1993) by highlighting the problems of greed and corruption, excessive central government interference facilitated through the powers of the Local Government Act, and the increasing failure of the city to pay its way. The "Nairobi we want" convention was an important social and political landmark, in that it brought together a wide range of actors from the public and private sectors. The resulting action plan covered all the major sectors of the city's development, and highlighted the need to restore and reinforce professionalism and ethics at City Hall. Although there has been no follow-up in terms of implementation, the convention created a forum that has remained an important pressure group on the need for change. Even after the former mayor was deposed, the new mayor has continued to crusade against corruption and has uncovered the "ghost" workers of the city. Recently, the mayor suspended several key officers of council, including the town clerk and chief planner (Karuga, 1993).

In Kampala, Uganda, there are interesting management innovations within the broader governance system that has been established. The Resistance Council System has offered opportunities to change the way both municipal and district councils function and has broadened their responsibilities and scope. Resistance Councils are democratically elected authorities whose jurisdiction covers socio-economic development. In terms of urban management, this innovation has strengthened bottom–up processes in the management of municipalities. There is no evidence yet of Resistance Councils strengthening the capacity for local revenue generation, but there is evidence of strong local-level participation in local-level (neighbourhood) development.

These examples point to some of the limited innovations occurring in the urban management sphere. There is still a major challenge to document them and to identify emerging models. There is, however, evidence of a shift towards a more public–private sector management model, away from the predominantly public sector approach.

Conclusions

The main conclusion of this chapter is that recent urban management experience in Africa clearly shows that changes are occurring in terms of who manages the cities and what objects are being managed. Although there has been significant documentation of the malaise found in many cities, there has not been enough documentation or conceptualization of the types of changes that are occurring. As a result, my conclusion that a changing model of urban management is emerging can be only provisional.

It is important that urban management, like economic management, be viewed first and foremost as the management of scarce resources in ways that are sustainable, equitable, and efficient. Traditional economic variables (land, labour, and capital) have to be understood within the framework of urban economies. Organization for city management should therefore have a significant economic and business orientation. This dimension has been lacking, resulting in a tendency to focus on the supply orientation of urban management. Another key variable is political organization. Any management process has a political base and in many cities of Africa it is vital that the base shifts away from central government to local government. This shift, if it occurs, will undermine the traditional top–down orientation and strengthen the role of democratically elected authorities and civil society generally. Those elected to manage the cities should be fully empowered to take responsibility for their actions and should have the freedom to appoint good managers, lawyers, planners, and accountants to manage city activities. All this points to a need to strengthen local autonomy and to tilt centre–local relationships in favour of the local level. Finally, in each case there is no escape from asking: What is being managed? Who is being managed? What is the formula for resource allocation and management? These are critical and fundamental questions and they have to be asked and answered in a holistic way. This is the challenge for urban management in Africa now and into the future.

Note

The views expressed in this paper are solely those of the author and should not be attributed to the United Nations Centre for Human Settlements or its officials or individuals acting on its behalf.

References

Alderfer, H. F. 1964. *Local Government in Developing Countries.* McGraw Hill, New York.

Amis, P. and P. Lloyd, eds. 1990. *Housing Africa's Urban Poor.* Manchester University Press, Manchester.

Anyumba, G. 1995. *Kisumu Town: History of the Built Form, Planning and Environment: 1890–1990.* Delft University Press, Delft.

Bahl, R. W. and J. F. Linn. 1992. *Urban Public Finance in Developing Countries.* Oxford University Press, Oxford.

Becker, C. M., A. M. Hamer, and A. R. Morrison. 1994. *Beyond Urban Bias in Africa.* Heinemann, Portsmouth, N.H.

Clarke, G. 1991. Urban management in developing countries. A critical role. *Cities* 8(2): 93–107.

Karuga, J. G., ed. 1993. *Actions Towards a Better Nairobi. Report and Recommendations of the Nairobi City Convention.* Nairobi City Council, Nairobi.

Mabogunje, A. L. 1990. Urban planning and the post-colonial state in Africa. A research overview. *African Studies Review* 33(2): 121–203.

Mabogunje, A. L. et al. 1990. United Republic of Tanzania. Managing sustainable growth and development in Dar-es-Salaam (URT/90/033). Field report of the evaluation team, UNDP/United Republic of Tanzania, Dar es Salaam.

Mattingley, M. 1994. Meaning of urban management. *Cities* 11(3): 201–205.

Mawhood, P., ed. 1983. *Local Government in the Third World. The Experience of Tropical Africa.* Wiley, Chichester; 2nd edn, Africa Institute, Pretoria, 1993.

Mbuyi, K. 1989. Problems of urban management, infrastructure and food provision. In: R. E. Stren and R. R. White, eds., *African Cities in Crisis: Managing Rapid Urban Growth.* Westview, Boulder, Colo., pp. 148–175.

Stren, E. R. 1993. Urban management in development assistance. An elusive concept *Cities* 10(2): 125–138.

Stren, R. E. and R. R. White, eds. 1989. *African Cities in Crisis: Managing Rapid Urban Growth.* Westview Press, Boulder, Colo.

UNCHS (Habitat). 1993a. Zambia: Human Settlements Sector Report for UNDP. UNCHS, Nairobi, mimeo.

———— 1993b. Improvement of municipal management. Report of the Executive Director. *Habitat International.* 17(1): 3–31.

———— 1995. *Sustainable City News* 1(1).

UNCHS/UNDP/World Bank. 1995. Urban Management Programme. Report of the mid-term evaluation/forward looking assessment mission. UNCHS/UNDP/World Bank, Nairobi/New York/Washington D.C., mimeo.

Wekwete, K. H. 1992. Urban local government finance. The case of Harare. *Public Administration and Development* 12: 97–110.

16

Conclusion

Carole Rakodi

Abstract

Ce dernier chapitre fait ressortir certains des principaux thèmes et des principales conclusions, en mettant d'abord l'accent sur les rapports entre mondialisation et urbanisation en Afrique, puis sur les caractéristiques du processus d'urbanisation des plus grandes villes, et enfin sur les questions qui se posent et les expériences acquises en matière de politique et de gestion. Les liens avec l'économie mondiale par le biais des investissements des sociétés transnationales sont surtout constitués par les exportations de produits primaires, même si le peu que les transnationales investissent dans les manufactures et les services se concentre dans les villes. Le consumérisme mondial est plus envahissant, favorisé par le contrôle que les transnationales exercent sur les médias et il en va de même pour l'influence des agences internationales. C'est pourquoi l'autonomie économique et politique de l'Afrique est handicapée par sa position dans le monde. Les effets des conditions en matière de politique imposées par les donateurs et les programmes de prêts se font fortement sentir, directement et indirectement, dans les zones urbaines. Les conditions des relations entre les pays d'Afrique et l'économie mondiale et la façon dont elles ont évolué avec le temps sont un des déterminants essentiels des modes d'urbanisation, mais pas le seul.

Malgré un ralentissement du rythme de la croissance urbaine, notamment dans la plupart des villes les plus importantes, au cours des dernières décennies et en particulier durant les années les plus sombres de la récession, ces villes continuent de se propager à un taux plus élevé que celui de la croissance naturelle. Les tendances de l'économie urbaine, notamment la stagnation ou le rétrécissement du secteur officiel de grande envergure au profit du secteur informel et du travail temporaire en même temps que la diversification et l'épanouissement du secteur informel, sont assez mal comprises. La tendance à une prédominance croissante de mécanismes officieux, voire illégaux, pour la division et l'aménagement des sols se fait sentir dans tout le continent. Face à la récession et à l'augmentation des inégalités, les ménages urbains ont réagi de diverses façons, tirant parti des stratégies de migration, des liaisons entre villes et campagnes, de l'esprit d'entreprise, du travail des femmes et de la culture des sols urbains disponibles. La libéralisation politique s'est traduite par une évolution de la recherche, qui met moins l'accent sur les aspects ethniques en eux-mêmes, les classes, la nature de l'État, les régimes autoritaires et les relations de patron à client que sur la résurgence de la société civile. Le chapitre décrit, document à l'appui, le rôle des organizations non-gouvernementales, et autres associations de la société civile, dans la vie et la gestion urbaine, quoiqu'il soit encore difficile de discerner si la prolifération de ces associations va avoir un impact à long terme et une signification politique majeure. Les mesures prises jusqu'à présent pour la gestion de la ville se sont avérées incapables de relever le défi de l'accélération de la croissance. L'échec de la décentralisation, de la réforme des structures et procédures administratives et de la révision des politiques, exacerbé par la récession et les programmes d'ajustement structurel, a provoqué une nette détérioration de la qualité de la vie, surtout chez les pauvres, et de la capacité des organismes urbains. Il va falloir changer les régimes politiques et administratifs des villes ainsi que les politiques et procédures de gestion urbaine, en particulier en matière de création de ressources, de développement économique, d'apport d'infrastructures et de services, de logements et de sols, de planification des sols, de réglementation et d'amélioration de l'environnement. Enfin, il faudrait déterminer quelles nouvelles données améliorées et quelles nouvelles recherches de fond nous permettraient de mieux comprendre l'économie et les sociétés urbaines, les marchés immobiliers, les mesures politiques et les effets des politiques et procédures de planification et de gestion.

Introduction

The first part of the concluding chapter draws out some of the main themes and findings of this volume, concentrating first on the relationships between globalization and urbanization in Africa, secondly on the characteristics of the urbanization process and the largest cities, and thirdly on policy and management issues and experience. Finally, some of the outstanding research needs and priorities are identified.

Global forces and Africa's future

Whatever the terms and outcomes of its integration into the world economy, world politics, and the cultural–ideological world system, Africa is, like it or not, part of that system. On balance, as discussed by Rakodi (chap. 2) and Simon (chap. 3) in this volume (see also Sklair, 1991; Brown, 1995), Africa has in the past and continues in the present to lose more than it gains: for much of the continent, dependency, marginalization, and a lack of policy autonomy are the main outcomes of its incorporation. The organizational framework for the global economy, as discussed in this volume, is comprised of two interlocking sets of institutions: the transnational corporations (TNCs) engaged in exploitation of primary resources, manufacturing, and services, as well as the institutions that enable them to carry out their activities, such as the major stock exchanges; and the international agencies, particularly the International Monetary Fund (IMF) and the World Bank, pulling in their wake smaller multilateral and bilateral agencies. External forces, be they TNCs or international agencies, call the shots, heavily influencing patterns of investment, preventing the write-off of debts, and dictating particular economic policy packages. Africa's bargaining power is so limited and the *developmental* effects of global economic changes and international agency policy conditionality so negligible for much of the continent that reductions in dependency, participation in growing and prosperous sectors of the global economy, and dynamic economic growth and development seem remote possibilities.

Though large parts of the economies of African countries, both rural and urban, do not come under the control of TNCs, almost none is immune from the effects of donor conditionality and aid, and global consumerism has penetrated even urban slums and remote rural areas, thanks to the power of the media and advertising. Links with

555

the global economy are particularly manifest in the cities, which are the locations within countries for much of whatever TNC investment in manufacturing has occurred, TNC administration and services, and the offices of international agencies and diplomats. In addition, their populations have easier access to imported goods and the media. Even in the cities, however, large parts of the economy, the spatial fabric, and the socio-political structure are not directly affected by the operations of TNCs, although many of these have been indirectly affected by the terms of the continent's integration into the world economy and culture.

At present, foreign direct investment continues to be interested primarily in the exploitation of primary resources (Seddon, 1995). There seems little prospect of investment in the more labour-intensive stages of the manufacturing process in profitable high-technology sectors flowing into Africa as it has into East and South-East Asia, leading Rogerson (chap. 10) to term Africa's current state "stalled globalization." Nevertheless, in some interesting quarters, including Japanese trading companies, Afro-American investors, and South African manufacturers, there is a spark of interest in further investment, perhaps because high profits may be made where the potential is unexploited and the risk high. However, poor transport and communications, inadequate infrastructure, labyrinthine and ineffective bureaucracies, and uneducated labour forces continue to deter large-scale foreign investment. Recent recognition of this by national governments, city administrations, and international agencies is already starting to bring about changes, and these are likely to accelerate, at least in some countries, in the next decade.

In addition, the increased cultural hegemony of global consumerism seems unstoppable, as transnational producers penetrate global markets with the aid of transnational-controlled media – media that have, with satellite technology, become more accessible to remote and low-income populations, as well as to the urban élite, in every African country. The demand for "global" consumer goods, from televisions to Coca Cola (see Simon in chap. 3), combined with IMF insistence on liberalization of import controls, has biased the composition of imports away from those needed for productive purposes towards consumer goods. Although import controls were undoubtedly in need of reform and streamlining, given the limited capacity of African countries to earn foreign exchange, such a wholesale abandonment of policy objectives in favour of free market economics has been extremely damaging to countries' fledgling manufacturing bases and other sectors such as transport. Even if liberalization is slowed and some protection sustained, as recommended, for example, by Riddell (1993), penetration by global consumer goods industries into African markets is likely to continue. Because of the coincidence of satellite-based media technology and political liberalization, it seems likely that the use of the media to foster consumerism, disseminate global culture, and even spread religious views will outweigh the potential advantages of more accessible media for educational and developmental purposes. In Ghana, for example, the government-controlled press, which might choose to use some of its capacity for civic education, is under attack in the name of political liberalization in favour of an ostensibly independent but in practice party-political press. However, increased access to global channels of communication also creates opportunities for easier interaction between academics and professionals, and especially between non-governmental organizations (NGOs), with unpredictable results.

The political game in Africa has changed, with the end of the Cold War, the collapse of communist regimes in Eastern Europe, and the association made by international agency economists and others between economic liberalization and political liberalization on a European–North American model. Although interference by the colonial powers, especially France, persists, there are signs of an increasing reluctance to prop up patrimonial rulers merely because of their Western sympathies, first because it is clear that development has not resulted from often protracted periods of such rule, and secondly because such personal authoritarian rule does not fit easily with the West's advocacy of greater political competition elsewhere in the continent. Although much of the explicit or implicit political policy conditionality is crass and superficial, and the type of political liberalization advocated may have economically and politically destabilizing effects, it is opening up political spaces that were constricted during the most authoritarian periods of one-party and military rule. Changes in international political forces are, therefore, provoking a widespread reconfiguration of domestic politics, with particular implications for urban areas that will be explored further below.

The pervasive but contradictory influences of the international agencies in Africa have been referred to again and again in this volume. The institutions themselves have, as a result of the far from uniformly successful and sometimes devastating effects of their policies, been under attack mainly, but not only, from recipient countries. Although criticism has led to some shifts in the policies advocated and ways of operating (Green, 1993; Ravenhill, 1993; Green and Faber, 1994), the basic rationale of the system and its neoclassical economic theory underpinnings remain unchanged. Until decision-making power in the institutions is more evenly distributed between backers and recipients, the hegemony of a theoretical world-view that is based on faith rather than empirical evidence is challenged (George and Sabelli, 1994), improved economic understanding is accompanied by more nuanced political and social analysis, and their mode of operation is less centralized and autocratic, the relationship between African countries and these institutions seems unlikely to change, despite attempts to negotiate more appropriate reforms (Aboyade, 1994).

However, it is wrong to be wholly pessimistic about the impact of global forces on the African continent: Egypt has benefited from its roles in Cold War politics and as a labour source for Middle Eastern countries, Libya from high oil prices, and other North African countries from their proximity to Europe and ties with the Arab world. Although their economies still have structural shortcomings, poverty is widespread, and urban problems unsolved, these benefits are manifest in economies that are more prosperous and diversified than in much of sub-Saharan Africa (SSA). In southern Africa, the achievement of political freedom in the continent's industrial giant has dramatically changed domestic and regional prospects for economic growth and development with, as yet, unpredictable consequences. Some smaller countries, notably Botswana, have achieved significant economic and social progress, and others, such as Uganda and Mozambique, have achieved peace after periods of civil war. Although Africans have in the recent past had little success in advancing their own alternatives to the stabilization and structural adjustment policies of the IMF and World Bank, convincing policy statements are starting to emerge, notably from the UN Economic Commission for Africa (Brown, 1995). Cooperation between African countries has been deterred by, for example, the concern of politicians in the immediate post-independence period to consolidate and sustain the nation-states based on artificial boundaries in which they took power, the varying colonial heritage, ongoing ties with the colonial powers, late struggles for independence in parts of the continent, and the effect of international Cold War politics. However, there are signs that some of the more recent groupings, such as the Southern Africa Development Conference (SADC), will be more enduring, thus potentially providing a basis for stronger and more diversified regional economies (Adedeji, 1993; Brown, 1995).

Urbanization

Urban population growth

The terms on which African countries interact with the world economy and the way in which these have changed over time are a major, but not the only, factor determining patterns of urbanization. The inherited colonial pattern of urbanization, designed to facilitate the exploitation of resources and administrative and political control, was developed from scratch in parts of the continent and overlain on older patterns of urban development in others, as sketched in chapter 2. The asymmetrical pattern, centred on ports, large-scale European commercial farming areas, mines, and the transport routes connecting these, has persisted. Indeed, the continued location of most capitals in the former colonial capital, accompanied by the state-centred model of development and centralized administrative and political systems that characterized countries in the decades after independence, and the continued dependence on exports of primary products and imports of most manufactured and all capital goods, reinforced the inherited pattern. Similarly, the constraints on development of secondary cities and small towns arising from colonial neglect of peasant agriculture and the exclusion of indigenous populations from many business activities were reinforced in the years after independence by continued neglect of peasant agriculture, state domination of agricultural input supply and marketing, and the obstacles placed in the way of budding entrepreneurs by the general shortage of credit, by poor infrastructure, and by heavy-handed government regulation. Making up in some cases for colonial/settler restrictions on rural–urban migration, and fuelled by the urban bias of investment and state activity, the largest cities grew extremely rapidly in the years immediately after independence. Since then, rates of urban growth have slowed down but, insofar as it is possible to tell in the absence of reliable and regular censuses, cities continued to grow at rates above already fast rates of natural increase. As discussed by Simon in chapter 3 and Potts in chapter 13, although there is some evidence of even slower rates of growth in the worst crisis years, typically in the 1980s, and in the urban settlements whose economic base has been hardest hit by recession and liberalization policies, it seems that such slow-downs were temporary. Even modest rates of growth in the largest cities, of course, represent large absolute population increases, and may reflect continued net in-migration, because there is evidence from some countries of lower fertility among urban populations.

The continued growth of large cities is partly due to the natural increase of their own populations and this is likely to decrease only slowly, despite the as yet unpredictable effects of AIDS. The continued attraction of the cities for rural migrants, in a context in which recession and liberalization policies have had an adverse effect on public and large-scale private sector employment and wages, while simultaneously favouring rural production, is more puzzling. In addition, urban management systems are generally unable to keep pace with infrastructure needs and, in some cases, have all but collapsed. Continued rural–urban migration in such apparently discouraging circumstances throws doubt on the validity of earlier models of migration and the urban economy. The experience of cities such as Lagos and Kinshasa, documented in this book, shows that it is unrealistic to anticipate any significant or permanent slow-down in rates of urban population growth. And should economies begin to recover, as a result of increased world demand for Africa's products or structural adjustment policies, cities are likely to grow even more rapidly. Although the attention to rural development and the agricultural sector that characterizes current policies in some countries, such as Ghana, may give an impetus to the growth of second- and third-tier settlements, the continued desire for industrialization and the political importance of urban populations will fuel large-city growth and will (and should) not permit urban neglect.

Urban economies

What is clear from the trends of urban development in the 1980s and 1990s is that our understanding of the economic dynamics of African cities is partial. In the 1970s, when the existence of an informal sector providing small-scale economic opportunities for the working poor was officially acknowledged, it seemed clear that demand generated by those working in the formal sector was what sustained informal sector activities. Indeed, Beavon's account of Johannesburg (chap. 5) and Dubresson's of Abidjan (chap. 8) in this volume still portray a dominant formal sector and an informal sector largely dependent on demand generated by formal economic activity and lacking an independent dynamic of its own. Rogerson (chap. 10), however, documents the increasing predominance of informal employment in many cities and draws on recent work, especially by the International Labour Office Jobs and Skills Programme for Africa (JASPA), to increase our understanding of the sector.

In both the global and domestic economies, it is clear that there are both formal and informal economic activities. Examples of informal activities in the global economy might include drug trafficking and smuggling. However, it is also clear, first, that there are continua within both sectors from illegal to legal and from profitable to marginal activities, which are not captured by the dualist conceptualization of the urban economy, and, secondly, that current trends include informalization and reduced dominance of the formal sector. There are, Rogerson notes, various layers of informalization, ranging from enterprises that simply operate without licences, pay no tax, or occupy a particular site without permission, to major corruption and crime. In addition, a distinction must be made between those enterprises that are dynamic, profitable, and have a potential for growth, and those that are involutionary – survivalist enterprises that help people cope with economic shocks but that are overcrowded and unprofitable. What is also clear from studies of recent changes in the organization of production and services is that increased use of subcontracting and processes of deskilling and casualization are creating forms of production that do not fit the common understanding of formal sector enterprises, shading as they do into small-scale, unprotected, and unenumerated sectors such as commission selling and home-work. Some of these changes, he suggests, create opportunities for clusters of small and medium enterprises that can then develop a growth dynamic of their own, although not yet in Africa.

During the 1980s open unemployment became more significant and visible, especially among young people. This illustrated not only the decline in formal wage employment but also, according to some authors, the growing inability of the informal sector to absorb more workers (Zeleza, 1994). However, with the decline in real public sector wages in the 1980s making them unimportant components of income for many households, not only is it less common than it ever was for households to rely solely on the formal sector for their livelihoods, but also, in many cities, it is apparent that the demand generated by either formal enterprises or formal sector wages is insufficient to explain the size, persistence, and diversification of the informal sector. Thus, not everyone agrees that the informal sector lacks potential. A study of five SSA countries (Botswana, Kenya, Malawi, Swaziland, and Zimbabwe) estimates that during the period from 1981 to 1990 over 40 per cent of the labour force increase was absorbed by small-scale non-primary enterprises, mostly through starts of new businesses but also by enterprise growth and graduation to the intermediate size category (50+) (Mead, 1994). Although less than a quarter of these were in the urban areas and the study was unable, because of the difficulty of collecting such information, to determine the level of profitability of the businesses surveyed, it implies a significant and dynamic small-scale sector, in which high failure rates amongst new businesses are more than compensated for by the number of start-ups. The jury is still out on the role and dynamics of the small-scale informal sector and its relationship to a declining or stagnant and partly informalized large-scale formal sector. What is certain is that available studies and published statistics are an inadequate base for analysis and understanding in either economic or spatial terms.

Economic activities occupy different areas of economic space, but they also have a physical manifestation. Whereas the organized employment centres of industrial areas and central business districts (CBDs) are well established in most African cities, and informal activities have been ubiquitous in some, the concentration of clusters of informal enterprises in particular urban spaces, as well as their proliferation throughout the city regardless of zoning, are more recent phenomena in many, as liberalization of both economic policies and restrictive regulations has proceeded. The significance of site and location to large-scale and formal enterprises is reasonably well understood, but the role of site, location, and proximity to companion or competing enterprises and customers for small-scale enterprises has been little studied.

Property markets

The mechanism through which economic and other activities occupy space and become manifest physically is the property market. My review of evidence on the real, as opposed to the theoretical, functioning of urban property markets in African cities in chapter 11 illustrates the prevalence of informal but not ill-organized transactions, although to a differing extent in different cities. Cities thus range from Harare, with universal private tenure and a formal land market, at one extreme; through the cities where the state struggles to maintain control over subdivision, issue of title, and construction in the face of increasingly prevalent illegal subdivision of privately or communally held land; to Kinshasa at the other extreme, where agents of the state have "privatized" land supply. The squatting that was prevalent in many cities in the 1960s and 1970s was less anarchic than it appeared to many analysts, drawing as it did on understandings of property rights embodied in communal tenure systems. In addition, access to urban land through the legitimate exercise of communal tenure rights was important, especially in cities that predated colonial rule. Both these ways of obtaining land have changed as urbanization has become more established, so that the predominant means of getting access to land in many cities today is through the illegal subdivision of legally owned communal or private land. Increasingly, those with claims to land have taken the law and procedures into their own hands, as the capacity of the state to facilitate and regulate land transactions has declined and land markets have become increasingly commercialized. Clearly, just as with most small-scale activity, some accommodation with the prevalent mechanisms for land and property development must be made by the state. This point will be returned to in the discussion of urban management below.

Social structures and processes in cities

As most clearly recognized by francophone analysts, land transactions and their outcomes, as well as the concepts of property on which they are based, reflect not merely economic but also social and political relations. Thus the claims of members of kinship networks to usufruct rights in land held under communal tenure, or of lineage members to accommodation rights in family houses, as in Ghana, are rooted in pre-existing social structures. The adaptation of social processes and patterns to the demands of urban development concerns both Aina and Potts, as well as a number of the authors of the city case-studies in this volume. While Aina in chapter 12 is more concerned with social networks and their intersection with political organization, Potts (chap. 13) focuses on the economic and social basis for urban livelihoods and thus shares an area of concern with Rogerson. Drawing on evidence from many parts of the continent, she demonstrates the increasing poverty and inequality that have accompanied recession and structural adjustment (see also O'Connor,

1991). Although the deliberate anti-urban bias of structural adjustment policies was in some respects justified, their economic rationale
and crude design failed to recognize both that urban populations
are differentiated and that reduced investment in infrastructure and
education would in the longer term adversely affect both existing
economic activities and the longer-term potential for recovery and
diversification. As a result, the already disadvantaged in urban areas
have been affected worst, although many of the waged lower middle
class have also been hard hit. Cairo is typical:

Cairo's overcrowdedness, deteriorating physical infrastructure and public
services are compounded for the majority of its population by glaring
inequalities of power and wealth. As there is struggle for Cairo's soul, there
is an even more intense struggle for the limited resources and privileges.
Cairo's elite (top 5 percent) in recent years has been oblivious to the fate
and conditions of the majority of the rest of the city's poorer quarters.... It
is the middle classes, especially the lower rungs, which feel the squeeze, and
the youngsters are steaming with frustration and anger. Much of Cairo's
future, and hence of Egypt's, may very well lie in their hands. (Eddin Ibrahim, 1987, pp. 225–226)

In these conditions, some analysts suggest, crime and prostitution
increase (see Obudho on Nairobi in chap. 9), while Touré et al.
(1992), in a study that emphasizes increased inequality and poverty,
discriminatory investment in infrastructure, and the precariousness
of life for the majority in Abidjan, also draw attention to a rise in
xenophobia in that cosmopolitan city, which they attribute to the
need to find scapegoats for economic hardship.

The reactions of urban households have been diverse and ingeni-
ous, drawing on migration strategies, rural–urban links, entrepreneurial skills, female labour, and access to unused urban land. Cultivation, of both rural land, to which many urban residents continue to
have rights, and undeveloped urban land, has been an important
component of the livelihood strategies for many urban residents, as
stressed by both Rogerson (chap. 10) and Potts (chap. 13). However,
Rogerson acknowledges that much of the evidence on the extent of
urban agriculture is impressionistic; that the dividing line between
urban cultivation, which is primarily for household consumption, and
peri-urban agriculture, which may be subsistence or commercial, is
unclear; and that information on its environmental implications is
lacking. It is clear from the city case-studies in this volume that the
extent of urban agriculture varies: unused land that can be cultivated

is less available in higher-density cities (such as Cairo) or parts of cities (such as the central areas of Lagos), in some of the cities with more commercialized land markets (although not Nairobi), and in cities where residents are predominantly renters rather than house-owners. Although most contributors acknowledge that urban culti-vation and sometimes animal rearing may be a significant element in the livelihood strategies of many (not always poor) urban house-holds, the contribution of such food production to the total city food supply is unknown and suspected by some (for example Piermay in the case of Kinshasa – chap. 7) to be limited. Analysis of the potential of and constraints on urban agriculture is lacking. The use of land for cultivation, especially on a permanent basis, has opportunity costs, while the effectiveness of support to urban agriculture compared with support to peri-urban agriculture or other types of small-scale enter-prise is not known. In addition, there has been little investigation of the environmental impacts of urban agriculture, both cultivation and livestock keeping, or the effects of air and water pollution on the products of urban gardens.

The last major aspect of urban development to be dealt with in a thematic chapter and to varying extents in the city case-studies is the social and political organization and processes that have come increasingly to be grouped under the term "civil society." Civil society is a general term that refers to social phenomena beyond for-mal state structures but not necessarily disconnected from the state (Woods, 1992). Subject to longstanding debate in the academic liter-ature, there seems to be no consensus on its precise meaning, boundaries, or relationship with the state (Aina in chap. 12; see also Woods, 1992; Mamdani, 1992). In African societies, certain compo-nents of society and politics other than the state have been important focuses of attention, in particular ethnicity and, more recently, class, as well as specific groups such as trade unions. These have not, on the whole, been theorized in terms of an over-arching concept of civil society that can be set against that of the state. Indeed, more recent analysts seem to disagree on which types of association should be regarded as part of civil society. Woods (1992), for example, appears to exclude pre-colonial ethnic and kinship groups, asserting that eth-nically based associations in urban areas, which were formed in the social space created by colonial urbanization, mark the emergence of civil society. The forms of political power and leadership that have predominated in post-independence Africa and the state-centred model of development that was adopted have resulted in most attention in the political science literature being given to the nature of the state, the characteristics and shortcomings of patrimonial rule, the rise of authoritarianism, and the prevalence of military regimes (Healey and Robinson, 1992). Relatively little attention has been given to either civil society or the particular characteristics of urban politics.

In part this can be explained by the nature of post-independence regimes and the political and developmental models they adopted. Authoritarian rule and state-centred development were accompanied by restrictions on the formation of NGOs and often repression of groups critical of the prevailing political and economic order. In addition, urban populations benefited from the jobs created in an expanding public sector and lacked avenues for accumulation that did not depend on access to state resources. Not until the 1980s, as the economic crisis threatened the accumulation strategies of the urban élite and middle class, did critical voices start seriously to challenge the political structures and economic policies (Woods, 1992; Chazan and Rothchild, 1993). This is as true in the cities of north Africa as elsewhere in the continent. Findlay (1994, p. 189) finds it unsurprising that cities in the Arab world have become the focus of unrest and protest:

[It is in cities that] inequalities within society are most starkly displayed ... and the contested images of Arab society are most powerfully portrayed in terms of the symbols of the built environment. And it is in the urban riot or demonstration that those without power can most forcefully challenge political decision makers about the future directions of state development policies.

The voluntary associations that have proliferated to articulate various interests, including professional associations, religious groups, and women's associations, interact with ascriptive groups including ethnic and kinship associations. Their interaction with each other and the state determines the characteristics and boundaries of civil society (Chazan and Rothchild, 1993). Although social structures based on ethnicity are associated predominantly with rural areas, and the emerging pluralistic associational movement is associated broadly with the urban middle class, overlaps are more significant and a crude rural–urban distinction is inappropriate. Traditional social structures are said to be underlain by values of solidarity and communitarian responsibility and to have advantages over imported social, economic, and political systems based on individualism and competition.

Said to have been undermined by urbanization, it is clear that, although rapid social change has occurred, ethnic allegiances and support systems remain significant for urban as well as rural people and are important influences on both urban politics and daily life. In addition, the growth of informal sector economic activity during the 1980s was accompanied by the development of collective organizations to cope with the scarcity of credit, establish alternatives to government monopoly trading networks, and provide services (Chazan and Rothchild, 1993; Stren et al., 1994). These are confined neither to the middle class nor to urban areas.

The increasing numbers of NGOs are, it is hypothesized, both an outcome of political and economic change and likely to contribute to political change and make it difficult to reverse. Fowler (1991) attempts to assess whether NGOs have, as expected, been a significant force in eastern and southern Africa's political liberalization. He concludes that, with the exception of South Africa, they have not, because fragmentation of the sector inhibits the formation of strong representative bodies to defend their interests and argue for them on development policy issues; there are still only a few strong mass membership organizations; there is little indication of a coalescence of community-level bodies into politically significant networks and broader independent associations; many are top–down, undemocratic, élitist organizations or consultants by another name; external funding is a mixed blessing because of the additional controls it implies and the ambivalent reaction of governments to its being channelled to NGOs; and governments disregard or discriminate against professional organizations such as lawyers' and journalists' associations. Thus, although the NGO sector has expanded, there is little evidence that this has encouraged political pluralism beyond whatever changes the state itself finds expedient and increasing evidence that "existing elites are both consolidating themselves within the voluntary sector and limiting its political impact by external controls" (Fowler, 1991, p. 74). In addition, while recognizing the continued significance of traditional social structures and their potential to provide alternative models of social and political organization, and the importance of social relationships based on trust and reciprocity in groups such as home town associations or rotating credit associations, care must be taken not to romanticize either ascriptive or voluntary groups in civil society. They are no more immune to patriarchy, clientelism, and venality than state bureaucratic or political interests. Nevertheless, the renewed attention that is being paid to urban social and political forces because of their significance in national political change is important because, it is suggested,

> the emergence of powerful forces at the local urban level within civil society, combined with both national and international support for the institutionalisation of decentralisation and democratisation, have led to new forms of local governance and local arrangements for solving urban problems. (Stren, 1995, p. 12)

To what extent do the arrangements for urban administration and the policies and practices of urban planning and management revealed in the city case-studies in this volume bear out Stren's assertion? Can the current arrangements for urban management cope with the challenge?

Coping with the challenge

The inherited legal, institutional, and financial arrangements for managing urban development, although different in many details in different African countries, have clearly been unable to cope with the challenge for decades. In part this has been due to the inappropriate laws, institutional and decision-making structures, and revenue-generating instruments on which they are based and the failure of post-independence governments to make significant and appropriate changes. In part it has been due to the stress imposed on *any* institutional structure by rapid and unpredictable growth and change. And in part it has been due to the contradictions inherent in a state-centred model of economic and political development.

The inability of many central states to raise sufficient resources, develop sufficient administrative capacity, and operate in a sufficiently flexible way to deliver their development promises at the local level was already becoming clear in the late 1960s. Decentralization has periodically formed part of the political rhetoric of central governments since then, and administrative reforms have been attempted in a number of countries. However, political rhetoric has not been accompanied by devolution of decision-making power and the decentralization of administrative responsibilities has not been matched by the development of administrative and financial capacity to fulfil them. Although the political importance of urban populations has been recognized in national policies, such as the cheap food policy pursued by many countries, the damaging results of such policies have outstripped any progress in generating resources within urban areas to finance and manage their own developmental needs. The result has been unaccountable and poorly coordinated urban administration; failures in service delivery, development promotion, and regulation; and the decreasing ability of the formal system of management to control more than a minor part of the urban sphere. The cities have shared in the general crisis of public administration (Mutahaba et al., 1993), as is clear from the accounts in this book. Practical failures of service delivery and daily administration have given rise to fiscal crises, crises of political legitimacy, and opportunities for mismanagement and corruption. More recently, cities have suffered considerably from the effects of economic policy reforms, illustrating that there are limits on the political influence of urban groups (Healey and Robinson, 1992).

The inability of central government and city administrations to cope with the challenge of growth has had adverse implications for the development of national and urban economies, for the stability of political systems, and for the lives of urban residents, as is clear from the accounts presented here. The solution is said to be improved urban management. In assessing the likelihood that the management systems of African cities can rise to the challenge in the next decade, both the political and institutional arrangements for governance and the functions and tasks to be performed by administrative agencies need to be considered. These will be discussed in turn.

Urban governance

The "good governance" debate in which the international agencies have engaged African governments is related to the economic and political liberalization agendas discussed above. By the end of the 1970s the state was diagnosed as being overburdened, and this was said to account for its failure to cope with demands, its reduced efficiency, and the bloated size of the public sector. Structural Adjustment Programmes were, therefore, associated with demands that the size and role of the public sector should be reduced and its efficiency increased via budgetary reform and the adoption of private sector management methods. Expenditure cut-backs, reductions in employment, and some privatization occurred, but there was little evidence of enhanced capacity in the administrative system because of a failure adequately to consider the new institutional capacities demanded by economic and political reform, defects in the process of policy management, and organizational dysfunctions, including a proliferation of agencies with poorly defined roles and inadequate coordination mechanisms, the stultification of local governance, and the neglect of NGOs (Mutahaba et al., 1993).

The extent to which the cities described in this volume have arrangements for local government – defined as "a broadly account-able system of governance with respect to a wide range of functions" (Stren, 1991, p. 15) – varies. In the francophone countries of Africa, urban government was established on the French model. The largest cities had elected councils and elected mayors, and were responsible for a significant range of local services. However, immediately on independence, the national governments of countries such as Senegal and Côte d'Ivoire took over control of the largest cities, explicitly because of their financial insolvency and administrative incom-petence but implicitly in order to establish control over potential political opposition. In anglophone Africa likewise, elected local councils had been put in place by the end of the colonial period, but their performance fell far short of their responsibilities and growing demands, and their political autonomy and fiscal base were pro-gressively eroded during the 1960s and 1970s, with few exceptions (Stren, 1991). Although the failure of city councils to deal with urban problems was bemoaned, central governments failed to give them adequate funds or revenue-raising powers or to ensure that they had sufficient decision-making powers and trained staff to improve the situation.

By the 1980s, however, a new recognition of the importance of effective municipal government seemed to be emerging. In Abidjan in 1980, for example, the City of Abidjan was established for the 10 communes, and a similar arrangement was made in Dakar in 1983. Local government was re-established in Dar es Salaam, Tanzania, and Kampala, Uganda. Increasingly, governments and international agencies seem to be recognizing that improved urban management, decentralization, and local democracy are interlinked.

Urban governance is concerned with the political arrangements to ensure that urban residents have a say in resource allocation, that decision-making is transparent, and that public agencies are account-able. It is, therefore, concerned with the roles and representation of a variety of actors and with informal as well as formal politics. It is also concerned with the relations between central and local government, which are typically contradictory and problematic. The variety of possible institutional arrangements for the management of urban growth and development is clear both from the city case-studies in this volume and from other research (Davey, 1993a,b). No single institutional arrangement is appropriate everywhere, and it is to be expected that political and institutional changes currently under way in many African countries will produce different institutional configurations and results.

Earlier attempts to decentralize had been ignored by most of the aid agencies and counteracted by the centralizing tendencies of one-party and military regimes. The practical results of more recent attempts to decentralize urban government, where these have occurred, have been limited. Kasfir (1993) considers that the new structures for participation introduced in the 1980s in Ghana, Burkina Faso, and Uganda "were given neither sufficient financial support nor political autonomy by national leaders" (Kasfir, 1993, p. 43). He expects new decentralized arrangements to continue to fail because of the contradictions inherent in central–local relations and deepening poverty. However, Stren (1995) suggests that various features of the current situation are more promising than hitherto, including the fact that reforms have been backed by the international agencies, are occurring in the context of a process of democratization, and are beginning to recognize the role of the associations of civil society (see also chaps. 14 and 15).

This is not to imply that forging new divisions of responsibility between central and local government, NGOs, community-based organizations (CBOs), and the private sector is unproblematic. In Nairobi, for example, the restitution of elected local government has not resolved the political rivalry between central government and Nairobi City Council that led to the suspension of the latter, and mechanisms have not evolved to coordinate the activities of the increasing numbers of NGOs. In Cairo, the lack of coordination between central government agencies and the three governorates into which the city is divided continues to hinder strategic planning and service delivery, while the role of Islamic organizations in providing welfare in a situation of increasing inequality adds to political/religious tensions. In Johannesburg, radical administrative and political reform is proceeding apace, but the large, diversified, and vibrant non-governmental sector is experiencing difficulties in making the adjustment from protest politics to partnership in urban administration.

Whereas some authors view the emergence or revitalization of local voluntary organizations capable of guaranteeing security, adequate incomes, and services in the face of government inability to do so as positive for both society and the state, averting even more of a legitimacy crisis than that to which it was already subject (Tripp, 1992), others fear that such associations, especially if based on ethnic or religious affiliations, will exacerbate conflict and polarization. Certainly, if the resources of all the actors on the urban scene are to be drawn upon in rising to the challenge posed by continued urban growth, explicit and directed attempts to define appropriate roles and forge appropriate relationships between the various actors in urban societies will be necessary (Halfani, 1995).

These relationships have both political components, defined in law and the constitution, expressed through electoral systems, and safeguarded through the courts and a lively civil society, and institutional components. City government, it is suggested, can provide effective leadership if it covers the whole built-up and developing area, has wide responsibilities for services related to the living environment, has a buoyant revenue base and well-qualified professional staff, and is politically accountable to the local population (Davey, 1993a,b). However, many systems of urban government are geographically fragmented (for example, Cairo and Johannesburg), functionally fragmented (Cairo, Lagos), or lack other of these attributes (Nairobi, Lagos, Kinshasa). Internal management, Davey concludes (1993a,b), seems to work best either where elected decision makers operating via a council and/or committees are backed by a professional administrator, whose department has corporate policy-making responsibility and capacity, or where political executive leadership encourages integrated management where there is functional fragmentation. In either case, forms of community representation and user participation are needed for local development, service provision, and management. There is, however, no consensus on the most appropriate administrative structure for large cities. Intra-city organization for area management and coordination of services, participation by community representatives in the direction of local services, representation of community interests to public agencies, or contribution to service provision may occur through administrative decentralization, separate municipal governments, publicly sponsored community representation structures, or independent community organizations. Delegated management of individual services to cost centres is increasingly being encouraged in order to improve efficiency. Davey advocates two-tier government for only the largest cities because of the resource requirements and risks of political conflict between the tiers, but does not recognize the problems that tend to arise if the city administration is too distant and centralized. He also comments apparently approvingly on the increasing prevalence and use of community-based structures (as do El-Shakhs, chap. 14, and Wekwete, chap. 15) without fully appreciating the potential difficulties created by the presence of a fragmented and competing set of community organizations that do not cover the whole metropolitan area.

Jaglin's evaluation (1994) of the government of Burkina Faso's attempt to mobilize residents of the peripheral areas of Ouagadougou to build or improve services is more perceptive of the drawbacks of reliance on CBOs as well as of the achievements. Between 1983 and 1990 in each neighbourhood, elected "revolutionary committees" organized land regularization and helped to mobilize and support improvements in local public facilities. Community labour and local financial levies helped to compensate for the lack of public sector resources, but attention was focused on the construction of water and social facilities, while operation and maintenance of these facilities and the organization and management of larger-scale initiatives and services, such as drainage and sanitation, were neglected. Other limitations of the system included the failure of the revolutionary committees to deal with large-scale infrastructure and long-term needs because it was possible to mobilize active community support only for short-term initiatives; and their inability to counteract inequalities within and between residential areas without public sector support.

Evolving political structures and processes that are accountable and stable at national level in African societies is proving difficult, so it is unsurprising that urban political systems are also unsatisfactory and volatile. The implications of current political trends for both urban governance and the tasks of urban management will need careful examination as they evolve.

Urban management

Traditional approaches to the management of urban development were fragmented, dividing responsibility for the operation and management of individual services (water, sanitation, transportation, health, etc.) sectorally and associating "planning" with physical planning. The results are well known: poor coordination between service providers, disjunctures between installation and operation and maintenance, and static blueprint land-use plans that were not implemented because of their reliance on (ineffective) controls over private sector development. Although exacerbated by the weakness of local government, tricky central–local relations, inadequate revenue bases, inherited land-use patterns, and widening inequalities between urban groups, approaches to the urban development process were conceptually and practically deficient (Stren and White, 1989; Devas and Rakodi, 1993a). Attempts to devise more adequate approaches have redefined "planning" and adopted it in tandem with "management" to embrace the full range of governmental interventions in the development and day-to-day operations of the city. Whereas urban planning is concerned primarily with anticipating and preparing for the future, and particularly with the spatial and land-use dimensions of urban development, urban management is concerned more with the operation of a range of public services and with a variety of interventions that affect urban conditions as a whole (Devas and Rakodi, 1993b, p. 44). Thus arguments are advanced for an integrated approach, in which responsibilities are clearly defined and allocation and coordination mechanisms established, as well as a dynamic approach, in which flexibility to respond to changing circumstances is built into planning, policy-making, and implementation by the institutionalization of monitoring and evaluation (see, for example, the approach advocated by McGill, 1994, based on experience in Malawi).

The approaches to urban management established in colonial days and promoted subsequently by donors, education and training, and research outputs have been subject to widespread criticism (Kironde, 1992; Okpala, 1987). In addition, problems with the design, implementation, and continued operation of externally financed urban projects in the 1970s (see chap. 2) led to some reconsideration of urban lending (World Bank, 1991). Although it is unanimously agreed that changes were and are needed, the adoption and promotion of "urban management" by the international agencies have been treated with considerable scepticism. Stren (1993) criticizes the World Bank and its partners in the Management Programme for failing to define the term. He explains this failure in terms of the need for an all-purpose concept that would, first, enable the agencies to move away from shelter projects to more institutional approaches; secondly, signal a shift from a public sector statist perspective of development to a neo-liberal perspective concerned with efficiency and the coordination of public and private sector activities; and, thirdly, maintain organizational flexibility to vary programme components. Jones and Ward (1994) take the critique further. Although applauding the shift from large-scale urban projects, in which government expects to be the provider, towards an enabling role for a more efficient and transparent public sector, they doubt whether the policy prescriptions advocated by the World Bank are likely to be effective. The approach is also criticized for being technocratic and still highly sectoral (Stren, 1991).

Effective urban management requires competence in running individual services, integrated approaches to redevelopment and development of new areas, and responses to overall challenges such as economic decline or environmental deterioration. Consideration must thus be given to the specific functions of an urban management system and also to mechanisms for decision-making and coordination. Administrative arrangements are needed to generate resources, define responsibilities, and provide staff, as well as to ensure the tasks of policy formulation, resource allocation, implementation, operation, maintenance, regulation, and promotion are carried out in an efficient and coordinated manner. Actions are needed with respect to urban economic development, physical and social infrastructure and services, land, shelter, and environmental problems.

The financial basis for urban administration

Typically the most buoyant taxes are retained by central government, and local authorities are left with less buoyant and politically more tricky revenue sources, such as property tax. This limited tax base, exacerbated by central government restrictions on rates, limited and erratic central–local transfers, poor performance with respect to collection and enforcement, out-of-date valuations, and the increasingly widespread occurrence of unenumerated property and economic activities, has meant that, invariably, the revenue available to local government has been insufficient for it to perform its functions (Stren, 1989a). As a result, it lacks legitimacy in the eyes of urban people and businesses, further curtailing its ability to generate revenue. Escape from this vicious circle requires political and legislative change, an injection of funds, and a more explicit political and practical strategy to deliver improved services, in order to increase legitimacy and thus increase the potential for further revenue generation and implementation of regulatory functions.

Both capital and revenue funds are needed for urban development. In the absence of well-developed capital markets, government action is essential to provide capital funds, although the transfer of responsibilities to local government without the powers and resources to fulfil these responsibilities, as Wekwete points out, is more typical. Backed by an injection of external funds and technical assistance to weaker local authorities, revolving municipal development funds administered by central government are a promising initiative in a number of countries including Nigeria and Zimbabwe, although Davey points out some of the pitfalls (Davey, 1993a,b). The promise of access to further borrowing in future provides a lever to improve local government financial management, although it can also be used to secure political compliance from elected local authorities. Revenue funding may be partly provided by central government transfers, especially if central government monopolizes most tax revenue, but the unpredictability of such transfers can hinder the planning and operation of local councils and so increased local resource mobilization is essential. Although there is insufficient space here to go into detail, research and guidance are emerging from the urban management programme (Bahl and Linn, 1992; Davey, 1993a,b). Both taxes on property and taxes on local economic activities are advocated.

Urban economic development

Economic activity located in urban areas is the driving force of urban growth and the jobs created the main attraction for rural migrants. Buoyancy in urban economies was taken for granted, especially in the years after independence, when expansion of the public sector and the pursuit of import substitution industrialization policies gave a boost to urban employment opportunities. Indeed, the economic pre-eminence of the largest cities was typically seen as a problem and measures (however ineffective) taken to divert investment elsewhere, either to rural development or to secondary cities and urban centres in rural areas.

Not until the drastic decline in urban infrastructural standards that followed recession and structural adjustment in the 1980s was the economic importance of adequate infrastructure widely recognized. This recognition was assisted by the continued failure of African cities to compete for international investment in manufacturing and services (especially compared with Pacific Rim Asian cities); by research that demonstrated the costs to manufacturers of poor infrastructure and the important contribution made by economic activities located in urban areas to national economic growth; and by pressure from a growing business lobby that, especially where entrepreneurs had emerged from the informal sector, was less dependent on the state for its access to the means of production and accumulation than before.

The health of city economies has not, except more recently in South Africa, been within either the legal remit or the area of concern of local government, or indeed of central agencies responsible for local services, which have been preoccupied with routine administration, service provision, and political survival (Harris, 1992). Analyses of city economies that chart trends in demand for the package of goods and services produced in the city, identify activities with current or future comparative advantage, pinpoint constraints on the productivity of economic enterprises and their labour force, and analyse the spatial distribution of economic activities in the city and the links between them, as a basis for formulating economic development policies, are rare. Rogerson in chapter 10 advocates such studies and a more proactive role for public agencies in local economic development. The "urban managers" in this context, Harris (1992) suggests, comprise the local authority, the chamber of commerce, and relevant industrial, commercial, financial, and professional associations (and, I would add, labour unions).

Some initiatives were mentioned in the case-studies, for example Nairobi's City Convention, the alliance between local government, big business, and inner-city residents to revitalize Johannesburg's CBD, and collaboration between local authorities, employers, and infrastructure companies to improve security and services in the Ikeja and Apapa areas of Lagos. The number and scope of such alliances in contemporary African cities compared with nineteenth-century and contemporary cities in, for example, the United States, Japan, or Europe are, however, limited. This reflects the absence of large-scale indigenous enterprises; governments' assumption that the management of the economy, installation and operation of infrastructure and services, and provision of housing were their responsibility; the lack of encouragement given to alternative associations during the authoritarian and statist post-independence decades; and the inheritance of good-quality infrastructure in the formally planned parts of cities, which, at least initially, was in working order. The forging of such alliances between local politicians and entrepreneurs (large and small scale), backed by officials more prepared to be proactive than traditional local government bureaucrats, can be expected to become more common in future, although the formation of politically strong local alliances in the largest cities is likely to provoke ambivalent reactions by central governments, even if they are committed to democratization and decentralization.

Infrastructure and services

One of the most visible and disturbing characteristics of the poorer cities ... is the decline of their infrastructural base. As urban populations grow, and as available resources decline, public infrastructure is being degraded to a point where cities are seriously losing their capacity to operate as productive entities ... In many African cities ... refuse is uncollected and piles of decaying waste are allowed to rot in the streets; schools are ... overcrowded; some urban roads deteriorate into quagmires in the rainy season, and are pitted with dangerous potholes during the dry season; ... private telephones ... are an impossible dream; public transport systems are becoming seriously overloaded; and more and more people are obliged to live in unserviced plots ... Not only is little new infrastructure constructed, but existing infrastructure is poorly maintained. (Stren, 1991, p. 7)

Stren's analysis refers to African cities in general. The situation he describes is characteristic of large parts of some of the cities described in this volume, especially Nairobi, Lagos, and Kinshasa, and is becoming increasingly widespread in lower-income areas of the others (see also Ngom, 1989, on Dakar; El Sammani et al., 1989, on Khartoum). The situation is even worse in many smaller cities and poorer countries (Onibokun, 1989).

Stren and White's research in the 1980s showed that most water and electricity supply agencies in African cities were either central government parastatals or attached to central government ministries. In most cases, supply has failed to keep pace with urban growth. Where local government continues to be responsible, experience varies, from Zimbabwe on the one hand, where the supply of water has generally kept pace with urban population growth, to Kenyan local authorities on the other. However, problems should be attributed not only to local government failings, but also to central government policies and inaction. In some francophone countries, the water supply function is contracted out to private companies. The Côte d'Ivoire's experience is that such an arrangement can be efficient if the company concerned is given adequate autonomy with respect to operation and pricing, although there can be difficulties in ensuring supply to low-income areas (Stren, 1989b). An intermediate arrangement, of a national (Ghana) or municipal (some Zambian local authorities) public sector company, is becoming more widespread, as countries attempt to improve efficiency without outright privatization.

Waste management arrangements in most cities are also far from satisfactory. Whereas anglophone countries rely on a public service, elsewhere solid waste collection may be subcontracted, to a single company as in Abidjan, or to local entrepreneurs (Stren, 1989b). Whatever the arrangement, effectiveness is inhibited by inappropriate collection arrangements and shortages of foreign exchange to import equipment, and equity is reduced by the lack of finance to subsidize services in low-income areas where necessary.

The failure of land subdivision and servicing programmes to keep pace with urban growth, which has led to widespread illegal and informal development, and not only of low-income areas (see below), has hindered the extension not only of water, electricity, and solid waste collection services but also of adequate sanitation arrangements and road networks to large areas of Africa's cities. In the absence of collective sanitation arrangements, households are forced to devise individual solutions suited to their incomes and physical circumstances. Reliance on pit latrine sanitation can give rise to groundwater pollution and problems occur as density rises, while the use of septic tanks needs to be backed up by private or public sludge removal services and suitably located disposal sites. Where waterborne sewage disposal to conventional treatment works is available, it is costly, limited in coverage, and poorly operated, because revenue and foreign exchange shortages have made it increasingly difficult to obtain spare parts and maintain systems. As densities increase, unacceptable levels of sharing occur, or residents cannot get access to any toilet facility and are forced to "use the bush" ("free range" in Accra). Both have adverse health and environmental implications.

In the early years after independence, public transport was typically a public monopoly, whether a parastatal bus company or a local government function. Invariably it was inadequate, owing to shortages of foreign exchange for parts and new buses and poor management. Increasingly, the public monopoly has been supplemented or replaced (legally or illegally) by private operators, a trend that increased its momentum with economic liberalization. Although the availability of public transport has generally improved as a result, the failure of the public sector to provide an adequate road network results in patchy coverage and high operating costs, while its inability to regulate the private sector has resulted in poor safety standards and sometimes violent competition to ply particular routes.

Conclusion

A review of the privatization of urban services in Asia suggests that the advantages, in theory, include competition, leading to lower production and delivery costs, increased efficiency, better access to current technology, greater capacity to obtain and maintain capital equipment, more flexibility and speed in decision-making, and reduced pressure on government. However, opposition is likely from political leaders who control patronage and from public sector unions, as well as from some consumer groups and low-income residents' organizations, who fear higher costs. In addition, private and NGO management skills may be poor and, where financial markets are undeveloped, private contractors may not be able to get access to capital. Finally, services that are collective goods, those that require lumpy investment, and those for which it is difficult to charge users directly are unsuitable for privatization. Privatization may occur through a variety of mechanisms, including sale of public assets, deregulation and liberalization, contracting out, public–private or public–NGO partnerships, transfer to NGOs, and government support for private providers (Rondinelli and Kasarda, 1993). Lessons from the Asian experience for African cities demonstrate the need to take care in designing the mechanisms for private/NGO involvement, to devise a workable regulatory framework, and to select only those services for which privatization is appropriate (for example, transport, housing, refuse collection, and perhaps aspects of health care) (see also Davey, 1993a,b). Institutional reforms related to service provision are under way in African cities. Wekwete, in chapter 15, describes a shift from a public sector-based approach to urban management to a public–private sector model. However, he stresses the uncertain future of the new approach, owing to its reliance on external funding, its dependence on cooperative relations between central and local government, and the lack of formal structures at city level through which NGOs and CBOs can be systematically involved in decision-making. In addition, he notes the lack of evaluation of recent attempts at privatization and related changes, to update the review carried out in the 1980s (Stren and White, 1989).

Housing, land, and planning
Public sector housing policies focused initially on the provision of complete house units, typically for public sector employees as well as low-income groups. To some extent this approach has been superseded by sites and services, but neither has succeeded in matching supply with demand, let alone need, for a variety of reasons, includ-

ing inadequate land administration systems, lags in infrastructure provision programmes, lack of capital, shortages of building materials, and limited capacity in the construction sector. As a result, most additions to the housing stock have been made by the private sector, with quantitatively by far the largest contribution coming from individual households and small landlords. Almost invariably, at least one aspect of this housing is illegal – lack of formal land tenure, failure to obtain development permission, failure to satisfy building regulations, or disregard of rent control. It is financed, built, and exchanged outside the formal systems for mortgage lending, construction, and sale.

Where pressures on land are greatest and infrastructure most deficient, the quality of accommodation can be appalling, but much of the housing produced is adequate to satisfy basic needs for shelter. Thus infrastructure improvements and provision of education and health services are much more important than improvements to the dwelling in improving the quality of the residential environment. Whereas regularization and upgrading programmes were accepted reluctantly by politicians and officials in the 1970s, there are signs of a new realism as the financial and administrative weakness of public agencies has become increasingly clear, and the potential of more participatory community-based approaches to infrastructure installation and operation is demonstrated in residential areas, often with donor and NGO assistance. The need to regularize informal tenure arrangements sufficiently for them to be used to generate revenue may assist in this process (Durand-Lasserve, 1993). However, it should be recognized that regularization of unplanned areas is no substitute for a rapid land subdivision and strategic infrastructure investment programme linked to a land-use planning process.

This is not to advocate a return to the land-use master plans of earlier decades, with their inappropriate levels of detail, inflexibility, dependence on foreign consultants for preparation, and lack of connection to resource allocation decisions. The assumptions on methods of implementation, administrative capacity, and planning standards built into that approach to planning are demonstrably inappropriate (Stren, 1989b; Devas and Rakodi, 1993b; see also Findlay and Paddison, 1986, on Tunis and Rabat; Dubresson, chap. 8 in this volume, and Attahi, 1991, on Abidjan). Strategic planning in which land-use and other policy proposals are linked to capital investment programmes is needed, together with more detailed guidance for development control in some areas, such as the CBD, and more action-oriented approaches to development or improvement in others. Increasingly, adaptive responses are becoming more common than coercive removal of offending structures or people, but there is still political and bureaucratic resistance to "lowering" of standards, while the flexibility of strategic planning frameworks compared with zoning maps also increases the opportunities for corruption in decision-making on development applications.

Environmental problems

Related to deficiencies in infrastructure provision and waste management, environmental problems also arise from the inability of public sector authorities to enforce regulations governing land development, industrial emissions, etc. The urban poor are most exposed to environmental hazards because they are most likely to depend on untreated water, to live in risky areas, to be unprovided with sanitation and solid waste collection services, to live in overcrowded conditions and work in unregulated enterprises, and to be exposed to high levels of indoor pollution from cooking fuels. Their vulnerability to ill health arising from environmental problems is increased by poor nutrition and inadequate access to health care. Action on environmental problems is more likely to occur, however, when the better-off are affected, as for example by air pollution, contaminated food, or bad effects on economic activities such as tourism. It may also follow disaster. Thus many unsustainable practices and environmental problems are not tackled until disaster occurs or until organized groups increase the pressure for change. Action is needed both to tackle negative externalities such as pollution directly and to monitor the upstream resource-using and downstream disposal or recycling of wastes in the city and its region.

Guiding and controlling urban growth

Should African countries try to restrain the growth of their largest cities? The largest cities probably *are* more expensive per head of population to service and may have absorbed a disproportionate share of public investment. However, they generally also contribute a major share of GDP. In addition, there is no evidence that, if given scope to raise revenue locally and use appropriate standards, they need be a drain on government resources or that disamenities are necessarily greater in very large cities (Richardson, 1993). Appropriate levels of investment and development programmes in rural areas are needed. There is also scope for increasing the attractiveness of secondary cities by supporting the development of economic activities linked to their hinterlands, investment in infrastructure, and development of greater institutional capacity. However, even if such programmes are successful, they are unlikely to have more than marginal effects on the rate of growth and size of the largest cities. More important for the latter, therefore, are improved management, some of the components of which have been discussed above, and spatial restructuring. The latter is one of the main concerns of El-Shakhs, who in chapter 14 advocates the acceptance and promotion of urbanized corridors, such as the one that is developing between Cairo and Alexandria, and decentralization of urban growth within city regions in preference to continuous expansion of the built-up area.

This volume has been concerned with both the dynamics of urban growth and development and its management. The summary of key trends and issues has, more than once, referred to incomplete knowledge and unanswered questions. Neither improved understanding nor more adequate responses to the challenge is possible without better data on and analysis of urban characteristics. The final section of this chapter will, therefore, outline some of the outstanding research needs that have been revealed.

Research priorities

As part of a large project funded by the Ford Foundation to review recent research on urban areas in the developing world, five regional reviews were carried out in Africa (Stren, 1994). While mainly concerned to identify and summarize research undertaken during the past 30 years, the project also aimed to outline a research agenda for the 1990s. The research priorities identified below arise from the experience of producing this volume for the United Nations University, but parallels with the views of contributors to that project will be noted.

The biggest problem in identifying the relationship between global forces and urbanization in Africa, trends in urbanization, the characteristics of cities, and the outcomes of policy and management interventions is the lack of both basic data and original research. This volume has been written in the absence of recent reliable census data for the majority of countries and cities considered. Ascertaining the dimensions of and trends in urbanization in the absence of such data is virtually impossible, hence the accounts are full of estimates, general statements, and alternative figures, where greater precision is desirable. Although urban trends and characteristics are better documented in some countries and cities than others, owing not only to the absence of census and other published data but also to the incomplete topic and disciplinary coverage of urban issues, nowhere is the level of knowledge satisfactory. The papers in this volume, especially but not only the thematic papers, were designed as reviews of existing knowledge and data. They are, indeed, valuable reviews and many draw on sources that are inaccessible to an international readership within and outside Africa. However, what can be learnt from existing work, which declined noticeably in the 1980s, especially in eastern Africa, has, in my view, largely been exhausted. The research priorities identified below cannot be addressed without substantive new research, drawing both on national data and on primary data collection designed to elucidate the specifically urban issues outlined. At both the national and city levels, better use needs to be made of available data, especially census data. However, formally collected data are not always suitable for addressing the critical issues identified below, and they need to be supplemented by both nation- and city-wide studies and smaller-scale quantitative and qualitative data-collection exercises. As donor and country interest in urban development increases, the need for improved knowledge of urban dynamics and the outcomes of policies and management practices poses a challenge for research funders and researchers alike.

The urban economy

A better understanding is needed of the dynamics of urban economies because, without this, it is impossible to judge the efficacy of any policies aimed at urban economic development and employment creation. Sector studies that embrace enterprises of all sizes are needed. They should explore the potential of and constraints on enterprises of different sizes, as well as links between them and with other sectors in terms of subcontracting, training, transfer, and labour movement. Obvious candidates are leather, food processing, textiles and clothing, wood processing and manufacturing, construction and building materials production, business services, and wholesale and retail trade. However, there is also some evidence to show that the potential of and constraints on enterprises of different sizes have some similarities. Thus there is also a need for intersectoral studies of large, intermediate, small, and micro-enterprises, in order to ascertain what the outcome of structural adjustment policies and past support programmes has been and what type of support programmes might be appropriate in future. Not only should business enterprises be studied as discrete units, but the associations between them, in addition to processes and procedures for operating contracts, accessing credit, and regulating malpractice, should also be examined. It is important to consider both formal and informal associations and procedures. First, associations of small-scale enterprises may come to be as significant as the traditional associations of large enterprises, such as employers' federations or chambers of commerce, in the less state-centred model of policy development likely to emerge in future years. Secondly, the procedures and operating practices evolved by small-scale businesses may be more appropriate and workable for African countries today than those that typify the large-scale sector, for example with respect to accessing credit (Tripp, 1992; Halfani, 1994, 1995; Attahi, 1994; Kharoufi, 1994; Onibokun, 1994).

As competition between the largest cities to benefit from trends in the global economy increases and becomes more explicit, studies of the comparative advantage of cities, the way in which stakeholders within them articulate their economic interests, and the scope for cooperation, if not at a continental then at a regional level, are needed. In addition, evaluations of the prospects for and components and outcomes of local economic development strategies are needed (Swilling, 1994).

Urban society, poverty, and equity

To underpin both economic development and urban politics and governance (see below), a deeper understanding is needed of the social changes taking place in cities, especially given the strains generated by the rapid socio-economic changes currently taking place and the importance of household structures and social networks in enabling urban residents to cope with economic deterioration and declining investment in social services. The themes to be investigated include the family and social networks, culture, community, and crime and insecurity (Halfani, 1994; Swilling, 1994). The social and cultural consequences of urbanization, in particular social disorder and urban violence, which appear to be on the increase, are also emphasized by Onibokun (1994), as is the need for study of social movements by Kharoufi (1994).

Attempts to improve understanding of urban poverty are under way (Rakodi, 1995a; Vanderschueren et al., 1996) and need to be taken further by assessments of whether the holistic conceptualization of urban poverty currently being advocated is an advance on earlier concentration on poverty lines, both analytically and in terms of policy formulation (Attahi, 1994; Onibokun, 1994). The implications of recession in general, structural adjustment policies in particular, and political changes for the extent and nature of urban inequality and poverty need more systematic consideration, drawing on the national poverty assessments that are increasingly being funded by the World Bank, UNICEF and others. The response to increasingly widespread evidence of increased hardship has typically been the design, limited funding, and partial implementation of programmes to ameliorate the adverse effects of Structural Adjustment Programmes rather than reconsideration and redesign of structural adjustment policies. Although the scope for such programmes to do more than tinker at the margins of poverty appears to be limited, their effects need to be evaluated.

Land and property markets

The importance of the land market processes by which agricultural land on the urban periphery is converted for urban use was noted in chapter 11. The extent to which this is a legal process varies from city to city, but, except in one or two countries, such as Zimbabwe and, to a lesser extent, South Africa, most of the land development processes under way operate wholly or partly outside the formal legal process. The scope for universalizing formal freehold or leasehold tenure systems and effectively controlling subdivision and development seems limited in most African countries. If ways of guiding development to avoid the worst impacts of unplanned development and unregistered land rights are to be found, it will be necessary to devise systems that can work alongside prevailing land markets and development processes rather than futilely attempt to control them. A start has been made in devising such systems, for example in countries such as Uganda and by some agencies, such as the World Bank/UNCHS/ UNDP Urban Management Programme for Africa (Durand-Lasserve, 1993), but, to make progress, a greater depth of understanding of existing informal and semi-formal processes is needed (see also Halfani, 1994; Onibokun, 1994). Such research should investigate the factors that determine processes and patterns of urbanization, including the tenure preferences of urban residents, property prices

586

in relation to incomes, tenure systems in the rural areas surrounding cities, and the institutional framework for land management in the city and its surrounding region. Institutions in this context include official land management agencies and planning authorities, arrangements for coordination between those administering the city and those responsible for the surrounding rural areas, and social relations governing the rights of indigenous individuals and groups to use and dispose of land.

The extent and nature of the impact of cities on their hinterlands are relevant to this topic as to others (Halfani, 1994; Onibokun, 1994) – changes in economic activities in response to urban opportunities may either intensify rural land uses, for example intensive vegetable production for urban markets, or disrupt them as labour is withdrawn from agricultural production and holdings are subdivided. In addition to land tenure, urban employment opportunities and transport links are important influences on the extent to which urban sprawl occurs and the ways in which economic and spatial patterns and relationships in the city region are transformed.

Although the conversion of agricultural land for urban use will continue to be very important, as cities mature, markets in undeveloped land and property within the broadly built-up area become increasingly important (see Kharoufi, 1994, on the need to study the dynamics of resident mobility and property markets in old city centres in north Africa). Identifying and explaining trends in these property markets is essential to an improved understanding of urban dynamics and to devising appropriate policies with respect to, for example, bringing forward undeveloped land for development, redevelopment, or densification. A range of interventions in urban land markets are currently being implemented or considered in one or more cities in Africa. At present, our understanding of their likely impacts is limited and evaluations of attempts to implement them are needed. Relevant policies include:
- the use of capital investment in major infrastructure to guide new development;
- the imposition of high rates of property tax to encourage the sale or development of undeveloped land;
- the use of financial incentives and regulatory changes to encourage densification;
- decontrol of rents;
- community land trusts as an alternative to private individual tenure, especially for regularization of informal settlement areas.

Urban politics and governance

The failure of public administrative systems to cope with the challenge of urban growth in Africa has been relatively well documented. The exceptional cases where there is considerable administrative capacity at the local urban level have also been analysed (see, for example, Rakodi, 1995b, on Harare, and Pasteur, 1992, on Bulawayo in Zimbabwe; Smith, 1992; Swilling et al., 1991; and Tomlinson, 1994, on South Africa). Elsewhere, the extent of change to urban politics and governmental arrangements varies from very little to quite extensive. The differences are a result partly of the "variation in the degree of institutionalisation and richness of civil society in different countries, reflecting both historical and cultural factors and the coercive power of the state" (Healey and Robinson, 1992). The latter in turn governs the strategies open to people to challenge the prevailing political order, which vary from open criticism and opposition to the expression of discontent through disengagement from the state or non-compliance with state policies. Until the 1980s, most institutional effort and research had been directed to the built environment and formal institutional arrangements for management and politics. The state was seen as the main agent directing urban change and the sphere outside the formalized sector as an unintended by-product or pathology of a formal process of urban development (Halfani, 1995). Anecdotal evidence reveals recent attempts to democratize local government (both non-party political, as in Ghana's district assemblies and Uganda's Resistance Councils, and party political, as in Lusaka or Nairobi); attempts to strengthen urban local government and its planning, revenue-raising, and management capacities; and attempts to develop partnerships with NGOs and CBOs (e.g. in Freetown or Lusaka) and with private sector service providers. Systematic documentation and evaluation of the structures, relationships, and processes involved and their outcomes is, however, limited (Halfani, 1994), and indeed the conceptual framework for doing this is undeveloped.

Hyden (1992) suggests a number of conditions that facilitate good governance and therefore effective problem-solving, which could form the basis for a set of evaluative criteria:

(a) citizen influence and oversight, determined by the scope for political participation, methods of preference aggregation, and the means of ensuring public accountability;

(b) responsive and responsible leadership, including the degree of respect evident for the public realm, adherence to the rule of law, and the openness of policy-making – Manor (1995) distinguishes in this respect between bureaucrats, who should be accountable to elected representatives, and elected representatives, who should be accountable to citizens;

(c) social reciprocity, including the degree of political equality, the extent of intergroup tolerance, and the degree of inclusiveness in associational membership.

In the 1960s and 1970s, as discussed in chapter 2, international lending was focused on urban projects and little attention was paid to developing institutional capacity. This has changed more recently, but evaluation of the role of the aid agencies in promoting and supporting political reform and institutional development at the urban level is lacking. The main conclusion of Healey and Robinson's (1992) review of the role of these agencies at national level is that they have been extremely vague with respect to their recommendations on appropriate reforms to institutional structures and processes. At this level there is no clear association between regime type and successful reform, or between political liberalization and improved economic performance. Early research into institutional reform, for example with respect to the water sector in Ghana, demonstrates that it has proceeded less rapidly than economic liberalization and less rapidly than hoped for by the lending agencies.

Healey and Robinson's (1992) research agenda related to democracy, governance, and economic policy at the national level has obvious urban counterparts. Comparative studies are needed of:

– the institutional and procedural context of policy-making in established democratic systems of local government, focusing on how interest groups are consulted;
– the outcomes of democratization for the operation of urban local governments and their relations with central government;
– the political implications of decentralization and its impact on policy-making, resource generation, and implementation;
– the nature of urban actors (including central and local political institutions and bureacracies, traditional authorities, NGOs, CBOs, informal associations of residents, and the large- and small-scale private sector) and of the evolving relationships between them, as illustrated by policy-making, implementation and service delivery, operation and maintenance, at community, district/neighbourhood, and city levels (see also Halfani, 1994; Swilling, 1994).

Thus evaluations are needed both of reforms of public sector arrangements for urban management and of mechanisms and forums designed to incorporate a wider range of actors into policy formulation and decision-making, such as the UNCHS-facilitated Sustainable Cities Programmes in Dar es Salaam and Accra, and the Local Forums and Commissions in South Africa. Without neglecting the politics of urban government, Halfani (1994), Attahi (1994), Onibokun (1994), and Swilling (1994) also stress the need for structural and functional analyses of the institutions responsible for urban management and the operating systems they employ. To address this more specific focus on evaluating the effectiveness of urban management systems and urban governmental institutions, Davey (1993a, pp. 1–2) suggests the use of six criteria:

(1) technical competence in the choice, design, and implementation of infrastructure investment, and its operation and maintenance;
(2) efficiency in the use of resources;
(3) financial viability based on local revenue generation and sound financial management;
(4) responsiveness to the needs arising from urban growth and the ability to plan the city and its services ahead of, or at least in pace with, demand;
(5) sensitivity to the needs of the urban poor and appropriate weighting of public interventions to promote their access to basic services, employment, and shelter;
(6) concern for environmental protection, through public service provision and regulation of the private sector.

To summarize, there is a need to assess effectiveness with respect to service delivery, regulation, overall economic and physical development of the city, poverty alleviation, and environmental protection (see also Halfani, 1994; Attahi, 1994). Healey and Robinson's (1992) call for studies of *how* particular policy changes were initiated, designed, and implemented is as relevant to the study of the processes involved in urban management as it is at the national level. Finally, cross cutting all the research themes identified above is the need to identify gender differentiation and relations with respect, first, to access to urban resources and decision-making, and, secondly, to the outcomes of policy and practice.

The project of which this volume is the outcome set out to describe and explain the evolution of some of the largest and most important cities in Africa; to investigate the linkages between these cities and global, continental, and national urban systems; to assess the policy implications of present and future patterns of large-city growth; and to assess the performance of urban management systems in coping with urban growth. The lack of adequate data and research studies on which to draw, and the enormous differences between the countries and cities of continental Africa, have hindered our achievement of these aims. However, the material drawn together in this volume will, we hope, make a significant contribution to contemporary analysis of urbanization in Africa.

References

Aboyade, O. 1994. Essentials for African economic transformation. *IDS Bulletin* 25(3): 73–78.

Adedeji, A. 1993. The case for remaking Africa. In: D. Rimmer, ed., *Action in Africa: The Experience of People Involved in Government, Business and Aid*. J. Currey, London, and Heinemann, Portsmouth, NH, pp. 43–57.

Attahi, K. 1991. Planning and management in large cities: A case study of Abidjan, Côte d'Ivoire. In: UNCHS, *Metropolitan Planning and Management in the Developing World: Abidjan and Quito*. United Nations Centre for Human Settlements, Nairobi, pp. 31–82.

——— 1994. Urban research in Francophone West Africa: Côte d'Ivoire, Senegal, Burkina Faso, Togo. In: R. Stren, ed., *Urban Research in the Developing World, Volume 2: Africa*. Centre for Urban and Community Studies, University of Toronto, Toronto, pp. 193–230.

Bahl, R. W. and Linn, J. F. 1992. *Urban Public Finance in Developing Countries*. Oxford University Press, New York.

Brown, M. B. 1995. *Africa's Choices after Thirty Years of the World Bank*. Penguin, Harmondsworth, Middx.

Chazan, N. and D. Rothchild. 1993. The political repercussions of economic malaise. In: T. M. Callaghy and J. Ravenhill, eds., *Hemmed in: Responses to Africa's Economic Decline*. Columbia University Press, New York, pp. 180–214.

Davey, K. 1993a. *Managing Growing Cities: Options for Urban Government*. Development Administration Group, Institute of Local Government Studies, University of Birmingham, Birmingham.

——— 1993b. *Elements of Urban Management*. World Bank/UNCHS/UNDP, Urban Management Programme Discussion Paper 11, Washington D.C.

Devas, N. and C. Rakodi, eds. 1993a. *Managing Fast Growing Cities: New Approaches to Urban Planning and Management in the Developing World*. Longman, London.

——— 1993b. Planning and managing fast growing cities. In: N. Devas and C. Rakodi, eds., *Managing Fast Growing Cities: New Approaches to Urban Planning and Management in the Developing World*. Longman, London, pp. 41–62.

Durand-Lasserve, A. 1993. *Conditions de mise en place des systèmes d'information foncière dans les villes d'Afrique sud-Saharienne francophone*. World Bank, UMP 8, Washington D.C.

Eddin Ibrahim, S. 1987. A sociological profile. In: A. Y. Saqqaf, ed., *The Middle East City: Ancient Traditions Confront a Modern World*. Paragon House, New York, pp. 209–226.

El Sammani, M. O., M. El Hadi Abu Sin, M. Talha, B. M. El Hassan, and I. Haywood. 1989. Management problems of Greater Khartoum. In: R. E. Stren and R. R. White, eds., *African Cities in Crisis: Managing Rapid Urban Growth.* Westview, Boulder, Colo., pp. 246–275.

Findlay, A. M. 1994. *The Arab World.* Routledge, London.

Findlay, A. M. and R. Paddison. 1986. Planning the Arab city: The cases of Tunis and Rabat. *Progress in Planning* 26(1): 1–82.

Fowler, A. 1991. The role of NGOs in changing state–society relations: Perspectives from Eastern and Southern Africa. *Development Policy Review* 9(1): 53–84.

George, S. and F. Sabelli. 1994. *Faith and Credit: The World Bank's Secular Empire.* Penguin, Harmondsworth, Middx.

Green, R. H. 1993. The IMF and the World Bank in Africa: How much learning? In: T. M. Callaghy and J. Ravenhill, eds., *Hemmed in: Responses to Africa's Economic Decline.* Columbia University Press, New York, pp. 54–89.

Green, R. H. and M. Faber. 1994. The structural adjustment of structural adjustment: Sub-Saharan Africa 1980–1993. *IDS Bulletin* 25(3): 1–8.

Halfani, M. 1994. Urban research in eastern Africa: Tanzania, Kenya and Zambia – towards an agenda for the 1990s. In: R. Stren, ed., *Urban Research in the Developing World, Volume 2: Africa.* Centre for Urban and Community Studies, University of Toronto, Toronto, pp. 113–192.

———— 1995. The governance of urban development in East Africa: An examination of the institutional landscape and the poverty challenge. Paper to the Global Urban Research Initiative/African Research Network for Urban Governance Workshop, Nairobi, November, mimeo.

Harris, N. 1992. Productivity and poverty in the cities of the developing countries. In: N. Harris, ed., *Cities in the 1990s: The Challenge for Developing Countries.* UCL Press, London, pp. 173–195.

Healey, J. and M. Robinson, 1992. *Democracy, Governance and Economic Policy: Sub-Saharan Africa in Comparative Perspective.* Overseas Development Institute, London.

Hyden, G. 1992. Governance and the study of politics. In: G. Hyden and M. Bratton, eds., *Governance and Politics in Africa.* Lynne Rienner, Boulder, Colo., pp. 1–26.

Jaglin, S. 1994. Why mobilise town dwellers? Joint management in Ouagadougou (1983–1990). *Environment and Urbanization* 6(2): 111–132.

Jones, G. A. and P. M. Ward. 1994. The World Bank's "new" Urban Management programme: Paradigm shift or policy continuity? *Habitat International* 18(3): 33–51.

Kasfir, N. 1993. Designs and dilemmas of African decentralization. In: P. Mawhood, ed., *Local Government in the Third World: Experience of Decentralization in Tropical Africa.* Africa Institute, Pretoria, pp. 24–48.

Kharoufi, M. 1994. Reflections on a research field: Urban studies in Egypt, Morocco and the Sudan. In: R. Stren, ed., *Urban Research in the Developing World, Volume 2: Africa.* Centre for Urban and Community Studies, University of Toronto, Toronto, pp. 47–112.

Kironde, J. M. L. 1992. Received concepts and theories in African urbanisation and management strategies: The struggle continues. *Urban Studies* 29(8): 1277–1292.

McGill, R. 1994. Integrated urban management: An operational model for third world city managers. *Cities* 11(1): 35–47.

Mamdani, M. 1992. Conceptualising state and civil society relations: Towards a methodological critique of contemporary Africanism. In: C. Auroi, ed., *The Role of the State in Development Processes*. Frank Cass, London, pp. 15–23.

Manor, J. 1995. Democratic decentralization in Africa and Asia. *IDS Bulletin* 26(2): 81–96.

Mead, D. C. 1994. The contribution of small enterprises to employment growth in southern and eastern Africa. *World Development* 22(12): 1881–1894.

Mutahaba, G., R. Baguma, and M. Halfani. 1993. *Vitalizing African Public Administration for Recovery and Development*. Kumarian, West Hartford, Conn.

Ngom, T. 1989. Appropriate standards for infrastructure in Dakar. In: R. E. Stren and R. R. White, eds., *African Cities in Crisis: Managing Rapid Urban Growth*. Westview, Boulder, Colo., pp. 176–202.

O'Connor, A. 1991. *Poverty in Africa: A Geographical Approach*. Belhaven, London.

Okpala, D. C. I. 1987. Received concepts and theories in African urbanisation studies and urban management strategies: A critique. *Urban Studies* 24: 137–150.

Onibokun, A. G. 1989. Urban growth and urban management in Nigeria. In: R. E. Stren and R. R. White, eds., *African Cities in Crisis: Managing Rapid Urban Growth*. Westview, Boulder, Colo., pp. 68–111.

—— 1994. Urban research in Anglophone West Africa: Towards an agenda for the 1990s. In: R. Stren, ed., *Urban Research in the Developing World, Volume 2: Africa*. Centre for Urban and Community Studies, University of Toronto, Toronto, pp. 231–282.

Pasteur, D. 1992. *Good Local Government in Zimbabwe: Bulawayo and Mutare*. Development Administration Group, School of Public Policy, University of Birmingham, Birmingham.

Rakodi, C. 1995a. Poverty lines or household strategies? A review of conceptual issues in the study of urban poverty. *Habitat International* 19(4): 407–426.

—— 1995b. *Harare. Inheriting a Settler-Colonial City: Continuity or Change?* Wiley, London.

Ravenhill, J. 1993. A second decade of adjustment: Greater complexity, greater uncertainty. In: T. M. Callaghy and J. Ravenhill, eds., *Hemmed in: Responses to Africa's Economic Decline*. Columbia University Press, New York, pp. 18–53.

Richardson, H. W. 1993. Efficiency and welfare in less developed country megacities. In: J. D. Kasarda and A. M. Parnell, eds., *Third World Cities: Problems, Policies, Prospects*. Sage, Newbury Park, Calif., pp. 32–57.

Riddell, R. 1993. The future of the manufacturing sector in Sub-Saharan Africa. In: T. M. Callaghy and J. Ravenhill, eds. *Hemmed in: Responses to Africa's Economic Decline*. Columbia University Press, New York, pp. 215–247.

Rondinelli, D. A. and J. D. Kasarda. 1993. Privatization of urban services and infrastructure in developing countries: An assessment of experience. In: J. D. Kasarda and A. M. Parnell, eds., *Third World Cities: Problems, Policies, Prospects*. Sage, Newbury Park, Calif., pp. 134–160.

Seddon, D. 1995. Economic prospects for Africa. *Review of African Political Economy* no. 64: 275–278.

Sklair, L. 1991. *Sociology of the Global System*. Harvester/Wheatsheaf, New York.

Smith, D. M., ed. 1992. *The Apartheid City and Beyond: Urbanization and Social Change in South Africa*. Routledge, London, and Witwatersrand University Press, Johannesburg.

Stren, R. E. 1989a. Urban local government in Africa. In: R. E. Stren and R. R. White, eds., *African Cities in Crisis: Managing Rapid Urban Growth*. Westview, Boulder, Colo., pp. 20–36.

―――― 1989b. The administration of urban services. In: R. E. Stren and R. R. White, eds., *African Cities in Crisis: Managing Rapid Urban Growth*. Westview, Boulder, Colo., pp. 37–68.

―――― 1991. Large cities in the Third World. In: UNCHS, *Metropolitan Planning and Management in the Developing World: Abidjan and Quito*. United Nations Centre for Human Settlements, Nairobi, pp. 1–30.

―――― 1993. "Urban management" in development assistance: An elusive concept. *Cities* 10(2): 125–139.

―――― ed. 1994. *Urban Research in the Developing World, Volume 2: Africa*. Centre for Urban and Community Studies, University of Toronto, Toronto.

Stren, R. 1995. The GURI project: Urban researchers on three continents focus on governance. Paper to the Global Urban Research Initiative Workshop/African Research Network for Urban Management, Nairobi, November, mimeo.

Stren, R. E. and R. R. White, eds. 1989. *African Cities in Crisis: Managing Rapid Urban Growth*. Westview, Boulder, Colo.

Stren, R., M. Halfani, and J. Malombe. 1994. Urban politics in Kenya and Tanzania. *The Urban Age* 2(2): 1–5.

Swilling, M. 1994. Towards an urban research agenda for southern Africa in the 1990s. In: R. Stren, ed., *Urban Research in the Developing World, Volume 2: Africa*. Centre for Urban and Community Studies, University of Toronto, Toronto, pp. 283–374.

Swilling, M., R. Humphreys, and K. Shubane. 1991. *Apartheid City in Transition*. Oxford University Press, Cape Town.

Tomlinson, R. 1994. *Urban Development Planning: Lessons for the Economic Reconstruction of South Africa's Cities*. Witwatersrand University Press, Johannesburg, and Zed Books, London.

Touré, M., S. Ouattara, and E. Annan-Yao. 1992. Population dynamics and development strategies in the Ivory Coast. In: M. Touré and T. O. Fadayomi, eds., *Migrations, Development and Urbanization Policies in Subsaharan Africa*. CODESRIA, Dakar, pp. 7–50.

Tripp, A. M. 1992. Local organizations, participation and the state in urban Tanzania. In: G. Hyden and M. Bratton, eds., *Governance and Politics in Africa*. Lynne Rienner, Boulder, Colo., pp. 221–242.

Vanderschueren, F., E. Wegelin, and K. Wekwete. 1996. *Policy Options for Urban Poverty Reduction: A Framework for Action at the Municipal Programme Level*. UNDP/UNCHS/World Bank, Urban Management Programme Policy Paper 20. World Bank, Washington D.C.

Woods, D. 1992. Civil society in Europe and Africa: Limiting state power through a public sphere. *African Studies Review* 35(2): 77–100.

World Bank. 1991. *Urban Policy and Economic Development: An Agenda for the 1990s*. World Bank, Washington D.C.

Zeleza, T. 1994. The unemployment crisis in Africa in the 1970s and 1980s. In: E. Osaghae, ed., *Between State and Civil Society in Africa: Perspectives on Development*. Council for the Development of Social Science Research in Africa, Dakar, pp. 75–122.

Contributors

Josephine Olu Abiodun
Professor, Department of Geography, Obafemi Awolowo University, Ile-Ife, Nigeria

Tade Akin Aina
Deputy Executive Secretary (Publications), Council for the Development of Social Science Research in Africa (CODESRIA), Dakar, Senegal

Tarek A. Aboul Atta
Associate Professor of Urban and Regional Planning, Cairo University, Egypt

Keith S. O. Beavon
Professor, Department of Geography and Environmental Studies, University of the Witwatersrand, Johannesburg, South Africa

Alain Dubresson
Professor, Department of Geography, Centre d'Etudes Géographiques sur l'Afrique Noire, University of Paris X, France

Salah El-Shakhs
Professor, Department of Urban Planning and Policy, Edward J. Bloustein School of Planning and Public Policy, Rutgers University, New Brunswick, N.J., USA

R. A. Obudho
Associate Professor, Department of Geography, University of Nairobi, Kenya

Jean-Luc Piermay
Professor, UFR de Géographie, Université Louis Pasteur, Centre National de la Recherche Scientifique, Strasbourg, France

Deborah Potts
Department of Geography, School of Oriental and African Studies, University of London, UK

Carole Rakodi
Professor of International Urban Development Planning, Department of City and Regional Planning, University of Wales, Cardiff, UK

Contributors

Christian M. Rogerson
Professor, Department of Geography,
University of the Witwatersrand,
Johannesburg, South Africa

David Simon
Reader in Development Geography, and
Director, Centre for Developing Areas
Research (CEDAR), Department of
Geography, Royal Holloway, University
of London, Egham, Surrey, UK

Kadmiel H. Wekwete
United Nations Centre for Human
Settlements (HABITAT), Nairobi,
Kenya

Mahmoud Yousry
Professor of Urban and Regional
Planning, Cairo University, Egypt

596

Index

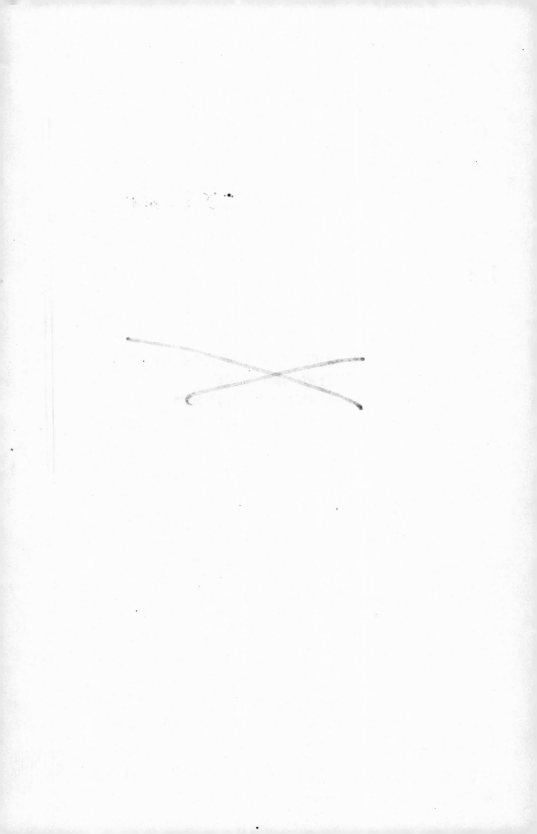

WARNER MEMORIAL LIBRARY
EASTERN UNIVERSITY
ST. DAVIDS, PA 19087-3696

Printed in the United States
24924LVS00001B/290

9 789280 809527